David M. Brownstone

Irene M. Franck

FACTS ABOUT AMERICAN IMMIGRATION

Reference Titles from H.W. Wilson

By David M. Brownstone and Irene M. Franck

Famous First Facts About Sports
The Wilson Chronology of Asia and the Pacific
The Wilson Chronology of Women's Achievements

Other Wilson Titles

Facts About Retiring in the United States
Facts About the Presidents, Seventh Edition
Famous First Facts About American Politics
Speeches of the American Presidents, Second Edition
Facts About the Supreme Court of the United States
Facts About the American Wars
Facts About the Cities
Facts About the Congress
Facts About the States, Second Edition
Facts About Canada, Its Provinces and Territories
Facts About China (forthcoming)
Facts About the British Prime Ministers
Facts About the 20th Century
Facts About the World's Languages
Facts About the World's Nations
Famous First Facts, Fifth Edition
Famous First Facts, International Edition
Famous First Facts About the Environment
The Wilson Chronology of the World's Religions

David M. Brownstone
Irene M. Franck

FACTS ABOUT AMERICAN IMMIGRATION

The H.W. Wilson Company
New York • Dublin
2001

Library of Congress Cataloging-in-Publication Data

Brownstone, David M.
    Facts about American immigration / by David M. Brownstone and Irene M. Franck.
        p.cm.
    Includes bibliographical references.
    ISBN 0-8242-0959-1 (alk. paper)
        1. United States—Emigration and immigration. 2. Immigrants—United States. 3. United States—Emigration and immigration—Statistics. 4. Immigrants—United States—Statistics. I. Franck, Irene M. II. Title.

JV6465 .B73 2001
304.873—dc21

00-053422

Printed in the United States of America

The H. W. Wilson Company
950 University Avenue
Bronx, NY 10452

Visit H.W. Wilson's Web site: www.hwwilson.com

Table of Contents

List of Tables

Part 3. Immigration from Africa

List of Graphs

Preface

In *Facts About American Immigration*, we have supplied a highly specific, substantial body of information and insight on the greatest migration in human history—the massive, worldwide emigration to what is now the United States that has been a major feature of world history for more than five centuries and continues today. To place that immigration in its full context, we have necessarily gone back to the First Americans, the Asian peoples who crossed the Bering Land Bridge into Alaska, probably by 12,000 to 15,000 B.C., though some believe that human settlement of the Americas came much earlier.

We have focused here on who came to the lands that became the United States and from where, their reasons for coming, the nature of their journey, where they settled, and the many efforts made to stop or divert them.

To that end, we have opened the book with general materials (Part I), to place the whole process of immigration in a wide historical context. These materials include an overview of immigration; a survey of the efforts to restrict immigration; a portrait of the immigrant journey over the centuries, including the passage through places such as Castle Garden, The Shed, Ellis Island, and Angel Island; a discussion of Native Americans and immigration; and a chronology of immigration. This section includes extensive statistical materials, which summarize in tables and graphs key information about overall immigration to the United States.

Following that section is the largest portion of the book (Parts II–VI), which is divided by region: Europe, Africa, Asia, the Americas, and Oceania. Each part begins with a brief introduction to the region, followed by a series of articles focusing on specific countries or groups of countries within that region. Articles include tables and graphs that summarize and portray statistical information relating to that group's immigration, as well as specific Internet and print resources. Each regional section concludes with tables and graphs summarizing the pattern of immigration from the region, plus regional Internet and print resources.

At the back of the book are two other sections. Part VII offers tables of annual immigration statistics covering the period 1820 to 1996. These are followed by extensive general notes about the immigration statistics used in the book.

Note that the tables in Part VII are drawn directly from the official figures generated by the Immigration and Naturalization Service. However, almost all of the other tables and graphs in this book are new; they have been developed by the authors especially for this work, drawing on Immigration and Naturalization Service data and U.S. Census Bureau data, some of which is not otherwise readily available. The result is a detailed picture, in tabular and graphic form, of the pattern of immigration from each country and region covered and of how it fits into the overall emigration to the United States.

Note also that the statistics in the body of the book run through 1996; that is because, at the time the book was being completed (Spring 1999), those were the latest official immigration figures available from the U.S. government. However, the statistics in Part VII have been updated through 1998, using the most current official immigration statistics available as of mid-2001. Although these figures arrived too late to be incorporated into the body of the book, readers will be able to find the most recent immigration data available on any nation or region of interest in Part VII. Updates to these immigration statistics are published annually by the Immigration and Naturalization Service, but (as the above indicates) the volumes are often two or even three years behind.

The final section of the book (Appendixes) begins with general Internet and print resources on immigration. This is followed by other useful immigration-related information, largely derived from government resources, including a summary of immigration and naturalization legislation, a discussion of estimates of emigration and illegal immigration, and tips on genealogical research. To the latter, we have appended a list of Internet and print resources for budding family historians and amateur genealogists. A glossary of immigration terms follows the Appendices.

Note that throughout the book, print resources have been listed in alphabetical order, in long lists grouped alphabetically under thematic subheads for ease of use. Internet resources, however, are listed in order of likely general usefulness, with the most wide-ranging Web sites listed first. These are also categorized under thematic subheads where a list includes many Internet resources.

Readers seeking information about specific countries or regions can look either at the detailed table of contents or in the index at the back of the book. Full lists of all the tables and graphs—well over 400 of them—also appear in the front of the book, following this Preface.

Our thanks, as always, to the librarians of the northeastern library network, and especially to the staff of the Chappaqua Library, in particular director Mark Hasskarl; the expert reference staff, including Martha Alcott, Maryanne Eaton, Carolyn Jones, Jane Peyraud, Paula Peyraud, Carolyn Reznick, and Michele Capozzella; and the circulation staff, headed by Marilyn Coleman and later Barbara Le Sauvage.

Our thanks also to the many people at H.W. Wilson—especially director of general publications Michael Schulze; former editor Hilary Claggett; editors Lynn Messina, Norris Smith, Gray Young, and Richard Stein; and the whole production staff—who helped see this work through from manuscript to published book; to Dan Essex, Reference Librarian at the U.S. Census Bureau, for locating for us some materials that were not otherwise generally available; to picture researcher Susan Hormuth; and to computer consultant Jim Mayers.

David M. Brownstone
Irene M. Franck
August 2001

Part I
Immigration

An Overview

In a very real sense, all of the peoples who came to live in what is now the United States were immigrants—although we quite properly describe those who came first as First Americans, Earliest Americans, or Native Americans. The latter is today by far the most widely used name, and the one used in this book.

All those who came to the Americas have shared an essential fact: that they have been fully formed modern humans, that is, *Homo sapiens.* All evolved elsewhere, in some part of the "Old World," where there were forerunners and variant branches of humanity. It is quite clear that all those who came to the Americas were indeed immigrants, who arrived at different times and developed different civilizations, while simultaneously being part of a worldwide human society.

Earliest Americans

When humans migrated from the Old World and where they migrated from have long been disputed matters. Almost all archaeologists and historians agree that by at least 11,000 B.C., Asian hunter-gatherers had migrated across the then-dry Bering Land Bridge between northeast Asia and Alaska. However, a substantial minority are convinced that settlement of the Americas began long before that. Some have based their views on finds at a wide range of 14,000- to 40,000-year-old archaeological sites scattered throughout the Americas, most notably in northeastern Brazil and the American Southwest. Most notable so far are southern Chile's Monte Verde site, verifiably dated at 12,000 to 11,500 B.C.; and the Meadowcroft site, near Pittsburgh, Pennsylvania, verifiably dated at 10,000 B.C. The dating of the latter is very controversial, however, for some claim it as proof of settlement dating back to 18,000 to 17,000 B.C.

There have also long been unverifiable claims about early peoples from East Asia and the South Pacific making sea voyages of thousands of miles to make landfall on South America's west coast, and others tra-versing the Atlantic from east to west, riding the same great east-west South Atlantic currents that would later take Columbus to America. Farther afield, some people are convinced that the Americas were settled by people who came from the legendary "lost" continents of Atlantis and Mu. However, no adequately reliable evidence has so far supported any of these more speculative theories.

In sum, there are great problems associated with dating the settlement of the Americas earlier than perhaps 12,000 to 14,000 B.C.—and that may take it back a bit farther than most archaeologists are so far willing to go. There is another problem as well: the earliest verifiable settlers of the Americas seem to have come from northeast Asia across the Bering Land Bridge. However, there is no known evidence that people lived in northeast Asia much earlier than 20,000 to 15,000 B.C. These are generally accepted to be the Asian hunter-gatherers who had been spreading into northeastern Asia as glacial ice sheets receded, following the mammoths, reindeer, and other large animals that were their primary food sources.

With the end of the final stage of the Wisconsin Glaciation came a major warming trend that caused the massive glaciers covering much of the Northern Hemisphere to recede, releasing huge quantities of water that raised sea levels as much as several hundred feet. One result was the flooding of the Bering Land Bridge, in approximately 8000 B.C., to form the modern Bering Strait and Aleutian Islands. By then, the Bridge had served as an Asia-to-North America migration route for at least 5,000 to 6,000 years.

So far, archaeological finds indicate that the main migrations to North America took place in two major waves, with those who became the "Indian" peoples of the Americas migrating out of Asia 13,000 to 14,000 years ago, and those who became the Inuit and Aleut peoples arriving more recently, by land near the end of the glaciation, or perhaps island-hopping across the Aleutian chain after the flooding of the land bridge.

The earlier of these two main migrations out of Asia was the genesis of the Native American peoples of the Americas, among them the earliest peoples in what would become the United States. For at least 13,000 years before the European conquest, they would spread and develop into hundreds of separate peoples and many cultures. Their long and complex course of development spans a period fully as long as the whole course of known Old World history, from Mesopotamian, Egyptian, and East Asian beginnings until now, and is far beyond the purposes of this work on American immigration history. Nor were they immigrants after the flooding of the Bering Land Bridge; rather, in all their diversity, they had become the Native Americans whose lands and cultures were conquered by European invaders starting in 1492 (see also "Native Americans and Immigration" on p. 73).

Other Early Contacts

Before Columbus arrived in 1492, other peoples from various continents at least visited North America. Most of these contacts have not been verified, but some may have validity. *The Great Chinese Encyclopedia*, a substantial historical work published early in the sixth century A.D., describes the sea journey of a group of Chinese Buddhist priests led by Hui Shen across the Pacific to the west coast of what may be North America, followed by a coastwise voyage south to what is now Mexico. Their name for the country they found was *Fusang*. In that period, Chinese seafarers might very well have achieved such a trip—and the great Chinese historians must be heard, as they are some of the most notable scholars in world history. It was also in that period that Polynesian seafarers, probably from the Marquesas, settled in Hawaii.

Until the "Little Ice Age" of the 12th through the 16th centuries, the easiest way by far to reach the Americas was by way of the North Atlantic. It is only about 200 miles from Bergen, Norway, to the Shetlands; another 200 miles from the Shetlands to the Faeroes; 400 more to Iceland; and only 200 more to Greenland and

the Americas. In those warmer centuries, there was during the summer little of the kind of subsurface ice that would in a later day sink even the *Titanic,* a massive steel ship. Sailing out of the Irish Sea past the Shetland Islands, or from the Norwegian coast past the Orkney Islands, off Scotland, seafarers could island-hop to the Faeroe Islands, to Iceland, and then on to Greenland and North America.

That is precisely what they did. Irish sea rovers moving out into the Atlantic settled in Iceland in the seventh and eighth centuries. Norse ships reached Iceland in the middle of the ninth century, and were followed by the first wave of immigrants in the 870s. By 900, the estimated Norse population of Iceland was 20,000; it reached 40,000 in 930.

In the 980s Erik the Red founded the first Norse Greenland colony, though he was not the first Norse seafarer to reach Greenland. He founded their second settlement a few years after that, in southeastern Greenland. A few years later, his son, Leif Eriksson, made the first recorded Norse landing on the mainland of North America, probably reaching the coast of Newfoundland, which the Norse called Vinland, after the grapevines they found there. The first known American-born child of European ancestry was a boy named Snorri, who was reportedly born in Vinland during the winter of 1003–1004.

A Norse settlement dating back to the 11th century, L'Anse aux Meadows, was discovered in 1960 on the northern tip of Newfoundland, at the entrance to the Strait of Belle Isle. The nature of the artifacts found there indicates that this was a ship repair and reprovisioning site, which implies that the Norse could and probably did explore considerably to the south on the North American coast, more than four centuries before Columbus.

Greenland's Norse settlements lasted at least 400 years, with peak populations in the 5,000–10,000 range. They may have lasted in much diminished form all the way into the mid-16th century. The advent and worsening of the "Little Ice Age" made travel and trade in the North Atlantic far more difficult, however. The Greenland settlements eventually ended, although the Iceland settlements went on without a break.

There was little, if any, pause in European contact with North America during the decades before Columbus "discovered" the New World. Portuguese vessels were probably fishing on the Grand Banks, off Newfoundland, in the final decades of the 15th century, and were soon joined by Basque, British, and Breton ships. Some vessels reportedly made landfall on what was probably Newfoundland; certainly those fishing in those waters were familiar with the Norse settlements on Iceland, and perhaps with those on Greenland as well. Like fishers throughout history, however, these visitors kept secret their favorite fishing grounds—and therefore most of what they knew about the lands they visited.

The Beginning of the European Invasion

Had it not been for the icing of the northern seas, European penetration of the New World might well have continued to come by the short, island-hopping route across the North Atlantic, to Greenland and Newfoundland and then south. As it was, an entirely different set of circumstances led to the European penetration and conquest of the Americas.

In 1453, Ottoman Turkish forces finally took Constantinople, after centuries of attacks on the failing Byzantine Empire. The Turks then blocked the major Asian-European trade routes, spurring new European efforts to find alternate trade routes to Asia. The Portuguese, who had been inching their way south along Africa's west coast since early in the 15th century, responded by accelerating their African explorations. Bartolomeu Dias rounded the Cape of Good Hope in 1487, while Vasco da Gama reached India in 1498, beginning the long European attack on and partial conquest of south and east Asia.

Spain responded by turning west. On August 3, 1492, Spanish-sponsored Italian seafarer Christopher Columbus sailed south out of Palos, Spain, caught the westbound winds and current at the Canary Islands, and rode them to the Caribbean, making landfall on San Salvador, in the Bahamas, on October 12, 1492. During this first visit, he took hostages, beginning the long European assault on the peoples of the Americas. He later made landfall on Cuba and Hispaniola (Santo Domingo), on the latter founding Navidad, the first post-Columbian European settlement in the Americas. At Navidad, the European conquest of the Americas can be said to have begun.

A second major event in the history of the Americas—and of Africa—also occurred on Hispaniola. In 1501, the first African slaves were brought to the island, beginning the east-west portion of the transatlantic slave trade, which was to cost millions of African lives (see "The Slave Trade" on p. 321). The Atlantic slave trade had begun 60 years earlier, in 1441, when the Portuguese had brought their first 10 black African slaves back to Portugal.

On the eve of the European invasion and conquest of the Americas, the Native American population of the Americas was probably in the 20 million to 25 million range. Of these, an estimated 1 million to 3 million lived in what would later become the United States. However, estimates vary widely, and no consensus exists as to preconquest populations.

A major and unknown factor is the number of Native Americans killed by plague during the conquest. The coming of the Europeans was marked by devastating plagues that apparently killed millions of Native Americans throughout the Americas, including at least some hundreds of thousands in what would become the United States. The Native Americans had no resistance to the diseases carried by the peoples of the Old World, for the Native Americans had developed largely in isolation since the flooding of the Bering Land Bridge 9,000 to 10,000 years before Columbus.

Early Europeans in the New World

The first European seafarer of his day known to have reached the North American mainland was Italian sailor John Cabot (Giovanni Caboto), who captained an English ship that reached Newfoundland and possibly Nova Scotia's Cape Bre-

This is an early artist's fanciful view of the arrival of Christopher Columbus's three ships in the Americas.

ton Island in 1497. He was followed by his son, Sebastian Cabot, who sailed an English ship into the approaches to Hudson Bay in 1509.

Juan Ponce de León was the first of the Spanish conquerors to reach North America, in 1513. This marked the beginning of the European conquest of North America, although settlement did not follow until mid-century. European penetration, though not settlement, also soon came in the north. Giovanni da Verrazano, another Italian leading an English expedition, explored the Newfoundland and Belle Isle coasts, as well as Narragansett and New York Bays, in 1524.

Ten years later, in 1534, Jacques Cartier led the first major French expedition to the New World, landing at Chaleur Bay, on the coast of New Brunswick. Cartier entered the Gulf of St. Lawrence through the Strait of Belle Isle, between Newfoundland and the Quebec mainland, and landed on New Brunswick's Gaspé Peninsula at Chaleur Bay. He returned to Canada in 1535 and this time sailed into the interior of North America, up the St. Lawrence River to the Native American village of Hochelaga, later the site of Quebec City, and farther on to the Lichine Rapids, later the site of Montreal.

Strong Spanish penetration into the North American mainland began with Hernando de Soto's 1539 expedition, which landed in Florida and traveled throughout the Southeast and mid-South, all the way to the Mississippi River in 1541. The de Soto expedition brought with it diseases that devastated many Native American tribes, among them the Mandans of the Mississippi basin, a highly cultured farming people.

Francisco Vásquez de Coronado led another Spanish expedition in 1540. This one went north out of Mexico into what would become the American Southwest. In July 1540, Coronado's forces took Zuni Pueblo and—with Native American guides—went on to reach the Grand Canyon. Of tremendous significance was Coronado's introduction of the horse to North America. With the horse came enormous changes in the lives of the Native American peoples of the Great Plains. In later centuries, these peoples would be joined by many other Native Americans from the eastern woodlands, as they were pushed farther west by the conquering Europeans, who by then had themselves become Americans.

Spanish seafarers also explored the Pacific coast of North America. Juan Cabrillo led the way, in 1542 exploring that coast from Navidad, near Acapulco, to Oregon. However, substantial European settlement of the Pacific coast would not come until the 1770s, and would become heavy only with the California Gold Rush of 1849.

These explorers—and the lands they claimed for their countries—laid the basis for the long European imperial contest for the Americas. Major players in the fight for North America would include Britain, France, the Netherlands, Spain, Russia, and later the United States, Mexico, and Canada.

Authors' Archives

The Mandan people who lived in the Mississippi Valley were largely destroyed by epidemics of diseases inadvertently introduced into the region by the de Soto expedition in 1541.

On the mainland of eastern North America, the European contest began in 1564, with France's establishment of Fort Caroline, on Florida's St. Johns River. Stung by the French initiative, Spanish forces took Fort Caroline in 1565, while Spanish settlers in that year also founded Florida's St. Augustine, the first permanent European settlement in what would later become the United States.

Nuevo Mexico

It was in the Southwest, however, that the main Spanish push into North America came. Spanish penetration roughly followed the course of North America's greatest migration route, the Old North Trail, which ran from northern Canada all the way to Chile along the eastern slope of the long chain of mountains that includes the Rockies and the Andes.

For the earliest Asian immigrants, who had crossed the Bering Land Bridge more than 10,000 years before, the Old North Trail had been the main route south. From approximately A.D. 300 until the early 15th century, the area that later became the American Southwest was home to some of North America's highest cultures. Among them were peoples called the Anasazi (Old Ones). They were so named by nomadic raiders from the north, whom the Anasazi called Apaches (Enemies). By the time of the Spanish conquest of the southwest, the Anasazi had all but disappeared. The peaceful Pueblo peoples were unable to resist the Spanish invaders, who enslaved them. Many other Native American peoples would continue to resist the invaders, however. In northern Mexico, they would fight a series of very substantial wars against Spain and Mexico all the way into the early 20th century. Apaches and Comanches also resisted Mexican and later U.S. forces, some late into the 19th century.

In August 1519, a little less than 27 years after Columbus made landfall on San Salvador, a Spanish force of only 600, led by Hernán Cortés, attacked and took Tenochtitlán (Mexico City). In 1521, after losing the city to an Aztec insurrection, they and local allies retook the city and killed Aztec emperor Montezuma. Spain then went on to take the entire Aztec empire and all of central America. By the 1580s, Spanish exploring and raiding expeditions had reached the Rio Grande.

The first successful major Spanish incursion into what would become the American Southwest occurred in 1598, when Don Juan de Oñate led a party of 200 settlers north on New Spain's El Camino Real (the Royal Road) on the main direct route north, reaching the Rio Grande (Río Bravo) south of El Paso (the Pass). The settlement survived its difficult early years; its capital, Santa Fe (Holy Faith), was founded in 1610. However, in 1680, a successful Pueblo insurrection drove out the Spanish colonists, who by then numbered 3,600. Spanish control was reestablished in 1693, with the area becoming the province of Nuevo México (New Mexico). The region would remain under Spanish and then Mexican control until 1848; then, after the Mexican War, the United States annexed the region, along with Texas, the rest of the American Southwest, and California.

Rivalry for Eastern North America

In the 17th century, European immigration to eastern North America began in earnest, spurred in part by imperial rivalries, and also by major European religious, political, and commercial developments. Within a single decade, France, England, and the Netherlands founded settlements that would grow into full-scale colonies.

Following the path taken by Cartier more than half a century earlier, French explorer Samuel de Champlain entered the interior of North America in 1603 via the St. Lawrence River, exploring south on the river as far as the Lichine Rapids. The first of the great French explorers of North America, he would reach Lake Huron in 1615. Jean Nicolet would reach Green Bay in 1634, and René-Robert Cavelier, Sieur de La Salle, would travel through the Great Lakes and the Mississippi Valley all the way to the mouth of the Mississippi in 1682. Together, these French explorers entirely opened up the interior of the conti-

Authors' Archives

The French made their first permanent settlement in the Americas at the Habitation, at Port Royal (Annapolis), in what is now Nova Scotia, in 1605.

nent to European conquest. However, New Orleans would not be founded until 1718, and then from the sea.

In 1605, Champlain established France's first successful Canadian settlement, the Habitation, at Port Royal (Annapolis), Nova Scotia. In 1608, Champlain founded Quebec City, which would become the center of French power in North America. French settlement in Canada would be slow until 1663, when the French government began to strongly encourage settlement.

The long English-French conflict in North America also began at Port Royal, in 1613. Only eight years after its founding, the settlement was captured and destroyed by English forces.

Early English Settlements

Meanwhile, the English were attempting to establish their own settlements. Several early colonizing attempts failed, most notably the one at Roanoke in 1587. The first successful English settlement in North America was established by London's Virginia Company in 1607 at Jamestown. The colony quickly and very lucratively turned to tobacco cultivation as its main source of income. The English took farmlands previously worked by the Powhatan confederation to form the Chesapeake Bay Tidewater plantations that became the basis of the early Greater Virginia economy. Two wars with the Powhatans resulted; the second, in 1644, featured a Powhatan massacre of some 500 English colonists, followed by an English massacre of most remaining Powhatans.

Although regarded as an addictive, cancer-causing substance in the late 20th century, tobacco was widely used in the Americas before Columbus, who encountered tobacco during his first voyage. Grown by European settlers in the Americas from the 1530s, it was introduced into continental Europe in the late 1550s and into England in 1565. Tobacco cultivation provided a staple cash crop and was a large source of profits for Virginia planters, spurring the growth of the southern English colonies after the difficult early years of the Virginia colony.

Tobacco cultivation also provided the prototype for the plantation system that was to play such a major role in the history of the American South. While drawing planters to the colonies, it also drew substantial numbers of indentured servants, immigrants who would work off their passage money over a period of years to win their freedom (see "The Journey" on p. 53).

The plantation system was also applicable to other labor-intensive crops, most notably cotton, and played a major role in the development of slavery in the American South. In 1619, the first 20 of 400,000 to 500,000 imported black African slaves arrived at Jamestown (see "The Slave Trade" on p. 321).

Motives for Migration

Much of the early English migration to the new North American colonies was generated by straightforward economic motives, as land, cash crops, and trade beckoned. Some English immigrants, especially in the southern colonies, came as large-scale farmers, who employed substantial numbers of poor English immigrants as indentured servants. There were many indentured servants in the northern colonies as well, though most English immigrants in the north came as small-scale farmers and businesspeople who largely worked their own lands and businesses.

English imperial motives also played a major role. England had just become a world power. After defeating the Spanish Armada in 1588, it turned to the worldwide seaborne expansion that would create the massive British empire. Imperial policy was to encourage colonization of the North American mainland, and in the process to take as much territory as possible.

Other substantial factors spurred migration to the English colonies. One major set of events, which had a great impact on the transatlantic migration, was the English "plantation" of Ireland, which greatly contributed to centuries of instability in Ireland and helped generate a long series of Irish-English wars.

Another major source of transatlantic migration was the growth of religious dissent and political disaffection in England itself, together with the English defeat of Scotland and the English Civil War. Linked to this was the long set of Protestant-Catholic religious wars in France, which resulted in the flight of scores of thousands of French Protestant Huguenots during the 16th and 17th centuries. Some Huguenots fled to England and later arrived in Britain's American colonies, while others went directly to North America. A greater, continent-wide, largely Catholic-Protestant conflict was the Thirty Years War (1618–1648), which cost an estimated 8 million lives, and triggered the first major migration of central Europeans, most of them Germans, to the new American colonies.

Plymouth and Freedom

It was religious dissent that spurred the first successful English settlement in New England, at Plymouth, in what later became Massachusetts, founded by the 101 Puritan dissenters who arrived aboard the *Mayflower*. They reached the tip of Cape Cod, at what is now Provincetown, on November 21, 1620, and settled at Plymouth Harbor a month later.

These English dissenters and earliest New Englanders brought with them something quite unusual—an idea of political equality that would permeate the further American experience. It was embodied in their Mayflower Compact, signed by all the able-bodied male immigrants in the party at Provincetown. The Compact provided for political equality only among the male colonists, leaving out the women in the party and thereby half of humanity. Its signers also did not address the issues of slavery, religious freedom, or several of the other freedoms that would be established by the Bill of Rights and later constitutional guarantees. They did, however, make a very substantial start on the ideas of freedom and equality, which with material prosperity would become central motives for the tens of millions of immigrants who would follow them to what would become the United States.

Early Dutch Settlements

At the turn of the 17th century, the Netherlands became a major player in the European invasion and partial conquest of south and east Asia, contesting Portuguese trading monopolies there and battling against the Portuguese in many areas. The Dutch soon began to move toward what would become control of the huge Indonesian archipelago, and with it domination of the lucrative spice trade.

In the same period, the Dutch also became a presence in the European contest for the New World, establishing colonies and contesting with Portuguese forces in Brazil, the Caribbean, and Central America, and planting a substantial settlement on North America's east coast.

In 1609, a Dutch expedition led by Henry Hudson sailed into what would become New York harbor and traveled some distance up the Hudson River, the natural mid-Atlantic gateway to North America. In 1612 the Dutch returned to establish the New Netherlands colony in the Hudson Valley, within two years moving north in the valley as far as the eastern end of the Mohawk Valley. In 1614 they established Fort Nassau, near modern Albany.

New Amsterdam (New York) was established in 1626 on Manhattan Island and began to grow into the major entry port it would later become. The colony did not receive the kind of imperial encouragement given to the French and English North American colonies, however, for the major Dutch imperial focus continued to be on the riches of Asia. The Dutch were also involved in the long series of Catholic-Protestant wars that enveloped most of Europe,

and in three Anglo-Dutch wars between 1652 and 1674, all of them connected with worldwide imperial rivalries.

Fort Christina

Sweden emerged as a major European power during the early 17th century and remained a powerful military force well into the 18th century. For a short time, the Swedes developed imperial ambitions in North America, and in 1638 established Fort Christina on the Delaware River.

Sweden's main focus during this period, however, was on a series of major European wars, including the Thirty Years War and wars against Russia and Poland. The Swedish presence in North America was a minor focus. In 1655 Dutch forces from New Amsterdam took Fort Christina, ending Sweden's involvement in the colonization of North America.

English Ascendancy

In 1664, during the Second Anglo-Dutch War, English forces took New Amsterdam and the entire New Netherlands colony, renaming it New York. Eight years later, in 1672, during the Third Anglo-Dutch war, the Dutch retook the city and colony, but then returned it permanently to the English in the worldwide Dutch-English settlement that was the Treaty of Westminster. The new English colony then became a fast-growing and central link in the chain of English North American colonies.

To the north and west, France held what would become Canada, and had outposts west of the Appalachians and settlements from New Orleans some distance north in the Mississippi basin. Spain held lightly populated settlements in Florida, Texas, the Southwest, and California.

The territories of the three remaining colonial powers would shift dramatically in the 18th century, after the Seven Years War (1756–1763), which was called in North America the French and Indian War (1754–1763). France lost Canada and all its territories east of the Mississippi except part of Louisiana to England. Spain took the rest of the North American mainland territories, including New Orleans and the rest of Louisiana, while transferring Florida to English rule.

Less than two decades later, the American Revolution established the new United States. In 1800, France took the formerly French mainland holdings back from Spain. Then in 1803, as part of the "Louisiana Purchase," France ceded to the United States huge quantities of land from the Mississippi to the Rockies, called the Louisiana Territory. The United States took Florida from Spain in 1819. North American mainland British colonial rule was now confined to Canada, while the new United States went on to build a massive, continent-wide world power based largely on British roots.

In reality, the great mass of the North American lands transferred in all of the above war settlements and purchases were Native American lands, which had been taken by the European powers and the United States.

The Balance of Population

During the late 18th century, immigration into what became the United States meant immigration into the English seacoast colonies, by white Europeans and black African slaves (called "Negroes" in U.S. census data). Native American, French, and Spanish population shifts within North America during this period and before these areas became part of the United States are not properly treated as "immigration"; as a practical matter, they are also not adequately verifiable.

U.S. Census Bureau estimates indicate that in 1670, after the English had taken New Netherland, the total population of the English colonies that would become the United States stood at a little less than 112,000 (not counting Native Americans). In 1780, during the American Revolution, the estimate had climbed to a little over 2,780,000. Of these, a little over 575,000, or 20.7 percent, were African Americans. The great majority of these were slaves, but some were free.

Authors' Archives

This is the earliest known view of New Amsterdam (later New York), from a book published in 1651.

The first U.S. Census, in 1790, estimated a population of 3,929,000, not counting Native Americans. Historians have later made estimates as to the ethnic origins of white Americans in this period, though not of the numbers of foreign-born whites.

The U.S. population in 1790 consisted of approximately 3,182,000 whites (81 percent) and 746,000 (19 percent) African Americans. Of the whites, a large majority (60.1 percent) were of English and Welsh origin (lumped together as English in the statistics). Within the states that in that period formed the United States, people of English-Welsh ancestry formed an absolute majority in all except two, with the highest concentration in Massachusetts, at 82 percent. The two exceptions were Pennsylvania and New Jersey. Large numbers of Germans were concentrated in Pennsylvania, along with more than average numbers of Irish and Scots. There were almost as many Germans (33.3 percent) as English-Welsh (35.3 percent) in Pennsylvania, a kind of balance that occurred

Table 1.1: Estimated Number and Percentage of Whites and Negroes in the Total White and Negro Population in the American Colonies, 1610–1780

Decade	Number of Whites and Negroes in the American Colonies	Number of Whites in the American Colonies	Percentage of Whites in the Total White and Negro Population of the American Colonies	Number of Negroes in the American Colonies	Percentage of Negroes in the Total White and Negro Population of the American Colonies
1610	350	350	100.00	0	0.00
1620	2,302	2,282	99.13	20	0.87
1630	4,646	4,586	98.71	60	1.29
1640	26,634	26,037	97.76	597	2.24
1650	50,368	48,768	96.82	1,600	2.24
1660	75,058	72,138	96.11	2,920	3.18
1670	111,935	107,400	95.95	4,535	4.05
1680	151,507	144,536	95.40	6,971	4.60
1690	210,371	193,642	92.05	16,729	7.95
1700	250,888	223,071	88.91	27,817	11.09
1710	331,711	286,845	86.47	44,866	13.53
1720	466,185	397,346	85.23	68,839	14.77
1730	629,445	538,424	85.54	91,021	14.46
1740	905,563	755,539	83.43	150,024	16.57
1750	1,170,760	934,340	79.81	236,420	20.19
1760	1,593,625	1,267,819	79.56	325,806	20.44
1770	2,148,076	1,688,254	78.59	459,822	21.41
1780	2,780,369	2,204,949	79.30	575,420	20.70

Note: Figures derived from estimates of the population of the 13 English colonies that would later become the United States, not counting Native Americans. White and Negro are the terms used in the source.

Source notes: Based on American Council of Learning Societies, "Report of Committee on Linguistic and National Stocks in the Population of the United States" (based on studies by Howard F. Barker and Marcus L. Hansen), *Annual Report of the American Historical Association*, 1931, Vol. I, Washington, D.C., 1932, p. 124. Distribution was made primarily on the basis of family names. For an explanation of the methods used, see source.

Source: Adapted from *Historical Statistics of the United States Bicentennial Edition*, U.S. Bureau of the Census, 1975, Chapter C 89–119.

Table 1.2: Estimated Percentage of Ethnic Ancestry in Total White Population of the United States, 1790

Nationality	Percentage of Total White Population of United States	Percentage of Total White Population of Northwest Territory	Percentage of Total White Population of Spanish-held Territories	Percentage of Total White Population of French-held Territories
English	60.9	29.8	2.5	11.2
Scotch	8.3	4.1	0.3	1.6
Irish: Ulster	6.0	2.9	0.2	1.1
Irish: Free State	3.7	1.8	0.1	0.7
German	8.7	4	0.4	8.7
Dutch	3.4	-	-	-
French	1.7	57	-	64.2
Swedish	0.7	-	-	-
Spanish	-	-	96.5	12.5
Unassigned	6.6	-	-	-

(-) Represents zero.

Note: The Northwestern Territory was the land west of Pennsylvania between the Ohio and Mississippi rivers.

Source: Adapted from *Historical Statistics of the United States Bicentennial Edition,* U.S. Bureau of the Census, 1975, Chapter Z 20–23.

nowhere else in the country. New Jersey and New York had relatively large populations of Dutch origin, as well as substantial German, Irish, and Scots ethnic groups. Many Scotch-Irish and Scots arriving in America soon headed through the Appalachians and out to the frontier.

Mass Immigration

One of the largest migrations in human history has been the movement of at least 70 million people to the United States during the past two centuries. Of these, more than 63 million were recorded as immigrants from 1820, when the United States first began to keep official immigration records, to 1996. At least 5 million more came as undocumented "illegals." Most of these arrived in the final decades of the 20th century, though a minimum of several hundred thousands came uncounted by land across the Mexican and Canadian borders before full counting began in 1908. Probably 3 million more documented immigrants have come between 1997 and 1999, their immigration not yet reported by the U.S. government. To all of these must be added those black African slaves who arrived as involuntary immigrants between the time of the American Revolution and the end of the Civil War. There was also substantial undercounting and failure to count at all for a variety of reasons in many periods. (See "General Notes on Immigration Statistics" on p. 684.)

Note that there has also been some substantial overcounting of immigrants, throughout the history of U.S. immigration, for those leaving the United States have in some periods and at some border crossings not been counted at all or been counted more than once, as when a migrant worker from Canada or Mexico crosses and recrosses a land border several times in the course of a single year.

The reasonably hard figures available indicate that from 1820 to 1996 the massive worldwide immigration into the United States has totaled more than 63.1 million. Of these, 38 million emigrated from Europe, 7.9 million from Asia, 16.2 million from the Americas, 530,000 from Africa (not including those entering as slaves), 241,000 from Oceania (including Australia), and 268,000 from unspecified locations.

Table 1.3: Number of Immigrants to the United States by Region of Last Residence by Decade, 1820–1996

Decade	Number of Immigrants to the United States from Europe	Number of Immigrants to the United States from Asia	Number of Immigrants to the United States from the Americas	Number of Immigrants to the United States from Africa	Number of Immigrants to the United States from Oceania	Number of Immigrants to the United States from Unspecified Regions	Total Number of Immigrants to the United States
1820	7,690	6	387	1	1	300	8,385
1821–1830	98,797	30	11,564	16	2	33,030	143,439
1831–1840	495,681	55	33,424	54	9	69,902	599,125
1841–1850	1,597,442	141	62,469	55	29	53,115	1,713,251
1851–1860	2,452,577	41,538	74,720	210	158	29,011	2,598,214
1861–1870	2,065,141	64,759	166,607	312	214	17,791	2,314,824
1871–1880	2,271,925	124,160	404,044	358	10,914	790	2,812,191
1881–1890	4,735,484	69,942	426,967	857	12,574	789	5,246,613
1891–1900	3,555,352	74,862	38,972	350	3,965	14,063	3,687,564
1901–1910	8,056,040	323,543	361,888	7,368	13,024	33,523	8,795,386
1911–1920	4,321,887	247,236	1,143,671	8,443	13,427	1,147	5,735,811
1921–1930	2,463,194	112,059	1,516,716	6,286	8,726	228	4,107,209
1931–1940	347,566	16,595	160,037	1,750	2,483	0	528,431
1941–1950	621,147	37,028	354,804	7,367	14,551	142	1,035,039
1951–1960	1,325,727	153,249	996,944	14,092	12,976	12,491	2,515,479
1961–1970	1,123,492	427,642	1,716,374	28,954	25,122	93	3,321,677
1971–1980	800,368	1,588,178	1,982,735	80,779	41,242	12	4,493,314
1981–1990	761,550	2,738,157	3,615,225	176,893	45,205	1,032	7,338,062
1990–1996	916,733	1,875,391	3,119,506	198,068	36,326	189	6,146,213
Total 1820–1996	38,017,793	7,894,571	16,187,054	532,213	240,948	267,648	63,140,227
Percentage of Total Immigration	60.2	12.5	25.6	0.84	0.38	0.42	

Source: Adapted from the *Statistical Yearbook of the Immigration and Naturalization Service*, 1996, Table 3.

Graph 1.1: Estimated Percentage of Ethnic Ancestry in Total White Population of the United States, 1790

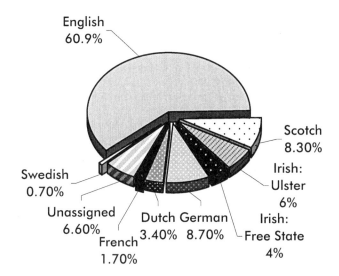

English
60.9%

Scotch
8.30%

Swedish
0.70%

Irish:
Ulster
6%

Unassigned
6.60%

Dutch German
3.40% 8.70%

Irish:
Free State
4%

French
1.70%

Motives for Emigration

From 1775 to 1815, immigration across the Atlantic to the United States was greatly limited by a series of wars that included the American Revolution, the Napoleonic Wars, and the War of 1812. Only after 1815, when peace came and the Congress of Vienna redrew the map of the world, did shipping across the North Atlantic pick up and substantial immigration to North America resume.

The European immigration to the United States was small at first, as recorded totaling less than 99,000 in the decade from 1821 to 1830. However, it was somewhat larger than that, for some thousands of immigrants crossed by land untabulated over the Canadian border, and many were "not specified" as to ethnic origin. Quite notably, almost 51,000, or 51.5 percent of those recorded as entering the United States from Europe from 1821 to 1830, were from Ireland, two decades *before* the Great Famine of the 1840s. In the same period, the recorded immigration to the United States from the United Kingdom totaled 25,000, half that from Ireland, though still 25 percent of the total number of European immigrants. (For overall decade-by-decade immigration figures, see Table 1.3, p. 14; for annual immigration figures; see Tables 7.1–5, p. 659–738.)

Seen clearly, the number of Irish and United Kingdom immigrants was a portent of things to come, in terms of immigration to the United States from all over the world in the 180 years that followed. Though largely Protestant northern Ireland had some developing landholding and the beginnings of industrial resources, Catholic Ireland was poverty-stricken and becoming ever poorer. It was experiencing enormous population growth, tenant farming remained the rule, and any profits flowed to often-absentee landowners, the same landowners who would continue to export food out of Ireland during the Great Famine. Nor did Catholic Ireland have anything at all significant in terms of industrial growth, so that very few jobs were available for the increasingly large numbers of unemployed and dispossessed. The best alternatives available both involved emigration, either to Britain or overseas to British territories or to the United States.

British immigrants faced a considerably different situation, for Britain was in the early stages of its Industrial Revolution, with its cities and industries growing by leaps and bounds. Huge population increases occurred in Britain as well. However, many of the people forced to leave the land migrated internally, to jobs newly opening up in Britain's industrial cities. Even so, a substantial and growing migration out of Britain also occurred, sometimes directly and sometimes following an internal move.

These early Irish and British patterns would be repeated for U.S. immigrants coming from throughout the world, though with substantial variations. Massive population increases and the accompanying flight to the cities and abroad would provide the substructure of the huge immigration to the United States that would follow during the balance of the 19th century and the first quarter of the 20th century. In some countries, as in northwestern Europe during the 19th century, the flight to the cities was often to a growing body of industrially based jobs in the migrants' home countries. However, in many other countries, as in much of southern and eastern Europe in the late 19th and early 20th centuries, the major response of those forced off the land was emigration abroad, though there was also a very substantial move to the cities.

The above is half of the basic immigration story, describing the key element of the "push" to emigrate from other countries to the United States. There were other key elements, certainly, for different peoples at different times, among them the ideas of democracy, of living with all of the freedoms and developing freedoms guaranteed by the U.S. Constitution and Bill of Rights, and much more. Many immigrants came as political refugees seeking asylum, others as persecuted religious dissenters.

For the mass of immigrants, however, the basic reasons for coming were economic. The United States offered land, jobs, and a open continent in which to find a seemingly limitless future. These were very attractive prospects. Until World War I, the flood of immigrants waxed and waned with United States economic conditions, but only as to amount of growth; underneath immigration grew and grew, as the United States expanded to the Pacific and simultaneously emerged as one of the world's most highly developed and productive industrial countries.

One of the greatest ironies in American history is that the seemingly limitless land that figured so largely in the 19th-century American expansion and in the enormous wave of immigration that accompanied it, was taken from the Native Americans, whose land it was before the Europeans and Americans came. In the process, the vast majority of Native Americans, from the Atlantic to the Pacific and from Canada to Mexico, were "cleared" from their ancestral lands. First there was a single large-scale clearance all the way west to the Mississippi, and then people by surviving people the remaining Native Americans were forced into "reservations," primarily between the Mississippi and the Pacific. Only a few small prior reservations survived east of the Appalachians, and only a portion of the Seminoles remained free in the Southeast, after successful resistance. Putting it a little differently, and in a world-historical context, the great majority of Native Americans living in the United States were the victims of "ethnic cleansing." (See "Native Americans and Immigration" on p. 73, for a more extended discussion.)

Pathways into North America

The great early-19th-century European immigrant pathway into the North American heartland was also by far the best of the four natural routes into North America.

The first of these routes was the earliest taken; it was Jacques Cartier's route from the north, up the St. Lawrence River to Quebec and Montreal. By taking the French through to the Great Lakes and

Graph 1.2: Percentage of Immigrants to the United States by Region of Last Residence in Total U.S. Immigration, 1820–1996

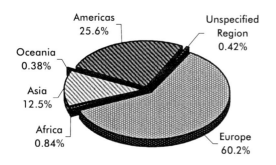

Americas 25.6%

Unspecified Region 0.42%

Oceania 0.38%

Asia 12.5%

Africa 0.84%

Europe 60.2%

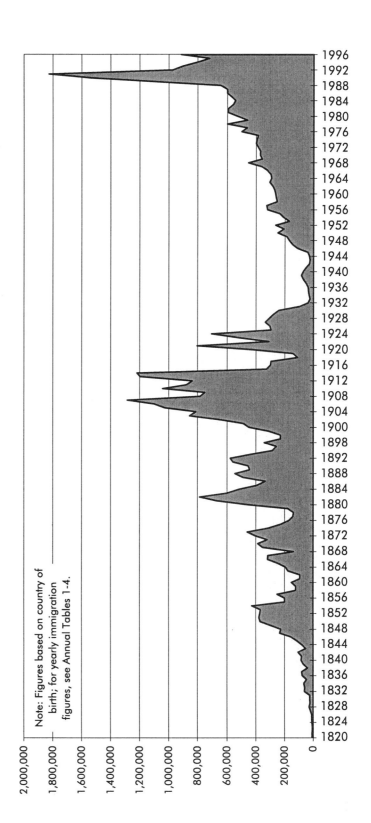

Graph 1.3: Number of Immigrants to the United States Annually, 1820–1996

Note: Figures based on country of
birth; for yearly immigration
figures, see Annual Tables 1-4.

Graph 1.4: Percentage of Immigrants to the United States per Decade in Total U.S. Population at End of Decade, 1820–1996

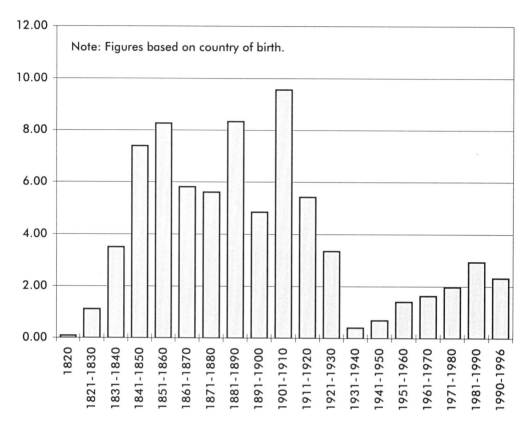

Note: Figures based on country of birth.

south to the mouth of the Mississippi, Cartier's route bypassed the natural and considerable barrier of the Appalachian Mountains stretching from New York to Georgia, and opened up the continent. A second main migration route ran south along the eastern slope of the Appalachians; from that route, Daniel Boone's party cut a path through the mountains at the Cumberland Gap in 1775, just before the start of the American Revolution. A third, less-used route ran farther south, swinging south of the Appalachians in Georgia.

The fourth—and by far the best—way west was the route that made New York one of the world's great cities. It began at

New York harbor and ran north on or along the Hudson River to Albany. The route then turned west, through the Mohawk Valley, the only large natural gap in the entire Appalachian chain, becoming a water-level route all the way to the Great Lakes and the open Midwest, so opening the continent to the Mississippi and beyond.

None of these routes beyond the Appalachians was open to mass immigration until after the American Revolution. That was because, during their long war for dominance in North America, France and Britain had made alliances with several Native American peoples. The colonial pol-

Graph 1.5: Number of Immigrants to the United States per Decade, 1820–1996

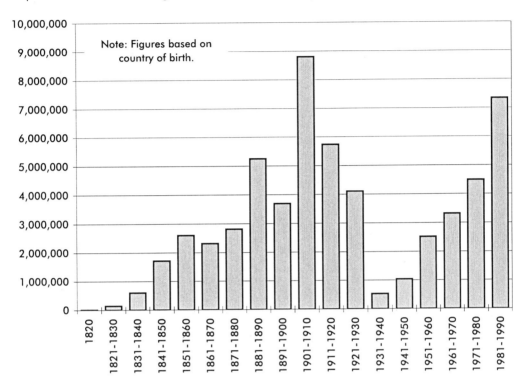

Note: Figures based on country of birth.

icies of both European powers therefore precluded any major attempt to take trans-Appalachian Native American lands.

After the American Revolution, all that changed. Many of Britain's Iroquois allies retreated to Canada, vacating the Mohawk Valley and much other land in and through the northern Appalachians. American immigrants began to pour through the Appalachians on Daniel Boone's Wilderness Road and farther south settled Georgia.

Several states began pushing Native American peoples west in the 1820s. In 1830, Congress passed the Indian Removal Act, providing for "an exchange of lands with the Indians residing in any of the states or territories, and for their removal west of the river Mississippi." By the early 1840s, that removal had been forcibly completed. The removal of the Cherokees in the murderous Trail of Tears expulsion was only part of a much larger story (see "Native Americans and Immigration" on p. 73).

With completion of the Erie Canal in 1825, linking the Hudson River and the Great Lakes, the main immigrant way west was open. Starting from New York City, it was a water-level route all the way, through which streamed millions of settlers. Millions more moved west on the trans-Appalachian Wilderness, National, and Pennsylvania roads. However, the northern route carried by far the greatest traffic in people and goods, for it was first a major water-level route and later the main railroad route west. (For information on the immigrants' routes to America and to the West, see "The Journey" on p. 53.)

Rising Immigration

With industrialization and the flight from the land to the cities and abroad accelerating in Europe, and the United States now a powerful magnet, a great flood of immigrants began to pour into the United States. From 1831 to 1840, almost 600,000 recorded immigrants entered the United States. Almost 500,000 of these were from Europe, with the largest single number, 207,000, coming from Ireland. Another 76,000 came from Britain, and the large German immigration to the United States was also beginning, with 152,000. An additional 70,000 were listed as of "unspecified" place of origin, and an undetermined number came unrecorded over the Canadian border, so that the recorded totals from Europe were clearly understated.

Still before the potato blight and Ireland's Great Famine, this immigration stemmed largely from population pressure, the availability of good land at little cost, and the lure of jobs in the expanding economy of the United States. Large numbers of Irish immigrants, for example, worked on the building of the Erie Canal from 1820 to 1825, just as successive waves of immigrants from Ireland and elsewhere would build the U.S. transcontinental road system and later the U.S. railway system.

In the 1830s, "immigrant chains" from northern and central Europe were being fully established, as young men and young families came to the United States from many countries and sent passage money home so that others might follow. "America letters" began to circulate in many countries, as immigrants extolled the virtues of their new country and urged others to come; they did, and would do so in great waves, for many generations. The immigrant chains would be a key element in the immigration of peoples from all over the world to the United States, and continue to be so today, as immigrants from the Americas, Asia, Africa, and Oceania replicate the earlier European-American experience. That is a worldwide migration pattern, and scarcely limited to the United States.

Immigration continued to rise in the early 1840s, then surged enormously in the late 1840s as the potato blight and its aftereffects hit many European countries. Ireland was hit earliest and hardest. Its disastrous Great Famine and accompanying plagues resulted in 1 to 1.5 million

Museum of the City of New York

New York City celebrated the opening of the Erie Canal in 1825; Fort Clinton, the circular structure at center left, would later become Castle Garden, the immigration station.

Graph 1.6: Percentage of Foreign-Born Immigrants by Region of Birth in Total Foreign-Born Americans, 1850

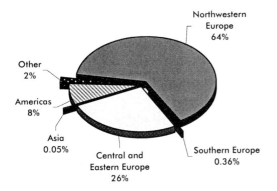

Northwestern
Europe
64%

Other
2%

Americas
8%

Asia
0.05%

Central and
Eastern Europe
26%

Southern Europe
0.36%

dead and 2 million more forced to flee abroad. Of the latter, 1.3 million Irish immigrants were recorded as reaching the United States from 1847 to 1854, with probably tens of thousands more coming undocumented via Canada.

Germany was also hit hard by the potato blight. German immigration to the United States ballooned in the 1840s and 1850s, with more than 500,000 immigrants reaching the United States in just three years, from 1852 to 1854. In all, more than 1.7 million immigrants reached the United States from 1841 to 1850, the vast majority of these from northern and central Europe. In the next decade an enormous 2.6 million recorded immigrants entered the United States.

These numbers of immigrants were even larger than they might seem, when viewed comparatively, for the United States they entered was numerically a far smaller country than it would become. The 1840s migration of 1.7 million entered a U.S. population of 23.2 million, and comprised 7.4 percent of the U.S. population in that period, while the 1850s migration comprised 8.3 percent of the U.S. population in that period. To reach those kinds of percentages in the 1990s, with the U.S. population at 270 million, immigrants would have had to number a huge 20 to 22 million. Only twice more would immigration reach similar heights, in the 1880s and from 1901 to 1910. In the latter decade, the recorded U.S. immigration of 8.8 million was into a population of 92 mil-

lion, and totaled 9.6 percent of the U.S. population. To reach that percentage in the 1990s, immigrants would have had to number more than 25 million.

Moving West

After the Mexican War, the United States forced the 1848 Treaty of Guadalupe-Hidalgo on defeated Mexico, taking an area of 1 million square miles, approximately half of what had been the nation of Mexico. Out of this territory would come the U.S. states of Texas, California, Arizona, New Mexico, Nevada, Utah, and half of Colorado, with the United States having reached to the Pacific.

In the same year, the discovery of gold at Sutter's Mill started the 1849 California Gold Rush, which quickly drew tens of thousands of gold seekers from all over the world. Tens of thousands emigrated west over the newly opened Oregon and California trails. At least as many came by sea, generally taking the overland path across Panama and then by sea again to San Francisco.

In longer terms, the Gold Rush triggered the United States settlement of California and the mountain states. It also initiated East Asian immigration into the United States, largely in the form of Chi-

Graph 1.7: Percentage of Immigrants by Region of Last Residence in Total U.S. Immigration, 1831–1860

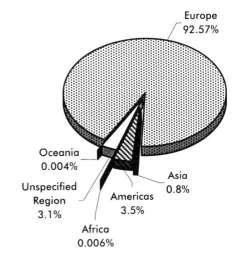

Europe
92.57%

Oceania
0.004%

Unspecified
Region
3.1%

Africa
0.006%

Americas
3.5%

Asia
0.8%

Table 1.4: Number and Percentage of Immigrants to the United States per Decade in Total U.S. Population at End of Decade, 1820–1996

Decade	Number of Immigrants to the United States	Total U.S. Population at End of Decade	Percentage of Immigrants to the United States in Total U.S. Population
1820	8,385	9,638,453	0.09
1821-1830	143,439	12,866,020	1.11
1831-1840	599,125	17,069,453	3.51
1841-1850	1,713,251	23,191,876	7.39
1851-1860	2,598,214	31,443,321	8.26
1861-1870	2,314,824	39,818,449	5.81
1871-1880	2,812,191	50,155,783	5.61
1881-1890	5,246,613	62,947,714	8.33
1891-1900	3,687,564	75,994,575	4.85
1901-1910	8,795,386	91,972,266	9.56
1911-1920	5,735,811	105,710,620	5.43
1921-1930	4,107,209	122,775,046	3.35
1931-1940	528,431	131,669,275	0.40
1941-1950	1,035,039	150,697,361	0.69
1951-1960	2,515,479	179,323,175	1.40
1961-1970	3,321,677	203,235,298	1.63
1971-1980	4,493,314	227,726,000	1.97
1981-1990	7,338,062	249,907,000	2.94
1990-1996	6,146,213	265,557,000	2.31

nese immigrants coming from Guangdong (Kwangtung or Canton) to Gum San, the land of the Mountains of Gold.

With California and the West fully opened to American conquest, the pattern of "ethnic cleansing" was repeated. By the late 1850s, the process of expelling Native Americans from their lands was well under way, with Native American forces offering sporadic—and in some instances temporarily effective—resistance to U.S. forces, as the final set of "Indian Wars" began. Effective Native American resistance west of the Mississippi would end in 1886, with the surrender of Apache forces led by Geronimo. In 1890, a minor and largely aborted Sioux rebellion called the Ghost Dance Wars resulted in the massacre of some hundreds of Sioux by U.S. forces at

Wounded Knee Creek, in South Dakota's Pine Ridge Indian Reservation. That effectively ended the Indian Wars.

In 1862, seeking European recruits for the Union Army, the U.S. Congress passed the Homestead Act, offering free land grants as a bonus for those who would sign up. Thousands of European men responded. The Homestead Act remained in force after the war and played a major role in drawing "homesteaders" to the West, among them many immigrants directly from Europe.

Immigration to the United States continued at high levels during the Civil War and the post–Civil War period, as the westward movement grew, the transcontinental railway system was set in place, and the first outlines of what would become industrial America began to appear. Large numbers of German, British, and Irish still

Table 1.5: Number of Foreign-Born Immigrants by Region of Birth at End of Decade, 1850–1990

Year	Number of Foreign-Born Immigrants Born in Europe	Number of Foreign-Born Immigrants Born in Northwestern Europe	Number of Foreign-Born Immigrants Born in Central and Eastern Europe	Number of Foreign-Born Immigrants Born in Southern Europe	Number of Foreign-Born Immigrants Born Elsewhere in Europe	Number of Foreign-Born Immigrants Born in Asia	Number of Foreign-Born Immigrants Born in North or South America	Number of Other Foreign Born Immigrants	Total Number of Foreign-Born Immigrants
1850	2,031,867	1,437,475	586,240	8,152	-	1,135	168,484	43,116	2,244,602
1860	3,805,701	2,472,211	1,311,722	20,365	1,403	36,796	288,285	7,915	4,138,697
1870	4,936,618	3,124,638	1,784,449	25,853	1,678	64,565	551,335	14,711	5,567,229
1880	5,744,311	3,494,484	2,187,776	58,265	3,786	107,630	807,230	20,772	6,679,943
1890	8,020,608	4,380,752	3,420,629	206,648	12,579	113,396	1,088,245	27,311	9,249,560
1900	8,871,780	4,202,683	4,136,646	530,200	2,251	120,248	1,317,380	31,868	10,341,276
1910	11,791,841	4,239,067	6,014,028	1,525,875	12,871	191,484	1,489,231	43,330	13,515,886
1920	11,882,053	3,830,094	6,134,845	1,911,213	237,950	237,950	1,727,017	73,672	13,920,692
1930	11,748,399	3,728,050	5,897,799	2,106,295	16,255	275,665	2,102,209	77,876	14,204,149
1940	(NA)	(NA)	(NA)	(NA)	(NA)	(NA)	(NA)	(NA)	11,656,641
1950	8,286,871	(NA)	(NA)	(NA)	185,685	275,990	1,655,324	202,723	10,420,908
1960	7,233,725	1,973,025	3,717,907	1,528,473	14,320	499,312	1,860,809	144,245	9,738,091
1970	5,712,026	1,536,722	2,811,094	1,343,510	20,700	824,887	2,616,391	465,998	9,619,302
1980	6,745,550	(NA)	(NA)	(NA)	(NA)	2,539,777	5,225,914	1,164,643	14,079,906
1990	4,016,478	(NA)	(NA)	(NA)	(NA)	4,979,037	7,161,754	(NA)	19,767,316

Source: Figure for 1850–1970 adapted from *Historical Statistics of the United States Bicentennial Edition*, U.S. Bureau of the Census, 1975, Chapter C 228–295. Figures for 1980 and 1990 drawn from other tables of the U.S. Census Bureau.

Graph 1.8: Percentage of Immigrants by Region of Last Residence in Total U.S. Immigration, 1861–1890

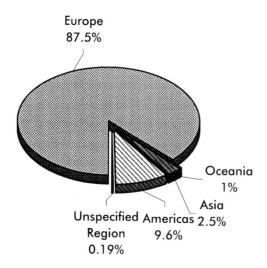

Europe
87.5%

Oceania
1%

Asia 2.5%

Unspecified Americas
Region   9.6%
0.19%

grated directly to the United States rather than first to their own growing industrial cities. Once in the United States, these people of the "new immigration" generally settled in urban industrial areas, working in a wide range of available jobs. In the final two decades of the 19th century, they included almost 1 million from Austria-Hungary, almost 1 million from Italy, and more than 1 million from Russia, including 150,000 from Poland, much of which was then part of Russia. Large numbers of the immigrants from eastern and southeastern Europe were Jews. Only small numbers of Chinese were included, as the 1882 Chinese Exclusion Act had largely cut off what had been a fast-growing emigration from China to the United States (see "Immigration Restrictions" on p. 47).

Some new immigrants were added to the United States by the stroke of a pen in 1867, when Alaska was acquired from the Russians. Though there had been Russian settlements in Alaska since 1784, their number was small. Approximately half of the Russian population returned to Russia; most of the rest stayed in Alaska, though some Russians moved south to northern California, where there were also Russian settlements. The number of Inuit and Aleuts in the region was somewhat greater, but the region was and would remain the least populated United States territory.

constituted the main mass of the immigrants; now they were also joined by substantial numbers of Canadians, Chinese, Swiss, and the beginnings of what would become the immense Italian immigration. Almost 53,000 Italian immigrants were recorded from 1871 to 1880, twice the total number of previous Italian immigrants into the United States.

In the two decades from 1881 to 1900, well over 9 million immigrants entered the United States, more than 8.9 million of them recorded and as many as several hundred thousand coming unrecorded across the Canadian border. In that number were almost 2 million immigrants from Germany in just 20 years, an average of 100,000 a year. Ireland and the United Kingdom also continued to be major immigration sources, with more than 1 million coming from each in those two decades. Scandinavia also became a major northern European source, with more than 1 million immigrants in 20 years.

At the same time, major new sources of immigration appeared, consisting largely of country and small-town people from eastern and southern Europe, who were part of fast-growing populations in countries late to begin their industrial revolutions. Many of these, like most Irish and Germans in the mid-19th century, immi-

Graph 1.9: Percentage of Foreign-Born Immigrants by Region of Birth in Total Foreign-Born Americans, 1890

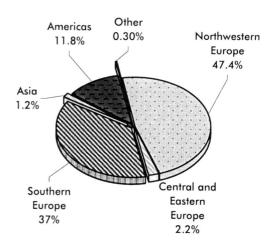

Americas
11.8%

Other
0.30%

Northwestern
Europe
47.4%

Asia
1.2%

Southern
Europe
37%

Central and
Eastern
Europe
2.2%

Graph 1.10: Percentage of Immigrants by Region of Last Residence in Total U.S. Immigration, 1891–1930

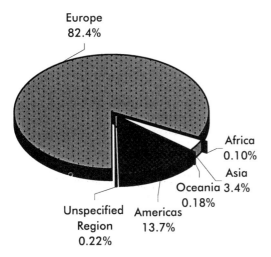

Europe
82.4%

Africa
0.10%

Asia
3.4%

Oceania
0.18%

Americas
13.7%

Unspecified Region
0.22%

Recorded immigration to the United States from other parts of North America and from the Caribbean also grew sharply, largely because of fuller tabulation by U.S. immigration authorities. Understatement continued, though, for full tabulation of land crossings did not start until 1908 and even then was inadequate.

The peak decade in U.S. immigration overall was 1901 to 1910, when almost 8.8 million immigrants arrived. The peak year within this main wave was 1907, when nearly 1.3 million immigrants were recorded. That number would not be exceeded until 1990 and 1991, when 1.5 million and 1.8 million immigrants respectively were tallied, though by then the population they were joining was far larger.

Choked off during World War I, immigration rose sharply again after 1918, with Europe and the Atlantic once more open to migration. However, it was then sharply curtailed as immigration restrictions took hold in 1921, with even more severe restrictions in 1924. Immigration to the United States from Europe greatly declined after that, totaling 1.5 million from 1921 to 1924, and only 1 million in the six years that followed, from 1925 to 1930. Immigration to the United States from elsewhere in the Americas was not affected by the restrictive new immigration laws and rose to 1.5 million in the same decade, though still with some undercounting.

More immigrants from newly acquired U.S. possessions were added to the mix after the Spanish-American War of 1898, when the United States took control of several former Spanish possessions, including Puerto Rico, the Philippines, and Guam. Puerto Rico and Hawaii became sources of internal U.S. migration, and were therefore not recorded as part of U.S. immigration. Puerto Rican immigrants would build very substantial communities in the New York metropolitan area, most notably following World War II.

Early 20th Century

From 1901 to 1914, when World War I effectively cut off most immigration to the United States from Europe, more than 13 million immigrants entered the United States. Almost 3 million of these were from northern and western Europe. But they were now overshadowed by the large numbers of immigrants from southern and eastern Europe, almost 3 million of them from Italy, 3 million from Austria-Hungary, and 2.5 million from Russia. Japanese immigration, which had started to swell at the turn of the century, was sharply cut off by the 1907 "Gentlemen's Agreement" between Japan and the United States (see "Immigration Restrictions" on p. 47).

Graph 1.11: Percentage of Foreign-Born Immigrants by Region of Birth in Total Foreign-Born Americans, 1930

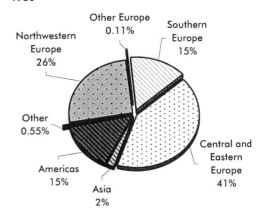

Other Europe
0.11%

Northwestern Europe
26%

Southern Europe
15%

Other
0.55%

Americas
15%

Asia
2%

Central and Eastern Europe
41%

Depression and War

With the onset of the worldwide Great Depression, immigration plummeted, as no more jobs were available in the United States than in the rest of the world. From 1931 to 1940 a total of only 528,000 immigrants entered the United States. That was the lowest total since the 1830s, and at 0.40 percent of the U.S. population the lowest rate since immigration figures had first been tabulated in the 1820s.

During World War II, immigration was even less, totaling only 151,000 from 1941 to 1945. Nor did immigration move up greatly during the postwar period, for the restrictive quotas set by the 1924 Immigration Act were still in place.

One major change did take place in 1943, when the Chinese Exclusion Acts were repealed. However, the action was more symbolic than substantial, as Chinese immigration quota was set at 105 per year.

In the years after World War II, Europe was awash with millions of refugees, including survivors of Nazi concentration camps and many who were unwilling or unable to return to their prewar homes. Among these were many people from eastern Europe who refused to accept Soviet domination of the region. In response to widespread pressure, especially from many first- and second-generation immigrants in America, the United States in 1948 passed the Displaced Persons Act, allowing more than 220,000 refugees to enter the United States. This was just the first of several such laws over the following years, often acts responding to specific international refugee crises. Later, in 1980, the U.S. Congress would finally pass the Refugee Act, establishing a general approach to dealing with refugees and asylees, instead of the previous case-by-case handling. (See "Appendix B: Immigration and Naturalization Legislation" on p. 723, for more on specific laws.)

Changes in Immigration

The great late-20th-century U.S. immigration change came with the 1965 Immigration Act, which abolished the restrictive national origins quota system set up in the 1924 Immigration Act. The new act set up a much less restrictive set of hemispheric and national quotas, and among other things established two categories that were not subject to numerical quotas at all. The first and by far most important of these categories covered the immediate relatives of U.S. citizens. It was this category that reopened the "golden door," for it allowed legal admission of hundreds of thousands of new immigrants per year, beyond the quotas.

The net effect of the 1965 Immigration Act was to allow the development of a legal immigration pattern based on the "immigrant chains." As in the past, some family members would come first as quota-allowed legal immigrants, ultimately gaining citizenship. They would then send for those of their immediate families not already legally in the United States. Later the 1990 Immigration Act, which would go into full effect in the mid-1990s, would establish a quite different pattern, setting up new maximum worldwide quotas. However, by then legal immigrants would be entering the United States at a rate of almost 1 million a year, along with large numbers of new illegal immigrants.

The post-1965 wave of immigration was quite different from previous waves, in that it drew its immigrants primarily from the Americas and Asia rather than from Europe, although substantial numbers of

Graph 1.12: Percentage of Immigrants by Region of Last Residence in Total U.S. Immigration, 1931–1960

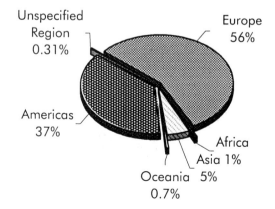

Unspecified Region 0.31%

Europe 56%

Americas 37%

Africa

Asia 1%

Oceania 5%
0.7%

Graph 1.13: Percentage of Foreign-Born Immigrants by Region of Birth in Total Foreign-Born Americans, 1960

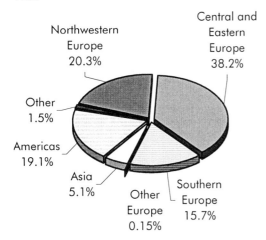

European immigrants did come from Poland and from Russia and the other countries of the former Soviet Union.

From the mid-1960s on, millions of legal immigrants arrived from south of the Rio Grande, and millions of "illegals" as well. From 1951 to 1996, some 3.5 million legal Mexican immigrants entered the United States, with at least 2.5 million illegals entering in the same period (see "Appendix C: Estimates of Emigration and Illegals" on p. 749). Not all of these illegal immigrants were Mexicans. Hundreds of thousands of immigrants had entered Mexico from the south and ultimately crossed into the United States. The U.S. government estimated that a total of 5 million "illegals" were living in the United States in 1996, 2.7 million of them from Mexico and the great majority of the rest from the Caribbean, Central America, and South America.

The great mass of these immigrants were pressed to emigrate by population increases, high unemployment rates, inflation, failed or barely existent social service networks, and widespread financial crises. For most, the United States seemed by far the best available choice. Many came directly from their rural homes. However, a good number had first tried the alternatives of flight to their own country's cities or abroad to neighboring countries. The latter course was especially the choice of emigrants fleeing war and political repres-

sion as well as economic misery, as in El Salvador, Guatemala, Cuba, Haiti, and Nicaragua.

Changing social attitudes also triggered some emigration, as people tried to escape traditional practices that could cripple their lives. Most notably, in the late 20th century some young women from Africa began to seek asylum to avoid the genital mutilation that was traditional in their cultures. Some were indeed granted asylum on those grounds, but only after long and bitter battles with the Immigration and Naturalization Service, during which they were often held in detention in camps or jails.

In the same period, millions of Asian immigrants arrived, among them more than 1 million Chinese, more than 650,000 Indians, 700,000 Koreans, and more than 1.35 million Filipinos. Very late in the 20th century, substantial immigration to the United States from Africa also began. Some Asian and African nationals emigrated to the United States to escape war and revolution at home, in Vietnam, Cambodia, Laos, or Lebanon, for instance. Others represented a kind of "brain drain," as millions of the world's best-educated and sometimes moneyed people fled to the stability and lifestyle of the United States, still by far the world's largest consumer. Other new arrivals, as from China, repre-

Graph 1.14: Percentage of Immigrants by Region of Last Residence in Total U.S. Immigration, 1961–1996

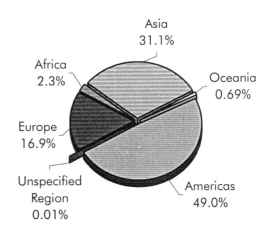

Graph 1.15: Percentage of Foreign-Born Immigrants by Region of Birth in Total Foreign-Born Americans, 1990

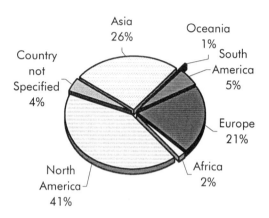

sented a continuation of immigrant chains long interrupted by U.S. immigration restrictions.

Beneath the surface fluctuations, in peace or war, the same population and economic pressures continued to build. Mexico, for example, at peace since the 1920s, had seen its population soar from 13.6 million to more than 100 million during the 20th century, an increase of 735 percent. That rate of growth proved entirely unsupportable, and despite mass deportations of illegal Mexican immigrants, millions of Mexicans continued to flood into the United States in the latter decades of the century, whether as legal or illegal immigrants.

As to the immigration to the United States from relatively affluent countries, the underlying adverse population and economic factors were in the vast majority of cases entirely the same. However, the U.S. immigration results have been so far more varied. That may be only a matter of timing; the millions of well-educated, often middle-class Indians, Iranians, Nigerians, Koreans, and others arriving in the early 21st century will also be trying to bring their families and extended families into the United States, no matter what the current immigration laws may be. The many immigrants and their families will exert increasing and quite possibly successful political pressure to make that possible, so continuing the old pattern of immigration chains into the United States.

At the turn of the 21st century, humanity numbered at least 6 billion people, and estimates indicated that this figure would double to at least 12 billion no later than midway into the 21st century. During the 1990s, the United States experienced strong economic growth, accompanied by low unemployment and a stock market boom, and was largely able to absorb its new wave of immigrants. However, there is no possibility at all that the United States will long be able to absorb anything remotely like the flood of immigrants being generated by the world's population pressures and its decreasing ability to handle the needs even of existing populations, much less the numbers that are expected. Clearly, any workable U.S. immigration policy must be part of a sustained global campaign to successfully address the world's massive population and related economic problems.

Note: For more on overall immigration, including year-by-year figures for selected countries, see "Annual Immigration Statistics" on p. 657; "General Notes on Immigration Statistics" on p. 684; and "General European Immigration Resources" on p. 317. See also chapters on specific countries that were major sources of immigration.

Graph 1.16: Percentage of Immigrants Admitted to the United States by Region of Birth in Total U.S. Immigration, 1986–1996

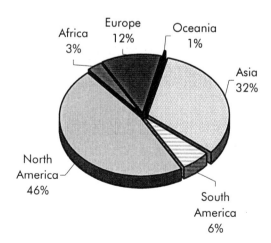

Statistical Overview

Table 1.6: Number and Percentage of Immigrants Arriving per Decade in Total U.S. Immigration by Decade, 1820–1996

Decade	Number of Immigrants to the U.S.	Percentage of New Immigrants per Decade in Total U.S. Immigration
1820	8,385	0.01
1821-1830	143,439	0.23
1831-1840	599,125	0.95
1841-1850	1,713,251	2.71
1851-1860	2,598,214	4.11
1861-1870	2,314,824	3.67
1871-1880	2,812,191	4.45
1881-1890	5,246,613	8.31
1891-1900	3,687,564	5.84
1901-1910	8,795,386	13.93
1911-1920	5,735,811	9.08
1921-1930	4,107,209	6.50
1931-1940	528,431	0.84
1941-1950	1,035,039	1.64
1951-1960	2,515,479	3.98
1961-1970	3,321,677	5.26
1971-1980	4,493,314	7.12
1981-1990	7,338,062	11.62
1991-1996	6,146,213	9.73
Total 1820-1996	63,140,227	100

Source: Adapted from the *Statistical Yearbook of the Immigration and Naturalization Service*, 1996, Table 2.

Table 1.7: Number and Percentage of Foreign-Born Immigrants in the United States by Decade in Total U.S. Immigration at End of Decade, 1850–1990

Decade	Number of Foreign-Born Immigrants in the United States	Total U.S. Population	Percentage of Foreign-Born Immigrants in the United States in Total U.S. Population
1850	2,244,602	23,191,876	9.7
1860	4,138,697	31,443,321	13.2
1870	5,567,229	39,818,449	14.0
1880	6,679,943	50,155,783	13.3
1890	9,249,560	62,947,714	14.7
1900	10,341,276	75,994,575	13.6
1910	13,515,886	91,972,266	14.7
1920	13,920,692	105,710,620	13.2
1930	14,204,149	122,775,046	11.6
1940	11,656,641	131,669,275	8.9
1950	10,420,908	150,697,361	6.9
1960	9,738,091	179,323,175	5.4
1970	9,619,302	203,235,298	4.7
1980	14,079,906	227,726,000	6.2
1990	19,767,316	249,907,000	7.9

Source: Figures for 1850–1970 adapted from *Historical Statistics of the United States Bicentennial Edition*, U.S. Bureau of the Census, 1975, Chapter C 228–295. Figures for 1990 drawn from other tables of the U.S. Census Bureau.

Table 1.8: Number of Immigrants Admitted to the United States by Region of Birth Annually, 1986–1996

Year	Number of Immigrants from Europe	Number of Immigrants from Asia	Number of Immigrants from Africa	Number of Immigrants from Oceania	Number of Immigrants from North America	Number of Immigrants from South America	Total Number of Immigrants Admitted to the United States
1986	62,512	268,248	17,463	3,894	207,714	41,874	601,705
1987	61,174	257,684	17,724	3,993	216,550	44,385	601,510
1988	64,797	264,465	18,882	3,839	250,009	41,007	642,999
1989	82,891	312,149	25,166	4,360	607,398	58,926	1,090,890
1990	112,401	338,581	35,893	6,182	957,558	85,819	1,536,434
1991	135,234	358,533	36,179	6,236	1,210,981	79,934	1,827,097
1992	145,392	356,955	27,086	5,169	384,047	55,308	973,957
1993	158,254	358,047	27,783	4,902	301,380	53,921	904,287
1994	160,916	292,589	26,712	4,592	272,226	47,377	804,412
1995	128,185	267,931	42,456	4,695	231,526	45,666	720,459
1996	147,581	307,807	52,889	5,309	340,540	61,769	915,895
Total 1986-1996	1,259,337	3,382,989	328,233	53,171	4,979,929	615986	10,619,645

Source: Adapted from the *Statistical Yearbook of the Immigration and Naturalization Service, 1996*, Table 3.

Graph 1.17: Number of Foreign-Born Immigrants in Total U.S. Population by Decade, 1850–1990

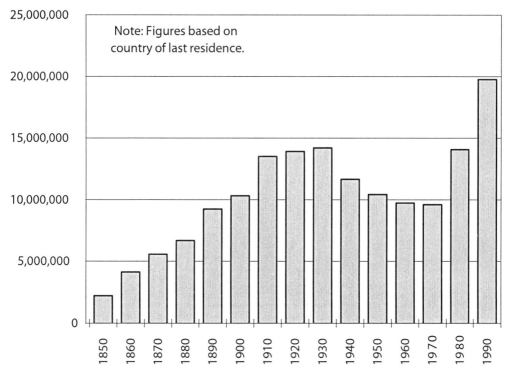

Graph 1.18: Percentage of Immigrants Arriving per Decade in Total U.S. Immigration by Decade, 1820–1996

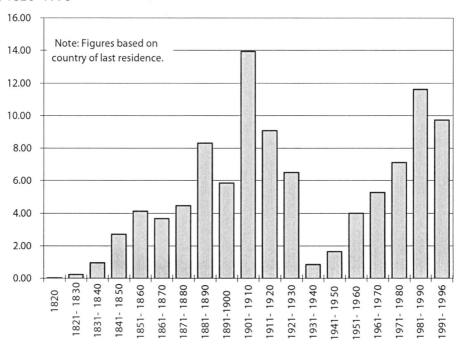

Graph 1.19: Number of Immigrants Arriving per Decade, 1820–1996

Graph 1.20: Percentage of Refugees and Asylees Granted Lawful Permanent Resident Status by Region in Total Refugees and Asylees Granted Status, 1946–1996

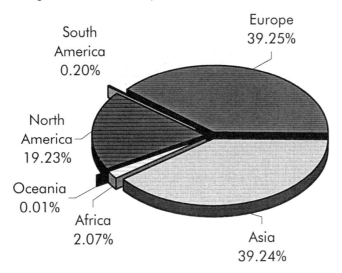

Note: Figures based on country of birth.

South
America
0.20%

Europe
39.25%

North
America
19.23%

Oceania
0.01%

Africa
2.07%

Asia
39.24%

Graph 1.21: Number of Foreign-Born Immigrants in the United States by Decade in Total U.S. Population at End of Decade, 1850–1990

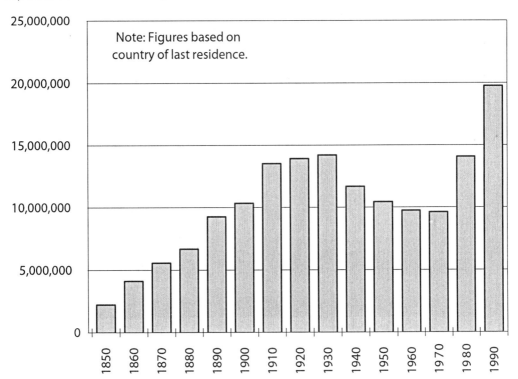

Note: Figures based on country of last residence.

Table 1.9: Number of Immigrants to the United States by Region and Selected Country of Last Residence by Decade, 1820–1996

Region and country of last residence (1): 1820-90	1820	1821-30	1831-40	1841-50	1851-60	1861-70	1871-80	1881-90
All countries	**8,385**	**143,439**	**599,125**	**1,713,251**	**2,598,214**	**2,314,824**	**2,812,191**	**5,246,613**
Europe	**7,690**	**98,797**	**495,681**	**1,597,442**	**2,452,577**	**2,065,141**	**2,271,925**	**4,735,484**
Austria-Hungary	(2)	(2)	(2)	(2)	(2)	(2)	7,800	353,719
Austria	(2)	(2)	(2)	(2)	(2)	(3) 7,124	72,969	226,039
Hungary	(2)	(2)	(2)	(2)	(2)	(3) 484	63,009	127,681
Belgium	1	27	22	5,074	4,738	6,734	7,221	20,177
Czechoslovakia	(4)	(4)	(4)	(4)	(4)	(4)	(4)	(4)
Denmark	20	169	1,063	539	3,749	17,094	31,771	88,132
France	371	8,497	45,575	77,262	76,358	35,986	72,206	50,464
Germany	968	6,761	152,454	434,626	951,667	797,468	718,182	1,452,970
Greece		20	49	16	31	72	210	2,308
Ireland (5)	3,614	50,724	207,381	780,719	914,119	435,778	436,871	655,482
Italy	30	409	2,253	1,870	9,231	11,725	55,759	307,309
Netherlands	49	1,078	1,412	8,251	10,789	9,102	16,541	53,701
Norway-Sweden	3	91	1,201	13,903	20,931	109,298	211,245	568,362
Norway	(6)	(6)	(6)	(6)	(6)	(6)	95,323	176,586
Sweden	(6)	(6)	(6)	(6)	(6)	(6)	115,922	391,776
Poland	5	16	369	105	1,164	2,027	12,970	51,806
Portugal	35	145	829	550	1,055	2,658	14,082	16,978
Romania	(7)	(7)	(7)	(7)	(7)	(7)	(7) 11	6,348
Soviet Union	14	75	277	551	457	2,512	39,284	213,282
Spain	139	2,477	2,125	2,209	9,298	6,697	5,266	4,419
Switzerland	31	3,226	4,821	4,644	25,011	23,286	28,293	81,988
United Kingdom (5) (8)	2,410	25,079	75,810	267,044	423,974	606,896	548,043	807,357
Yugoslavia	(9)	(9)	(9)	(9)	(9)	(9)	(9)	(9)
Other Europe	3	3	40	79	5	8	1,001	682
Asia	**6**	**30**	**55**	**141**	**41,538**	**64,759**	**124,160**	**69,942**
China (10)	1	2	8	35	41,397	64,301	123,201	61,711
Hong Kong	(11)	(11)	(11)	(11)	(11)	(11)	(11)	(11)
India	1	8	39	36	43	69	163	269
Iran	(12)	(12)	(12)	(12)	(12)	(12)	(12)	(12)
Israel	(13)	(13)	(13)	(13)	(13)	(13)	(13)	(13)
Japan	(14)	(14)	(14)	(14)	(14)	186	149	2,270
Korea	(15)	(15)	(15)	(15)	(15)	(15)	(15)	(15)
Philippines	(16)	(16)	(16)	(16)	(16)	(16)	(16)	(16)
Turkey	1	20	7	59	83	131	404	3,782
Vietnam	(11)	(11)	(11)	(11)	(11)	(11)	(11)	(11)
Other Asia	3		1	11	15	72	243	1,910

Region and country of last residence (1): 1820–90

	1820	1821-30	1831-40	1841-50	1851-60	1861-70	1871-80	1881-90
North America	**387**	**11,564**	**33,424**	**62,469**	**74,720**	**166,607**	**404,044**	**426,967**
Canada & Newfoundland (17) (18)	209	2,277	13,624	41,723	59,309	153,878	383,640	393,304
Mexico (18)	1	4,817	6,599	3,271	3,078	2,191	5,162	(19) 1,913
Caribbean	**164**	**3,834**	**12,301**	**13,528**	**10,660**	**9,046**	**13,957**	**29,042**
Cuba	(12)	(12)	(12)	(12)	(12)	(12)	(12)	(12)
Dominican Republic	(20)	(20)	(20)	(20)	(20)	(20)	(20)	(20)
Haiti	(20)	(20)	(20)	(20)	(20)	(20)	(20)	(20)
Jamaica	(21)	(21)	(21)	(21)	(21)	(21)	(21)	(21)
Other Caribbean	164	3,834	12,301	13,528	10,660	9,046	13,957	29,042
Central America	**2**	**105**	**44**	**368**	**449**	**95**	**157**	**404**
El Salvador	(20)	(20)	(20)	(20)	(20)	(20)	(20)	(20)
Other Central America	2	105	44	368	449	95	157	404
South America	**11**	**531**	**856**	**3,579**	**1,224**	**1,397**	**1,128**	**2,304**
Argentina	(20)	(20)	(20)	(20)	(20)	(20)	(20)	(20)
Colombia	(20)	(20)	(20)	(20)	(20)	(20)	(20)	(20)
Ecuador	(20)	(20)	(20)	(20)	(20)	(20)	(20)	(20)
Other South America	11	531	856	3,579	1,224	1,397	1,128	2,304
Other America	(22)	(22)	(22)	(22)	(22)	(22)	(22)	(22)
Africa	**1**	**16**	**54**	**55**	**210**	**312**	**358**	**857**
Oceania	**1**	**2**	**9**	**29**	**158**	**214**	**10,914**	**12,574**
Not specified (22)	300	33,030	69,902	53,115	29,011	17,791	790	789

(1) Data for years prior to 1906 relate to country whence alien came; data from 1906–79 refer to country of last permanent residence; and data for 1980–93 refer to country of birth. Because of changes in boundaries, changes in lists of countries, and lack of data for specified countries for various periods, data for certain countries, especially for the total period 1820–1996, are not comparable throughout. Data for specified countries are included with countries to which they belonged prior to World War I.
(2) Data for Austria and Hungary not reported until 1861.
(3) Data for Austria and Hungary not reported separately for all years during the period.
(4) No data for Czechoslovakia until 1920.
(5) Prior to 1926, data for Northern Ireland included in Ireland.
(6) Data for Norway and Sweden not reported separately until 1871.
(7) No data available for Romania until 1880.
(8) Since 1925, data for United Kingdom refer to England, Scotland, Wales, and Northern Ireland.
(9) In 1920, a separate enumeration was made for the Kingdom of Serbs, Croats, and Slovenes. Since 1922, the Serb, Croat, and Slovene Kingdom recorded as Yugoslavia.
(10) Beginning in 1957, China includes Taiwan. As of January 1, 1979, the United States has recognized the People's Republic of China.
(11) Data not reported separately until 1952.
(12) Data not reported separately until 1925.

Table 1.9 Continued

Region and country of last residence (1): 1891–1970	1891-1900	1901-10	1911-20	1921-30	1931-40	1941-50	1951-60	1961-70
All countries	**3,687,564**	**8,795,386**	**5,735,811**	**4,107,209**	**528,431**	**1,035,039**	**2,515,479**	**3,321,677**
Europe	**3,555,352**	**8,056,040**	**4,321,887**	**2,463,194**	**347,566**	**621,147**	**1,325,727**	**1,123,492**
Austria-Hungary	(23) 592,707	(23) 2,145,266	(23) 896,432	63,548	11,424	28,329	103,743	26,022
Austria	(3) 234,081	(3) 668,209	453,649	32,868	(24) 3,563	(24) 24,860	67,106	20,621
Hungary	(3) 181,288	(3) 808,511	442,693	30,680	7,861	3,469	36,637	5,401
Belgium	18,167	41,635	33,746	15,846	4,817	12,189	18,575	9,192
Czechoslovakia	(4)	(4)	(4) 3,426	102,194	14,393	8,347	918	3,273
Denmark	50,231	65,285	41,983	32,430	2,559	5,393	10,984	9,201
France	30,770	73,379	61,897	49,610	12,623	38,809	51,121	45,237
Germany	(23) 505,152	(23) 341,498	(23) 143,945	412,202	(24) 114,058	(24) 226,578	477,765	190,796
Greece	15,979	167,519	184,201	51,084	9,119	8,973	47,608	85,969
Ireland (5)	388,416	339,065	146,181	211,234	10,973	19,789	48,362	32,966
Italy	651,893	2,045,877	1,109,524	455,315	68,028	57,661	185,491	214,111
Netherlands	26,758	48,262	43,718	26,948	7,150	14,860	52,277	30,606
Norway-Sweden	321,281	440,039	161,469	165,780	8,700	20,765	44,632	32,600
Norway	95,015	190,505	66,395	68,531	4,740	10,100	22,935	15,484
Sweden	226,266	249,534	95,074	97,249	3,960	10,665	21,697	17,116
Poland	(23) 96,720	(23)	(23) 4,813	227,734	17,026	7,571	9,985	53,539
Portugal	27,508	69,149	89,732	29,994	3,329	7,423	19,588	76,065
Romania	12,750	53,008	13,311	67,646	3,871	1,076	1,039	2,531
Soviet Union	(23) 505,290	(23) 1,597,306	(23) 921,201	61,742	1,370	571	671	2,465
Spain	8,731	27,935	68,611	28,958	3,258	2,898	7,894	44,659
Switzerland	31,179	34,922	23,091	29,676	5,512	10,547	17,675	18,453
United Kingdom (5) (8)	271,538	525,950	341,408	339,570	31,572	139,306	202,824	213,822
Yugoslavia	(9)	(9)	(9) 1,888	49,064	5,835	1,576	8,225	20,381
Other Europe	282	39,945	31,400	42,619	11,949	8,486	16,350	11,604
Asia	**74,862**	**323,543**	**247,236**	**112,059**	**16,595**	**37,028**	**153,249**	**427,642**
China (10)	14,799	20,605	21,278	29,907	4,928	16,709	9,657	34,764
Hong Kong	(11)	(11)	(11)		(11)	(11)	(11) 15,541	75,007
India	68	4,713	2,082	1,886	496	1,761	1,973	27,189
Iran	(12)	(12)	(12)	(12) 241	195	1,380	3,388	10,339
Israel	(13)	(13)	(13)	(13)	(13)	(13) 476	25,476	29,602
Japan	25,942	129,797	83,837	33,462	1,948	1,555	46,250	39,988
Korea	(15)	(15)	(15)	(15)	(15)	(15) 107	6,231	34,526
Philippines	(16)	(16)	(16)	(16)	(16) 528	4,691	19,307	98,376
Turkey	30,425	157,369	134,066	33,824	1,065	798	3,519	10,142
Vietnam	(11)	(11)	(11)	(11)	(11)	(11)	(11) 335	4,340
Other Asia	3,628	11,059	5,973	12,739	7,435	9,551	21,572	63,369

Region and country of last residence (1): 1891-1970

	1891-1900	1901-10	1911-20	1921-30	1931-40	1941-50	1951-60	1961-70
North America	38,972	361,888	1,143,671	1,516,716	160,037	354,804	996,944	1,716,374
Canada & Newfoundland (17)(18)	3,311	179,226	742,185	924,515	108,527	171,718	377,952	413,310
Mexico (18)	1	4,817	6,599	3,271	3,078	2,191	5,162	(19) 1,913
Caribbean	33,066	107,548	123,424	74,899	15,502	49,725	1,325,727	1,123,492
Cuba	(12)	(12)	(12)	(12) 15,901	9,571	26,313	78,948	208,536
Dominican Republic	(20)	(20)	(20)	(20)	(20) 1,150	5,627	9,897	93,292
Haiti	(20)	(20)	(20)	(20)	(20) 191	911	4,442	34,499
Jamaica	(21)	(21)	(21)	(21)	(21)	(21)	(21) 8,869	74,906
Other Caribbean	33,066	107,548	123,424	58,998	4,590	16,874	(21) 20,935	58,980
Central America	549	8,192	17,159	15,769	5,861	21,665	44,751	101,330
El Salvador	(20)	(20)	(20)	(20)	(20) 673	5,132	5,895	14,992
Other Central America	549	8,192	17,159	15,769	5,188	16,533	38,856	86,338
South America	1,075	17,280	41,899	42,215	7,803	21,831	91,628	257,940
Argentina	(20)	(20)	(20)	(20)	(20) 1,349	3,338	19,486	49,721
Colombia	(20)	(20)	(20)	(20)	(20) 1,223	3,858	18,048	72,028
Ecuador	(20)	(20)	(20)	(20)	(20) 337	9,841	9,841	36,780
Other South America	1,075	17,280	41,899	42,215	4,894	12,218	44,253	99,411
Other America	(22)	(22)	(22)	(22) 31	25	29,276	59,711	19,644
Africa	350	7,368	8,443	6,286	1,750	7,367	14,092	28,954
Oceania	3,965	13,024	13,427	8,726	2,483	14,551	12,976	25,122
Not specified (22)	14,063	(25) 33,523	1,147	228	—	142	12,491	93

(13) Data not reported separately until 1949.
(14) No data available for Japan until 1861.
(15) Data not reported separately until 1861.
(16) Prior to 1934, Philippines recorded as insular travel.
(17) Prior to 1920, Canada and Newfoundland recorded as British North America until 1948.
(18) Land arrivals not completely enumerated until 1948.
(19) No data available for Mexico from 1886–1894.
(20) Data not reported separately until 1932.
(21) Data for Jamaica not collected until 1953. In prior years, consolidated under British West Indies, which is included in "Other Caribbean."
(22) Included in countries "Not Specified" until 1925.
(23) From 1899–1919, data for Poland included in Austria-Hungary, Germany, and the Soviet Union.
(24) From 1938–45, data for Austria included in Germany.
(25) Includes 32,897 persons returning in 1906 to their homes in the United States.

NOTE: From 1820–67, figures represent alien passengers arrived at seaports; from 1868–91 and 1895–97, immigrant aliens arrived; from 1892–94 and 1898–1996, immigrant aliens admitted for permanent residence. From 1892–1903, aliens entering by cabin class were not counted as immigrants. Land arrivals were not completely enumerated until 1908.

See Glossary for fiscal year definitions. For this table, fiscal year 1843 covers 9 months ending September 1843; fiscal years 1832 and 1850 cover 15 months ending December 31 of the respective years; and fiscal year 1868 covers 6 months ending June 30, 1868.

Table 1.9 Continued

Region and country of last residence (1): 1971-96	1971-80	1981-90	1991-92	1993	1994	1995	1996	Total 177 years 1820-1996
All countries	4,493,314	7,338,062	2,801,144	904,292	804,416	720,461	915,900	63,140,227
Europe	800,368	761,550	299,931	165,711	166,279	132,914	151,898	38,017,793
Austria-Hungary	16,028	24,885	8,389	2,914	2,123	2,190	2,325	4,360,723
Austria	9,478	18,340	6,406	1,880	1,314	1,340	1,182	(3) 1,841,068
Hungary	6,550	6,545	1,983	1,034	809	850	1,143	(3) 1,673,579
Belgium	5,329	7,066	1,658	776	621	694	802	215,107
Czechoslovakia	6,023	7,227	1,499	792	759	1,057	1,299	151,207
Denmark	4,439	5,370	1,398	762	639	588	795	374,594
France	25,069	32,353	8,470	3,959	3,592	3,178	3,896	810,682
Germany	74,414	91,961	23,762	9,965	8,940	7,896	8,365	7,142,393
Greece	92,369	38,377	5,097	2,460	2,539	2,404	2,394	718,799
Ireland (5)	11,490	31,969	16,643	13,396	16,525	4,851	1,611	4,778,159
Italy	129,368	67,254	42,278	3,899	2,664	2,594	2,755	5,427,298
Netherlands	10,492	12,238	2,990	1,542	1,359	1,284	1,553	382,960
Norway-Sweden	10,472	15,182	4,092	2,253	1,804	1,607	2,015	2,157,725
Norway	3,941	4,164	1,344	713	515	465	552	(6) 804,813
Sweden	6,531	11,018	2,748	1,540	1,289	1,142	1,463	(6) 1,292,657
Poland	37,234	83,252	41,597	27,288	27,597	13,570	15,504	731,892
Portugal	101,710	40,431	7,350	2,075	2,163	2,611	3,024	518,484
Romania	12,393	30,857	11,693	4,517	2,932	4,565	5,449	233,997
Soviet Union	38,961	57,677	68,626	59,949	64,502	54,133	61,895	3,752,811
Spain	39,141	20,433	4,704	1,791	1,756	1,664	1,970	297,033
Switzerland	8,235	8,849	2,306	1,263	1,183	1,119	1,344	366,654
United Kingdom (5) (8)	137,374	14,667	38,692	20,422	17,666	14,207	15,564	5,225,701
Yugoslavia	30,540	18,762	5,543	2,781	3,183	7,828	10,755	166,361
Other Europe	9,287	8,234	3,144	2,907	3,732	4,874	8,583	205,214
Asia	1,588,178	2,738,157	686,959	345,425	282,449	259,984	300,574	7,894,571
China (10)	124,326	346,747	53,549	57,775	58,867	41,112	50,981	1,176,660
Hong Kong	113,467	98,215	32,697	14,026	11,953	10,699	11,319	(11) 382,924
India	164,134	250,786	77,548	38,653	33,173	33,060	42,819	680,969
Iran	45,136	116,172	16,922	8,908	6,998	5,646	7,299	(12) 222,624
Israel	37,713	44,273	11,054	5,216	3,982	3,188	4,029	(13) 165,009
Japan	49,775	47,085	17,335	7,673	6,974	5,556	6,617	(14) 506,399
Korea	267,638	333,746	44,164	17,320	15,417	15,053	17,380	(15) 751,582
Philippines	354,987	548,764	132,228	63,406	52,832	49,696	54,588	(16) 1,379,403
Turkey	13,399	23,233	6,669	3,487	3,880	4,806	5,573	436,742
Vietnam	172,820	280,782	46,019	31,894	32,387	37,764	39,922	(11) 646,263
Other Asia	244,783	648,354	248,774	97,067	55,986	53,404	60,047	1,545,996

Region and country of last residence (1): 1971-96	1971-80	1981-90	1991-92	1993	1994	1995	1996	Total 177 years 1820-1996
North America	1,982,735	3,615,225	1,742,774	361,476	325,173	282,270	407,813	16,187,054
Canada & Newfoundland (17) (18)	169,939	156,938	41,472	23,898	22,243	18,117	21,751	4,423,066
Mexico (18)	640,294	1,655,943	1,162,051	126,642	111,415	90,045	163,743	5,542,625
Caribbean	741,126	872,051	234,536	98,185	103,750	96,021	115,991	3,351,660
Cuba	264,863	144,578	20,364	12,976	14,216	17,661	26,166	(12) 840,093
Dominican Republic	148,135	252,035	83,370	45,464	51,221	38,493	36,284	(20) 764,968
Haiti	56,335	138,379	57,802	9,899	13,166	13,872	18,185	(20) 347,681
Jamaica	137,577	208,148	41,257	16,761	13,909	16,061	18,732	(21) 536,220
Other Caribbean	134,216	128,911	31,743	13,085	11,238	9,934	16,624	862,698
Central America	134,640	468,088	168,669	58,666	40,256	32,020	44,336	1,163,575
El Salvador	34,436	213,539	73,000	26,794	17,669	11,670	17,847	(20) 421,647
Other Central America	100,204	254,549	95,669	31,872	22,587	20,350	26,489	741,928
South America	295,741	461,847	136,033	54,077	47,505	46,063	61,990	1,595,971
Argentina	29,897	27,327	8,314	2,972	2,474	2,239	2,878	(20) 149,995
Colombia	77,347	122,849	32,157	12,597	10,653	10,641	14,078	(20) 375,479
Ecuador	50,077	56,315	17,284	7,400	5,943	6,453	89348	(20) 201,195
Other South America	138,420	255,356	78,278	31,108	28,435	26,730	36,686	869,302
Other America	995	458	13	8	4	4	2	110,157
Africa	80,779	176,893	58,249	25,532	24,864	39,818	49,605	532,213
Oceania	41,242	45,205	13,055	6,144	5,647	5,472	6,008	240,948
Not specified (22)	12	1,032	176	4	4	3	2	267,648

(-) Represents zero.

Source: *Statistical Yearbook of the Immigration and Naturalization Service,* 1996, Table 3.

Authors' Note: Totals given for individual countries in some cases do not match the actual sum of the figures given by decade or year. Where the two disagree we have, in country-by-country tables in this book, used the actual sum by adding the figures given by decade or year rather than the country's total given in the table.

Table 1.10: Foreign-Born Population of the United States by Country of Birth by Decade, 1850–1970

Country of Birth	1850	1860	1870	1880	1890	1900	1910	1920	(15)1930	(3)1950	(2)1960	(1)1970
All countries	2,244,602	4,138,697	5,567,229	6,679,943	9,249,560	10,341,276	13,515,886	13,920,692	14,204,149	10,420,908	9,738,091	9,619,302
Northwestern Europe	1,437,475	2,472,211	3,124,638	3,494,484	4,380,752	4,202,683	4,239,067	3,830,094	3,728,050	(NA)	1,973,025	1,536,722
England	278,675	433,494	555,046	664,160	909,092	840,513	877,719	813,853	809,563	846,570	528,205	458,114
Scotland	70,550	108,518	140,835	170,136	242,231	233,524	261,076	254,570	354,323		213,219	170,134
Wales	29,868	45,763	74,533	83,302	100,079	93,586	82,488	67,066	60,205		23,469	17,014
Northern Ireland									178,832		68,162	40,837
Ireland (Eire)	961,719	1,611,304	1,855,827	1,854,571	1,871,509	1,615,459	1,352,251	1,037,234	744,810	505,285	338,722	251,375
Norway	12,678	43,995	114,246	181,729	322,665	336,388	403,877	363,863	347,852	202,448	152,698	97,243
Sweden	3,559	18,625	97,332	194,337	478,041	582,014	665,207	625,585	595,250	325,118	214,491	127,070
Denmark	1,838	9,962	30,107	64,196	132,543	153,690	181,649	189,154	179,474	107,982	85,060	61,410
Iceland									2,764		2,780	2,895
Netherlands	9,848	28,281	46,802	58,090	81,828	94,931	120,063	131,766	133,133	102,224	118,415	110,570
Belgium	1,313	9,072	12,553	15,535	22,639	29,757	49,400	62,687	64,194	(NA)	50,294	41,412
Luxembourg			5,802	12,836	2,882	3,031	3,071	12,585	9,048	(NA)	4,360	3,531
Switzerland	13,358	53,327	75,153	88,621	104,069	115,593	124,848	118,659	113,010	71,636	61,568	49,732
France	54,069	109,870	116,402	106,971	113,174	104,197	117,418	153,072	135,592	108,547	111,582	105,385
Central and Eastern Europe	586,240	1,311,722	1,784,449	2,187,776	3,420,629	4,136,646	6,014,028	6,134,845	5,897,799	(NA)	3,717,907	2,811,094
Germany	583,774	1,276,075	1,690,533	1,966,742	2,784,894	(5)2,663,418	2,311,237	1,686,108	1,608,814	991,321	989,815	832,965
Poland			7,298	48,557	147,440	383,407	(5)937,884	1,139,979	1,268,583	861,655	747,750	548,107
Czechoslovakia								362,438	491,638	278,438	227,618	160,899
Austria	946	25,061	70,797	124,024	241,377	432,798	(5)845,555	575,627	370,914	409,043	304,507	214,014
Hungary			3,737	11,526	62,435	145,714	495,609	397,283	274,450	268,183	245,252	183,236
Yugoslavia								169,439	211,416	144,070	165,798	153,745
Russia/U.S.S.R.	1,414	3,160	4,644	35,722	182,644	(5)423,726	(5)1,184,412	1,400,495	1,153,628	896,000	(6)690,598	(6)463,462
Latvia									20,673		50,681	41,707
Estonia									3,550		13,991	12,163
Lithuania								135,068	193,606	147,872	121,475	76,001
Finland						62,641	129,680	149,824	142,478	95,686	67,624	45,499
Romania									146,393	85,230	84,575	70,687
Bulgaria									9,399	(NA)	8,223	8,609
Turkey in Europe	(7)106	(7)128	(7)302	(7)1205	(7)1,839	(7)9,910	(8)32,230	5,284	2,257	(7)	(7)	(7)
Southern Europe	8,152	20,365	25,853	58,265	206,648	530,200	1,525,875	1,911,213	2,106,295	(NA)	1,528,473	1,343,510
Greece	86	328	390	776	1,887	8,515	(8)101,282	175,976	174,526	169,335	159,167	177,275
Albania							(8)	5,608	8,814	9,618	9,180	
Italy	3,679	11,677	17,157	44,230	182,580	484,027	1,343,125	1,610,113	1,790,429	1,427,952	1,256,999	1,008,533
Spain	3,113	4,244	3,764	5,121	6,185	7,050	22,108	49,535	59,362	(NA)	44,999	57,488
Portugal	1,274	4,116	4,542	8,138	15,996	30,608	59,360	69,981	73,164	56,591	57,690	91,034
Other Europe		1,403	1,678	3,786	12,579	2,251	12,871	5,901	16,255	(9)185,685	14,320	20,700
Danzig								2,049	1,483			
Europe, not specified		1,403	1,678	3,786	12,579	2,251	(10)12,871	3,852	14,772			

Country of Birth	1850	1860	1870	1880	1890	1900	1910	1920	(15) 1930	(3) 1950	(2) 1960	(1) 1970
Asia	1,135	36,796	64,565	107,630	113,396	120,248	191,484	237,950	275,665	(7) 275,990	(7) 499,312	(7) 824,887
Armenia	-	-	-	-	-	-	-	36,628	32,166	(NA)	(6)	(6)
Palestine	-	-	-	-	-	-	-	3,203	6,137	(NA)	(11)	(11)
Syria	-	-	-	-	-	-	59,729	51,901	57,227	(NA)	16,717	14,962
Turkey in Asia	(7)	(7)	(7)	(7)	(7)	(7)	(7)	11,019	46,654	(NA)	(7) 52,228	(7) 48,085
China	758	35,565	63,042	104,468	106,701	81,534	56,756	43,560	46,129	(NA)	99,735	172,132
Japan	-	-	73	401	2,292	24,788	67,744	81,502	70,993	(NA)	109,175	120,235
India	-	-	586	1,707	2,143	2,031	4,664	4,901	5,850	(NA)	12,296	51,000
Korea	-	-	-	-	-	-	-	-	-	(NA)	11,171	38,711
Philippines	-	-	-	-	-	-	-	-	-	(NA)	104,843	184,842
Other Asia	377	1,231	864	1,054	2,260	11,895	2,591	5,236	10,509	(NA)	(11) 93,147	(11) 194,920
America	168,484	288,285	551,335	807,230	1,088,245	1,317,380	1,489,231	1,727,017	(9) 2,102,209	(9) 1,655,324	1,860,809	2,616,391
Canada-French	147,711	249,970	493,464	717,157	(12) 302,496	(12) 395,126	385,083	307,786	370,852	1,003,038	952,500	812,421
Canada-Other	-	-	-	-	(12) 678,442	(12) 784,796	819,554	817,139	915,537	(NA)	-	-
Newfoundland	-	-	-	-	(12)	(12)	5,080	13,249	23,980	(NA)	-	-
Cuba	5,772	7,353	5,319	6,917	23,256	11,081	15,133	14,872	18,493	(NA)	79,150	439,048
Other West Indies	-	-	6,251	9,484	-	14,354	32,502	64,090	87,748	(NA)	(13) 114,772	(13) 34,513
Mexico	13,317	27,466	42,435	68,399	77,853	103,393	221,915	486,418	641,462	454,417	575,902	759,711
Central America	141	233	301	707	1,192	3,897	1,736	4,912	10,514	(NA)	48,949	315,460
South America	1,543	3,263	3,565	4,566	5,006	4,733	8,228	18,551	33,623	(NA)	89,536	255,238
All other	43,116	7,915	14,711	20,772	27,311	31,868	43,330	73,672	77,876	(9) 202,723	144,245	465,998
Africa	551	526	2,657	2,204	2,207	2,538	3,992	5,781	8,859	(NA)	18,737	61,463
Australia	-	1,419	3,118	4,906	5,984	6,807	9,035	10,914	12,816	(NA)	22,209	24,271
Azores	-	1,361	4,434	7,641	9,739	9,768	18,274	33,995	35,611	(NA)	22,586	28,865
Other Atlantic Islands	588	721	910	1,953	3,369	2,013	2,415	10,345	9,467	(NA)	8,302	18,680
Pacific Islands	-	-	954	-	479	2,546	2,687	3,712	4,527	(NA)	(14) 12,521	(14) 8,680
Country not specified	41,977	1,366	2,638	4,068	5,533	8,196	6,927	3,589	1,588	89,691	59,890	323,849
Born at sea	-	2,522	-	-	-	-	-	5,336	5,008	-	-	-

NA = Not available

(-) Represents zero.

(1) Based on 15-percent sample.
(2) Based on 25-percent sample.
(3) Based on complete count.
(4) Listed as Holland prior to 1910.
(5) Persons reported in 1910 as of Polish mother tongue born in Austria, Germany, and U.S.S.R. have been deducted from their respective countries and combined as Poland.
(6) Armenia included with "Other Asia" for 1920–1950; included with U.S.S.R. beginning 1960.
(7) Turkey in Asia included with Turkey in Europe; 1930 and 1940, with "Other Europe."
(8) Albania included with Turkey in Europe; 1930 and 1940, with "Other Europe."
(9) Included countries for which figures are not shown separately.
(10) Includes persons born in Serbia and Montenegro, which became part of Yugoslavia in 1918.
(11) Palestine included with "Other Asia."
(12) Newfoundland included with Canada prior to 1910.
(13) Excludes U.S. outlying areas.
(14) Includes New Zealand and Trust Territories of the Pacific Islands, but excludes outlying areas of the U.S.
(15) There were 11,656,641 total foreign-born persons in 1940; data by country of birth are not available.

Note: Data are given for each country for all census years since 1850 for which figures are available. For information on the statistics used for this table, see General Notes on Immigration Statistics, under "Foreign-Born Population, by Country of Birth, 1850–1970."

Source: *Historical Statistics of the United States Bicentennial Edition*, U.S. Bureau of the Census, 1975, Chapter C 228–295.

Table 1.11: Foreign-Born Population of the United States by Country of Birth by Decade, 1980 and 1990

Country of Birth	1980	1990
All countries	14,079,906	19,767,316
Europe	6,745,550	4,016,478
England, Scotland, Wales, and Northern Ireland	669,149	640,145
England	442,499	
Scotland	142,001	
Wales	13,528	
Northern Ireland	19,831	
Ireland (Eire)	197,817	169,827
Norway	63,316	42,240
Sweden	77,157	53,676
Denmark	42,732	34,999
Netherlands	103,136	96,198
Belgium	36,487	34,366
Switzerland	42,804	39,130
France	120,215	119,233
Germany	849,384	711,929
Poland	418,128	388,328
Czechoslovakia	112,707	87,020
Austria	145,607	87,673
Hungary	144,368	110,337
Yugoslavia	152,967	141,516
U.S.S.R.	406,022	333,725
Latvia	34,349	26,179
Estonia		9,210
Lithuania	48,194	29,745
Finland	29,172	22,313
Romania	66,994	91,106
Greece	210,998	177,398
Italy	831,922	580,592
Spain	73,735	76,415
Portugal	177,437	210,122
Azores	32,531	
Other Europe	62,244	
Asia	2,539,777	4,979,037
Syria		36,782
Turkey in Asia	51,915	55,087
China	286,120	529,837
Japan	221,794	290,128
India	206,087	450,406
Korea	289,885	568,397
Philippines	501,440	912,674
Iran	121,505	210,941
Israel	66,961	86,048
Lebanon	52,674	86,369
Thailand	54,803	106,919
Vietnam	231,120	543,262
Hong Kong	80,380	147,131
Afghanistan		28,444
Burma		19,835
Cambodia		118,833
Indonesia		48,387
Iraq		44,916
Jordan		31,871
Laos		171,577
Malaysia		33,834
Pakistan		91,889
Saudi Arabia		12,632
Taiwan		244,102
Other Asia	375,093	

Country of Birth	1980	1990
America		
North and Central America	4,664,903	
North America		8,124,257
Canada-French and other	842,859	744,830
Barbados	26,847	43,015
Cuba	607,814	736,971
Dominican Republic	169,147	347,858
Haiti	92,395	225,393
Jamaica	196,811	334,140
Trinidad and Tobago	65,907	115,710
West Indies	1,258,363	
Other West Indies	99,442	
Caribbean		1,938,348
Bahamas		21,633
Grenada		17,730
Mexico	2,199,221	4,298,014
Central America		1,133,978
El Salvador	94,447	465,439
Guatemala	63,073	225,739
Belize		29,957
Costa Rica		43,530
Honduras		108,923
Nicaragua		168,659
Panama		85,737
Other North and Central America	204,940	
South America	561,011	1,037,497
Argentina	68,887	92,563
Brazil	40,919	82,489
Colombia	143,508	286,124
Ecuador	86,128	143,314
Guyana	48,608	120,698
Peru	55,496	144,199
Bolivia		31,303
Chile		55,681
Uruguay		20,766
Venezuela		42,119
Other South America	117,465	
All other	1,164,643	
Africa	199,723	363,819
North Africa	71,450	
Egypt	43,424	66,313
Other Africa	128,273	
Cape Verde		14,368
Ethiopia		34,805
Ghana		20,889
Morocco		15,541
Nigeria		55,350
South Africa		34,707
Australia	42,267	
Oceania		101,145
New Zealand		15,415
Azores	32,531	
All other countries	78,896	
Country not specified	886,024	808,158

Source: U.S. Census Bureau.

Authors' Note: This table was drawn from U.S. Census Bureau tables that broke down the data somewhat differently, so the two periods are not fully comparable for all countries.

Table 1.12: Number of Refugees and Asylees Granteed Lawful Permanent Resident Status by Region and Country of Birth, 1946–1996

Region and country of birth	Total (1)	1946-1950	1951-1960	1961-1970	1971-1980 (2)	1981-1990 (2)	1994	1995	1996
All countries	3,219,750	213,347	492,371	212,843	539,447	1,013,620	121,434	114,664	128,565
Europe	1,263,549	211,983	456,146	55,235	71,858	155,512	54,978	46,998	51,977
Albania	7,151	29	1,409	1,952	395	353	733	314	154
Austria	17,460	4,801	11,487	233	185	424	25	15	15
Bulgaria	7,030	139	1,138	1,799	1,238	1,197	138	105	100
Czechoslovakia	37,928	8,449	10,719	5,709	3,646	8,204	41	38	25
Estonia	11,935	7,143	4,103	16	2	25	176	83	98
Germany	101,777	36,633	62,860	665	143	851	84	61	90
Greece	31,506	124	28,568	586	478	1,408	65	50	33
Hungary	76,401	6,086	55,740	4,044	4,358	4,942	37	28	40
Italy	63,615	642	60,657	1,198	346	394	11	7	17
Latvia	40,474	21,422	16,783	49	16	48	568	387	359
Lithuania	28,356	18,694	8,569	72	23	37	214	151	136
Netherlands	17,638	129	14,336	3,134	8	14	3	-	-
Poland	210,030	78,529	81,323	3,197	5,882	33,889	334	245	183
Portugal	5,077	12	3,650	1,361	21	21	2	3	1
Romania	75,144	4,180	12,057	7,158	6,812	29,798	1,199	592	447
Soviet Union, former	412,804	14,072	30,059	871	31,309	72,306	50,756	40,120	42,356
Russia	37,245	x	x	x	x	x	10,359	8,176	9,745
Ukraine	67,916	x	x	x	x	x	19,366	14,937	16,636
Uzbekistan	13,088	x	x	x	x	x	3,211	3,258	4,144
Other republics	40,675	x	x	x	x	x	12,101	8,689	8,528
Unknown republic	253,880	14,072	30,059	871	31,309	72,306	5,719	5,060	3,303
Spain	10,731	1	246	4,114	5,317	736	55	33	46
Yugoslavia	97,762	9,816	44,755	18,299	11,297	324	506	4,744	7,920
Other Europe	10,730	1,082	7,687	778	382	541	31	22	57
Asia	1,263,323	1,106	33,422	19,895	210,683	712,092	45,768	43,314	42,076
Afghanistan	32,554	-	-	-	542	22,946	1,665	616	369
Cambodia	127,891	-	-	-	7,739	114,064	557	268	210
China (3)	44,422	319	12,008	5,308	13,760	7,928	774	805	847
Hong Kong	9,123	-	1,076	2,128	3,468	1,916	82	48	47
Indonesia	17,692	-	8,253	7,658	222	1,385	41	62	30
Iran	67,631	118	192	58	364	46,773	2,186	1,245	1,212
Iraq	29,104	-	130	119	6,851	7,540	4,400	3,848	3,802
Japan	4,544	-	3,803	554	56	110	4	2	-
Korea	4,631	3	3,116	1,316	65	120	3	5	4
Laos	198,355	-	-	-	21,690	142,964	4,482	3,364	2,155

Region and country of birth

Region and country of birth	Total (1)	1946-50	1951-60	1961-70	1971-80 (2)	1981-90 (2)	1994	1995	1996
Syria	4,950	4	119	383	1,336	2,145	34	258	208
Thailand	50,851	–	15	13	1,241	30,259	3,076	2,932	1,940
Turkey	7,068	603	1,427	1,489	1,193	1,896	156	58	42
Vietnam	644,288	–	2	7	150,266	324,453	27,318	28,595	29,700
Other Asia	20,219	59	3,280	862	1,890	7,593	990	1,208	1,510
Africa	66,638	20	1,768	5,486	2,991	22,149	6,078	7,527	5,464
Egypt	8,894	8	1,354	5,396	1,473	426	37	29	66
Ethiopia	36,233	–	61	2	1,307	18,542	2,730	2,006	1,053
Other Africa	21,511	12	353	88	211	3,181	3,311	5,492	4,345
Oceania	348	7	75	21	37	22	23	63	56
North America	619,279	163	831	132,068	252,633	121,840	14,204	16,265	28,070
Cuba	572,817	3	6	131,557	251,514	113,367	11,998	12,355	22,542
El Salvador	5,052	–	–	1	45	1,383	275	283	262
Nicaragua	26,883	1	1	3	36	5,590	966	727	766
Other North America	14,527	159	824	507	1,038	1,500	965	2,900	4,500
South America	6,484	32	74	123	1,244	1,986	383	497	922
Chile	1,066	–	5	4	415	532	8	10	21
Colombia	1,038	(NA)	(NA)	(NA)	217	350	70	102	116
Peru	1,668	(NA)	(NA)	(NA)	132	251	153	241	568
Venezuela	1,301	(NA)	(NA)	(NA)	83	407	91	95	150
Other South America	1,411	32	69	119	397	446	61	49	67
Unknown or not reported	129	36	55	15	1	19	–	–	–

(1) Includes data for fiscal years 1991–93, not shown separately.
(2) Data for fiscal years 1971–90 have been adjusted.
(3) Includes People's Republic of China and Taiwan.

Note: See Glossary for fiscal year definitions. The data no longer includes Cuban/Haitian entrants granted immigration status.

(-) Represents zero.

NA = Not available

X = Not applicable.

Source: *Statistical Yearbook of the Immigration and Naturalization Service, 1996,* Table 3.

Table 1.13: Resident Population of the United States, by Region, Race, and Hispanic Origin, 1990

Race and Hispanic Origin	Population (in Thousands)					Percent Distribution			
	United States	Northeast	Midwest	South	West	Northeast	Midwest	South	West
Total	248,710	50,809	59,669	85,446	52,786	20.4	24.0	34.4	21.2
White	199,686	42,069	52,018	65,582	40,017	21.1	26.0	32.8	20.0
Black	29,986	5,613	5,716	15,829	2,828	18.7	19.1	52.8	9.4
American Indian, Eskimo, Aleut	1,959	125	338	563	933	6.4	17.2	28.7	47.6
American Indian	1,878	122	334	557	866	6.5	17.8	29.7	46.1
Eskimo	57	2	2	3	51	2.9	3.5	4.9	88.8
Aleut	24	2	2	3	17	8.1	8.1	11.5	72.3
Asian or Pacific Islander	7,274	1,335	768	1,122	4,048	18.4	10.6	15.4	55.7
Chinese	1,645	445	133	204	863	27.0	8.1	12.4	52.4
Filipino	1,407	143	113	159	991	10.2	8.1	11.3	70.5
Japanese	848	74	63	67	643	8.8	7.5	7.9	75.9
Asian Indian	815	285	146	196	189	35.0	17.9	24.0	23.1
Korean	799	182	109	153	355	22.8	13.7	19.2	44.4
Vietnamese	615	61	52	169	334	9.8	8.5	27.4	54.3
Laotian	149	16	28	29	76	10.7	18.6	19.6	51.0
Cambodian	147	30	13	19	85	20.5	8.8	13.1	57.7
Thai	91	12	13	24	43	12.9	14.2	26.0	46.8
Hmong	90	2	37	2	50	1.9	41.3	1.8	55.0
Pakistani	81	28	15	22	17	34.3	18.9	26.5	20.4
Hawaiian	211	4	6	12	189	2.0	2.6	5.8	89.6
Samoan	63	2	2	4	55	2.4	3.6	6.4	87.6
Guamanian	49	4	3	8	34	7.3	6.4	16.8	69.5
Other Asian or Pacific Islander	263	49	34	54	126	18.6	12.9	20.5	48.0
Other races	9,805	1,667	829	2,350	4,960	17.0	8.5	24.0	50.6
Hispanic Origin (1)	22,354	3,754	1,727	6,767	10,106	16.8	7.7	30.3	45.2
Mexican	13,496	175	1,153	4,344	7,824	1.3	8.5	32.2	58.0
Puerto Rican	2,728	1,872	258	406	192	68.6	9.4	14.9	7.0
Cuban	1,044	184	37	735	88	17.6	3.5	70.5	8.5
Other Hispanic	5,086	1,524	279	1,282	2,002	30.0	5.5	25.2	39.4
Not of Hispanic Origin	226,356	47,055	57,942	78,679	42,680	20.8	25.6	34.8	18.9

(1) Persons of Hispanic origin may be of any race.

Source: U.S. Bureau of the Census, 1990 Census of Population, General Population Characteristics, United States (CP-1-1), No. 30.

Immigration Restrictions

Until the mid-1850s, no major legal restrictions were placed on immigration into the United States. Restrictions did legally occur in some states in some periods, because the states controlled immigration until 1875. In addition, citizenship—though not immigration—was denied to persons of color by the 1790 Naturalization Act, a matter which it took the Union victory in the Civil War to change. There was certainly a great deal of antialien sentiment in the United States, most notably directed at Catholics, the objects of bigotry since early colonial times.

The first national attempt to control and at the same time restrict immigration came in 1864, with congressional passage of a statute that attempted to take over control of immigration from the states. A second major provision of the law authorized "contract labor" arrangements, under which immigrants agreed to pay back their passage money from their later earnings. Largely because of the opposition of U.S. labor organizations, the law was repealed in 1868. The federal government took control of immigration in 1875, after the U.S. Supreme Court reversed an earlier position that had left control in the hands of the states.

Anti-Asian Actions

Racism coupled with a campaign attacking Chinese immigration as a threat to "American" jobs was at the root of the first major successful attempt to restrict U.S. immigration. From the early 1850s, the arrival of Chinese immigrants triggered a massive surge of anti-Chinese, anti-"colored" bigotry that brought murderous violence to goldfields and silver mines throughout the West. It also brought legalized discrimination: Chinese were treated as "colored" and denied elementary legal protections.

Anti-Chinese hysteria also brought many attempts by the state of California to stop Chinese immigration. From 1868 to 1880 that proved impossible, because the 1868 China–United States Burlingame Treaty provided for unrestricted immigration both ways between the two nations.

However, in 1880 the United States forced an increasingly weaker China to renegotiate that treaty. The new treaty allowed the United States to restrict Chinese immigration, and in 1882 Congress did so, passing the Chinese Exclusion Act, the first of a series of anti-Chinese acts that together largely cut off Chinese immigration until the 1950s.

Controlling Immigration

With the massive immigration from eastern and southeastern Europe that began in the 1880s came another surge in antialien sentiment. This was again fueled by opposition from the labor movement, which succeeded in securing the anti–contract labor laws of 1885, 1887, and 1888. From then on, the immigration process became a cat-and-mouse game: immigrants who in reality were coming to take promised jobs had to deny they were doing so, while at the same time proving that they had the means to support themselves while looking for work in the United States. (For more on labor arrangements, see "The Journey" on p. 53.)

Pressure for immigration restriction grew. Indeed, it was one of the main reasons for the establishment of the federally controlled Ellis Island immigration station, which because of much more restrictive federal policies made it far more difficult for many immigrants to enter the United States than had been so through the New York State–operated Castle Garden immigration station.

The Immigration Acts of 1891, 1893, and 1903 added many more restrictions, establishing whole new classes of inadmissible aliens. Would-be immigrants could be rejected for a wide range of reasons, among them a considerable range of health problems, previous criminal convictions, inability to support themselves, and political views. In 1910 the Mann White Slavery Traffic Act, aimed at ending the importation of women to work as prostitutes, had the practical effect of making it far more difficult than before for single women to enter the United States.

American Museum of Immigration, Statue of Liberty National Monument, National Park Service, U.S. Department of the Interior

The Ellis Island inspection station was established to assert federal control over immigration, in the wake of several immigration restriction acts.

A second major Asian exclusion action occurred in 1907, when Japan and the United States made the "Gentlemen's Agreement," which resulted in sharp Japanese government restriction of the number of Japanese allowed to emigrate to the United States. In addition, President Theodore Roosevelt, by executive order, blocked Hawaiian Japanese from moving to the United States.

Although Asian exclusion was largely effective, immigration to the United States from eastern and southeastern Europe continued to soar. In a further attempt to restrict that immigration, the 1917 Immigration Act introduced a long-resisted literacy test, which excluded illiterate aliens from entry into the United States. That had some impact, but after World War I ended in 1918, immigration to the United States from eastern and southeastern Europe again moved up sharply. The 1917 Immigration Act also worsened Asian exclusion, establishing a "barred zone" that extended over most of Asia, from which all immigration to the United States was prohibited.

National Quotas

In the bitterly anti-immigrant atmosphere of the 1920s, the U.S. Congress passed the greatly restrictive 1921 Immigration Act, which for the first time set up numerical quotas and limits on immigration. Immigration of each nationality was limited to 3 percent of the number of foreign-born persons of that nationality living in the United States in 1910. This law sharply cut immigration to the United States from southern and eastern Europe. Immigration to the United States from the Western Hemisphere was not limited.

Immigration from southern and eastern Europe—and immigration overall—was cut even more sharply with passage of the 1924 Immigration Act. The 1924 Act set up the national origins quota system, limiting immigration to 2 percent of the number of foreign-born persons of each nationality living in the United States in 1890. Again, Western Hemisphere immigration was not limited. With minor later amendments, the highly restrictive quota system established by the 1924 Immigration Act remained in effect until 1952, as did other restrictive provisions such as the Asian "barred zone."

After World War II, with the European colonial system being dismantled and the Cold War in full swing, U.S. immigration policy began to present a different face to the world. The Immigration and Nationality Act of 1952 eliminated racial bars to citizenship and declared sexual discrimination in immigration to be at an end. While not changing the basic quota system, it eliminated much of its bias against eastern and southern Europeans. It also retained separate, discriminatory treatment for countries in the "barred zone," but allowed small numbers of people from Asia to immigrate.

The 1965 Immigration Act

A sweeping change occurred in 1965. Following through on President John F. Kennedy's announced intention of easing immigration restrictions and providing a level playing field for worldwide immigration into the United States, President Lyndon B. Johnson pushed through the 1965 Immigration Act, which became effective in 1968. This major new law retained some numerical limits on immigration but abolished the national origins quota system set up in 1924, setting a numerical cap of 290,000 immigrants per year.

However, the new law also succeeded in reopening the long-closed Golden Door, by establishing no numerical limit on the immediate relatives of U.S. citizens who could legally become U.S. immigrants, thereby opening the way to a flood of new immigrants. Immigration figures began to climb again, by 1989 once again topping 1 million a year.

Library of Congress

One of the first things inspectors checked as immigrants arrived in Ellis Island was their eyes, for some eye diseases could lead to instant rejection and return.

Later Immigration Laws

The 1965 law, however, did not in any way seriously limit the flood of illegal, or undocumented, immigrants, millions of whom poured into the United States in the decades that followed. (See "Appendix C: Estimates of Emigration and Illegals" on p. 749.) A whole body of new, often contradictory immigration laws and regulations followed, accompanied by greatly increased attempts to control illegal immigration. These were all in aggregate quite ineffective, while at the same time often generating shockingly inhumane treatment of many of those attempting to enter the United States.

The 1986 Immigration Act was an attempt to more fully control immigration, while at the same time solving the problems posed by the millions of "illegals" then living in the United States by declaring an amnesty for those who had been living in the United States since January 1, 1982. The law did succeed in legalizing millions of illegals. However, it did not in any way succeed in stemming the growing flow of new undocumented immigrants, who continued to arrive by the millions.

The 1990 Immigration Act seemed largely an attempt to partially close the open door created by the 1965 Immigration Act. It established a new total immigration cap of 675,000 immigrants per year. These were to consist of 480,000 family-sponsored immigrants (rather than the unlimited number allowed by the 1965 law), who were to be admitted via a complex set of preferences; 140,000 employment-based immigrants; and 55,000 others. The law did not work. In the mid-1990s, legal immigrants were still pouring into the United States at the rate of almost 1 million per year. Nor was the flow of illegals impeded.

The 1996 Immigration Act, titled the Illegal Immigration Reform and Immigrant Responsiblity Act, was yet another attempt to stem and reverse the continuing flow of illegal immigrants into the United States. By that time, the U.S. government estimated, 5 million illegal immigrants were residing in the United States. The 1996 law greatly expanded enforcement efforts, making it possible for U.S. immigration authorities to refuse entry and to deport aliens without effective opposition or guarantees of legal process. It also introduced several other new bars aimed at reducing the numbers of new illegal immigrants and deporting those already residing in the United States. The 1996 law greatly expanded enforcement efforts, making it possible for U.S. immigration authorities to refuse entry and to deport aliens without effective opposition or guarentees of legal process. It also introduced several new bars aimed at reducing the numbers of new illegal immigrants and deporting those already residing in the United States.

At the close of the 20th century, the effectiveness of the new enforcement efforts was still very much in question. In early 1999, the U.S. Immigration and Naturalization Service reported that it had turned back 300,000 illegal immigrants attempting to enter in the previous two years, while deporting 78,000 already living in the United States. Yet that agency also reported that illegal immigrants were entering the United States at the rate of 275,000 per year (or 550,000 in two years), while many other reports indicated that the flow of illegal immigrants was in fact much higher than that.

By 1999, in addition to long-standing and intensifying charges of inhumanity in dealing with immigrants, the immigration service faced massive criticism for alleged incompetence. By then a backlog of 1.8 million citizenship applications had developed, despite the agency's repeated promises to develop new and improved ways of handling those applications. The growing numbers of people imprisoned by the immigration authorities made overcrowded conditions increasingly common in detention facilities.

As the dawn of a new century approached, it seemed clear that current efforts to restrict U.S. immigration had not been successful in any significant way.

For more on the key laws affecting immigration, see "Appendix B: Immigration and Naturalization Legislation" on p. 723.

National Archives

Under increasingly restrictive laws, many immigrants arrived in the United States only to be held in detention camps, such as this one for Cuban refugees, or even in jails.

The Journey

Throughout the history of immigration to what became the United States, from the earliest colonies to the end of the late 20th century, most people arrived by sea. Some walked overland, of course, including many (if not all) Native Americans, as well as immigrants from Canada in the north and Mexico and Central America in the south. But before the mid-20th century, when airplane travel became widespread, most people arrived by boat.

In the earliest days of immigration to North America, immigrants were most likely to be drawn from the regions around the main seaports which served as departure points. Land travel then was often slow, expensive, and difficult, so people who lived far inland, remote from the ports, had a much longer, harder journey.

Early Ships

Colonial immigrants generally chartered ships to bring them and their supplies to the New World, for there would be no regularly scheduled sailings until the 19th century. The earliest colonists had to bring with them everything they thought they would need, for one or more years might go by before another ship came with relief supplies.

In the 16th and 17th centuries, the journey across the Atlantic took as long as two or three months, in often rough seas. The *Mayflower*, for example, left Plymouth, England, on September 16, 1620, and did not make its first landfall in New England, at Provincetown, on Cape Cod, until November 21. These very early settlers arrived at Plymouth Rock a month later, and there lived on the ship for several weeks until they had built shelters on shore. The *Mayflower* returned to England in April 1621.

In those early centuries, immigrants sailed on all-purpose cargo ships, not designed to carry passengers. The *Mayflower,* for example, had earlier been used to transport wine. The ships were also small. The *Mayflower* was only 90 feet long, less than the length of a modern basketball court, and 26 feet across in its midsection. In this relatively small space, it carried 101 passengers and a crew of 20 to 30. Some ships were even smaller. The *Restaurationen*, which brought a party of 52 Norwegian immigrants to America in 1825, was only a quarter of the size of the *Mayflower*.

By the 1820s, many transatlantic ships would be in the 1,000-ton range. Ships that carried cotton, flax, and other goods from America to Liverpool might return with a "cargo" of as many as 1,000 immigrants.

Leaving Home

In many countries, citizens could not emigrate without the government's permission—sometimes no easy matter to obtain. Often people had to collect a fistful of permits from the local and national authorities, as well as certification that they did not owe any money or taxes. Sometimes even announcing an intention to emigrate could call forth penalties, which might include being evicted from housing and dismissed from work. Such penalties were common even in the late 20th century, in some Soviet-dominated countries of eastern Europe.

Young men were not usually allowed to leave the country until they had performed mandated military service. Over the centuries, many left illegally to avoid serving in the military. Just before World War I, for example, hundreds of thousands of young men left Europe to avoid serving in the armies of their imperial oppressors, among them Russia, Austria-Hungary, and Turkey.

In some countries, emigrants were required to give up their citizenship on leaving. Some countries forbade emigration absolutely, most notably Manchu-ruled China. Illegal Chinese emigrants—or even those trying to return after previously leaving illegally—faced possible beheading, though the prohibition and punishment were little enforced in the later years of emigration.

For most emigrants over the centuries, leaving home meant saying good-bye to family, friends, and places they would never see again. Though some would come back, for a visit or to stay, most never returned. Some slipped away to avoid detection, saying their good-byes privately, especially those leaving without government permission, but for many the start of the journey was marked by a procession of relatives and friends saying tearful farewells.

The journey generally began with a long walk, as emigrants headed for the nearest seaport, often with a backpack or handcart. Those far from the sea would—if they could afford it—head for a riverboat or stagecoach to bridge the distance, with water routes in the early days being easi-

NovA BRITANNIA.

OFFERING MOST

Excellent fruites by Planting in
VIRGINIA.

Exciting all such as be well affected
to further the same.

LONDON
Printed for SAMVEL MACHAM, and are to be sold at
his Shop in Pauls Church-yard, at the
Signe of the Bul-head.
1 6 0 9.

Authors' Archives

This 1609 advertisement for people going to Virginia shows how small boats of the day were.

est. Only in the mid-19th century would trains make such overland journeys faster and easier.

People traveling across several countries generally had the most difficulty. All their goods and papers were inspected at every major point, so they faced danger and delays not just at national borders but also sometimes from city to city and province to province. Corrupt officials often demanded bribes, while others tried to obstruct the emigrants' passage. In some cases emigrants were imprisoned for having defective papers or sent back home—a disaster for those who had already been forced to give up their citizenship. Those leaving illegally were at special risk, but most emigrants—generally relying on reports of those who had gone before—sought for routes where they could expect to encounter the least trouble.

With the slow pace of travel and all the delays, the journey to America—which now might take half a day by plane—could take months, depending on how far emigrants had to travel to the seaports (see "Traveling from Germany in 1750" on p. 55).

Part of the emigrants' journey was spent waiting in port. The cargo ships on which early emigrants sailed did not have fixed schedules, but would leave only after they had filled their holds with appropriate cargo. As a result, emigrants might spend days or weeks waiting in port for a ship. Often they lived in tent camps; these were desperate places, full of diseases such as typhus and cholera, where many people died. Boardinghouses and hotels sprang up to meet the demand for food and shelter but often exploited the helpless emigrants. Even in the 19th century, after regular sailings were common, emigrants often had to wait in port.

Many emigrants ended up spending all their money on the journey to the port, or were robbed or swindled on arrival. At that point, some emigrants returned home; others tried to find ways to earn money for the fare.

Some emigrants, in fact, arrived in port as a result of fraud. In early 19th-century Germany, for example, unscrupulous coach drivers, boatmen, and shipping agents sometimes persuaded emigrants that, at ports such as Rotterdam or Amsterdam, they would be given food, cash, free pas-

Traveling from Germany in 1750

This [whole] journey lasts from the beginning of May until the end of October, that is, a whole six months, and involves such hardships that it is really impossible for any description to do justice to them. . . . At each [customs house] all the ships must be examined, and these examinations take place at the convenience of the customs officials. Meanwhile, the ships with the people in them are held up for a long time. This involves a great deal of expense for the passengers; and it also means that the trip down the Rhine alone takes from four to six weeks.

During the journey the ship is full of pitiful signs of distress—smells, fumes, horrors, vomiting, various kinds of sea sickness, fever, dysentery, headaches, heat, constipation, boils, scurvy, cancer, mouth-rot, and similar afflictions, all of them caused by the age and the highly-salted state of the food, especially of the meat, as well as by the very bad and filthy water, which brings about the miserable destruction and death of many. Add to all that shortage of food, hunger, thirst, frost, heat, dampness, fear, misery, vexations, and lamentation as well as other troubles. Thus, for example, there are so many lice, especially on the sick people, that they have to be scraped off the bodies. All this misery reaches its climax when in addition to everything else one must also suffer through two or three days and nights of storm, with everyone convinced that the ship with all aboard is bound to sink. In such misery all the people on board pray and cry pitifully together.

Gottlieb Mittelberger

sage across the Atlantic, and free land in the United States. Small numbers of Protestant refugees from Catholic countries did receive help from prosperous Protestants in Britain or the Netherlands. But for most the promise of aid was a cruel hoax.

Indentured Servants

One alternative for penniless emigrants was to come as *indentured servants*. Such people signed a contract to work for a specified number of years in exchange for passage across the Atlantic. In a variation on this theme, British and Dutch shippers developed a system called *redemption*. They would ship emigrants across the Atlantic without payment, if the emigrant signed a contract agreeing to repay, or *redeem*, the loan within a short time after arrival. If he or she could not do so, as was usually the case, the captain would sell the contract at auction to the highest bidder. The immigrant then would be required to work for the contract holder as an indentured servant until the loan was paid off.

The term of work varied. It often ranged from three to eight years; however, children were obliged to work until they were 21. For indentured servants from the British Isles, the term was generally fixed before sailing, but for redemption contracts, especially from Dutch ports, the term was often not specified until arrival.

Indentured servants were little more than slaves, the main difference being that their time of service was limited. But, like slaves, they could be sold from one person to another, and family members were often widely separated. Some immigrants who were sick and therefore found no one to buy their contracts remained on the ship until they were well or, in some cases, were taken to a hospital on shore. If they survived, their indenture contracts were then sold.

Even death did not cancel redemption contracts. Surviving family members were obligated to pay the fare for anyone who died. Orphaned children might be indentured for their dead parents' fares, in addition to their own.

Some Americans protested the practice of redemption, forming organizations to pay the fares for some poor newcomers.

However, there were far too many to help directly in this way, so such organizations worked to ban the practice. They finally succeeded in 1819.

Sailors and Brides

Healthy young people also had other ways of reaching America, even if they lacked the fare. Men could come as sailors and women as brides.

From the earliest times, many men came to America as sailors. Some signed on board ship specifically to reach the New World, while others decided only later to settle in America. That would remain true right through the 20th century. How many sailors became immigrants is unknown, for those who left ship in port were never properly counted in U.S. immigration figures.

In most communities of new immigrants, from the earliest times until now, single men predominated. Many preferred to marry someone of their own ethnic and religious background, and marriageable women were always in short supply. As a result, some women were imported as brides-to-be.

The original 1607 settlement at Jamestown, Virginia, for example, was all male. One woman and her maid arrived the following year, with more than a hundred women coming in 1609. Seeking more women for the colony, the Virginia Company posted advertisements, offering free passage and free land to women who would come to Virginia. When some of these immigrant women chose to work the land themselves rather than marry, the company ceased to offer free land, but continued to recruit women. On arrival in America, women would line up on board ship; male colonists would board, select the woman they wished to marry, and pay her fare. If a woman chose not to marry the man who chose her, she sometimes worked to pay off her fare or chose another man to be her husband and pay her fare.

The practice of importing women to marry male immigrants would remain common through the coming centuries. In the late 19th century, after the development of photography, single women from abroad would often be selected on the basis of photographs they sent to potential husbands. As a result, they would be called "picture brides" or "mail order brides." Many hundreds of women over the centuries, from all around Europe and from Asia, especially Japan and China, would come to America as picture brides to marry men they had never met.

Some women were also imported to be prostitutes—including some who thought they were coming to America to be married. That would remain a special hazard for women, especially in the great 19th-century wave of immigration. As a result, in the early 20th century, the immigration authorities would become very strict in the handling of female immigrants; generally a single woman would be allowed to enter only if she married her would-be husband on the spot or if a responsible person or agency took charge of her.

The Crossing

Emigrants crossing from Europe sailed east to west across the North Atlantic, fighting the prevailing east-flowing winds and currents all the way. The main current was the Gulf Stream, which traveled in a great clockwise movement north along the North American coast, east across the North Atlantic, then south from the British Isles along the European coast, then west across the southern Atlantic to the Caribbean, before swinging north again to ports such as Savannah, Charleston, Baltimore, Philadelphia, New York, and Boston. The southern route was the route of Columbus, and would be the main route of the slave ships (see "The Slave Trade" on p. 321) and also of many early ships headed for ports in the Caribbean and the Gulf of Mexico, or on the southern East Coast. However, most emigrants from Europe crossed the North Atlantic, through some of the world's roughest, stormiest seas.

Emigrants crossing from Asia were not faced with the same contrary winds, but had far longer journeys and sometimes found their sailing ships becalmed in too-quiet seas. The main route taken by Chinese emigrants was directly across the Pacific, from South China to San Francisco. Many American China traders were New Englanders, so small numbers of

Asian immigrants came with them to ports such as Boston or Salem. Some went southwest from East Asia across the Indian Ocean, around the Cape of Good Hope at the tip of southern Africa, and then north across the whole expanse of the Atlantic. Others went from East Asia across the Pacific, all the way south to the tip of South America to round Cape Horn, and then back north to New England. That route only fell out of regular use after the Panama Canal was opened in 1914, eliminating the long detour.

Whatever their route, passengers faced the danger that their ship might be lost at sea. The fragile wooden craft might easily be ripped apart by a storm at sea, wrecked on rocks or icebergs, or consumed by fire. If they were near land, some passengers might be saved by rescuers from ashore, and if they were in the shipping lanes, another ship might arrive to rescue some of them. But for most people, such disasters at sea spelled death. Between 1847 and 1853 alone, a reported 59 emigrant ships sank in the North Atlantic.

Even if the ship survived, many immigrants did not, for their traveling conditions were abysmal. As cargo ships, these craft had no special arrangements for carrying passengers and little or no concern for sanitation or hygiene. (On return trips to Europe, many ships would carried raw or semifinished goods, such as tobacco, cotton, flax, timber, and furs.) Immigrants were packed tightly into unventilated cargo holds; these upper holds were called *steerage* because they were near the ship's steering mechanism. In ships carrying as many as 600 passengers, the immigrants were crowded together as closely as possible, with small sleeping spaces perhaps measuring two by six feet. Though the ships generally provided food and water, these were almost always in short supply and of poor quality.

Under such conditions, diseases spread quickly and many people died. Young children were especially at risk, but people of all ages were vulnerable; many were weakened and sick with diseases caught en route before they even boarded the ship. The risk of death overall was enormous. In 1710, on one six-month-long journey from Germany to America, 446 people died out of 2,814 in the original party, a death rate of more than 15 percent.

The crossing was the worst for black Africans who had been kidnapped and transported in ships against their will. Destined for slavery, they were brought across the mid-Atlantic in chains, packed literally like cargo, with humans sometimes interspersed with bags of rice and other commodities. Heat, disease, and lack of proper food, water, and sanitation combined with these conditions to produce a death rate estimated at 15 to 20 percent on the "Middle Passage," the sea journey between Africa and the Americas (see "The Slave Trade" on p. 321).

The Pacific journey had its own hazards. The crossing from East Asia to California might take two months or more. Many ships made no stops en route, so—in the absence of rain—water was often in extremely short supply. Though passing through warmer climes, passengers faced the same problems of overcrowding and poor sanitation.

Far fewer immigrants arrived across the Pacific than across the Atlantic. The first of them arrived in 1564, after Spanish navigators opened the transpacific route of the China trade (see "Immigrants from China" on p. 365). After that, Spanish galleons sailed between Acapulco, Mexico, and Manila, in the Philippines, sometimes with stops in California, sometimes bringing with them small numbers of Asian immigrants.

By the 18th century, the China trade was no longer in Spanish hands, and most Asian immigrants to the United States crossed in American ships. At the time of the 1849 California Gold Rush, they might travel in anything from a small, overcrowded cargo ship up to a large transpacific clipper ship in the China trade. The trip from China to San Francisco cost $50 to $200—an enormous amount in those days, when Chinese laborers generally earned only $1 to $2 a week, out of which many had to pay back the money borrowed for their fare. Long after regularly scheduled steamships became standard in the Atlantic, most immigrants from Asia crossed in the cargo holds of the older-style sailing ships (see "Traveling from China in 1868" below). That was true for many of the Asians who came at the time of the 1849 California Gold Rush and would remain true for decades after.

Packets

Early emigrants from Europe might sail from any port large enough to handle oceangoing cargo ships. However, in the early 19th century some shipping lines began to see emigrants as big business, building ships specifically designed to carry emigrants and setting regular sailing schedules. The first of these regularly scheduled liners, called *packets*, began sailing between Liverpool and New York in 1818. This and other early packet lines were run primarily by Americans.

Regular schedules cut the amount of time emigrants needed to wait in ports. As a result, people from many parts of northern Europe made Liverpool their destination. From all around the Baltic and North Seas, they crowded into short-haul cargo ships that would take them to Liverpool for the transatlantic crossing. For many, this was the worst part of the journey, no matter how short the distance. On some such short-haul boats, emigrants did not even have any protection from the elements, as

in the open cattle boats that brought Irish emigrants across the Irish Sea to Liverpool.

Packet liners were faster than the cargo ships, crossing the North Atlantic in as little as 35 days from Liverpool. As the number of emigrants swelled, packet lines began to sail from other ports as well, most notably the northern European ports of Le Havre (France) and Bremen and Hamburg (Germany). The ocean voyage took longer from the more distant ports, approximately 50 to 60 days from Hamburg and Bremen, for example. However, many emigrants from continental Europe, as from Scandinavia and the Baltic countries, preferred to sail from the German ports. The Hamburg-American Line, in particular, was well run and had large facilities for housing emigrants in port.

Transatlantic fares dropped by half in the early 19th century. In 1819, passage from Liverpool across the Atlantic to New York in steerage might cost 10 to 12 pounds, perhaps a little less for the slowest ships, but by 1832 that had dropped to 6 pounds. Cargo ships, which by the 1830s charged just 4 pounds, would continue to attract the poorest emigrants. Fares from Britain to Canada were even cheaper, at

---

Traveling from China in 1868

Finally the day was set for the ship to sail. We were two full months or more on our way. I do not know what route we took, but it was warm all the time, and we stopped at no intermediate port. When the wind was good and strong, we made much headway. But for days there would be no wind, the sails and ropes would hang lifeless from the masts, and the ship would drift idly on the smooth sea, while the sailors amused themselves by fishing. Occasionally, head winds became so strong as to force us back. Once we thought we were surely lost, for it was whispered around that the officers had lost their bearings. There was plenty of foodstuff on board, but fresh water was scarce and was carefully rationed. Not a drop was allowed to be wasted for washing our faces, and so, when rain came we eagerly caught the rain water and did our washing.

On a clear, crisp, September morning in 1868, or the seventh year of our Emperor T'ung Chih, the mists lifted, and we sighted land for the first time since we left the shores of Kwangtung [Guangdong] over sixty days before. To be actually at the "Golden Gate" of the land of our dreams! The feeling that welled up in us was indescribable. . . . We rolled up our bedding, packed our baskets, straightened our clothes, and waited.

Huie Kin

Traveling from Ireland in 1847

Before the emigrant has been a week at sea he is an altered man. How can it be otherwise? Hundreds of poor people, men, women, and children of all ages, from the drivelling idiot of ninety to the babe just born, huddled together without light, without air, wallowing in filth and breathing a fetid atmosphere, sick in body, dispirited in heart, the fever patients lying between the sound, in sleeping places so narrow as almost to deny them the power of indulging, by a change of position, the natural restlessness of the disease; by their ravings disturbing those around, and predisposing them, through the effects of the imagination, to imbibe the contagion; living without food or medicine, except as administered by the hand of casual charity, dying without the voice of spiritual consolation, and buried in the deep without the rites of the Church.

The food is generally ill-selected and seldom sufficiently cooked, in consequence of the insufficiency and bad construction of the cooking places. The supply of water, hardly enough for cooking and drinking, does not allow washing. In many ships the filthy beds, teeming with all abominations, are never required to be brought on deck and aired; the narrow space between the sleeping berths and the piles of boxes is never washed or scraped, but breathes up a damp and fetid stench.

The meat was of the worst quality. The supply of water shipped in board was abundant, but the quantity served out to the passengers was so scanty that they were frequently obliged to throw overboard their salt provisions and rice . . . because they had not water enough for the necessary cooking and the satisfying of their raging thirst afterwards. They could only afford water for washing by withdrawing it from cooking of their food. I have known persons to remain for days together in their dark, close berths because they suffered less from hunger.

—An anonymous Irish emigrant

more like 2 pounds, so many of the poorest emigrants took timber ships to Quebec and then went south into the United States.

Though the packet ships had better accommodations for first- and second-class passengers, the conditions for emigrant passengers in steerage were still terrible (see "Traveling from Ireland in 1847" above). In 1847, during the great exodus from Ireland, of the 90,000 emigrants who sailed from Liverpool to Quebec, more than 15,000 died, either at sea or soon after in hospital, or more than 16 percent.

In 1847, the U.S. Congress passed a law designed to improve emigrant ships. The new law specified that 14 square feet be allotted to each passenger, with bunks to be at least 6 feet long and 18 inches wide. It also required, for the first time, that men and women be given separate sleeping areas, toilets, and entrances. However, even when shipping lines observed the law, the ships were still grossly overcrowded.

Sometimes passengers even had to sleep in hallways or on deck in crudely built shacks.

Disease and death continued to be common on emigrant ships. As late as 1867, a report to an immigrant aid society put it this way: "If crosses and tombstones could be erected on the water, the routes of the emigrant vessels from Europe to America would long since have assumed the appearance of crowded cemeteries."

Steamers

Conditions for emigrants did not begin to change until the late 19th century, as steamships became widespread. Steam-assisted ships had sailed the North Atlantic from 1818, with full steamships coming in the 1830s and 1840s. These were small ships, however. Not until the late 1850s did steamships begin to have a major impact on the emigrants' journey. By then, steamships in the 3,000 to 4,000-ton range were crossing the Atlantic in just 10 to 12 days. Within two decades, the fastest ships were crossing in a week, with some ships making the trip in just five days by 1906, and fares kept dropping for steerage passengers. Even so, into the 1890s at least, the poorest immigrants to cross the Atlantic continued to arrive in slow sailing ships.

Steamships came to the Pacific somewhat later. The Pacific Mail Steamship Company did not begin carrying Chinese immigrants until 1866, but it was soon joined by many competitors. Fares soon dropped sharply, with the fare from China to San Francisco costing as little as $13 to $15, down from the $50 to $200 of Gold Rush days. As in the Atlantic, the steamships were much faster than the sailing ships, with the crossing taking about a month, instead of two. Many steamers put in at Hawaii for coal and supplies.

The main route for European immigrants continued to be out of the major ports of northwestern Europe. In the late 19th century, during the huge flood of emigration, many ships also sailed from Mediterranean ports, such as Piraeus, Greece; Naples, Italy; and Marseilles, France. These ships carried many people of the "new immigration," primarily poor people from southern and eastern Europe. Even in this period, however, many people from southeastern Europe preferred to go by train across Europe to sail out of northwestern ports.

The late 19th and early 20th centuries were the age of the great ocean liners. While people with money sailed in luxury above, as many as 2,000 immigrants might be jammed into steerage below. Water was still limited and the food poor, often consisting primarily of herring and potatoes. Disease was still widespread and death not uncommon, though the faster voyage cut the immigrants' death rate considerably.

Emigrants who had money to pay the higher fare could travel in more comfort in second-class or first-class quarters. But even they faced hazards at sea. In a marine disaster, passengers of all classes would be at risk. The *Titanic*, which in 1912 sank after hitting an iceberg, carried people of all classes—including hundreds of emigrants—to their deaths.

Trains and Canals

Two other innovations dramatically changed the emigrants' journey in the 19th century: canals and railroads. After the Napoleonic Wars ended, in 1815, Europe saw an explosion of canal-building. Primarily built to facilitate the transport of cargo, canals also allowed emigrants to reach main seaports more quickly and easily.

Canals were also widely built in the eastern United States. The most important of these for immigrants was the Erie Canal, which opened in 1825. This connected the Hudson River with the Great Lakes, providing a convenient water-level route to the Midwest. Emigrants headed for the heartland no longer had to take tortuous routes through the Appalachian Mountains. Instead, from the port of New York, they could board canal boats that would take them all the way to the Great Lakes and on to port cities such as Chicago. This route was so convenient that by the 1840s New York had replaced Philadelphia as the dominant port of entry from Europe.

Canals would serve for decades, but they were soon overtaken in convenience by railroads. First developed in Britain in 1825, railroads quickly spread, first in western Europe and the United States, then in southern and eastern Europe, and then somewhat later elsewhere around the world. As railroads reached into the interior of Europe and other continents, they allowed people from rural areas to emigrate more easily.

Agents and Contractors

From the days of indentured contracts, shipping agents had been employed to encourage immigration to North America. With the rise of packet ships and then steamers, agents became even more important. With posters, leaflets, and other advance publicity, agents would travel far into the countryside to speak about the

Philadelphia, shown here, in 1800, with a ship at dock, was the main early immigration port on the East Coast.

wonders of America. Many of the Old World's poor had, by the mid-19th century, already heard much about the New World, often through the "America letters" sent by friends and relatives who had gone before, which were often published in local newspapers. Sometimes agents would arrive to find hundreds of people awaiting them, some of whom had already sold their goods and were ready to leave immediately for America.

As emigration grew in the late 19th century, the agent's role expanded. Certainly many agents continued to be employed directly by shipping lines. However, some began to work as travel agents, who specialized in arranging the whole trip, including not just the ocean voyage but also train rides on either end. Immigrants already in America would pay such agents to provide the complete set of tickets for other family members to follow. Sometimes the packet of tickets was not sent directly to the family but held at some convenient point to be picked up. That was especially true for people emigrating ille-

gally. Some of these left with no more than the shirts on their backs, giving border guards no indication that they were not returning. They would then go on to pick up tickets awaiting them at a port such as Hamburg.

From the late 19th century, some governments required shipping lines to provide room and board for emigrants awaiting ships bound for America. Sometimes emigrants were housed in private boardinghouses, often run by people from the emigrants' homeland, who therefore spoke their language. However, some shipping companies built their own facilities, such as the emigrant halls of the Hamburg-American Line, which carried emigrants from all over Europe.

Some people worked as "professional emigrants." Often people who had earlier gone to America, they were paid to return to their homeland and lead parties of new emigrants on the journey. These were especially important in regions where emigration was illegal, such as Russia or Turkey, for they would handle the bribing of the border guards and the safehouses along the route, as well as keeping emigrants from the clutches of robbers and swindlers on the way.

As the United States was settling the Midwest and the Great Plains, many states employed agents to attract new immigrants. Railroads, too, employed agents, for they wanted immigrants to settle the land in those regions, providing goods to ship on their trains.

To help build the country, including the railroad lines, many companies also employed agents to provide immigrants as laborers. Their arrangements varied widely and went by many names, but the system was generally known as *contract labor* or, in the Italian term, the *padrone* system. An agent who spoke the language would arrange for workers to come to America to do specific work, sometimes transporting them across country to the work site and arranging for food and shelter, in exchange for a percentage of their earnings. A party of Greek or Italian workers, for example, might be taken to Salt Lake City to help build a railroad.

Many American workers fought against the contract labor system, however, believing that immigrants took jobs that should have been theirs. At their urging a series of laws was passed, starting in 1885, banning contract labor. As a result, when immigrants were examined on arrival, they had to be careful not to say they had jobs waiting for them (even if they did) or they

risked being returned as contract laborers (Note: For more on overall immigration, including year-by-year figures for selected countries, see "Annual Immigration Statistics" on p. 657; "General Notes on Immigration Statistics" on p. 684; and "Appendix A: General Immigration Resources" on p. 716. See also chapters on specific countries that were major sources of immigrants.)

Ship's Manifests

Ships normally recorded what they carried on lists called *manifests*. For emigrants, these ships' manifests were essentially passenger lists. Before 1820, these were not standardized, and so varied by shipping line or country of origin. They generally included the name of the ship and the captain, the ports and dates of departure and arrival, and the names of passengers, though these sometimes might be general, such as "John Doe with wife and two children." They sometimes also gave information about each passenger's age, country of origin, occupation, and baggage. One major exception was slave ships, on which the unwilling passengers were listed as cargo, generally just by age and sex, but without individual names or other information.

Starting in 1820, the U.S. government required ships to keep standardized lists of passengers, which were to be filed with the Bureau of Customs. These called for the name, age, sex, occupation, and nationality

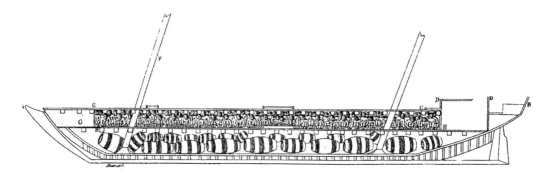

This is a drawing of a Spanish slave ship en route to the Americas from Africa in 1822, carrying 216 male slaves jammed into the hold along with sacks of rice.

National Archives

These refugees arriving in New York City in 1940 were lucky to escape Europe, then being overrun by the Germans.

of each passenger, along with the name of the ship and captain, and the ports and dates of departure and arrival. These passenger lists were filed at the customs house of any of the more than 100 ports on the east and west coasts of the United States.

From 1891, the U.S. government required even more detailed passenger lists. In addition to the above information, the ship's manifests were required to include:

- country of last residence
- destination in the United States
- whether the passenger had previously entered the country, with details of when, where, and length of visit
- if going to a relative, details such as name, address, and relationship to the relative
- whether the immigrant could read and write
- whether the immigrant had a train ticket to the intended destination
- who paid for the train ticket
- how much money the immigrant was carrying
- information on the immigrant's state of health

- whether the immigrant had ever been in a prison, almshouse, or mental asylum, or was a polygamist

Starting in 1903, the federal government required yet more information, including race and ethnic origin. From 1906, place of birth was required, and such personal information as height, complexion, color of hair and eyes, and identifying characteristics. From 1907, the name and address of the immigrant's oldest living relative at home were also required.

It is from passenger lists such as these that basic immigration figures have been derived. Genealogists and family historians today rely on such lists in seeking information about individual immigrants. Unfortunately, these records were often kept inconsistently.

Names were a particular problem. Especially where immigrants could not speak English or could not read and write, the immigration inspectors sometimes had to approximate the spelling of their names, often shortening or simplifying them in the process. This meant that immigrants from the same family, arriving at different times, might have variously spelled last

District of New York—Port of New York.

... Master of the Ship ... do solemnly, sincerely and truly ... that the following List or Manifest, subscribed by me, and now delivered by me to the Collector of the Customs of the Collection District of New York, list of all the passengers taken on board of the said ... said Ship ... has now arrived ... and that on said list is truly designed the age, the sex, and the occupation of each of said ... of the vessel occupied by each during the passage, the country to which each belongs, and also the country of which it is intended by each to become an ... said List or Manifest truly sets forth the number of said passengers who have died on said voyage, and the names and ages of those who died ...

Sworn to this ... July 3d ... 1863 ...

List or Manifest of ALL THE PASSENGERS taken on board the ... is Master, from ... burthen ...

NAMES.	Age Years.	Months.	SEX.	OCCUPATION.	The country to which they severally belong.	The country in which they intend to become inhabitants.	Died on the voyage.
Mary Austin	50		F	None	England	United States of America	
Mary Ann Turner	27		F	do	do	do	
Arthur B. Austin	10		M	do	do	do	
Charles E. Austin			M	do	do	do	
Richard Ralph	33		M	Bootmaker	do	do	
Jane Ralph	28		F	Milliner	do	do	
Royce Vince	27		M	Sugar maker	Holland	do	
Martha Vince	22		F	None	England	do	
Nathan Vince	4		M	do	do	do	
Louis Vince	2		M		do	do	
Rosa Vince	inft		F		do	do	
Lucy Cox	29		M	Pedlar	Holland	do	
Isaac Schmerls	26		M	Sugar maker	do	do	
Mina Vince	28		F	Servant	Holland	U.S. America	
Ezekiel Nykerk	54		M	Sugar maker	do	do	
Elizabeth Nykerk	50		F	None	do	do	
Esther Nykerk	8		F		do	do	
Louis Nykerk	3		M		do	do	
Morris Nykerk	1		M		do	do	
Morris Vampray	31		M	Sugar maker	do	do	
Amelia Vampray	28		F	None	do	do	
Soloman Vampray	4		M		do	do	
David Vampray	3		M		do	do	
Martha Vampray	2		F		do	do	
Caroline Vampray	inft		F		do	do	
Edward Lyons	48		M	Bootmaker	do	do	
Rosetta Lyons	38		F	None	do	do	
Rachael Lyons	1		F		England	do	

This is a sample of a ship's manifest from 1863, showing the kind of passenger information recorded at the time.

Authors' Archives

From 1855 to 1892, most immigrants who arrived in New York City passed through Castle Garden (right). Many transferred directly to barges, as shown here in 1869, for the trip up the Hudson and westward on the Erie Canal.

names in the United States (see "Appendix F: Guide to the Soundex System" on p. 766, for how genealogists get around that problem). Sometimes, when the last name was unclear, the immigrants would be given the name of their hometown as a last name. Some inspectors also changed names deliberately, and even maliciously, so a Ukrainian immigrant might be renamed "O'Day," for example.

Many of the records from the 19th century are lost. While records from some ports are nearly complete, those from others are incomplete or missing altogether. Accident took many of them. In particular, an 1897 fire at Ellis Island destroyed all New York City's immigration records from 1855 to 1897. This has enormously complicated the process of researching immigrant family histories (see "Appendix D: Tips on Genealogy" on p. 756).

The Arrival

Immigrants to the United States might arrive at any of more than 100 United States ports. Whatever the port of entry,

the ship's passenger lists would be presented at the local customs houses, and the immigrants themselves would be examined. In the early years, most people who wished to enter the United States were allowed to do so. From the second half of the 19th century, however, the United States began to turn back some people as unwanted immigrants after examining them at immigrant receiving stations. (Note: For more on overall immigration, including year-by-year figures for selected countries, see "Annual Immigration Statistics" on p. 657; "General Notes on Immigration Statistics" on p. 684; and "Appendix A: General Immigration Resources" on p. 716. See also chapters on specific countries that were major sources of immigrants.)

From the 1840s on, the main East Coast port was New York City. From 1855, the immigration receiving station there was Castle Garden, a circular building on a small island off the Battery, in lower Manhattan. More than 7.5 million immigrants passed through Castle Garden between

Library of Congress

These Chinese immigrants, just arriving from Asia, were going through immigration inspection at the custom house in San Francisco in 1877.

then and 1890. As U.S. immigration swelled, Castle Garden became totally inadequate.

It was replaced by Ellis Island, a much larger structure on an island farther out in New York harbor. Ellis Island formally opened on January 1, 1892, when the first immigrant to pass through was Annie Moore, from Ireland. The station was not fully completed until June 13, 1897, but just a day later its wooden buildings were completely destroyed by fire, which consumed immigration records back to 1855.

In its place, a new, fire-resistant brick structure was built, opening in December 1900. The complex at Ellis Island would be much expanded over the coming years, including not only processing centers but also detention centers and hospitals. It would operate as an immigrant reception station until 1932 and would finally be closed in 1954.

Immigration policy was strongly class-conscious. People arriving as first- or second-class passengers were examined aboard ship—in most cases, barely examined at all. They were able to land directly from the ship, when it docked in the har-

bor. As a result, if a family could afford it, they would sometimes buy a second-class ticket for someone with questionable health, such as an ill grandmother.

However, immigrants traveling third-class (steerage) were subjected to a rigorous inspection. They were offloaded from the ship onto a ferryboat, which took them to Ellis Island. There as many as two percent would be rejected by the immigration inspectors. While that percentage may, in one sense, seem small, it amounted to 250,000 people during the Ellis Island years. They were forced to return to their port of departure, often arriving penniless and ill, far from the homelands from which they had come. The human tragedy was enormous. If a child was sent back, the tragedy could be double, for an adult was required to accompany the child.

On the West Coast, the main immigration port was San Francisco. Most early immigrants were examined at the customs house there. However, after the Chinese Exclusion Act of 1882 and subsequent anti-Asian laws, Chinese and other Asian immigrants were held, often for months, ostensibly for immigration hearings.

Their detention center was "The Shed," a rough warehouse on San Francisco's Pacific Mail Steamship Company wharf, with men kept on one floor and women on the other. Conditions there were as bad as on the worst immigrant ships, in such matters as overcrowding, poor food, and terrible sanitation—so bad that some immigrants committed suicide in despair.

In 1910 San Francisco's immigration inspection and detention center was shifted to Angel Island, a small island in San Francisco Bay. Physical conditions were little improved, and anti-Asian discrimination remained strong. Unlike Ellis Island, where almost all of the immigrants passed through into America, Angel Island was always linked with detention and exclusion. Some would-be immigrants were held there for as long as two years. In 1919 and in the 1920s, detainees rioted several times, after which conditions improved somewhat, with immigrants being held for shorter periods of time. Angel Island would not finally be closed until 1940. To avoid detention and rejection in this period, some Asian immigrants instead went to Canadian ports, most notably to Vancouver, then crossed into the United States illegally.

Inspection Abroad

From 1891 on, the U.S. government required that shipping companies vaccinate, disinfect, and examine emigrants before they boarded the ship, to cut down on the number of people rejected in U.S. ports. Some major lines, such as Germany's Hamburg-American Line, developed extensive quarters for disinfecting and examining passengers; these also offered protection from the thieves, swindlers, and other hazards awaiting emigrants in port cities. However, most shipping lines carried out only a cursory examination. Even though the law required shippers to pay for housing detained immigrants and provide free return passage for those rejected, many shippers found that cost acceptable—and were heedless of the human cost for those who might be returned penniless.

National Archives

These European emigrants are standing outside the extensive complex of buildings created by the Hamburg-American Line for housing and examining emigrants.

American Museum of Immigration, Statue of Liberty National Monument, National Park Service, U.S. Department of the Interior

During its years of use, the Ellis Island immigration station grew into a massive complex, including not only the Great Hall (top right) but also hospitals and administration buildings.

One man helped change that system. As U.S. consul in Fiume, Italy, from 1903 to 1906, Fiorello La Guardia insisted that emigrants receive a careful medical examination before being allowed to board ships for the United States. His approach proved so successful that it was adopted by Italy and then by other countries, especially in northern Europe after World War I.

The U.S. Congress made that official in 1924, formally shifting the main medical examination abroad. The 1924 law also required that immigrants apply to the U.S. consul for a visa to enter the United States. In that same period, starting in 1921, immigration restrictions sharply cut the number of immigrants allowed to enter the United States. The result of these changes was that mass use of immigration stations such as Ellis Island ended. Some would remain open for decades, but with the main inspection being carried on abroad, they were increasingly used as detention centers, for people subject to possible deportation, rather than as immigrant processing centers.

Modern Journeys

The next major change in the immigrant journey came with air travel. Regular transatlantic and transpacific air service began in 1939, but few emigrants would arrive by air in this period, except some affluent refugees fleeing the conflict that would become World War II. Jets came into use after the war, but it was not until the 1960s, with the introduction of larger jets and the lowering of air fares, that large numbers of people began to fly. Even so, air fares were high enough so that they were out of the reach of the poorest immigrants. However, in the classic way of immigrant chains, those who were already in the United States and earning money began to build up enough savings to bring other family members in by air.

By the 1990s, most immigrants who formerly would have arrived by ship were arriving in the United States by air. That included many immigrants who arrived ostensibly as tourists and simply stayed as immigrants—in official government parlance called *overstays* (see "Appendix C: Estimates of Emigration and Illegals" on p. 749).

By the 1990s, immigrants by the hundreds of thousands were also arriving by the oldest means known—by foot. Many immigrants had always arrived across the borders with Canada and Mexico; they were not even regularly counted until 1908. But in the late 20th century, the United States became such a magnet for poor people from Mexico and Central America that many walked across the border on foot. Because many of them waded across the Rio Grande (Río Bravo), the border between the United States and Texas, they were often called "wetbacks."

From the 1950s, the U.S. government mounted increasingly intensified efforts to slow or halt these illegal crossings, stepping up patrols across the borders. Such efforts have done little to slow the immigration—especially because work is readily available for these illegal immigrants—but they have made the passage far more dangerous. To try to avoid detection, many immigrants pay people to smuggle them across the border. Unfortunately, the immigrants are often placed in severe and sometimes deadly danger. Unknown numbers have died after being dumped in a desert near the border, or trapped in overcrowded, unventilated trucks or railroad cars, hot enough to become lethal ovens.

Other illegals have turned to small cargo ships to help them enter the United States. On such ships, conditions may be as bad as—or even worse than—those on the early sailing cargo ships. How many and how often such ships bring in immigrants we do not know, for many are small enough to anchor offshore, with immigrants expected to swim to land. We only know of the ships that get caught, such as the *Golden Venture*, which ran aground off Long Island in 1993, carrying 282 Chinese emigrants who said they were fleeing their country's forced abortion and sterilization policies.

Even smaller craft have been employed by many refugees around the world, from the Vietnamese "boat people" to the Mariel

California Historical Society, San Francisco

From 1910 until it was closed in 1940, many Chinese immigrants were detained at Angel Island, like these Chinese women and children waiting with a social worker.

National Archives

The Vietnamese "boat people" crowded into tiny wooden boats like these and headed out into the South China Sea, hoping to be spotted by rescuers in larger, more seaworthy ships.

Cubans, also labeled "boat people." From small motorized boats to homemade rafts, desperate refugees have often chosen hazards at sea over the dangers at home. If they are lucky, they are picked up by a larger boat. Many from Vietnam were rescued and taken to refugee centers, with some later flown to the United States. In the waters near the United States, the lucky ones were rescued by the Coast Guard, though certainly some perished. Some even made it all the way to the United States in manifestly unseaworthy boats. On some occasions, notably in regard to Cuba, governments have allowed private boats to enter ports legally and take away people wishing to immigrate to the United States. Many refugees have been grossly disappointed, however. Instead of being allowed to enter, they have been held in detention camps or even jails, sometimes for months or years, while the U.S. government decided whether or not to allow them to enter legally.

In the years after the communist revolution in Cuba, many thousands of refugees took boats like these across the 90 miles of water to refuge in the United States.

Native Americans and Immigration

The European conquerors of the Americas called the peoples they first encountered in the Americas "Indians," for they had set out to reach the East Indies and for a little while thought they had succeeded. Today the peoples they found and conquered are generally described as Native Americans, though some prefer First Americans or Earliest Americans. In a very real sense, Native Americans can also be described as Former Asians, for northeast Asia is the probable geographical and ethnic origin of the earliest known settlers of the Americas. (See "An Overview" on p. 2, for a discussion of early Native American history.)

At the beginning of the European conquest, more than 200 peoples or tribes in at least 60 major groups occupied what would later become the United States. Among them were 10 to 12 language groups. Today these peoples are quite diversely distributed, reflecting preconquest migrations and the many migrations that occurred as Native Americans were forced out of their territories by invading Europeans. Estimates vary widely, but of the 20 to 25 million Native Americans in the Americas at that time, approximately 1 to 3 million are believed to have lived in what is now the United States. By the beginning of the 20th century, that number would be down to an estimated 235,000 to 240,000.

Early Conflicts

There were several substantial European–Native American conflicts on the East Coast during the colonial period, as the colonizing Europeans penetrated and took Native American lands. However, both England and France cultivated Native American allies during their long war for North America. Most notably, the Iroquois and the British became allies. Several Native American peoples in what is now Canada even more easily allied themselves with the French, who had not aggressively attacked them, at least partly because French North American colonial populations were so much smaller than those of the British. Until after the Revolutionary War, these alliances barred major attempts to invade lands west of the Appalachian Mountains.

In Spanish-held Texas, the Southwest, and California, on the other hand, Spain pursued very aggressive policies, as it did throughout its American colonies. These resulted in the effective enslavement of the Pueblo peoples, despite a major revolt during the 1680s. The Apaches and other southwestern peoples successfully resisted until the Native American defeat by U.S. forces late in the 19th century.

Ethnic Cleansing

In the early history of Native American–European conflict, by far the most significant event directly affecting the fortunes of masses of Native Americans was the American Revolution. It set in motion a series of developments that would, by 1860, bring more than 5 million immigrants to the United States, while at the same time generating an internal migration westward, which brought millions more into what had been Native American lands. A major effect of this huge westward movement was the "ethnic cleansing" of Native Americans all the way to the Mississippi. (See

Graph 1.22: Percentage Distribution of Americans of Native American Origin by Region in the United States, 1990

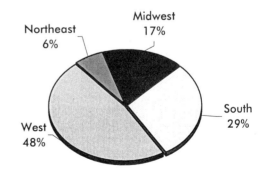

Authors' Archives

As Americans pushed the Native Americans farther west, they carried out many massacres, like this one of Cheyenne villagers on the Washita River in 1868.

"An Overview" on p. 2, for a wider discussion of the westward movement and immigration.)

With the end of the American Revolution and the flight of Britain's Iroquois allies north into Canada, the new U.S. government took Iroquois lands, opening the Mohawk Valley to westward migration all the way to the Great Lakes and from there to the Mississippi. With the flat route north on the Hudson and west to the Great Lakes open, it became possible for internal and international migrants to travel easily into the heart of the continent on the most natural of all U.S. routes into North America. From 1825 on, with the Erie Canal in place, that route westward also became a water route all the way. All that, in turn, triggered a flood of millions of migrants west, with no natural obstacles in their path. Only the Native American peoples of the region barred the way.

To the south, a far less natural but entirely feasible route through the Appalachians also became available, once British colonial policy was set aside. The route opened by Daniel Boone through Cumberland Gap became the Wilderness Road, through which millions of internal migrants would move west into Kentucky

and Tennessee following the Revolution, with again only the Native American peoples in the way.

Farther south still, where the Appalachians ended, there was no natural barrier at all, and no longer any British colonial policy barring the westward movement. Only the Creeks, Cherokees, and other Native American peoples of that region blocked further westward settlement.

The result was at least "ethnic cleansing." For some Native American peoples, it was also genocide. Beginning in the 1820s, Native American peoples in some parts of the South and the northern Midwest (then called the Old Northwest) were forced by several state governments to move to "Indian territories" farther west. In 1830, the policy became openly national, when the U.S. Congress passed the Indian Removal Act, which mandated "an exchange of lands with the Indians residing in any of the states or territories, and for their removal west of the river Mississippi."

It was done, and by force. Most Native American peoples were not able to resist. A few did; in the South, the Seminoles and some Creeks took up arms, while the Cherokees tried to resist by using the U.S. legal system. The Creeks were defeated by far stronger and better armed U.S. forces, led by Andrew Jackson. The Cherokees were forcibly removed in the winter of 1838–39, at the cost of thousands of lives, their journey soon becoming known as the Trail of Tears. Only some of the Seminoles won, led by Osceola; they would never be defeated by U.S. forces.

In the north, as in the south, most Native American peoples did not resist their forcible removal. A few peoples did unsuccessfully take up arms against U.S. forces, most notably the Sauk and Fox, led by Black Hawk. None were successful; by 1833, even the Sauk and Fox had vacated their lands.

Once established, the pattern was repeated west of the Mississippi. Reneging on all Native American–United States treaties, the U.S. government encouraged and protected the westward movement. By the 1840s, immigrant trains were moving west on the Oregon and California trails, and the long series of western Native American–United States wars had started.

These would ultimately constitute another "ethnic cleansing" in the American West, again often accompanied by genocide.

Large numbers of new or recent immigrants were part of that migration, notably those who responded to the pull of free land. The U.S. Homestead Act of 1862 was enacted during the Civil War as part of a successful attempt to recruit Europeans who would enlist in the Union Army in return for land grants, or "homesteads." It remained in force after the war, then becoming a major factor in drawing immigrants who would settle the western United States.

The number of Native Americans in the United States reached a probable low point of perhaps 215,000 to 220,000 in 1910. After that, the population began to rise again, as infant mortality rates began to drop and life expectancies lengthened. By the end of the 20th century, the estimated Native American population in the United States was approximately 1 million. As of 1990, almost half, or 47 percent, lived in the West and 29 percent in the South, with only 17 percent in the Midwest and 6 percent in the Northeast.

Authors' Archives

Native Americans in Virginia grew corn, melons, squash, sunflower, tobacco, and other crops shown in a drawing based on a 1585 sketch by Englishman John White.

Resources

Internet Resources

Native American Genealogy
(*hometown.aol.com / bbbenge /
front.html*) Web site containing many
files on family and tribal genealogy,
and links to many other Native
American genealogy sites.

Native American Indian Genealogy
Webring Homepage
(*members.tripod.com / ~kjunkutie /
natvrng.htm*) A "circle of knowledge"
Web site for anyone seeking
information about Native American
genealogy, with links to many Web
sites.

Cyndi's List—Native American
(*www.cyndislist.com / native.htm*) Part
of the WorldGenWeb project, linking
genealogical research sites around the
world, by region.

Genealogy (*www.coax.net / people / lwf /
genes.htm*) Privately maintained Web
site provides links to state, family, and
other sites related to genealogy and
history, primarily of African Americans
but also Native Americans, including
sources of records and other materials,
newsletters, archives of discussion
groups, and related organizations.

Bill's Aboriginal Links: Canada and U.S.
(*www.bloorstreet.com / 300block /
aborcan.htm*) Wide range of links,
including historical resources such as
texts of treaties.

Print Resources

General Works

Axtell, James. *Beyond 1492: Encounters in
Colonial North America.* New York:
Oxford University Press, 1992.

Ballantine, Betty, and Ian Ballantine, eds.
*The Native Americans: An Illustrated
History.* Atlanta: Turner, 1993.

Calloway, Colin G. *New Worlds for All:
Indians, Europeans, and the Remaking
of Early America.* Baltimore: Johns
Hopkins University Press, 1997.

*Cambridge History of the Native Peoples of
the Americas.* New York: Cambridge
University Press, 1996– .

Champagne, Duane, ed. *Chronology of
Native North American History: From
Pre-Columbian Times to the Present.*
Detroit: Gale, 1994.

Champagne, Duane, and Michael A. Pare,
eds. *Native North American
Chronology.* New York: U.X.L., 1995.

Cordoba, Maria. *Pre-Columbian Peoples of
North America.* Chicago: Children's
Press, 1994.

Dennis, Henry C., ed. *The American
Indian, 1492–1970: A Chronology and
Fact Book.* 2d ed. Dobbs Ferry, N.Y.:
Oceana, 1977.

Fitzhugh, William W., ed. *Cultures in
Contact: The Impact of European
Contacts on Native American Cultural
Institutions, A.D. 1000–1800.*
Washington, D.C.: Smithsonian
Institution Press, 1985.

Francis, Lee. *Native Time: A Historical
Time Line of Native America.* New
York: St. Martin's Press, 1996.

Gallant, Roy A. *Ancient Indians: The First
Americans.* Hillside, N.J.: Enslow,
1989.

Georgakas, Dan. *The Broken Hoop: The
History of Native Americans from 1600
to 1890, from the Atlantic Coast to the
Plains.* Garden City, N.Y., Zenith, 1973.

Gibson, Arrell Morgan. *The American Indian: Prehistory to the Present.* Lexington, Mass.: Heath, 1980.

Hakim, Joy. *The First Americans.* 2d ed. New York: Oxford University Press, 1999.

Harvey, Karen D., and Lisa D. Harjo. *Indian Country: A History of Native People in America.* Golden, Col.: North American Press, 1994.

Hatt, Christine. *The Peoples of North America Before Columbus.* Austin, Tex.: Raintree Steck-Vaughn, 1999.

Hazen-Hammond, Susan. *Timelines of Native American History: Through the Centuries with Mother Earth and Father Sky.* New York: Berkley, 1997.

Heard, J. Norman. *Handbook of the American Frontier: Four Centuries of Indian-White Relationships.* 5 vols. Metuchen, N.J.: Scarecrow, 1987–1998.

Hernandez, Jose. *Conquered Peoples in America.* 5th ed. Dubuque, Iowa: Kendall/Hunt, 1994.

Hoxie, Frederick E., and Peter Iverson, eds. *Indians in American History: An Introduction.* 2d ed. Wheeling, Il.: Harlan Davidson, 1998.

Jaffe, A. J. *The First Immigrants from Asia: A Population History of the North American Indians.* New York: Plenum Press, 1992.

Jennings, Francis. *The Founders of America: How Indians Discovered the Land, Pioneered in It, and Created Great Classical Civilizations . . . .* New York: Norton, 1993.

Jones, Jayne Clark. *The American Indians in America.* Minneapolis: Lerner, 1991.

Jones, Constance. *The European Conquest of North America.* New York: Facts on File, 1995.

Josephy, Alvin M. *500 Nations: An Illustrated History of North American Indians.* New York: Knopf, 1994.

Larsen, Clark Spencer, ed. *Native American Demography in the Spanish Borderlands.* New York: Garland, 1991.

Legay, Gilbert. *Atlas of Indians of North America.* Hauppauge, N.Y.: Barron's, 1995.

MacLeish, William H. *The Day Before America.* Boston: Houghton Mifflin, 1994.

Moquin, Wayne, comp. *Great Documents in American Indian History.* New York, Praeger, 1973.

Nies, Judith. *Native American History: A Chronology of the Vast Achievements of a Culture and Their Links to World Events.* New York: Ballantine Books, 1996.

Stuart, Paul. *Nations Within a Nation: Historical Statistics of American Indians.* New York: Greenwood, 1987.

Swisher, Karen Gayton, and AnCita Benally. *Native North American Firsts.* Detroit: Gale, 1998.

Underhill, Ruth Murray. *Red Man's America: A History of Indians in the United States.* Rev. ed. Chicago: University of Chicago Press, 1971.

Vogel, Virgil J. *This Country Was Ours: A Documentary History of the American Indian.* New York: Harper & Row, 1972.

Washburn, Wilcomb E., comp. *The American Indian and the United States: A Documentary History.* New York: Random House, 1973.

Genealogical Works

Byers, Paula K., ed. *Native American Genealogical Sourcebook.* New York: Gale, 1995.

Carpenter, Cecelia Svinth. *How to Research American Indian Blood Lines: A Manual on Indian Genealogical Research.* Orting, Wash.: Heritage Quest, 1987.

Kavasch, E. Barrie. *A Student's Guide to Native American Genealogy.* Phoenix: Oryx, 1996.

Kirkham, E. Kay. *Our Native Americans and Their Records of Genealogical Value.* 2 vols. Logan, Utah: Everton Publishers, 1980–1984.

McClure, Tony Mack. *Cherokee Proud: A Guide for Tracing and Honoring Your Cherokee Ancestors.* Somerville, Tenn.: Chunannee Books, 1996.

Pangburn, Richard L. *Indian Blood.* 2 vols. Louisville: Butler Books, 1993, 1996.

Chronology of Immigration

15,000 B.C.

The first fully verifiable emigration from Asia across the Bering Land Bridge (now Bering Strait) brought hunter-gatherers into Alaska, probably in pursuit of large game (by ca. 15,000–12,000 B.C.). Many believe that immigration to the Americas began much earlier, but fully acceptable verification has not yet been found. Some believe that emigration began as early as 50,000–45,000 B.C.; however, modern humans are not known to have reached Central Asia before 32,000 B.C. or northeastern Asia before 20,000 B.C. From the Bering Land Bridge, they would gradually spread throughout the Americas, becoming the many and varied peoples today known as the Native Americans.

A.D. 450

Voyagers from Polynesia, probably from the Marquesan Islands, settled in Hawaii (ca. 450).

500

Chinese sources describe the voyage of a group of Chinese Buddhist priests across the Pacific to a place they called *Fusang*, which may have been the west coast of North America, and then south to the west coast of Mexico (before ca. 500).

870

Norse explorers reached Iceland, with settlers soon following (ca. 870).

980

Norse explorers and settlers reached Greenland, among them Erik the Red and his father, Thorvald (ca. 980).

1000

Norse explorers and settlers reached North America (by ca. 1000), settling on the northern Newfoundland coast, in at least one known site, L'Anse aux Meadows.

1189

The Norse made their last recorded visit to Greenland, although their Greenland colony may have survived until the 15th century or even later.

1200

A second wave of Polynesian voyagers arrived in Hawaii, probably from Tahiti (ca. 1200).

1441

Portuguese ships that had sailed south of Muslim-held territory in West Africa returned to Portugal with 10 black African slaves. This began the Atlantic slave trade, originally headquartered on Arguin Island, off the coast of Mauretania.

1453

Ottoman Turkish forces finally took Constantinople, after centuries of attacks on the Byzantine Empire. The Turks then blocked the major Asian-European trade routes, generating new European efforts to find alternate trade routes to Asia.

1480

Portuguese, Basque, British, and Breton ships were probably fishing on the Grand Banks, off Newfoundland. Some reportedly made landfall on what was probably Newfoundland (ca. 1480–1500).

1490

On the eve of the European invasion, an estimated 1 million to 3 million Native Americans lived in what would later become the United States, part of a total population of 20 million to 25 million for the Americas as a whole (ca. 1490).

1492

On his first voyage to the Americas (August 3, 1492–March 15, 1493), Christopher Columbus reached San Salvador (probably Watling Island) in the Bahamas (October 12, 1492) and also visited Cuba and Hispaniola, where he founded Navidad, beginning the European conquest of the Americas.

1492

Tens of thousands of Jews were expelled from Spain, fleeing north to the Low Countries and to many countries bordering on the Mediterranean. The first Jewish communities in the New World would come from the Jewish communities in the Netherlands.

1493

On his second voyage to the Americas, Columbus explored Dominica, Puerto Rico, parts of the Antilles, and Jamaica.

1493

Pope Alexander VI granted Spain exclusive rights to American lands west of a specified line of demarcation, beyond the Azores and Cape Verde Islands.

1494

In the treaty of Tordesillas, Spain and Portugal agreed on what was essentially a partition of the colonial world between them.

1497

John Cabot (Giovanni Caboto), an Italian in English service, made landfall in North America, probably on Cape Breton Island and Newfoundland.

1497

Thousands of Jews were expelled from Portugal.

1498

Portuguese navigator Vasco da Gama led the first European expedition to sail around Africa to India and back, reaching Calicut in 1498 and starting the European assault on South and East Asia.

1498

On his third voyage to the Americas, Columbus discovered Trinidad Island and explored the South American coast, south to the Orinoco River (1498–1499).

1499

Alonso de Ojeda and Amerigo Vespucci explored the east coasts of South and North America, discovering the mouth of the Amazon River (1499–1500). The new lands were named after Vespucci, one of the first to recognize that the Americas were a New World, not part of Asia.

1500

Portuguese explorer Pedro Cabral reached Brazil.

1501

The first black African slaves were brought to Hispaniola, beginning the east-west portion of the transatlantic slave trade, which would cost millions of black African lives.

1502

On his fourth and last voyage to the Americas, Columbus explored the western Caribbean and coastal regions of Central America, including what are now Honduras, Nicaragua, Costa Rica, and Panama (1502–1504).

1508

Spanish forces conquered Puerto Rico (1508–1511).

1509

Sebastian Cabot, son of John Cabot, sailed an English ship into the strait opening into Hudson Bay.

1513

Spanish explorer Juan Ponce de León landed in Florida, beginning the European conquest of North America.

1513

Spanish explorer Vasco Nuñez de Balboa reached the Pacific Ocean at Panama.

1519

Spanish-sponsored Portuguese sailor Ferdinand Magellan rounded Cape Horn and entered the Pacific, on the first round-the-world voyage.

1519

Spanish forces of 600, led by Hernán Cortés, reached Tenochtitlán (Mexico City). Received peacefully as the incarnation of the god Quetzalcoatl, Cortés later took Aztec emperor Montezuma prisoner and held him as a hostage.

1520

Spanish and allied Native American forces put down an Aztec rising, killed Montezuma, and went on to conquer the entire Aztec Empire.

1521

Ferdinand Magellan reached the Philippines, where he was killed in a skirmish. Spain began its conquest of the Philippines.

1524

Giovanni Verrazano, leading an English expedition, explored the coast of Newfoundland and the Strait of Belle Isle.

1524

Spanish forces took northern Mexico, which then included part of what would become the American Southwest (1524–1555).

1534

Jacques Cartier landed on the Gaspé Peninsula, at Chaleur Bay, New Brunswick, beginning the French conquest of Canada.

1535

Returning to North America, Jacques Cartier sailed up the St. Lawrence River to the Native American village of Hochelaga, later the site of Quebec City, and on to the Lichine Rapids, later the site of Montreal.

1539

Hernando de Soto led a Spanish expedition that landed in Florida, and then explored through the South, reaching the Mississippi River in 1541. His party unknowingly carried European diseases that would destroy great numbers of Native Americans.

1540

Francisco Vásquez de Coronado led a Spanish expedition into northern Mexico, en route taking Zuni Pueblo and then reaching the Grand Canyon. He introduced the horse into North America, which had a major impact on Native American history.

1542

Juan Cabrillo led a Spanish expedition that explored the Pacific coast of North America from Mexico as far north as Oregon.

1564

French forces established Fort Caroline, on Florida's St. Johns River. It was taken by Spanish forces in 1565.

1565

St. Augustine, Florida, was founded by the Spanish; it was the first successful mainland European settlement in what would become the United States.

1587

English settlers founded a settlement on Roanoke Island, off Virginia. When a relief ship returned in 1590, the settlers had disappeared.

1588

England defeated the Spanish Armada, fully opening the way for English colonial expansion throughout the world.

1592

Spanish-sponsored Juan de Fuca (possibly a Greek sailor originally named Ioannis Phocas) discovered the strait south of Vancouver Island, now called the Strait of Juan de Fuca.

1598

Don Juan de Oñate led 200 settlers north to the Rio Grande (Río Bravo) south of modern El Paso (The Pass).

1603

Exploring south on the St. Lawrence River, Samuel de Champlain reached the Lichine Rapids, at present-day Montreal.

1605

The French established their first permanent North American settlement, at the Habitation, Port Royal (Annapolis), Nova Scotia.

1607

London's Virginia Company established England's first successful North American settlement, at Jamestown, Virginia.

1608

The French under Samuel de Champlain founded Quebec City.

1609

Henry Hudson's Dutch expedition entered the mouth of the Hudson River, then sailed north on the Hudson.

1610

Spanish settlers founded Santa Fe (Holy Faith), in what is now New Mexico.

1612

Dutch settlers founded the New Netherlands colony, in what is now New York.

1613

English forces took and destroyed Port Royal (Annapolis), Nova Scotia, beginning a long English-French battle for North America.

1614

The Dutch founded Fort Nassau, near Albany, New York.

1615

French explorer Samuel de Champlain reached Lake Huron.

1618

In Europe the continent-wide Catholic-Protestant Thirty Years War (1618–1648) began. It would cost an estimated eight million lives and triggered the first major immigration of central Europeans, most of them Germans, to the new American colonies.

1619

Twenty black African slaves arrived and were sold at Jamestown. They were the first of what would eventually be 400,000 to 500,000 people imported as slaves into North America.

1620

Puritan dissenters arrived in New England aboard the *Mayflower*. The 101 Pilgrims landed first at Provincetown, at the tip of Cape Cod, then at Plymouth Harbor, where they settled.

1622

Powhatan-English war began in Virginia, with Powhatan attacks on Jamestown and other English settlements that killed more than 350. It ended in 1625, with the massacre of an estimated 1,000 Powhatans.

1626

The Dutch founded New Amsterdam (New York).

1634

French explorer Jean Nicolet reached Green Bay, Wisconsin.

1638

Swedish colonists made the first European settlements along the Delaware River, including Fort Christina (now Wilmington, Delaware).

1654

The French frigate *St. Catherine* arrived in New Amsterdam harbor, carrying 23 Jewish immigrants who had fled from Brazil after the Portuguese had taken the Dutch settlements there. These 23 and two other Jews who arrived that year established the first Jewish community in North America.

1655

Dutch forces took Fort Christina, on the Delaware River, ending any substantial Swedish penetration into North America.

1664

English forces took New Amsterdam (New York) and much of the New Netherlands colony.

1670

The estimated total population of England's mainland American colonies was a little less than 112,000, counting slaves and free blacks, but not counting Native Americans.

1672

Dutch forces retook New York (New Amsterdam) and much of the New Netherlands colony, but they were returned to the English under the Treaty of Westminster, which ended the Third Anglo-Dutch War.

1679

French explorer René-Robert Cavelier, Sieur de La Salle, traveled through the Great Lakes and the Mississippi Valley, to the mouth of the Mississippi.

1680

Popé led a successful Native American insurrection against Spanish colonists in Santa Fe, killing 400 and forcing 1,200 to flee to El Paso. Spain would retake the area in the early 1690s.

1683

Led by Francis (Franz) Daniel Pastorius, the first primarily German group of immigrants arrived in Pennsylvania, on the *Concord*, the German equivalent of the *Mayflower*. They settled in Germantown, then a little north of Philadelphia.

1685

Thousands of French Huguenots immigrated to the English colonies after France revoked the Edict of Nantes, which had protected French Huguenots from Catholic persecution. An estimated 15,000 immigrated from 1685 to 1750, most to South Carolina.

1709

The first group of Palatine Germans arrived in the English colonies, settling in the Hudson Valley.

1718

French settlers founded New Orleans.

1727

Vitus Bering, a Dane in Russian service, discovered and named the Bering Strait.

1733

Substantial numbers of English settlers began moving into the Carolinas.

1741

Vitus Bering claimed the Aleutian Islands for Russia.

1755

The British forcibly expelled 6,000 French Canadians from Acadia (later Nova Scotia), shipping many to the British East Coast colonies.

1759

In the decisive battle of the French and Indian War, English forces besieged and took Quebec. They took Montreal in 1760, ending the war.

1775

Daniel Boone led a party through the Appalachian Mountains via the Cumberland Gap, establishing the Wilderness Road, through which millions of settlers would pour following the American Revolution.

1778

English seafarer James Cook led the first European expedition known to have reached the Hawaiian Islands.

1780

The estimated population of the British East Coast colonies was a little over 2,780,000, not counting Native Americans. Of these, a little over 575,000 (21

percent) were African Americans, the great majority of whom were slaves.

1781

British forces surrendered at Yorktown, effectively ending the American Revolution.

1784

On Kodiak Island, off Alaska, Russians founded their first permanent settlement in North America.

1790

The first U.S. Census, in 1790, estimated a population of 3,929,000, not counting Native Americans.

1791

Catherine the Great's deeply anti-Jewish policies forced most Russian Jews into the Pale of Settlement, which included much of Ukraine and all of the Russian-occupied part of Poland.

1798

The U.S. government first ordered the collection of information on "alien arrivals." However, the law expired two years later.

1799

The Russian-American Company founded Fort St. Michael, near present-day Sitka, Alaska. The settlement was destroyed by the Tlingits in 1802.

1803

The United States acquired the Louisiana Territory from France. In this "Louisiana Purchase," France ceded to the United States huge areas of land from the Mississippi to the Rockies.

1804

The Russians reestablished their fort near Sitka (New Archangel), which became the capital of Russian America.

1807

The United States formally banned the slave trade. However, slaves continued to be imported into southern ports until the Civil War.

1809

Kamehameha, founder of the Kamehameha dynasty (1795–1872), completed the conquest and unification of the Hawaiian Islands.

1814

Russians founded Fort Stawianski (Fort Ross), a fortified trading post in northern California.

1815

With the end of the Napoleonic Wars, shipping across the North Atlantic picked up and substantial immigration to North America resumed.

U.S. forces attacked and took Florida; Spain ceded Florida to the United States in 1819.

The first regularly scheduled liners, called *packets*, began sailing between Liverpool and New York; they were soon followed by many others. Before then, emigrants had to wait in port until the next cargo ship was ready to sail.

1819

The U.S. government mandated the keeping of continuous official records of immigration information, with summaries published from 1820.

1820

The number of immigrants recorded in the first year of official U.S. immigration tabulation was 8,385.

1825

The Erie Canal was completed, fully opening the main immigrant way west. Millions of United States and European immigrant settlers would follow this water-level route into the Midwest.

1830

From 1821 to 1830, recorded immigrants to the United States numbered 143,439.

Congress passed the Indian Removal Act, providing for "an exchange of lands with the Indians residing in any of the states or territories, and for their removal west of the river Mississippi." By the early 1840s, that removal had been forcibly completed.

1835

Seminole and escaped slave forces began a partially successful defense of their lands against attacking U.S. forces.

1836

United States settlers won their war of independence from Spain, establishing a republic in Texas.

1838

The Cherokees were forcibly removed from their lands in the winter of 1838–1839, at the cost of thousands of lives. Their journey soon became known as the Trail of Tears.

1840

From 1831 to 1840, recorded immigrants to the United States numbered 599,125.

After China attempted to stop the British-run opium trade, British forces attacked and defeated China, in the Opium War. That began more than 70 years of European domination of an increasingly helpless China and sparked the beginning of massive emigration out of China, largely to southeast Asia, the Pacific, and the Americas.

1841

Russians sold Fort Ross, California, and other lands in the area to John Augustus Sutter, and left California.

1842

The annual number of recorded immigrants to the United States topped 100,000 for the first time.

1843

Part of the Seminole nation, as well as some former slaves and their descendants, successfully held their territory in the Everglades against attacking U.S. forces and were never defeated. Many other Seminoles were forcibly removed to Oklahoma, in one of the final acts of "ethnic cleansing" east of the Mississippi.

1845

A potato blight caused crop failures across Europe. The worst effects were felt in Ireland, where crops failed three times (1845–1847) and even the seed potatoes for the 1847 crop were lost. The result was Ireland's Great Famine accompanied by several plagues and widespread evictions of tenants. In all, an estimated 1 to 1.5 million died of famine and plague, while an estimated

2 million fled abroad, 1.3 million of them to the United States.

1845

Substantial Chinese immigration to the Americas began. Many Chinese became Peruvian gold mine and Cuban sugarcane plantation contract laborers.

1846

The British-American Oregon Treaty expanded United States lands to include much of Oregon, Washington, and other territories in the Pacific Northwest.

U.S. forces successfully attacked Mexico, beginning the Mexican-American War (1846–1848). United States settlers took California, while U.S. forces attacked overland across New Mexico and Arizona into California, and U.S. seaborne forces landed on the Pacific coast. The war effectively ended in 1847, when U.S. seaborne forces took Mexico City.

1848

Under the Treaty of Guadalupe Hidalgo, the United States annexed an area of one million square miles, approximately half of what had been Mexico, taking the United States to the Pacific. These lands would become the states of Texas, California, Arizona, New Mexico, Nevada, Utah, and half of Colorado.

Many liberals ("the Forty-Eighters") emigrated in the wake of failed revolutions across Europe, especially from Germany and Austria.

1849

Immigrants from around the world poured into California during the Gold Rush of 1849, which followed the discovery of gold at Sutter's Mill near Sacramento.

1850

From 1841 to 1850, recorded immigrants to the United States numbered 1,713,251.

The U.S. Census Bureau first started to track information about the national origin of foreign-born immigrants in the United States.

The Taiping Rebellion (1850–1966) against the Manchu rulers began in

Guangxi (Kiangsi), China. The massive civil war would cost 20 million to 40 million lives, destroy China's remaining ability to resist European penetration, and generate heavy emigration out of China.

U.S. immigration statistics first began to include arrivals in West Coast ports; previously only arrivals in East Coast or Gulf Coast ports had been counted.

1853

Mindful of the example of China, which by then had lost the first Opium War and seen the beginning of the massive Taiping Rebellion, Japan reopened itself to Western trade, after being almost completely closed to the West since 1637. The issue was forced by the entry into Tokyo Bay of a flotilla of four U.S. ships commanded by Commodore Matthew Perry (July 8, 1853).

1855

Castle Garden, a circular building on a small island off the Battery, in lower Manhattan, began being used as the main immigration station for New York harbor. From 1855 to 1890, more than 7.5 million immigrants would pass through Castle Garden.

1860

From 1851 to 1860, recorded immigrants to the United States numbered 2,598,214.

1862

The U.S. Congress passed the Homestead Act, offering free land grants as a bonus for those who would sign up in the Union Army, drawing many thousands of immigrants from Europe.

1864

The U.S. Congress made the first national attempt to control and restrict immigration, passing a statute that attempted to take over control of emigration from the states. A second major provision of the law authorized "contract labor" arrangements, under which immigrants could agree to pay back their passage money from their later earnings. The law was repealed in 1868, largely because of opposition from U.S. labor organizations.

1866

The Pacific Mail Steamship Company began carrying Chinese immigrants to the United States; it was soon joined by many competitors between Asia and the U.S. West Coast.

1867

Russia sold the entire Alaska Territory to the United States.

1868

The 1868 China–United States Burlingame Treaty provided for unrestricted immigration both ways between the United States and China, frustrating many attempts by the state of California to stop Chinese immigration.

1870

From 1861 to 1870, recorded immigrants to the United States numbered 2,314,824.

1875

The federal government took control of immigration, after the U.S. Supreme Court reversed an earlier position that had left control in the hands of the states.

1877

Anti-Chinese riots flared in San Francisco, as anti-Asian bigotry grew throughout the West.

1880

From 1871 to 1880, recorded immigrants to the United States numbered 2,812,191.

The United States forced China to renegotiate the Burlingame Treaty; the new treaty allowed the United States to restrict Chinese immigration.

1881

The annual number of recorded immigrants topped 500,000 for the first time, reaching almost 670,000.

Russian czar Alexander II was assassinated, ending the period of reform he had started in 1855, which had included laws easing discrimination against Russian Jews. Major anti-Jewish riots throughout southern Russia and Poland occurred in the spring of 1881. In May 1882, the harshly repressive May Laws were introduced, triggering massive Russian Jewish immigration to the United States.

1882

The Chinese Exclusion Act effectively banned Chinese immigration into the United States; it was the first of a series of anti-Chinese acts that together effectively cut off Chinese immigration until the 1950s.

The San Francisco immigration station called "The Shed" opened. This dilapidated warehouse on a San Francisco wharf was used for 28 years (1882–1910) to detain Chinese immigrants, in miserable conditions, often for months, and on a host of pretexts.

1884

A second Chinese Exclusion Act was passed.

1885

Anti-Chinese attacks in Rock Springs, Wyoming, killed 28 Chinese Americans.

The U.S. Congress adopted a law against contract labor, especially aimed at immigrants; other anticontract labor laws were passed in 1887 and 1888.

1886

Effective Native American resistance west of the Mississippi ended, with the surrender of Apache forces led by Geronimo.

1888

The Scott Act barred 20,000 Chinese immigrants, who had been in China visiting their families, from returning to the United States.

1890

From 1881 to 1890, recorded immigrants to the United States numbered 5,246,613.

U.S. forces massacred a captive Sioux band of 350, consisting of 230 women and children and 120 men, at Wounded Knee Creek, in South Dakota's Pine Ridge Sioux reservation. It was the last "battle" of the "Indian Wars."

1891

The U.S. Congress passed the first comprehensive immigration restriction law. Immigrants could be classed as "inadmissible aliens" and barred from entry for many reasons, including that they were likely to become public charges, suffered from certain contagious diseases, had been convicted of crimes or misdemeanors, were polygamists, or had received assistance in payment of their passage. The law also outlawed advertisements encouraging immigration and provided for the deportation of immigrants who entered illegally.

1892

The immigration station at Castle Garden was replaced by the federally run Ellis Island, a much larger structure on an island in New York harbor. The first immigrant to pass through, after its formal opening on January 1, 1892, was Annie Moore, from Ireland.

1893

The Immigration Act of 1893 required the reporting of additional information about immigrants, including occupation, marital status, ability to read or write, amount of money in possession, and physical and mental health. This information was used in expanding the classification of immigrants as "inadmissible aliens," with special boards of inquiry to review their status. The records of those who passed through would be useful to later genealogists and family historians.

A United States–backed revolution deposed Liliuokalani, the last monarch of Hawaii. A U.S.-dominated republic was then established.

The Panic of 1893 in the United States slowed emigration from many countries.

1898

Under the Treaty of Paris following the Spanish-American War, Spanish forces left Cuba, which became a U.S. protectorate. The United States also took control of Puerto Rico, Guam, and the Philippines, though a Philippine independence movement led by Emilio Aguinaldo continued.

The United States annexed Hawaii.

1900

From 1891 to 1900, recorded immigrants to the United States numbered 3,687,564.

Hawaii became a U.S. territory.

1901

Emilio Aguinaldo, president of the Philippines, was captured by U.S. forces and subsequently signed an oath of allegiance to the United States, ending the main phase of the failed Philippine War of Independence. The Philippines became a U.S. protectorate.

1903

The Immigration Act of 1903 expanded still further the list of reasons for classing an immigrant as an "inadmissible alien," in particular for the first time excluding "anarchists, or persons who believe in, or advocate, the overthrow by force or violence the government of the United States."

After the murders of thousands of Jews during the pogroms that began at Kishinev in 1903, the exodus of Jews from Russia increased enormously. From 1900 to 1914, an estimated 1,447,000 Russian Jews immigrated to the United States.

1905

The annual number of recorded immigrants to the United States topped 1 million for the first time.

1906

The Naturalization Act of 1906 required that immigrants had to know English to become naturalized citizens.

1907

The Immigration Act of 1907 expanded yet again the possible classifications of "inadmissible aliens," including people with physical or mental problems that might adversely affect their ability to make a living, children unaccompanied by their parents, and women immigrating for "immoral purposes." For the first time the law required those arriving to declare whether they intended to stay or only to visit, classifying them as immigrants and nonimmigrants accordingly.

U.S. president Theodore Roosevelt and the Japanese government negotiated a "Gentlemen's Agreement" providing that the Japanese would, in essence, limit Japanese immigration to the

United States in return for protection against anti-Japanese U.S. legislation. In addition, by executive order, Roosevelt blocked the immigration of Japanese to the United States from Hawaii.

1907

The annual number of recorded immigrants reached a peak of 1,285,349. That yearly total would not be exceeded until 1991.

1910

From 1901 to 1910, recorded immigrants to the United States numbered 8,795,386. That would be by far the largest number of immigrants per decade before the 1990s, being almost 14 percent of the total immigration between 1820 and 1996.

"The Shed" was succeeded by Angel Island, an equally infamous U.S. immigration station in San Francisco Bay, where from 1910 to 1940 Chinese immigrants were held, some of them for as long as two years.

The Mexican Revolution (1910–1920), which cost the lives of approximately 1 million people, spurred an estimated 1 million Mexican refugees to enter the United States, filling available jobs throughout the growing American economy.

The Mann White Slavery Traffic Act prohibited the importation or interstate transportation of women for immoral purposes. Directed against the importation of women to work as prostitutes, in practice the law made it far more difficult than before for single women to enter the United States.

1914

Many emigrants fled from Europe to avoid the coming war, among them many young men facing conscription, who fled as "illegals" across closed borders. Once war started, immigration to the United States dropped sharply.

1917

The 1917 Immigration Act introduced the long-resisted literacy test, which excluded illiterate aliens from entry into the United States. The act also expanded anti-Asian exclusion, establishing a "barred zone" that included most of Asia, from which all immigration to the United States was prohibited.

1920

From 1911 to 1920, recorded immigrants to the United States numbered 5,735,811.

1921

The 1921 Immigration Act for the first time established numerical quotas and limits on immigration. Immigration was limited to 3 percent of the foreign-born persons of each nationality living in the United States in 1910; this favored emigration from northern and western Europe, sharply cutting immigration to the United States from southern and eastern Europe. The limitations did not apply to people who had lived for a year (extended to five years in 1922) in the Western Hemisphere or to countries where immigration was covered by treaty.

1924

The 1924 Immigration Act established the national origins quota system, limiting immigration to 2 percent of the foreign-born persons of each nationality living in the United States in 1890, even more heavily favoring northern and western Europe as against southern and eastern Europe. Again, Western Hemisphere immigration was not limited. With minor later amendments, including modification of quotas in 1929, the highly restrictive quota system established by the 1924 Immigration Act remained in effect until 1952, as did other restrictive provisions such as the Asian "barred zone." In another major change, the examination of both immigrants and nonimmigrants was shifted abroad; those wishing to enter the country had to apply to a U.S. consul's office for a visa. That would end the mass use of Ellis Island and similar stations, which came to be employed primarily as places of detention for deportees.

The U.S. Border Patrol was established.

1929

The Immigration Act of 1929 made it a felony (punishable by fine or imprisonment or both) for immigrants to enter the United States by fraud or at other than a designated place.

1929

The Crash of 1929 ushered in the Great Depression; the lack of jobs would sharply cut immigration, for many countries below even the low quotas established by the 1924 Immigration Act.

1930

From 1921 to 1930, recorded immigrants to the United States numbered 4,107,209.

1933

The annual number of recorded immigrants dropped to 23,068, the lowest it had been since 1831.

1934

The Tydings-McDuffie Independence Act granted the Philippines commonwealth status, making it possible to declare Filipinos aliens. The law set a quota of 50 Filipino admissions per year, effectively stopping immigration to the United States from the Philippines.

1937

The 1937 Immigration Act allowed for the deportation of any immigrant who had obtained an entry visa through a fraudulent marriage.

1940

From 1931 to 1940, recorded immigrants to the United States numbered 528,431, the lowest total for a decade since 1830. It would remain low throughout World War II.

The 1940 Alien Registration Act provided for the registration of all resident aliens, and past or present membership in proscribed or "subversive" organizations was made a deportable offense, as was the smuggling in of illegal aliens.

1941

The 1941 Public Safety Act authorized U.S. consular offices abroad to deny visas to any aliens who might endanger the safety of the United States.

1943

The Chinese Exclusion Act was effectively repealed. However, a quota of only 105 per year was set for the whole of China.

The U.S. Congress passed a law allowing for the temporary importation of agricultural laborers from elsewhere in the Americas; this was later expanded into the *bracero* program.

1945

The War Brides Act of 1945 waived visa requirements and immigration restrictions as they applied to foreign-born spouses of members of U.S. armed services. The G.I. Fiancées Act of 1946 and a law applying to Chinese wives of U.S. citizens would similarly ease admission.

1948

The 1948 Displaced Persons Act was the first law allowing for admission of people fleeing persecution. This and succeeding laws would allow admission of several hundred thousand refugees in the next few years.

1949

Alaska became the 49th state in the United States.

1950

From 1941 to 1950, recorded immigrants to the United States numbered 1,035,039.

1951

During the Korean War, Mexico and the United States negotiated a *bracero,* or guest worker, agreement that from 1951 to 1965 brought a total of 4.5 million Mexican workers into the United States, an average of 300,000 per year.

1952

The Immigration and Nationality Act of 1952 eliminated racial bars to citizenship, and declared sexual discrimination in immigration to be at an end. The quota system was revised to eliminate much of its bias against eastern and southern Europeans. It also retained separate, discriminatory treatment for countries in the "barred zone," but allowed for entry of small numbers of immigrants from Asia. The law also set up a system giving preferred quota status to people with urgently required skills, while ending the ban on contract labor, in existence since 1868.

1953

The U.S. Congress passed the Refugee Relief Act of 1953, allowing immigration of many Dutch refugees, some of the thousands who had fled to the Netherlands after Indonesia won independence from Dutch rule (1949–1950).

1954

A 41-year-long guerrilla insurrection began in Guatemala after a right-wing United States–backed military takeover. The conflict would generate hundreds of thousands of emigrants, many of them Mayan refugees from the government's reign of terror in the countryside. Many Guatemalan refugees reached the United States as "illegal" immigrants.

The United States carried out "Operation Wetback," a major but ultimately unsuccessful attempt to cut the flow of illegal immigrants from Mexico. Operation Wetback came at the end of a series of increasingly punitive efforts to curb illegal Mexican immigration. From 1950 to 1955 an estimated 3 million to 4 million Mexicans were deported, approximately 1.1 million of them without hearings and appeals during Operation Wetback. The flow of illegal immigrants was affected for a few years but then picked up again, for conditions in Mexico changed only for the worse, and United States growers continued to provide seasonal jobs for those who made it across the border.

1957

With the dictatorship of François "Papa Doc" Duvalier (1957–1971), thousands fled Haiti, a flow that would eventually reach an estimated 1 million emigrants from 1957 to 1996. Of these, an estimated 500,000 would reach the United States, at least 200,000 of them as "illegals." Many of these arrived by small boat and were therefore called the "Haitian boat people." Some perished en route, in one of the most poignant of the 20th century's multitude of refugee stories.

1959

Fidel Castro's forces took Havana and with that took power in Cuba on January 8, 1959. They soon turned Cuban society upside down, building a Soviet-allied Communist state and triggering a set of mass refugee migrations out of Cuba, mainly to the United States. The first major wave of Cuban refugees numbered approximately 150,000 from 1959 to 1962, when it was cut off by the Cuban Missile Crisis.

Hawaii became the 50th state in the United States.

1960

From 1951 to 1960, recorded immigrants to the United States numbered 2,515,479.

1961

In a series of modifications to the 1952 Immigration Act, the quota ceiling of 2,000 for the whole Asia-Pacific triangle was lifted, with a quota of at least 100 established for each newly independent nation.

1962

Britain passed the Commonwealth Immigrants Act, sharply limiting immigration to Great Britian from countries that had been part of the British Empire. As a result, many emigrants from these regions, most notably from the Caribbean, went instead to the United States.

1965

The second wave of Cuban refugees began to reach the United States, starting with 5,000 evacuated by sea from Camarioca, with many more being evacuated by a U.S.-financed airlift. More than 250,000 refugees reached the United States from 1965 to 1972.

The 1965 Immigration Act abolished the restrictive national origins quota system originally set up by the 1924 Immigration Act. In its place, the law established a much less restrictive set of hemispheric and national quotas. The act also established two categories that were not subject to any numerical quotas. The first and by far most important of these covered the immediate relatives of U.S. citizens, and it was this category that reopened the "golden door," as it allowed the legal admission of hundreds of thousands of new immigrants per year, beyond the quotas. The other category was a small class of special immigrants, such as former employees of the U.S. government abroad.

1966

The Freedom of Information Act provided that aliens (or their attorneys) have access to their Immigration and Naturalization records, with copies of decisions to be made available to the public.

1970

From 1961 to 1970, recorded immigrants to the United States numbered 3,321,677.

1975

Two years after withdrawal of U.S. troops ended the wider Vietnam War, the continuing north-south civil war ended with the fall of Saigon to the North Vietnamese. Approximately 130,000 South Vietnamese refugees fled to the United States in the following year. Several laws were passed to aid in their immigration and resettlement.

The Cambodian Civil War (1969–1975) ended with victory by the Khmer Rouge, who carried out wholesale relocation and massacres in which 2 million to 3 million Cambodians died, in what is rightly called the Cambodian Holocaust (1975–1978). Massive flight from Cambodia followed, much of it to the United States.

1978

Hundreds of thousands of Vietnamese fled Vietnam (1978–1982) by boat (and so were called the "Vietnamese boat people"). Many of them ethnic Chinese Vietnamese, they often reached the United States after internment in countries neighboring Vietnam.

Hundreds of thousands of refugees flooded out of Nicaragua following the outbreak of the Nicaraguan civil war (1978–1988), many of them reaching the United States as "illegal" immigrants.

1979

During El Salvador's long, exceedingly "dirty" civil war (1979–1992), an estimated 600,000 to 750,000 Salvadorans fled the country as right-wing death squads killed tens of thousands. An estimated 500,000 Salvadorans entered the United States, most of them as "illegal" immigrants who made their way north through Mexico and then across the U.S. border.

1980

From 1971 to 1980, recorded immigrants to the United States numbered 4,493,314.

From April to September, an estimated 125,000 people were evacuated from Cuba, after that country opened the port of Mariel to ships that would take them out. Popularly called the "Mariel boat people," most ultimately were accepted as refugees by the United States.

The 1980 Refugee Act established a general and systematic approach to international refugees and asylees, instead of the case-by-case laws of the past, though there would be continuing controversy over who was or was not to be classified as a refugee.

1986

The 1986 Immigration Reform and Control Act (IRCA) attempted to more fully control immigration, while also solving the problems posed by millions of "illegals," by declaring an amnesty for those who had been living in the United States since January 1, 1982. The law legalized millions of illegals but did not in any way stem the growing flow of new undocumented immigrants, who continued to arrive by the millions.

1989

The annual number of recorded immigrants topped 1 million for the first time since 1914, at the start of World War I.

1990

From 1981 to 1990, recorded immigrants to the United States numbered 7,338,062.

The 1990 Immigration Act attempted to partially close the open door created by the 1965 Immigration Act, establishing a new total immigration cap of 675,000 immigrants per year. These would consist of 480,000 family-sponsored immigrants (rather than the unlimited number allowed by the 1965 law), who were to be admitted via a complex set of preferences; 140,000 employment-based immigrants; and 55,000 others. Legal immigrants continued to enter the United States at an average of more than 1 million per year, as did millions of "illegals."

1991

The number of recorded immigrants reached an all-time annual high of 1,827,167.

1996

From 1991 to 1996, recorded immigrants to the United States numbered 6,146,213.

The Antiterrorism and Effective Death Penalty Act focused on countering terrorism, expanding procedures for identifying possible terrorists from among refugees and for expediting the deportation of people identified as terrorists and criminals. The law came to be used far beyond this original intention, with some immigrants being deported for extremely minor legal infractions.

The Personal Responsibility and Work Opportunity Reconciliation Act sharply restricted public assistance benefits for immigrant residents and barred illegal and some other immigrants from receiving most types of public benefits, on the federal, state, and local levels.

The Illegal Immigration Reform and Immigrant Responsibility Act was yet another attempt to stem and reverse the continuing flow of illegal immigrants into the United States. By 1996, the U.S. government estimated that 5 million illegal immigrants were residing in the United States (see "Appendix C: Estimates of Emigration and Illegals" on p. 749). This law greatly expanded U.S. enforcement efforts, making it possible for U.S. immigration authorities to refuse entry and deport aliens without effective opposition or guarantees of legal process, and introduced several other new bars aimed at reducing the numbers of new illegal immigrants and deporting those already residing in the United States.

For more on laws relating to immigration, see "Appendix B: Immigration and Naturalization Legislation" on p. 723.

Part II

Immigration from

Europe

Introduction

Europe has been by far the largest source of immigrants to the United States. Between 1820 (when the United States began keeping official immigration statistics) and 1996, more than 63 million recorded immigrants entered the United States. Of these, 60.21 percent were from Europe. In reality, the percentage is even higher, for an undetermined but substantial number of immigrants to Canada were actually "sojourners," passing through Canada on their way from Europe to the United States.

In terms of ethnic origins, the numbers become overwhelming, as massive European immigration came first, long before the late-20th-century bulge of emigration from Asia and the Americas. Therefore, the greatest part, by far, of the natural increase in the U.S. population occurred in its European ethnic groups. In addition, many of the new immigrants from the Americas were also of European ethnicity.

As the figures below indicate, European immigration predominated in every decade until the 1920s, though because immigration overland to the United States from Canada and Mexico was not fully recorded until 1908, the immigration figures from those countries are understated. However, the restrictive immigration laws of 1921 and 1924 sharply cut southern and eastern European immigration, while not affecting emigration from the Americas. That helped shift immigration balances toward the Americas.

European immigration to the United States plummeted during the Great Depression and World War II. During this period, immigrants from the Americas for the first time came to outnumber those from Europe.

A decisive change occurred after passage of the 1965 Immigration Act, which opened the United States to immigrants from the Eastern Hemisphere for the first time. Immigration to the United States from the Americas skyrocketed, as enormous population pressures, coupled with economic crises and political instability, drove millions to enter the United States, legally and illegally. In the same period, immigration to the United States from Europe slackened, as population pressures subsided and much of Europe prospered. European immigration to the United States in the 1980s hit its lowest level, at only 10.38 percent of the total immigration, far behind the percentage of immigration to the United States from Asia and the Americas. In the 1990s, European immigration reached only 14.92 percent.

Following are country-by-country treatments of the main sources of immigration to the United States from Europe. These are followed by the overall recorded U.S. immigration statistics for Europe and general resources on European immigration.

Immigrants from Britain

Although an English expedition led by John Cabot (Giovanni Caboto) made landfall on Newfoundland in 1497, and English sailors may have been fishing off the Grand Banks even earlier, English settlement in what would become the United States began more than a century later, with the settlement of Jamestown in 1607. We tell the story of the early English North American settlements in an earlier chapter (see "An Overview" on p. 2), within the context of the European imperial rivalries of that time and the European conquest of the Americas. (See also "Native Americans and Immigration" on p. 73, for the disastrous impact of the European conquest on the earlier inhabitants of North America, and "The Slave Trade" on p. 321, for the development of the slave trade that would have such a major influence on the course of American history.)

Colonial Times

During the 17th century, the largest source of immigration into England's North American colonies was England itself, though some of those recorded as "English" were from Scotland and Wales. In the southern colonies, the greatest number of English immigrants came for economic reasons, the minority as entirely free people and the majority as indentured servants or redemptioners, encumbered by the need to repay passage money and other debts before they could be free to make their own lives in a new land (see "The Journey" on p. 53). Some also came as bonded servants for stated periods of time; among these were deported convicts. Later in the century, the numbers of indentured servants and bonded servants immigrating into the southern colonies diminished somewhat, as the numbers of black slaves sharply increased in the southern plantation system. However, a majority of English immigrants to the southern colonies continued to be indentured servants.

In New England, the picture was quite different. There most early English immigrants were Puritans, many of them skilled people with some capital, whose religious beliefs caused them to want to leave England, where the government was unfriendly to their views. Only later in the 17th century were they joined in any substantial numbers by those immigrants coming to New England and the other northern and mid-Atlantic colonies for largely economic reasons, among them farmers and many Londoners. Emigration for religious reasons sharply diminished after 1689, when the Protestant triumph in England and the accession of William and Mary brought more religious freedom for Puritans and other Protestant Dissenters.

In the 18th century, the British emigration picture widened. While most of those emigrating across the Atlantic from Britain continued to be English, substantial numbers of Scots and Welsh also began to come to the British colonies, though good information is not available as to how many of each group came to the British colonies during the colonial period. The majority of English immigrants to the southern colonies continued to be indentured servants. However, New England strongly discouraged such immigrants, on several occasions turning away immigrant ships carrying indentured servants; indenture contracts were finally outlawed in 1819.

Sorting out how many British immigrants came from England, Scotland, or Wales during the colonial period is nearly impossible. Colonial immigration statistics do not provide that information, instead lumping all three together as British immigrants. For that matter, neither do most later immigration statistics. At best, some estimates are possible, as in the first U.S. census from 1790. Beyond that, reconstruction is sometimes partly—though not very reliably—possible by study of ships' manifests (see "The Journey" on p. 53) and other records in the immigrants' countries of origin.

The matter of usable statistics is even more complicated than that, for many of the almost 200,000 Scotch-Irish immigrants estimated to have come to the British colonies from the 1690s to 1790 have, in a sense, been double-counted. Researchers studying emigration out of Scotland have

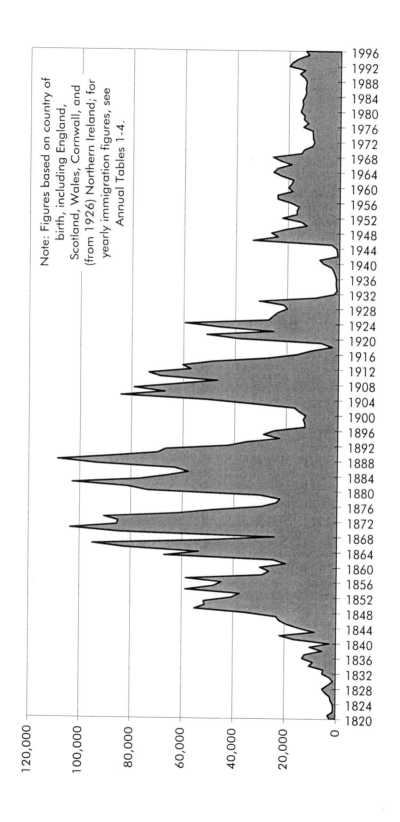

Graph 2.1: Number of Immigrants from Great Britain Annually, 1820–1996

Note: Figures based on country of birth, including England, Scotland, Wales, Cornwall, and (from 1926) Northern Ireland; for yearly immigration figures, see Annual Tables 1–4.

The Puritan immigrants known as the Pilgrims were more than two months at sea in the Mayflower *before they landed in New England in 1620, a scene depicted here.*

often counted some of those 200,000 as Scots immigrants, while in official U.S. immigration statistics they have also been counted as Scotch-Irish. Even beyond that, an unknown but apparently sizable number of early Catholic Irish immigrants changed their names and religions on arrival in the New World, appreciably throwing off British, Irish, and Scotch-Irish immigration figures.

Some thousands of Scots, most of them from the Highlands, emigrated to the British colonies during the late 17th and early 18th centuries, largely to North Carolina and Georgia. Among them were many deported as civil criminals and as rebels against British rule. The greatest mass of Scottish emigrants in colonial times, an estimated 20,000 to 25,000 in all, came between the early 1760s and the outbreak of the American Revolution in 1775. They had been forced out of Scotland because of increased land rents in the Highlands. The majority of these late Scottish immigrants supported the Loyalist side in the Revolution and were forced to emigrate once again after British defeat. At that point, most of them went to Canada, though some returned to Britain.

Immigrants from Wales, counted as part of the British immigration, began to reach the colonies in organized groups late in the 17th century, but not in very large numbers until the early 19th century. A group of Welsh Quakers reached Pennsylvania in 1681, and Welsh farming communities then began to be established in the mid-Atlantic colonies. Following establishment of the new United States, Welsh settlers were an integral part of the trans-Appalachian movement westward.

In the New United States

By 1780, the best available estimate of ethnic origins in the emerging United States indicated that 60.9 percent of the white population was of English origin. That figure included people of Welsh and Cornish origin. Scotch ethnic origin was attributed to 8.3 percent of the white population, and Scotch-Irish origin to 6.0 percent. By that time, however, a great deal of ethnic mixing had already occurred within the North American population, especially among immigrants originally from the British Isles.

New England's Pilgrims came to America seeking religious freedom, but did not always grant it; Anne Hutchinson, shown here, was expelled from Massachusetts for her preaching.

Many people fled the crowded cities of Britain, such as London, shown here in the late 19th century, for the wide open spaces of the United States.

During the 40 years between the beginning of the American Revolution and the end of the Napoleonic Wars (1775–1815), which included the War of 1812 (1812–1814), the North Atlantic crossing was very unsafe indeed, and very few immigrant-carrying ships even tried to reach North America from Britain. Nor did Britain encourage immigration to the United States. The 1803 Passenger Vessel Act, ostensibly passed to relieve the terrible conditions on immigrant ships, was primarily used to limit immigration to the new United States, by driving up the price of passage. Further Passenger Acts in 1816, 1817, 1823, and 1825 had the same effect; they also encouraged immigration to British colonies by making passage to them cheaper than to the United States. However, many immigrants took the cheaper passage to Canada, and then entered the United States from there.

British immigration is often described as having been rather limited in the early decades of the 19th century. However, that is not entirely so, for the percentage of British immigrants in the total U.S. immigration remained very substantial and rather steady from 1820 to 1890, averaging 17.6 percent during that 70-year period. There was a single sag in the 1830s and a single surge after the Civil War, as the American West was fully opened and the new industrial United States began to emerge.

Later Immigration

The numbers of British immigrants did drop significantly during the late 1890s, but surged in the peak years of the pre–World War I migration, averaging more than 60,000 per year from 1903 to 1914. Relatively few British immigrants entered the United States during World War I, but

Graph 2.2: Percentage of Immigrants from England, Scotland, and Wales in Total Foreign-Born Immigrants from Great Britain, 1850

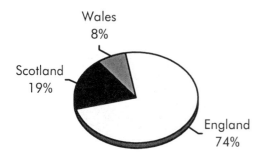

Note: Figures based on country of birth.

an average of almost 34,000 a year did so in the prosperous 1920s. They were able to enter freely, for British immigration was not at all affected by the restrictive 1924 U.S. Immigration Act, which favored admission of immigrants from northern Europe.

The Great Depression and World War II brought British immigration down very sharply: an average of only 2,400 British immigrants per year entered the United States from 1932 to 1945. After a brief surge into the 20,000 to 30,000 range in the early postwar period, British immigration was for two decades in the 15,000 to 25,000 per year range. From 1970 to 1975, it dropped into the 10,000 to 11,000 per year range, and from then on never reached 20,000 per year.

Overall Impact

U.S. immigration records indicate that a total of more than 5 million British immigrants entered the United States from 1820 to 1996. That would be the fourth-largest national total for that period, after Germany, Mexico, and Italy. The figure must be considered approximate, though, for in some periods passengers traveling first- or second-class were not adequately counted or not counted at all as immigrants. In addition, many immigrants arriving in Canada and then entering over the Canadian border are not to be found in the official totals, especially because most people arriving by land were not counted

before 1908. Beyond that, the 1820–1996 figures do not include immigrants arriving before 1820; in the case of the British, that means most of the founding European settlers of the United States, at least some hundreds of thousands in number. The British, then, are clearly the second most numerous of American immigrant groups, after the Germans, while the first in every other significant way, for with their language, culture, and political ideas, they laid the basis for what would become the defining culture of the United States.

During the 19th century, British immigrants settled throughout the United States, for they were settling into their own society and culture, without any of the language or cultural adjustment problems faced by so many other immigrant groups. That was not true of all English speakers, however; poor Irish immigrants fleeing the effects of the mid-19th-century potato famine faced deep problems of discrimination (see "Immigrants from Ireland" on p. 109).

Britain's industrial revolution, which came some decades before that of even the rest of western Europe, enabled large numbers of British immigrants to play a crucial role in the development of the United States as an advanced industrial nation. Had that not been so, the balance of population, industrial strength, and military power between North and South might

Graph 2.3: Percentage of Immigrants from England, Scotland, Wales, and Northern Ireland in Total Foreign-Born Immigrants from Great Britain, 1930

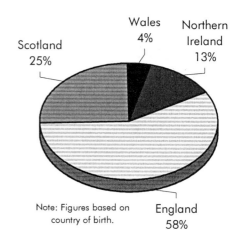

Note: Figures based on country of birth.

Table 2.1: Number and Percentage of Immigrants from Great Britain in Total U.S. Immigration by Decade, 1820–1996

Decade	Number of Immigrants from Great Britain	Total U.S. Immigration	Percentage of Immigrants from Great Britain in Total U.S. Immigration
1820	2,410	8,385	28.74
1821-1830	25,079	143,439	17.48
1831-1840	75,810	599,125	12.65
1841-1850	267,044	1,713,251	15.59
1851-1860	423,974	2,598,214	16.32
1861-1870	606,896	2,314,824	26.22
1871-1880	548,043	2,812,191	19.49
1881-1890	807,357	5,246,613	15.39
1891-1900	271,538	3,687,564	7.36
1901-1910	525,950	8,795,386	5.98
1911-1920	341,408	5,735,811	5.95
1921-1930	339,570	4,107,209	8.27
1931-1940	31,572	528,431	5.97
1941-1950	139,306	1,035,039	13.46
1951-1960	202,824	2,515,479	8.06
1961-1970	213,822	3,321,677	6.44
1971-1980	137,374	4,493,314	3.06
1981-1990	14,667	7,338,062	0.20
1991-1996	106,551	6,146,213	1.73
Total 1820-1996	5,081,195	63,140,227	8.05

Note: Data include England, Scotland, Wales, and (from 1926) Northern Ireland.

Source: Adapted from Table 2, Immigration by Region and Selected Country of Last Residence, Fiscal Years 1820–1996, from the *Statistical Yearbook of the Immigration and Naturalization Service*, 1996.

Table 2.2: Number and Percentage of Foreign-Born Immigrants from Great Britain by Decade in Total U.S. Population at End of Decade, 1850–1990

Decade	Number of Foreign-Born Immigrants from Great Britain	Total U.S. Population	Percentage of Foreign-Born Immigrants from Great Britain in Total U.S. Population
1850	379,093	23,191,876	1.63
1860	587,775	31,443,321	1.87
1870	770,414	39,818,449	1.93
1880	917,598	50,155,783	1.83
1890	1,251,402	62,947,714	1.99
1900	1,167,623	75,994,575	1.54
1910	1,221,283	91,972,266	1.33
1920	1,135,489	105,710,620	1.07
1930	1,224,091	122,775,046	1.00
1940	(NA)	131,669,275	(NA)
1950	846,570	150,697,361	0.56
1960	833,055	179,323,175	0.46
1970	686,099	203,235,298	0.34
1980	669,149	227,726,000	0.29
1990	640,145	249,907,000	0.26

NA = Not available

Note: Includes figures for immigrants from England, Scotland, Wales, and (from 1926) Northern Ireland (previously included under Ireland).

Source: Adapted from Series C 228–295, Foreign-Born Population, by Country of Birth: 1850–1970, in *Historical Statistics of the United States, Colonial Times to 1970, Bicentennial Edition*, and other updating tables from the U.S. Census Bureau.

Graph 2.4: Number of Immigrants from Great Britain by Decade, 1820–1996

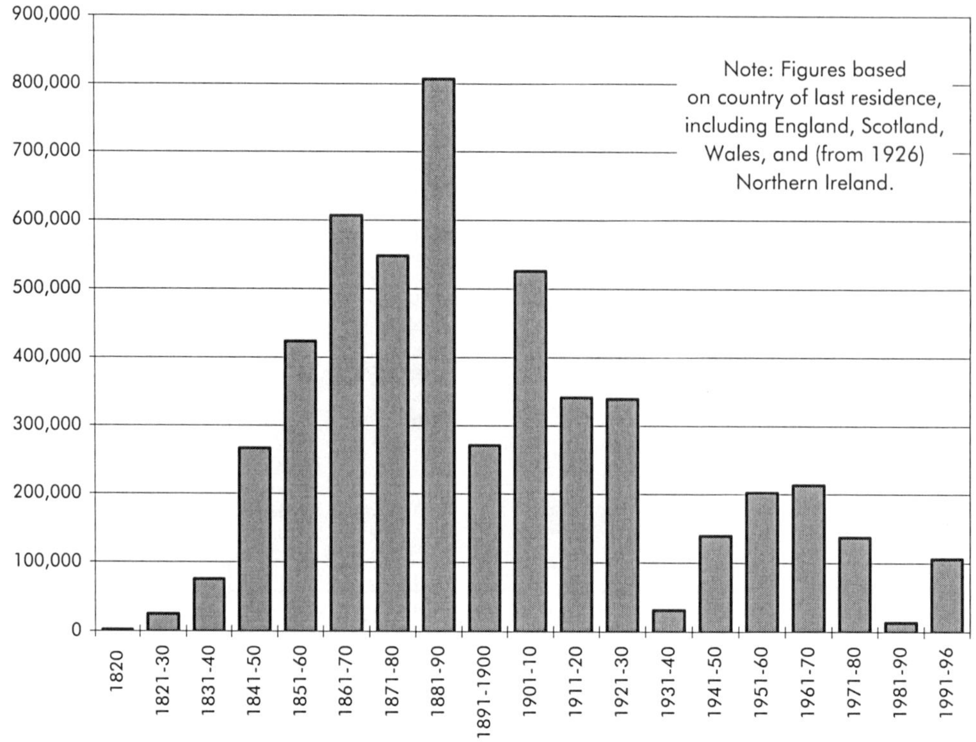

Note: Figures based on country of last residence, including England, Scotland, Wales, and (from 1926) Northern Ireland.

have been greatly different as the defining argument over slavery and secession developed, with incalculable consequences.

As it had in Britain, the textile industry nearly led the way toward the American industrial revolution, starting in New England, side by side with the development of the canal, road, and railway networks that would knit together a continent-wide industrial nation. English and Scottish textile workers began emigrating from the industrial north of Britain in the 1820s, to skilled textile industry mill jobs and supervisory positions in such New England towns as Lowell, Fall River, and New Bedford. They were later joined by many Irish millhands, and afterwards by many immigrants from southern and eastern Europe. However, these highly skilled British textile workers, among them spinners and weavers, supplied much of the necessary skills base from which the American textile industry would develop. They continued to come in substantial numbers well into the 1880s and to work well into the 20th century.

From the 1820s on, skilled Welsh, English, and Scottish workers also played a major role in the growth of the American coal mining industry, while skilled Cornish tin and copper miners immigrated to the United States to extract iron, copper, and lead, tunneling deep into ore deposits. In the early 1900s, however, open-pit mining replaced the Cornish-dug tunnels, a development that took much longer in coal. From the mid-1830s, metalworking also drew large numbers of British workers to America, to help make and work pig iron, coke, and steel. Late in the century, large numbers of Welsh tinplating workers transplanted their whole industry to the United States. Many skilled British metalworkers also worked in American iron and steel fabrication shops.

British immigrants helped build a substantial number of other industries, among them pottery, quarrying, granite and slate cutting, shipbuilding, and all the skilled building trades. Many other English, Welsh, and Scottish immigrants became farmers, as they had been in Europe.

Skilled people continued to come to the United States from Britain, especially in the years after World War II, as Britain's economy became weaker. Scientists, acade-micians, and other highly trained British immigrants constituted a significant "brain drain" from their homeland in the late 20th century.

Graph 2.5: Percentage of Immigrants from Great Britain in Total U.S. Immigration by Decade, 1820–1996

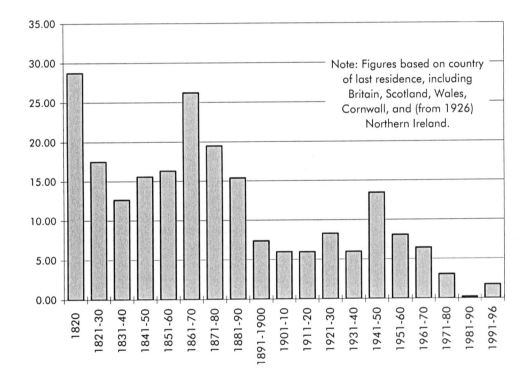

Note: Figures based on country of last residence, including Britain, Scotland, Wales, Cornwall, and (from 1926) Northern Ireland.

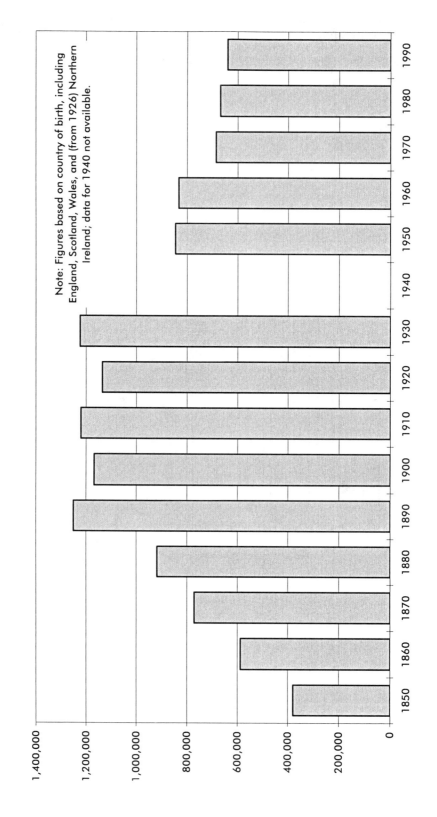

Graph 2.6: Number of Foreign-Born Immigrants from England, Scotland, Wales, and Northern Ireland in Total U.S. Population by Decade, 1850–1990

Note: Figures based on country of birth, including England, Scotland, Wales, and (from 1926) Northern Ireland; data for 1940 not available.

Table 2.3: Number and Percentage of Foreign-Born Immigrants from England, Scotland, Wales, and Northern Ireland in Total U.S. Immigration from Great Britain by Decade, 1850–1980

Year	Number of Foreign-Born Immigrants from England	Percentage of Foreign-Born Immigrants from England in Total Foreign-Born Immigrants from Great Britain	Number of Foreign-Born Immigrants from Scotland	Percentage of Foreign-Born Immigrants from Scotland in Total Foreign-Born Immigrants from Great Britain	Number of Foreign-Born Immigrants from Wales	Percentage of Foreign-Born Immigrants from Wales in Total Foreign-Born Immigrants from Great Britain	Number of Foreign-Born Immigrants from Northern Ireland	Percentage of Foreign-Born Immigrants from Northern Ireland in Total Foreign-Born Immigrants from Great Britain	Total Number of Foreign-Born Immigrants from Great Britain (England, Scotland, Wales, and Northern Ireland)
1850	278,675	73.51	70,550	18.61	29,868	7.88	(NA)	(NA)	379,093
1860	433,494	73.75	108,518	18.46	45,763	7.79	(NA)	(NA)	587,775
1870	555,046	72.05	140,835	18.28	74,533	9.67	(NA)	(NA)	770,414
1880	664,160	72.38	170,136	18.54	83,302	9.08	(NA)	(NA)	917,598
1890	909,092	72.65	242,231	19.36	100,079	8.00	(NA)	(NA)	1,251,402
1900	840,513	71.98	233,524	20.00	93,586	8.02	(NA)	(NA)	1,167,623
1910	877,719	71.87	261,076	21.38	82,488	6.75			1,221,283
1920	813,853	71.67	254,570	22.42	67,066	5.91			1,135,489
1930	809,563	66.14	354,323	28.95	60,205	4.92	178,832	14.61	1,224,091
1940	(NA)	(NA)	(NA)	(NA)	(NA)	(NA)	(NA)	(NA)	(NA)
1950	(NA)	(NA)	(NA)	(NA)	(NA)	(NA)	(NA)	(NA)	846,570
1960	528,205	63.41	213,219	25.59	23,469	2.82	68,162	8.18	833,055
1970	458,114	66.77	170,134	24.80	17,014	2.48	40,837	5.95	686,099
1980	442,499	66.13	142,001	21.22	13,528	2.02	19,831	2.96	669,149

NA = Not available

Note: Before 1926, Northern Ireland included in Ireland. Data for 1940 not available; only total data available for 1950.

Source: Adapted from Series C 228–295, Foreign-Born Population, by Country of Birth: 1850–1970, in *Historical Statistics of the United States, Colonial Times to 1970, Bicentennial Edition*, and other updating tables from the U.S. Census Bureau.

Resources

Internet Resources

GENUKI Home Page (*http://www.genuki.org.uk/*) Web site of the the United Kingdom and Ireland Genealogical Information Service (GENUKI); includes tips on getting started and on doing genealogical research from abroad; prime source for links to history, chronologies, bibliographies, and records of all sorts; has sections focusing on particular regions, including Scotland (*http://www.genuki.org.uk/big/sct*) and Wales (*http://www.genuki.org.uk/big/wal*).

UKGenWeb (*http://pa-roots.com/britishisles/*) Part of the WorldGenWeb project, linking genealogical research sites around the world, by region, offering information and links by county, including parish, census, and other records, as well as historical and geographical information by region; has sections focusing on particular regions, including England (*http://www.rootsweb.com/~engwgw/index.html*), Scotland (*http://www.rootsweb.com/~sctwgw*), and Wales (*http://www.rootsweb.com/~engwales*).

British Isles Family History Society—USA (*http://www.rootsweb.com/~bifhsusa*) Web site of organization offers tips on research, information on publications, and related links. (Address: 2531 Sawtelle Boulevard, #134, Los Angeles, CA 90064-3163)

Cyndi's List—United Kingdom & Ireland Index (*http://www.cyndislist.com/uksites.htm*) Lists of on-line genealogical resources by region, maintained by genealogical author Cyndi Howells, with sublists by region, including England (*http://www.cyndislist.com/england.htm*),

Scotland (*http://www.cyndislist.com/scotland.htm*), Ireland and Northern Ireland (*http://www.cyndislist.com/ireland.htm*), and Wales (*http://www.cyndislist.com/wales.htm*).

A Celebration of the Family: English Genealogical Resources for the Family Historian (*http://hometown.aol.com/JLajza/index.html*) Wide collection of resources and links.

South and West Wales Genealogical Index (*http://members.aol.com/swalesidx*) Offers information on resources and related links, including to professional researchers. (Address: R James [WWW], P.O. Box 41, Llanelli, Carmarthenshire, SA15 2YF, UK E-mail: SWalesidx@aol.com)

All about Scottish Heritage USA (*http://www.sandhills.org/shusa*) Web site of organization focusing on Scottish-American ancestry; offers information, programs, and Scottish Web links. (Address: Contact: Jacqueline Stewart, Scottish Heritage USA, P.O. Box 457, Pinehurst, NC 28370-0457; Phone: 910-295-4448; Fax: 910-295-3147; E-mail: SHUSA@pinehurst.net)

Brits Abroad (*http://www.geocities.com/TheTropics/2865/index.htm*) Web site for expatriates and others interested in British culture, including historical and other information.

National Welsh-American Foundation (NWAF) (*http://www.wales-usa.org*) Organization Web site, with links. (Address: Dept. I, 24 Carverton Road, Trucksville, PA 18708; Phone: 570-696-NWAF)

Celtic Heritage Magazine (http://www.celticheritage.ns.ca/) On-line magazine on Celtic ancestry, including immigration to North America.

Print Resources

General Works

Ashton, E. T. *The Welsh in the United States*. Hove, Sussex: Caldra House, 1984.

Berthoff, Rowland. *British Immigrants in Industrial America, 1790–1950*. New York: Russell & Russell, 1968. Reprint of 1953 ed. of Cambridge: Harvard University Press.

Blumenthal, Shirley, and Jerome S. Ozer. *Coming to America: Immigrants from the British Isles*. New York: Delacorte, 1980.

Coleman, Terry. *Going to America*. Baltimore: Genealogical Publishing, 1987. Originally published London: Hutchinson/New York: Pantheon, 1972.

De Wolfe, Barbara, ed. *Discoveries of America: Personal Accounts of British Emigrants to North America During the Revolutionary Era*. New York: Cambridge University Press, 1997.

Dobson, David. *Scottish Emigration to Colonial America, 1607–1785*. Athens: University of Georgia Press, 1994.

Dollarhide, William. *British Origins of American Colonists, 1629–1775*. Bountiful, Utah: Heritage Quest Genealogical Service, 1997.

Donaldson, Gordon. *The Scots Overseas*. Westport, Conn.: Greenwood, 1976. Reprint of 1966 ed. published by R. Hale, London.

Erickson, Charlotte. *Invisible Immigrants: The Adaptation of English and Scottish Immigrants in Nineteenth-Century America*. Ithaca, N.Y.: Cornell University Press, 1990. Originally published Coral Gables, Fla.: University of Miami Press, 1972.

Erickson, Charlotte. *Leaving England: Essays on British Emigration in the Nineteenth Century*. Ithaca, N.Y.: Cornell University Press, 1994.

Hanna, Charles A. *The Scotch-Irish; or, The Scot in North Britain, North Ireland, and North America*. 2 vols. Baltimore: Genealogical Publishing, 1968. Reprint of the 1902 ed.

Hartmann, Edward George. *Americans from Wales*. New York: Octagon Books, 1978. Reprint of 1967 ed. published by Christopher Publishing House, Boston.

Hill, Douglas Arthur. *The English to New England*. London: Gentry Books, 1975.

Johnson, James E. *The Scots and Scotch-Irish in America*. Rev. ed. Minneapolis: Lerner, 1991.

Johnson, Stanley Currie. *A History of Emigration from the United Kingdom to North America, 1763–1912*. New York: A. M. Kelley, 1966. Reprint of New York: Dutton/London: Routledge, 1913.

Landsman, Ned C. *Scotland and Its First American Colony, 1683–1765*. Princeton, N.J.: Princeton University Press, 1985.

Leyburn, James Graham. *The Scotch-Irish: A Social History*. Chapel Hill: University of North Carolina Press, 1962.

Lines, Kenneth. *British and Canadian Immigration to the United States Since 1920*. San Francisco: R & E Research Associates, 1978.

Rodgers, John. *The Common Bond*. Paisley, Scotland: Wilfion Books, 1980.

Rowe, John. *The Hard-Rock Men: Cornish Immigrants and the North American Mining Frontier*. Liverpool: Liverpool University Press, 1974.

Rowse, A. L. *The Cousin Jacks: The Cornish in America*. London: Macmillan/New York: Scribner, 1969.

Scotland and the Americas, 1600 to 1800. Providence, R.I.: John Carter Brown Library, 1995.

Shepperson, Wilbur Stanley. *British Emigration to North America: Projects and Opinions in the Early Victorian Period*. Oxford: Blackwell, 1957.

Thomas, R. D. *A History of the Welsh in America*. Lanham, Md.: University Press of America, 1983. Translation by Phillips G. Davies of *Hanes Cymry America*, 1872.

Van Vugt, William E. *Britain to America: Mid-Nineteenth-Century Immigrants to the United States*. Urbana: University of Illinois Press, 1999.

Williams, David. *Cymru ac America (Wales and America)*. Cardiff: University of Wales Press, 1975. Originally published 1946. In English and Welsh.

Genealogical Works

Baxter, Angus. *In Search of Your British and Irish Roots: A Complete Guide to Tracing Your English, Welsh, Scottish, and Irish Ancestors*. Rev. ed. Baltimore: Genealogical Publishing, 1989.

Campbell, R. G. *Scotch-Irish Family Research Made Simple*. 2d ed. Munroe Falls, Ohio: Summit Publications, 1982.

Coppage, A. Maxim. *Searching for Scottish Ancestors*. Utica, Ky.: McDowell Publications, 1983.

Cox, Jane. *Never Been Here Before? A First Time Guide for Family Historians at the Public Record Office*. London: PRO Publications, 1993.

Goldie, Douglas Bruce. *In Search of Hamish McBagpipes: A Concise Guide to Scottish Genealogy*. Bowie, Md.: Heritage Books, 1992.

Johnson, Anne E. *A Student's Guide to British American Genealogy*. Phoenix: Oryx, 1996.

Konrad, J. *English Family Research*. Munroe Falls, Ohio: Summit Publications, 1979.

Moscinski, Sharon. *Tracing Our English Roots*. Santa Fe, N.M.: J. Muir, 1995.

Turk, Marion G. *The Quiet Adventurers in North America*. Bowie, Md.: Heritage Books, 1992.

Weaver, Jack W., and DeeGee Lester, comps. *Immigrants from Great Britain and Ireland: A Guide to Archival and Manuscript Sources in North America*. Westport, Conn.: Greenwood, 1986.

For more resources, see "General European Immigration Resources" on p. 317.

Immigrants from Ireland

More than four centuries of turbulent Irish history have run side by side with four centuries of colonial and United States history, from the time of the "plantation" of Ireland and the establishment of the first English North American settlements, near the turn of the 17th century, until today. In that period, more than 5 million Catholic and Protestant Irish immigrants entered what would become the United States, along with the English, Scots, and Welsh immigrants from Britain who dominated the earliest European immigration to the area. The European histories of all these groups were intertwined, as were their American histories, and the conflicts they brought with them from the Old World played a major role in the way their histories developed on both sides of the Atlantic. In 1829, Andrew Jackson became the first U.S. president of Scotch-Irish Protestant descent. He was followed by four more: James K. Polk, James Buchanan, William McKinley, and Woodrow Wilson. In 1961, John F. Kennedy became the first U.S. president of Irish Catholic descent.

Irish Background

In 1607, the year of England's settlement in Jamestown, Virginia, Ulster (Northern Ireland) saw the "Flight of the Earls," led by Hugh O'Neill, leader of the major failed Ulster rising of 1604. The conquering English confiscated the large landholdings of those who had fled and on them "planted" thousands of Scottish colonists, creating the "plantation" of a Protestant majority in northern Ireland. Catholic Ireland rose again in 1641, massacring thousands of Protestants in the civil war that followed.

English forces led by Oliver Cromwell retook the country in 1648, with even larger massacres, this time of Catholics. A final and decisive war came in 1689, as part of a series of Catholic-Protestant European wars. It was settled at the Battle of the Boyne, in 1690. There a Protestant army drawn from all over Europe and led by William of Orange, the new Dutch king of England, smashed an Irish-French Catholic army. England would then rule a rebellious, defeated Ireland for 230 years; the form of the even longer Catholic-Protestant conflict in Northern Ireland had been firmly set.

Early Immigration

Many Catholics fled Ireland for Europe and the Americas as the above events unfolded. These were Ireland's "wild geese," some of whom became the earliest Irish Catholic American immigrants. Most of these Irish Catholics came as penniless indentured servants or redemptioners, who had to pay off their borrowed passage costs and related expenses before winning their freedom (see "The Journey" on p. 53). Even larger numbers of Protestants came in this early immigration. Most arrived with some assets to use in starting farms and businesses, though many also came as indentured servants and redemptioners.

A good many of the early Irish Catholics who emigrated declared themselves Protestants after arriving in the North

Library of Congress

The son of Irish immigrant parents, John Sullivan became a general in the Revolutionary War; a delegate to the Continental Congress, he was later New Hampshire's first governor.

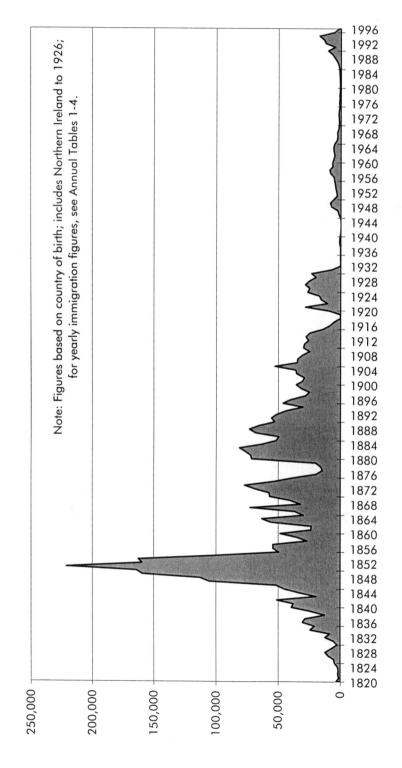

Graph 2.7: Number of Immigrants from Ireland Annually, 1820–1996

Note: Figures based on country of birth; includes Northern Ireland to 1926; for yearly immigration figures, see Annual Tables 1-4.

Graph 2.8: Percentage of Immigrants from Ireland in Total U.S. Immigration by Decade, 1820–1996

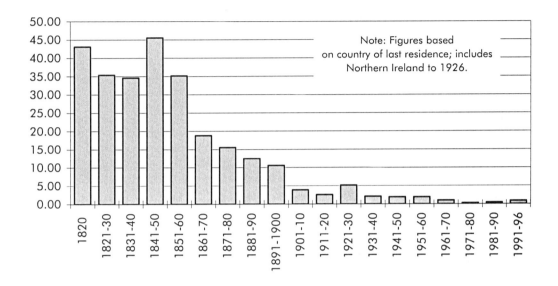

Note: Figures based on country of last residence; includes Northern Ireland to 1926.

Graph 2.9: Number of Immigrants from Ireland by Decade, 1820–1996

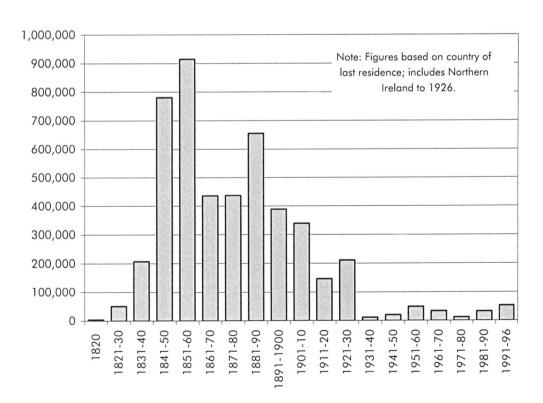

Note: Figures based on country of last residence; includes Northern Ireland to 1926.

American colonies, for they encountered widespread discrimination in the colonies. This was partly due to English colonial laws and policies and partly because of the Protestant-Catholic conflict in Ireland, which both sides brought with them to the New World. Therefore, although the first U.S. Census estimates in 1790 indicated a roughly five-to-three ratio of Irish-American Protestants to Irish-American Catholics, the ratios were probably somewhat closer to even. The barriers created by discrimination against Irish Catholics did not disappear in fact in the new United States, but did disappear in law. That made an enormous difference, helping pave the way for greatly increased Irish Catholic immigration during the 19th century.

Many of the Irish Protestants who emigrated during and after the colonial period came seeking economic opportunity, though they were also fleeing religious and economic discrimination against them by the English rulers of Ireland. Most were Presbyterians, and therefore Dissenters subject to discrimination, as well as the victims of laws and policies favoring absentee English landlords.

For most Irish Protestant immigrants, before and after the Revolution, America was a land of greater freedom and opportunity than Ireland had offered. Many came to America, prospered, and sent home money that paid for the passage of their families. They also sent home "America letters" that drew many others from their extended families, villages, and towns. In short, they began the kinds of "immigrant chains" that became the classic pattern of immigrants from many countries.

The Main Wave of Irish Immigration

During the American Revolution, the North Atlantic was an unsafe place for immigrant ships, as Britain, France, and the United States were at war. After a very short break, the Napoleonic Wars began,

Table 2.4: Number and Percentage of Immigrants from Ireland in Total U.S. Immigration by Decade, 1820–1996

Decade	Number of Immigrants from Ireland	Total U.S. Immigrants	Percentage of Immigrants from Ireland in Total U.S. Immigration
1820	3,614	8,385	43.10
1821-1830	50,724	143,439	35.36
1831-1840	207,381	599,125	34.61
1841-1850	780,719	1,713,251	45.57
1851-1860	914,119	2,598,214	35.18
1861-1870	435,778	2,314,824	18.83
1871-1880	436,871	2,812,191	15.53
1881-1890	655,482	5,246,613	12.49
1891-1900	388,416	3,687,564	10.53
1901-1910	339,065	8,795,386	3.86
1911-1920	146,181	5,735,811	2.55
1921-1930	211,234	4,107,209	5.14
1931-1940	10,973	528,431	2.08
1941-1950	19,789	1,035,039	1.91
1951-1960	48,362	2,515,479	1.92
1961-1970	32,966	3,321,677	0.99
1971-1980	11,490	4,493,314	0.26
1981-1990	31,969	7,338,062	0.44
1991-1996	53,026	6,146,213	0.86
Total 1820-1996	4,778,159	63,140,227	7.57

Note: Prior to 1926, data for Northern Ireland included in Ireland.

Source: Adapted from Table 2, Immigration by Region and Selected Country of Last Residence, Fiscal Years 1820–1996, from the *Statistical Yearbook of the Immigration and Naturalization Service,* 1996.

and from 1793 to 1815, the Atlantic was again unsafe. Immigration to the United States from Ireland was very small during the whole period, although a few immigrant ships carrying Ulster Protestants made the journey to the New World.

Catholic immigration to the United States from Ireland began to pick up during the 1820s, as transatlantic fares began to come down on the new "packet ships" that sailed to America on a regularly scheduled basis, many of them from British ports (see "The Journey" on p. 53). Immigration statistics began to be kept by the U.S. government in 1820. These showed that more than 35 percent of immigrants from 1821 to 1830 came from Ireland. Total immigration soared to almost 600,000 from 1831 to 1840, with more than 207,000 Irish immigrants, or a little under 35 percent of the total immigration for the period. Irish immigration picked up even more in the decade that followed, with almost 240,000 immigrants from Ireland arriving in America from 1841 to 1846 alone.

Throughout the period Irish immigration was understated, for many immigrants from Ireland traveled to the United States via Canada and then came uncounted across the Canadian border. By the 1820s, a substantial transatlantic trade in Canadian timber had started, and emigrants from Britain traveling west across the Atlantic in returning timber ships paid half the price or less than those traveling directly to New York and other United States East Coast ports. British government policy encouraged this, by driving up the price of passage to the United States, while making passage to the British colonies less expensive. One result of the British policy was that in the first half of the 19th century, including Ireland's famine and plague years, most Irish emigrants had to first cross the Irish Sea to Liverpool, often in open cattle boats, and then wait for a ship to America (see "The Journey" on p. 53).

Famine and Plague

In the mid-1840s, famine and plague came to an overpopulated Ireland, dependent for most of its food on its potato crop. From 1690 to 1840, the Irish population had grown by more than four times, from an estimated 2 million people to 8.2 million.

Library of Congress

After the potato crops failed in the 1840s, Ireland's poor faced starvation, disease, and eviction from their homes, as depicted here.

Graph 2.10: Percentage of Foreign-Born Immigrants from Ireland by Decade in Total U.S. Population at End of Decade, 1850–1990

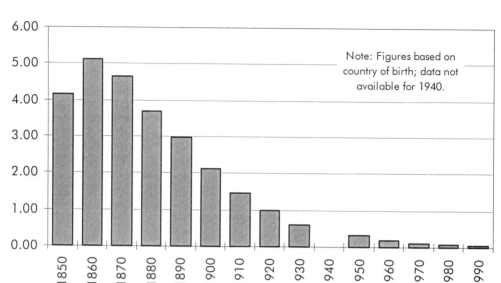

Note: Figures based on country of birth; data not available for 1940.

Most were poor subsistence farmers, working very small plots of land, with little or no resources or reserves of any kind.

In 1845, the European potato crop was infected and partially destroyed by a potato disease that had earlier appeared in North America. In 1846, the Irish potato crop was hit very hard by the disease, failing so badly that even most seed potatos for the 1847 crop were lost. The crop failed again almost completely in 1847 and partly in 1848, largely coming back in 1849.

The result was Ireland's Great Famine, together with a series of plagues. As landowners continued to export food out of Ireland, hundreds of thousands starved and became vulnerable to disease. The massive typhus epidemic of 1847 followed, along with epidemics of relapsing fever, dysentery, scurvy, and many other diseases. On top of that, hundreds of thousands of tenants were evicted from their lands for nonpayment of rent. In all, an estimated 1 to 1.5 million died of famine and plague, while an estimated 2 million fled abroad.

From 1847 to 1854, some 1.3 million Irish emigrants fled to the United States, in a floodtide of immigration that averaged 130,000 a year, and comprised one-third of all immigrants into the United States in those years. By 1860, more than 1.6 million, or more than 5 percent of the United States population, were Irish-born.

After the famine and plague years, the Irish kept on coming to America, for although the famine ended, Ireland was still poor and ruled by Britain, while the United States was full of Irish Americans who built massive immigrant chains that drew millions from their homeland to the New World. From 1855 until World War I temporarily shut off North Atlantic emigration in 1914, another 2.5 million Irish immigrants crossed the sea to the United States.

In relative terms, the Irish immigration became much smaller, so that from 1901 to 1910 "only" 3.85 percent of all U.S. immigrants came from Ireland. In numbers, however, the flow of Irish immigrants to the United States continued to be very substantial.

Modern Immigration

With the onset of the Atlantic conflict between German submarine forces and Allied navies during World War I, immigrant traffic on the North Atlantic slowed to a trickle. After the war, immigration to

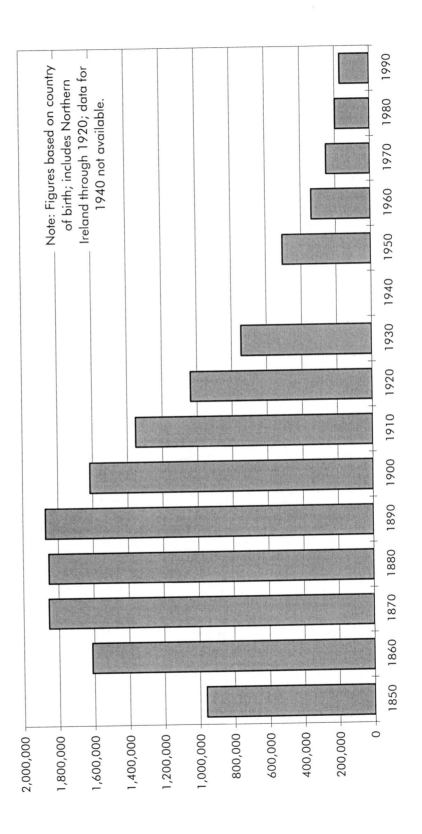

Graph 2.11: Number of Foreign-Born Immigrants from Ireland in U.S. Population by Decade, 1850–1990

Note: Figures based on country of birth; includes Northern Ireland through 1920; data for 1940 not available.

the United States from southern and eastern Europe was largely cut off by the U.S. restrictive immigration laws of 1921 and 1924. However, these laws greatly favored admission of immigrants from northern Europe. As a result, Irish emigration from 1921 to 1930 totaled more than 211,000. When compared with earlier figures, it was even larger than that, because after 1926, immigration to the United States from Northern Ireland was not included, being recorded separately with other regions of Great Britain.

With the onset of the Great Depression and its tens of millions of unemployed, immigration to the United States declines sharply. Irish immigrants from 1931 to 1940 totaled a little less than 11,000. Nor did their numbers increase until after World War II, when the Atlantic once again opened to normal shipping. Then Irish immigration increased but remained under 10,000 a year until 1990. It peaked again in 1994, with more than 17,000 Irish immigrants, as Ireland endured a substantial recession, spurring many young people to leave for the United States to seek jobs. However, in the late 1990s, with European Union subsidies encouraging economic growth in Ireland, immigration to the United States diminished sharply, to a few thousand a year.

In addition to the legal immigration to the United States from Ireland, there were substantial numbers of "illegals," many of them officially classed as *overstays*, people who came in on a tourist visa and just stayed. As of 1996, the Immigration and Naturalization Service estimated that there were approximately 30,000 illegal immigrants from Ireland (see "Appendix C: Estimates of Emigration and Illegals" on p. 749).

In the United States

Most Irish immigrants in colonial times were Ulster Protestant farmers, who sought productive farmland and several kinds of freedom in America. They took passage largely to the main East Coast ports, and especially to Philadelphia, Baltimore, and the coastal towns of the Carolinas. There they were made welcome by expanding colonial governments and land speculators alike, all eager to sell and settle expanding frontiers. As a result, transatlantic fares cost least on ships headed for those ports, and frontier land was readily available at low prices. The Scotch-Irish Presbyterian Dissenters of Northern Ireland were especially attracted to Pennsylvania, where they found a great measure of religious freedom, far more than in largely intolerant Puritan New England. Not that the Scotch-Irish were particularly tolerant themselves; they made war very readily against the Native Americans whose lands they took (see "Native Americans and Immigration" on p. 73), and were far from welcoming to the Catholic Irish who came to America after them.

Large numbers of 18th-century Scotch-Irish immigrants who arrived in Philadelphia settled nearby, and soon went on into the Cumberland Valley and then west through the Allegheny Mountains and into central and western Pennsylvania. In the process, they created the Pennsylvania Road, from Philadelphia to Pittsburgh. After the American Revolution, these

Table 2.5: Number and Percentage of Foreign-Born Immigrants from Ireland by Decade in Total U.S. Population at End of Decade, 1850–1990

Decade	Number of Foreign-Born Immigrants from Ireland	Total U.S. Population	Percentage of Foreign-Born Immigrants from Ireland in Total U.S. Population
1850	961,719	23,191,876	4.15
1860	1,611,304	31,443,321	5.12
1870	1,855,827	39,818,449	4.66
1880	1,854,571	50,155,783	3.70
1890	1,871,509	62,947,714	2.97
1900	1,615,459	75,994,575	2.13
1910	1,352,251	91,972,266	1.47
1920	1,037,234	105,710,620	0.98
1930	744,810	122,775,046	0.61
1940	(NA)	131,669,275	(NA)
1950	505,285	150,697,361	0.34
1960	338,722	179,323,175	0.19
1970	251,375	203,235,298	0.12
1980	197,817	227,726,000	0.09
1990	169,827	249,907,000	0.07

NA = Not available

Note: Figures include Northern Ireland through 1920.

Source: Adapted from Series C 228–295, Foreign-Born Population, by Country of Birth: 1850–1970, in *Historical Statistics of the United States, Colonial Times to 1970, Bicentennial Edition*, and other updating tables from the U.S. Census Bureau.

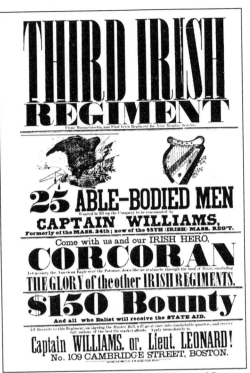

During the American Civil War, many Irish immigrants joined all-Irish regiments, often responding to posters such as this one for the Union side.

would be among the first of the millions of Americans who would pour through Pittsburgh on the way west.

Tens of thousands of other Scotch-Irish immigrants—and their American-born children—pushed the frontier south and west along the east slope of the Appalachian Mountains, creating the Pennsylvania Wagon Road. Beginning in 1775, they also pushed west through the Appalachians, following the Wilderness Road through Cumberland Gap opened by Daniel Boone. On this route, too, they were among the first of millions of Americans who headed west after the Revolution.

A third, somewhat smaller stream of Scotch-Irish immigrants continued to move southeast of the Appalachians, ultimately going through and around the mountain chain via Alabama and Mississippi, on the way to Texas, the Southwest, and California.

Irish-American Catholics

For the main body of Irish Catholic immigrants, New York was the main port of entry into the United States, with smaller but substantial numbers still arriving at Philadelphia, Baltimore, Boston, and other East Coast cities. Some Irish Catholic immigrants also arrived through New Orleans, as well as through Canada.

The great majority of Catholic Irish immigrants had been subsistence farmers in Ireland; however, probably less than 10 percent became farmers in the United States. That was true even though many of them headed westward from New York City, along with millions of other 19th-century immigrants. The best and easiest way west ran from New York City north through the Hudson Valley to the Mohawk Valley, where it turned due west through New York State to the Great Lakes and the Midwest. It was a water-level route all the way, and from 1825, when the Erie Canal was completed, it was a wide open path west.

Catholic Irish immigrants played a major role in building the Erie Canal, as well as many of the other canals and roads heading west. They played an equally

Irish-born John Hughes, who attended a Pennsylvania seminary, became the first Roman Catholic archbishop of New York in 1850.

important role in building the web of American railroads that soon knit the entire country together. In the process, Irish communities were established in many of the growing cities fed by the new transportation system, such as Albany, Rochester, Buffalo, and Chicago. Other Irish immigrants headed farther west, many of them seeking gold in California and silver in the mountain states.

Why the Catholic Irish became largely city dwellers in the United States is still a matter of conjecture and debate. They did encounter deep-seated and long-term discrimination, which always tends to push those discriminated against into tight, defensive communities. Examples of anti-Catholic bigotry include the 1824 burning of the Ursuline Convent, near Boston, and the Philadelphia riots of 1844. As late as 1928, anti-Catholic bigotry helped defeat Democratic presidential candidate Al Smith. Another major factor may have been lack of capital to buy land, coupled with the availability of nonfarm jobs in transportation and in the cities. A third may have been the growth of city-based "immigrant chains" that welcomed arriving Irish immigrants in the cities. Whatever the reason, Catholic Irish immigrants and their children would become major factors in several city-based industries, and would provide major political bases for the new Irish Catholic politicians who came to dominate political life in many urban areas.

Library of Congress

In the late 19th century, many Irish coal miners tried to organize groups to better their working conditions, such as the Molly Maguires group shown here.

Resources

Internet Resources

GENUKI: Ireland (*http://www.genuki.org.uk/*) Ireland home page of the United Kingdom and Ireland Genealogical Information Service (GENUKI); includes tips on getting started and on doing genealogical research from abroad; prime source for links to history, chronologies, bibliographies, and records of all sorts.

Irish Ancestors (*http://www.ireland.com/ancestor/*) Web site maintained by the *Irish Times*, providing information about history, emigration, place names, maps, and genealogical records, including on-screen forms for finding information about ancestors.

Ireland Genealogy Projects (*http://www.irelandgenweb.com*) Part of the WorldGenWeb project, linking genealogical research sites around the world, by region; offers information and links by county within Ireland; provides tips for getting started on Irish and Scotch-Irish genealogical research.

Ireland GenWeb (*http://www.irelandgenweb.com*). As a branch of the BritishIslesGenWeb, part of WorldGenWeb project, linking genealogical research sites around the world, by region, offering information and links by country, including parish, census, and other records, as well as historical and geographical information by region.

Irish Family History Society (*http://www.irishroots.net*) Web site of the organization; sponsors the Irish Family History Foundation for Irish Roots (*http://www.mayo-ireland.ie/roots.htm*), which coordinates genealogical research centers in both Eire and Northern Ireland; offers tips on research, links to resources by county and to professional research services. (Address: P.O. Box 36, Naas, County Kildare, Ireland; E-mail: heueston@iol.ie)

National Archives of Ireland: Family History and Genealogy (*http://www.nationalarchives.ie/genealogy.html*) Web site offers tips on research, bibliographies, and links to related sites and services. (Address: Bishop Street, Dublin 8, Ireland; Phone: + 353 (1) 407-2300; Fax: + 353 (1) 407-2333; E-mail: mail@nationalarchives.ie)

The Irish Ancestral Research Association (TIARA) (*http://tiara.ie*) Web site of organization concerned with Irish genealogy and history, offering information, publications, and related links. (Address: Dept. W, P.O. Box 619, Sudbury, MA 01776)

Irish Genealogy on the Web (*http://www.rootsweb.com/~irish/index.html*) Web site offered by the Irish Genealogical Society International offers tips on research, including computer disasters, and geographic links. (Address: P.O. Box 16585; St. Paul, MN 55116-0585)

Irish Genealogy: The Celtic Connection (*http://www.geocities.com/Heartland/Prairie/8088/ire.html*) Web site offering Web links to genealogical societies for all of Ireland and resources and links by county, as well as family home pages and connections to professional researchers.

Cyndi's List—Ireland & Northern Ireland (*http://www.cyndislist.com/ireland.htm*) List of on-line genealogical resources for the regions, maintained by genealogical author Cyndi Howells.

Irish Genealogy (*http://www.irish-insight.com/a2z-genealogy/index.html*) "A to Z of Irish Genealogy Web Sites."

American Irish Historical Society (*http://www.aihs.org*) Web site offers articles about Irish-American history, bibliographies about Irish immigration and Irish in America, information about the organization's archives, and related links. (Address: 991 Fifth Ave., New York, NY 10028; Phone: 212-288-2263; Fax: 212-628-7927)

Ancient Order of Hibernians in America (*http://www.aoh.com*) Web site of the Irish-American organization, founded in 1836; offers links to national and international Irish sites.

IrishNet (*http://www.ceolas.org/ IrishNet/*) Searchable on-line directory of Irish connnections in the United States.

Celtic Heritage Magazine (*http:// www.celticheritage.ns.ca/*) On-line magazine on celtic ancestry, including immigration to North America.

Print Resources

General Works

Brownstone, David M. *The Irish-American Heritage*. New York: Facts on File, 1989.

Coffey, Michael, ed. *The Irish in America*. New York: Hyperion, 1997.

Cromie, Howard. *Ulster Settlers in America*. Rev. ed. Belfast, Northern Ireland: Irish Mission Publications, 1984.

Diner, Hasia R. *Erin's Daughters in America: Irish Immigrant Women in the Nineteenth Century*. Baltimore: Johns Hopkins University Press, 1983.

Fitzgerald, Margaret E., and Joseph A. King. *The Uncounted Irish in Canada and the United States*. Toronto: P. D. Meany, 1990.

Gribben, Arthur, ed. *The Great Famine and the Irish Diaspora in America*. Amherst: University of Massachusetts Press, 1999.

Johnson, James E. *The Scots and Scotch-Irish in America*. Rev. ed. Minneapolis: Lerner, 1991.

Johnson, James E., and Jack Kavanagh. *Irish in America*. Rev. ed. Minneapolis: Lerner, 1994.

Laxton, Edward. *The Famine Ships: The Irish Exodus to America, 1846–51*. London: Bloomsbury, 1996; New York: Holt, 1997.

Marshall, William F. *Ulster Sails West: The Story of the Great Emigration from Ulster to North America in the 18th Century. . . .* Baltimore: Genealogical Publishing, 1977. Reprint of the 3d ed. published in 1950 in Belfast.

McCaffrey, Lawrence John. *The Irish Catholic Diaspora in America*. Washington, D.C.: Catholic University

of America Press, 1997. Revised ed. of *The Irish Diaspora in America,* Bloomington: Indiana University Press, 1976; reprinted by Catholic University of America Press, 1984.

Miller, Kerby A. *Emigrants and Exiles: Ireland and the Irish Exodus to North America*. New York: Oxford University Press, 1985.

Miller, Kerby A., and Paul Wagner. *Out of Ireland: The Story of Irish Emigration to America*. Washington, D.C.: Elliott & Clark, 1994.

Nolan, Janet. *Ourselves Alone: Women's Emigration from Ireland, 1885–1920*. Lexington: University Press of Kentucky, 1989.

O'Hanlon, Ray. *The New Irish Americans*. Boulder, Col.: Roberts Rinehart, 1998.

Sawyer, Kem Knapp, ed. *Irish Americans*. Carlisle, Mass.: Discovery Enterprises, 1998.

Schrier, Arnold. *Ireland and the American Emigration, 1850–1900*. Chester Springs, PA: Dufour Editions, 1997.

Wittke, Carl Frederick. *The Irish in America*. New York: Russell & Russell, 1970. Reprint of 1956 ed.

Genealogical Works

Baxter, Angus. *In Search of Your British and Irish Roots: A Complete Guide to Tracing Your English, Welsh, Scottish, and Irish Ancestors*. Rev. ed. Baltimore: Genealogical Pub. Co., 1989.

Begley, Donal F. *The Ancestor Trail in Ireland: A Companion Guide*. Dublin, Ireland: Heraldic Artists, 1982.

Begley, Donal F., ed. *Handbook on Irish Genealogy: How to Trace Your Ancestors and Relatives in Ireland*. 6th ed. Dublin, Ireland: Heraldic Artists, available from Genealogy Bookshop, 1984.

Betit, Kyle J., and Dwight A. Radford. *Ireland: A Genealogical Guide for North Americans*. 2d ed. Salt Lake City: Irish at Home and Abroad, 1995.

Campbell, R. G. *Scotch-Irish Family Research Made Simple*. 2d ed. Munroe Falls, Ohio: Summit Publications, 1982.

Glynn, Joseph Martin, Jr., comp. *Manual for Irish Genealogy: A Guide to Methods and Sources for Tracing Irish Ancestry*. 2d ed. Newton, Mass: Irish Family History Society, 1982.

Handbook on Irish Genealogy: How to Trace Your Ancestors and Relatives in Ireland. Rev. ed. Dublin: Heraldic Artists, 1976.

McKenna, Erin. *A Student's Guide to Irish American Genealogy*. Phoenix: Oryx, 1996.

Medley, Eileen. *Helpful Suggestions for Irish Research*. Sudbury, Mass.: TIARA, 1989.

Moscinski, Sharon. *Tracing Our Irish Roots*. Santa Fe, N.M.: J. Muir, 1993.

O'Laughlin, Michael C. *The Complete Book for Tracing Your Irish Ancestors*. Kansas City, Mo.: Irish Genealogical Foundation, 1980.

Weaver, Jack W., and DeeGee Lester. *Immigrants from Great Britain and Ireland: A Guide to Archival and Manuscript Sources in North America*. Westport, Conn.: Greenwood, 1986.

For more resources, see "General European Immigration Resources" on p. 317.

Immigrants from Spain

The Spanish portion of the European settlement of North America is best seen as part of the European conquest of the continent, set within the context of worldwide European imperial rivalries. We discuss the Spanish imperial thrust into North America in an earlier chapter (see "An Overview" on p. 2).

Just as it was a Spanish expedition under Christopher Columbus that "discovered" the Americas, so Spain was the earliest of the European powers to penetrate the mainland of North America. Hernando de Soto's expedition landed in Florida in 1539 and reached the Mississippi River two years later, while in 1540 Francisco Vásquez de Coronado's expedition moved north through what would become New Mexico to the Grand Canyon. By 1565, the Spanish had founded Florida's St. Augustine, the first permanent European settlement on the North American mainland. In 1598, nine years before England's Jamestown settlement, a party of 200 emigrants journeyed north to found New Mexico's first Spanish settlements.

During the course of the three centuries that followed, Spain would add Texas and California to its territories. In 1822, these Spanish-Mexican territories became independent Mexico. The estimated 80,000 Mexicans in Texas, California, and the American Southwest became a conquered people in 1848, after the Mexican–United States War (see "Immigrants from Mexico" on p. 491). Estimates of how many of their descendants now describe themselves as Spanish Americans or Hispanic Americans vary widely, but generally run in the 800,000 to 900,000 range, though it is equally possible to describe these people as part of the much larger Mexican-American ethnic group.

Early Immigration

U.S. immigration records show only small numbers of immigrants coming directly from Spain during the 19th century. However, Spanish-born immigrants may be undercounted, with some arriving from south of the Rio Grande either not counted at all or treated as part of the much larger Mexican immigration. U.S. records show a total of only a little over 41,000 Spanish immigrants for the entire 19th century, an average of a little more than 500 per year.

Immigration to the United States from Spain jumped very substantially from 1901 to 1930, even though immigration quotas greatly cut Spanish immigration after 1921. From 1901 to 1930, a total of more than 125,000 immigrants entered the United States from Spain, a very small part of the 18,638,000 European immigrants to the United States in that period.

After 1921, and until the abolition of the quota system in 1965, few immigrants entered the United States from Spain, as the 1921 restrictive immigration law established a quota of only 931 yearly admissions from Spain. The even more restrictive 1924 immigration law cut that annual quota to 131 Spanish immigrants per year. Some of the most notable Spanish immigrants of this period entered the United States as political refugees after the Republican side was defeated by the Fascists in the Spanish Civil War (1936–1939).

Modern Immigration

After the abolition of the restrictive quotas in 1965, immigration to the United States from Spain grew substantially, averaging more than 4,000 per year from 1961 to 1980. In the 1980s and 1990s, as the Spanish economy improved, it dropped into the very modest range of 1,500 to 2,000 per year.

During most of the 19th century, immigrants from Spain tended to settle into established Spanish-speaking communities, especially in the Southwest and California, with a substantial minority also building a Spanish-American community in and around New York City. Late in the century, many Spanish cigar makers also immigrated to Tampa, Florida, building a community there.

During the relatively heavy immigration of the first three decades of the 20th century, Spanish immigrants spread out

Authors' Archives

Spanish priest Junipero Serra founded a string of missions in California, starting with this one at San Diego in 1769.

Authors' Archives

Throughout Spain's American territories, Spanish priests established missions such as this one in California.

considerably, working in the growing industrial areas of the northeast and northern Midwest. Post–World War II Spanish immigrants followed similar patterns.

Among the immigrants from Spain, especially in the 19th and 20th centuries, there have been some thousands of Basques, an ethnic minority living primarily in northern Spain. Many of them became sheepherders working in California from the 1850s and in the mountain states from the 1870s. How many Basques came to the United States is a matter of conjecture, as most were classified for immigration purposes as Spanish or French, with some coming from other European countries. Some Basque sailors had also been among the Europeans fishing on the Grand Banks of Newfoundland from at least the 1480s, before Columbus arrived in the Americas.

Table 2.6: Number and Percentage of Immigrants from Spain in Total U.S. Immigration by Decade, 1820–1996

Decade	Number of Immigrants from Spain	Total U.S. Immigrants	Percentage of Immigrants from Spain in Total U.S. Immigration
1820	139	8,385	0.00
1821-1830	2,477	143,439	1.73
1831-1840	2,125	599,125	0.35
1841-1850	2,209	1,713,251	0.13
1851-1860	9,298	2,598,214	0.36
1861-1870	6,697	2,314,824	0.29
1871-1880	5,266	2,812,191	0.19
1881-1890	4,419	5,246,613	0.08
1891-1900	8,731	3,687,564	0.24
1901-1910	27,935	8,795,386	0.32
1911-1920	68,611	5,735,811	1.20
1921-1930	28,958	4,107,209	0.71
1931-1940	3,258	528,431	0.62
1941-1950	2,898	1,035,039	0.28
1951-1960	7,894	2,515,479	0.31
1961-1970	44,659	3,321,677	1.34
1971-1980	39,141	4,493,314	0.87
1981-1990	20,433	7,338,062	0.28
1991-1996	11,885	6,146,213	0.19
Total 1820-1996	297,033	63,140,227	0.47

Source: Adapted from Table 2, Immigration by Region and Selected Country of Last Residence, Fiscal Years 1820–1996, from the *Statistical Yearbook of the Immigration and Naturalization Service, 1996.*

Graph 2.12: Number of Foreign-Born Immigrants from Spain in Total U.S. Population by Decade, 1850–1990

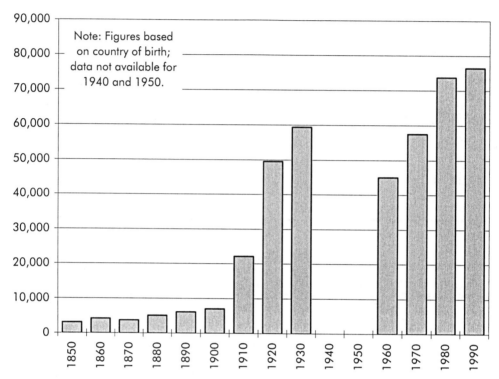

Graph 2.13: Number of Immigrants from Spain by Decade, 1820–1996

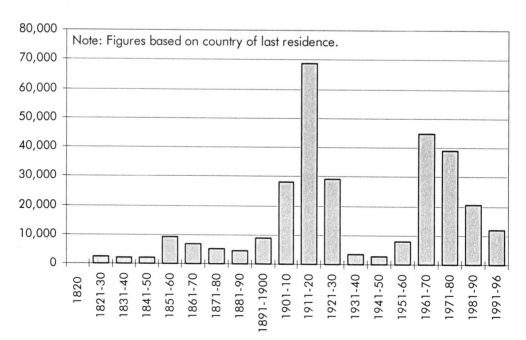

Resources

Internet Resources

WorldGenWeb Project—Spain (*http://members.aol.com/balboanet/spain/index.html*) Web site offering tips on Spanish genealogy, maps, historical information, and resources by region, as well as links to related sites; part of the wider MediterraneanGenWeb (*http://www.mediterraneangenweb.org*), in turn part of the WorldGenWeb project, linking genealogical research sites around the world, by region, with resources by individual country and links to neighboring regions of the world.

Cyndi's List—Spain, Portugal & the Basque Country / España, Portugal y El País Vasco (*http://www.cyndislist.com/spain.htm*) List of on-line genealogical resources for the regions, maintained by genealogical author Cyndi Howells.

Print Resources

Cortes, Carlos E., ed. *Portuguese Americans and Spanish Americans.* New York: Arno Press, 1980. Reprints of articles originally published between 1892 and 1969.

Fernandez-Florez, Dario. *The Spanish Heritage in the United States.* New York: Arno Press, 1980.

Fernandez-Shaw, Carlos M. *The Hispanic Presence in North America from 1492 to Today.* Updated ed. New York: Facts on File, 1999.

Lick, Sue Fagalde. *The Iberian Americans.* New York: Chelsea House, 1990.

Natella, Arthur A., ed. *The Spanish in America, 1513–1979: A Chronology and Fact Book.* Rev. ed. Dobbs Ferry, N.Y.: Oceana, 1980.

Spain: A Country Study. 2d ed. Eric Solsten and Sandra W. Meditz, eds. Washington, D.C.: Federal Research Division, Library of Congress, 1990. (Available on-line at *http://lcweb2.loc.gov/frd/cs*)

Stein, R. Conrad. *The Spanish West.* New York: Benchmark Books, 1999.

For more resources, see "General European Immigration Resources" on p. 317. For Hispanic Americans, see "General Immigration Resources for the Americas" on p. 632.

Immigrants from Portugal

During the European search for a route to Asia, which led to the "discovery," invasion, and conquest of the Americas, the main Portuguese thrust was to the east, around Africa and into the Indian Ocean. After more than a century of exploration and conquest that took the Portuguese the length of Africa, around the Cape, and into the Indian Ocean, Portuguese navigator Vasco da Gama led the first expedition to sail from Europe to India and back, reaching Calicut in 1498 and returning to Lisbon in 1499. After him came the explorers and conquerors of many European nations, pursuing the conquest and exploitation of much of Asia and the Pacific.

Portuguese and Spanish expeditions also sailed westward, across the Atlantic, beginning what might have become a series of worldwide imperial wars between the two countries. In 1427, Portuguese pilot Diogo de Senill (or Sevilha) discovered and claimed the Azores Islands, almost 1,000 miles west of Portugal in the Atlantic; these would become the source of most of the early Portuguese immigration into the United States. In 1420 Portuguese navigator João Gonçalves Zarco claimed the Madeira Islands; these would be another source of Portuguese immigration. In 1461,

the Portuguese claimed the Cape Verde Islands, almost 400 miles off the West African coast, a third source of future immigrants. From 1500, the Portuguese claimed Brazil, which they held against Spanish and later Dutch claims; it was into Brazil that they would import 4 million to 5 million black African slaves (see "The Slave Trade" on p. 321). The Portuguese had actually begun the Atlantic slave trade in 1441, when they brought 10 black Africans back to Portugal as slaves.

Worldwide war between Spain and Portugal, the two great imperial powers of the 15th century, was averted by papal intervention. That ultimately resulted in the landmark 1494 Treaty of Tordesillas, in which rival Spanish and Portuguese imperial claims were settled by dividing the world between them. By the terms of that agreement, Portugal recognized Spanish claims in South America (except Brazil) and the Pacific, while Spain recognized Portuguese claims in the Indian Ocean and Asia. By at least the 1480s, Portuguese as well as northern European ships were fishing on the Grand Banks of Newfoundland, but this generated no Portuguese territorial claims.

Table 2.7: Number and Percentage of Immigrants from Portugal in Total U.S. Immigration by Decade, 1820–1996

Decade	Number of Immigrants from Portugal	Total U.S. Immigrants	Percentage of Immigrants from Portugal in Total U.S. Immigration
1820	35	8,385	0.00
1821-1830	145	143,439	0.10
1831-1840	829	599,125	0.14
1841-1850	550	1,713,251	0.03
1851-1860	1,055	2,598,214	0.04
1861-1870	2,658	2,314,824	0.11
1871-1880	14,082	2,812,191	0.50
1881-1890	16,978	5,246,613	0.32
1891-1900	27,508	3,687,564	0.75
1901-1910	69,149	8,795,386	0.79
1911-1920	89,732	5,735,811	1.56
1921-1930	29,994	4,107,209	0.73
1931-1940	3,329	528,431	0.63
1941-1950	7,423	1,035,039	0.72
1951-1960	19,588	2,515,479	0.78
1961-1970	76,065	3,321,677	2.29
1971-1980	101,710	4,493,314	2.26
1981-1990	40,431	7,338,062	0.55
1991-1996	17,223	6,146,213	0.28
Total 1820-1996	518,484	63,140,227	0.82

Source: Adapted from Table 2, Immigration by Region and Selected Country of Last Residence, Fiscal Years 1820–1996, from the *Statistical Yearbook of the Immigration and Naturalization Service*, 1996.

Graph 2.14: Number of Foreign-Born Immigrants from Portugal in Total U.S. Population by Decade, 1850–1990

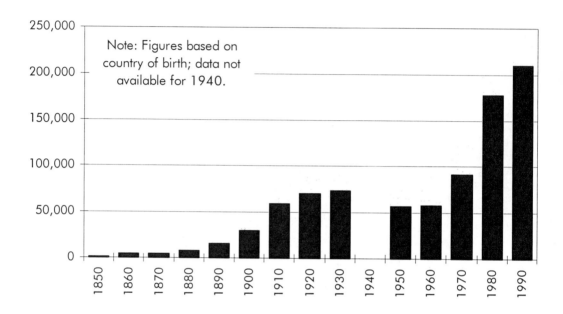

Graph 2.15: Number of Immigrants from Portugal by Decade, 1820–1996

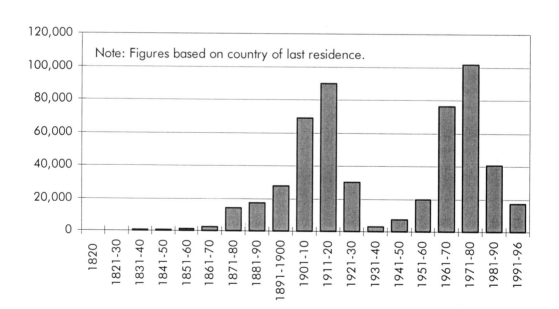

Early Immigration

Early Portuguese migration into what would later become the United States was small. In New England and southern Louisiana, some hundreds of Portuguese sailors are estimated to have settled by the time of the American Revolution. Most of them were originally picked up as crew members of American whaling ships using the Azores as a base in the Atlantic. Some Portuguese sailors were also picked up as crew members in the Cape Verde Islands.

In the early and mid-19th century, a small Portuguese Protestant community from the island of Madeira, faced with Catholic persecution, relocated to Trinidad, and then made their way to Springfield, Illinois. Some Portuguese sailors became prospectors for gold during the California Gold Rush, and small numbers arrived in Louisiana as plantation workers before the Civil War.

Estimates vary. In all, approximately 9,000 foreign-born Portuguese Americans were living in the United States in 1870.

At most half were from Portugal itself; probably more than half were from the Azores, Madeira, and the Cape Verde Islands.

Somewhat more substantial immigration to the United States from Portugal and the Atlantic islands began in the 1870s. However, from 1871 to 1900 a total of only 59,000 Portuguese immigrants arrived in the United States, an average of 2,000 a year. Most settled in the New England coastal towns and cities that by then already had established Portuguese communities. Many Portuguese ultimately moved out to California, and many worked in the fishing and canning industries on both coasts.

In New England, some Portuguese later became farm laborers, but most moved into relatively better-paid factory work in the region's growing textile industry. In California, the move was from sea-based industries to farming, with many Portuguese becoming farm laborers and then farmers working their own land. California's Portuguese farmers soon became a major factor

Authors' Archives

The Atlantic slave trade was started by Portuguese traders, such as this one examining black Africans being held for possible transport to become slaves.

in the state's dairy industry. In Hawaii, the great majority of Portuguese immigrants became plantation laborers, and later went into a wide range of other occupations.

Modern Immigration

The first three decades of the 20th century saw far greater Portuguese immigration, as well-established Portuguese communities and expanding industrial America drew millions of immigrants from all over Europe. From 1901 to 1930, some 189,000 Portuguese immigrants entered the United States, following the settlement patterns established late in the 19th century.

Immigration to the United States from Portugal was sharply reduced by the restrictive 1921 Immigration Act, and then cut even more by the 1924 Immigration Act, which set a yearly quota of just 503 admissions from Portugal, reduced to 440 a year in 1929. During the Great Depression and World War II, in the 1930s and 1940s, the annual number of immigrants did not always reach even that small number. Portuguese immigration rose considerably only after passage of the 1958 Azorean Refugee Act, which followed the disastrous 1957–1958 Azores earthquakes.

Late-20th-century Portuguese immigration surged after passage of the 1965 Immigration Act, which generated large-scale immigration into the United States from many countries. From 1968 to 1980, more than 229,000 Portuguese immigrants arrived. The great majority came for purely economic reasons, for Portugal had experienced an economic crisis as the country fought multiple wars in a futile effort to hold on to its African colonies. That crisis deepened after the 1974 democratic revolution, the end of the colonial wars, and the return of former Portuguese colonials to their homeland.

As conditions at home improved, emigration slackened, and total Portuguese immigration to the United States dropped. From 1981 to 1996, only a little over 57,000 arrived, an average of less than 4,000 per year.

Meanwhile, immigrants of Portuguese descent continued to arrive from various Atlantic islands. Between 1971 and 1996, nearly 19,000 arrived from the Cape Verde Islands alone, and U.S. Census figures showed that more than 32,000 foreign-born immigrants from the Azores were living in the United States in 1980.

Table 2.8: Number and Percentage of Foreign-Born Immigrants from Portugal by Decade in Total U.S. Population at End of Decade, 1850–1990

Decade	Number of Foreign-Born Immigrants from Portugal	Total U.S. Population	Percentage of Foreign-Born Immigrants from Portugal in Total U.S. Population
1850	1,274	23,191,876	0.01
1860	4,116	31,443,321	0.01
1870	4,542	39,818,449	0.01
1880	8,138	50,155,783	0.02
1890	15,996	62,947,714	0.03
1900	30,608	75,994,575	0.04
1910	59,360	91,972,266	0.06
1920	69,981	105,710,620	0.07
1930	73,164	122,775,046	0.06
1940	(NA)	131,669,275	(NA)
1950	56,591	150,697,361	0.04
1960	57,690	179,323,175	0.03
1970	91,034	203,235,298	0.04
1980	177,437	227,726,000	0.08
1990	210,122	249,907,000	0.08

NA = Not available

Note: Figures include Northern Ireland through 1920.

Source: Adapted from Series C 228–295, Foreign-Born Population, by Country of Birth: 1850–1970, in *Historical Statistics of the United States, Colonial Times to 1970, Bicentennial Edition*, and other updating tables from the U.S. Census Bureau.

Table 2.9: Number and Percentage of Immigrants from Cape Verde in Total U.S. Immigration Annually, 1971–1996

Year	Number of Immigrants from Cape Verde	Total U.S. Immigration	Percentage of Immigrants from Cape Verde in Total U.S. Immigration
1971	183	370,473	0.05
1972	248	384,685	0.06
1973	214	400,063	0.05
1974	122	394,861	0.03
1975	196	396,194	0.05
1976	1,110	502,289	0.22
1977	964	462,315	0.21
1978	941	601,442	0.16
1979	765	460,348	0.17
1980	788	530,639	0.15
1981	849	596,600	0.14
1982	852	594,131	0.14
1983	594	559,763	0.11
1984	591	543,903	0.11
1985	627	570,009	0.11
1986	760	601,708	0.13
1987	657	601,516	0.11
1988	921	643,025	0.14
1989	1,118	1,090,924	0.10
1990	907	1,536,483	0.06
1991	973	1,827,167	0.05
1992	757	973,977	0.08
1993	936	904,292	0.10
1994	810	804,416	0.10
1995	968	720,461	0.13
1996	1,012	915,900	0.11
Total 1971-1996	18,863	17,987,584	0.10

Sources: *Statistical Yearbook of the Immigration and Naturalization Service*, 1980, Table 13; *Statistical Yearbook of the Immigration and Naturalization Service*, 1986, Table 3; *Statistical Yearbook of the Immigration and Naturalization Service*, 1996, Table 3.

Resources

Internet Resources

LusaWeb: Portuguese-American Communities on the World Wide Web (*http://www.lusaweb.com*) Searchable Web site offering information and resources on immigration and genealogy. (Address: P.O. Box 5223; El Dorado Hills, CA 95762-5223)

MediterraneanGenWeb (*http://www.mediterraneangenweb.org*) Part of the WorldGenWeb project, linking genealogical research sites around the world, by region, with resources by individual country and links to neighboring regions of the world.

Cyndi's List—Spain, Portugal & the Basque Country / España, Portugal y El País Vasco (*http://www.cyndislist.com/spain.htm*) List of on-line genealogical resources for the regions, maintained by genealogical author Cyndi Howells.

Print Resources

Almeida, Raymond A., et al. *Cape Verdeans in America: Our Story.* Boston: Tchuba, the American Committee for Cape Verde, 1978.

Amaral, Pat. *They Ploughed the Seas: Profiles of Azorean Master Mariners.* St. Petersburg, Fla.: Valkyrie Press, 1978.

Baganha, Maria Ioannis Benis. *Portuguese Emigration to the United States, 1820–1930.* New York: Garland, 1990.

Cardozo, Manoel Da Silveira, ed. *The Portuguese in America, 590 B.C.–1974: A Chronology and Fact Book.* Dobbs Ferry, N.Y.: Oceana, 1976.

Halter, Marilyn. *Between Race and Ethnicity: Cape Verdean American Immigrants, 1860–1965.* Urbana: University of Illinois Press, 1993.

Lick, Sue Fagalde. *The Iberian Americans.* New York: Chelsea House, 1990.

Mira, Manuel. *The Forgotten Portuguese: The Melungeons and Other Groups.* Franklin, N.C.: Portuguese-American Historical Research Foundation, 1998.

Pap, Leo. *The Portuguese in the United States: A Bibliography.* Staten Island, N.Y.: Center for Migration Studies, 1976.

———. *The Portuguese-Americans.* Boston: Twayne, 1981.

———. *Portugal: A Country Study.* 2d ed. Eric Solsten, ed. Washington, D.C.: Federal Research Division, Library of Congress, 1993. (Available online at: *http://lcweb2.loc.gov/frd/cs*)

Rogers, Francis Millet. *Atlantic Islanders of the Azores and Madeiras.* North Quincy, Mass.: Christopher Publishing, 1979.

Williams, Jerry R. *And Yet They Come: Portuguese Immigration from the Azores to the United States.* Staten Island, N.Y.: Center for Migration Studies, 1982.

Wolforth, Sandra. *The Portuguese in America.* San Francisco: R & E Research Associates, 1978.

For more resources, see "General European Immigration Resources" on p. 317.

Immigrants from Germany

Germans were a key part of what historians call the "old immigration," primarily from northern and western Europe. They began to arrive in the 17th century, soon after northern Europeans started settling on the eastern coast of North America. They continued to come in large numbers throughout the 19th century, with newer waves also in the 20th century. In fact, though early English colonial settlement determined that the main language and culture of the American colonies would be English, the Germans formed the largest group of immigrants overall, numbering more than 7 million between 1820 (when official U.S. immigration records began to be kept) and 1996 alone.

That is so even though, until 1871, there was no single country called "Germany." The people's unity lay in their common language, culture, and customs. Indeed, the figures for German immigration are somewhat misleading, for they generally include only those Germans who were actually born in the territory known as Germany. However, many people who spoke primarily German and regarded themselves as Germans lived in other countries, including Austria, Switzerland, Poland, Alsace-Lorraine (disputed borderlands between France and Germany), Russia, and Czechoslovakia. (See separate chapters on emigration from those regions.)

On the other hand, some people who later lived within the borders of Germany did not consider themselves German, such as many Poles. Jews formed a special category. Many found refuge in Germany from the mid-17th century on, and their descendants often came to regard themselves as "German." A significant number of the immigrants counted as German were Jews, especially in the 19th and 20th centuries (see "Jewish Immigrants" on p. 297).

Early German Immigrants

The first German in North America may have come with the Vikings (see "Immigrants from Scandinavia" on p. 165). Norse sagas tell of a man named Tyrker the German, who early in the 11th century discovered the grapevines that gave the continent its Viking name: Vinland. After Columbus "discovered" America, some Germans may have been in early Spanish and Portuguese settlements.

However, we cannot firmly document the arrival of German immigrants until 1607. Some Germans, mostly carpenters and other artisans, were in the party of English settlers who founded Jamestown, Virginia. That same year, others joined a short-lived French Huguenot settlement at Port Royal, in South Carolina.

Another German, Peter Minuit (born Minnewit), led the Dutch group that founded New Amsterdam (later New York). Forced out of that colony in 1632, he returned with a mostly Swedish-sponsored group, which also included some other Germans. These were the first European-born immigrants to settle on the lower Delaware River, in what are now Pennsylvania, Delaware, New Jersey, and Maryland.

The first primarily German group arrived in Pennsylvania on the *Concord*, the German equivalent of the *Mayflower,* in 1683, a date many historians use to mark the beginning of German immigration. Led by Francis (Franz) Daniel Pastorius, they settled in Germantown, north of Philadelphia.

Many early German immigrants came to North America seeking religious freedom. The Protestant Reformation had been sparked in the early 16th century by German priest Martin Luther. By the 17th century, much of Europe was ravaged by religious conflict, most notably the Thirty Years War (1618–1648). Under the Treaty of Westphalia ending the war, each of the many German states was to follow the religion of its ruler—Lutheran, Roman Catholic, or Reformed (Calvinist). Followers of other religions were often persecuted, such as Anabaptists, who believed in adult baptism only (a heresy at the time) and questioned the power of the state, and Quakers, converted to that faith by English missionaries. Many smaller religious groups, such as the Mennonites and the Amish, were Anabaptist in origin.

It was the Quaker connection that first drew the Pastorius party—primarily Mennonites and Quakers—to Pennsylvania. They would be followed by many others. Because the Germans called themselves "Deutsch," in America they became known collectively as the "Pennsylvania Dutch."

Many German Protestants sought support from England's Queen Anne, and some received it. Among them were many Palatine Germans (from the Palatinate, a state along the Rhine River), who arrived in America in 1709 and settled in the Hudson River valley. Many later settled in the fertile Schoharie and Mohawk valleys of upstate New York, making them a breadbasket for the Americans during the Revolutionary War. Other Palatine Germans went to Virginia and the Carolinas.

Many Germans from Salzburg, Austria, went to Georgia starting in 1734. In the same period, German immigrants also settled in Maryland and New England, while others joined French colonies in the Mississippi valley, north of New Orleans.

Meanwhile, German immigrants continued to arrive in the mid-Atlantic regions. By 1776, at the start of the Revolutionary War, Benjamin Franklin estimated that one out of every three Pennsylvania residents was of German ancestry.

Many early Germans chafed at British colonial control. They often sought more freedom by moving into the frontier lands along the Appalachian Mountains. Some missionaries, especially pacifist Moravians, reached beyond the Appalachians into Ohio and Kentucky.

While members of smaller religious groups would continue to arrive, from the 1740s on most German immigrants would be members of the main Protestant churches: Lutheran or Reformed. These new German immigrants contributed enormously to the development of American culture. Many were highly educated, and their skills and learning were important in the new settlements. They established

Authors' Archives

Many Hessian soldiers were taken into the army—despite protests by their families, as here—and then sent to the New World to fight for the British during the American Revolution.

Library of Congress

Among the early German immigrants to the American colonies were Mennonites, followers of the German religious reformer Menno Simons.

schools, newspapers, musical groups, churches, and businesses, and often served as doctors, lawyers, and ministers.

In this period, many of the poorer German immigrants—who could not otherwise afford the fare—came to the American colonies as indentured servants or "redemptioners" (see "The Journey" on p. 53). That would be true until the practice was banned in 1819.

Revolution and Expansion

During the Revolutionary War, some 30,000 Germans came to America involuntarily, as soldiers "rented" by their rulers to the British army. Some of these Hessians—so called because so many came from the state of Hesse—went over to the American rebels. After the war, some 5,000 to 6,000 Hessians later became citizens of the new United States.

Experienced German officers also joined the Continental Army. The most important of these was Baron Friedrich

Wilhelm von Steuben, whose Prussian-style discipline helped the American army survive the terrible winter of 1778 at Valley Forge. Some German officers also fought on the British side, a few later going over to the Americans. The so-called Kentucky rifle was actually developed by German gunsmiths for German troops who rejected the standard army musket.

After the war, German immigrants as well as longtime German Americans were a major part of the move west, beyond the Appalachian Mountains, often coming into sharp conflict with the Native Americans. They helped shape the culture and industry of the trans-Appalachian regions, founding many new towns, often with German names such as Berlin, Winesburg, Potsdam, and Frankfort.

More established German Americans often founded organizations to help newer German immigrants adjust to American life. This tradition went back to at least 1784, with the founding of the *Deutsche*

Library of Congress

German pastor Heinreich Muhlenberg helped organize the Lutheran Church in America, after he arrived in Pennsylvania in 1741.

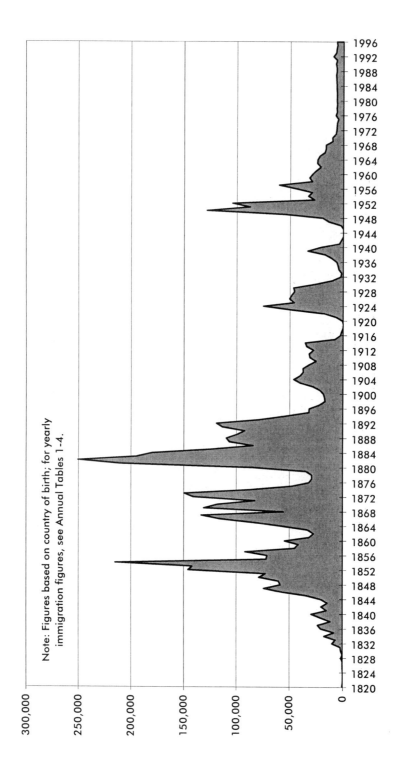

Graph 2.16: Number of Immigrants from Germany Annually, 1820–1996

Note: Figures based on country of birth; for yearly immigration figures, see Annual Tables 1-4.

Gesellschaft (German Society) in New York, and would continue into the 20th century.

19th-Century Immigration

Early in the 19th century, immigration to the United States was hindered by the Napoleonic Wars, which devastated much of Europe and made the Atlantic dangerous. However, when the wars ended, in 1815, a new wave of Germans was drawn to America, joining the great flood of pioneers settling the heartland of North America. Many arrived at the East Coast ports, pushing on through Ohio and Kentucky to the Mississippi, while others came to ports on the Gulf of Mexico. Many went to Missouri, having read glowing reports in a book by German immigrant Gottfried Duden.

Germans often emigrated in groups, sometimes forming colonizing societies for the purpose. Some such societies were primarily religious, hoping to found a "new Jerusalem" in America. Others wanted to create a new German state, perhaps in Missouri or Texas. One of the most successful German colonies was at New Braunfels, Texas. It was named for Prince Carl von Solms-Braunfels, a key leader of the *Adelsverein* (Noblemen's Society), which sent almost 7,400 German colonists to Texas in the mid-1840s.

Many German immigrants settled in the Midwest, especially in Illinois, Iowa, and Wisconsin. There they opened up more new farmlands and helped grow the young cities of the region, such as Chicago, Milwaukee, Des Moines, Davenport, Dubuque, and Sheboygan. By 1850, Germans made up an estimated 40 percent of the population of Milwaukee, which called itself the "German Athens." By then, overall, the United States had more than 580,000 people who were German-born.

Many of these German immigrants were Protestants. Among the newcomers in the late 1830s were many "Old Lutherans," who resisted the forced merger of the Lutheran and Reformed churches in Prussia. However, significant numbers of German Catholics also emigrated, most notably to Wisconsin. From the 1840s on,

large numbers of German Jews also arrived (see "Jewish Immigrants" on p. 297).

The immigrants of this period included farmers, unskilled laborers, and a whole range of skilled workers. Some initially worked as peddlers, supplying the needs of pioneers. A smaller but influential group of newcomers were highly educated people and aristocrats, including liberal reformers forced to leave Germany after failed revolts against political oppression. Called "Latin farmers," because of their education, many had little notion of how to go about clearing and cultivating frontier land. Some, however, would become political, cultural, artistic, and intellectual leaders in the United States.

Some small religious colonies would maintain their culture and often their language for many decades, in some cases right into the late 20th century. However, many German immigrants from this time on rather quickly adopted English and merged with the others in the frontier lands and cities, soon becoming simply "Americans."

Table 2.10: Number and Percentage of Immigrants from Germany in Total U.S. Immigration by Decade, 1820–1996

Decade	Number of Immigrants from Germany	Total U.S. Immigrants	Percentage of Immigrants from Germany in Total U.S. Immigration
1820	968	8,385	11.54
1821-1830	6,761	143,439	4.71
1831-1840	152,454	599,125	25.45
1841-1850	434,626	1,713,251	25.37
1851-1860	951,667	2,598,214	36.63
1861-1870	797,468	2,314,824	34.45
1871-1880	718,182	2,812,191	25.54
1881-1890	1,452,970	5,246,613	27.69
1891-1900	505,152	3,687,564	13.70
1901-1910	341,498	8,795,386	3.88
1911-1920	143,945	5,735,811	2.51
1921-1930	412,202	4,107,209	10.04
1931-1940	114,058	528,431	21.58
1941-1950	226,578	1,035,039	21.89
1951-1960	477,765	2,515,479	18.99
1961-1970	190,796	3,321,677	5.74
1971-1980	74,414	4,493,314	1.66
1981-1990	91,961	7,338,062	1.25
1991-1996	58,928	6,146,213	0.96
Total 1820-1996	7,142,393	63,140,227	11.31

Notes: For 1899–1919, data for Poland included in Austria-Hungary, Germany, and the Soviet Union. For 1938–45, data for Austria included in Germany.

Source: Adapted from Table 2, Immigration by Region and Selected Country of Residence, Fiscal Years 1820–1996, from the *Statistical Yearbook of the immigration and Naturalization Service,* 1996.

American Museum of Immigration, Statue of Liberty National Monument, National Park Service, U.S. Department of the Interior; Photo: Lewis W. Hine

Many German immigrants brought with them valuable skills, such as this printer (photographed by Lewis Hine in 1905), who later taught printing in an elementary school.

The Great Wave

By 1850, perhaps a quarter of the population of the United States was of German ancestry. That would rise to 30 percent by 1860, as nearly a million new German immigrants arrived. They were part of the great wave of European immigration which would last through the end of the 19th century. In the 1850s alone, it brought more than 2.8 million people to the United States, more than 34 percent of them Germans.

One key trigger for this mid-century emigration was famine. In the 1840s, a potato blight swept across Europe, from Ireland to Russia. Facing starvation, German farm families by the thousands headed to America, if they could scrape together money for the fare. They were often drawn by the many books and letters being written about the "Golden Land" of America.

Political upheaval also spurred emigration. Continuing battles for political reform led to revolution in 1848. When this failed, many highly educated immigrants, called forty-eighters, left Germany for the United States, where they would become powerful liberal figures. Many became active in the fight against slavery, and some were also early supporters of women's equality, including the right to vote. These political refugees included professionals, such as doctors, lawyers, physicians, pharmacists, horticulturists, scientists, professors, and teachers, and many other highly skilled people, including machinists, traders, and industrialists.

Gold drew many German immigrants and German Americans, after its discovery in 1848 near a California mill owned by Swiss-born German immigrant John A. Sutter. Gold-seekers called forty-niners flooded to the West Coast by land and by sea, via Cape Horn or Panama.

During the 1860s, many young German men came to fight in the Civil War, among them German-trained military officers. Most fought on the Union side, attracted by promises of citizenship and free land in the West. German immigrants and German Americans sometimes formed all-German-speaking regiments. Out of some 2 million Union soldiers, an estimated

Table 2.11: Number and Percentage of Foreign-Born Immigrants from Germany in Total U.S. Population by Decade, 1850–1990

Decade	Number of Foreign-Born Immigrants from Germany	Total U.S. Population	Percentage of Foreign-Born Immigrants from Germany in Total U.S. Population
1850	583,774	23,191,876	2.52
1860	1,276,075	31,443,321	4.06
1870	1,690,533	39,818,449	4.25
1880	1,966,742	50,155,783	3.92
1890	2,784,894	62,947,714	4.42
1900	2,663,418	75,994,575	3.50
1910	2,311,237	91,972,266	2.51
1920	1,686,108	105,710,620	1.60
1930	1,608,814	122,775,046	1.31
1940	(NA)	131,669,275	(NA)
1950	991,321	150,697,361	0.66
1960	989,815	179,323,175	0.55
1970	832,965	203,235,298	0.41
1980	849,384	227,726,000	0.37
1990	711,929	249,907,000	0.28

NA = Not available

Note: 1910 figure excludes Polish-speakers.

Source: Adapted from Series C 228–295, Foreign-Born Population, by Country of Birth: 1850–1970, in *Historical Statistics of the United States, Colonial Times to 1970, Bicentennial Edition*, and other updating tables from the U.S. Census Bureau.

These settlers were arriving in Cincinnati, a town largely founded by German immigrants, in 1802, crossing the Ohio River on a flatbed ferry.

500,000 to 600,000 were of German descent and about 176,000 were German-born.

Though immigration by German families slowed during the Civil War, it boomed again from 1865 until 1873, when the United States had an economic depression. The number of German immigrants rose again in the 1880s, reaching an all-time high of more than 250,000 in 1882.

Among the 1870s immigrants were Germans from Russia. They had maintained their language and culture in distinct communities in Russia, especially along the Volga River, and initially did the same in the United States, especially in Nebraska and the Dakotas, before spreading throughout the Great Plains and all the way to the West Coast.

Large numbers of German immigrants in this period also settled in the mid-Atlantic states, as many as 30 percent of them in New York State after 1850. Among these were some who had enormous cultural influence on the region, such as Leopold Damrosch, who helped found the Philharmonic Society and the Metropolitan Opera Company, and Albert Bierstadt, who as a painter helped shape the American vision.

They were also extremely influential in this period in education at all levels and in politics, including the labor movement.

Large numbers of Germans would continue to come to America through the early part of the 20th century, though another economic depression in 1893 helped slow that immigration somewhat. By late in the 19th century, Germans and other immigrants from northern and western Europe began to be outnumbered by the flood of immigrants from southern and eastern Europe, which historians call the "New Immigration."

From the earliest times, most Germans had immigrated to America as families. However, from the 1890s on, a large proportion of immigrants were single workers, usually men. Many of them came to earn money in American industries, and some later returned to Germany.

In all, between the end of the Napoleonic Wars (1815) and the beginning of World War I (1914), more than 5 million immigrants came to America from various German states. Another 1 to 2 million Germans came from other countries, notably Austria, Switzerland, and Russia.

War and Depression

During World War I, German immigration slowed to a trickle. The German government wanted to keep young men as soldiers. Anti-German feeling among many Americans also discouraged German immigration.

Early in the war, some German immigrants in America continued to support the land of their birth. However, many later dropped obvious ties to German culture, especially after the 1915 sinking of the *Lusitania,* in which 1,100 people, including many Americans, died. Many German-language publications and organizations were closed, teaching and speaking German was curbed or banned, German music was rejected, some German towns were renamed, and some German Americans were personally attacked.

When the United States entered the war, in 1917, most German-Americans supported the Allied side, even when they had relatives fighting for Germany. Opera star Ernestine Schumann-Heink, for example, had become an American citizen in 1908; she actively supported the war, and four of her sons fought for the Allies, but another was killed fighting in the Austrian army. After Germany lost the war, many Germans left their devastated country for America, through the 1920s and early 1930s. But as the full effects of the Great Depression came to be felt, immigration slowed sharply.

In Germany, conditions changed in the mid-1930s with the rise of the Nazis. Adolf Hitler and his Nazi Party built a dictatorship that glorified the military and the German ethnic heritage, while fostering hatred and persecution of other peoples, especially Jews. This caused a new exodus of people who were anti-Nazi or who were the targets of Nazi attacks. Among these were some highly talented, often well-educated Germans, including conductor Bruno Walter, composer Kurt Weill, actresses Lotte Lenya and Marlene Dietrich, architects Walter Gropius and Ludwig Mies van der Rohe, painter Josef Albers, mathematician Richard Courant, physicists Albert Einstein and Hans Bethe, and film director Erich von Stroheim. However, many people who wanted to leave Germany could not do so because no other country would take them; this included the United States, which had established immigration quotas in the 1920s (see"Annual Immigration Statistics" on p. 657; "General Notes on Immigration Statistics" on p. 684; and "General European Immigration Resources" on p. 317. See also chapters on specific countries that were major sources of immigrants).

American Museum of Immigration, Statue of Liberty National Monument, National Park Service, U.S. Department of the Interior; Photo: Lewis W. Hine

Many 20th-century German immigrants were rather prosperous and well-educated, like this group at Ellis Island in 1926.

Some of the early settlers of the German community at New Braunfels, Texas, posed in front of the dilapidated remains of the first structure they had built there.

Graph 2.17: Number of Immigrants from Germany by Decade, 1820–1996

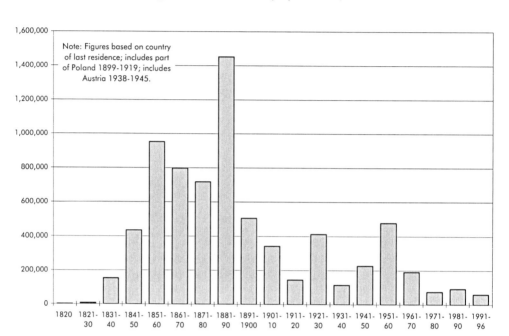

Many who were thus trapped in Germany would die during the terrible war years (1939–1945), either as a direct result of the conflict or in one of the Nazi concentration camps where millions of people perished, most of them Jews.

War's end found Germany, like much of Europe, devastated. Many Germans—including Jews who had survived the Holocaust and ethnic Germans from the Slavic and Baltic states—became refugees and were admitted to the United States as such. Also among the immigrants were numerous rocket scientists (including some Nazi supporters), who—led by Wernher von Braun—would form the core of the U.S. space program. The exact number of postwar refugees from Germany is unclear, for after World War II national borders shifted. Germany lost territories to its victorious neighbors, and the remainder was split into two parts: East Germany and West Germany.

The split in Germany reflected the Cold War, as East Germany came under Communist control, while West Germany was drawn into the group of Western democracies. West Germany developed a strong economy, so the number of new immigrants from there to America was relatively small from the 1970s on. East Germany became a closed society; especially after the building of the Berlin Wall in 1961, its citizens were unable to emigrate or even travel freely. That would remain true until 1989, when the Berlin Wall came down and East Germans were once more free to emigrate.

East and West Germany were reunited the following year, in 1990. Though the reunion caused some economic and political difficulties, West Germany had in the previous decades built up a strong enough economy to bear the burden, so there was little impulse to emigration. By the 1990s, less than 1 percent of immigration to the United States came from Germany.

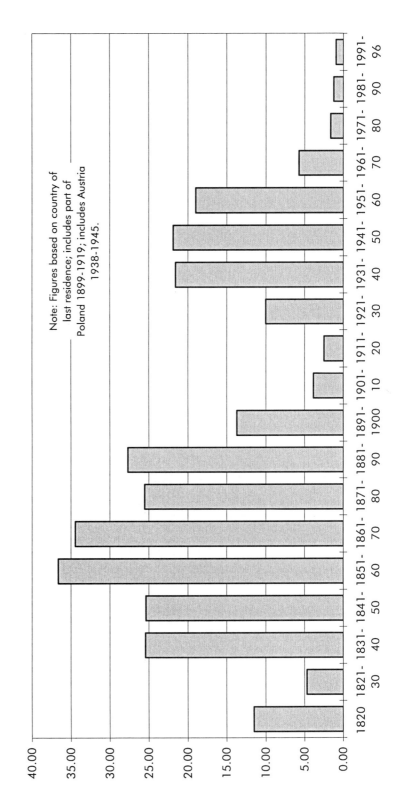

Graph 2.18: Percentage of Immigrants from Germany in Total U.S. Immigration by Decade, 1820–1996

Note: Figures based on country of last residence; includes part of Poland 1899-1919; includes Austria 1938-1945.

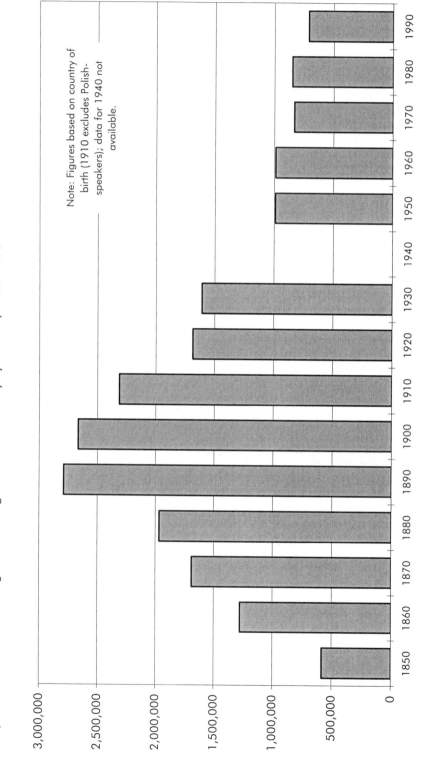

Graph 2.19: Number of Foreign-Born Immigrants from Germany by Decade, 1850–1990

Note: Figures based on country of birth (1910 excludes Polish-speakers); data for 1940 not available.

Resources

Internet Resources

German Corner (*http://www.germanheritage.com*) Contains full text of some works on German-American history (such as Adams, below), capsule biographies, bibliographies, teaching resources, information on German-American organizations, and links to other German-American Web sites. Hosted by IUPUI (Indiana University–Purdue University Indianapolis).

German-American Center (*http://www-lib.iupui.edu/kade*) Hosted by IUPUI (see above) and the Society for German-American Studies (see below); run at one of several Max Kade Institutes devoted to German-American research. Includes an international bibliography and yearbook; indexes to German-American historic sites, museum, libraries, archives, programs, and societies; full text of works on German-American history; teaching resources; special events; and links to other sites.

Society for German-American Studies (SGAS) (*http://andretti.iupui.edu/kade/sgasin.html*) Publishes quarterly newsletter and yearbook; cosponsors Web site (see above). (Address: c/o LaVern J. Rippley, German Department, St. Olaf's College, Northfield, MN; Telephone: 507-646-3223; Fax: 507-646-3732; e-mail: rippley@stolaf.edu)

GermanyGenWeb (*http://www.rootsweb.com/~wggerman/*) Part of the WorldGenWeb project, linking genealogical research sites around the world, by region, providing information by states or provinces.

Internet Sources of German Genealogy (*http://www.bawue.de/~hanacek/info/edatbase.htm*) Web site for amateur genealogists, providing information on how to access archives, links to newsgroups and reading lists, and CDs and software to help in genealogical searches, including links to archives (*http://www.bawue.de/~hanacek/info/earchive.htm*).

Cyndi's List—Germany/Deutschland (*http://www.cyndislist.com/germany.htm*), Cyndi's List—Mennonite (*http://www.cyndislist.com/menno.htm*), Cyndi's List —Germans from Russia (*http://www.cyndislist.com/germruss.htm*) Lists of on-line genealogical resources maintained by genealogical author Cyndi Howells.

Palatines to America (*http://palam.org*) Web site of organization focused on research of German ancestry, not just from the Palatinate; offers information and Web links.

German Genealogy Links (*http://www.justgen.com*) Web site offering numerous links.

Germans in America (*http://www.serve.com/shea/germusa/germusa.htm*) Collection of links to German-American resources.

American Historical Society of Germans from Russia (*http://www.ahsgr.org*) Web site offering information, resources, and related links. (Address: 631 D Street, Lincoln, NE 68502-1199; Phone: 402-474-3363; Fax: 402-474-7229; E-mail: AHSGR@aol.com)

Germans from Russia Heritage Society (*http://www.grhs.com*) Web site of organization for Americans of German-Russian ancestry. (Address: 1008 East Central Avenue, Bismarck, ND 58501; Phone: 701-223-6167; E-mail: grhs@btigate.com)

Steuben Society of America (*http://www.steubensociety.org*) Web site for organization. (Address: National Offices, 6705 Fresh Pond Road, Ridgewood, NY 11385; Phone: 718-381-0900; Fax: 718-628-4874)

Deutsch-Amerikanische Nationalkongress (DANK) (German American National Congress) (*http://www.dank.org*)

Organization Web site offering membership application. (Address: 4740 North Western Avenue, Chicago, IL 60625-2097; Phone: 773-275-1100; Fax: 773-275-4010)

Print Resources

General Works

Adams, Willi P. *The German-Americans: An Ethnic Experience*. Indianapolis: Max Kade German-American Center and IUPUI (see above), 1993. Available on-line at *www.germanheritage.com* (see German Corner, above).

Bailyn, Bernard. *From Protestant Peasants to Jewish Intellectuals: The Germans in the Peopling of America*. New York: Oxford University Press, 1988.

Brown, Liane I. *From Fear to Freedom*. Hobe Sound, Fla.: FEA Publishing, 1993.

Franck, Irene M. *The German-American Heritage*. New York: Facts on File, 1988.

Eric Solsten, ed. *Germany: A Country Study*. 3d ed. Washington, D.C.: U.S. Government Printing Office, 1996.

Haller, Charles R. *Across the Atlantic and Beyond: The Migration of German and Swiss Immigrants to America*. Bowie, Md.: Heritage Books, 1993.

Kunz, Virginia Brainard. *The Germans in America*. Minneapolis: Lerner, 1966.

Luebke, Frederick C. *Germans in the New World: Essays in the History of Immigration*. Urbana: University of Illinois Press, 1990.

Museums, Sites, and Collections of Germanic Culture in North America: An Annotated Directory of German Immigrant Culture in the United States and Canada. Westport, Conn.: Greenwood, 1980.

O'Connor, Richard. *The German-Americans: An Informal History*. Boston: Little, Brown, 1968.

Parsons, William T. *The Pennsylvania Dutch: A Persistent Minority*. Boston: Twayne, 1976.

Rippley, LaVern J. *The German-Americans*. Boston: Twayne, 1976.

Schouweiler, Tom. *Germans in America*. Minneapolis: Lerner, 1994.

Tolzmann, Don H. *The German-American Experience: A History of German Immigration, Settlement, and Influences in the United States*. Atlantic Highlands, N.J.: Humanities, 1998.

Totten, Christine M. *Roots in the Rhineland: America's German Heritage in Three Hundred Years of Immigration, 1683–1983*. New York: German Information Center, 1988.

Trommler, Frank, and Joseph McVeigh, eds. *America and the Germans: An Assessment of a Three-Hundred-Year History*. 2 vols. Vol. 1: *Immigration, Language, Ethnicity*. Vol. II: *The Relationship in the Twentieth Century*. Philadelphia: University of Pennsylvania Press, 1985.

Genealogical Works

Baxter, Angus. *In Search of Your German Roots: A Complete Guide to Tracing Your Ancestors in the Germanic Areas of Europe*. Baltimore: Genealogical Publishing, 1994. Original ed. 1991.

Brandt, Edward R. *Germanic Genealogy: A Guide to Worldwide Sources and Migration Patterns*. St. Paul: Germanic Genealogy Society, 1995. Includes chapter on Jewish genealogy by George E. Arnstein.

Reed, Robert D., and Danek S. Kaus. *Finding Your German-American Roots: A Guide to Researching Your Ethnic-American Cultural Heritage.* Saratoga, Calif.: R & E Publishers, 1993.

Schweitzer, George Keene. *German Genealogical Research.* Knoxville, Tenn.: G. K. Schweitzer, 1992.

Silver, Leda. *Tracing Our German Roots.* Santa Fe, N.M.: J. Muir, 1994.

Wellauer, Maralyn A. *German Immigration to America in the Nineteenth Century: A Genealogist's Guide.* Milwaukee: Roots International, 1985.

For more resources, see "General European Immigration Resources" on p. 317.

Immigrants from France

French fishing boats sailing out of Saint-Malo and Dieppe, in northern France, were fishing the Grand Banks off Newfoundland during the first decade of the 16th century. So were Portuguese, Basque, and British sailors, all of whom dried their cod on the Newfoundland shore and traded for furs with the local Native Americans. But they did not stay. Exploration came only later, starting with Jacques Cartier's 1534 and 1535 journeys into the Gulf of St. Lawrence and south to Hochelaga and the Lichine Rapids, the sites of what would become Quebec City and Montreal.

In 1605, French explorer Samuel de Champlain founded the first lasting French North American settlement, at Port Royal, Nova Scotia. Three years later, in 1608, he founded Quebec City, which would become the capital of New France. Only five years after that, in 1613, the long French-English battle for North America began, with English destruction of the Port Royal settlement.

The Battle for North America

In territory, New France grew quickly. By 1615, Champlain had reached Lake Huron; by 1679, René-Robert Cavelier, Sieur de La Salle reached the mouth of the Mississippi. On the other hand, the French population of New France grew very slowly, numbering only approximately 3,000 in 1663. However, in that year New France became a royal province, signaling a policy change toward encouragement of immigration. From 1663 to 1672, some 30,000 more French settlers immigrated into Quebec. However, the population and resources of English North America were far greater than those of New France. The population of the English colonies numbered an estimated 1.5 million during the French and Indian War (1754–1763), which was also the worldwide Seven Years War (1756–1763), while that of New France numbered only an estimated 50,000. During the war, in 1755, after the English took Acadia

(later Nova Scotia), they forcibly evacuated many French settlers from the region (see "Immigrants from Canada" on p. 483).

At the end of that war, France lost its North American holdings. Its territories in Canada were taken by the English. The French settlements in the Mississippi Basin, from the Canadian border to New Orleans, went to Spain, which would cede them back to France in 1800. The French settlers in the Mississippi Basin, then numbering an estimated 10,000, became part of the United States in 1803, when it purchased the Louisiana Territory from France.

After the English took Canada, a distinctly French-Canadian population evolved. It would later became a major source of immigrants into the United States, especially into New England (see "Immigrants from Canada" on p. 483).

Authors' Archives

French explorer La Salle traveled from the Great Lakes to the mouth of the Mississippi River in 1682, claiming for France the vast region he called Louisiana.

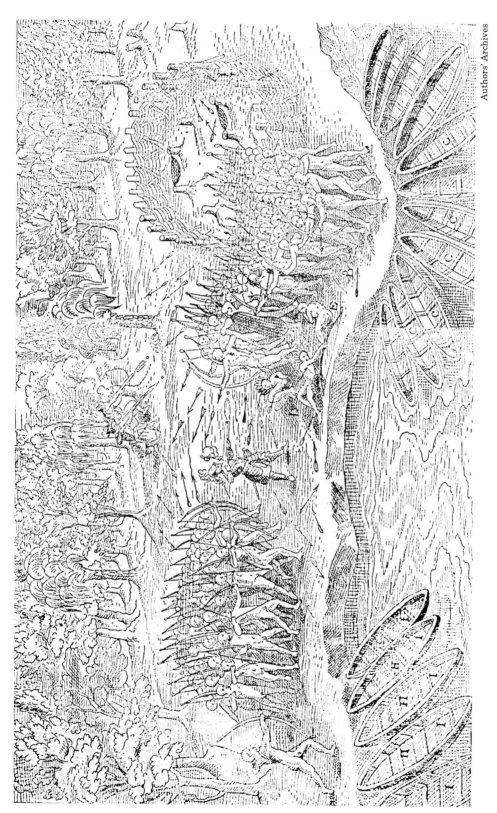

This drawing shows the French, led by Samuel de Champlain, in their first battle with the Iroquois in 1609.

Table 2.12: Number and Percentage of Immigrants
from France in Total U.S. Immigration by Decade,
1820–1996

Decade	Number of Immigrants from France	Total U.S. Immigrants	Percentage of Immigrants from France in Total U.S. Immigration
1820	371	8,385	4.42
1821-1830	8,497	143,439	5.92
1831-1840	45,575	599,125	7.61
1841-1850	77,262	1,713,251	4.51
1851-1860	76,358	2,598,214	2.94
1861-1870	35,986	2,314,824	1.55
1871-1880	72,206	2,812,191	2.57
1881-1890	50,464	5,246,613	0.96
1891-1900	30,770	3,687,564	0.83
1901-1910	73,379	8,795,386	0.83
1911-1920	61,897	5,735,811	1.08
1921-1930	49,610	4,107,209	1.21
1931-1940	12,623	528,431	2.39
1941-1950	38,809	1,035,039	3.75
1951-1960	51,121	2,515,479	2.03
1961-1970	45,237	3,321,677	1.36
1971-1980	25,069	4,493,314	0.56
1981-1990	32,353	7,338,062	0.44
1991-1996	23,095	6,146,213	0.38
Total 1820-1996	810,682	63,140,227	1.28

Source: Adapted from Table 2, Immigration by Region and
Selected Country of Last Residence, Fiscal Years 1820–
1996, from the *Statistical Yearbook of the Immigration and
Naturalization Service, 1996.*

Other Early French Immigrants

There were other early sources of French
immigration as well, directly into the
English colonies and later into the United
States. Chief among these were French
Protestant Huguenot refugees who left
France during the Catholic-Protestant
Huguenot Wars (1562–1628). Huguenots
began arriving in New Netherlands (later
New York) and the English colonies in the
mid-1650s. They formed a substantial por-
tion of the New Netherlands colony, just
before it was taken by the English in 1664.

A major wave of Huguenots began
arriving in 1685, after France revoked the
Edict of Nantes, which had protected
French Huguenots from Catholic persecution. An estimated 15,000 Huguenots
immigrated to England's American colonies from 1685 to 1750. Though most went
to South Carolina, they spread throughout
the colonies.

In 1790, the first U.S. Census estimated a French-born U.S. population of
almost 55,000. Among these were some

French democrats, along with aristocratic
French army officers who had fought on
the American side during the Revolutionary War. That population was quickly aug-
mented by the arrival of an estimated
10,000 to 20,000 refugees from 1790 to
1800. Some of these were fleeing from
France during the French Revolution and
others fleeing anti-colonial revolutions in
Santo Domingo and other French Caribbean areas. Other French refugees from
the Caribbean arrived during the first
decade of the 19th century. Many of these
Caribbean refugees did not stay on to
become Americans, instead ultimately
returning to France or moving on to other
French-speaking areas.

After the end of the Napoleonic Wars in
1815, French immigrants to the United
States included an unknown number of
former Napoleonic soldiers, many of whom
settled in French-speaking Louisiana.
These probably numbered in all no more
than 2,000.

Table 2.13: Number and Percentage of Foreign-Born
Immigrants from France in Total U.S. Population by
Decade, 1850–1990

Decade	Number of Foreign-Born Immigrants from France	Total U.S. Population	Percentage of Foreign-Born Immigrants from France in Total U.S. Population
1850	54,069	23,191,876	0.23
1860	109,870	31,443,321	0.35
1870	116,402	39,818,449	0.29
1880	106,971	50,155,783	0.21
1890	113,174	62,947,714	0.18
1900	104,197	75,994,575	0.14
1910	117,418	91,972,266	0.13
1920	153,072	105,710,620	0.14
1930	135,592	122,775,046	0.11
1940	(NA)	131,669,275	(NA)
1950	108,547	150,697,361	0.07
1960	111,582	179,323,175	0.06
1970	105,385	203,235,298	0.05
1980	120,215	227,726,000	0.05
1990	119,233	249,907,000	0.05

NA = Not available

Source: Adapted from Series C 228–295, Foreign-Born
Population, by Country of Birth: 1850–1970, in *Historical
Statistics of the United States, Colonial Times to 1970,
Bicentennial Edition,* and other updating tables from the
U.S. Census Bureau.

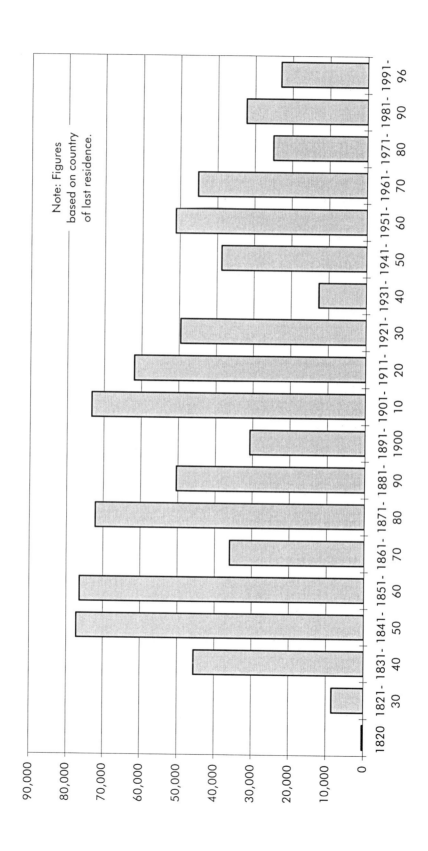

Graph 2.20: Number of Immigrants from France by Decade, 1820–1996

Note: Figures based on country of last residence.

Later French Immigration

U.S. immigration statistics were systematically compiled from 1820. These show a comparatively slow pace of immigration into the United States from France, as compared with the massive immigration to the United States from many other European countries. French immigration showed no great surge in any period and seemed closely related to the economic opportunities offered by the United States, rising in periods of prosperity and declining in hard times.

There were some variations in the French immigration pattern that flowed from other factors. One bulge in immigration occurred in the late 1840s and early 1850s, as an estimated 20,000 to 30,000 French immigrants joined the great California Gold Rush.

A second bulge in French immigration, this one unestimated, occurred after the Republican revolution of 1848, when some monarchists and others associated with the defeated government became political refugees. The same revolution brought the flight of many former slaveholders and plantation owners from the French Caribbean.

A third bulge came in the 1870s, primarily triggered by the Franco-Prussian War (1870–1871). A large part of the emigration from this period was of French people from the province of Alsace-Lorraine, which was taken by the Germans. Alsace-Lorraine was returned to France at the end of World War I.

From 1820 to 1996, a total of almost 811,000 French immigrants are recorded as having entered the United States. This figure does not include French Canadians, who are recorded as part of the Canadian immigration. All U.S. immigration figures are approximate, due to several kinds of undercounting and overcounting; but the French immigration is probably more approximate than some others. Overcounting occurred because many French immigrants reportedly returned to France, but U.S. immigration figures in some periods did not take returnees into account. On the other hand, undercounting also occurred, as an unusually large number of French immigrants arrived via cabin class, rather

Graph 2.21: Number of Foreign-Born Immigrants from France in Total U.S. Population by Decade, 1850–1990

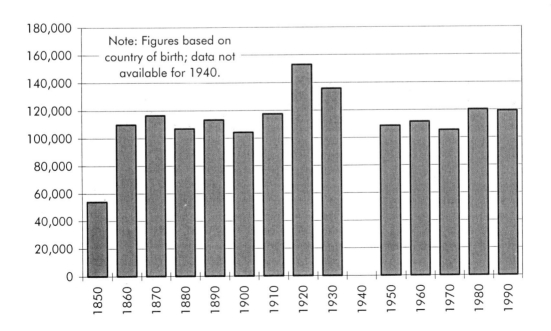

Note: Figures based on country of birth; data not available for 1940.

than in steerage; cabin-class passengers in some periods were not counted as immigrants.

The restrictive 1921 and 1924 U.S. immigration laws did not greatly affect the numbers of French immigrants reaching the United States. On the other hand, the Great Depression did; like immigrants from many countries, the French were deterred by hard times as bad in the United States as in their homeland. Only a little under 13,000 French immigrants are recorded as having entered the United States from 1931 to 1940. Nor was there a surge after World War II. Fewer than 39,000 French immigrants came from 1941 to 1950. From 1951 to 1996, French immigration was modest, averaging a little less than 4,000 per year.

Graph 2.22: Percentage of Immigrants from France in Total U.S. Immigration by Decade, 1820–1996

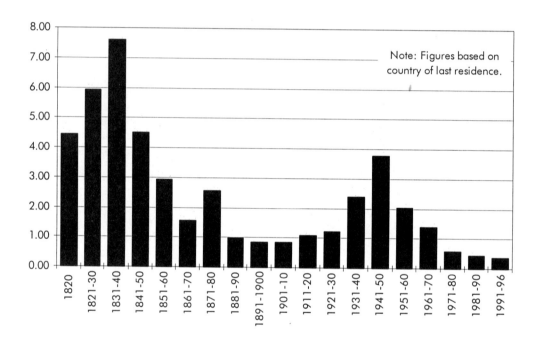

Note: Figures based on country of last residence.

Resources

Internet Resources

American-French Genealogical Society (*http://www.afgs.org*) Web site providing information about the organization's activities and links to useful genealogical Web sites, mailing lists, and newsgroups. (Address: P.O. Box 2113GH, Pawtucket, RI 02861; Phone/Fax: 401-765-6141)

Cyndi's List—France (*http://www.cyndislist.com/france.htm*), Cyndi's List—Huguenot (*http://www.cyndislist.com/huguenot.htm*), Cyndi's List—Acadian, Cajun & Creole (*http://www.cyndislist.com/acadian.htm*) Lists of on-line genealogical resources for France and French Americans, maintained by genealogical author Cyndi Howells.

National Huguenot Society (*http://huguenot.netnation.com*) Web site of an American organization focused on the history of the Huguenots and their experiences in America (Address: National Huguenot Society, 9033 Lyndale Avenue South, #108, Bloomington, MN 55420)

FranceGenWeb (*http://francegenweb.org*) A French-language Web site, part of MediterraneanGenWeb (*http://www.mediterraneangenweb.org*), itself part of the WorldGenWeb project, linking genealogical research sites around the world.

Print Resources

Avery, Elizabeth Huntington. *The Influence of French Immigration on the Political History of the United States.* San Francisco: R & E Research Associates, 1972. Reprint of author's thesis.

Brasseaux, Carl A. *The "Foreign French": Nineteenth-Century French Immigration into Louisiana.* 3 vols. Lafayette, La.: Center for Louisiana Studies, University of Southwestern Louisiana, 1990–1993.

Colletta, John Philip, comp. *A Select Bibliography of Works in the Collection of the Library of Congress Relating to French-American Genealogy: Including Library of Congress Card Catalog Numbers.* Washington, D.C.: J. P. Colletta, 1986.

Hafen, LeRoy R., ed. *French Fur Traders and Voyageurs in the American West.* Lincoln: University of Nebraska Press,

1997. Previously published Spokane, Wash.: A. H. Clark, 1995. Earlier part of 10-volume set: *The Mountain Men and the Fur Trade of the Far West.*

Holbrook, Sabra. *The French Founders of North America and Their Heritage.* New York: Atheneum, 1976.

Morrice, Polly Alison. *The French Americans.* New York: Chelsea House, 1988.

Pula, James S., ed. *The French in America, 1488–1974: A Chronology and Factbook.* Dobbs Ferry, N.Y.: Oceana, 1975.

Stone, Amy. *French Americans.* New York: Marshall Cavendish, 1995.

For French-Canadian resources, see also "Immigrants from Canada" on p. 483; for more resources, see "General European Immigration Resources" on p. 317.

Immigrants from the Netherlands

The estimated population of the Dutch North American colony of New Netherlands, which included New Amsterdam (later New York), stood at a little more than 5,000 in 1660, four years before British forces took it in the worldwide Second Anglo-Dutch War. The political fate of the city and colony were sealed in 1672, when the Netherlands ceded the colony to Britain in the Treaty of Westminster, which ended the worldwide Third Anglo-Dutch War. (See "An Overview" on p. 2, for a discussion of the founding and early years of the New Netherlands colony, within the context of the European imperial rivalries of the time.)

From 1664 until the 1840s, Dutch immigration to North America was negligible, although the numbers of Americans of Dutch or partly Dutch ethnic origin grew sharply, due to natural increase. In 1790, the year of the first U.S. census, very approximate estimates indicated that there were 100,000 Americans of at least all or partly Dutch ethnic origin.

The Main Wave

Several factors caused a substantial rise in Dutch immigration to the United States from the 1840s through the 1860s. Chief among these were the repeated failures of the European potato crop in the mid-1840s; though the effect was worst in Ireland, the failure affected many countries, including the Netherlands. A minor but substantial factor in emigration from the Netherlands was a series of splits within the Dutch Reformed Church, and between that church and the Dutch monarchy.

From 1841 to 1880, an estimated 44,000 Dutch immigrants entered the United States, approximately 80 percent of them Protestant and the rest Catholic. The overwhelming majority of these were farmers, forced to emigrate because of hard times. Some of those who emigrated earliest were religious dissidents (Seceders), many of whom settled in large groups that formed closely knit New World communities. In the late 1840s, three of the most notable of these communities were those at Calumet and High Prairie, near Chicago, Illinois; the New Holland area of Michigan;

Library of Congress

Heading a Dutch expedition, Peter Minuit purchased Manhattan Island, a 1626 event shown here, then founded New Amsterdam (later New York).

Graph 2.23: Percentage of Immigrants from the Netherlands in Total U.S. Immigration by Decade, 1820–1996

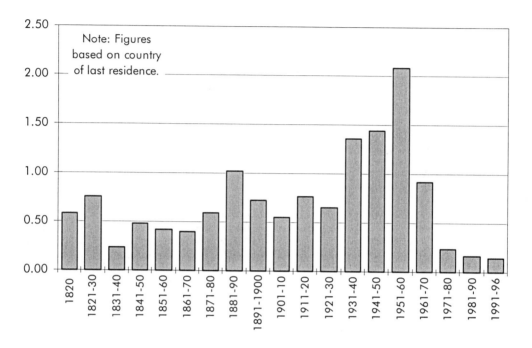

Graph 2.24: Number of Foreign-Born Immigrants from the Netherlands in Total U.S. Population by Decade, 1850–1990

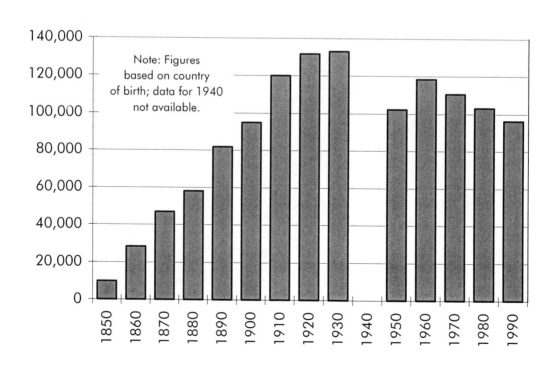

and Pella, Iowa. All served as centers from which later Dutch immigrants expanded into wider areas.

Nineteenth-century Dutch immigration peaked from the early 1880s until the United States Panic of 1893, which slowed immigration to the United States from many countries. In that period, Dutch farmers—once again hit hard by hard times—emigrated in large numbers. Some 80,000 reached the United States from 1881 to 1900, despite a sharp decline after the 1893 panic. Many had been attracted by the "America letters" sent back to the Netherlands by earlier immigrants, which encouraged them to join families and friends in America. These immigrants, new and old, made up the "immigrant chains" common to almost all immigrant groups coming to America.

In the early 20th century, the Dutch immigrant wave that had been somewhat reduced in the 1890s continued, as part of the huge European emigration of the era. From 1901 to 1930, some 117,000 more Dutch immigrants arrived in the United States, even though there was a very sharp interruption during World War I, and another sharp drop after restrictive immigration quotas went into effect in 1924 (see "Immigration Restrictions" on p. 47).

Table 2.14: Number and Percentage of Foreign-Born Immigrants from the Netherlands by Decade in Total U.S. Population at End of Decade, 1850–1990

Decade	Number of Foreign-Born Immigrants from the Netherlands	Total U.S. Population	Percentage of Foreign-Born Immigrants from the Netherlands in Total U.S. Population
1850	9,848	23,191,876	0.04
1860	28,281	31,443,321	0.09
1870	46,802	39,818,449	0.12
1880	58,090	50,155,783	0.12
1890	81,828	62,947,714	0.13
1900	94,931	75,994,575	0.12
1910	120,063	91,972,266	0.13
1920	131,766	105,710,620	0.12
1930	133,133	122,775,046	0.11
1940	(NA)	131,669,275	(NA)
1950	102,224	150,697,361	0.07
1960	118,415	179,323,175	0.07
1970	110,570	203,235,298	0.05
1980	103,136	227,726,000	0.05
1990	96,198	249,907,000	0.04

NA = Not available

Source: Adapted from Series C 228–295, Foreign-Born Population, by Country of Birth: 1850–1970, in *Historical Statistics of the United States, Colonial Times to 1970, Bicentennial Edition*, and other updating tables from the U.S. Census Bureau.

Table 2.15: Number and Percentage of Immigrants from the Netherlands in Total U.S. Immigration by Decade, 1820–1996

Decade	Number of Immigrants from the Netherlands	Total U.S. Immigrants	Percentage of Immigrants from the Netherlands in Total U.S. Immigration
1820	49	8,385	0.58
1821-30	1,078	143,439	0.75
1831-40	1,412	599,125	0.24
1841-50	8,251	1,713,251	0.48
1851-60	10,789	2,598,214	0.42
1861-70	9,102	2,314,824	0.39
1871-80	16,541	2,812,191	0.59
1881-90	53,701	5,246,613	1.02
1891-1900	26,758	3,687,564	0.73
1901-10	48,262	8,795,386	0.55
1911-20	43,718	5,735,811	0.76
1921-30	26,948	4,107,209	0.66
1931-40	7,150	528,431	1.35
1941-50	14,860	1,035,039	1.44
1951-60	52,277	2,515,479	2.08
1961-70	30,606	3,321,677	0.92
1971-80	10,492	4,493,314	0.23
1981-90	12,238	7,338,062	0.17
1991-96	8,728	6,146,213	0.14
Total 1850-1996	382,960	63,140,227	0.61

Source: Adapted from Table 2, Immigration by Region and Selected Country of Last Residence, Fiscal Years 1820–1996, from the *Statistical Yearbook of the Immigration and Naturalization Service*, 1996.

Later Immigration

After 1924, and through 1953, Dutch immigration was small, being limited by the Great Depression of the 1930s, World War II, and continuing restrictive quotas. After the war, emigration pressure grew, with tens of thousands in the Netherlands waiting for places in the small American immigration quota, which was limited to 3,136 per year.

Dutch emigration pressure became massive after Indonesia won independence from Dutch rule (1949–1950), and more than 300,000 Dutch Indonesians fled to the Netherlands. The United States responded with the Refugee Relief Act of 1953, which allowed 17,000 more Dutch immigrants into the United States. Further refugee relief acts followed, in 1958 and 1962. In all, a surge of 83,000 new Dutch immigrants entered the United States from 1951 to 1970.

This wave of Dutch immigrants settled largely in East and West Coast urban areas, most notably in southern California and the New York City area. The 19th- and early-20th-century Dutch immigrants, largely rural and self-contained, had settled largely in farming areas in the Midwest, forming tight, often insulated communities. The new Dutch immigrants of the late 20th century, while settling in well-defined urban areas, spread out far more quickly in American society, soon becoming part of the mainstream.

Immigration to the United States from the Netherlands diminished in the 1980s and 1990s. Only 21,000 Dutch immigrants were recorded as entering the United States from 1981 to 1996, a generally prosperous and stable period in the Netherlands.

Graph 2.25: Number of Immigrants from the Netherlands by Decade, 1820–1996

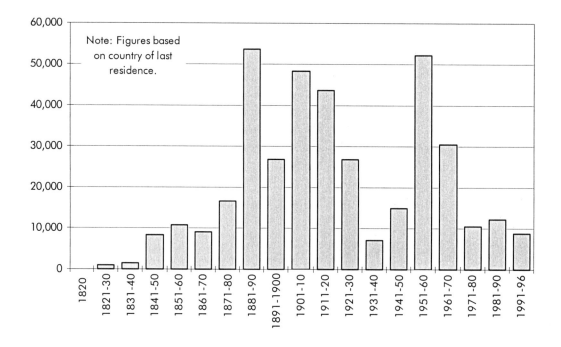

American Museum of Immigration, Statue of Liberty National Monument, National Park Service, U.S. Department of the Interior

Many immigrants had large families; this photograph shows Dutch mother Johanna Dÿkhoff and her 11 children en route to Minnesota.

Resources

Internet Resources

New Netherlands Project (*http://www.nnp.org*) Web site about this project focusing on transcription, translation, and publication of documents from the early Dutch colony, sponsored by various organizations, including the Friends of New Netherland (*http://www.nnp.org/fnn/index.html*; address: Box 2536, Empire State Plaza Station, Albany, NY 12220-0536).

Holland Society of New York (*http://members.aol.com/hollsoc*) Web site of organization of descendants of New Amsterdam settlers before 1675. (Address: 122 E. 58th St., New York, NY 10022)

Cyndi's List—Netherlands / Nederland (*http://www.cyndislist.com/nether.htm*) List of on-line genealogical resources for the Netherlands, maintained by genealogical author Cyndi Howells.

Wortels naar het verleden, "Roots to the past" (*http://members.tripod.com/~westland/index.htm*) Part of the WorldGenWeb project, linking genealogical research sites around the world, by region, providing information about and links to information on emigration, history, and genealogy, including maps and ship passenger lists.

Print Resources

De Jong, Gerald Francis. *The Dutch in America, 1609–1974.* Boston: Twayne, 1975.

Galema, Annemieke. *Frisians to America, 1880–1914: With the Baggage of the Fatherland.* Detroit: Wayne State University Press, 1996.

Ganzevoort, Herman, and Mark Boekelman, eds. *Dutch Immigration to North America.* Toronto: Multicultural History Society of Ontario, 1983.

Hinte, Jacob van. *Netherlanders in America: A Study of Emigration and Settlement in the Nineteenth and Twentieth Centuries in the United States of America.* Grand Rapids, Mich.: Baker Book House, 1985.

Kroes, Rob, et al., eds. *The Dutch in North America: Their Immigration and Cultural Continuity.* Amsterdam: VU University Press, 1991.

Lucas, Henry Stephen. *Netherlanders in America: Dutch Immigration to the United States and Canada, 1789–1950.* Grand Rapids, Mich.: W. B. Eerdmans, 1989.

———. *Dutch Immigrant Memoirs and Related Writings.* Rev. ed. Grand Rapids, Mich.: W. B. Eerdmans, 1997.

Smit, Pamela, and J. W. Smit, comps. *The Dutch in America, 1609–1970: A Chronology and Fact Book.* Dobbs Ferry, N.Y.: Oceana, 1972.

Swierenga, Robert P., ed. *The Dutch in America: Immigration, Settlement, and Cultural Change.* New Brunswick, N.J.: Rutgers University Press, 1985.

TenZythoff, Gerrit J. *The Dutch in America.* Minneapolis: Lerner, 1969.

Wabeke, Bertus Harry. *Dutch Emigration to North America, 1624–1860: A Short History.* Freeport, N.Y.: Books for Libraries Press, 1970. Reprint of the 1944 ed.

For more resources, see "General European Immigration Resources" on p. 317.

Immigrants from Scandinavia

The first Europeans to land in North America may well have been Scandinavian. Viking sagas record that around the turn of the 11th century A.D., Norse explorers led by Leif Eriksson landed in a place they named Vinland, and that a baby boy named Snorri was born there in the winter of 1003–1004, probably the first child of European descent born in America. Scholars disagree on precisely where Vinland was, but most believe it to have been somewhere between New York harbor and the coast of Labrador.

The Norse Vikings had settlements throughout the North Atlantic, including some along the North American coast, such as the one discovered in 1960 at L'Anse aux Meadows on the northern coast of Newfoundland. But as the earth grew colder with the Little Ice Age that started in the 12th century, the Norse gradually withdrew from the mainland, though their colonies in Greenland may have survived as late as the 15th century or even beyond.

When European settlers again began to settle in northeastern North America, starting in the 17th century, Scandinavians were among them. However, the main Scandinavian immigration would not come until the mid-19th century. Then Scandinavians became a major part of the flood of northwestern Europeans called the "old immigration."

Scandinavian Background

For more than a thousand years, the Scandinavians have had an intertwined history. From about A.D. 800, Scandinavians from Norway, Denmark, and Sweden led a massive expansion from their northern homelands. These Vikings (a term originally meaning "invaders") penetrated deep into Europe and established colonies across the Atlantic in this period. Swedish Vikings swept through the region of Finland and later established the state of Rus (modern Russia), while Norse and Danish Vikings took sizable parts of France and the British Isles.

Norse Vikings seeking independence from Norway fanned out in the Atlantic from the mid-9th century. They settled Iceland in the 870s, forming the main population of the island, though some Celts had arrived there before them. They also settled in Greenland and elsewhere. These island colonies remained independent for some centuries, but by the 13th century had come under the rule of Norway.

However, by the late 14th century Norway was so weakened that it and its Atlantic colonies fell under the domination of Denmark. In the Union of Kalmar (1397), Denmark and Norway were joined by Sweden, which then included Finland and some lands that are now part of Russia.

Sweden pulled out of the Scandinavian union in 1523 and began to build its own empire. In Finland and other eastern territories, Swedish speakers formed an elite. Most Finnish-speaking Finns were poor and ill educated, which would remain true into modern times. Finland was also devastated by a series of wars between Sweden and Russia from the 17th through the mid-20th centuries. In 1809, Russia took con-

Authors' Archives

In ships like these, Norse Vikings crossed the North Atlantic; when they made landfall, the ship continued to be their shelter, often topped with a tentlike covering.

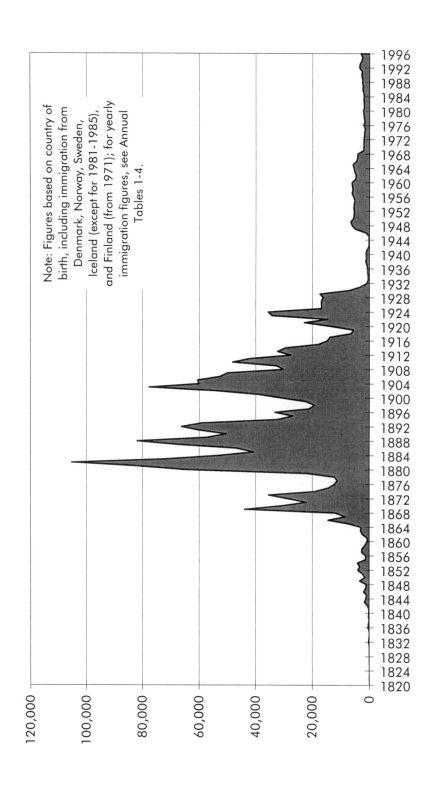

Graph 2.26: Number of Immigrants from Scandinavia Annually, 1820–1996

Note: Figures based on country of birth, including immigration from Denmark, Norway, Sweden, Iceland (except for 1981-1985), and Finland (from 1971); for yearly immigration figures, see Annual Tables 1-4.

trol of Finland, which did not become independent again until after the 1917 Russian Revolution.

Denmark remained powerful. By 1537, Norway had become a province of the Danish empire, which included Iceland and other North Atlantic colonies. The Danes would even establish a toehold in the Caribbean, in the Danish West Indies, now called the Virgin Islands. However, Denmark would gradually lose power, especially after the Napoleonic Wars. In 1815, Denmark lost Norway to Sweden, and in the 1860s lost a costly war against Prussia and Austria.

From 1815, Norway was reluctantly yoked in a dual kingdom dominated by Sweden. This was finally dissolved peacefully in 1905, with Norway becoming an independent monarchy.

Iceland long remained dominated by Denmark. It became a separate state tied to the Danish crown in 1918, but did not become fully independent until 1944.

In the 17th century, Scandinavia became strongly Protestant and Sweden especially became a haven for Protestants during Europe's many religious wars.

It was against this background that many Scandinavians immigrated to America. Some sought personal and political

Like other early immigrants, Scandinavians often centered their communities on churches, like this one in Wilmington, Delaware (originally Sweden's Fort Christina), built in 1698.

freedom. Others sought religious freedom. Sometimes the two were intertwined. The Lutheran church dominated in Scandinavia and was closely tied to the state. People who followed other religions were often persecuted, even arrested. That included other Protestants, among them Quakers, Mormons, and Methodists, many of whom left their homelands because of religious repression.

Many left Scandinavia for economic opportunity. Wars, crop failures, famine, high taxes, and political repression all combined to make life hard for poor people. Added to that was the enormous pressure of rising population throughout the region. In Norway alone, the population more than doubled between the late 17th century and 1815.

Scandinavians could leave the country only with special permission from the government, which was not readily granted. Restrictions were tightest in Sweden, Finland, and Iceland, with Danes and Norwegians being able to gain the required permission more easily. Restrictions were not eased until the 1840s.

Early Immigrants

The first Scandinavian immigrants in the post-Columbus era were a party of Swedes led by German-born Peter Minuit, former governor of the New Netherlands colony. Their two ships arrived on the Delaware River in 1638, where they founded the colony of New Sweden, centered on Fort Christina (now Wilmington, Delaware), named for the Swedish queen. On land purchased from Native Americans, they settled along Delaware Bay and inland along the Delaware River, as far north as Philadelphia and Trenton, becoming the first European settlers in the region.

The first Swedish trading company did not succeed, but the new settlers did recognize the fertility of the land. They became farmers, and the Swedish government sent out additional farmers, other skilled workers, and Lutheran ministers. It also sent some Swedes and Finns convicted of minor crimes, such as adultery, failure to pay debts, or clearing the land by burning (a tradition in Finland, but against Swedish law).

Some hundreds of additional Swedish and Finnish settlers arrived by the 1650s. However, the Swedish colonies had rivals: the Dutch and the English. In the end, the Swedes lost to the Dutch, who in turn lost to the English. After 1653, no more Swedish parties arrived, and the early Swedish settlers blended into the general population of the new America. Later some of them would help form the new United States, such as John Morton (Mortenson), who signed the Declaration of Independence, and John Hanson, who would be the first chief executive of the new nation, until George Washington took office.

In the same period, some Danish and Norwegian immigrants arrived in America with Dutch colonists. Many of these were sailors or clerks who had traveled to the Netherlands to look for work or to the Danish West Indies and then on to America. The first known family of Danes to arrive in North America was that of Jan Jansen Van Breestede, who came to the New Netherlands in 1636. Among those who followed was Jonas Bronck, who in 1639 bought a large farm in New Amsterdam—and gave his name to the modern Bronx.

Many of these early immigrants were Lutherans, who joined with other northern Europeans in Lutheran churches in the New World. However, starting in the 1740s, some Scandinavian Protestants came to America because their form of

Library of Congress

John Hanson, descendant of the earliest Swedish immigrants, was the first chief executive of the new United States, before George Washington became president.

Protestantism was banned at home. The first group was composed of Danish Moravians, who joined other Moravians in Bethlehem, Pennsylvania, in 1742. Whole shiploads followed, including Norwegian Moravians.

Apart from such groups, relatively few Scandinavians arrived in America during the late 18th and early 19th centuries. However, some skilled and educated Danes arrived just after the American Revolution, among them teachers, doctors, ministers, and merchants.

The Main Wave

Scandinavian immigration to the United States began to build slowly in the years following the end of the Napoleonic Wars, in 1815. The first notable Norwegian party—52 emigrants, including 10 married couples and many children, plus an additional child born at sea—arrived in 1825 in the *Restaurationen.* They left from Stavanger, which would be a key emigration port for Norwegians, and after three months arrived in New York by way of England and Spain. Their tiny ship was the Norwegian equivalent of the *Mayflower,* but it had only a quarter of the size of that more famous ship, and was therefore even more crowded.

Many of these early Norwegian immigrants were Quakers, who received help from American Quakers in settling on the New York shore of Lake Ontario. The year they arrived, 1825, the Erie Canal opened, making this route up the Hudson River and then west on the canal the main migration route into the heart of the continent. Some of these early Norwegian immigrants followed the route themselves, to places such as Illinois and Wisconsin. Their letters to family and friends back home, popularly called "America letters," were widely circulated, and helped to attract others to follow them to the United States. The numbers tell the tale: the combined immigration to the United States from Norway and Sweden (which meant primarily Norway at that time) was 91 from 1821 to 1830, but it jumped to 1,201 in the following decade (1831–1840).

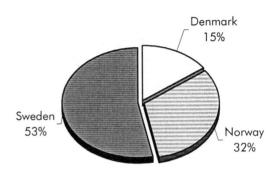

Graph 2.27: Percentage of Immigrants from Denmark, Norway, and Sweden in Total Immigration from Scandinavia, 1871–1996

Denmark
15%

Sweden
53%

Norway
32%

Note: Figures based on country of last residence; Finland not included in these figures.

Danish emigration also grew in these decades, as Denmark suffered economic and territorial losses because of its alliance with defeated France. Many of these Danes headed west, some right across the continent. Danish blacksmith Peter Lassen led one party all the way to northern California, opening a new pathway through the Sierra Nevada, past the mountain now named for him: Lassen Peak.

Religion spurred an increase in Danish emigration in the 1850s. Mormon missionaries in Denmark from 1850 converted many Danes, especially those from small villages. Within the next decade, more than 3,000 Danish Mormons would immigrate to America. They generally traveled on chartered ships from the ports of Hamburg, Germany, or Liverpool, England, with New York and New Orleans the main ports of arrival (see "The Journey" on p. 53). Many paid their own way, but the emigrants also received aid from the Mormons, including loans from church funds and agents to guide them across the continent to the Mormon settlements in Utah, which were desperate for their labor and skills.

The cross-country trip was brutal; immigrants often carried their goods on handcarts or ox-drawn wagons, with sickness and bad weather being major hazards. Many died on the way; one 1854 party of 680 Danish Mormons lost 160 members to

This party of Swedish immigrants formed a parade as they passed through Boston in 1852, on their way west.

Library of Congress

Table 2.16: Number and Percentage of Immigrants from Scandinavia in Total U.S. Immigration by Decade, 1820–1996

Decade	Number of Immigrants from Scandinavia	Total U.S. Immigration	Percentage of Immigrants from Scandinavia in Total U.S. Immigration	Number of Immigrants from Denmark	Number of Immigrants from Norway-Sweden	Number of Immigrants from Norway	Number of Immigrants from Sweden
1820	23	8,385	0.27	20	3	—	—
1821-1830	230	143,439	0.16	169	91	—	—
1831-1840	2,264	599,125	0.38	1,063	1,201	—	—
1841-1850	14,442	1,713,251	0.84	539	13,903	—	—
1851-1860	24,680	2,598,214	0.95	3,749	20,931	—	—
1861-1870	126,392	2,314,824	5.46	17,094	109,298	—	—
1871-1880	243,016	2,812,191	8.64	31,771	—	95,323	115,922
1881-1890	656,494	5,246,613	12.51	88,132	—	176,586	391,776
1891-1900	371,512	3,687,564	10.07	50,231	—	95,015	226,266
1901-1910	505,324	8,795,386	5.75	65,285	—	190,505	249,534
1911-1920	203,452	5,735,811	3.55	41,983	—	66,395	95,074
1921-1930	198,210	4,107,209	4.83	32,430	—	68,531	97,249
1931-1940	11,259	528,431	2.13	2,559	—	4,740	3,960
1941-1950	26,158	1,035,039	2.53	5,393	—	10,100	10,665
1951-1960	55,616	2,515,479	2.21	10,984	—	22,935	21,697
1961-1970	41,801	3,321,677	1.26	9,201	—	15,484	17,116
1971-1980	14,911	4,493,314	0.33	4,439	—	3,941	6,531
1981-1990	20,552	7,338,062	0.28	5,370	—	4,164	11,018
1991-1996	15,953	6,146,213	0.26	2,784	—	2,245	1,463
Total 1820-1996	2,532,289	63,140,227	4.01	373,196	145,427	755,964	1,248,271

(-) Represents zero.

Notes: Data for Norway and Sweden not reported separately until 1871. Figures for Finland not reported separately in three tables.

Source: Adapted from Table 2, Immigration by Region and Selected Country of Last Residence, Fiscal Years 1820–1996, from the *Statistical Yearbook of the Immigration and Naturalization Service*, 1996.

cholera. They also faced attacks by other anti-Mormon settlers. In all, the journey from Denmark to Utah could take five months or more. Some chose not to complete the journey, settling instead on the Great Plains, most notably in Iowa and Nebraska.

Life in Utah was hard for the new arrivals. Many Danish immigrants wrote about their dissatisfaction with conditions there, so Danish Mormon emigration later slowed. Indeed, some Danish immigrants called "backtrailers" left Utah and returned to settle in the Great Plains, especially around Omaha, Nebraska.

Meanwhile, other Danes were immigrating to the United States. Many of these were Lutherans, who would often join in Scandinavian congregations in the United States. Danish minister Claus Laurits Clausen led a largely Norwegian congregation. His "America letters" were widely reprinted in Danish newspapers, attracting many new immigrants. Other Danes wrote guidebooks for emigrants or led parties themselves. Such writings attracted many to Wisconsin, which then had the largest number of Danish immigrants of any state, and later to other states in the upper Midwest, notably Michigan. Other

Graph 2.28: Percentage of Foreign-Born Immigrants from Denmark and Iceland, Finland, Norway, and Sweden in Total Foreign-Born Immigrants from Scandinavia by Decade, 1850–1990

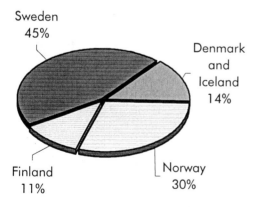

Sweden
45%

Denmark
and
Iceland
14%

Finland
11%

Norway
30%

Note: Figures based on country of birth; data for Finland included from 1900 only.

religious and political groups also came, including Danish Baptists and Socialist reformers. In 1867, Danish Americans founded the Dania Society to help new immigrants learn English and settle into their new homes.

Norwegians, too, continued to arrive. Many of the mid-century immigrants settled in Illinois and Wisconsin, though one notable Norwegian community was established in Texas. In addition, many Norwegians were to be found in U.S. port cities. Some of the Norwegian immigrants came for religious reasons, such as the Norwegian Moravians who came to Green Bay, Wisconsin, in 1850.

Swedes, too, began to emigrate in larger numbers. In the 1840s, many of these were Swedes from Finland, which had been lost to the Russians. Notable Finnish-Swedish leader Gustav Unonius led a party of affluent families to Wisconsin. They were ill prepared for the hard life there, and Unonius later moved to Chicago in 1849 and back to Sweden in 1859. However, during these years he wrote many "America letters" for Swedish newspapers, attracting new immigrants.

New immigrants often encountered problems in the United States. Some were unable to find the communities they sought, while others were robbed en route. To help such travelers, two Swedish brothers, converts to Methodism, founded an immigrant support network. From the mid-1840s, Olaf Hedstrom would help new immigrants from his series of missions, often demasted ships, in New York. Olaf himself had been robbed of all his money when he first arrived as a sailor in New York in the late 1820s. He would guide immigrants to Chicago, where his brother, Jonas Hedstrom, lived. Largely through their efforts, many thousands of Swedes settled in Illinois.

Many of the mid-century Swedish immigrants sought religious freedom. Lutheranism was still the state-sponsored religion, and members of other religious groups were persecuted and even arrested for holding prayer meetings in their homes. The famous Bishop Hill community, originally a commune, was established in 1846 by one of those groups, directed to Illinois by Olaf Hedstrom.

Many Scandinavians were drawn by America's promise of political freedom. With political power in their homelands in the hands of rich and powerful elites, they were attracted to the possibility of establishing a "New Norway" or a "New Sweden" in America. In the 1840s, these visions were part of a wider reform movement that led to a failed series of revolutions throughout Europe in 1848.

These revolutions gave an economic boost to emigration, for turmoil in Europe caused a depression in Scandinavia. Many unemployed workers looked to America, among them dockworkers, woodworkers, factory workers, builders, loggers, and sailors. They were among the many Scandinavian immigrants touched by gold fever. After gold was discovered in California in 1848, many Scandinavians booked passage across the Atlantic—and many sailors jumped ship in American ports. Some stayed briefly and then went home, a few with modest fortunes, while others settled permanently in the United States. Either way, their experiences continued to generate interest in America.

Shipping lines had also begun to see the possibility of reaping substantial profits from carrying emigrants. Unlike in earlier times, when emigrants had to buy or charter ships for themselves, or wait for space on cargo vessels, regularly scheduled boats called *packets* linked northern Europe and America ("The Journey" on p. 53).

Shipping lines also hired recruiting agents to help sell transatlantic tickets to emigrants. Such recruiters often exaggerated the nature of their ships and of life in America, and Scandinavian newspapers warned potential emigrants against such "soul-buyers." However, the "America letters" still made America enormously attractive. One such recruiting agent, Oscar Malmborg, a Swedish soldier who had fought for the U.S. Army during the Mexican War, found an audience of more than 2,000 people in Wrigstad, Sweden, when he arrived in 1861. Many of them were farmers who had already sold their land and packed their goods before Malmborg arrived.

Some states also hired recruiting agents. Wisconsin, Minnesota, Michigan, and Maine were among those who actively recruited Scandinavians to settle their lands, sometimes offering land, jobs, and other aid as inducements.

Graph 2.29: Number of Foreign-Born Immigrants from Scandinavia in Total U.S. Population by Decade, 1850–1990

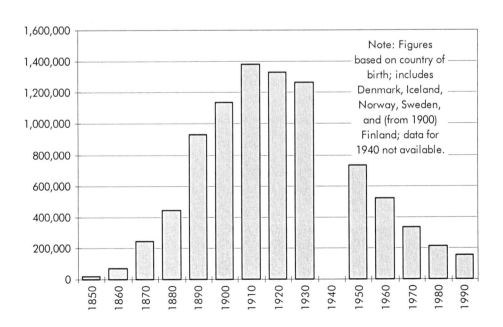

Note: Figures based on country of birth; includes Denmark, Iceland, Norway, Sweden, and (from 1900) Finland; data for 1940 not available.

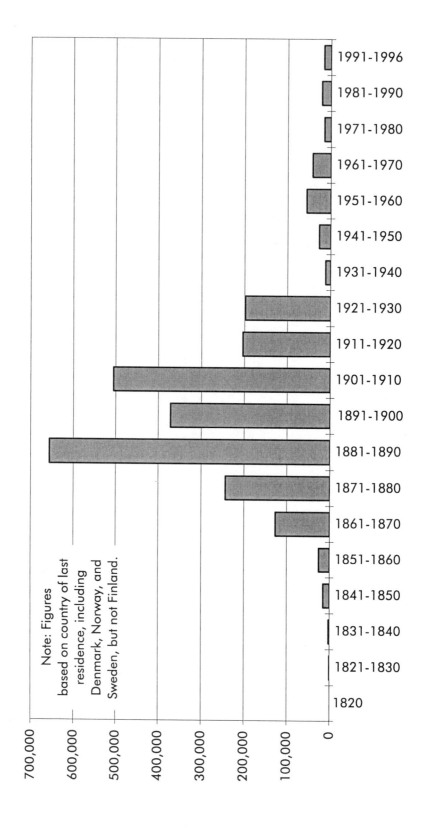

Graph 2.30: Number of Immigrants from Scandinavia in Total U.S. Immigration by Decade, 1820–1996

Note: Figures based on country of last residence, including Denmark, Norway, and Sweden, but not Finland.

National Archives

In the early years, Scandinavian and other pioneers on the Great Plains often lived in sod houses, like this one in the Dakota Territory in 1885.

A different kind of recruitment began in the 1860s. Seeking soldiers to fight in the Union Army during the Civil War, the federal government actively recruited in Europe. The Homestead Act of 1862 offered free land—160 acres—to people who would settle and work it, an offer extended to immigrant recruits. In 1862, President Abraham Lincoln sent 30 consular officials to Sweden alone, to recruit settlers and soldiers. The response was especially strong because of a series of crop failures, especially in Sweden, and because America and Russia were supplying grain more cheaply than Scandinavia could do, with its marginal farms. Some Scandinavians turned instead to dairy farming or animal husbandry, especially in Denmark, but others found themselves simply growing poorer.

Some parts of Scandinavia, especially Sweden, were also affected by an enclosure movement. Lands once held and worked in common by people in a village were converted into small farms, with many people in the process being thrown off the land, with no work available for them.

Added to the mix of motives for emigration from Scandinavia was enormous population pressures, as the death rate fell with better medical care. In Sweden, the population was 3 million in 1815; by 1900 it had doubled, even though the country had sent hundreds of thousands of emigrants to America. Norway's population had doubled from the late 1600s, to reach 886,000 by 1815. But the population kept rising, reaching 2,221,000 by 1900, even though nearly a million Norwegians would immigrate to America between the 1820s and the 1920s. No country except Ireland has sent a larger proportion of its population to America than Norway.

The pressures at home and the attractions of America combined to produce a massive emigration by the mid-19th century. It would reach its peak in the 1880s, when more than 650,000 Scandinavians were recorded as arriving in the United States, the peak year being 1882, with 105,326. These were almost all from Denmark, Norway, and Sweden.

How many Finnish immigrants came in these decades is unclear, for Finland was held by Russia, and Finnish immigrants were counted as Russians. Their numbers were not great, however. Some Finns joined the Russians in Alaskan settlements in the early 19th century ("Immigrants from Russia and the Commonwealth States" on p. 277), with two of them later serving as governors of Alaska. They are credited with building the first Protestant church on the Pacific Northwest coast, in Sitka, by the 1840s. Finnish sailors were among the gold-seeking forty-niners heading to California, while some also fled to America to avoid having to fight for Russia in the Crimean War (1854–1856).

Finns began to arrive in larger numbers in the 1860s, at first from the coastal regions, later from inland areas. Often they had left the land and gone to the city in search of work. Many of these were recruited, such as the Finns brought in to work in the copper mines of northern Michigan. One earlier Finnish immigrant, Carl Sjödahl (known in America as Charles Linn), brought a number of Finns to Alabama, including some young women to work as maids.

Finnish immigration continued to build until it was slowed by the 1893 U.S. depression. Through the 1860s, most Finnish immigrants were Swedish speakers, but after that the immigration was split more equally between them and Finnish speakers. By 1914, an estimated 300,000 Finns had come to America.

Emigration from Iceland also began late, for the island was still tightly controlled by Denmark. The first two known Icelandic immigrants were Thorarinn Haflidason Thorason and Gudmund Gudmundsson, Mormon converts who in the mid-1850s led an Icelandic Mormon party to Utah.

Other Icelandic immigrants began to come in the 1860s, following a series of widely circulated "America letters" written by Danish clerk William Wickham to his former employer, an Icelandic merchant. They came in small numbers, mostly settling in Wisconsin, where Wickham lived. Because of Danish restrictions, Icelandic immigrants had to travel eastward across the Atlantic to Europe to catch a ship for America. Many sailed from Liverpool to Quebec, then went by train to Milwaukee, while others came through New York. Some Icelanders ended up staying in Canada, which employed agents offering land and aid to new immigrants. Some later settled in northern Minnesota, the Dakotas, Alaska, and Canada, often attracted by cool climates.

Library of Congress

Danish-born Jacob Riis became a noted American reformer, through his photographs and writings exposing the terrible living and working conditions of late-19th-century immigrants.

Scandinavian immigration was heaviest in the decade from 1881 to 1890, when more than 650,000 immigrants arrived (not counting Finns from Russia), forming 12.5 percent of the total immigration for the period. The peak year was 1882, when more than 100,000 Scandinavians arrived. Scandinavians still formed 10 percent of the total immigration for 1891 to 1900. However, from then on they formed a much smaller proportion of the total immigration, as the so-called "new immigration," primarily from southern and eastern Europe, began to dominate.

The numbers of Scandinavian immigrants living in the United States reached a peak in 1910, when the census tallied more than 1,380,000 foreign-born Scandinavians in the U.S. population. Of these, more than 665,000 were born in Sweden, more than 403,000 in Norway, more than 181,000 in Denmark, and more than 129,000 in Finland. The latter two groups peaked in the following decade, when the 1920 census recorded more than 189,000 foreign-born Danish Americans and nearly 149,000 foreign-born Finnish Americans.

Modern Immigration

Scandinavians continued to come to America in substantial numbers through the 1920s. Immigration quotas somewhat restricted the flow of Scandinavian immigrants from the early 1920s (Note: For more on overall immigration, including year-by-year figures for selected countries, see "Annual Immigration Statistics" on p. 657; "General Notes on Immigration Statistics" on p. 684; and "General European Immigration Resources" on p. 317. See also chapters on specific countries that were major sources of immigrants), though the number of immigrants from Sweden and Iceland remained below the quota. Some Finns, Norwegians, and Danes who could not enter went instead to other countries, especially Canada. Even so, because the quotas were designed to favor "desirable" immigrants from northern and western Europe, nearly 200,000 more Scandinavians arrived between 1921 and 1930.

With the Crash of 1929 and the onset of the Depression, Scandinavian immigration plummeted, to just over 11,000 for 1931–1940. It remained low during World War II, and although it increased after the war was over, it never returned to pre-1929 levels. The peak year for Scandinavian immigration after 1929 was 1949, which saw a total of 6,665 immigrants to the United States. From the 1970s on, immigration from Scandinavia settled at an even lower level.

Many Scandinavian immigrants in the early 20th century settled in the cities, and many descendants of earlier Scandinavian immigrants also migrated to the cities. Swedes congregated in the upper Midwest, in cities such as Chicago, Minneapolis and St. Paul, Madison, and Duluth. In the 1920s, Chicago had the third largest Swedish population of all the cities in the world.

Many Swedes also settled in the East, most notably in New York, Boston, Worcester, Hartford, and Providence.

Many Norwegians settled in the eastern states as well, most notably in New York, which had more than 30,000 Norwegian immigrants in the mid-20th century. Norwegians settled around the country, too, in cities such as Chicago, Minneapolis, and Seattle, and in many smaller cities and towns.

Many Danes continued to settle in Utah. Even in the decade after World War II, some 900 Danish immigrants migrated there. Iowa also continued to attract large numbers of Danes. However, other Danish immigrants settled widely around the country, especially in industrial cities. The largest concentration of Danish immigrants was in Chicago, which in the 1930s had more Danes than any city outside Denmark.

Finnish immigrants also settled widely around the country, but especially favored the north. Many worked as miners and loggers in states such as Michigan, Minnesota, Montana, Wisconsin, California, Oregon, and Washington. Others settled and worked near the fishing and canning industries of the Pacific Northwest, as well as the mills and factories of the East.

Icelandic immigrants settled primarily in northern areas, especially in North Dakota. Though early immigrants frequently settled on farms, their descendants more often moved into the cities, as many later immigrants did.

Overall, from 1820, the year that the U.S. government began tracking immigration, more than 2.5 million immigrants arrived from Scandinavia (not counting many Finns, recorded under Russia). These formed 4 percent of the total immigration between 1820 and 1996.

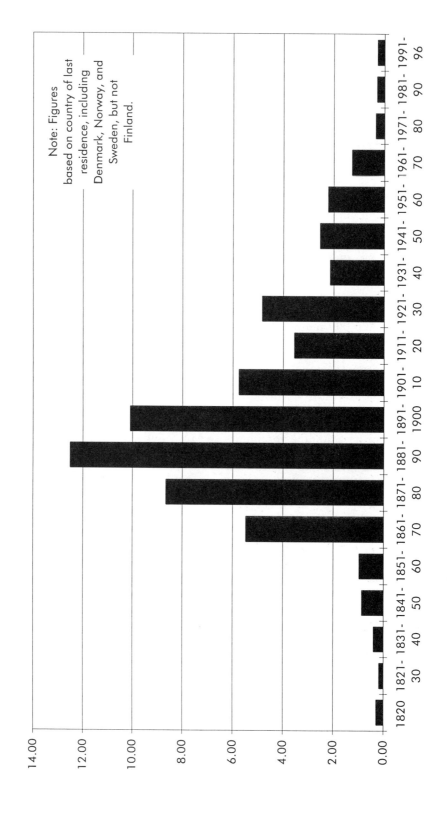

Graph 2.31: Percentage of Immigrants from Scandinavia in Total U.S. Immigration by Decade, 1820–1996

Note: Figures based on country of last residence, including Denmark, Norway, and Sweden, but not Finland.

Table 2.17: Number and Percentage of Foreign-Born Immigrants from Scandinavia by Decade in Total U.S. Population at End of Decade, 1850–1990

Decade	Total U.S. Population	Number of Foreign-Born Immigrants from Scandinavia	Foreign-Born Immigrants from Scandinavia in Total U.S. Population	Number of Foreign-Born Immigrants from Denmark and Iceland	Number of Foreign-Born Immigrants from Denmark	Number of Foreign-Born Immigrants from Iceland	Number of Foreign-Born Immigrants from Finland	Number of Foreign-Born Immigrants from Norway	Number of Foreign-Born Immigrants from Sweden
1850	23,191,876	18,075	0.08	1,838	—	—	—	12,678	3,559
1860	31,443,321	72,582	0.23	9,962	—	—	—	43,995	18,625
1870	39,818,449	241,685	0.61	30,107	—	—	—	114,246	97,332
1880	50,155,783	440,262	0.88	64,196	—	—	—	181,729	194,337
1890	62,947,714	933,249	1.48	132,543	—	—	—	322,665	478,041
1900	75,994,575	1,134,733	1.49	153,690	—	—	62,641	336,388	582,014
1910	91,972,266	1,380,413	1.50	181,649	—	—	129,680	403,877	665,207
1920	105,710,620	1,328,426	1.26	189,154	—	—	149,824	363,863	625,585
1930	122,775,046	1,267,818	1.03	.	179,474	2,764	142,478	347,852	595,250
1940	131,669,275	(NA)	—	.	(NA)	(NA)	(NA)	(NA)	(NA)
1950	150,697,361	731,234	0.49	.	107,982	(NA)	95,686	202,448	325,118
1960	179,323,175	522,653	0.29	.	85,060	2,780	67,624	152,698	214,491
1970	203,235,298	334,117	0.16	.	61,410	2,895	45,499	97,243	127,070
1980	227,726,000	212,377	0.09	.	42,732	(NA)	29,172	63,316	77,157
1990	249,907,000	153,228	0.06	.	34,999	(NA)	22,313	42,240	53,676

NA = Not available

Note: Includes figures for immigrants born in Denmark, Norway, Sweden, Iceland, and (from 1900) Finland.

Source: Adapted from Series C 228–295, Foreign-Born Population, by Country of Birth: 1850–1970, in *Historical Statistics of the United States, Colonial Times to 1970, Bicentennial Edition*, and other updating tables from the U.S. Census Bureau.

Resources

Internet Resources

Cyndi's List—Scandinavia & the Nordic Countries Index (*http://www.cyndislist.com/scan.htm*) List of on-line genealogical resources for the region, maintained by genealogical author Cyndi Howells.

CenEuroGenWeb (*http://www.rootsweb.com/~ceneurgw*) Part of the WorldGenWeb project, linking genealogical research sites around the world, by region, with resources by individual Scandinavian and Baltic countries, including Denmark, Finland, and Iceland.

American-Scandinavian Foundation (*http://www.amscan.org*) Web site of organization seeking to promote cultural exchange and understanding between the United States and Denmark, Finland, Iceland, Norway, and Sweden. (Address: 15 East 65th Street, New York, NY 10021; Phone: 212-879-9779; Fax: 212-249-3444; E-mail: asf@amscan.org)

Genealogy Research Denmark (*http://www.ida.net/users/really*) Privately maintained Web site focusing on Danish genealogy; contains some emigration records and notes on doing Danish genealogical research, plus links to related Web sites.

Genealogy Resource Index for Denmark (GRID) (*http://www.genealogyindex.dk*) Web site offering links to genealogical resources on the Internet, including databases, indexes, periodicals, and personal home pages, as well as discussion groups, software, transcribed sources, and links to research help.

Finnish-American Resource Site (*http://members.home.net/finnsite*) Privately maintained site offering materials on Finnish history, genealogy, and language; excerpts from the Finnish-American Reporter, an English-language newspaper; information on Finnish foreign exchange experiences; and links to other resources about Finland, with materials on Finnish emigration history scheduled to be added.

Genealogia (*http://www.genealogia.org/indexe.htm*) Web site offering links to sites offering information on Finnish genealogical research, including genealogical societies; records of births, marriages, and deaths; information on emigration; tips on Finnish genealogical research; and links to professional researchers.

Institute of Migration (*http://www.utu.fi/erill/instmigr*) Web site in Finnish, Swedish, and English offering information on Finnish emigration, including statistics, articles, research tips, an emigrant register, and related Web links.

Norwegian Historical Data Centre (NHDC) (*http://draug.rhd.isv.uit.no/rhd/indexeng.htm*) Government-sponsored, university-run Web site offering searchable censuses, tips on research, information on parish registers, and related links. (Address: The Faculty of Social Sciences, University of Tromsø, N-9037 Tromsø, Norway; Phone: +47 77 64 41 77)

Norwegian Emigration and Genealogy Center (*http://www.utvandrersenteret.no/index.htm*) Official Web site offers on-line forms for requesting information on Norwegian emigration studies and travel to Scandinavia. (Address: Strandkaien 31, N-4005 Stavanger, Norway; Phone: +47 5153 8860; Fax: +47 5153 8863; E-mail: detnu@online.no)

Ancestors from Norway (*http://members.xoom.com/follesdal*) Privately maintained Web site focusing on Norwegian genealogy and immigration history; includes articles on tracing Norwegian ancestry, genealogical resources, and related Web links, as well as a chat room and bookstore.

Swedish Council of America (*http://www.swedishcouncil.org*) Web site of a network of Swedish organizations in America; provides links to regional groups and publications on Swedish Americans.

American Swedish Institute (*http://www.americanswedishinst.org*) Web site of a museum on Swedish culture; includes information about its archives and library, and links to related Web sites. (Address: 2600 Park Avenue, Minneapolis, MN 55407; Phone: 612-871-4907)

Suomen Sukututkimusseura (Genealogical Society of Finland) (*http://www.genealogia.fi/index.htm*) Web site for Finnish genealogy, in Finnish and English; provides information on immigrants plus tips, resources, and links related to family history research.

Emigration from Iceland to North America (*http://nyherji.is/~halfdan/westward/vestur.htm*) Web site offers information about Icelandic settlers, names, and ancestry, with poems, photos, and links to other sites.

Icelandic GenWeb (Íslenski Ættfræ›ivefurinn) (*http://nyherji.is/~halfdan/aett/aettvef.htm*) Genealogical Web site in Icelandic, with English version planned.

Sons of Norway (*http://www.SofN.com*) Web site of the organization for men and women, including links. (Address: 1455 West Lake Street, Minneapolis, MN 55408; Phone: 800-945-8851 or 612-827-3611)

Viking Connection (*http://members.aol.com/ivolut/welcome.html*) Web site focusing on Scandinavian and Estonian "society, culture, and heritage," with links by region.

Print Resources

General Works

Andersen, Arlow W. *The Norwegian-Americans*. Boston: Twayne, 1974.

Anderson, Wilford Raymond. *Norse America, Tenth Century Onward*. Evanston, Ill: Valhalla Press, 1996.

Arnason, David, and Vincent Arnason, eds. *The New Icelanders: A North American Community*. Winnipeg, Manitoba, Canada: Turnstone Press, 1994.

Benson, Adolph B., and Naboth Hedin. *Americans from Sweden*. Philadelphia: Lippincott, 1950.

Carlsson, Sten. *Swedes in North America, 1638–1988: Technical, Cultural, and Political Achievements*. Stockholm, Sweden: Streiffert, 1988.

Finland: A Country Study. 2d ed. Eric Solsten and Sandra W. Meditz, eds. Washington, D.C.: Federal Research Division, Library of Congress, 1990. (Available on-line at *http://lcweb2.loc.gov/frd/cs*)

Fiske, Arland O. *The Scandinavian World*. Minot, N. Dak.: North American Heritage Press, 1988.

Franck, Irene M. *The Scandinavian-American Heritage*. New York: Facts on File, 1988.

Hale, Frederick, ed. *Danes in North America*. Seattle: University of Washington Press, 1984.

Hoglund, A. William. *Finnish Immigrants in America, 1880–1920*. New York: Arno Press, 1979. Originally published Madison: University of Wisconsin Press, 1960.

Holland, Ruth Robins. *Vikings of the West: The Scandinavian Immigrants in America*. New York, Grosset & Dunlap, 1968.

Kastrup, Allan. *The Swedish Heritage in America: The Swedish Element in America and American-Swedish Relations in Their Historical Perspective*. Minneapolis: Swedish Council of America, 1975.

Kero, Reino. *The Finns in North America: Destinations and Composition of Immigrant Societies in North America Before World War I*. Turku, Finland: Turun Yliopisto, 1980.

Larsen, Birgit Flemming, and Henning Bender, eds. *Danish Emigration to the U.S.A.* Aalborg, Denmark: Danes Worldwide Archives and Danish Society for Emigration History, 1992.

Lovoll, Odd S. *The Promise of America: A History of the Norwegian-American People.* Minneapolis: University of Minnesota Press and the Norwegian-American Historical Association, 1984.

———. *Nordics in America: The Future of Their Past.* Northfield, Minn.: Norwegian American Historical Association, 1993.

———. *The Promise Fulfilled: A Portrait of Norwegian Americans Today.* Minneapolis: University of Minnesota Press, 1998.

Malmberg, Carl. *America Is Also Scandinavian.* New York: Putnam, 1970.

Moberg, Vilhelm. *The Unknown Swedes: A Book About Swedes and America, Past and Present.* Carbondale: Southern Illinois University Press, 1988.

Nielsen, George R. *The Danish Americans.* Boston: Twayne, 1981.

Norman, Hans, and Harald Runblom. *Transatlantic Connections: Nordic Migration to the New World After 1800.* Oslo: Norwegian University Press. Distributed outside Scandinavia by Oxford University Press, 1988.

Paananen, Eloise. *Finns in North America.* Annapolis, Md.: Leeward Publications, 1975.

Qualey, Carlton. *Norwegian Settlement in the United States.* New York: Arno Press, 1970. Originally published 1938.

Semmingsen, Ingrid. *Norway to America: A History of the Migration.* Minneapolis: University of Minnesota Press, 1978.

For Young People

Cornelius, James M. *The Norwegian Americans.* New York: Chelsea House, 1989.

Engle (Paananen), Eloise. *The Finns in America.* Minneapolis: Lerner, 1977.

Hillbrand, Percie V. *The Norwegians in America.* Minneapolis: Lerner, 1991.

McGill, Allyson. *The Swedish Americans.* New York: Chelsea House, 1988.

Mussari, Mark. *The Danish Americans.* New York: Chelsea House, 1988.

Petersen, Peter L. *The Danes in America.* Minneapolis: Lerner, 1987.

Genealogical Works

Carlberg, Nancy Ellen. *Beginning Swedish Research.* Anaheim, Calif.: Carlberg Press, 1989.

———. *Beginning Norwegian Research.* Anaheim, Calif.: Carlberg Press, 1991.

Carlberg, Nancy Ellen, and Norma S. Keating. *Beginning Danish Research.* Anaheim, Calif.: Carlberg Press, 1992.

Colling, Joyce. *Swedish Family Research.* Burbank, CA: Southern California Genealogical Society, 1989.

Hjelm, Dennis J. *Especially for Swedes.* Basalt, Idaho: D. J. Hjelm, 1985.

Jonasson, Eric. *Tracing Your Icelandic Family Tree.* Winnipeg, Manitoba, Canada: Wheatfield Press, 1975.

Olsson, Nils William. *Tracing Your Swedish Ancestry.* Rev. ed. Stockholm: Ministry for Foreign Affairs, 1985.

Paddock, Lisa Olson, and Carl Sokolnicki Rollyson. *A Student's Guide to Scandinavian American Genealogy.* Phoenix: Oryx, 1996.

Reed, Robert D. *How and Where to Research Your Ethnic-American Cultural Heritage.* Saratoga, Calif.: R. D. Reed, 1979.

Ross, Carl, and Velma M. Doby. *Handbook for Doing Finnish American Family History.* 2d ed. Minneapolis: Minnesota Finnish American Family History Project, 1980.

Searching for Your Danish Ancestors: A Guide to Danish Genealogical Research in the United States and Denmark. St. Paul: Danish Genealogy Group of the Minnesota Genealogical Society, 1989.

Swedish Genealogical Resources. St. Paul: Swedish Genealogy Group, Minnesota Historical Society, 1987.

Thomsen, Finn A. *Scandinavian Genealogical Research Manual.* 3 vols. Bountiful, Utah: Thomsen's Genealogical Center, 1980.

Vincent, Timothy Laitila, and Rick Tapio. *Finnish Genealogical Research.* New Brighton, Minn.: Finnish Americana, 1994.

Wellauer, Maralyn A. *Tracing Your Norwegian Roots*. Milwaukee: Wellauer, 1979.

For more resources, see "General European Immigration Resources" on p. 317.

Immigrants from Belgium

Between 1830, when Belgium declared its independence from the Netherlands, and 1996, a little more than 215,000 immigrants entered the United States from Belgium. Their numbers were small until the 1880s, grew into the modest 2,000-per-year range during the next two decades, and then swelled into the 4,000-per-year range from 1900 until the outbreak of World War I, in 1914. Belgian immigration increases somewhat after World War I, diminished to a few hundred a year during the Great Depression, and again rebounded after World War II, into the 3,000-per-year range. It sharply declined in the 1960s and remained small through the mid-1990s, with only 17,000 Belgian immigrants reaching the United States between 1971 and 1996.

Belgium is a small, heavily industrialized country which began its industrialization early in the 19th century. It is also a country that has long been split between its Flemish Dutch speakers, living in Flanders, in the north and west of the country, and its French speakers, since the mid-1840s called Walloons, living largely in the south and east of the country. In Brussels, the Belgian capital, both languages are spoken. The two groups are distinct in more than language, for the economies of the two regions have also developed somewhat differently, a matter that has had much bearing on Belgian immigration to the United States.

The earliest substantial Belgian immigration began in the mid-1840s and consisted largely of Dutch-speaking Flemish farmers who had been hit hard by the same potato blight that brought the Great Famine and its accompanying set of plagues to Ireland, and that also impelled hundreds of thousands of German and other mainland European farmers to immigrate to the United States.

Approximately 10,000 of those forced off the land in Belgium immigrated to the United States. That was only a very small proportion of those who left Belgian farms and villages in those years. The great majority of dispossessed Flemish farmers emigrated to the Netherlands and other countries in the region, often settling in urban areas; many of those who remained in Belgium also joined the growing move from countryside to city, the pattern everywhere as the Industrial Revolution took hold. Dispossessed French-speaking Walloon farmers were able to migrate internally within Belgium even more easily, for coal mining, metalworking, and other heavy industries came to their area faster than to the Flemish north and west. As a result, fewer Walloon Belgians immigrated to the United States.

Beyond the potato blight, the forces that spurred migration continued throughout the 19th century in Belgium and throughout much of western Europe, as the Industrial Revolution and the simultaneous flights to the cities and to America accelerated. In Belgium, an additional factor was that the Flemish population of Flanders increased far more rapidly than the Walloon population. In 1860, the population of Flanders was only slightly larger than that of Walloonia, but by the end of the century the gap had widened consider-

Table 2.18: Number and Percentage of Immigrants from Belgium in Total U.S. Immigrants by Decade, 1820–1996

Decade	Number of Immigrants from Belgium	Total U.S. Immigrants	Percentage of Foreign-Born Immigrants from Belgium in Total U.S. Immigration
1820	1	8,385	0.01
1821-1830	27	143,439	0.02
1831-1840	22	599,125	0.00
1841-1850	5,074	1,713,251	0.30
1851-1860	4,738	2,598,214	0.18
1861-1870	6,734	2,314,824	0.29
1871-1880	7,221	2,812,191	0.26
1881-1890	20,177	5,246,613	0.38
1891-1900	18,167	3,687,564	0.49
1901-1910	41,635	8,795,386	0.47
1911-1920	33,746	5,735,811	0.59
1921-1930	15,846	4,107,209	0.39
1931-1940	4,817	528,431	0.91
1941-1950	12,189	1,035,039	1.18
1951-1960	18,575	2,515,479	0.74
1961-1970	9,192	3,321,677	0.28
1971-1980	5,329	4,493,314	0.12
1981-1990	7,066	7,338,062	0.10
1991-1996	4,551	6,146,213	0.07
Total 1820-1996	215,107	63,140,227	0.34

Source: Adapted from Table 2, Immigration by Region and Selected Country of Last Residence, Fiscal Years 1820–1996, from the *Statistical Yearbook of the Immigration and Naturalization Service*, 1996.

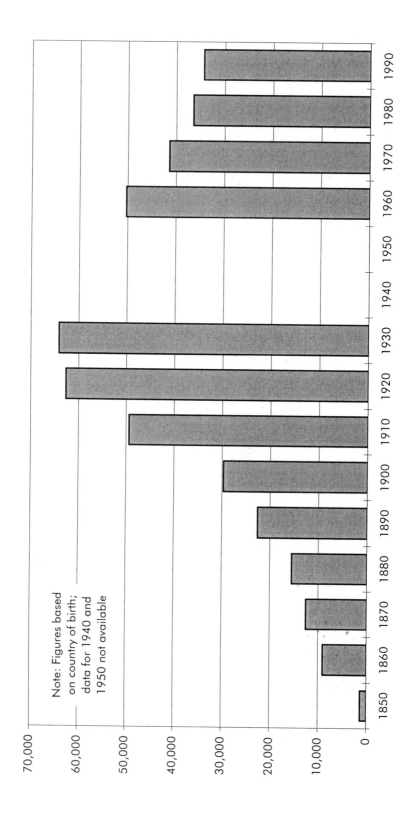

Graph 2.32: Number of Foreign-Born Immigrants from Belgium in Total U.S. Population by Decade, 1850–1990

Note: Figures based on country of birth; data for 1940 and 1950 not available

ably. By 1970, there were almost twice as many Flemish Belgians as Walloon Belgians.

The peak years of the Belgian immigration, in the early 20th century, coincided with the peak years of the total immigration to the United States from Europe, although by then total immigration was largely from eastern and southeastern Europe. Belgian immigration was a more matter of "pull" to the United States than of "push" out of Belgium, for in that period the development of the United States as an industrial nation and world power was an immense magnet for immigrants from many countries. By the early 1900s, Belgium's own industries and cities had absorbed most of its rural migrants, and its population had largely stabilized. Most of the relatively large numbers of Belgians who immigrated to the United States in that period were skilled workers and businesspeople, seeking economic opportunities in the prosperous United States.

Between the mid-1840s and the mid-1920s, most Belgian immigrants into the United States settled in the northern Midwest, with heavy early concentrations in upper Michigan, which spread out into neighboring states as the frontier pushed west. Other Belgians, especially many French-speaking Walloons, initially settled in French Canada and then later joined the French-Canadian immigration into New England and the northern Midwest. Some of these found their way into New England's growing textile industry, where as a practical matter they tended to become part of the large French-Canadian component of that industry's workforce. That was especially so for Flemish Belgians who had worked in Belgium's developing textile industry, which had been centered in Flanders, rather than in Walloonia, where heavy industry predominated. After each of the 20th century's world wars, a substantial part of the postwar Belgian immigration was composed of the country's most highly educated and skilled people, seeking new lives in the United States.

Table 2.19: Number and Percentage of Foreign-Born Immigrants from Belgium by Decade in Total U.S. Population at End of Decade, 1850–1990

Decade	Number of Foreign-Born Immigrants from Belgium	Total U.S. Population	Percentage of Foreign-Born Immigrants from Belgium in Total U.S. Population
1850	1,313	23,191,876	0.01
1860	9,072	31,443,321	0.03
1870	12,553	39,818,449	0.03
1880	15,535	50,155,783	0.03
1890	22,639	62,947,714	0.04
1900	29,757	75,994,575	0.04
1910	49,400	91,972,266	0.05
1920	62,687	105,710,620	0.06
1930	64,194	122,775,046	0.05
1940	(NA)	131,669,275	(NA)
1950	(NA)	150,697,361	(NA)
1960	50,294	179,323,175	0.03
1970	41,412	203,235,298	0.02
1980	36,487	227,726,000	0.02
1990	34,366	249,907,000	0.01

NA = Not available

Source: Adapted from Series C 228–295, Foreign-Born Population, by Country of Birth: 1850–1970, in *Historical Statistics of the United States, Colonial Times to 1970, Bicentennial Edition*, and other updating tables from the U.S. Census Bureau.

Until 1830, Belgium was part of the Netherlands; this 1650 view of New Amsterdam (now New York) is from a book called Novum Belgii (1651–55).

Resources

Internet Resources

Genealogy in Belgium (*http://
users.skynet.be/sky60754/
familiekunde/*) Searchable Web site
offering information about doing
genealogical research in Belgium;
focuses on the Dutch-speaking section,
with links (in French) to the French-
speaking part; provides information on
Belgian history, links to genealogical
societies and archives, searchable
databases, genealogical software, and
links to international sites.

Genealogy Benelux Web Ring (*http://
www.dijkgraaf.org/benelux.htm*) Site
linking sites related to genealogy in
Belgium, the Netherlands, and
Luxembourg, in Dutch, French, and
English.

Cyndi's List—Belgium / Belgique / België
(*http://www.cyndislist.com/
belgium.htm*) List of on-line
genealogical resources for the region,
maintained by genealogical author
Cyndi Howells.

Print Resources

Belgians in the United States. Brussels:
Ministry of Foreign Affairs, External
Trade, and Cooperation in
Development, 1976.

The Belgian Texans. San Antonio:
University of Texas at San Antonio,
Institute of Texan Cultures, 1975.

Belgium: A Country Study. 2d ed. Stephen
B. Wickman, ed. Washington, D.C.:
Federal Research Division, Library of
Congress, 1985.

Verslype, Henry A. *The Belgians of
Indiana, with a Brief History of the
Land from Which They Came.*
Mishawaka, Ind.: H. A. Verslype, 1987.

For more resources, see "General European Immigration Resources" on p. 317.

Immigrants from Switzerland

Switzerland is a small, mountainous, land-locked country, with very little in the way of natural resources or the kind of arable land that lends itself to efficient large-scale farming. It has no coal, nor does it have any of the other resources that would allow it to build heavy industry. It is necessarily a trading country, yet surrounded by larger nations, and entirely vulnerable to tariff barriers erected by other European countries, as well as to highly competitive lower-priced farm products from abroad. In self-defense, the Swiss in the 19th century did harness their fast-flowing streams to produce hydroelectric power and built an efficient railway system, as well as developing a substantial textile industry, especially in embroidery. Late in the century, the Swiss developed a highly respected machine tool industry, and moved from by-then uncompetitive grain production to effective dairy farming, producing cheese for export as a substantial cash farm product.

Yet the net effect of the country's total 19th-century economic situation, coupled with a substantial natural population increase, was that by the 1850s Switzerland was also exporting large numbers of its people to neighboring countries and to the Americas, primarily to the United States. Many Swiss farmers were of necessity leaving their farms and villages to seek jobs in the growing Swiss cities. However, Switzerland was not developing the kinds of basic industries that could absorb the combination of flight from the land and population increase; nor did it do so during the rest of the 19th century.

In Switzerland, as throughout western and central Europe, "America fever" was very much in the air. Those already in the United States were sending "America letters" home, extolling the virtues and limitless promise of their huge, rich new land. Immigrant chains were forming, and millions of Europeans were immigrating to the United States.

Starting in the 1850s, peaking in the 1880s, and continuing through the 1920s, the Swiss—and especially the roughly 75 percent who were German speakers—joined the mass European immigration to

the United States. From 1850 to 1930, more than 277,000 Swiss immigrants entered the United States.

Long before the 1850s, small numbers of Swiss had immigrated to the United States. The first substantial numbers were the more than 10,000 Swiss Mennonites, most of them farmers, who began settling in Pennsylvania early in the 18th century. From there, many moved south into the Shenandoah Valley, after the American Revolution becoming part of the huge westward migration beyond the Appalachians into what became the Midwest.

By the middle of the 18th century, these and other Swiss religious dissenters were joined by an estimated 20,000 more Swiss, most of them also farmers. They, too, tended to move south and west in the United States.

From 1820 to 1850, Swiss immigration into the United States was small, in all totaling only a little more than 11,000. After that, considerable Swiss immigration developed, as immigrant chains and "America fever" grew, along with the flight from the land and population increases. From 1851 to 1880, the number of Swiss immigrants to the United States averaged more than 12,500 per year.

During the 1880s, with American industrialization and the settling of the West in full swing, Swiss immigration totaled almost 82,000, an average of 8,200 people per year. Among them were Italian-speaking Swiss immigrants who settled in California, some of them farmers who played a major role in building California's winemaking industry. Many skilled Swiss artisans settled in the cities. In addition, some Swiss immigrants who were originally farmers in the United States joined the move to the new industrial cities that swiftly grew after the Civil War.

Swiss immigration slowed to a trickle in the 1930s. It never again rose to pre-1930s levels, for Switzerland became a very prosperous country, which itself imported large numbers of low-paid "guest workers" after World War II. From 1931 to 1996, Swiss immigration into the United States totaled only 76,000, fewer than 1,200 per year .

Table 2.20: Number and Percentage of Immigrants from Switzerland in Total U.S. Immigration by Decade, 1820–1996

Decade	Number of Immigrants from Switzerland	Total U.S. Immigrants	Percentage of Immigrants from Switzerland in Total U.S. Immigration
1820	31	8,385	0.00
1821-1830	3,226	143,439	2.25
1831-1840	4,821	599,125	0.80
1841-1850	4,644	1,713,251	0.27
1851-1860	25,011	2,598,214	0.96
1861-1870	23,286	2,314,824	1.01
1871-1880	28,293	2,812,191	1.01
1881-1890	81,988	5,246,613	1.56
1891-1900	31,179	3,687,564	0.85
1901-1910	34,922	8,795,386	0.40
1911-1920	23,091	5,735,811	0.40
1921-1930	29,676	4,107,209	0.72
1931-1940	5,512	528,431	1.04
1941-1950	10,547	1,035,039	1.02
1951-1960	17,675	2,515,479	0.70
1961-1970	18,453	3,321,677	0.56
1971-1980	8,235	4,493,314	0.18
1981-1990	8,849	7,338,062	0.12
1991-1996	7,215	6,146,213	0.12
Total 1820-1996	366,654	63,140,227	0.58

Source: Adapted from Table 2, Immigration by Region and Selected Country of Last Residence, Fiscal Years 1820–1996, from the *Statistical Yearbook of the Immigration and Naturalization Service*, 1996.

Graph 2.33: Number of Immigrants from Switzerland by Decade, 1820–1996

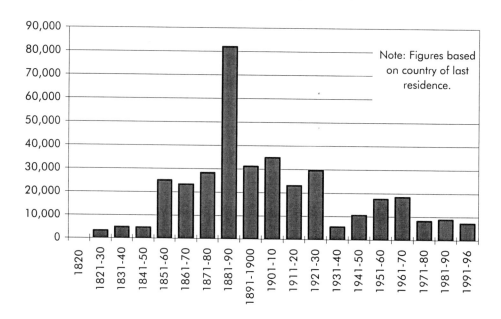

Note: Figures based on country of last residence.

Graph 2.34: Number of Foreign-Born Immigrants from Switzerland in Total U.S. Population by Decade, 1850–1990

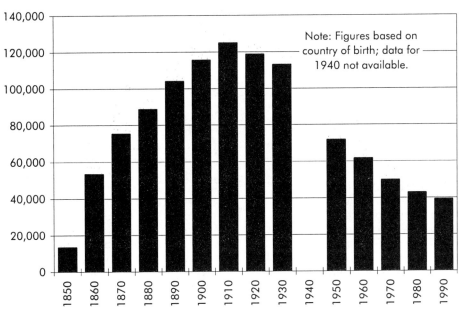

Note: Figures based on country of birth; data for 1940 not available.

Table 2.21: Number and Percentage of Immigrants from Switzerland in Total U.S. Immigration by Decade, 1820–1996

Decade	Number of Foreign-Born Immigrants from Switzerland	Total U.S. Population	Percentage of Foreign-Born Immigrants from Switzerland in Total U.S. Population
1850	13,358	23,191,876	0.06
1860	53,327	31,443,321	0.17
1870	75,153	39,818,449	0.19
1880	88,621	50,155,783	0.18
1890	104,069	62,947,714	0.17
1900	115,593	75,994,575	0.15
1910	124,848	91,972,266	0.14
1920	118,659	105,710,620	0.11
1930	113,010	122,775,046	0.09
1940	(NA)	131,669,275	(NA)
1950	71,636	150,697,361	0.05
1960	61,568	179,323,175	0.03
1970	49,732	203,235,298	0.02
1980	42,804	227,726,000	0.02
1990	39,130	249,907,000	0.02

NA = Not available

Source: Adapted from Series C 228–295, Foreign-Born Population, by Country of Birth: 1850–1970, in *Historical Statistics of the United States, Colonial Times to 1970, Bicentennial Edition*, and other tables from the U.S. Census Bureau.

Resources

Internet Resources

Swiss-American Genealogy (*http://
www.usaswiss.org/swissweb/
genealog.html*) Web site of the National
Center for Swiss-American Studies,
offering bibliographies, indexes to
Swiss archives and libraries, and links
to useful genealogical sites. (Address:
P.O. Box 2642, Fairfax, VA 22031;
Phone: 800-475-7947 or 206-748-1434;
E-mail: swissweb@usaswiss.org)

SwitzerlandGenWeb (*http://
www.rootsweb.com/~chewgw/*) Part of
the WorldGenWeb project, linking
genealogical research sites around the
world, by region, providing information
by provinces or cities; includes
chronology, surname dictionary, and
links to related sites.

Swiss Genealogy on the Internet (*http://
www.eye.ch/swissgen*) Web site
associated with the Swiss Genealogical
Society, in English, German, French,
and Italian, offering Swiss genealogical
links, including information on
individual cantons and related
organizations.

Cyndi's List—Switzerland / Suisse /
Schweiz (*http://www.cyndislist.com/
swiss.htm*) List of on-line genealogical
resources for Switzerland, maintained
by genealogical author Cyndi Howells.

Genealogy in French-Speaking
Switzerland (*http://www.unige.ch/
biblio/ses/jla/gen/swiss-e.html*) Web
site offering information,
bibliographies, and other resources, in
English and French, plus links to
related sites, including those for
elsewhere in Switzerland and other
French-speaking sites.

Graubünden Genealogy (*http://
www.mindspring.com/~philipp/
che.html*) Web site focusing on German-
speaking portions of Switzerland;
provides bibliographies and links to
useful related sites.

Print Resources

Bly, Daniel W. *From the Rhine to the
Shenandoah: Eighteenth Century Swiss
and German Pioneer Families in the
Central Shenandoah Valley of Virginia
and Their European Origins.* 2 vols.
Baltimore: Gateway Press, 1993–1996.

Haller, Charles R. *Across the Atlantic and
Beyond: The Migration of German and
Swiss Immigrants to America.* Bowie,
Md.: Heritage Books, 1993.

For more resources, see "General European Immigration Resources" on p. 317.

Immigrants from Austria

For centuries, Austria was at the heart of a major European empire, with Vienna as its capital. *Austrian* was not an ethnic designation, but rather a label applied to the many and varied inhabitants of the Austrian Empire. (The name originally referred to an eastern portion of the empire: Österreich, or Eastern Realm, anglicized to Austria.) That remained true in modern times, when immigrants tallied as "Austrian" in U.S. immigration records could be from any number of ethnic groups, including Germans, Czechs, Slovaks, Hungarians, Poles, Jews, Ukrainians, and many others who lived within Austria's borders.

Immigration figures for Austria are more than usually unreliable because of its extremely complicated modern political history, including sharply changing borders, and because information was gathered and kept inconsistently. Immigrants recorded as Austrian included not only people born within the empire but also some who had been born in other countries and had come to Austria as a place of temporary refuge. That would remain true through the end of the 20th century.

Austrian Background

The Austrian-based empire was known as the Holy Roman Empire in the Middle Ages, but was later called the Hapsburg Empire, after the imperial throne began to pass by heredity to the Hapsburg line of rulers. This multinational empire spread so widely across Europe that in 1556 it was divided between two Hapsburg lines, the Spanish and the Austrian. Still multinational, the Austrian Hapsburg Empire stretched from the North Sea to northern Italy. As the Ottoman Turks weakened and were pushed south in the 17th century, the Hapsburgs expanded into the Balkans. Late in the 18th century, they also expanded to the northeast, gaining the Polish region of Galicia when they joined with the Prussians and Russians in the partition of Poland.

Wars and political changes in Europe began to weaken the empire, however. Austria led in the defeat of France in the Napoleonic Wars, ending in 1815, but later lost power and influence. The widespread revolutionary movements of 1848 were defeated, though they spurred some reforms in Austria, which that year had its first parliament. Hungary declared its independence from the empire in the same period; though Austria reasserted its control, it was forced to create a dual monarchy in 1867, which became known as Austria-Hungary or the Austro-Hungarian Empire. In the same period, Austria fought and lost a brief war against many small German states that had traditionally been part of the Austrian empire. Led by Prussia, they formed their own German empire in 1871.

At that time, Austria-Hungary was still far larger than it is now, including territories such as northern Italy, Czechoslovakia, Romania, and the northern Balkans, most notably Croatia, Slovenia, and Bosnia and Herzegovina (see separate articles on these regions, including "Immigrants from the Yugoslav (South Slav) States" on p. 259). Austria-Hungary also sought more territories in the Balkans, which it was seeking to divide with Russia as Turkish power diminished. Struggles over the Balkans would help lead Europe into World War I, after the 1914 assassination of Franz Ferdinand, heir to the Hapsburg throne, in Sarajevo by Bosnian-supported nationalists. The defeat of the Central Powers in World War I spelled the end of the Hapsburg Empire.

A new and much smaller Austrian Republic emerged after that war, with Poland, Czechslovakia, and Romania becoming independent, and farther-flung territories also being stripped away. The republic had a short life, however, for the Austrian branch of the Nazi Party— inspired by Hitler's German Nazis— showed real strength by the early 1930s. In 1938, Austria was annexed by Nazi Germany and ceased to exist.

A second Austrian Republic was formed after the end of World War II. In the postwar world, Austria became a neutral coun-

nd Ich habe noch andere Schaaffe die find nicht
us diesem Stall und dißelben mus Ich herführen
sie werden meine Stimme hören, u. wird ein Heerde
u. ein Hirt werden.

Die Unterweisung der Eltern an ihre
Kinder Zu der Evangl. Religion

Die Verbrennug der Evangl. Bücher.

Die um der Evangl. Religion bekennent ge
fangene Saltzburger.

Authors' Archives

*Salzburg Lutherans like these worshipping at home (top right), shown in a 1732 German
book, were some of the many Protestants to leave Austria because of persecution.*

try, often acting as a place of refuge, as a pathway for people fleeing Soviet bloc countries, and as a bridge between eastern and western Europe.

Early Immigrants

We do not know when the first Austrian immigrants arrived in North America. Some came during the colonial period, generally as individuals or small parties with larger groups from other countries.

The first notable group of Austrians were Protestants from Salzburg. In the early days of the Reformation, from the 1520s, many people from the Austrian Empire became Protestants. As Catholics later mounted a Counter-Reformation, religious battles raged throughout the empire, including the Europe-wide Thirty Years War (1618–1648). That ended with the Peace of Westphalia, which allowed rulers to decide which would be the official religion in their state or principality. For most Hapsburg territories, this meant Catholicism. Over the next century, tens of thousands of Protestants fled into exile. Many found refuge in other Protestant states, most notably in Germany, Scandinavia, and England. One party of Protestants from Salzburg, Austria—some 50 families—migrated to the new colony of Georgia in 1734, settling near Savannah.

Other immigrants arrived in America from the Austrian Empire in the late 18th and early 19th centuries, but their numbers were small. They often went to large cities, especially those with substantial German-speaking populations, such as New York and St. Louis. Among them were some 100 to 200 Catholic priests sent by the Leopoldine Society of Vienna after its 1829 founding. They served as anchors for German Catholic immigrant communities in the East and Midwest, in this period running German-language parochial schools. A number of Austrians were also among the "48ers," the political refugees who fled Europe after the failed revolutions of 1848.

By 1850, when the U.S. Census Bureau began to track such information, fewer than 1,000 foreign-born immigrants from Austria were recorded as living in the United States. The government did not begin to keep separate data on immigrants from Austria until 1861; even after that the figures were distorted because they included large numbers of immigrants from Austrian-held parts of Poland. Beyond that, information was recorded inconsistently. Total figures are given for Austria-Hungary as a whole, but figures for Austria and Hungary were not kept separately in all years.

The Main Wave

The late 19th century saw the main wave of immigration into the United States from Austria. Between 1861 and 1870, some 7,800 immigrants from the Austro-Hungarian Empire entered the country, more than 90 percent of them from Austria itself. The number of immigrants from Austria then jumped dramatically, with more than 226,000 for 1871–1880 and a similar number for 1881–1890.

By 1891–1900, the number of immigrants from the Austro-Hungarian Empire overall was more than 592,000, which was approximately 16 percent of the total immigration for the decade. The peak decade was 1901–1910, when the empire sent a total of more than 2.1 million immigrants to the United States; in that period, nearly one in every four U.S. immigrants was from Austria-Hungary.

It is hard to identify how many of these immigrants came from Austria itself, because immigration figures for Austria were still not being separately recorded for all years. Also, some hundreds of thousands of immigrants from the Austrian-held portion of Poland were included in the figures for 1899–1919. However, we can say that at least 234,091 immigrants arrived from Austria proper during 1891–1900 and 668,209 in 1901–1910; the latter alone was more than 7 percent of the total immigration for the period. The percentage of immigrants from Austria was even higher for 1911–1920, when Austria's more than 450,000 immigrants made up nearly 8 percent of the total U.S. immigration.

But even these figures do not tell us about the ethnic background of the immigrants. Though many were Austrian Germans, many were of other backgrounds, including Hungarians, Romanians, Czechs, Slovaks, Romanians, Ukrainians, Poles, Jews, Gypsies, and Slavs.

The huge and diverse Austrian immigration to the United States stemmed from the same combination of population pressures and country-to-city flight encountered by most European emigrants of the 19th and early 20th centuries. As huge population increases occurred and the Industrial Revolution simultaneously spread throughout Europe, millions of Austrians left the land to seek work in the cities and abroad, spurred by the ever-shrinking size of inherited farms, cut up by heirs into smaller and smaller plots. At the same time, mechanization began to come to the land, with large-scale farming beginning to drive out family farmers. Nor were there enough jobs in the cities; population pressures quickly outstripped the numbers of new industrial jobs available. The net effect was enormous pressure to emigrate, and the fast-growing United States economy, with its developing industries and its

abundance of free and nearly free land, became the world's greatest emigrant magnet.

In the early part of this main wave of Austrian immigration to the United States, many immigrants from Austria settled on the land, often becoming small farmers in mid-America. However, the rapidly industrializing cities soon attracted large numbers, who would help build the country's economy, while establishing new lives for themselves.

This pattern of emigration would be sharply broken with the start of World War I. Indeed, in the years just before 1914, many men emigrated from Austria to avoid military service. During the war, emigration was almost nil, especially after the United States joined the Allies.

At war's end, Austria was no longer an empire but a small republic, with far less territory and population. Its future was uncertain and America still held promise, so emigration resumed. Soon, however, Austrians faced immigration restrictions. More people wished to enter the United

Graph 2.35: Number of Immigrants from the Austro-Hungarian Empire by Decade, 1861–1920

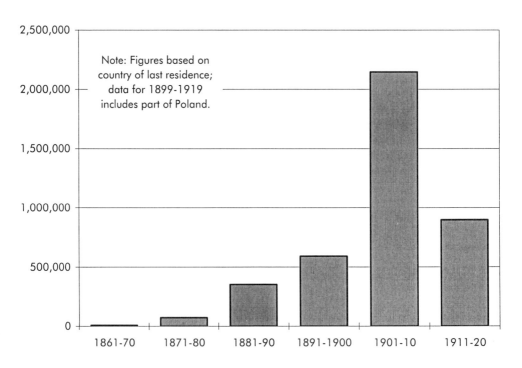

Graph 2.36: Percentage of Immigrants from the Austro-Hungarian Empire in Total U.S. Immigration by Decade, 1861–1920

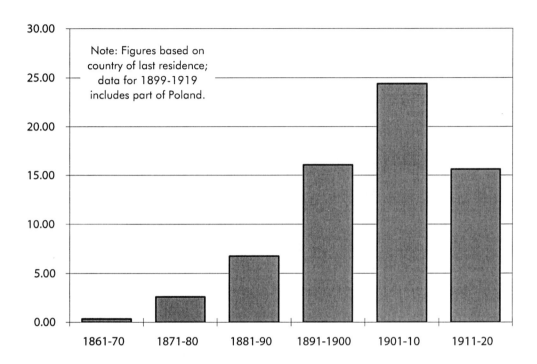

Note: Figures based on country of last residence; data for 1899-1919 includes part of Poland.

States from Austria than were able to do so, because the U.S. quotas were set so low, at only 785 a year from 1924 and 1,413 from 1929.

After the Crash of 1929, the promise of America faded badly, and emigration for economic reasons dropped off sharply. But the events of the 1930s—the rise of the Nazis and the German annexation of Austria—produced a wave of political refugees. Approximately 80 percent of these Austrian refugees were Jews, fleeing the anti-Semitism that had strengthened with the rise of the Nazis. They were generally well educated, bringing considerable resources and skills to their new country. Among them were some internationally known figures, such as composer Arnold Schönberg, pianist Artur Schnabel, conductor Erich Leinsdorf, psychoanalyst Bruno Bettelheim, Nobel Prize–winning physicist Viktor Hess, and director-producers Billy Wilder, Max Reinhardt, and Otto Preminger.

However, only a few of these Austrian refugees were able to enter the United States. Quota restrictions barred most of them. Some went to other countries, such as Canada, Argentina, and Brazil. Others remained in Austria; many of the Jews among them would die in German concentration camps. Almost all of Austria's Jews had emigrated or been killed by the end of the war.

Later Immigration

At the end of World War II, large parts of Europe were devastated, and there were millions of refugees. Austria alone served as a refuge for more than 1.6 million displaced persons. Many of these were ethnic Germans, including some who had lived in the former Austrian provinces of northern Italy or in areas that became part of Yugoslavia, and some who had fled from many countries in eastern Europe ahead of the Soviet army at war's end. A substantial

Graph 2.37: Percentage of Immigrants from Austria in Total U.S. Immigration by Decade, 1861–1996

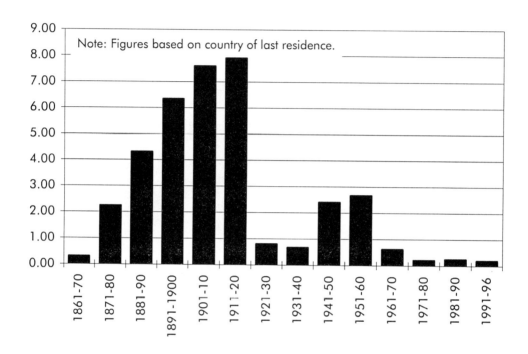

Graph 2.38: Number of Immigrants from Austria by Decade, 1861–1996

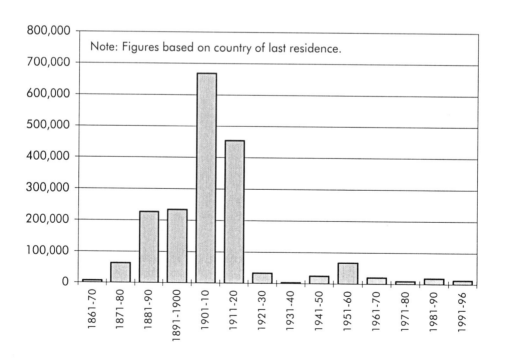

Table 2.22: Number and Percentage of Immigrants from Austria and Hungary in Total U.S. Population by Decade, 1861–1996

Decade	Number of Immigrants from Austria and Hungary	Total U.S. Immigrants	Percentage of Immigrants from Austria and Hungary in Total U.S. Immigration	Number of Immigrants Identified as Specifically from Austria	Percentage of Immigrants from Austria in Total U.S. Immigration	Number of Immigrants Identified as Specifically from Hungary	Number of Immigrants not Specifically Identified as from Austria or Hungary
1861-1870	7,800	2,314,824	0.34	7,124	0.31	484	192
1871-1880	72,969	2,812,191	2.59	63,009	2.24	9,960	0
1881-1890	353,719	5,246,613	6.74	226,039	4.31	127,680	0
1891-1900	592,707	3,687,564	16.07	234,081	6.35	181,288	177,338
1901-1910	2,145,266	8,795,386	24.39	668,209	7.60	808,511	668,546
1911-1920	896,432	5,735,811	15.63	453,649	7.91	442,693	90
1921-1930	63,548	4,107,209	1.55	32,868	0.80	30,680	0
1931-1940	11,424	528,431	2.16	3,563	0.67	7,861	0
1941-1950	28,329	1,035,039	2.74	24,860	2.40	3,469	0
1951-1960	103,743	2,515,479	4.12	67,106	2.67	36,637	0
1961-1970	26,022	3,321,677	0.78	20,621	0.62	5,401	0
1971-1980	16,028	4,493,314	0.36	9,478	0.21	6,550	0
1981-1990	24,885	7,338,062	0.34	18,340	0.25	6,545	0
1991-1996	17,941	6,146,213	0.29	12,122	0.20	5,819	0
Total 1820-1996	4,360,723	63,140,227	6.91	1,841,069	2.92	1,673,578	846,166

Notes: Data for Austria and Hungary not reported until 1861, and not reported separately for all years 1861–1870 and 1891–1910. For 1899–1910, data for Austria include part of Poland. For 1938–1945, data for Austria included in Germany.

Source: Adapted from Table 2, Immigration by Region and Selected Country of Last Residence, Fiscal Years 1820–1996, from the *Statistical Yearbook of the Immigration and Naturalization Service*, 1996.

number of these displaced persons eventually came to the United States, generally admitted under special laws, starting with the 1948 Displaced Persons Act.

Immigration quota restrictions remained in effect until 1965. Until then, the number of Austrian emigrants exceeded the Austrian quota, and some Austrians instead went to other countries, such as Canada and Australia. As their country prospered, however, fewer Austrians wished to emigrate, and U.S. immigration figures from Austria fell.

Throughout the last half of the 20th century, Austria continued to be a temporary haven for refugees, especially those fleeing the Eastern European countries dominated by the Soviet Union. As large numbers of Jews were allowed to leave the Soviet Union in the 1980s, many traveled first to Austria, generally en route to Israel, though some came instead to the United States. This pattern was demonstrated most dramatically in the early 1990s, with the breakup of the Soviet bloc, as people from countries with newly open borders flowed through Austria.

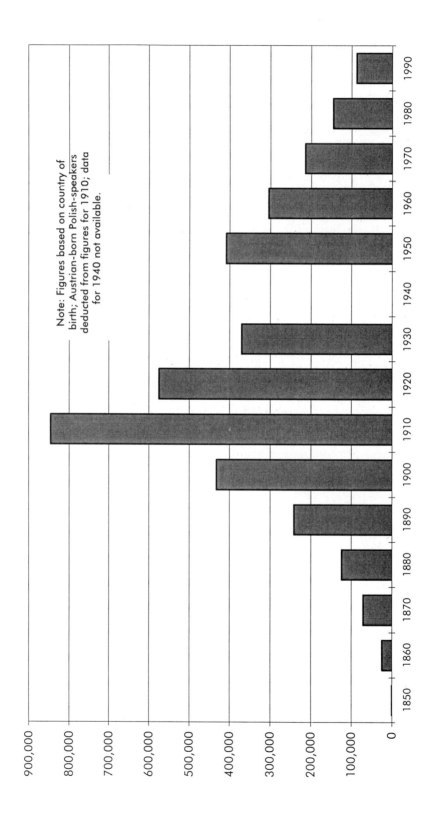

Graph 2.39: Number of Foreign-Born Immigrants from Austria in Total U.S. Population by Decade, 1850–1990

Note: Figures based on country of birth; Austrian-born Polish-speakers deducted from figures for 1910; data for 1940 not available.

These members of the von Trapp family were among the many to flee Austria when the Nazis came to power there; their story was told in The Sound of Music *(Maria is second from right, front row).*

Table 2.23: Number and Percentage of Foreign-Born Immigrants from Austria in Total U.S. Population at End of Decade, 1850–1990

Decade	Number of Foreign-Born Immigrants from Austria	Total U.S. Population	Percentage of Foreign-Born Immigrants from Austria in Total U.S. Population
1850	946	23,191,876	0.00
1860	25,061	31,443,321	0.08
1870	70,797	39,818,449	0.18
1880	124,024	50,155,783	0.25
1890	241,377	62,947,714	0.38
1900	432,798	75,994,575	0.57
1910	845,555	91,972,266	0.92
1920	575,627	105,710,620	0.54
1930	370,914	122,775,046	0.30
1940	(NA)	131,669,275	(NA)
1950	409,043	150,697,361	0.27
1960	304,507	179,323,175	0.17
1970	214,014	203,235,298	0.11
1980	145,607	227,726,000	0.06
1990	87,673	249,907,000	0.04

NA = Not available

Note: Polish-speakers excluded in 1910.

Source: Adapted from Series C 228–295, Foreign-Born Population, by Country of Birth: 1850–1970, in *Historical Statistics of the United States, Colonial Times to 1970, Bicentennial Edition*, and other updating tables from the U.S. Census Bureau.

Resources

Internet Resources

AustriaGenWeb (*http://www.rootsweb.com/~autwgw/*) Part of the WorldGenWeb project, linking genealogical research sites around the world, by region, providing information by current provinces and by links to former provinces now in other countries; includes

LowerAustriaGenWeb (*http://www.rootsweb.com/~autnoe/index.htm*).

Cyndi's List—Austria / Österreich (*http://www.cyndislist.com/austria.htm*) List of on-line genealogical resources for the region, maintained by genealogical author Cyndi Howells.

Print Resources

Austria: A Country Study. 2d ed. Eric Solsten and David E. McClave, eds. Washington, D.C.: Federal Research Division, Library of Congress, 1994. (Available on-line at *http://lcweb2.loc.gov/frd/cs*)

For more resources, see "General European Immigration Resources" on p. 317.

Immigrants from Italy

Many of the key explorers who opened up the Americas for European colonization were Italian sailors searching for a route to Asia. Christopher Columbus (born Cristoforo Colombo), who "discovered" the Americas in 1492, was a Genoese sailor leading a Spanish-sponsored expedition. Venetian sailor John Cabot (born Giovanni Caboto) headed the English expedition that made the first documented post-Columbian landfall on mainland North America in 1497, laying the basis for English claims to North America. His son Sebastian Cabot, also Venetian-born, explored the coast of North America as far south as Virginia for the English, later for a time serving the Spanish.

Amerigo Vespucci, born in Florence, explored the coast of South America for the Spanish and the Portuguese. He recognized that this land was not Asia but a new continent (which would be named after him: America). Another Florentine, Giovanni da Verrazano, explored Narragansett Bay and New York harbor in 1524. His name is celebrated by the Verrazano Narrows bridge over New York harbor.

However, relatively few Italians arrived to settle in America in the early centuries. Not until the 1880s did the number of Italian immigrants to the United States exceed 10,000 a year. But then their numbers swelled. From 1900 to 1914, and again in 1921, they reached well over 100,000 a year. That made Italians a major factor in what historians call the "new immigration," primarily of poor people from southern and eastern Europe, during the late 19th and early 20th centuries.

Early Italian Immigrants

The earliest Italian immigrants to North America were few in number and arrived with parties of colonists from other countries. From the 16th century, Italian soldiers, sailors, and missionaries were part of Spanish settlements, most notably in Florida and in the American Southwest. Others joined French explorations, such as Enrico de Tonti, who explored the Mississippi Valley with the La Salle expedition in 1678 and eventually settled in Alabama. Italians with skills such as winemaking, glassmaking, and silk cultivation were imported into English colonies, from as early as 1610 in Virginia.

In this period, there was no single country called Italy. Instead, the land that had once been the center of the huge Roman Empire was made up of many small states and principalities. By the 17th century, many of these had fallen under the control of other nationalities, including the French, Spanish, and Austrians.

Italy was also a land divided in its economy. Northern Italy had been the home of the European Renaissance, the cultural flowering that began in the 14th century and then spread across Europe; in later centuries, it would grow and develop economically. However, southern Italy was little touched by these developments, remaining generally poor and deprived. These north-south divisions would persist through the 20th century and would help determine the pattern of Italian emigration.

Most early Italian immigrants to America came from northern Italy. Often cultured and well educated, Italian artists, musicians, teachers, writers, physicians, merchants, weavers, cabinetmakers, gardeners, and other skilled workers were highly prized in the Americas, as they were in many parts of Europe in that period.

Among these early Italian immigrants were Catholic missionaries in the Spanish territories. Father Marcos de Niza, based in northern Mexico, explored the area now called Arizona and New Mexico in 1539. A century and a half later, between 1698 and 1711, Jesuit priest Eusebio Francisco Kino (Chino) founded two dozen missions in northern Mexico and southern Arizona, helping to map the region and to establish ranching and fruit farming there. Vincentian (Lazarist) missionaries were notable for their work in the Louisiana Territory from 1816. Other Italian Catholic missionaries worked in California and Oregon, founding early missions, colleges, and vineyards.

CAV. JOHN FOSTER CARR

GUIDA

DEGLI STATI UNITI

PER

L'IMMIGRANTE ITALIANO

PUBBLICATA A CURA

DELLA

SOCIETA' DELLE FIGLIE DELLA RIVOLUZIONE AMERICANA

SEZIONE DI CONNECTICUT.

IMMIGRANT EDUCATION SOCIETY

241 Fifth Avenue. New York

1913.

Authors' Archives

Like other immigrant groups, Italian Americans published guidebooks for other Italians seeking to emigrate, such as this 1913 guide.

Italian Jews and Protestants came to some early American colonies, especially Maryland, Georgia, the Carolinas, and New Amsterdam (later New York). Among the Italian Protestants were French-speaking Waldensians, who had long lived in northern Italy.

Notable Italian immigrants to Maryland included the Paca family, who became wealthy plantation owners by the late 17th century. One descendant, William Paca, became a revolutionary leader, signed the Declaration of Independence, and was elected as the third governor of Maryland in 1782, the first Italian-American governor in the United States.

In these early times, colonies sometimes recruited settlers from abroad. More than a hundred Italians were among the Mediterranean immigrants in the colony of

New Smyrna in Florida in the mid-18th century. That later failed, and by 1777 many of the settlers had migrated to the St. Augustine area.

From about 1750, many Italians fought to reform and unify their homeland. Called the Risorgimento, this movement would not succeed until 1870. During that period many intellectuals and revolutionaries were forced into exile, some temporarily, some permanently. They were often drawn to Ameria, with its promise of freedom.

The most noted of these Risorgimento immigrants was probably the physician Philip (Filippo) Mazzei, who corresponded with his friend Thomas Jefferson on questions of religious tolerance, political freedom, and horticulture. Mazzei was employed by the young state of Virginia from 1779 until 1784, when he returned to

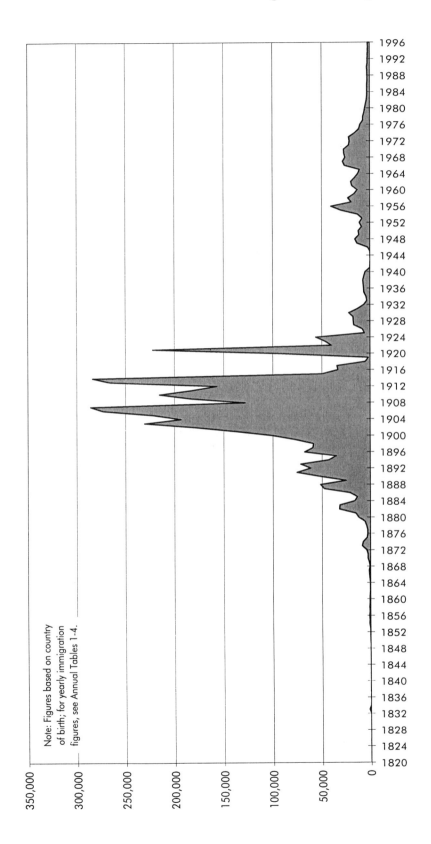

Graph 2.40: Number of Immigrants from Italy Annually, 1820–1996

Note: Figures based on country of birth; for yearly immigration figures, see Annual Tables 1-4.

Italy. He encouraged many other Italians to go to America, some of whom fought for the Americans in the Revolutionary War. When Jefferson became president, he engaged Mazzei to send some Italian sculptors, to help create properly grand public buildings for the still-new nation in Washington, D.C.

Italian musicians tried to establish Italian opera in the new United States in the 1830s and 1840s. In particular Lorenzo Da Ponte established the Italian Opera House in New York City in 1832. However, these attempts largely failed, though their successors would later succeed.

The numbers of Italian immigrants were still small. In 1820, when the United States began tracking immigration, the government recorded the arrival of only 30 immigrants from Italy. By 1850, the total number of Italian-born immigrants was 3,679, only .02 percent of the total United States population. Except for a spike in 1833, the number of Italian immigrants would not exceed 1,000 annually until 1854.

Immigration to the United States from Italy grew slightly in the 1850s, topping one thousand for five years during that decade. Even so, the 1860 census found fewer than 12,000 foreign-born Italian Americans, only .04 percent of the total U.S. population.

A significant number of the Italian immigrants in this period were skilled, cultured people. They established schools, teaching subjects such as music, dancing, painting, writing, foreign languages, history, and geography. Many were artists, including some imported in the 1850s to help with the expansion of the Capitol. Among them were Constantine Brumidi, who painted notable frescoes in the Capitol Rotunda—though in this period "Know Nothing" Americans began to sharply criticize employing foreign artists for public buildings. Many Italian immigrants were musicians of all sorts, playing in operas, theaters, and street bands, including the marching bands of the U.S. Army, Navy, and Marines. Many worked in other highly skilled occupations, as musical-instrument makers, cabinetmakers, carpenters, stonecutters, and the like.

By the mid-19th century, however, the range of Italian immigrants had become wider, including merchants, miners, farmers, fishers, tailors, barbers and hairdressers, and bakers. Though Italian immigrants were by now to be found throughout the country, they were especially concentrated in California, New York, and Louisiana, often in or near large cities. Many of these newer immigrants were poorer than the earlier Italian arrivals, though they were still generally from northern Italy.

Back in Italy, the Risorgimento movement began to have striking success. By 1860, the revolution had succeeded in unifying large parts of Italy, establishing a new kingdom under King Victor Emmanuel. However, many of the revolutionaries found themselves unwelcome in the new government.Revolutionaries continued the fight to oust foreign rulers from other parts of Italy, but some turned their eyes to America. President Abraham Lincoln offered revolutionary leader Giuseppe Garibaldi a command in the Union Army during the American Civil War (1861–1865). Garibaldi declined, but many other revolutionaries accepted.

The Main Wave

The unification of Italy was effectively completed in 1870. However, the benefits that resulted—especially wider education, industrialization, and expansion of opportunities—were largely felt in the north. The poor people of southern Italy found their lives little improved. As a result, large numbers of southern Italians began streaming across the Atlantic to America, primarily to the United States. They would form the main wave of Italian immigration.

From 1871 to 1880 well over 55,000 Italian immigrants arrived in the United States. By the 1880s that had jumped to more than 300,000, topping 650,000 in the 1890s. The first decade of the 20th century saw the heaviest influx of Italian immigrants, with more than 2 million arriving. The peak year overall was 1907, when 285,731 recorded immigrants arrived from Italy. From 1901 to 1910, Italians formed more than 23 percent of the total U.S.

immigration. The following decade (1911–1920) saw another 1.1 million Italians arrive, with another annual peak at 283,738 in 1914. Immigration to the United States from Italy (as from Europe altogether) dropped off sharply during World War I, but peaked again in 1922 at 222,260, before being sharply restricted by U.S. quota laws (see "Immigration Restrictions" on p. 47).

Most of the immigrants in this main wave left through the port of Naples, which also became a major gathering place for others making the journey to America from places farther east in the Mediterranean and from southeastern Europe. They generally traveled on the great ocean liners, most of them in the crowded quarters known as steerage (see "The Journey" on p. 53).

Poverty, disease, and natural disasters such as earthquakes and volcanic eruptions all helped spark emigration from Italy. Many Italians also sought more personal freedom than they could find in their native land—freedom from landlords and employers, but also sometimes freedom from parental and societal restrictions. Some young men emigrated to avoid compulsory military service, while others left Italy after serving in the military—and after seeing that they could have a better life than the grinding poverty they had known at home.

Especially from the 1870s on, the steamship companies actively solicited emigrant business, sending agents into the Italian countryside as recruiters. Labor agents called *padroni* also combed the land for emigrants who could be sent to the United States as cheap laborers. Both portrayed America as a golden land. Many poor Italian immigrants found it was not so and suffered enormous hardships in the early years. However, many others found that even a modest American wage was far more than they might have earned in Italy.

Table 2.24: Number and Percentage of Immigrants from Italy in Total U.S. Immigration by Decade, 1820–1996

Decade	Number of Immigrants from Italy	Total U.S. Immigrants	Percentage of Immigrants from Italy in Total U.S. Immigration
1820	30	8,385	0.36
1821-1830	409	143,439	0.29
1831-1840	2,253	599,125	0.38
1841-1850	1,870	1,713,251	0.11
1851-1860	9,231	2,598,214	0.36
1861-1870	11,725	2,314,824	0.51
1871-1880	55,759	2,812,191	1.98
1881-1890	307,309	5,246,613	5.86
1891-1900	651,893	3,687,564	17.68
1901-1910	2,045,877	8,795,386	23.26
1911-1920	1,109,524	5,735,811	19.34
1921-1930	455,315	4,107,209	11.09
1931-1940	68,028	528,431	12.87
1941-1950	57,661	1,035,039	5.57
1951-1960	185,491	2,515,479	7.37
1961-1970	214,111	3,321,677	6.45
1971-1980	129,368	4,493,314	2.88
1981-1990	67,254	7,338,062	0.92
1991-1996	54,190	6,146,213	0.88
Total 1850-1996	5,427,298	63,140,227	8.60

Source: Adapted from Table 2, Immigration by Region and Selected Country of Last Residence, Fiscal Years 1820–1996, from *Statistical Yearbook of the Immigration and Naturalization Service,* 1996.

Table 2.25: Number and Percentage of Foreign-Born Immigrants from Italy in Total U.S. Population by Decade, 1850–1990

Decade	Number of Foreign-Born Immigrants from Italy	Total U.S. Population	Percentage of Foreign-Born Immigrants from Italy in Total U.S. Population
1850	3,679	23,191,876	0.02
1860	11,677	31,443,321	0.04
1870	17,157	39,818,449	0.04
1880	44,230	50,155,783	0.09
1890	182,580	62,947,714	0.29
1900	484,027	75,994,575	0.64
1910	1,343,125	91,972,266	1.46
1920	1,610,113	105,710,620	1.52
1930	1,790,429	122,775,046	1.46
1940	(NA)	131,669,275	(NA)
1950	1,427,952	150,697,361	0.95
1960	1,256,999	179,323,175	0.70
1970	1,008,533	203,235,298	0.50
1980	831,922	227,726,000	0.37
1990	580,592	249,907,000	0.23

NA = Not available

Source: Adapted from Series C 228–295, Foreign-Born Population, by Country of Birth: 1850–1970, in *Historical Statistics of the United States, Colonial Times to 1970, Bicentennial Edition*, and other updating tables from the U.S. Census Bureau.

The proof could be seen in the steady stream of checks sent back from America to Italy. The first to leave were generally young single or married men. After settling in the United States, often in a job gained through the *padrone* network, they would send money home, to help support their families and to build up savings so other family members could join them. In time whole families would cross the Atlantic by ones and by twos, with sons and brothers often followed by wives and younger children, then parents.

Poorer regions of Italy greatly benefited from "remittance money" sent by immigrants. As early as 1877, the Italian and U.S. governments reached an agreement to make it easier for immigrants to send small amounts of money back home safely. Later laws, most notably Italy's 1910 Emigration Law, made the transmission more secure and less expensive.

Early immigrants were exploited by the *padroni*, who were paid a commission on the immigrants' wages. The *padrone* system declined in the early 20th century, as laws were passed limiting their activities. With large Italian communities in the United States, family and regional networks often helped new arrivals get settled in work and housing.

Though many early Italian immigrant laborers experienced extreme hardship and exploitation, the late 19th and early 20th centuries saw enormous economic expansion in the United States. Italians were among the peoples from southern and eastern Europe, many of them unskilled workers, who helped fuel this expansion with their cheap labor. They built railroads and dams, dug canals, laid water and sewage lines, and worked on major construction projects around the country. Italian communities followed the route of such

American Museum of Immigration, Statue of Liberty National Monument, National Park Service, U.S. Department of the Interior; Photo: Lewis W. Hine

These Italian men were waiting at Ellis Island in 1905 for connections to the railroad that would take them west.

work all across the country. The immigrants worked in factories of all sorts, making clothing, shoes, steel, matches, or whatever required large numbers of workers. Many also cut timber, worked as migrant laborers, and became gardeners, but relatively few became farmers. The main exception was in California, where Italians became major vegetable and fruit farmers. Most notably, an Italian-Swiss colony helped to establish the modern grape-growing and winemaking industries in Sonoma County.

Though Italian immigrants were to be found throughout the land, with a significant impact in California, in 1900 more than 70 percent of them lived in the Northeast: in New York, New Jersey, Pennsylvania, and New England. Though many had come from the land, the majority of them lived in the cities. Of the many "Little Italy" communities around America, by far the largest was in New York City, with more than 145,000 Italian immigrants in 1900. By 1910, New York City had an Italian immigrant population numbering more than 340,000—larger than the populations of Florence, Venice, and Genoa combined.

Other major Italian communities were found in cities such as Chicago, St. Louis, Newark, New Orleans, and San Francisco.

At first, immigrants would often settle near people from their home village or region, so the "Little Italy" sections of many major cities were initially made up of many subcommunities. Sometimes each would have its own Catholic church, with Italian priests, featuring the patron saint of their region. Later, however, such regional distinctions generally broke down—though distinctions between northern and southern Italians persisted (as they do in Italy itself today).

Most Italian immigrants were Catholic, but a significant minority were Jews (most of whom would arrive later) and Protestants. From the 1870s American Protestants, especially Baptists, Methodists, and Presbyterians, had active missions in Italy. Some of their converts later came to the United States.

Not all Italian immigrants stayed in America. Significant numbers earned some money in the United States and returned home to make their lives in Italy. Others

In the late 19th and early 20th centuries, newly arrived immigrants often crowded together in "Little Italy" sections of major cities.

Graph 2.41: Number of Immigrants from Italy by Decade, 1820–1996

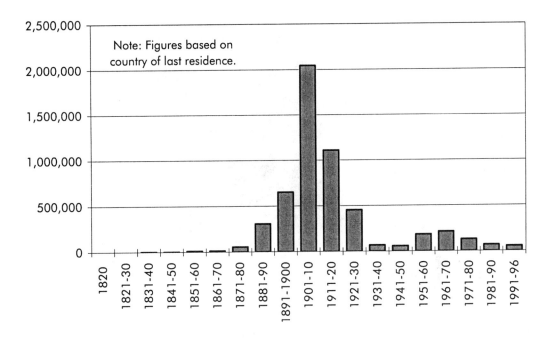

Graph 2.42: Number of Foreign-Born Immigrants from Italy in Total U.S. Population by Decade, 1850–1990

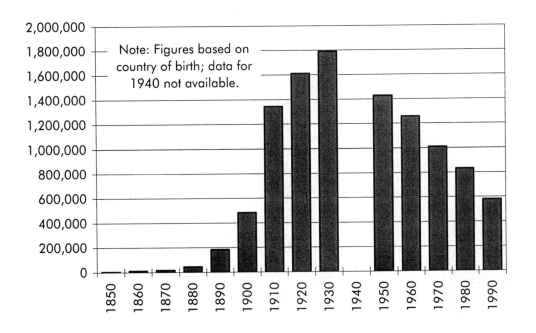

American Museum of Immigration, Statue of Liberty National Monument, National Park Service, U.S. Department of the Interior; Photo: Lewis W. Hine

Many Italian immigrant men worked in construction and transportation, like this one who was working on the New York Barge Canal system in 1912.

traveled back and forth several times, often bringing family members or additional workers with them.

For those who did stay, Italians (like other immigrant groups) established mutual aid societies, to help newcomers make their way in the new world and to help them bring other family members across the ocean to join them.

Depression and War

Restrictive immigration laws in the 1920s sharply curtailed immigration to the United States from Italy ("Immigration Restrictions" on p. 47). The Depression of the 1930s slowed immigration even further, for America—like the rest of the world—was in deep economic trouble.

However, political turbulence in Italy once again began to spur the emigration of well-educated, cultured, and often affluent Italians. Benito Mussolini, who had become Italy's prime minister in 1922, fashioned a Fascist dictatorship that would see Italy invade and take Abyssinia (now Ethiopia) in 1935 and then enter World War II (1939–1945) as an ally of Adolf Hit-

ler's Nazi Germany. Many political liberals fled from Fascist Italy in these years. In addition, some Jews, rightly fearing the Fascists' anti-Jewish activities, also fled to America, though some who wished to do so were barred by U.S. immigration restrictions. Perhaps the most notable emigrant of this period was the physicist Enrico Fermi, who in America would be a major figure in the development of nuclear physics. Overall, though the total number of U.S. immigrants shrank to just 528,431 from 1931 to 1940, more than 68,000, or nearly 13 percent, were from Italy.

During World War II, with the United States and Italy fighting on opposite sides, and with the Atlantic Ocean a major battleground, the number of Italian immigrants was very small, reaching a low of just 49 in 1943. After war's end, in 1945, the number of Italian immigrants started to rise again. Though they never reached the huge numbers of early in the century, Italians made up more than 7 percent of the total immigrants from 1951 to 1960 and only a little less in the following decade, with the peak year in this period being 1956, when 40,430 immigrants arrived from Italy.

From then on the numbers of Italian immigrants began to fall. By the 1980s and 1990s, other immigrant groups dominated, with Italian immigrants making up less than 1 percent of the total immigrants in these decades. Overall, from 1820 to 1996, the U.S. government recorded 5,427,298 immigrants from Italy, nearly 9 percent of the total immigrants to the United States in that period.

Resources

Internet Resources

Order Sons of Italy in America (*http://www.osia.org*). Web site of major Italian-American organization includes articles from *Italian America* magazine; a virtual reference library, including Italian studies, genealogical resources, books, related Web links, and special features. (Address: 219 E St., NE, Washington, DC 20002; Phone: 202-547-2900, Fax: 202-546-8168, E-mail: osianat@aol.com)

National Italian American Foundation (*http://www.niaf.org*). Web site of organizations seeking to preserve and protect Italian culture and heritage, to enhance the image of Italian Americans, and to strengthen ties between Italy and the United States. Offers on-line research guides, including fact sheets, statistics, bibliographies, and related Web links. (Address: 1860 19th Street, NW, Washington, DC 20009; Phone: 202-387-0600; Fax: 202/387-0800)

Italian Genealogy (*http://www.regalis.com/italgen.htm*) An Italian-based guide to Italian genealogical research and related topics.

ItalianGenWeb (*http://www.rootsweb.com/~itawgw/index.html*) Part of the MediterraneanGenWeb, in turn part of the WorldGenWeb project, linking genealogical research sites around the world, by region; provides resources by province, including searchable databases and query boards, and links to other sites, including related regions, such as Vatican City and San Marino.

Cyndi's List—Italy / Italia (*http://www.cyndislist.com/italy.htm*) List of on-line genealogical resources for Italy, maintained by genealogical author Cyndi Howells.

Print Resources

General Works

Barolini, Helen. *Images, a Pictorial History of Italian Americans.* New York: Center for Migration, 1986.

Capozzola, Richard A., comp. *Five Centuries of Italian-American History, 1492–1992: A Chronology of Events, Little Known Facts, and Stories about a People Who Contributed to the Greatness of America.* New Orleans: American Italian Renaissance Foundation, 1992.

Di Franco, J. Philip. *The Italian American Experience.* New York: T. Doherty, 1988.

Gallo, Patrick J. *Old Bread, New Wine: A Portrait of the Italian-Americans.* Chicago: Nelson-Hall, 1981.

Giovannetti, Alberto. *The Italians of America.* New York: Manor Books, 1979.

Iorizzo, Luciano J. *The Italian Americans.* Boston: Twayne, 1980.

Italy: A Country Study. 2d ed. Rinn S. Shinn, ed. Washington, D.C.: U.S. Government Printing Office, 1985.

Mangione, Jerre. *America Is Also Italian.* New York: Putnam, 1969.

———. *La Storia: Five Centuries of the Italian American Experience.* New York: HarperCollins, 1992.

Moquin, Wayne, ed. *A Documentary History of the Italian Americans.* New York: Praeger, 1974.

Nelli, Humbert S. *From Immigrants to Ethnics: The Italian Americans.* New York: Oxford University Press, 1983.

Null, Gary, and Carl Stone. *Italian-Americans*. Harrisburg, Pa.: Stackpole, 1976.

Rolle, Andrew F. *The Italian Americans: Troubled Roots*. New York: Free Press, 1980.

Scarpaci, Vincenza. *A Portrait of the Italians in America*. New York: Scribner, 1982.

Schiavo, Giovanni. *Four Centuries of Italian American History*. New York: Vigo Press, 1952.

Schoener, Allon. *The Italian Americans*. New York: Macmillan, 1987.

Works for Young People

Di Franco, J. Philip. *The Italian Americans*. Rev. ed. New York: Chelsea House, 1996.

Grossman, Ronald P., with Martha Savaglio. *Italians in America*. Rev. ed. Minneapolis: Lerner, 1993.

Hoobler, Dorothy, and Thomas Hoobler. *The Italian American Family Album*. New York: Oxford University Press, 1994.

Washburne, Carolyn Kott. *Italian Americans*. New York: Marshall Cavendish, 1995.

Witkoski, Michael. *Italian Americans*. Vero Beach, Fla.: Rourke, 1991.

Genealogical Works

Brockman, Terra. *A Student's Guide to Italian American Genealogy*. Phoenix: Oryx, 1996.

Carmack, Sharon DeBartolo. *Italian-American Family History: A Guide to Researching and Writing About Your Heritage*. Baltimore: Genealogical Publishing, 1997.

Cole, Trafford. *Italian Genealogical Records: How to Use Italian Civil, Ecclesiastical and Other Records in Family History Research*. Salt Lake City, Utah: Ancestry, 1995.

Colletta, John Philip. *Finding Italian Roots: The Complete Guide for Americans*. Baltimore: Genealogical Publishing, 1993.

DeAngelis, Priscilla Grindle. *Italian-American Genealogy: A Source Book*. Rockville, Md.: Noteworthy Enterprises, 1994.

Konrad, J. *Italian Family Research*. Munroe Falls, Ohio: Summit Publications, 1980.

Lee, Kathleen. *Tracing Our Italian Roots*. Santa Fe, N.M.: J. Muir, 1993.

Nelson, Lynn. *A Genealogist's Guide to Discovering Your Italian Ancestors: How to Find and Record Your Unique Heritage*. Cincinnati: Betterway, 1997.

Reed, Robert D. *How and Where to Research Your Ethnic-American Cultural Heritage: Italian Americans*. Saratoga, Calif.: Reed, 1979.

For more resources, see "General European Immigration Resources" on p. 317.

Immigrants from Greece

Greek civilization gave democracy to the world, but the Greek people were ruled by others from long before the birth of Christ until 1829, when Greece won its independence from the Turkish empire. The Greeks maintained their language and culture, however, even though they lived in several countries, primarily in the eastern Mediterranean. Large numbers of Greeks lived in Turkey, Egypt, Romania, Albania, Crete, Cyprus, and the Aegean islands, some of which became part of the modern nation of Greece.

Figures for Greek immigration to the United States are very misleading. From 1829, they show the number of immigrants from the nation of Greece. However, that nation's boundaries changed dramatically between 1829 and 1948, so that the country's size was nearly doubled. In addition, many Greeks were counted in the immigration figures for other countries, most notably Turkey.

Greeks did not come to America in large numbers until the late 19th century, with most arriving in the first two decades of the 20th century. They were a key part of what historians call the "new immigration," primarily of poor people from southern and eastern Europe.

Early Immigrants

The earliest Greeks came to America as individuals or in small groups, often as explorers or adventurers. One Greek sailor, John Griego, is believed to have sailed with Christopher Columbus in his 1492 "discovery" of the Americas. Other Greeks sailed with the Spanish; among them was Don Teodoro, who in 1528 was reputedly the first Greek to land on the American mainland. The Spanish-sponsored sailor Juan de Fuca—who in 1592 discovered the strait south of Vancouver Island now named for him—may have been a Greek sailor originally named Ioannis Phocas.

In the mid-18th century, several hundred Greeks came to Florida with a Mediterranean party to found the settlement of New Smyrna (named after the ancient Greek city of Smyrna, now Izmir, on the coast of Turkey). The colony failed, and in 1777 most of the settlers moved into the colony of St. Augustine.

Greek immigration was not counted separately until Greece became independent in 1829. U.S. immigration records show that 20 Greek immigrants arrived in 1829–1830. Their numbers remained small for decades. As late as 1870, fewer than

Authors' Archives

Many emigrants from Greece and nearby regions sailed out of Piraeus, the port of Athens.

400 foreign-born Greek Americans were recorded in the census (though these figures would not include Greeks from Turkey).

Among the Greek emigrants in this early period were some boys orphaned during the struggle for Greek independence, who were adopted by sympathetic Americans. One of these boys was George M. Colvocoresses, who later became a commander in the Civil War. Another was Lucas Miltiades Miller, raised by his adopted family in Vermont, who in 1853 was elected to the Wisconsin legislature. In 1891, he became the first Greek American to be elected to the U.S. Congress.

The Main Immigration

A somewhat larger and steadier flow of Greek immigrants began in the 1880s. Greece was extremely poor, and many Greek men traveled around the Mediterranean looking for work. A notable example was Christos Tsakonas, who is credited with sparking emigration from Greece. Like many Greeks, he traveled to Piraeus (the port of Athens) and then to Alexandria, Egypt, seeking his fortune. Unusually, he then went to America, in 1873. After a visit back to Greece in 1875, he returned to America bringing with him several other Greeks. Many more would follow.

Most of these emigrants came from southern Greece, and that would remain the case. However, by 1890, Greeks were also emigrating from all the other parts of Greece and from the eastern Mediterranean. In the classic immigrant pattern, Greeks sent money back home to their families. This "remittance money" helped to ease the terrible poverty of the region. The Greek government's own records showed that in the late 19th and early 20th centuries the most prosperous regions of Greece were those receiving the most money from the United States. Sometimes a family's property was mortgaged to raise the fare for one or more emigrants, who would help to pay off the mortgage with money earned in the United States.

As in many other European countries, steamship agents and labor bosses traveled around Greece, encouraging emigration—and business for themselves. The immigrants were often exploited, paying the bosses a substantial portion of their earnings.

Through 1910, males made up as much as 95 percent of the Greek immigrants to the United States. Many arrived as part of an immigrant chain, getting their first jobs and places to stay through relatives or friends from their home region. Though many came from rural areas, in the United States most settled in cities. Many unskilled immigrants worked as manual laborers, establishing communities around the country, wherever they found work, such as along the railroad lines. The largest Greek community was that in New York City. Greeks also formed notable communities in other large cities such as Chicago, Salt Lake City, and Milwaukee, and smaller ones such as Spartanburg, South Carolina, and Tarpon Springs, Florida, where they founded a sponge industry.

At first these communities were largely male. Perhaps half of these early emigrants would return home, after earning some money in America. That would change later as more Greek women and children came. Some arrived to join their

Table 2.26: Number and Percentage of Immigrants from Greece in Total U.S. Immigration by Decade, 1820–1996

Decade	Number of Immigrants from Greece	Total U.S. Immigrants	Percentage of Immigrants from Greece in Total U.S. Immigration
1820	—	8,385	0.00
1821-1830	20	143,439	0.01
1831-1840	49	599,125	0.01
1841-1850	16	1,713,251	0.00
1851-1860	31	2,598,214	0.00
1861-1870	72	2,314,824	0.00
1871-1880	210	2,812,191	0.01
1881-1890	2,308	5,246,613	0.04
1891-1900	15,979	3,687,564	0.43
1901-1910	167,519	8,795,386	1.90
1911-1920	184,201	5,735,811	3.21
1921-1930	51,084	4,107,209	1.24
1931-1940	9,119	528,431	1.73
1941-1950	8,973	1,035,039	0.87
1951-1960	47,608	2,515,479	1.89
1961-1970	85,969	3,321,677	2.59
1971-1980	92,369	4,493,314	2.06
1981-1990	38,377	7,338,062	0.52
1991-1996	14,894	6,146,213	0.24
Total 1820-1996	718,798	63,140,227	1.14

Source: Adapted from Table 2, Immigration by Region and Selected Country of Last Residence, Fiscal Years 1820–1996, from the *Statistical Yearbook of the Immigration and Naturalization Service*, 1996.

husbands or fathers who had come to America first, in the classic immigrant pattern. Other women came as brides, for many single Greek males sought wives from their homelands. Some of these women came to America as "picture brides," chosen from photographs, to marry men they had never met. Like other immigrant groups, Greeks established mutual aid societies and Greek-language publications, which helped ease the immigrants into their new lives.

From 1910 on, a larger number of single women began to immigrate to America on their own. Some came to seek husbands, especially women who were too poor to have the traditional dowry and so might well have remained unmarried in Greece. In the United States, where dowries were not needed and Greek women were scarce, they had a better chance of finding a husband, usually from among the Greek community. Indeed, some of the immigrants' remittance money was used to provide dowries for their unmarried sisters and daughters back home—or to provide them with tickets to the United States.

Table 2.27: Number and Percentage of Foreign-Born Immigrants from Greece in Total U.S. Population at End of Decade, 1850–1990

Decade	Number of Foreign-Born Immigrants from Greece	Total U.S. Population	Percentage of Foreign-Born Immigrants from Greece in Total U.S. Population
1850	86	23,191,876	0.00
1860	328	31,443,321	0.00
1870	390	39,818,449	0.00
1880	776	50,155,783	0.00
1890	1,887	62,947,714	0.00
1900	8,515	75,994,575	0.01
1910	101,282	91,972,266	0.11
1920	175,976	105,710,620	0.17
1930	174,526	122,775,046	0.14
1940	(NA)	131,669,275	(NA)
1950	169,335	150,697,361	0.11
1960	159,167	179,323,175	0.09
1970	177,275	203,235,298	0.09
1980	210,998	227,726,000	0.09
1990	177,398	249,907,000	0.07

NA = Not available

Source: Adapted from Series C 228–295, Foreign-Born Population, by Country of Birth: 1850–1970, in *Historical Statistics of the United States, Colonial Times to 1970, Bicentennial Edition*, and other updating tables from the U.S. Census Bureau.

The second decade of the 20th century saw the largest Greek immigration to the United States. Between 1911 and 1920, more than 184,000 came from Greece itself, forming more than three percent of the U.S. immigration for the period. Many Greeks also emigrated from other countries, most notably Turkey. Often they sought to escape compulsory military service in a "foreign" army, especially to avoid being forced to fight against other Greeks. This was a real possibility, because Greece and Turkey fought on opposite sides during World War I and the Greco-Turkish War that followed it. Greece lost that war, during which the Turks destroyed the large Greek section of Smyrna on the Turkish coast in 1922.

Under the 1923 Treaty of Lausanne, the two countries then had a massive exchange of populations. Nearly 1.3 million Greeks left Turkey for Greece, while some 400,000 Turks left Greece for Turkey. This enormous number of refugees greatly strained the resources of Greece, which at the time had only 4.5 million people. Most refugees had little or no money, but many of those who had the fare, such as business owners or professionals, immigrated to the United States.

Starting in 1921, U.S. immigration laws set quotas that sharply restricted the number of immigrants from Greece, as from many other countries (see "Immigration Restrictions" on p. 47). Many of the Greek immigrants in this period were still largely unskilled. However, a significant number of the newer immigrants, both women and men, were well educated or had valuable technical skills.

Later Immigration

The Depression of the 1930s and the turmoil of World War II caused immigration to drop off sharply, from Greece as from many other countries. During much of the war, Greece was occupied by German, Italian, and Bulgarian forces, with many Greeks fighting in the resistance. When the occupying forces pulled out in 1944, the country plunged into a civil war, led by rival resistance groups, which lasted until

Graph 2.43: Percentage of Immigrants from Greece in Total U.S. Immigration by Decade, 1821–1996

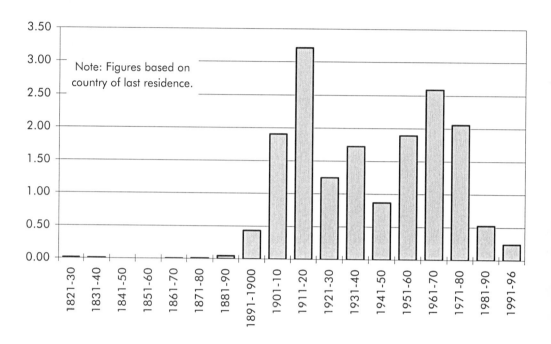

Note: Figures based on country of last residence.

Graph 2.44: Number of Immigrants from Greece by Decade, 1821–1996

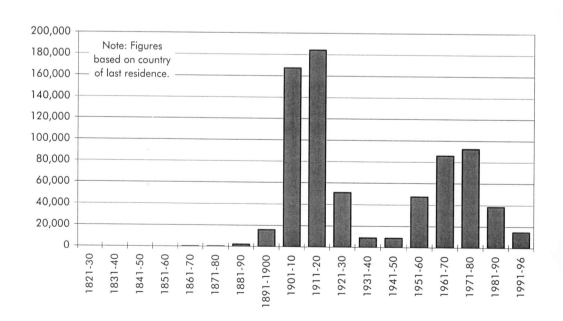

Note: Figures based on country of last residence.

1949. Even during the civil war, some Greeks arrived in the United States as displaced persons.

After the civil war ended, Greek immigration rose again. Unlike many earlier immigrants, these newer arrivals often arrived in families intending to settle permanently, rather than to earn money and then return to their homeland. Far from being unskilled, many of them were highly educated professionals, including a significant number of women. During the 1950s and 1960s, Greek emigration included numerous engineers, physicians, surgeons, and other scientific professionals. They constituted a significant "brain drain" from their homeland.

Later troubles at home would also spur immigration to America, most notably the military dictatorship that ruled Greece from 1967 to 1974. More Greeks were allowed to enter also after the 1965 Immigration Act took effect in 1968, ending the quota system that had severely restricted their numbers. The postwar peak decade was 1971–1980, when 92,369 immigrants were recorded from Greece alone.

From early in the 20th century, many Greeks had worked in the restaurant business. Why this happened is unclear, though some suggest it was because early male immigrants frequently congregated in Greek cafés. In any case, it remained so. While some highly skilled and educated Greeks continued to arrive, many young, unskilled Greek immigrants in the late 20th century continued to find their way into America by working in one of the innumerable Greek restaurants dotting the land.

Overall from 1829, the U.S. immigration records record 718,799 immigrants from Greece, a little over 1 percent of the total immigration since 1820. How many more Greeks came from other countries is unclear.

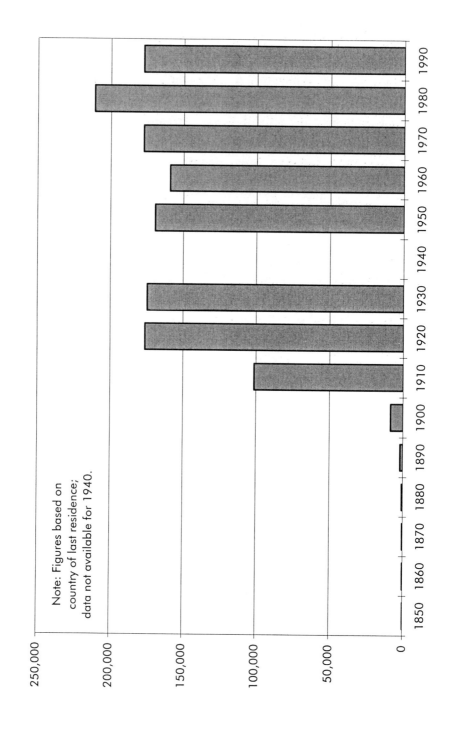

Graph 2.45: Number of Foreign-Born Immigrants from Greece in Total U.S. Population by Decade, 1850–1990

Note: Figures based on country of last residence; data not available for 1940.

National Archives, Farm Security; Photo: Dorothy Lange

During the Depression of the 1930s people looked for work wherever they could find it; this Greek immigrant was living in a migrant labor camp in California in 1936.

Resources

Internet Resources

American Hellenic Educational Progressive Association (AHEPA), (*http://www.ahepa.org*). Web site operated by the Greek Club at the University of California at Los Angeles for this major Greek-American heritage organization. Includes information about events, news from Greece, and local and national organizations. (Address: AHEPA Headquarters, 1909 Q Street, NW, Suite 500, Washington, DC 20009. Telephone: 202-232-6300; Fax: 202-232-2140)

Hellenic-American Union (*http://www.hau.gr*). Web site in Greek and English versions offers news, educational programs, a library, and publications.

Archive of Hellenism (*http://www.me.wustl.edu/ME/faculty/add/hellas/archell.htm*) On-line index of information and sources relating to Greek immigration, history, and culture.

Print Resources

Burgess, Thomas. *Greeks in America*. New York: Arno Press, 1970. Originally published Boston: Sherman, French & Co., 1913.

Callinicos, Constance. *American Aphrodite: Becoming Female in Greek America*. New York, N.Y.: Pella Publishing, 1990.

Greece: A Country Study. 4th ed. Curtis, Glenn E., ed. Washington, D.C.: U.S. Government Printing Office, 1995.

Hecker, Melvin, and Heike Fenton, eds. *The Greeks in America, 1528–1977: A Chronology and Fact Book*. Dobbs Ferry, N.Y.: Oceana, 1978.

Jones, Jayne Clark. *The Greeks in America*. Rev. ed. Minneapolis: Lerner, 1990.

Koken, Paul, et al. *A History of the Greeks in the Americas, 1453–1938*. Ann Arbor, Mich.: Proctor Publications, 1995.

Mazacoufa, Demetrius. *The Story of the Greeks in America*. Atlanta: Argonne Press, 1977.

Monos, Dimitris. *The Greek Americans*. New York: Chelsea House, 1988.

Moskos, Charles C., Jr. *Greek Americans, Struggle and Success*. Englewood Cliffs, N.J.: Prentice-Hall, 1980.

Phillips, David, and Steven Ferry. *Greek Americans*. Tarrytown, N.Y.: Benchmark, 1996.

Saloutas, Theodore. *Greeks in the United States*. Cambridge, Mass.: Harvard University Press, 1964.

Scourby, Alice. *The Greek Americans*. Boston: Twayne, 1984.

For more resources, see "General European Immigration Resources" on p. 317.

Immigrants from Hungary

Hungary has a long history, but for many centuries it was part of larger empires. Only in the 20th century has it become once again an independent nation, and even then it was largely controlled by other powers until late in the century.

Hungary was traditionally multiethnic. The dominant group was the Magyars, a Central Asian people who arrived on the Danube in the late 9th century. Other Europeans called them Hungarians (from a Turkic word meaning "ten tribes"). Immigrants from Hungary were part of the "new immigration," largely from southern and eastern Europe, in the late 19th and early 20th centuries.

Hungarian Background

By the early 10th century, the Magyars had conquered large parts of what would become Hungary. Though they raided westward, they were blocked in the late 10th century by the Carolingian Empire, out of which would emerge the Holy Roman Empire, later called the Hapsburg Empire after the Hapsburgs established a hereditary claim on the imperial throne. The Magyars adopted Christianity in the 11th century, establishing closer ties with the rest of Europe.

In the early 16th century, Hungary was made part of the Hapsburg Empire by a dynastic marriage. However, the Hapsburgs soon lost much of Hungary to the Ottoman Turks, who in that period were expanding into southeastern Europe. Hungary was partitioned between the Hapsburgs and the Turks. Territories near Austria and part of northwestern Croatia remained under Hapsburg control, as a region named Royal Hungary. The rest of Hungary, including Transylvania, fell under Turkish domination, with parts being directly incorporated into the Turkish empire in 1603. Hungary remained a battleground between Christian Europe and the Muslim Turks, until the late 17th century, when the Hapsburgs finally recaptured almost all of Hungary.

A strong nationalist current animated Hungarian politics throughout the period of Hapsburg domination, along with considerable Protestant Hungarian resistance to Catholic Austrian rule. Many Hungarians had become Protestants with the start of the Reformation in the early 16th century, though many had converted back to Catholicism during the Counter-Reformation. Those who remained Protestant were persecuted by the strongly Catholic Hapsburgs. Protestant or Catholic, very substantial Hungarian resistance to autocratic Austrian rule generated a long series of insurrections and reform movements in Hungary, though with little effect until the 19th century.

The southern parts of Hungary had been devastated by the Austrian-Turkish wars, and during the 18th century the Hapsburgs brought in many settlers from elsewhere, most notably Slovaks, Serbs, Croatians, and Germans, who were joined by many Jews from Austria and Poland. With a combination of natural increase and immigration to Hungary from other regions, the population of Hungary more than tripled during the 18th century, to some 8 million, while in the same period the percentage of Magyars fell to below 40 percent.

Hungarian unrest culminated in the revolution of 1848, one of many European democratic revolutions at the time. Though initially successful, Hungary's revolution failed and was harshly suppressed. But the Hapsburg Empire was weakening, and in an 1867 compromise Austria and Hungary formed a dual monarchy, variously called Austria-Hungary or the Austro-Hungarian Empire. In 1872, the Danube cities of Buda and Pest united to form Hungary's modern capital, Budapest.

Hungary was the weaker partner, however, and faced substantial social and economic problems. Not the least of these was population pressure, as the country's population soared from 13 million to 20 million between 1850 and 1910, including approximately 900,000 Jews, who were vitally important in the business and financial communities. In rural areas, farms subdivided among families could no longer support the rising population. These population pressures and rural economic problems laid the basis for the massive wave of emigration from Hungary in the late 19th century.

Early Immigrants

The first known Hungarian to visit America was Stephen Parmenius of Buda, a poet and classical scholar who sailed with Sir Humphrey Gilbert to Newfoundland in 1583, dying on the return voyage. Some other Hungarians came to the New World in the 17th and early 18th centuries, but they were relatively few and most came as individuals. Among them were the Reformed Protestant minister Istvan Zador, who arrived in Boston in 1682; Johannes Kelp, a Pietist who led a group of Transylvanian Saxons to Pennsylvania in 1694; and two Jesuit missionaries, Johannes Rarkay and Ferdinand Konsag, who—in the late 17th and early 18th centuries respectively—spent time exploring the Southwest. The writings of these and other Jesuits began to introduce Hungarians to the wonders of the new continent.

Many reform-minded Hungarians were sympathetic to the American revolutionary cause, and some crossed the Atlantic to fight in the colonial army. Colonel Michael Kovats served in the noted Pulaski Legion, dying in battle at Charleston in 1779. Major John Ladislaus Pollereczky commanded French forces, including Hungarians, on the revolutionary side; he later settled in Maine.

In the 19th century, Hungarians in Europe learned about the new United States through translations such as William Robertson's 1807 *History of America* and the writings of Hungarian travelers, most notably Sandor Böloni-Farkas's 1834 *Journey to North America* and Agoston Haraszthy's 1844 *Journey in North America*. Haraszthy eventually settled in the United States, helping to found Sauk City, Wisconsin, before moving on to California's Sonoma Valley, where he introduced Tokay grapes, helping to establish the winemaking industry there.

The first large number of Hungarians did not come to the United States until after the failure of the 1848 revolution. In the next few years, an estimated 4,000 Hungarian political refugees arrived, including the revolution's leader, Louis Kossuth. He and some others would return to Europe, to continue fighting for Hungarian independence. The rest chose to make new lives in America. They settled throughout the country, from the northeastern cities to the western plains, establishing the first Hungarian-American organizations and laying the basis for later Hungarian immigrant communities.

Another 4,000 or so Hungarians arrived in the 1860s, at the time of the Civil War. Some 800 of these served in the Union Army, including almost 100 officers, highly prized for their military experience. They were some of the many Europeans recruited by President Abraham Lincoln. Hungarians served in multiethnic regiments from Chicago and New York, and in local regiments drawn from many parts of the country, though they were too few in number to form all-Hungarian regiments. Notable Hungarians in the Civil War included Major General Julius H. Stahel (born Gyula Szamvald), who won the Congressional Medal of Honor; Major General Alexander Asboth, who later became U.S. minister to Argentina; and Colonel Géza Mihalotzy, who led the Lincoln Riflemen, a noted brigade from Chicago, which included a number of Hungarians. A few Hungarians served on the Confederate side, the best known being Colonel Béla Estván of the Virginia Cavalry.

The U.S. government did not begin tracking immigration to the United States from Hungary until 1861. Even then, the figures were highly unreliable and inconsistent. In some years the figures for Hungary were not broken out but were simply included in the overall data for Austria-Hungary. The census figures for the number of foreign-born immigrants are somewhat more reliable. As of 1870, they show 3,737 foreign-born immigrants from Hungary living in the United States. The figures do not, however, show the ethnic background of the immigrants, who might have been Magyar, Slovak, Croatian, German, Jewish, or any of several other ethnic minorities then living within the borders of Hungary.

The Main Wave

The main wave of Hungarian immigration began in the 1880s. The new immigrants were quite different from their earlier counterparts. Most were poor and had little education. Many came from the land, either emigrating directly from rural areas or from cities in Hungary or elsewhere in Europe, to which they had initially gone seeking work.

Most Hungarian immigrants in this period were young, single men looking for work. Often they planned to go back to Hungary, once they had earned enough money to buy their own land. Some—perhaps 20 percent—did just that, while others went back and forth several times (which skewed the immigration statistics). But most decided to stay in America, building new lives. Though most had been farmers in Hungary, large numbers would settle in cities, where they provided labor and skills for the country's rapidly expanding industries. They began to build Hungarian communities around the nation, but especially in the industrial cities in the northeastern states. There they would be joined by relatives, friends, and others from their hometowns and regions, building classic immigrant chains.

Table 2.28: Number and Percentage of Immigrants from Hungary in Total U.S. Immigration by Decade, 1861–1996

Decade	Number of Immigrants from Hungary	Total U.S. Immigrants	Percentage of Immigrants from Hungary in Total U.S. Immigration
1861-1870	484	2,314,824	0.02
1871-1880	9,960	2,812,191	0.35
1881-1890	127,681	5,246,613	2.43
1891-1900	181,288	3,687,564	4.92
1901-1910	808,511	8,795,386	9.19
1911-1920	442,693	5,735,811	7.72
1921-1930	30,680	4,107,209	0.75
1931-1940	7,861	528,431	1.49
1941-1950	3,469	1,035,039	0.34
1951-1960	36,637	2,515,479	1.46
1961-1970	5,401	3,321,677	0.16
1971-1980	6,550	4,493,314	0.15
1981-1990	6,545	7,338,062	0.09
1991-1996	5,819	6,146,213	0.09
Total 1820-1996	**1,673,579**	**63,140,227**	**2.65**

Note: Data for Hungary not reported until 1861, and not reported separately for all years 1861–1870 and 1891–1910.

Source: Adapted from Table 2, Immigration by Region and Selected Country of Last Residence, Fiscal Years 1820–1996, from the *Statistical Yearbook of the Immigration and Naturalization Service*.

Emigration fever was often fanned by "America letters," reports about the United States written by immigrants to family and friends back in Hungary. As elsewhere in Europe, agents of shipping companies also roamed the land, praising America to drum up business. But the prosperity of many who returned, to visit or to stay, sent perhaps the strongest message to potential emigrants.

As Hungarian-American communities became more settled, more whole families emigrated, though frequently one or more males would come to America first. By 1913, on the eve of World War I, female immigrants would come to slightly outnumber males, indicating that more wives, children, and mothers were coming to join the earlier arrivals.

American statistics on Hungarian immigration were rather unreliable before World War I, not least because the data for Hungary was not always separately broken out. Even so, the figures are striking. From under 10,000 in the 1871–1880 period, the number of immigrants from Hungary jumped to more than 127,000 in the following decade. From 1901 to 1910, the number of Hungarian immigrants tallied was a phenomenal 808,511, more than 9 percent of the total U.S. immigration for the period. The peak year was 1907; in that year alone, some 185,000 came, nearly 1 percent of Hungary's population at the time.

The ethnic background of these immigrants from Hungary is less clear. In those decades, Magyar speakers made up about half of the population of Hungary. However, the percentage of Magyar speakers in the total Hungarian emigration seems to have been lower than that, possibly even as low as 30 percent. Some have suggested that this was because the Magyars were the ruling elite of the country and were somewhat less likely to grant exit permits to Magyars than to people of other ethnic groups. In all, under 4 percent of Hungary's Magyars emigrated during this great wave.

By contrast, a little over 20 percent of Hungary's Slovaks emigrated, though they made up less than 11 percent of the country's population. Other ethnic groups strongly represented in Hungary's emigration were Carpatho-Rusyns or Ruthenians

Graph 2.46: Number of Immigrants from Hungary by Decade, 1861–1996

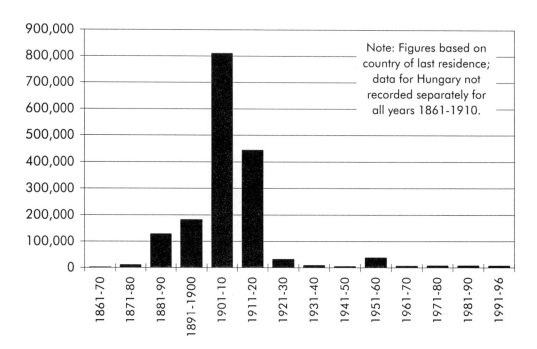

Graph 2.47: Percentage of Immigrants from Hungary in Total U.S. Immigration, 1861–1996

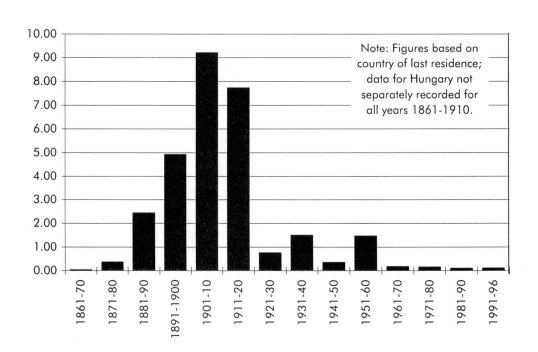

Table 2.29: Number and Percentage of Foreign-Born Immigrants from Hungary by Decade in Total U.S. Population at End of Decade, 1870–1990

Decade	Number of Foreign-Born Immigrants from Hungary	Total U.S. Population	Percentage of Foreign-Born Immigrants from Hungary in Total U.S. Population
1870	3,737	39,818,449	0.01
1880	11,526	50,155,783	0.02
1890	62,435	62,947,714	0.10
1900	145,714	75,994,575	0.19
1910	495,609	91,972,266	0.54
1920	397,283	105,710,620	0.38
1930	274,450	122,775,046	0.22
1940	(NA)	131,669,275	(NA)
1950	268,183	150,697,361	0.18
1960	245,252	179,323,175	0.14
1970	183,236	203,235,298	0.09
1980	144,368	227,726,000	0.06
1990	110,337	249,907,000	0.04

NA = Not available

Source: Adapted from Series C 228–295, Foreign-Born Population, by Country of Birth: 1850–1970, in *Historical Statistics of the United States, Colonial Times to 1970, Bicentennial Edition*, and other updating tables from the U.S. Census Bureau.

(see "Immigrants from Russia and the Commonwealth States" on p. 277), ethnic Germans, Romanians, and Jews, with smaller numbers of Serbs, Croats, Gypsies, and other groups.

Immigration to the United States from Hungary was sharply cut off after World War I began in 1914. After the United States joined the Allies in 1917, Hungarian Americans found themselves divided from their homeland, which (as Austria-Hungary) was part of the Central Alliance.

At war's end, the Austro-Hungarian Empire was dismembered. Several new independent nations were formed that included territory previously held by Hungary, including Czechoslovakia, Yugoslavia, and Romania. In all, Hungary lost more than two-thirds of its former territory and 60 percent of its population, as well as much of its natural resources. The country's ethnic composition changed as well. Some 90 percent of the country was now made up of ethnic Hungarians (Magyars), with another 6 to 8 percent of German ancestry. Of the approximately 10 million ethnic Hungarians, perhaps one third now found themselves living outside Hungary.

The new, smaller Hungary was independent for the first time in centuries. But the country, devastated by the effects of the war, was in turmoil. A democratic republic was established in 1918, but was replaced by a Communist government in 1919. This, in turn, was quickly replaced by an anti-Communist government, which instituted a "white terror" campaign of torture, imprisonment, and summary execution of leftists and political dissidents, as well as Jews.

Under these circumstances, emigration picked up again. Nearly 100,000 people fled during the white terror alone, and many of them came to the United States. But starting in 1921 the United States put restrictive immigration quotas into place, with even tighter restrictions in 1924. More Hungarians wished to enter from then on than were able to do so—though some continued to enter illegally.

The Depression that followed the Crash of 1929 was even more effective at discouraging immigration to America. During the 1930s the nature of Hungary's emigration also changed again. Many of the emigrants in this period were political refugees, fleeing Hungary's fascist Horthy government, which forged ever closer ties with Nazi Germany. Among them were some of Hungary's Jews, faced with rising anti-Semitism. U.S. immigration quotas remained in place, however, and few Hungarian Jews found refuge in the United States.

During World War II, Hungary was allied with Germany. Widely devastated, it lost an estimated 5 percent of its population during the war, which in 1941 had been approximately 9.3 million. A great many of those lost were Jews, the victims of German mass murders.

Immediately after World War II, many Hungarians fled their country, becoming displaced persons. Starting in early 1947, after the demise of the short-lived democratic Hungarian Republic (1946–1947), more Hungarians fled, to be joined by still more after Communist rule was formally established in 1949 by the founding of the Hungarian People's Republic. From 1945 to 1956, an estimated 25,000 to 27,000 Hungarian refugees entered the United States.

After the failed Hungarian Revolution of 1956, a second wave of Hungarian refugees entered the United States. Approximately 48,000 more Hungarian refugees entered the country from 1956 to 1960.

American Museum of Immigration, Statue of Liberty National Monument, National Park Service, U.S. Department of the Interior

Many immigrant groups were largely male, like these from the steamship Prinzess Irene *boarding the ferry to Ellis Island; they would often bring their families over later.*

Emigration from Communist Hungary itself remained low throughout the post–World War II period, as Hungary was a highly restricted society, from which citizens could not emigrate freely. Even though quota restrictions were lifted in 1965, immigration to the United States from Hungary continued to be low. Indeed, the government used forced emigration, or exile, as a punishment against political dissidents, some of whom found their way to the United States. After the end of Soviet control, emigration remained light, as most Hungarians were focused on building a new nation.

Overall, Hungary sent an estimated 1.7 million people to America between 1820 and 1996, or roughly 3 percent of the total immigration to the United States.

Graph 2.48: Number of Foreign-Born Immigrants from Hungary in Total U.S. Population by Decade, 1870–1990

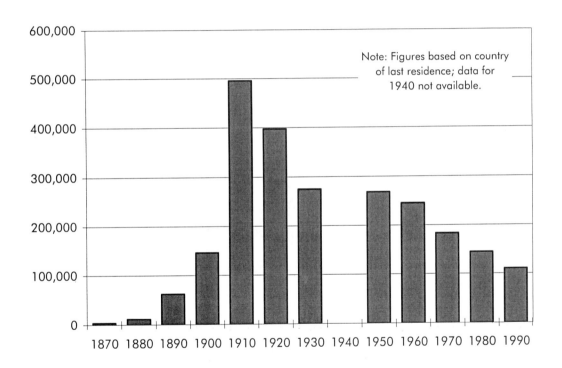

Resources

Internet Resources

Hungarian/American Friendship Society (HAFS) (*http://www.dholmes.com/hafs.html*) Web site of organization focusing on Hungarian and Slovak ancestry; provides information about translations and links. (Address: 2701 Corabel Lane #34, Sacramento, CA 95821-5233; Phone: 916-489-9599; E-mail: HAFS@dholmes.com)

Cyndi's List—Eastern Europe (*http://www.cyndislist.com/easteuro.htm*) List of on-line genealogical resources for eastern Europe, including Hungary, maintained by genealogical author Cyndi Howells.

Print Resources

The Hazardous Quest: Hungarian Immigrants in the United States, 1895–1920: A Documentary. Budapest, Hungary: Corvina, 1993. Edited and translated by Albert Tezla.

Hungary: A Country Study. 2d ed. Stephen R. Burant, ed. Washington, D.C.: Federal Research Division, Library of Congress, 1990. (Available on-line at *http://lcweb2.loc.gov/frd/cs*)

Perlman, Robert. *Bridging Three Worlds: Hungarian-Jewish Americans, 1848–1914*. Amherst: University of Massachusetts Press, 1991.

Puskas, Julianna. *Ties That Bind, Ties That Divide: 100 Years of Hungarian Experience in the United States*. New York: Holmes & Meir, 1997.

Suess, Jared H. *Handy Guide to Hungarian Genealogical Records*. Logan, Utah: Everton Publishers, 1980.

Vardy, Steven Bela. *The Hungarian-Americans*. Boston: Twayne, 1985.

———. *The Hungarian Americans: The Hungarian Experience in North America*. New York: Chelsea House, 1990.

For more resources, see "General European Immigration Resources" on p. 317.

Immigrants from Poland

Polish immigrants have played a role in American life since the days of the Jamestown settlements, in the early 17th century. However, for much of the past three centuries, Poland itself was ruled by others, and for long periods it was effectively wiped from the map.

Polish Background

The history of Poland traditionally has been dated back to 966, when the country's ruler converted to Christianity. Poland's greatest days were from the 14th to the 16th century, but by the end of the 17th century it had become weakened by internal struggles and Europe's wider political battles. Largely controlled by Russia from 1700 on, the country lost major portions of its territory to Russia, Austria, and Prussia in 1772–73, in the First Partition. It lost still more territory in the Second Partition of 1792 and then was completely divided by the three countries in the Third Partition of 1795. The country would not be even nominally independent again until the 20th century, and then it was dominated by Russia (and the Soviet Union) for most of the century, until 1989.

During the years of foreign rule, Poles continued to hold to their own language and culture, despite active campaigns to repress them, especially in areas under German and Russian influence. German and Russian settlers were often moved into these areas, to provide support for the occupying powers. In some times and places education in Polish was banned and Polish books had to be hidden and read in secret.

The troubled and tangled history of Poland means that its emigration and immigration figures are more than usually misleading and unreliable. The borders of the country have shifted markedly in the past two centuries, and some population shifts have involved hundreds of thousands of people. Many who spoke Polish and regarded themselves as Polish were counted, on arriving in America, as coming from Austria, Germany, or Russia. On the other hand, many who were counted as coming from Poland did not regard themselves as Polish; they included German and Russian colonists, Jews, Lithuanians, Gypsies, Ukrainians, and other ethnic minorities from the region.

Many early Polish immigrants came to America as a result of their country's struggles for independence. The main wave

Authors' Archives

The first certain Polish immigrants to North America were timberworkers imported in 1608 to Jamestown, Virginia, shown here in a drawing based on a 1622 print.

of Polish immigrants, who came more often for economic reasons, began to arrive in the late 19th and early 20th centuries. They formed a major part of what historians call the "new immigration," primarily of poor people from southern and eastern Europe.

Early Immigrants

Some historians have suggested that one or more Poles came to America with Columbus or even earlier with the Vikings. However, the first certain Polish immigrants in America were timberworkers imported to Jamestown, Virginia, in 1608, a year after the colony's establishment. Few others followed in the late 17th and early 18th centuries.

Starting in the 1770s, Polish revolutionaries fought to regain their independence from foreign rulers; many also wanted to establish a more democratic society, inspired by the American and French Revolutions. Many of these revolutionaries were forced into exile, often to France, and some found their way to America. Among these were two recruited in Paris by Benjamin Franklin: Tadeusz Kosciuszko (actually of Lithuanian ancestry) and Count Casimir Pulaski. Kosciuszko, an expert in military fortification, helped supervise the building of West Point and became a brigadier general with the Americans in the Revolutionary War, before returning to lead Polish revolutionaries. Pulaski organized and led an American cavalry and light infantry corps known as Pulaski's Legion, and later led French and American cavalry troops at Savannah, Georgia, where he was killed.

A larger group of Polish revolutionaries came to America following the failure of the November Uprising of 1830–31, which had been sparked by cadets from the Warsaw Military Academy. Forced to leave their temporary haven in Austria, 234 of them chose to come to America, and nearly 200 more would follow. The exiles had considerable American support for their cause, but that did not translate readily into material help and their hope of establishing a unified Polish community failed. Some returned to Europe, but about a third of them settled in New York, while the rest were scattered from Boston to Washington, D.C., and westward as far as Illinois.

Most of these revolutionary immigrants had been people of education and social standing in Poland. Many had to work as manual laborers at first, but as soon as they learned English most were able to put their education and skills to use in America. In particular, they were employed in the military, in business or agriculture, in surveying and mapmaking, or as teachers, especially of drawing, dancing, fencing, music, and languages.

Poles were sharply divided about whether or not these exiles should settle in America. Many felt that their emigration was costing the Polish revolution some of its natural leaders. Bertold Wiercinski, one who returned to Europe, put it this way in his *Kronika Emigracji (Emigration Chronicle)*: "Every Pole going to the United States sins not only against himself but against his obligations to his fatherland." However, many Poles decided to stay in America, putting Europe's battles behind them, though often continuing to support the revolutionaries from afar. At least 50 Poles settled in New Orleans, partly because they were familiar with French, then the prime language of culture in Europe. Some of these newcomers were associated with Polish emigration groups in Europe, most notably Zjednoczenie Emigracji Polskiej (United Polish Emigration), which also had an American branch.

Revolutionary exiles tended to split into factions, which would weaken their communities in both Europe and America. However, these emigrés provided a chain of contacts and support for later immigrants. These included several hundred more Polish revolutionaries, who came after the failure of revolts in the Austrian- and Prussian-held parts of Poland in 1846.

Poland was largely Roman Catholic, and that connection brought the first large group of poor Polish immigrants to the United States. Polish-born priest Leopold Moczygeba was sent to work with German settlers near Galveston, Texas. In what became a classic immigrant pattern, he wrote many letters to family and friends in Poland about his new life. These writings, popularly called "America letters," sparked some 800 Poles, in approximately 100 fam-

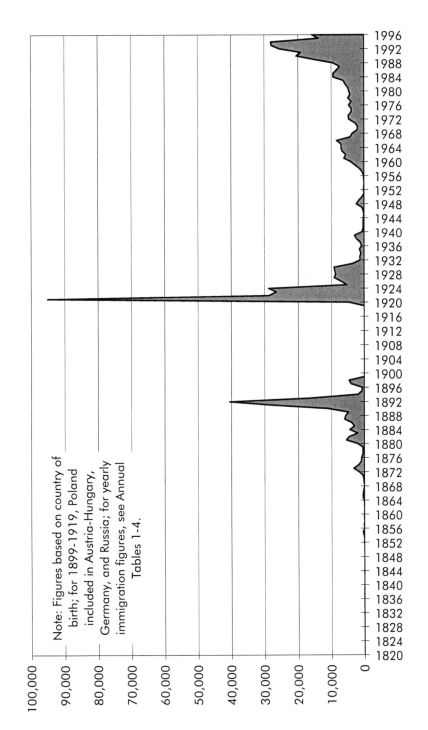

Graph 2.49: Number of Immigrants from Poland Annually, 1820–1996

Note: Figures based on country of birth; for 1899-1919, Poland included in Austria-Hungary, Germany, and Russia; for yearly immigration figures, see Annual Tables 1-4.

ilies, to settle in Panna Marya, Texas, in 1854. They found the life harder than he had described, but they succeeded in establishing the first substantial permanent Polish settlement in America.

As noted above, official figures for Polish immigration are notoriously unreliable. The U.S. Census Bureau's estimates of foreign-born immigrants suffered from the same problems, but may be somewhat more reliable. As of 1860, the census figures showed nearly 7,300 Polish-born immigrants, a figure that would nearly double by 1870.

The 1860s were a difficult time for Poles in both Europe and America. In the United States, the Civil War split the country—including Polish Americans. Though some were against slavery and supported the Union side, others—especially those in New Orleans and Texas—supported the South. Then in 1863 a new Polish revolt, the January Insurrection, began in Russian-held Poland. This again split the Polish-American community, as some went back to fight for Polish freedom while others remained in the United States. A further complication was that Russia, against

which the revolutionaries were fighting, was one of the Union's few European allies. In the end the Polish revolt failed, ending that country's major 19th-century revolutionary efforts. Poles in America increasingly turned to establishing their lives in their new homeland.

The Main Wave

From the late 1860s, the nature of Polish emigration changed. Increasingly emigrants left for economic, rather than political, reasons. That would remain the case during the main wave of Polish immigration of the late 19th and early 20th centuries.

Poles in Europe faced a rapidly changing world in this period. After the failure of the 1863 revolt, Russia freed the serfs (which had been a key aim of the revolutionaries) and allowed some measure of local self-rule in Russian-held Poland. However, it also began an active campaign of Russification, gradually eliminating Russian Poland as a separate political entity. The Russian government also

Graph 2.50: Number of Immigrants from Poland by Decade, 1820–1996

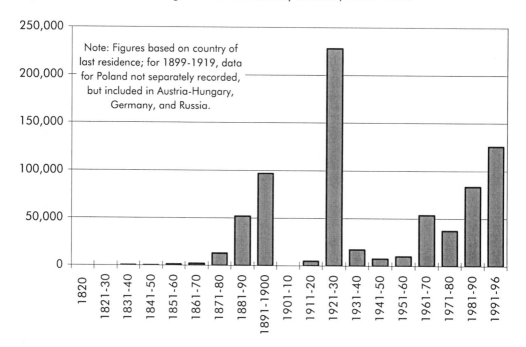

Note: Figures based on country of last residence; for 1899-1919, data for Poland not separately recorded, but included in Austria-Hungary, Germany, and Russia.

banned Polish in the schools, tried to limit the power of Polish priests, and sought to repress Polish culture in general.

The German empire, newly formed in 1871, also sought to totally absorb its Polish territories. Actively attacking Polish Catholicism, the Germans sought to replace Polish priests with German ones and to end the church's dominance of Polish education. They banned solely Polish papers, requiring that they be bilingual, and required the use of German, rather than Polish, place-names. Polish priests were forbidden to engage in political activities and were jailed for disobedience.

In the Austrian-held portion of Poland, known as Galicia, Poles were not subject to the same religious or cultural persecution. The region also retained some political autonomy within what was then called Austria-Hungary.

Underneath all this was the pressure of rapidly rising population, which was felt in Poland, as all across Europe. With families too large to be supported by small farms, and with many farm laborers thrown off the land, many Poles left home in search of work, part of the wider European move-ment from the country to the cities. Since the cities in central and eastern Europe could not support them all, many made their way to the United States, which sought workers to build its rapidly growing economy.

In the 1870s, the main Polish emigra-tion came from German-held areas, most notably Poznania, Silesia, and East and West Prussia. These regions had experi-enced economic decline, with increasing amounts of land and resources being taken out of Polish hands, and heavy population growth. Accurate figures are virtually impossible, but some estimate that as many as 150,000 Poles emigrated from this region to the United States in this period.

Followed by many more in succeeding decades, these immigrants would form the core of the Polish communities in major American cities, such as New York and Chicago. Partly because of their experi-ences with German religious persecution, these Polish immigrants held tightly to their Polish Catholic clergy and their paro-chial schools, which were often taught in Polish. This helped them keep the Polish communities distinct, but it also kept them

Graph 2.51: Percentage of Immigrants from Poland in Total U.S. Immigration, 1820–1996

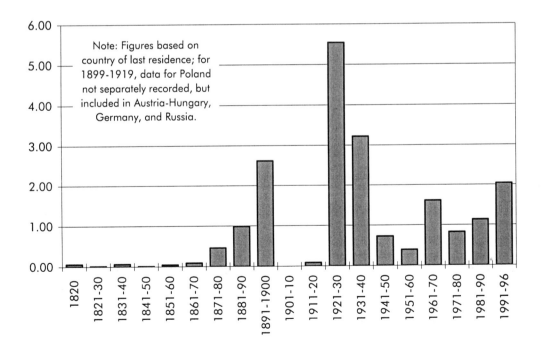

Note: Figures based on country of last residence; for 1899-1919, data for Poland not separately recorded, but included in Austria-Hungary, Germany, and Russia.

from fully integrating into American society for several generations. In all, between 1840 and 1910, an estimated 1 million to 1.5 million Poles immigrated to the United States from German Poland alone.

Emigration from Russian-held Poland was spurred partly by economic troubles, especially in the northern provinces. Approximately 40,000 Poles are estimated to have emigrated from there in the 1880s and another 134,000 in the 1890s.

Poles in Galicia were not actively persecuted by the Austrian government. However, the area was extremely poor and becoming more so with the rise in population. These conditions spurred the immigration of an estimated 82,000 Poles to the United States in the 1880s and some 340,000 in the 1890s.

In the early part of this main wave of immigration, starting in the 1870s, many Polish immigrants were young single males. Often they planned to work in the United States for a few years and then go home to buy property with their earnings. Some did just that, but an estimated three-quarters of them ended up staying in the United States.

While the majority came from German Poland in the 1870s, by the end of the century less than 5 percent of the Polish immigrants were from that region. The rest were roughly split between Russian Poland and Galicia, though emigration from Russian areas continued to increase, reaching nearly two-thirds of the total by 1913, on the eve of World War I.

World War I, a major disaster for Europe, found Poles fighting on both sides, as Russia was an ally of Britain and France against the Central Powers, led by Austria and Germany. Much of the war on the Eastern Front was fought on Polish soil, and Polish lands were also devastated by scorched-earth policies. Hundreds of thousands of refugees fled Poland.

Table 2.30: Number and Percentage of Foreign-Born Immigrants from Poland by Decade in Total U.S. Population at End of Decade, 1860–1990

Decade	Number of Foreign-Born Immigrants from Poland	Total U.S. Population	Percentage of Foreign-Born Immigrants from Poland in Total U.S. Population
1860	7,298	31,443,321	0.02
1870	14,436	39,818,449	0.04
1880	48,557	50,155,783	0.10
1890	147,440	62,947,714	0.23
1900	383,407	75,994,575	0.50
1910	937,884	91,972,266	1.02
1920	1,139,979	105,710,620	1.08
1930	1,268,583	122,775,046	1.03
1940	(NA)	131,669,275	(NA)
1950	861,655	150,697,361	0.57
1960	747,750	179,323,175	0.42
1970	548,107	203,235,298	0.27
1980	418,128	227,726,000	0.18
1990	388,328	249,907,000	0.16

NA = Not available

Note: 1910 figures are for Polish-speakers born in Austria, Germany, and Russia.

Source: Adapted from Series C 228–295, Foreign-Born Population, by Country of Birth: 1850–1970, in *Historical Statistics of the United States, Colonial Times to 1970, Bicentennial Edition*, and other updating tables from the U.S. Census Bureau.

Immigration History Research Center, University of Minnesota

Some immigrants returned home with the money they made in America. This Polish farmer has built a large new house (left), across from his old one.

In 1918, Bolshevik Russia withdrew from World War I. After German and Austrian defeat, a new Polish republic was established and immediately tried to regain traditional Polish territories from Russian control. However, when the Russo-Polish War ended in 1921, many of these territories remained in Russian hands. Poland's borders were shifted to the west to include territories from defeated Germany. These major border changes spurred massive population shifts, involving some hundreds of thousands of Poles, Germans, Ukrainians, and other minorities. Even so, nearly one-third of the population of the new Poland was composed of non-Polish minorities, including many Jews.

Though Poland was once again free and independent, the land was still greatly troubled. In addition to the devastation and the many refugees, the government of the new republic, modeled on France, was unstable and ineffectual. In the decade following independence, more than 200,000 Poles came to the United States, forming more than five percent of the total immigration from 1921 to 1930. Most of these

came before the drastic immigration cuts established by the 1921 and 1924 Immigration Acts.

Many of these new immigrants were coming to join relatives in established Polish-American communities. Indeed, some of those relatives had originally intended to return home; unable to do so because of the war, they had instead made new lives in America.

Later Immigration

Although the 1921 and 1924 Immigration Acts sharply cut immigration to the United States from Poland, as from many other parts of Europe (see "Immigration Restrictions" on p. 47), the Great Depression of the 1930s slowed immigration even more. The number of immigrants from Poland dropped below 20,000 from 1931 to 1940, as Europe moved toward World War II.

That second world war brought even more devastation to Poland. The conflict was formally triggered when Germany invaded Poland in September 1939. The

American Institute of Physics Emilio Segrè Visual Archives, Physics Today Collection

Many highly talented scientists arrived in the United States in the 1930s, including Polish physicist Maria Goeppert-Mayer (left foreground), who later won a Nobel Prize, and Italian physicist Enrico Fermi (center).

country was rapidly and crushingly defeated and then divided between Germany and the Soviet Union.

The Germans made their portion of Poland the site of numerous concentration camps, in which millions of people were killed, especially Jews, many of them from Poland itself. More than 2 million Poles were put into forced labor camps. Going beyond occupation, Germany also brought in large numbers of German settlers, attempting to wipe out Poland and incorporate it into Germany.

The Soviet Union, too, moved large numbers of Poles into forced labor camps, perhaps as many as 1.5 million. They also murdered many Polish prisoners of war, most notably some 4,000 military officers killed in Katyn Forest in 1940. Then in 1941 Germany invaded the Soviet Union, establishing an even more savage occupation. Poles resisted; some fought with the Soviets against Germany on the Eastern Front, while others joined with the western Allies, making a key contribution by capturing Germany's top-secret coding machine, Enigma. Poland was finally freed by Soviet troops.

By the end of the war in 1945, the Germans had killed nearly all the Jews in Poland, an estimated 3 million of them. Another 3 million Poles died in battle and under the occupation. That was a loss of perhaps 17 percent of Poland's total population, which had been approximately 35 million in 1939.

After the war, Poland's borders were again shifted to the west, with eastern regions being incorporated into the Soviet Union and western regions added from defeated Germany. Again, this was accompanied by massive population shifts. Some 3 million Poles moved out of territories taken by the Soviet Union. Many of these were settled in newly acquired western lands, while some 2 million Germans moved over the border into Germany. Large numbers of non-Polish ethnic minorities remained in the eastern territories taken by the Soviet Union (which in the 1990s would become part of Ukraine and Belarus). The result of these shifts and the war losses combined to radically change the ethnic makeup of Poland, which became more than 98 percent ethnically Polish and more than 90 percent Catholic.

Graph 2.52: Number of Foreign-Born Immigrants from Poland in Total U.S. Population by Decade, 1860–1990

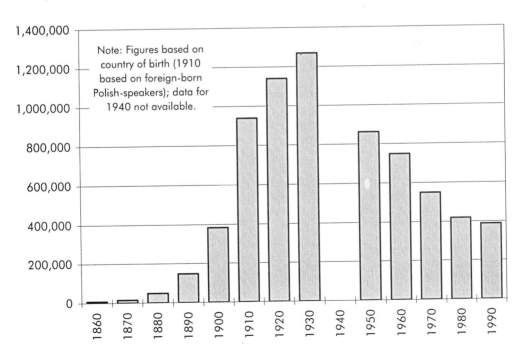

Note: Figures based on country of birth (1910 based on foreign-born Polish-speakers); data for 1940 not available.

Poland again effectively lost its independence, falling under the domination of the Soviet Union.

During and after the war, thousands of people left Poland for the United States. Many of the refugees early in the war were well-educated professionals, though some were briefly confined to low-level work until they learned English. In 1942, refugee scholars such as anthropologist Bronislaw Malinowski and sociologist Feliks Gross formed the Polish Institute of Arts and Sciences in America, an American branch of the Polish Academy, which would become a notable force in Polish-American intellectual life.

At war's end, hundreds of thousands of Poles were gathered in refugee camps in western Europe. More than 700,000 of them were forced to return to Soviet-controlled Poland against their will. However, after intensive lobbying by Polish Americans, the U.S. Congress finally passed the Displaced Persons Act of 1948, to allow immigration of some refugees from now-Communist areas of central and eastern Europe. In addition, a 1950 law allowed for immigration of veterans of the Polish army. Aside from this, the annual quota of Polish immigrants allowed was, in this period, only a little over 6,500. This period also saw a high proportion of well-educated immigrants, with less than one in five being unskilled. These were almost all permanent immigrants, with no notion of returning to Poland later in their lives.

Under Soviet control, Poland began to make the difficult transition from a largely rural society to a modern industrial one, in the process ending the traditional land-holding aristocracy. The country was at first kept tightly controlled, and the number of Polish immigrants coming to America was small. That began to change in the late 1960s, when Poland began to be affected by the widespread movement for social and economic reform, which in Europe was labeled the Prague Spring because of its roots in Czechoslovakia.

Through the 1970s, many Poles worked to reform and free their country. These movements led to some easing of repression by the Soviet Union and to the formation of the reform group Solidarity in 1980,

led by Lech Walesa. By 1989, Polish reformers had won legal recognition of Solidarity, which in free elections went on to defeat the Communists and win control of Poland. The Soviet Union was forced to accept the loss of Poland, which led the way for other central and eastern European countries to throw off Communist rule.

During these turbulent events, as restrictions eased, the number of Polish emigrants began to increase again. According to official records, more than 83,000 Poles arrived in America from 1981 to 1990, while another 125,000 arrived in just the six years from 1991 to 1996.

But even these figures do not tell the whole story, for tens of thousands more came to America as illegal immigrants. Immigration experts estimate that, as of 1996, there were approximately 70,000 illegal Polish immigrants in the United States (see "Appendix C: Estimates of Emigration and Illegals" on p. 749). In official parlance, they are called *overstays*, people who enter the country legally as temporary visitors and then simply stay, sometimes permanently.

Many of these later Polish immigrants were far better educated than their predecessors, for Poland by 1990 had a literacy rate of 98 percent and nearly one in five Poles had some college training. Many of them were young people, for more than 60 percent of Poland's population was under 40, the result of one of the highest birth rates in Europe—itself the result of Poland's staunch Catholicism.

From 1820, when the United States first began tracking immigration, official records tally more than 731,000 legal immigrants from Poland, or a little over 1 percent of the total U.S. immigration from 1820 to 1996. That number is far too small, but more accurate figures are hard to come by. The U.S. Census Bureau began tracking foreign-born immigrants in 1850. Their figures show more than 1.2 million foreign-born Polish Americans at its peak in 1930. Estimates of the total number of Polish immigrants go as high as 2 million, while the number of Americans with Polish ancestry has been variously estimated at 6 million to 10 million.

National Archives, Farm Security Administration; Photo: Jack Delano

Many Poles settled in Pennsylvania, like this family living in Mauch Chunk in 1940.

Resources

Internet Resources

Polish Genealogical Society of America (PGSA) (*http://www.pgsa.org*) Web site offers information on ships and immigration, maps, history, and heraldry, as well as resource centers and links, including searchable databases. (Address: 984 North Milwaukee Avenue, Chicago, IL 60622)

Polish American Association (*http://www.polish.org*) Provides information about immigration, genealogy, resources, cultural services. (Address: 3834 North Cicero Avenue, Chicago, IL 60641; Telephone: 773-282-8206; Fax: 773-282-1324)

American Polish Institute (*http://www.ampolinstitute.org*) Provides information on Polish history and links to other Web sites about Polish culture. (Address: The American Institute of Polish Culture, Inc., 1440 79th Street Causeway, Suite 117, Miami, FL 33141; Telephone: 305-864-2349; Fax: 305-865-5150; E-mail: info@ampolinstitute.org)

Kosciuszko Foundation (*http://www.kosciuszkofoundation.org*) Promotes increased understanding of Polish culture in America and cultural exchanges between the United States and Poland. (Address: 15 East 65th St., New York, NY 10021-6595; Telephone: 212-734-2130; Fax: 212-628-4552; E-mail: thekf@pegasusnet.com)

PolandGenWeb (*http://www.rootsweb.com/%7Epolwgw/polandgen.html*) Part of the WorldGenWeb project, linking genealogical research sites around the world, by region, with information provided overall and by region; provides useful directories, including lists of translations and changes in geographical names and historical maps, along with mailing lists and query boards, and links to related sites.

Federation of Eastern European Family History Societies (FEEFHS) (*http://www.feefhs.org*) Web site offers searchable index, resource guide, Internet journal, research notes, links to professional databases, map indexes, and specialist cross-indexes for individual ethnic groups. (Address: P. O. Box 510898, Salt Lake City, UT 84151-0898)

Cyndi's List—Poland / Polska (*http://www.cyndislist.com/poland.htm*) List of on-line genealogical resources for Poland, maintained by genealogical author Cyndi Howells.

Carpatho-Rusyn Genealogy Web Site Home Page (*http://www.rusyn.com*) Web site focusing on immigration and genealogy of people of Carpatho-Rusyn ancestry, who came from the region "primarily where Poland, Slovakia, the Ukraine, and Hungary adjoin or nearly adjoin"; offers searchable name lists, maps, photographs, links, information about villages and genealogy, and other information.

Carpatho-Rusyn Knowledge Base (*http://www.carpatho-rusyn.org*) Web site offering a wide range of information and resources relating to Carpatho-Rusyn ancestry and immigration, including maps, name lists, village information, photographs, tips on genealogy, and related links.

Carpathian Connection (*http://www.tccweb.org*) Web site focused on people from "former Carpathian territories or of Carpathian-Rusyn heritage," offering general historical and cultural information, information about notable settlements in eastern Europe, including Slovakia, and the United States, tips on researching family history, and related links.

Print Resources

General Works

Dolan, Sean. *The Polish Americans*. New York: Chelsea House, 1997.

Gabor, Al. *Polish Americans*. New York: Marshall Cavendish, 1995.

Kruszka, Waclaw. *A History of the Poles in America to 1908*. Washington, D.C.: Catholic University of America Press, 1993.

Kuniczak, W. S. *My Name Is Million: An Illustrated History of the Poles in America*. Garden City, N.Y.: Doubleday, 1978.

Lopata, Helena Znaniecka. *Polish Americans*. 2d ed. New Brunswick, N.J.: Transaction, 1994.

Poland: A Country Study. 3d ed. Glenn E. Curtis, ed. Washington, D.C.: Federal Research Division, Library of Congress, 1994. (Available on-line at *http://lcweb2.loc.gov/frd/cs*)

Pula, James S. *Polish Americans: An Ethnic Community*. New York: Twayne, 1995.

Toor, Rachel. *The Polish Americans*. New York: Chelsea House, 1988.

Wytrwal, Joseph Anthony. *The Polish-Americans*. Detroit: Endurance Press, 1977.

Genealogical Works

Moscinski, Sharon. *Tracing Our Polish Roots*. Santa Fe, N.M.: John Muir, 1994.

Rollyson, Carl Sokolnicki. *A Student's Guide to Polish American Genealogy*. Phoenix: Oryx, 1996.

Wellauer, Maralyn A. *Tracing Your Polish Roots*. Milwaukee: M. A. Wellauer, 1991.

For more resources, see "General European Immigration Resources" on p. 317.

Immigrants from the

Czech Republic and Slovakia

The Czech Republic and Slovakia are two of the newest nations in the world, having been formed only at the beginning of 1993. Even their previous joint nation of Czecho-slovakia had had a rather brief life. It came into existence in 1918, after the end of World War I, and during much of the 20th century it was under either German or Soviet occupation or control.

However, the histories of the Czechs and Slovaks reach back into the Middle Ages. Both are from the western branch of the Slavic peoples, originally from Central Asia, who arrived in Central Europe in the fifth century. Buffeted by other European invaders for some centuries, the Czechs founded the Moravian empire early in the ninth century, soon after that converting to Christianity. The Moravian empire was ended late in that century by invasions of Magyars (ethnic Hungarians). Some

Czechs migrated a little westward to found the Bohemian empire in about 900, which soon fell under German domination. The rest of the Czechs and most of the Slovaks and other groups in the region stayed in what became the kingdom of Hungary. They would remain largely under Hungarian control until the 20th century. From the 16th century on, this meant that they—and also Bohemia—were effectively controlled by the Hapsburg Empire, which in 1867 became the Austro-Hungarian Empire.

As a result, before 1920 immigrants from what became Czechoslovakia were counted in U.S. immigration records as coming from Austria-Hungary (see "Immigrants from Austria" on p. 195, and "Immigrants from Hungary" on p. 229). We have little good information about how many of them were Czechs, Slovaks, or of other eth-

Table 2.31: Number and Percentage of Immigrants from the Czech Republic and Slovakia (Former Czechoslovakia) in Total U.S. Immigration by Decade, 1920–1996

Decade	Number of Immigrants from the Czech Republic and Slovakia (Former Czechoslovakia)	Total U.S. Immigrants	Percentage of Immigrants from the Czech Republic and Slovakia (Former Czechoslovakia) in Total U.S. Immigration
1920	3,426	5,735,811	0.06
1921-1930	102,194	4,107,209	2.49
1931-1940	14,393	528,431	2.72
1941-1950	8,347	1,035,039	0.81
1951-1960	918	2,515,479	0.04
1961-1970	3,273	3,321,677	0.10
1971-1980	6,023	4,493,314	0.13
1981-1990	7,227	7,338,062	0.10
1991-1996	1,499	6,146,213	0.02
Total 1820-1996	151,207	63,140,227	0.24

Note: Separate data not available for Czechoslovakia until 1920.

Source: Adapted from Table 2, Immigration by Region and Selected Country of Last Residence, Fiscal Years 1820–1996, from the *Statistical Yearbook of the Immigration and Naturalization Service*, 1996.

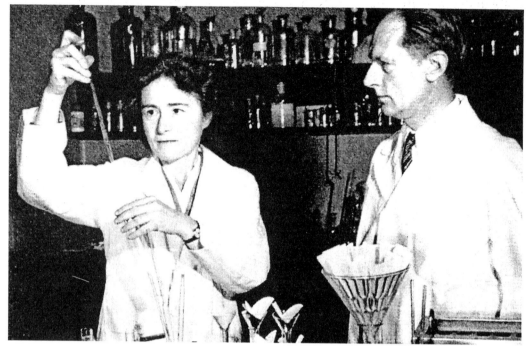

Library of Congress

Gerty Radnitz Cori (left) and Carl Ferdinand Cori, Czech immigrants to the United States in 1922, shared the 1947 Nobel Prize for physiology with Argentine biochemist Bernardo Houssay.

nic groups. Some researchers have used other records, including European statistical archives, to gauge the number of immigrants. They estimate that between 1850 and 1950, more than 393,000 Czechs came to the United States. Figures for Slovak immigration are spongier, but are estimated at approximately 500,000 in the late 19th and early 20th centuries. Many of these came from beyond the borders of what is now Slovakia.

Czechs began emigrating to North America quite early, primarily as religious refugees. Many Czechs in the 17th century were Protestants. They had developed a religious reform movement, led by the martyred Jan Hus, more than a century before Martin Luther sparked the Reformation. However, during the Counter-Reformation, the strongly Catholic Hapsburgs launched a major assault on Czech Protestants, closing churches and defeating their supporters at the Battle of White Mountain in 1620. After that, an estimated 36,000 Czech families emigrated to Protestant countries, including many of the most educated and cultured people of the region.

Some of these Czech Protestant refugees arrived in America with Dutch and Swedish colonists. The first Czech recorded was Augustine Herman, who came to the colony of New Amsterdam in 1633, later settling in Maryland. Others followed, with many of them joining German Protestants in Moravian settlements, such as that at Bethlehem, Pennsylvania (see "Immigrants from Germany" on p. 135). They were joined in the mid-19th century by Czech political refugees fleeing Europe after the failure of the 1848 revolutions. They would lay the basis for later Czech immigration.

The Slovak immigration began somewhat later, in the late 19th century. Slovak immigrants were generally poorer and less well educated than the Czech immigrants of the time. Part of what historians call the "new immigration," the Slovaks generally emigrated for the classic economic reasons of the day. Their region was experiencing an enormous population increase, while farms—frequently subdivided among heirs in a family—were too small to support families depending on them and were also

Table 2.32: Number and Percentage of Foreign-Born Immigrants from the Czech Republic and Slovakia (Former Czechoslovakia) by Decade in Total U.S. Population at End of Decade, 1920–1990

Decade	Number of Foreign-Born Immigrants from the Czech Republic and Slovakia (Former Czechoslovakia)	Total U.S. Population	Percentage of Foreign-Born Immigrants from the Czech Republic and Slovakia (Former Czechoslovakia) in Total U.S. Population
1920	362,438	105,710,620	0.34
1930	491,638	122,775,046	0.40
1940	(NA)	131,669,275	(NA)
1950	278,438	150,697,361	0.18
1960	227,618	179,323,175	0.13
1970	160,899	203,235,298	0.08
1980	112,707	227,726,000	0.05
1990	87,020	249,907,000	0.03

NA = Not available

Source: Adapted from Series C 228–295, Foreign-Born Population, by Country of Birth 1850–1970, in *Historical Statistics of the United States, Colonial Times to 1970, Bicentennial Edition*, and other updating tables from the U.S. Census Bureau.

unable to compete with larger farms, such as those in America and Russia. As was happening all across Europe, Slovaks left the land seeking work, often going first to the cities of their region, and then finding their way to America, where many of them settled in industrial cities needing their labor. By the late 19th century, shipping agents were also actively soliciting their business.

This main wave of immigration lasted until the start of World War I. Slovak immigration peaked in 1905, with an estimated 50,000 immigrants, while the much smaller Czech peak was in 1907, at more than 13,500. In these years, many young men emigrated to avoid military service in the Austro-Hungarian army, as rumbles of war spread across Europe. When war came in 1914, some refused to fight in a conflict not of their desire or making. Some revolutionaries were arrested, while others fled to France and elsewhere. There they helped shape plans for the new country of Czechoslovakia, created in 1919.

Fewer Czechs and Slovaks emigrated in the years after the war, partly because their country was independent for the first time in centuries. However, for many poor people, the situation was no better. Many of these came over in the early 1920s, before U.S. immigration quotas went into effect in 1921 and were then set even lower in 1924, sharply restricting their numbers.

The Depression of the 1930s slowed immigration to the United States from around the world, including Czechoslovakia. Of the relatively small number of immigrants arriving in that period, many were Jews seeking refuge from the anti-Semitism raging in Hitler's Germany and beyond. Their fears were well founded. In a futile effort to avoid war, Britain and France agreed not to contest Hitler's claim to Czechoslovakia, and in 1939 German troops marched into the country, making it a "protectorate." During the war that followed, at least 250,000 to 350,000 of Czechoslovakia's population died.

Graph 2.53: Number of Immigrants from the Czech Republic and Slovakia (Former Czechoslovakia) by Decade, 1920–1996

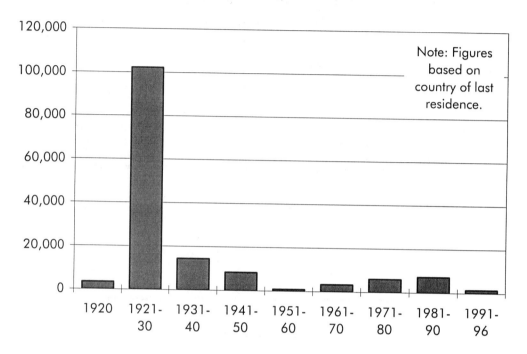

Graph 2.54: Number of Foreign-Born Immigrants from the Czech Republic and Slovakia (Former Czechoslovakia) in Total U.S. Population by Decade, 1920–1990

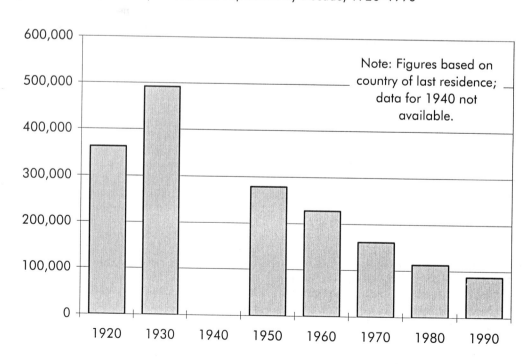

At war's end, Soviet troops from the east and Allied troops from the west joined in freeing Czechoslovakia from German control, but the country soon fell under Soviet domination, with the Communists taking full control in 1948. A new wave of Czech and Slovak immigration to America resulted, primarily of well-educated, highly skilled political refugees.

Czechoslovakia became a tightly restricted society, from which people could not travel freely. In the following years, the relatively small number of emigrants included some political dissidents who were forced to leave the country and were stripped of their passports. This was especially true after 1968, when Czechoslovakian attempts at liberal reform, called the Prague Spring, were ended by the arrival of Soviet troops. The country then was even more tightly controlled.

However, liberalization gradually came all across Communist eastern Europe. In 1989, in an extraordinarily peaceful movement called the Velvet Revolution, Czechs and Slovaks eased the Communists out of office—without a Soviet military reaction—and established a freely elected democratic government, headed by longtime Slovak leader Alexander Dubcek and leading Czech dissident Václav Havel. The new country lasted only until 1993, when the Slovaks initiated the separation of their region as independent Slovakia. Throughout this period, emigration remained relatively low, as many Czechs and Slovaks chose to stay and build their lives in their newly free countries.

American Museum of Immigration, Statue of Liberty National Monument, National Park Service, U.S. Department of the
Interior; Photo: Lewis W. Hine

Among Lewis Hine's many photographs of immigrants was this one of a Slovak woman at Ellis Island in 1905.

Resources

Internet Resources

CzechGenWeb (*http://
www.rootsweb.com/~czewgw/*) Part of
the WorldGenWeb project, linking
genealogical research sites around the
world, by region, providing information
by states or provinces within the Czech
Republic.

Slovak Republic GenWeb (*http://
www.rootsweb.com/~svkwgw/*) Part of
the WorldGenWeb project, linking
genealogical research sites around the
world, by region, providing information
by provinces or cities; provides help on
research and links to related sites.

Cyndi's List—Eastern Europe (*http://
www.cyndislist.com/easteuro.htm*) List
of on-line genealogical resources for
central and eastern Europe, including
the Czech Republic and Slovakia,
maintained by genealogical author
Cyndi Howells.

Eastern Slovakia, Slovak and Carpatho-
Rusyn Genealogy Research (*http://
www.iarelative.com/slovakia.htm*) Web
site offering tips, resources, and links
for people seeking to research ancestry
in these areas.

Czech Republic, Bohemia, and Moravia
Genealogy Research (*http://
www.iarelative.com/czech*) Web site
offering tools, tips, resources,
information, and links related to
researching Czech ancestry.

Slovak & Ruysn Roots; Getting Started—
Hudick's Home Page (*http://
dcn.davis.ca.us/go/feefhs/socslav/
hudick1.html*) On-line guide to
genealogical research, with links to
related U.S. family history societies.

Hungarian/American Friendship Society
(HAFS) (*http://www.dholmes.com/
hafs.html*) Web site of organization
focusing on Hungarian and Slovak
ancestry; provides information about
translations and links. (Address: 2701
Corabel Lane #34, Sacramento, CA
95821-5233; Phone: 916-489-9599; E-
mail: HAFS@dholmes.com)

Slovak Surname Location Reference
Project (SLRP) (*http://feefhs.org/
slovak/frg-slrp.html*) Web site offering
a database of Slovak immigrants to the
United States, including where they
settled, and related links. (Address: P.
O. Box 31831, Cleveland, OH 44131-
0831; Phone: 216-524-3037; Fax: 216-
642-8954; E-mail:
110066.1473@compuserve.com)

Print Resources

Chada, Joseph. *The Czechs in the United
States.* Washington, D.C.: SVU Press,
1981.

Czechoslovakia: A Country Study. 3d ed.
Ihor Gawdiak, ed. Washington, D.C.:
Federal Research Division, Library of
Congress, 1989. (Available on-line at
http://lcweb2.loc.gov/frd/cs)

Habenicht, Jan. *History of Czechs in
America.* St. Paul: Czechoslovak
Genealogical Society International,
1996.

Hudak, Andrew F., Jr. *Slovaks in Florida.*
Winter Park, Fla.: Agency DaVel, 1991.

Laska, Vera, ed. *The Czechs in America,
1633–1977: A Chronology and Fact
Book.* Dobbs Ferry, N.Y.: Oceana, 1978.

*Panorama: A Historical Review of Czechs
and Slovaks in the United States of
America.* Cicero, Ill.: Czechoslovak
National Council of America, 1970.

Roucek, Joseph Slabey. *The Czechs and
Slovaks in America.* Minneapolis:
Lerner, 1967.

Schlyter, Daniel M. *A Handbook of
Czechoslovak Genealogical Research.*
Buffalo Grove, Ill.: Genun Publishers,
1985.

Stasko, Joseph. *Slovaks in the United States of America: Brief Sketches of Their History, National Heritage and Activities.* Cambridge, Ontario, Canada: Dobra Kniha, 1974.

Stein, Howard F. *An Ethno-Historic Study of Slovak-American Identity.* New York: Arno Press, 1980.

Stolarik, M. Mark. *The Slovak Americans.* New York: Chelsea House, 1988.

———. *Immigration and Urbanization: The Slovak Experience, 1870–1918.* New York: AMS Press, 1989.

———. *Slovaks in Canada and the United States, 1870–1990: Similarities and Differences.* Ottawa, Canada: Chair in Slovak History and Culture, Dept. of History, University of Ottawa, 1992.

For more resources, see "General European Immigration Resources" on p. 317.

Immigrants from the Yugoslav (South Slav) States

The Yugoslavs (literally, South Slavs) are united by related languages and a largely shared ethnic ancestry. However, they are sharply and often bitterly divided by centuries of religious and political strife in the Balkan region of southeastern Europe. In the 20th century alone, they have been involved in two world wars—the first of which was started by a 1914 Serbian nationalist assassination in Sarajevo—and in bloody ethnic and religious strife at the end of the century.

The South Slavs were primarily part of what historians call the "new immigration," largely made up of poor people from southern and eastern Europe in the late 19th and early 20th century. However, some South Slavs, most notably Croatians, were among the earliest European settlers in the Americas.

South Slav Background

Lying at the crossroads of Europe and Asia, the Balkan region has long been a pathway for migrations and invasions. As a result, the people of the Balkans—like most peoples of Eurasia—are of mixed ethnic ancestry.

In the last several centuries, the main imperial contestants for the Balkans have been the Austrians, Hungarians, Turks, and Russians, with most South Slav countries being parts of competing empires. The exception was mountainous Montenegro, which largely kept its independence. Each shift of imperial borders brought shifts of population and religion, as conquerors brought in new colonists; as many peoples adopted the conquerors' religion and language; and as many others fled or strongly resisted losing their ethnic and religious identity in a foreign empire. The result was a highly checkered set of populations and cultures in the Balkans.

Among the South Slavs, the Slovenians occupied a relatively prosperous region at the northeast head of the Adriatic Sea, with its major city of Ljubljana. With strong historical links to western Europe, they became part of the Holy Roman Empire, which became the Hapsburg (later Austro-Hungarian) Empire. Many Slovenians became Protestants in the 1500s, but were then strongly persecuted by the Catholic Hapsburgs during the Counter-Reformation of the 1600s. During this period, some Slovenians fled north to Protestant states, especially in Germany, with a number of these later making their way to America, along with German Protestants seeking religious freedom.

Croatia occupied a much larger area to Slovenia's south, including the long coastal region of Dalmatia along the Adriatic Sea. Croatia was an independent maritime state during the 10th and 11th centuries, but much of the country was then conquered by Hungary and later incorporated into the Hapsburg Empire, which ruled it until 1918. However, the major Dalmatian port of Dubrovnik, earlier known as Ragusa, was for some centuries an independent commercial republic, akin to Venice. Other parts of Croatia were in some periods ruled by Venice and Turkey. With its seafaring tradition, Croatia sent immigrants to the New World earlier than did the other South Slav states.

Lying inland from Croatia was Serbia, long a power among the South Slavs. Strongly influenced by the Byzantine Empire, the Serbs adopted the Eastern Orthodox form of Christianity. They were at the height of their power in the early 14th century, but in 1389 lost the Balkans to the Ottoman Turks on the Field of the Blackbirds, in Kosovo. Serbia remained part of the Turkish empire until 1878. During this long period, many Serbs fled to other regions, most notably Croatia and Hungary, while keeping alive Serbian nationalism. When an independent kingdom (later called Yugoslavia) was formed from several South Slav states after World War I, Serbia became its center, with its capital at Belgrade. However, its continued desire to dominate clashed with other Slavs' desire for independence, leading to a series of wars in the 1990s.

Bosnia was under Eastern influence for many centuries. It annexed neighboring Herzegovina in the 15th century, but both soon came under Turkish control. Some Slavs chose to convert to Islam, the religion of their Turkish overlords. The Turks also brought colonists into the region, not only Muslims but also some Eastern Orthodox Christians. Later, as the Turks weakened, Bosnia-Herzegovina fell under the influence of the strongly Catholic Austro-Hungarian Empire, especially in the 19th century, a status made formal in 1908. As a result, the ethnic and religious composition of the region changed markedly over the centuries.

The small, poor, isolated region of Montenegro was also attacked by the Turks but was never fully conquered, becoming a refuge for some of the other Balkan peoples, among them many Serbians and Albanians.

The Bulgarians are another group of South Slavs. Originally from the region of the Volga River (from which the name Bulgar comes) in southern Russia, they gradually merged with the Slavs living in what is now Bulgaria, with the name then being applied to all. The Bulgarians had their own kingdom for several centuries, at times dominated by the Byzantine Empire and including large parts of Macedonia.

In 1389, Bulgaria was taken by the Turks and was then held for five centuries. During that time many Bulgarians adopted Islam, while others resisted, with many immigrating to southern Russia and the Hapsburg Empire. As the Ottomans weakened, Bulgarians finally in 1872 won the right to have their own Bulgarian Orthodox church, rather than the Turkish-controlled Greek Orthodox church. After a failed Bulgarian uprising in 1876, the Turks massacred thousands of Bulgarians, sparking international protests. The Russians, seeking influence in the Balkans, fought and defeated Turkey, establishing an independent Bulgaria as a Russian protectorate in 1878.

At that point, the region of Macedonia—in earlier times the homeland of Alexander the Great—was still under Turkish rule. The Macedonians, another South Slav people, hoped to establish their own independent state, but that was not to be. Macedonia was freed from the Turks during the Balkan Wars of 1912 and 1913, but after World War I the region was divided among Yugoslavia, Greece, and Bulgaria, which continued to fight over Macedonia through the 20th century.

The result of this tangled history was a highly volatile ethnic and religious mix throughout the Balkans. In Herzegovina, for example, the population at the turn of the 20th century was approximately 40 percent Eastern Orthodox, 40 percent Muslim, and 20 percent Roman Catholic, with ethnic groups and languages also mixed—a recipe for future trouble. Even a shared language could cause problems; though they spoke a common language, Serbo-Croatian, the Catholic Croats wrote in the Latin alphabet, while the Orthodox Serbs used the Cyrillic (Russian) alphabet.

Early Immigrants

The earliest South Slav immigrants to North America—and the most numerous overall—were the Croatians. One or more Croatians, as well as a Bulgarian sailor named Dragan, reportedly sailed with Columbus in 1492. By the mid-1500s, as merchant ships from Ragusa (Dubrovnik) plied Spanish routes, some Croatian sailors apparently also settled in the New World.

During the colonial period, some South Slav immigrants arrived as missionaries in the Spanish territories. Among them were Slovenian Jesuit priest Mark Anton Kapus, who explored northern Mexico and Arizona with Father Francisco Kino between 1687 and 1717, and Croatian Jesuit priest Fernando Consag (born Ferdinand Konscak), who served in Baja California from 1733, where he oversaw the building of the San Ignacio mission. Some Croatian and Slovenian Protestants, having fled north to Germany, are also believed to have been among the European Protestants who in 1715 went to the English-sponsored colony of Georgia.

Other early immigrants were sailors, serving either in foreign ships or as independent merchant-adventurers. By the early 1700s, Ragusan ships were sailing

American Museum of Immigration, Statue of Liberty National Monument, National Park Service, U.S. Department of the Interior

Immigrants from the South Slav countries included members of various ethnic minorities, such as this family of Gypsies from Serbia.

regularly into Philadelphia, New York, and various Caribbean ports. During the 1700s and early 1800s some Croatian sailors made their way around South America to California, a region they reportedly found attractive because of its similarities to Dalmatia. Other Croatians settled in coastal regions in the South, especially around the Gulf of Mexico, in places such as Tampa, Florida; Mobile, Alabama; and Galveston and Brownsville, Texas.

Some Slovenian Protestants also arrived in the American colonies in the late 1700s, having earlier immigrated to German states to escape Catholic persecution. Some of them fought with the Continental Army in the Revolutionary War.

Independent Dubrovnik was one of the first states to recognize the new United States, in 1783. But it lost its own independence in 1815, when the whole coastal region, including Slovenia and Croatia, was made part of the Hapsburg Empire (from 1867 the Austro-Hungarian Empire). More South Slav emigrants left for the United States in this period; among them were some families, not just lone men, joining relatives who had preceded them. How many is unclear, because from 1820—when the United States began to keep official immigration records—these immigrants were counted as coming from Austria-Hungary. In addition, sailors who left their ships and stayed were generally not counted in immigration figures at all. Many Croatian immigrants continued to settle in the South, especially in or near New Orleans. Some worked on the water, as sailors, fishers, shrimpers, and harbor pilots, while others established plantations and other businesses, and entered a wide range of other occupations.

Graph 2.55: Number of Immigrants from the Yugoslav (South Slav) States by Decade, 1920–1996

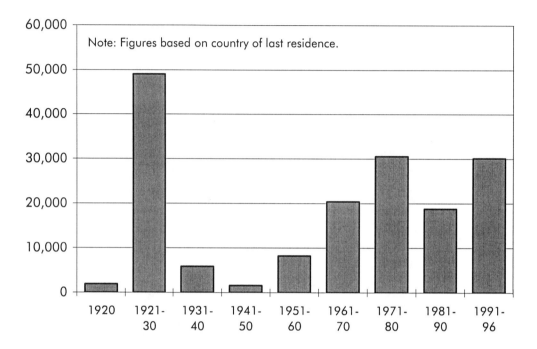

Table 2.33: Number and Percentage of Immigrants from the Yugoslav (South Slav) States in Total U.S. Immigration by Decade, 1920–1996

Decade	Number of Immigrants from the Yugoslav (South Slav) States	Total U.S. Immigrants	Percentage of Immigrants from the Yugoslav (South Slav) States in Total U.S. Immigration
1920	1,888	5,735,811	0.03
1921-1930	49,064	4,107,209	1.19
1931-1940	5,835	528,431	1.10
1941-1950	1,576	1,035,039	0.15
1951-1960	8,225	2,515,479	0.33
1961-1970	20,381	3,321,677	0.61
1971-1980	30,540	4,493,314	0.68
1981-1990	18,762	7,338,062	0.26
1991-1996	30,090	6,146,213	0.49
Total 1820-1996	166,361	63,140,227	0.26

Note: In 1920, the Kingdom of Serbs, Croats, and Slovenes was separately recorded. From 1922, it was recorded as Yugoslavia. Figures do not include Bulgaria.

Source: Adapted from Table 2, Immigration by Region and Selected Country of Last Residence, Fiscal Year 1820–1996, from the *Statistical Yearbook of the Immigration and Naturalization Service, 1996*.

More skilled and literate than many later immigrants, these early South Slavs often ranged widely and became fully integrated into American life. For example, George Fisher (born Djordje Sagic), a Serb from Hungary who arrived in Philadelphia in 1815, fought for Texan independence, helped establish the Texas supreme court, and later served as a land commissioner, judge, and finally in 1870 Greek consul in California. Croatian immigrant John Dominis (originally Gospodnetic) arrived in Boston in the 1820s, where he married a woman of Pilgrim ancestry and moved to Hawaii, where he became active in the China trade, building a mansion that later served as the governor's residence. Their son John, later governor of Oahu and adviser to four Hawaiian kings, married Liliuokalani, who would become the last queen of Hawaii.

By the early 1860s, an estimated 3,000 Croatian immigrants lived in the South, along with much smaller numbers of other South Slavs, most notably Montenegrins. Some hundreds of them served in the Confederate Army, jokingly calling themselves "Johnny Reboviches." After the South lost the Civil War, a good many of these South Slav Americans joined in the exodus to the West.

Those who went all the way to California found Croatian Americans from earlier times. Some had been there since the region was under Spanish rule, while others had come when the United States took control of the region in 1848. When gold was discovered in California in 1848, some Croatians were already working at Sutter's Mill. Many others would join the 1849 Gold Rush, including some who jumped ship in California ports. Hundreds settled in San Francisco, where they often ran restaurants, bars, and produce stores.

Some Slovenians, Montenegrins, and Serbs also joined the Gold Rush and settled in San Francisco. They were later joined in California by some Slovenians who had fought in Hapsburg armies in Mexico in the 1860s. A good number of Serbs and Montenegrins became ranchers and farmers in California's fertile San Joaquin Valley.

South Slav immigrants were drawn by other precious metals besides gold. Many went to Nevada after the discovery of silver

there in the late 1850s, while others found their way to mining towns in Montana and Idaho. Some of these would later make their way to the Pacific Northwest and even to Alaska.

Meanwhile, other South Slavs had continued to arrive in the early 19th century. Among them were a number of missionaries, such as those sponsored by the Vienna-based Leopoldine Society. These included Croatian Joseph Kundek, who went to Indiana in 1838, and Slovenian Frederick Baraga, who settled in Michigan in 1831, becoming bishop of Marquette. After the failed European revolutions of 1848, South Slavs were among the many who fled to America, especially Slovenians and Croatians from the Austro-Hungarian Empire.

Slovenians in the mid-19th century were especially drawn to the midwestern states. Some began their working lives in America as peddlers, selling goods from backpacks or carts, later establishing permanent businesses. Many were also drawn to the fertile farmlands of the region.

How many South Slavs had come to America by the mid-19th century is extremely hard to estimate. However, in 1869, when Austria started to tally emigrants, officials there estimated that nearly 20,000 people had by then left for America from Dalmatia alone.

The Main Wave

The main wave of immigration to the United States from southern and eastern Europe began in the 1870s, but the main wave of the South Slav immigration came a bit later, starting in the 1890s. Unlike the earlier South Slav immigrants, these were mostly poor people from rural areas. As in other parts of Europe, rising populations, changes in land ownership, competition from larger farms such as those in America and Russia, and the shrinking of family farms through subdivision at inheritance, all combined to make it harder for farmers and rural laborers to support their families. Some went first to nearby cities to look for work—as part of the 19th century's major social shift from country to city—and only then went on to America, where jobs were plentiful. Soon many people were leaving directly for America, attracted by

Table 2.34: Number and Percentage of Foreign-Born Immigrants from the Yugoslav (South Slav) States by Decade in Total U.S. Population at End of Decade, 1920–1990

Decade	Number of Foreign-Born Immigrants from the Yugoslav (South Slav) States	Total U.S. Population	Percentage of Foreign-Born Immigrants from the Yugoslav (South Slav) States in Total U.S. Population
1920	169,439	105,710,620	0.16
1930	211,416	122,775,046	0.17
1940	(NA)	131,669,275	(NA)
1950	144,070	150,697,361	0.10
1960	165,798	179,323,175	0.09
1970	153,745	203,235,298	0.08
1980	152,967	227,726,000	0.07
1990	141,516	249,907,000	0.06

NA = Not available

Note: Figures do not include Bulgaria.

Source: Adapted from Series C 228–295, Foreign-Born Population, by Country of Birth: 1850–1970, in *Historical Statistics of the United States, Colonial Times to 1970, Bicentennial Edition,* and other updating tables from the U.S. Census Bureau.

the glowing "America letters" sent by previous immigrants and by stories of riches told by agents drumming up business for the major shipping lines.

How many South Slavs left in this period is not clear, for their numbers were still buried in those for larger empires. In addition, official immigration figures were confusingly kept in overlapping categories by regions of birth and ethnic groups. However, of the more than 3.6 million immigrants from the Austro-Hungarian Empire between 1891 and 1920, at least 10 percent are estimated to have been Croatians, still the largest group of South Slav emigrants. In this same period, thousands of Muslims left the Balkans, most for Turkey but others for America, for they faced persecution and massacres after strongly Catholic Austria-Hungary took Bosnia-Herzegovina in 1878.

Between 1899 and 1910 alone, U.S. immigration records tallied more than 355,000 Croatians and Slovenians, nearly 51,000 of them women. Between then and 1923, another 225,000 were counted. Some of the Croatians who stayed behind

lamented, "Our strength and youth lie beyond the sea," as whole regions became depopulated.

Smaller numbers of Serbs, Montenegrins, Bulgarians, and Macedonians arrived during this wave of immigration. Some thousands of these would later return to fight against Turkey in the Balkan Wars of 1912–1913 and in World War I. In this main wave, Serbs were only about 15 percent of the South Slav immigrants in the United States. Even fewer immigrants came from lightly populated Montenegro; they often formed separate communities and mutual aid societies in the United States.

Before 1912, many Bulgarian immigrants came from Turkish-held territories, especially from Macedonia, and were counted in Turkish immigration figures. Among them were many Protestants, who had been converted by missionaries active in the Ottoman Empire from the 1860s. Some converts were sent to the United States to attend Protestant colleges. Most such students returned to Europe, especially after Bulgaria was freed from the

Turks in 1878, but significant numbers stayed in the United States. Through both groups, Bulgarians learned more about America, with increased emigration resulting.

In 1893, Macedonian nationalists rose up against Turkish rule. Their revolt was brutally suppressed, with some 5,000 Macedonians killed and many others made homeless. This prompted many Macedonians to immigrate to America, though many others chose to stay and fight. Other nationalist revolts through World War I would cause still more emigrants to flee the Balkans.

Many South Slav immigrants in this main wave went to mining or industrial towns in states such as Pennsylvania, New York, Ohio, Illinois, New Jersey, Michigan, Wisconsin, Minnesota, Colorado, and Montana, working especially in mines, steel mills, railroads, construction, and other heavy industry. Pennsylvania, sometimes called "the most Slavic of states," received tens of thousands of South Slav immigrants, including an estimated 150,000

between 1899 and 1908, more than half of them Croatians. Some were drawn by the 1898 gold rush to Alaska, including one Croatian whose son, Mike Stepovich, would become the first governor of Alaska after it became a state.

Most newcomers in this period went to established immigrant communities, often at first staying in Slavic boardinghouses in industrial towns, generally run by women immigrants. At first, the majority of the new immigrants were men, but as the communities became more established more immigrants brought their families over to join them. Single men sometimes brought over a bride from the old country, many of them "picture brides," so called because they were often selected by photograph (see "The Journey" on p. 53).

Modern Immigration

World War I changed everything for the South Slavs. After the war, Austria-Hungary was dissolved, and the Ottoman

Graph 2.56: Number of Foreign-Born Immigrants from the Yugoslav (South Slav) States in Total U.S. Population by Decade, 1920–1990

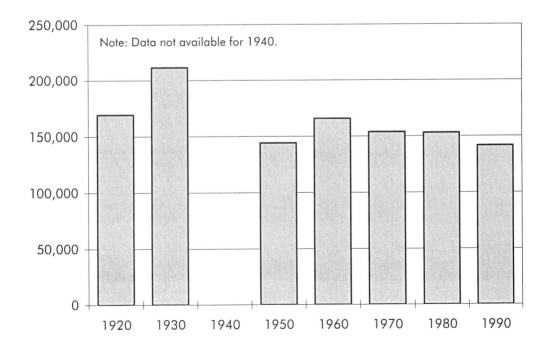

Table 2.35: Number and Percentage of Immigrants from the Yugoslav (South Slav) States Annually, 1992–1996

Year	Number of Yugoslav (South Slav) Immigrants Identified as from Bosnia-Herzegovina	Number of Yugoslav (South Slav) Immigrants Identified as from Croatia	Number of Yugoslav (South Slav) Immigrants Identified as from Macedonia	Number of Yugoslav (South Slav) Immigrants Identified as from Slovenia	Number of Yugoslav (South Slav) Immigrants not Separately Identified by State	Total Number of Immigrants from the Yugoslav (South Slav) States	Total U.S. Immigration	Percentage of Immigrants from the Yugoslav (South Slav) States in Total U.S. Immigration
1992	15	77	—	8	2,504	2,604	973,977	0.27
1993	159	370	—	50	2,230	2,809	904,292	0.31
1994	521	412	367	67	2,038	3,405	804,416	0.42
1995	4,061	608	666	65	2,907	8,307	720,461	1.15
1996	6,499	810	863	77	3,605	11,854	915,900	1.29
Total 1992-96	11,255	2,277	1,896	267	13,284	28,979	4,319,046	0.67

Source: Adapted from *Statistical Yearbook of the Immigration and Naturalization Service*, 1996, Table 3.

Empire greatly diminished. In the Balkans, two independent South Slav nations emerged. One was the Kingdom of Serbs, Croats, and Slovenes—renamed Yugoslavia in 1929—which included Slovenia, Croatia, Bosnia-Herzegovina, Serbia, Montenegro, and part of Macedonia. The other was Bulgaria, which included a small part of Macedonia, most of which was divided between Greece and Yugoslavia.

Emigration of South Slavs continued high after the war, with some going to other parts of Europe but many to the United States. Between 1920 and 1930, more than 51,000 arrived in the United States from Yugoslavia alone. Most of these came early in the decade, for the United States established restrictive immigration quotas that went into effect in 1921, with even tighter restrictions imposed in 1924 (see "Immigration Restrictions" on p. 47). Thereafter South Slav immigration was largely choked off, at first by the quotas and later also by the Great Depression of the 1930s and World War II.

World War II again brought harsh, divisive times to the Balkans. Bulgaria sided with Germany, as it had in World War I. Their joint forces attacked and took much of Yugoslavia in 1941, while the rest was occupied by the Italians. Many South Slavs fought against the Nazi-led powers, both at home and from exile abroad. However, these resistance groups also fought each other, especially the Serbian nationalists, called Chetniks; the Communist partisans, led by Josip Broz Tito; and various Croat-ian nationalist groups, who sought an independent state formed of Croatia and Bosnia-Herzegovina. Some South Slavs allied themselves with the fascist powers, including some Croatian fascists, who had been increasingly unhappy with the Serb-dominated government of Yugoslavia and had declared an independent Croatia. During and after the war, the region was devastated by continuing battles, not only between major armies but also between the various ethnic and political groups.

In the end, the area was liberated by Soviet troops, joined by Tito's Communist partisan forces. But it was a liberation in name only, for the whole region then came under Soviet Communist domination. Many South Slavs fled before the Soviet troops. Some of these refugees were returned against their will, and many were killed by the Communist forces. Others found a temporary haven in refugee camps in Austria, Germany, or Italy. Americans of South Slav ancestry, moved by their plight, strongly supported passage of the 1948 Displaced Persons Act, which allowed many refugees to find asylum in the United States after the war. South Slav Americans also sent aid to families, friends, and others still living in Yugoslavia. Some had hopes of the new Yugoslavia, and even returned to the Balkans to build a new and better society there. Most were bitterly disappointed, and some of those later returned, often leaving behind them everything they owned.

Despite continuing ethnic and religious divisions, Tito held Yugoslavia together for decades. Of all the states under Soviet influence, Yugoslavia was the most independent, and its people were able to emigrate relatively freely. As a result, the number of immigrants from Yugoslavia began to rise again. They did not approach the numbers of earlier times, being held in check by continuing quota restrictions until 1965 and then by other kinds of restrictions. Even so, immigration to the United States from Yugoslavia topped 20,000 in the 1960s and 30,000 in the 1970s. Primarily from Croatia and Slovenia, these new immigrants constituted a real "brain drain," for many were skilled, educated young people, including professionals such as physicians, engineers, and scientists.

Bulgaria, also under Soviet domination, was far more tightly controlled, and its people were generally unable to emigrate freely. During the 1970s, U.S. records show only approximately 2,300 Bulgarian immigrants.

With the death of Tito in 1980, Yugoslavia lost the central force holding it together, and the country's deep ethnic,

political, and religious strains came to the surface. In 1990, while several other countries in the Soviet bloc were breaking free of the Soviet Union, Yugoslavia held its first multiparty elections since World War II. Except in Serbia and Montenegro, the Communists were defeated.

In 1991 Croatia, Slovenia, Bosnia-Herzegovina, and Macedonia seceded from Yugoslavia. The federation's weakness was made clear when the Yugoslav army made only minimal military attempts to bar Slovenia from leaving—though it was by far the richest of the former Yugoslav republics. In Croatia, however, it was a different matter. There a Serbian minority attempted to secede from the new state and set up its own independent republic. In the resulting civil war, they were supported by the Yugoslav army, which was mostly Serbian. Following a temporary ceasefire in 1992, monitored by United Nations troops, war broke out again in 1995, at which time the Croats drove the Serbs out of all but a small portion of Croatia. By the time the fighting stopped, the percentage of Serbs in Croatia had

Table 2.36: Number and Percentage of Immigrants from Bulgaria in Total U.S. Immigration Annually, 1986–1996

Year	Number of Immigrants from Bulgaria	Total U.S. Immigration	Percentage of Immigrants from Bulgaria in Total U.S. Immigration
1986	221	601,708	0.04
1987	205	601,516	0.03
1988	217	643,025	0.03
1989	265	1,090,924	0.02
1990	428	1,536,483	0.03
1991	623	1,827,167	0.03
1992	1,049	973,977	0.11
1993	1,029	904,292	0.11
1994	981	804,416	0.12
1995	1,797	720,461	0.25
1996	2,066	915,900	0.23
Total 1971-96	8,881	17,987,584	0.05

Source: *Statistical Yearbook of the Immigration and Naturalization Service*, 1996, Table 3.

dropped from 12 percent to 2 to 3 percent, as hundreds of thousands of refugees fled into Serbia.

Bitter fighting also spread to Bosnia-Herzegovina, devastating the region, including the capital of Sarajevo. This generated more refugees, some thousands of whom found their way to the United States. In an attempt to keep the fighting from spreading, United Nations troops were also put into Macedonia, the poorest of the former Yugoslav republics.

Yugoslavia was now made up of only two republics: Serbia, with some 9.8 million people, and Montenegro, with just over 620,000. While other republics had broken away, the Serbs tightened their hold on their remaining territories. This included two formerly autonomous regions: Kosovo and Vojvodina. With a population that was 90 percent ethnic Albanian, however, Kosovo sought its own independence. Unwilling to grant that, the Serbs began trying to clear Kosovo of Muslim Albanians, driving them into Macedonia and Albania. The result was a humanitarian disaster, as hundreds of thousands of refugees overwhelmed the local ability to feed, shelter, and care for them. Some were admitted to the United States, with preference being given to those who already had family connections there. After NATO forces took control of Kosovo in 1999, many refugees returned home. At century's end, however, the Balkans were still the tinderbox of Europe.

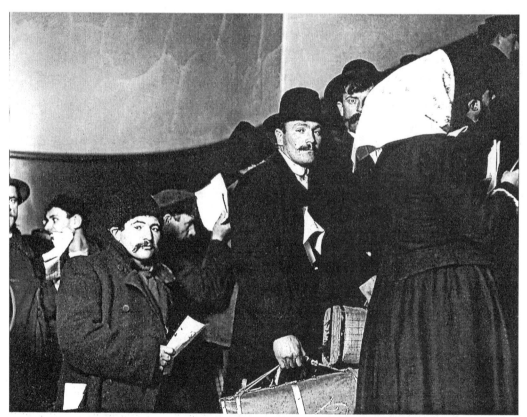

American Museum of Immigration, Statue of Liberty National Monument, National Park Service, U.S. Department of the Interior; Photo: Lewis W. Hine

These Slavic immigrants, just arrived in America, were climbing the steps into Ellis Island's Great Hall for their inspection.

Resources

Internet Resources

Cyndi's List—Eastern Europe (*http://www.cyndislist.com/easteuro.htm*) List of on-line genealogical resources for eastern Europe, including the Balkan countries, maintained by genealogical author Cyndi Howells.

CroatiaGenWeb (*http://www.rootsweb.com/~hrvwgw/index.htm*) Part of the WorldGenWeb project, linking genealogical research sites around the world, by region; provides searchable name databases, query boards, and other Croatia-related information, plus links to related sites.

Genealogy and Heraldry in Slovenia (SloveniaGenWeb) (*http://genealogy.ijp.si/*) Part of the WorldGenWeb project, linking genealogical research sites around the world, by region; provides searchable databases and references works; historical and genealogical materials; and links to related resources.

Croatian Culture and History on the Web (*http://www.romwell.com/travel/advisory/europe/croatia/culturecro/*

shtml) Part of a travel advisory site; includes many links to information and sites about Croatian life, culture, language, and history.

Slovene Archives (*http://www.pokarh-mb.si/home.html*) Web site offering information about and links to Slovenian archives.

Montenegrin Association of America (*http://www.montenegro.org*) Organization Web site offering information about the history and culture of Montenegro and links to related sites. (Address: 805 Magnolia St., Menlo Park, CA 94025)

Bulgarian-American Society (*http://www.basnet.org*) Organization Web site seeking to foster cultural exchange. (Address: 1020 16th Street, NW, Suite 200, Washington, D.C. 20036)

Bosnet (*http://www.bosnet.org*) Web site on Bosnia-Herzegovina, including news, information on the history and culture of the region, and links to related sites.

Print Resources

Altankov, Nikolay G. *The Bulgarian-Americans.* Palo Alto, Calif.: Ragusan Press, 1979.

Bulgaria: A Country Study. 2d ed. Glenn E. Curtis, ed. Washington, D.C.: Federal Research Division, Library of Congress, 1993. (Available online at *http://lcweb2.loc.gov/frd/cs*)

Carlson, Claudia, and David Allen. *Bulgarian Americans.* New York: Chelsea House, 1990.

Eterovich, Adam S. *Croatians from Dalmatia and Montenegrin Serbs in the West and South, 1800–1900.* San Francisco: R and E Research Associates, 1971.

———. *A Guide and Bibliography to Research on Yugoslavs in the United States and Canada.* San Francisco: R and E Research Associates, 1975.

———. *Croatian Pioneers in America, 1685–1900.* Palo Alto, Calif.: Ragusan Press, 1980.

Gakovich, Robert P., and Milan M. Radovich, comps. *Serbs in the United States and Canada: A Comprehensive Bibliography.* Minneapolis: Immigration History Research Center, University of Minnesota, 1976.

Ifkovic, Edward. *The Yugoslavs in America.* Minneapolis: Lerner, 1977.

Karlo, Milan, and Helen Karlo. *Early Days: Serbian Settlers in America: Their Life and Times.* Tucson: M. Karlo, 1984.

Kisslinger, Jerome. *The Serbian Americans.* New York: Chelsea House, 1990.

Kraljic, Frances. *Croatian Migration to and from the United States 1900–1914.* Palo Alto, Calif.: Ragusan Press, 1978.

Prpic, George J. *The Croatian Immigrants in America.* New York: Philosophical Library, 1971.

——. *South Slavic Immigration in America.* Boston: Twayne, 1978.

Shapiro, E. *The Croatian Americans.* New York: Chelsea House, 1989.

Silverman, Robin Landew. *A Bosnian Family.* Minneapolis: Lerner, 1997.

Stipanovich, Joseph, and Maria K. Woroby. *Slavic Americans: A Study Guide and Source Book.* San Francisco: R & E Research Associates, 1977.

Tekavec, Valerie. *Teenage Refugees from Bosnia-Herzegovina Speak Out.* New York: Rosen, 1995.

Yugoslavia: A Country Study. 3d ed. Glenn E. Curtis, ed. Washington, D.C.: Federal Research Division, Library of Congress, 1992. (Available on-line at *http://lcweb2.loc.gov/frd/cs*)

For more resources, see "General European Immigration Resources" on p. 317.

Immigrants from Romania

Romanians have been living in their portion of southeastern Europe since the classical era, when they were apparently known as the Dacians. However, their country's location just west of the Black Sea put it squarely across a major invasion route from Central Asia to Europe, and as a result various ethnic groups settled in the area over the centuries. Romania has been held as part of many different empires. As recently as the 19th century, large parts of what are now Romania—primarily the regions of Moldavia, Walachia, and Transylvania—were held by the Austro-Hungarian Empire and Russia, while other parts had long been held by the Ottoman Turkish Empire.

What this all meant was that many immigrants from what is now Romania were counted in the U.S. immigration records as coming from other countries, especially Austria, Hungary, Russia, and Turkey. In addition, though all the citizens of the country were Romanians in a political sense, many were not ethnically Romanian but were of other ethnic backgrounds, including Hungarians, Germans, Jews, Gypsies, Ukrainians, Serbs, Croats, Turks, and Russians.

Romanian immigrants came late to America. Before the 1870s, relatively few Romanians are known to have arrived, and they generally came as individuals. Some came to join the California Gold Rush in 1849. Others fought in the Civil War, among them Captain Nicolae Dunca, who died in battle in 1862, and General Gheorghe Pomutz, the first Romanian-American brigadier general, who was later U.S. consul general to Russia.

Romanians began to arrive in substantial numbers in the 1870s, but separate data on Romanian immigration was not kept until 1880. Even that was unreliable because of the complicated political and ethnic composition of the region. More than 12,000 Romanians arrived in the 1890s, a figure that jumped to more than 53,000 in the following decade.

The early members of this migration were generally skilled and somewhat educated artisans, often moving their whole families. But after 1895 that pattern changed. Then most Romanian immigrants were single men, or married men without their families, with little or nothing in the way of skills and education. Like many others in the "new immigration" from

Graph 2.57: Number of Immigrants from Romania by Decade, 1880–1996

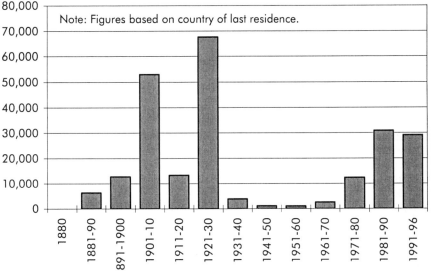

Note: Figures based on country of last residence.

Table 2.37: Number and Percentage of Immigrants from Romania in Total U.S. Immigration by Decade, 1880–1996

Decade	Number of Immigrants from Romania	Total U.S. Immigrants	Percentage of Romanians in Total U.S. Immigration
1880	11	2,812,191	0.00
1881–1890	6,348	5,246,613	0.12
1891–1900	12,750	3,687,564	0.35
1901–1910	53,008	8,795,386	0.60
1911–1920	13,311	5,735,811	0.23
1921–1930	67,646	4,107,209	1.65
1931–1940	3,871	528,431	0.73
1941–1950	1,076	1,035,039	0.10
1951–1960	1,039	2,515,479	0.04
1961–1970	2,531	3,321,677	0.08
1971–1980	12,393	4,493,314	0.28
1981–1990	30,857	7,338,062	0.42
1991–1996	29,156	6,146,213	0.47
Total 1820–1996	233,997	63,140,227	0.37

Note: Separate data not available for Romania until 1880.

Source: Adapted from Table 2, Immigration by Region and Selected Country of Last Residence, Fiscal Years 1820–1996, from the *Statistical Yearbook of the Immigration and Naturalization Service*, 1996.

southern and eastern Europe, they came from rural areas, often impoverished by rising populations and farms too small to support families. Some went initially to European cities looking for work, before being drawn to America—often by shipping agents drumming up business for the transatlantic liners. And work there was, drawing Romanian immigrants to the major industrial cities of the Northeast and Midwest.

Many Romanian immigrants in the late 19th and early 20th centuries intended to earn some money and then return home. As many as two-thirds of them did so, a much higher proportion than in most other ethnic groups. This was especially true in the years just after World War I, when Romania became independent and began to institute land reforms.

Even while some were returning, however, the years after World War I saw a new and even larger wave of Romanians coming to America. From 1921 to 1930, they numbered more than 67,000, which amounted to nearly 2 percent of the total U.S. immigration for the period. Most of these immigrants arrived early in the decade, for the United States began put-

ting in restrictive immigration quotas in 1921 and even tighter restrictions in 1924, with the Romanian quota set at only 603 a year (see "Immigration Restrictions" on p. 47).

The Depression of the 1930s cut immigration more effectively than any quota. When Hitler's Germany plunged Europe into World War II in 1939, Romania tried at first to remain neutral, but in vain. By 1940, Romania had been partially dismembered, losing the regions of Bessarabia and Bukovina to the Soviet Union, southern Dobrudja to Bulgaria, and northern Transylvania to Hungary. These were largely recovered soon afterward, when the German-supported Iron Guard took over, allying Romania with Germany and beginning widespread attacks on Jews and political dissidents. In all, some 260,000 Jews were killed in Bessarabia and Bukovina, and another 120,000 from Transylvania were killed or deported to concentration camps. Even so, Romanians did not carry out mass deportations of Jews from throughout the country, as desired by the Germans, so large numbers of Romanian Jews survived the war.

Table 2.38: Number and Percentage of Foreign-Born Immigrants from Romania by Decade in Total U.S. Population at End of Decade, 1950–1990

Decade	Number of Foreign-Born Immigrants from Romania	Total U.S. Population	Percentage of Foreign-Born Immigrants from Romania in Total U.S. Population
1950	85,230	150,697,361	0.06
1960	84,575	179,323,175	0.05
1970	70,687	203,235,298	0.03
1980	66,994	227,726,000	0.03
1990	91,106	249,907,000	0.04

NA = Not available

Source: Adapted from Series C 228–295, Foreign-Born Population, by Country of Birth: 1850–1970, in *Historical Statistics of the United States, Colonial Times to 1970, Bicentennial Edition*, and other updating tables from the U.S. Census Bureau.

Graph 2.58: Number of Foreign-Born Immigrants from Romania in Total U.S. Population by Decade, 1950–1990

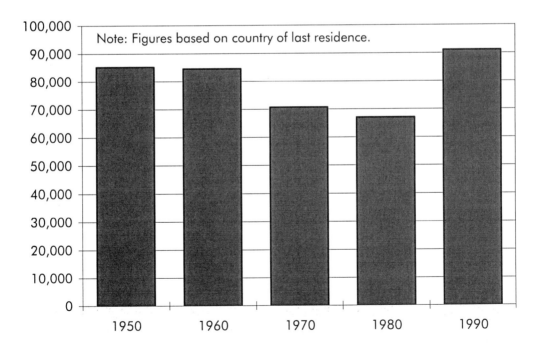

Note: Figures based on country of last residence.

As German forces withdrew in defeat, Soviet troops took Romania in 1944. Romania was again stripped of Bessarabia and Bukovina and fell under Soviet control. It would remain so until 1989. The country was devastated, not only by war losses but by hefty reparations to the Soviet Union. In the years just after the war some Romanians came to the United States under the Displaced Persons Act.

Soon, however, emigration was not so easy, for the country came under Communist rule. Though Romania was less restrictive of emigration than some other Soviet bloc countries, the process was enormously costly and difficult. From at least the late 1970s, Romania's government began an antiemigration campaign. Even ethnic minorities were strongly discouraged from emigrating, although the government's stated desire was for an "ethnically pure" Romania. People who asked for permission to emigrate were branded as traitors, frequently lost their jobs or were demoted, were denied medical care and other social benefits, including education for their children, and often were evicted from their homes as well. The government also required emigrants to pay up to $20,000 in U.S. dollars (supposedly as reimbursement for the cost of their education), though they were not legally allowed to hold foreign money. This "tax" was officially withdrawn after international protests, but was still unofficially present in the form of bribes for permission to emigrate. Someone caught trying to emigrate illegally could face three years in prison.

Despite these hazards, many people did emigrate from Romania. Some of these were ethnic Germans, most of whom immigrated to West Germany. Another major group of emigrants were Romanian Jews. More than 200,000 Jews emigrated between 1948 and 1970, many of them to Israel, and nearly half of the remaining 43,000 would emigrate by the end of the 1980s. Some of these Romanian Jews found their way to America. In the late 1980s, ethnic Hungarians also began to emigrate from Romania, mostly to Hungary, sparking international protests about Romania's persecution of minorities.

In the country itself, many people who had remained in Romania were unhappy with Communist rule. This would lead, in 1989, to the violent overthrow of the Ceaucescu regime. This, in turn, led to a new wave of immigration to the United States. Between 1971 and 1996, more than 90,000 immigrants arrived from Romania, with a peak of more than 8,000 in 1991 alone. Based on country of birth, these figures include some who were born in Romania but lived elsewhere before emigrating, for the figures based on country of last residence show only some 72,400 immigrants.

Resources

Internet Resources

Romania World GenWeb (*http://www.rootsweb.com/~romwgw/*) Part of the WorldGenWeb project, linking genealogical research sites around the world, by region, providing information by province.

Silent Echoes (*http://pages.nyu.edu/~am14*) Web site offering links to Romanian resources.

Print Resources

Diamond, Arthur. *The Romanian Americans*. New York: Chelsea House, 1988.

Hategan, Vasile. *Romanian Culture in America*. Cleveland: V. Hategan, 1988.

Romania: A Country Study. 2d ed. Ronald D. Bachman, ed. Washington, D.C.: Federal Research Division, Library of Congress, 1991. (Available on-line at *http://lcweb2.loc.gov/frd/cs*)

Thigpen, Kenneth A. *Folklore and the Ethnicity Factor in the Lives of Romanian-Americans*. New York: Arno Press, 1980. Originally presented as the author's thesis, Indiana University, 1973.

For more resources, see "General European Immigration Resources" on p. 317.

Immigrants from Russia and the Commonwealth States

Russia was long called a "prisonhouse of nations," and it was from its many minorities, especially those in its borderlands, that most Russian immigrants to the United States originally came. Immigration to the United States from Russia followed a great curve, rising to its peak between 1901 and 1910, when nearly 1.6 million people arrived, an estimated two-thirds of them Jews and Poles. Later, after a long period of largely closed borders, immigration would rise to a much smaller peak in the 1990s, with more than 300,000 people arriving between 1991 and 1996 from what was by then a much-diminished Russia and a host of other states, called the Commonwealth.

The Background

Russia—today known more formally as the Russian Federation—is the largest country in the world. During the 19th century, it expanded its empire from the Baltic Sea to the Pacific Ocean. It remained the largest even in the 1990s, when the Soviet Union broke up and many of its former borderlands became independent Commonwealth states, including Armenia, Azerbaijan, Belarus, Georgia, Kazakhstan, Kyrgyzstan, Moldova, Russia, Tajikistan, Turkmenistan, Ukraine, and Uzbekistan.

The many peoples of the region are widely mixed in ethnic origin and religion, for the Russian steppe has been a migration and invasion route for thousands of years. The name *Russia* comes from the Swedish Vikings, called Varangians or Rus, who conquered the region around Kiev in the ninth century and established the kingdom of Russia. They merged with the peoples of the region, who were primarily Eastern Slavs. Over the centuries some of these peoples were absorbed, but others kept their ethnic and cultural identity, even when they did not have a state of their own.

Among the most notable of the Eastern Slav peoples today, apart from the Russians and Poles, are the Ukrainians and Belarussians, both of whom finally gained their own states in the 1990s. Another notable Eastern Slav group is the Carpatho-Rusyns (also called Ruthenians, Carpatho-Ukrainians, Uhro-Rusyns, or Rusnaks), who had centuries before migrated to the region of the Carpathian Mountains, into lands now largely in Ukraine, Poland, and Slovakia, but in the past often controlled by Austria-Hungary. These other Eastern Slav peoples came to differ from the Russians in various ways, including language, cultural traditions, and religion. From the 18th century, aggressively imperial Russia also held other peoples in countries that are now fully independent, including Poland, Finland, and the Baltic states (see "Immigrants from Poland" on p. 237; "Immigrants from Scandinavia" on p. 165; and "Immigrants from the Baltic States: Estonia, Latvia, and Lithuania" on p. 291).

All of these peoples were prime targets for attack during frequent Russification campaigns, which aimed at stamping out ethnic, religious, and cultural differences within Russia's political borders. Ethnic minorities were often barred from using their languages in schools and churches; they often had to hide their books and study them in secret. From 1840 the name *Belarus* was banned entirely.

In matters of religion, Russia succeeded in converting many of its Slav minorities to the Orthodox form of Christianity. However, many Poles and Lithuanians continued to follow Roman Catholicism, many Ukrainians followed their own form of Orthodoxy, and many Estonians and Latvians remained Protestants.

A special group was the Jews, who faced widespread anti-Semitism. In the late 18th century, most Jews in the Russian Empire were forced into a region of western Russia then called the Pale of Settlement, which included parts of Poland, Ukraine, and several smaller areas. They

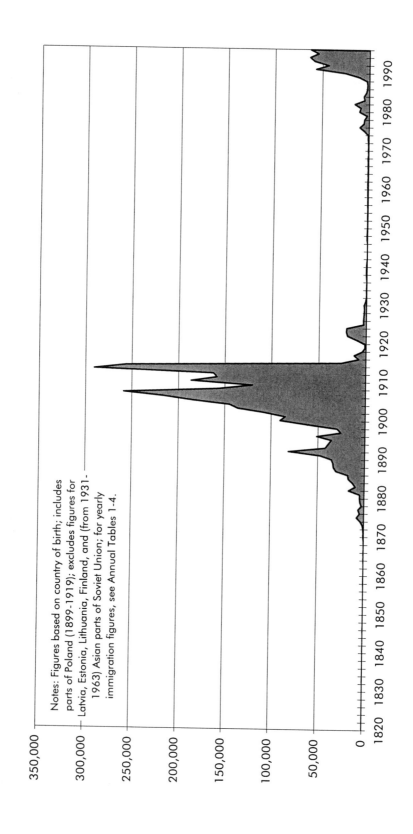

Graph 2.59: Number of Immigrants from Russia and the Commonwealth States (Former Soviet Union) Annually, 1820–1996

Notes: Figures based on country of birth; includes parts of Poland (1899-1919); excludes figures for Latvia, Estonia, Lithuania, Finland, and (from 1931-1963) Asian parts of Soviet Union; for yearly immigration figures, see Annual Tables 1-4.

were subjected not only to Russification but also to outright physical attacks, called *pogroms* (see "Jewish Immigrants" on p. 297).

As part of their campaign for control, the Russian authorities often moved large numbers of peoples into internal exile. The Molokans, for example, were exiled to the region of the Caucasus Mountains because they rejected the Russian Orthodox religion. Some would later emigrate to the United States.

Early Immigrants

A few Eastern Slavs immigrated early to the New World. Some Ukrainians settled in New Amsterdam (later New York) when it was still under Dutch control, and some later served in the Revolutionary War.

However, the earliest significant number of immigrants from Russia to North America came not to the East Coast but to the West, as part of Russia's imperial expansion to the Pacific. Vitus Bering, a Dane in Russian service, discovered and named the Bering Strait in 1727 and claimed the Aleutian Islands for Russia in 1741. From the 1760s, Russian hunters and fur traders worked in the region, by 1784 establishing their first permanent colony on Kodiak Island, off Alaska. In succeeding decades, they founded a string of settlements, most notably Sitka and New Archangel in Alaska, stretching south along the coast all the way to Fort Stawianski (Fort Ross), in northern California. Originally trading forts, these would become small communities, with their own churches. As the fur trade became less profitable, however, Russia withdrew from the region, selling Alaska to the United States in 1867. Perhaps half of the Alaskan colonists returned to Russia; the others stayed, though some eventually moved south to California. Russian holdings there had been sold to John Augustus Sutter in 1814. (Discovery of gold on Sutter's land in 1848 would spark California's famous Gold Rush in 1849.)

Only occasional Russian immigrants arrived on the east coast of North America, and these primarily as individuals. Among the earliest was Prince Demetrius Gallitzin, who came to Baltimore in 1792; after converting to Roman Catholicism, he was a missionary in western Pennsylvania—then a frontier region—for four decades.

The number of immigrants from Russia did not top 600 per decade until the period from 1861 to 1870, during which more than 2,500 immigrants arrived. That number jumped to more than 39,000 in the decade following, from 1871 to 1880.

The Main Wave

The main wave then began, with the number of immigrants from Russia exceeding 213,000 from 1881 to 1890, and in the following decade more than doubling to top 505,000. Immigration to the United States from Russia tripled in the decade that followed, peaking at 1.6 million from 1901 to 1910. Between 1911 and 1920, more than 921,000 came, despite the fact that World War I largely cut off immigration in the latter half of the decade. The peak individual year was 1913, with immigration of more than 258,000, but immigration also exceeded 255,000 in both 1907 (the peak year for U.S. immigration overall) and 1914 (the second-highest year for overall immigration). In the period between 1899 and 1919, these figures include immigrants from Russian-held portions of Poland, the source of most of the immigrants.

Russia's captive minorities formed the overwhelming majority of the immigrants that came to the United States from Russia in the main wave of the late 19th and early 20th centuries. By far the largest group in that emigration were the Jews. At the height of the migration, in the first decades of the 20th century, nearly six out of every ten immigrants to the United States from Russia were Jewish, while one in ten was Polish and a little under one in ten was German. Substantial numbers also migrated to the United States from Ukraine, the Baltic states, Moldova, and several other parts of the Russian empire. Only an estimated 17 percent were ethnic Russians.

Many of these immigrants were certainly fleeing ethnic and religious attacks. That was a major factor causing Jews to leave Russia. Most others left Russia for the same combination of fundamental rea-

Table 2.39: Number and Percentage of Immigrants from Russia and the Commonwealth States (Former Soviet Union) in Total U.S. Immigration by Decade, 1820–1996

Decade	Number of Immigrants from Russia and the Commonwealth States (Former Soviet Union)	Total U.S. Immigrants	Percentage of Immigrants from Russia and the Commonwealth States (Former Soviet Union) in Total U.S. Immigration
1820	14	8,385	0.17
1821-1830	75	143,439	0.05
1831-1840	277	599,125	0.05
1841-1850	551	1,713,251	0.03
1851-1860	457	2,598,214	0.02
1861-1870	2,512	2,314,824	0.11
1871-1880	39,284	2,812,191	1.40
1881-1890	213,282	5,246,613	4.07
1891-1900	505,290	3,687,564	13.70
1901-1910	1,597,306	8,795,386	18.16
1911-1920	921,201	5,735,811	16.06
1921-1930	61,742	4,107,209	1.50
1931-1940	1,370	528,431	0.26
1941-1950	571	1,035,039	0.06
1951-1960	671	2,515,479	0.03
1961-1970	2,465	3,321,677	0.07
1971-1980	38,961	4,493,314	0.87
1981-1990	57,677	7,338,062	0.79
1991-1996	309,105	6,146,213	5.03
Total 1820-1996	3,752,811	63,140,227	5.94

Note: For period 1899–1919, data for parts of Poland included in Russia.

Source: Adapted from Table 2, Immigration by Region and Selected Country of Last Residence, Fiscal Years 1820–1996, from the *Statistical Yearbook of the Immigration and Naturalization Service*, 1996.

sons that spurred others in the massive "new immigration," primarily from southern and eastern Europe. They were poor people from the land, with little prospect of improving their lives within the Russian empire. Many came from increasingly uneconomic small farms. Russian serfs had been freed in 1863, but the farms they later worked as landowners or free laborers were often too small to support their large families—and became smaller when subdivided in succeeding generations. In the new international markets, they could not compete in quality or in price with the products of large, fertile farms in North America or elsewhere in Russia. Rapidly rising populations increased the pressure on the poor, in the countries and the cities.

Among the rural poor, some headed first for nearby cities, looking for work, as part of the massive country-to-city shift then taking place in developing countries all across Europe. However, the Russian empire was still lightly industrialized and offered few industrial jobs. While some of the poor went to cities in western Europe, they soon learned that America offered them far more opportunities. They read "America letters," in which earlier immigrants told of the "golden streets" of America; they saw for themselves the prosperity of occasional returning immigrants; and they heard tales—often much exaggerated—told by agents drumming up business for the great transatlantic shipping lines.

Beyond that, the Russian empire was in ferment. From the 1860s at least, large numbers of people were involved in political actions against the czar and the aristocracy, with frequent violent attacks and revolts. Each revolt or failed terrorist attack sent more people fleeing from the turmoil, most notably after the failed revolution of 1905.

American Museum of Immigration, Statue of Liberty National Monument, National Park Service, U.S. Department of the Interior; Photo: Lewis W. Hine

Many new immigrants at first stayed in boardinghouses run by earlier immigrants, such as this Russian steelworker playing his accordion in Homestead, Pennsylvania, in 1909.

The shadows of approaching war also caused many people to leave Russia, often fleeing illegally across the border. It is no accident that 1913 saw the largest number of immigrants to the United States from Russia. People were frightened by the possibility of war sweeping across the land. Young men—especially Poles, Ukrainians, Jews, and other minorities—also left to avoid serving in the Russian army, the hated force of their oppressors. Among those who fled to avoid military service were pacifist Molokans from the Caucasus, who emigrated after the group's young men were threatened with induction into the army. Some of them went directly to California, while others first lived for some years in Iran.

When it did come in 1914, World War I proved devastating to Russia, especially in the western borderlands, where much of the fighting took place. Emigration to the United States was largely choked off, not only during World War I but also in the wars that followed.

Russia withdrew from the war in 1918, after the 1917 Bolshevik Revolution. Five years of nationwide civil war followed, in which "White" royalist-nationalist forces, often with international support, fought "Red" Communist forces. Russia and Poland also went to war, as did Russia and several ethnic minorities trying to assert their independence, among them the Ukrainians, Finns, Latvians, Lithuanians, and Estonians.

In these years, some hundreds of thousands of people fled Russia. Many of them settled in Europe, especially in France, Germany, and various eastern European countries. At least 30,000 of these refugees came to the United States in the early 1920s, some with aid from the Red Cross. Small numbers of Russian refugees also made their way to the United States in the 1930s.

The pre–World War I immigrants were quite different from those who came after the war. Before the war, most immigrants from Russia were poor, and many had little or no education. In the United States, they tended to settle in the industrial regions, especially in states such as Pennsylvania, New York, New Jersey, Connecticut, Ohio, and Illinois. Many worked in mines, mills, and factories of all sorts, from Chicago's slaughterhouses to New York's garment factories. Immigrants from Russia were found all across the country, however, with some settling in California and the Pacific Northwest.

Some immigrants in the late 19th and early 20th centuries—most of them ethnic Russians—were religious dissidents, such as the Russian Old Believers. Often settling first in California or Canada, some of these groups later established separate utopian communities in rural areas, especially in the Pacific Northwest.

Though many poor people continued to arrive, after World War I the immigrants from Russia included many more highly educated people, who had left in opposition to Communist rule. These included professionals, intellectuals, military officers, and religious leaders, as well as members of the

Immigration History Research Center, University of Minnesota

This 1911 issue of Emigrant *urged Ruthenian emigrants: "Do not forsake your homeland for always! When fate forces you to emigrate, at least don't sell your lands, so that you will have something to come back to. Go for the sake of making money. . . . Return with the money earned and use it to improve your farms/households."*

Graph 2.60: Number of Immigrants from Russia and the Commonwealth States (Former Soviet Union) by Decade, 1820–1996

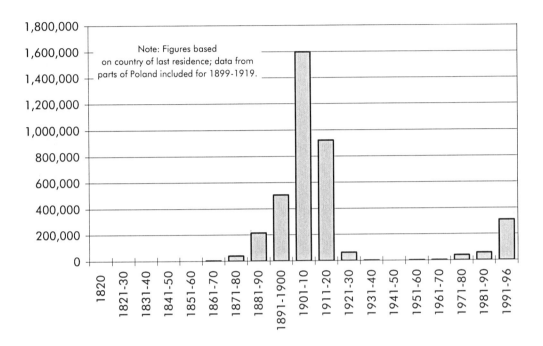

Note: Figures based on country of last residence; data from parts of Poland included for 1899-1919.

Graph 2.61: Percentage of Immigrants from Russia and the Commonwealth States (Former Soviet Union) in Total U.S. Immigration by Decade, 1820–1996

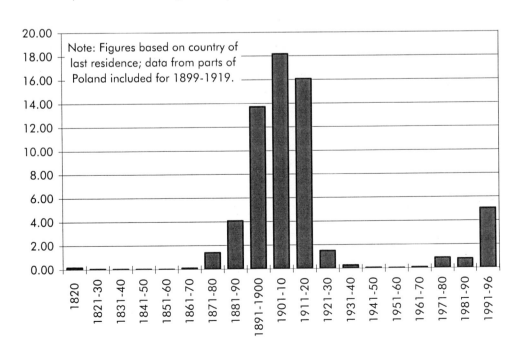

Note: Figures based on country of last residence; data from parts of Poland included for 1899-1919.

empire's former aristocracy. Some of these immigrants had difficulties at the start, and often initially had to work at low-level jobs, but once they learned English many were able to establish comfortable lives in the United States.

Later Immigration

From 1931 to 1970, direct immigration to the United States from the Soviet Union was negligible, totaling a little over 5,000 for the entire 40-year period. After World War II, some tens of thousands of refugees from Russia were admitted to the United States. However, many of these had spent years living in other countries and were often counted in the immigration totals from those countries, rather than from the Soviet Union. That would remain so throughout the Soviet period. In particular, large numbers of Jews emigrated from the Soviet Union and lived for a time in Israel, before emigrating from there to the United States (see "Jewish Immigrants" on p. 297). They were some of the few people allowed out of the Soviet Union in this period—and even they obtained permission

Table 2.40: Number and Percentage of Foreign-Born Immigrants from Russia and the Commonwealth States (Former Soviet Union) in Total U.S. Population by Decade, 1850–1990

Decade	Number of Foreign-Born Immigrants from Russia and the Commonwealth States (Former Soviet Union)	Total U.S. Population	Percentage of Immigrants from Russia and the Commonwealth States (Former Soviet Union) in Total U.S. Population
1850	1,414	23,191,876	0.01
1860	3,160	31,443,321	0.01
1870	4,644	39,818,449	0.01
1880	35,722	50,155,783	0.07
1890	182,644	62,947,714	0.29
1900	423,726	75,994,575	0.56
1910	1,184,412	91,972,266	1.29
1920	1,400,495	105,710,620	1.32
1930	1,153,628	122,775,046	0.94
1940	(NA)	131,669,275	(NA)
1950	896,000	150,697,361	0.59
1960	690,598	179,323,175	0.39
1970	463,462	203,235,298	0.23
1980	406,022	227,726,000	0.18
1990	333,725	249,907,000	0.13

NA = Not available

Notes: Figures include data for Latvia and Estonia (1850–1920) and Lithuania (1850–1990). Figures for 1910 exclude Polish-speakers.

Source: Adapted from Series C 228–295, Foreign-Born Population, by Country of Birth: 1850–1970, in *Historical Statistics of the United States, Colonial Times to 1970, Bicentennial Edition*, and other updating tables from the U.S. Census Bureau.

Graph 2.62: Number of Foreign-Born Immigrants from Russia and the Commonwealth States (Former Soviet Union) in Total U.S. Population by Decade, 1850–1990

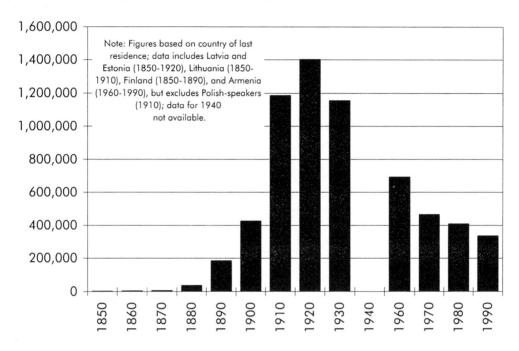

Note: Figures based on country of last residence; data includes Latvia and Estonia (1850-1920), Lithuania (1850-1910), Finland (1850-1890), and Armenia (1960-1990), but excludes Polish-speakers (1910); data for 1940 not available.

Graph 2.63: Number of Immigrants from Russia and the Commonwealth States (Former Soviet Union), 1992–1996

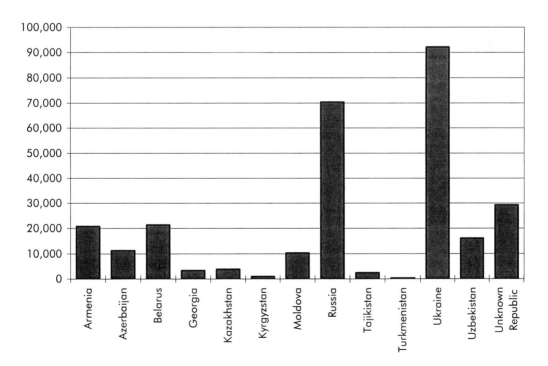

Table 2.41: Number of Immigrants from Russia and the Commonwealth States (Former Soviet Union) in Total U.S. Immigration Annually, 1992–1996

	1992	1993	1994	1995	1996	Total 1992-1996
Armenia	6,145	6,287	3,984	1,992	2,441	20,849
Azerbaijan	1,640	2,943	2,844	1,885	1,991	11,303
Belarus	3,233	4,702	5,420	3,791	4,268	21,414
Georgia	426	429	652	710	1,157	3,374
Kazakhstan	506	628	750	840	1,089	3,813
Kyrgyzstan	134	124	226	209	280	973
Moldova	1,705	2,646	2,260	1,856	1,849	10,316
Russia	8,857	12,079	15,249	14,560	19,668	70,413
Tajikistan	186	336	568	706	634	2,430
Turkmenistan	34	48	68	84	121	355
Ukraine	14,383	18,316	21,010	17,432	21,079	92,220
Uzbekistan	1,712	2,664	3,435	3,645	4,687	16,143
Unknown Republic	4,653	7,369	6,954	6,784	3,513	29,273
Total	43,614	58,571	63,420	54,494	62,777	282,876

Source: Adapted from Table 3, Immigrants Admitted by Region and Selected Country of Birth, Fiscal Years 1986–1996, from the *Statistical Yearbook of the Immigration and Naturalization Service*, 1996.

to leave only with great difficulty—for the country was a tightly closed society, with emigration largely banned.

That began to change somewhat in the 1970s. From then through the 1980s, direct immigration to the United States from the Soviet Union grew substantially, totaling almost 97,000 in those two decades. After the breakup of the Soviet Union, it grew greatly, to a total of 309,000 between 1991 and 1996. Part of this major increase in emigration was still an exodus of Jews, for historic anti-Semitism was openly resurgent in Russia and the Commonwealth states (which together had made up the former Soviet Union).

Much of the emigration in this period, however, reflected the terrible state of the economies and social systems of these countries, and most notably of Russia itself. Throughout the countries of the former Soviet Union, a health crisis deepened, as life expectancy dropped sharply, with rapidly rising death rates, including infant mortality rates. The health system had largely failed, with great increases in infectious disease and multiple epidemics. The environment had been catastrophically degraded during the Soviet period; for example, 75 percent of Russia's groundwater was reportedly polluted, while polluted waterways contributed to the steep rise in epidemic diseases, as did widespread radioactive contamination. There were major shortages of food, fuel, and medical supplies, while millions of workers remained unpaid for long periods. Crime became widespread and was often highly organized.

Much of the emigration in the 1990s continued to be from the former Russian borderlands. Ukraine contributed fully one third of the immigrants between 1992 and 1996, and only one quarter came from Russia itself. As a new century dawned, massive flight from the region could only be expected to increase.

Graph 2.64: Percentage of Immigrants from Russia and the Commonwealth States in Total U.S. Immigration from the Former Soviet Union, 1992–1996

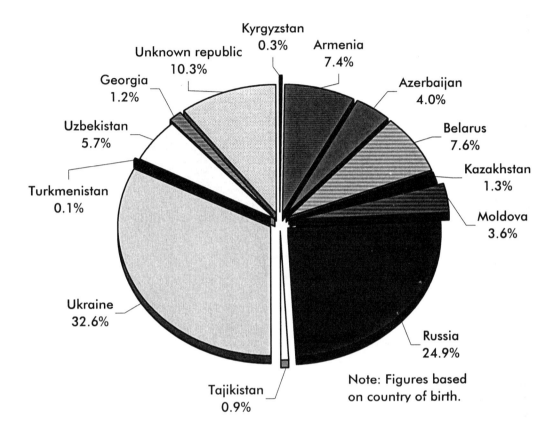

Kyrgyzstan 0.3%

Armenia 7.4%

Unknown republic 10.3%

Azerbaijan 4.0%

Georgia 1.2%

Belarus 7.6%

Uzbekistan 5.7%

Kazakhstan 1.3%

Turkmenistan 0.1%

Moldova 3.6%

Ukraine 32.6%

Russia 24.9%

Tajikistan 0.9%

Note: Figures based on country of birth.

In the Great Hall at Ellis Island, Ukrainians gave a concert on a Sunday in 1916, during World War I.

American Museum of Immigration, Statue of Liberty National Monument, National Park Service, U.S. Department of the Interior

Resources

Internet Resources

EastEuropeGenWeb (*http://www.rootsweb.com/~easeurgw/*) Part of the WorldGenWeb project, linking genealogical research sites around the world, by region, with resources by individual country and links to other parts of Europe; also offers links to other general resources and mailing lists.

Federation of Eastern European Family History Societies (FEEFHS) (*http://www.feefhs.org*) Web site offers searchable index, resource guide, Internet journal, research notes, links to professional databases, map indexes, and specialist cross-indexes for individual ethnic groups. (Address: P. O. Box 510898, Salt Lake City, UT 84151-0898)

InfoUkes—Information Resource about Ukraine and Ukrainians (*http://www.infoukes.com/*) Web site that covers all aspects of Ukraine, including history and genealogy, as well as current news and links to related sites.

Ukraine World GenWeb (*http://www.rootsweb.com/~ukrwgw/index.html*) Part of the WorldGenWeb project, linking genealogical research sites around the world, by region; provides information by oblast (county or province); offers tips on research, query boards, historical material, Ukrainian news, and links to related resources.

BRAMA—History of Ukraine (*http://www.brama.com/ukraine/history/index.html*) Chronological tables on Ukrainian history; part of a wider site: BRAMA—Gateway Ukraine (*http://www.brama.com/index.html*).

Belarusian Genealogy (*http://www.belarusguide.com/genealogy1/Genelgy.html*) Part of the WorldGenWeb project, linking genealogical research sites around the world, by region; part of a wider site: Virtual Guide to Belarus (*http://www.belarusguide.com/main/index.html*).

Carpatho-Rusyn Genealogy Web Site Home Page (*http://www.rusyn.com*) Web site focusing on immigration and genealogy of people of Carpatho-Rusyn ancestry, who came from the region "primarily where Poland, Slovakia, the Ukraine, and Hungary adjoin or nearly adjoin"; offers searchable name lists, maps, photographs, links, and other information.

Carpatho-Rusyn Knowledge Base (*http://www.carpatho-rusyn.org*) Web site offering a wide range of information and resources relating to Carpatho-Rusyn ancestry and immigration, including maps, name lists, village information, photographs, tips on genealogy, and related links, including information on Ukrainian archives.

Carpathian Connection (*http://www.tccweb.org*) Web site focused on people from "former Carpathian territories or of Carpathian-Rusyn heritage," offering general historical and cultural information, information about notable settlements in Eastern Europe and the United States, tips on researching family history, and related links.

Print Resources

Armenia, Azerbaijan, and Georgia: Country Studies. Glenn E. Curtis, ed. Washington, D.C.: Federal Research Division, Library of Congress, 1995. (Available as separate countries on-line at *http://lcweb2.loc.gov/frd/cs*)

Belarus and Moldova: Country Studies.
Helen Fedor, ed. Washington, D.C.:
Federal Research Division, Library of
Congress, 1995. (Available as separate
countries on-line at *http://*
lcweb2.loc.gov/frd/cs)

Dushnyck, Walter, and Nicholas L. Fr.-
Chirovsky, eds. *The Ukrainian Heritage*
in America. New York: Ukrainian
Congress Committee of America, 1991.

Ferry, Steven. *Russian Americans.*
Tarrytown, N.Y.: Benchmark Books,
1996.

Halich, Wasyl. *Ukrainians in the United*
States. New York: Arno Press, 1970.

Hardwick, Susan Wiley. *Russian Refuge:*
Religion, Migration, and Settlement on
the North American Pacific Rim.
Chicago: University of Chicago Press,
1993.

Kazakhstan, Kyrgyzstan, Tajikistan,
Turkmenistan, and Uzbekistan:
Country Studies. Glenn E. Curtis, ed.
Washington, D.C.: Federal Research
Division, Library of Congress, 1997.
(Available as separate countries on-line
at *http://lcweb2.loc.gov/frd/cs*)

Kuropas, Myron B. *The Ukrainian*
Americans: Roots and Aspirations,
1884–1954. Toronto and Buffalo:
University of Toronto Press, 1991.

———. *Ukrainians in America.* Rev. ed.
Minneapolis: Lerner, 1996.

Magocsi, Paul R. *The Russian Americans.*
New York: Chelsea House, 1996.
Originally published 1989.

Osborn, Kevin. *The Ukrainian Americans.*
New York: Chelsea House, 1989.

Russia: A Country Study. Glenn E. Curtis,
ed. Washington, D.C.: Federal Research
Division, Library of Congress, 1998.
(Available on-line at *http://*
lcweb2.loc.gov/frd/cs)

Soviet Union: A Country Study. 2d ed.
Raymond E. Zickel, ed. Washington,
D.C.: Federal Research Division,
Library of Congress, 1991. (Available
on-line at *http://lcweb2.loc.gov/frd/cs*)

Stefaniuk, Myroslava. *Ukrainian-*
Americans in the United States: An
Annotated Bibliography and Guide to
Research Facilities. Detroit: Ethnic
Studies Division, Center for Urban
Studies, Wayne State University, 1977.

Stolarik, M. Mark. *Immigration and*
Urbanization: The Slovak Experience,
1870–1918. New York: AMS Press,
1989.

Ukrainian Academy of Arts and Sciences
in the United States. *A Guide to the*
Archival and Manuscript Collection of
the Ukrainian Academy of Arts and
Sciences in the U.S., New York City: A
Detailed Inventory. Edmonton:
Canadian Institute of Ukrainian
Studies, University of Alberta, 1988.

Wertsman, Vladimir, ed. *The Russians in*
America: A Chronology and Fact Book.
Dobbs Ferry, N.Y.: Oceana, 1976.

For more resources, see "General European Immigration Resources" on p. 317.

Immigrants from the Baltic States: Estonia, Latvia, and Lithuania

The peoples of the Baltic states—Estonia, Latvia, and Lithuania—were for many centuries ruled by other, larger neighboring states. Their emigration from the region has often coincided with attempts to stamp out their culture and with failed revolts against foreign rule. Only in the 20th century have they had brief periods of independence, most recently with the liberation movements that began in 1989 and resulted in freedom.

Baltic Background

The Indo-European-speaking Latvians and Lithuanians and the Finno-Ugric-speaking Estonians arrived in the Baltic region as early as 3000 B.C., where they merged with earlier inhabitants of the area. Gradually developing distinct cultures, the Estonians were centered just south of the Gulf of Finland, the Latvians south of them, and the Lithuanians farther south, in the south-

east corner of the Baltic Sea, surrounded by Poland, Russia, and (since the 1990s) Belarus.

The Baltic peoples lived in small principalities until the 13th century, when the crusaders known as the Teutonic Knights invaded the region, taking political control and forcibly converting many inhabitants to Christianity. The Estonians came to be dominated by German and Danish overlords, with most Estonians becoming serfs, tied to the land. The Latvians were also largely confined to serfdom, with their overlords including Germans, Danes, Prussians, Swedes, Russians, Poles, and Lithuanians. Neither would again be free until the 20th century.

Lithuania, the largest of the Baltic states, had a somewhat different fate. United behind a strong king in the early 13th century, it largely held off the Teutonic Knights and built its own small empire, including parts of Latvia. Finally unable to stand alone, Lithuania formed

Library of Congress

This smiling young woman was one of 1,000 "picture brides"—so-called because they were often selected from photographs—who arrived in the United States on the steamship Baltic *to marry men they had never met.*

Table 2.42: Number and Percentage of Foreign-Born Immigrants from the Baltic States (Estonia, Latvia, and Lithuania) at End of Decade in Total U.S. Population 1920–1990

Decade	Number of Foreign-Born Immigrants from the Baltic States	Total U.S. Population	Percentage of Immigrants from the Baltic States in Total U.S. Population
1920	135,068	105,710,620	0.13
1930	217,829	122,775,046	0.18
1940	(NA)	131,669,275	(NA)
1950	147,872	150,697,361	0.10
1960	186,147	179,323,175	0.10
1970	129,871	203,235,298	0.06
1980	82,543	227,726,000	0.04
1990	65,134	249,907,000	0.03

NA = Not available

Notes: Figures for 1920 and 1950 are for Lithuania only. Estonia not included in 1980.

Source: Adapted from Series C 228–295, Foreign-Born Population by Country of Birth: 1850–1970, in *Historical Statistics of the United States, Colonial Times to 1970, Bicentennial Edition*, and other updating tables from the U.S. Census Bureau.

an alliance with Poland in 1386; the Lithuanian king was given the Polish crown in exchange for his conversion to Christianity. The Lithuanian-Polish empire successfully stopped the eastward expansion of the Teutonic Knights. The Lithuanian-Polish union was made formal in 1569, but Lithuania later declined into a mere province of Poland.

In all three Baltic states, foreign over-lords became the ruling elites, with the Estonian, Latvian, and Lithuanian languages and cultures being associated with the poorer, weaker classes. Lithuania became largely Roman Catholic, while Estonia and Latvia, largely dominated by the Swedes and the Germans, became primarily Protestant.

Early Immigrants

It was the Swedish-German connection that brought some of the earliest Baltic emigrants to America. Some Latvians and Estonians joined a party of Swedes who settled in Delaware and Pennsylvania in 1640. Others, who had initially settled on the Caribbean island of Tobago, came to Boston in 1687. Small numbers of Baltic immigrants continued to arrive in the following years, including some sailors, who arrived in America and decided to stay.

In the 18th century, the Baltic states fell under the control of Russia, which began an active Russification campaign, seeking to stamp out other cultures. Education, publishing, and religious activities in the Estonian, Latvian, and Lithuanian languages were discouraged or banned altogether. This spurred many Baltic peo-

Table 2.43: Number and Percentage of Immigrants from Estonia, Latvia, and Lithuania (the Baltic States) in Total U.S. Immigration Annually, 1986–1996

Year	Number of Immigrants from Estonia	Number of Immigrants from Latvia	Number of Immigrants from Lithuania	Total Number of Immigrants from the Baltic States	Total U.S. Immigration	Percentage of Immigrants from the Baltic States in Total U.S. Immigration
1986	6	26	49	81	601,708	0.01
1987	15	23	37	75	601,516	0.01
1988	11	31	47	89	643,025	0.01
1989	14	57	63	134	1,090,924	0.01
1990	20	45	67	132	1,536,483	0.01
1991	23	86	157	266	1,827,167	0.01
1992	194	419	353	966	973,977	0.10
1993	191	668	529	1,388	904,292	0.15
1994	272	762	663	1,697	804,416	0.21
1995	205	651	767	1,623	720,461	0.23
1996	280	736	1,080	2,096	915,900	0.23
Total 1986-1996	1,231	3,504	3,812	8,547	10,619,869	0.08

Source: *Statistical Yearbook of the Immigration and Naturalization Service, 1996,* Table 3.

Graph 2.65: Number of Immigrants from Estonia, Latvia, and Lithuania (the Baltic States) Annually, 1986–1996

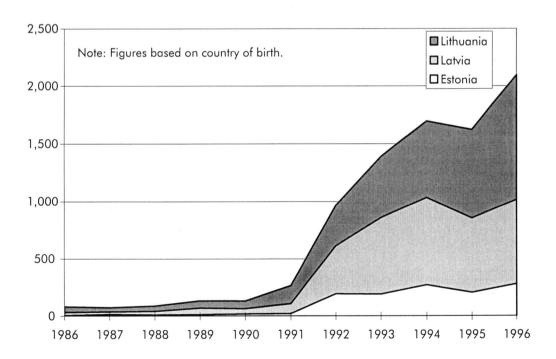

ples to join independence movements, sometimes with Poles. A series of failed revolts followed, and many of the revolutionaries were forced to flee the region. Some of these ended up in North America. Some even fought in the Revolutionary War, including Tadeusz Kosciuszko, a Lithuanian born in Poland, who became a brigadier general and helped supervise the building of West Point.

Relatively small numbers of Estonians, Latvians, and Lithuanians continued to find their way to the United States in the 19th and early 20th centuries. Their numbers are unclear, because they were counted as arriving from Russia, Germany, or Scandinavia. Some came after failed revolts, especially the 1905 revolution in Russia.

Sharply rising population pressure also spurred emigration. As elsewhere in Europe, a rising birth rate and the inability of small, subdivided farms to support expanding populations led to sharply increased emigration from the Baltic region, as part of what historians call the "new immigration" from southern and eastern Europe. Some initially emigrated to other parts of Europe, seeking work in the cities, as part of a worldwide country-to-city shift. Many of these emigrants ended up coming to America, and increasing numbers would come directly from the Baltic states. Many young men emigrated to avoid service in the hated Russian army. Among the emigrants in this period were many Jews, who were widely persecuted (see "Jewish Immigrants" on p. 297).

In the United States, most of the Baltic immigrants settled in the major industrial cities of the northeastern and midwestern states. Many immigrants in this period were males, some of whom stayed only long enough to earn some money and then returned to their homelands. Later many immigrants brought their families to America, establishing stable communities. By 1920, the United States census tallied more than 135,000 foreign-born immigrants from Lithuania alone, with thousands more from Estonia and Latvia.

By then the Baltic states had become independent. Occupied by the Germans for a time during World War I, then briefly by Soviet Russia in 1918, Estonia, Latvia, and Lithuania then declared their indepen-

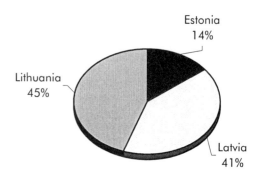

Graph 2.66: Percentage of Immigrants from Estonia, Latvia, and Lithuania in Total U.S. Immigration from the Baltic States, 1986–1996

Estonia 14%
Lithuania 45%
Latvia 41%

Note: Figures based on country of birth.

dence, which was affirmed by the international community. The pace of Baltic immigration slowed somewhat after that, as sharply restrictive immigration quotas went into place in 1921 and even tighter ones in 1924 and as the world slid into a Depression after 1929. Even so, the number of foreign-born Estonian, Latvian, and Lithuanian immigrants in the United States was nearly 218,000 by 1930 (see "Immigration Restrictions" on p. 47).

War and After

Some fled the Baltic region as war approached in 1939, but many would be trapped in harm's way. As part of a secret Nazi-Soviet pact, the two powers divided much of northeastern Europe between them. Under it, the Soviet Union annexed the Baltic states in 1940 and quickly began to suppress Estonian, Latvian, and Lithuanian nationalism, deporting tens of thousands of leaders to Siberian labor camps. Then came the German occupation (1941–1945), during which many thousands were killed, including an estimated 85 percent of Lithuania's Jewish population, numbering nearly 200,000 before the war.

As Soviet troops approached to retake the region at war's end, tens of thousands of people fled the Baltic region into western Europe as refugees. Many of these were later allowed to enter the United

Graph 2.67: Number of Foreign-Born Immigrants from the Baltic States (Estonia, Latvia, and Lithuania) in Total U.S. Population by Decade, 1920–1990

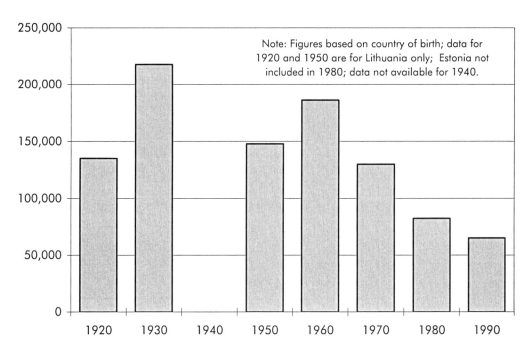

Note: Figures based on country of birth; data for 1920 and 1950 are for Lithuania only; Estonia not included in 1980; data not available for 1940.

States under the Displaced Persons Act of 1948. Among these were more than 40,000 from Latvia alone. By 1960, the number of foreign-born immigrants from Baltic states was more than 186,000. Under Soviet domination, the Baltic nationalism was once again suppressed and the region's peoples were not able to travel or emigrate freely, as was true of almost all Soviet states.

Modern Immigration

In the late 1980s, as the Soviet Union liberalized and weakened, Baltic independence movements reasserted themselves. Estonia was the first, in 1989 annulling its 1940 annexation by the Soviet Union. Latvia and Lithuania followed suit in 1990. The Soviet Union attempted to stop their secession, with economic blockades and troops in the Baltic states, but in the wake of a failed coup attempt in Moscow itself in 1991, it reluctantly accepted the independence of the three states.

Emigration was freer in this period, and thousands came from the Baltic states to America in the 1990s. Between 1986 and 1996, official U.S. records tallied more than 8,500 Baltic immigrants, including more than 3,800 from Lithuania, 3,500 from Latvia, and more than 1,200 from Estonia.

Many of the immigrants in the 1990s, as well as those just after World War II, were well educated and brought with them valuable skills, unlike those in the late 19th and early 20th centuries who largely came with strength and determination, learning necessary skills only after they arrived in America. Among the modern immigrants from the region were some Russians, who now formed minorities in states they had formerly dominated; as late as 1989, Russians made up more than 30 percent of the population of Estonia, nearly 34 percent of Latvia, and more than 8 percent of Lithuania.

Resources

Internet Resources

BalticSeaGenWeb Project (*http://
www.worldgenweb.org/eurogenweb/
bsgw.html*) Part of the WorldGenWeb
project, linking genealogical research
sites around the world, by region, with
resources by individual Baltic and
Scandinavian country.

Federation of Eastern European Family
History Societies (FEEFHS) (*http://
www.feefhs.org*) Web site offers
searchable index, resource guide,
Internet journal, research notes, links
to professional databases, map indexes,
and specialist cross-indexes for
individual ethnic groups. (Address: P.
O. Box 510898, Salt Lake City, UT
84151-0898)

Cyndi's List—Eastern Europe (*http://
www.cyndislist.com/easteuro.htm*) List
of on-line genealogical resources for
Eastern Europe, including the Baltic
countries, maintained by genealogical
author Cyndi Howells.

Global Resources for Lithuania (*http://
www.infowest.com/personal/d/
diogenes*) Web site focusing on
Lithuanian heritage worldwide,
offering genealogical and other
information and links.

American Latvian Association (*http://
www.alausa.org*) Organization Web site
offering publications and links.
(Address: 400 Hurley Avenue,
Rockville, MD 20850; Phone: 301-340-
1914; Fax: 301-340-8732)

Print Resources

Budreckis, Algirdas M., ed. *The
Lithuanians in America, 1651–1975: A
Chronology and Fact Book.* Dobbs
Ferry, N.Y.: Oceana, 1976.

*Estonia, Latvia, and Lithuania: Country
Studies.* Walter R. Iwaskiw, ed.
Washington, D.C.: Federal Research
Division, Library of Congress.
(Available on-line by individual state at
http://lcweb2.loc.gov/frd/cs)

Fainhauz, David. *Lithuanians in the USA:
Aspects of Ethnic Identity.* Chicago:
Lithuanian Library Press, 1991.

Karklis, Maruta, et al, eds. *The Latvians in
America, 1640–1973: A Chronology and
Fact Book.* Dobbs Ferry, N.Y.: Oceana,
1974.

Kucas, Antanas. *Lithuanians in America.*
Boston: Encyclopedia Lituanica, 1975.

Maldonado, Sigrid Renate. *Estonian
Experience and Roots: Ethnic Estonian
Genealogy . . . .* Fort Wayne, Ind.: As
Was Publishers, 1996.

Pennar, Jaan, et al., eds. *The Estonians in
America, 1627–1975: A Chronology and
Fact Book.* Dobbs Ferry, N.Y.: Oceana,
1975.

Van Reenan, Antanas J. *Lithuanian
Diaspora: Konigsberg to Chicago.*
Lanham, Md.: University Press of
America, 1990.

Jewish Immigrants*

In September 1654, the French frigate *St. Catherine* arrived in New Amsterdam (later New York) harbor, carrying 23 Jewish immigrants who had fled from Dutch settlements in Brazil, after those settlements were taken by the Portuguese. These 23, plus two other Jews who had arrived in New Amsterdam in the same year, established the first Jewish community in North America.

These Dutch Jews from Brazil were the descendants of the tens of thousands of Jews who had been expelled from Spain in 1492 and from Portugal in 1497. These Jewish refugees had established communities in the Protestant countries of western Europe, in North Africa, and in Turkey and other Middle Eastern countries. Indeed, in 1492, on the journey that "discovered" the Americas, Columbus had been forced to sail from the small Spanish port of Palos, because Cádiz and other major Spanish ports were too crowded with ships transporting expelled Jews out of Spain.

Nor did the story of their immigration to North America end on arrival in New Amsterdam, for then-governor Peter Stuyvesant attempted to expel them from there as well, because they were Jews. They were allowed to stay only because of powerful support in the Netherlands Jewish community, many of whose members were stockholders in the government-controlled Dutch East India Company.

The arrival of these first Jewish immigrants is symbolic of the history of Jewish immigration to the area that would later become the United States. In the centuries that followed, the great majority of Jews arriving in the United States came seeking more freedom than was available to them in their lands of origin. More often than not, that was their primary reason for emigrating, though like most other immigrants they also came to America for its promise of a better material life. In the three and a half centuries of Jewish immigration to the United States, Jews have come from dozens of countries and all over the world, and always for the same promises of freedom and a better life.

There were three main waves of Jewish immigration into what would become the United States. From 1654, when the first recorded Jewish immigrants landed in New Amsterdam, through the late 1990s, an estimated 2.7 to 3 million Jews reached the United States. Except for the late-20th-century immigration to the United States from Israel, that number can only be an estimate, for immigrants were recorded by recognized nationality, rather than by faith, no matter how they may have identified themselves as a people. Therefore, for example, a Jew from the Netherlands or Germany was classified in the U.S. records as Dutch or German, and were therefore counted as that nationality for statistical purposes.

Jewish Background

The great majority of Jewish immigrants thought of themselves—and were seen by others—as Jews. That is a matter of history, a long, complex history that extends back more than three millennia, to the Jewish migration from Egypt to Palestine led by Moses (ca. 1250 B.C.), told in the Old Testament as a story of exodus from Egypt and ultimate arrival in the Promised Land. Then a major expulsion occurred almost 2,600 years ago, when a failed Jewish revolt against Babylon in 586 B.C. ended with the destruction of Jerusalem and the

---

* The Jewish community is international, with Jews having been dispersed around the world over many centuries. As a result, Jewish immigrants have arrived in the United States from many parts of the world, and most Jewish immigrants have been counted not separately as Jews, but rather in the immigration figures of many other countries. Only during the latter half of the 20th century have some Jews been counted separately, as immigrants from Israel. We have included this article on Jewish immigrants in the section on Europe because by far the largest number of Jews came from that region, and Jewish immigration plays a very substantial role in the overall history of European immigration into the United States.

deportation of thousands of Jews to Babylon. That began the "Babylonian captivity" (586 B.C.–538 B.C.) and the dispersal (Diaspora) of the Jewish people from their homeland.

Even without the Diaspora, however, Jews would have lived and worked throughout the ancient world, for there were substantial Jewish trading communities in Phoenicia and Babylonia as long as 3,000 years ago. Jews were with the Phoenician traders who crossed the Mediterranean to settle in Spain as early as 1000 B.C.

A second major dispersal, this time forced by the Romans, occurred after a later failed rising, in Judaea (A.D. 132–135).

Massive persecution of Jews, however, came much later—not with the crucifixion of Jesus Christ in Roman-occupied Judaea (ca. 28–33), but more than six centuries beyond, with the triumph of Catholicism in mainland Europe. A pattern of anti-Jewish persecution then developed that would last in most of Europe for more than 1,300 years.

Authors' Archives

This is a rubbing from the tombstone of a Jewish woman who died in Newport, Rhode Island, in 1764.

This drawing portrays the Beth Israel Synagogue, founded in Philadelphia in 1747.

Anti-Jewish persecution was interrupted in France and Germany briefly during the reign of Charlemagne (768–814). In the same period, the conversion of the Khazars to Judaism (ca. 740) created a Jewish state astride the great Silk Road, north of the Black Sea.

With the Muslim conquest of Spain (711) came a long period of tolerant rule, during which a Spanish Jewish Golden Age developed. That lasted until the Christian reconquest of Spain, which was completed late in the 15th century. There were large-scale massacres of Jews in Castile in 1391, with torture and murder becoming commonplace in many Christian-held Spanish states during the 15th century, especially after the Catholic Inquisition was established in Spain in 1478. Jews were forced to renounce their faith and convert to Christianity, and many did so. Those who did not were expelled from Spain in 1492 and from Portugal in 1497. However, the Inquisition continued. Many converted Jews, who had stayed in Spain and Portugal, were suspected of secretly continuing in their religion, and many were tortured and murdered because of those suspicions.

In the rest of Europe, anti-Jewish persecution never really stopped, despite Charlemagne's brief respite. In 1096, during the First Crusade, Christian forces slaughtered tens of thousands of Jews on their march across Europe, going on to the mass murder of thousands of Jews in Jerusalem in 1099. Four more centuries of mass murders, expulsions, and many other attacks on Jews throughout Europe would follow. The expulsions from Spain and Portugal were late in the process; Jews were expelled from England in 1290; from the Holy Roman Empire (including Germany) in 1298 and 1348; from France in 1306, 1326, and 1394; and from Austria in 1421.

The 16th century brought another respite, as Jewish communities were built in the Protestant Netherlands, Denmark, and some Italian city-states. In 1657, Oliver Cromwell welcomed Jews back to England, after almost four centuries of exclusion.

During the period of the most intense and widespread attacks in western Europe, from the 12th to the 16th centuries, a major Jewish refuge had developed in Poland. By mid-17th century, the Jewish community there numbered more than 500,000. Although Polish Jews encountered a great deal of anti-Semitism, including confinement to ghettos in many cities, they were a good deal freer and safer than the Jews in most other parts of Europe.

However, that safety lasted only until the mid-17th-century Cossack risings against the Poles, which included massacres of tens of thousands of Polish Jews. These were followed by local anti-Jewish massacres in Poland during the several Swedish-Polish and Russo-Polish wars that followed. Beginning late in the 18th century, widespread and violent anti-Jewish campaigns within the Russian Empire would help trigger the huge emigration out of Russia and eastern Europe (see "Immigrants from Russia and the Commonwealth States" on p. 277), which would become the third main wave of Jewish immigration to the United States.

Nor did anti-Jewish persecution end in the modern period. The deaths of the 6 million Jews of the Holocaust were in a very real sense an extension of fourteen centuries of European anti-Jewish hate. It is this history that European Jews brought to America.

Sephardic Jews

The first main wave of Jewish immigration, from 1654 through the end of the 18th century, was by far the smallest of the three, numbering only a few thousand in all. By 1776, there were an estimated 2,000 to 3,000 Jews in the new United States.

These Jewish immigrants came largely from Brazil, the Netherlands, and Britain, and were composed mainly of descendants of the Spanish and Portuguese Jews who had been expelled by Spain in 1492 and Portugal in 1497. These were *Sephardic* Jews, who maintained the religious rites that had been practiced in Spain. All other Jews were described as *Ashkenazic* Jews, who maintained the German Jewish religious rites. A small number of the Sephardic Jews who emigrated from Catholic countries during the early colonial period came as *conversos* (New Christians); these were Jews who had formally converted to the Catholic faith to escape the Inquisition. Most of them converted back to Judaism as soon as they could after arriving in the British and Dutch American colonies.

New Amsterdam's Jewish community grew on a very small scale during the period of Dutch rule, as did New Amsterdam itself. After British conquest in 1664, New Amsterdam became New York, and the city began to develop its role as a mid-Atlantic gateway to North America.

After Jews were welcomed back in England by Oliver Cromwell in 1657, many Sephardic Jews settled in the British colony of Rhode Island, from 1658 on. The largest Jewish community in British North America grew at Newport, while other substantial Jewish communities were established in Philadelphia, Savannah, and Charleston.

Ashkenazic Jews also began to emigrate from Germany and other central and eastern European countries in this period, crossing the North Atlantic on British ships. Britain's Naturalization Act of 1740 brought a substantial increase in immigration into British North America, because

for the first time immigrants could become citizens of the colonies after seven years' residence.

American Jews fought on both sides during the American Revolution, as they would later during the Civil War. With independence, and with full religious freedom and the other guarantees embodied in the Constitution and its Bill of Rights, came federal legal equality. However, that did not always extend to social equality, or to the discriminatory laws of many of the states of the new United States. A great deal of struggle lay ahead for Jews in the new nation.

Nor did this new freedom, and later the reopening of the North Atlantic after the end of the Napoleonic Wars, in 1815, immediately translate into a large influx of European Jewish immigrants. That would come a little later, as part of the huge German immigration that developed in the 1830s.

German Jews

From 1830 to 1900, more than 5 million Germans immigrated to the United States (see "Immigrants from Germany" on p. 135). An estimated 250,000 to 300,000 of these were Jews. The German Jewish immigration into the United States therefore was approximately 100 times as large as the earlier Sephardic Jewish immigration.

Even before this wave of German Jewish immigration, the small American Jewish population included many German-speakers, most of whom had come through England from Germany and other central and eastern European countries. With large numbers of German-speakers immigrating to the United States, however, the number of German-American Jews shot up dramatically. From 1831 to 1840, more than 152,000 German immigrants entered the United States, and by 1840 the United States Jewish population had jumped from a few thousand to an estimated 15,000, most of them German-speakers. In the next decade the German immigration rose to almost 435,000, including an estimated 50,000 German-American Jews. By the 1880s, there were an estimated 250,000 to 300,000 Jews in the United States, the

Many early German Jews began their lives in America as peddlers, like this one selling goods from a wagon in about 1850.

great majority of them German-speakers or their descendants, including large numbers of American-born children and grandchildren of German-born Jews.

The huge German emigration of the early 1850s was caused largely by the potato blight that struck Europe in that period, essentially the same potato disease that struck Ireland and triggered the potato famine, mass deaths, and large-scale Irish emigration. Germany was different from Ireland, though, in that it did not suffer from Ireland's one-crop and subsistence farming, or from absentee landowners who would allow food to be exported while millions starved. There was certainly hardship in Germany, however, accompanied by great economic loss, and all at a time when opportunity beckoned from across the sea.

By the 1850s, large numbers of Germans, among them substantial numbers of German Jews, had already immigrated to the United States. They sent back home widely circulated "America letters," urging family and friends to join them in America for great new opportunities. "Immigrant chains" and a web of helpful organizations

had already been established. The result of all this push-and-pull to America was a major emigration across the Atlantic, which in only three years (1852–1854) brought more than 500,000 Germans to the United States, including tens of thousands of German Jews.

That dramatic rise in immigration slackened from 1854 to 1860, but continued at a significant pace even during the Civil War, sharply rising again in the postwar period. It became massive again in the early 1880s, with more than 730,000 Germans emigrating from 1881 to 1884, and then diminished more permanently.

More than a thousand years of bitter anti-Jewish prejudice in central Europe expressed itself in many ways. One very significant kind of discrimination related to the skills and professions that Jews were able to develop. Many Jews had been traders and businesspeople in the ancient world. In Europe they were for long periods actually barred from certain occupations, including many skilled crafts and farming. Instead, Jews in Germany and in many other countries were forced into such occupations as peddling and moneylending.

Therefore, although large numbers of Germans came to America as farmers and craftspeople, most German Jews, especially in the early years, came to America as peddlers. They followed the great multinational wave of European migration west with the frontier, in the process becoming peddlers and then storekeepers and traders, as well as moneylenders who went into a wide range of financial businesses.

After the American Revolution, the new United States had rapidly expanded west, with hundreds of thousands of settlers pouring through Daniel Boone's Wilderness Road into Kentucky and Tennessee, while even larger numbers moved north through the Hudson Valley and then wheeled west through the Mohawk Valley to Ohio and the Great Lakes. By 1860, the United States, a country of almost 3 million people at the time of the Revolution, had become a nation ten times as large, with almost half of its 31 million people living west of the Appalachians. Especially in the earliest days of the German Jewish emigration, many of those who came to the United States were young single men. They seized opportunity by becoming ped-

dlers, selling their goods while backpacking on foot through the countryside. In time, many moved up to horses and wagons and then became storekeepers, including the founders of many of the Jewish merchant and financial houses that devleoped in mid-century and beyond. Joseph Seligman, who started in 1837 as a backpacking Pennsylvania peddler, founded a national chain of stores and ultimately moved into banking, as did such families as the Lehmans, Guggenheims, and Loebs. Tombstone, Arizona, had three Jewish mayors, as the Wild West became a settled part of the United States.

Many of the young, single German Jews who followed the frontier west simply became part of the population of the United States, marrying people of other ethnic and religious backgrounds, including Native Americans and African Americans. Most, however, maintained a strong sense of Jewish identity, and often of German identity as well. By the mid-1850s, with large numbers of German Jews still arriving in the United States, many substantial Jewish communities had developed. Jewish congregations numbered

Authors' Archives

Jews in Russia were subjected to violent attacks, called pogroms, *and were sometimes driven from their homes, like these in 1881.*

American Museum of Immigration, Statue of Liberty National Monument, National Park Service, U.S. Department of the Interior

This family fled Russia for America in 1908, after the children's mother was killed in a pogrom.

more than 100, most of them led by ordained German Jewish rabbis who had emigrated from central Europe.

From the 1840s until huge numbers of Orthodox Jews from eastern Europe began to arrive late in the century, German Jews were in numbers and influence dominant in American Jewish life. Reform Judaism was the main force in American Jewish religious observance. In Europe, the movement had originated with Moses Mendelssohn and his colleagues before the French Revolution. It came to the United States with the German Jewish immigration of the early 19th century, and was firmly planted by the 1840s, led by such German immigrant rabbis as David Einhorn, Kaufmann Kohler, Isaac Mayer Wise, and Max Lilienthal.

German-American Jews fought on both sides during the Civil War, although by far the greatest number of Germans, including German Jews, were antislavery, and fought for the Union. After the war, as the West was settled, some recent Jewish immigrants moved directly to the West, though many of the new arrivals settled at the start largely where they already had families and friends.

Eastern European Jews

The third and by far the largest wave of Jewish immigrants into the United States came out of eastern Europe between 1882 and 1924, with a long pause during World War I. During that period, an estimated 2.5 million Jews emigrated from eastern Europe to the United States. Most of them were bitterly persecuted Jews from czarist Russia, which included most of occupied Poland, with smaller numbers coming out of Romania and several of the Balkan countries then occupied by the Austro-Hungarian Empire.

During the 19th century, Russia and Russian-occupied Poland had by far the largest Jewish community in the world. That had been so since the partition of Poland among Russia, Prussia, and Austria in 1772 and 1795. In 1791, the Russian empress Catherine the Great's deeply anti-Jewish government forced most Russian Jews into the Pale of Settlement, which included much of Ukraine and all of the Russian-occupied part of Poland. Severe anti-Jewish laws were eased somewhat during the Napoleonic Wars, but were reinstated and intensified from 1815 on. Jews in Russia were barred from farming and from many trades, and were discriminated against in law and in every aspect of social life. Physical attacks on Jews were common, with severe penalties for resistance.

In 1855, as liberal democratic ideas spread in Europe, Czar Alexander II made many reforms in Russia, among them laws easing discrimination against Russian Jews. However, the reform period ended sharply with his assassination in March 1881. A new and much more repressive era began, starting with major anti-Jewish riots throughout southern Russia and Poland in the spring of 1881. In May 1882, the repressive May Laws were introduced.

The immediate effect on Russian Jews was immense. Hopes of reform died, to be replaced by two very different motives: the will to resist, which would take large numbers of Russian and Polish Jews into two Russian revolutions (1905 and 1917); and the will to escape, which would carry millions of Russian Jews to the United States. A much smaller number decided to flee in a different direction—to Zionism and the ultimate creation of the state of Israel.

The immediate result was a sharp increase in Russian Jewish immigration to the United States. Emigration from Russia tripled from 1881 to 1882, going from a little over 5,000 to almost 17,000. By 1887, Russian immigration—most of it Jewish—had topped 30,000 a year, and it continued to rise through the 1890s as developing "immigrant chains" beckoned and then assisted new immigrants.

In the early 20th century, Russian Jews were subjected to widespread violent attacks and massacres, called *pogroms*. After the murders of thousands during the pogroms that began at Kishinev in 1903, the exodus of Jews from Russia increased enormously. From 1900 to 1914, an estimated total of 1,447,000 Russian Jews immigrated to the United States.

After World War I, heavy Jewish immigration resumed, with 119,000 reaching the United States in 1921. The restrictive American immigration law of 1921 then sharply cut Jewish immigration, along with all eastern and southern European immigration. Even so, 153,000 more Jews managed to enter the United States before the 1924 immigration law cut eastern and southern European immigration even more severely.

Russian and other eastern European Jews made a very different set of adjustments to America from the German Jews who preceded them. The great majority of Russian Jews arrived without resources, education, or saleable skills. Nor was there any longer a frontier they might follow westward. Instead, they entered an industrial America and lived as they could in the big cities, clustering in such Jewish neighborhoods as New York's Lower East Side. By 1914, New York City had by far the largest Jewish population in the world.

What the newcomers did have, however, was a passionate will to survive. Unlike many other European immigrants, who thought of returning home, eastern European Jews—especially Russian Jews—looked back at the Old World only as a place from which to extricate as many of their loved ones as possible. They also had an ardent desire to educate their children.

To further both ends, the vast majority of the new eastern European Jewish immigrants worked, saved, sent back money for the passage of other family members, strongly stressed the education of themselves and their children, and in the process built a very successful set of new Jewish-American communities. Many went into their own small businesses, even in the early years; many more became garment workers, hatters, and furriers, or entered other trades. They often played major roles in organizing successful unions that would provide some of the most memorable events in American labor history.

Later Jewish Immigration

During the Great Depression, Jewish emigration from Eastern Europe slowed to a trickle, for there were very few ways to make a living for new immigrants in the United States. Nor did many Jews fleeing Nazi Germany reach the United States; American failure to offer a safe haven for Jewish refugees fleeing Nazi persecution was one of the great failings of the otherwise rather humane Roosevelt administra-

Many Jews in Poland's Warsaw Ghetto fought long and hard against the Germans, but the survivors were eventually driven out of the Ghetto, and many of them later died in concentration camps.

tion. Some of those who survived the Holocaust found their way to America during the postwar period.

A new Russian Jewish emigration began in the late 1960s, when some Jews were allowed to leave the Soviet Union in response to growing international pressure. In 1974, in return for being granted a favorable trade status by the United States, the Soviet Union began to allow substantial numbers of Jews to emigrate. Many of these, along with some other dissidents, sought political asylum in the United States. From the late 1960s through 1996, approximately 385,000 people were recorded as having immigrated into the United States from Russia and the former Soviet Union, many of them Jews.

Another stream of Jewish immigrants came to the United States from Israel. From 1948, when the state of Israel was established, through 1996, 165,000 Israelis were recorded as immigrating into the United States. Many of these were Russian Jews who had gone first to Israel and then later went on to the United States. The figures may be somewhat misleading, because they include many people who emigrated from several countries to Israel after World War II. The figures do not distinguish between "sojourners," for whom Israel was only a way station en route to the United States, and those who immigrated to Israel by choice but later decided to move on to the United States.

Many refugees and immigrants became U.S. citizens after World War II, including Albert Einstein (center) and his stepdaughter Margot (left).

Table 2.44: Number and Percentage of Immigrants from Israel Annually, 1971–1996

Year	Number of Immigrants from Israel	Total U.S. Immigration	Percentage of Immigrants from Israel in Total U.S. Immigration
1971	1,739	370,473	0.47
1972	2,099	384,685	0.55
1973	1,917	400,063	0.48
1974	1,998	394,861	0.51
1975	2,125	396,194	0.54
1976	3,827	502,289	0.76
1977	3,008	462,315	0.65
1978	3,276	601,442	0.54
1979	3,093	460,348	0.67
1980	3,517	530,639	0.66
1981	3,542	596,600	0.59
1982	3,356	594,131	0.56
1983	3,239	559,763	0.58
1984	3,066	543,903	0.56
1985	3,113	570,009	0.55
1986	3,790	601,708	0.63
1987	3,699	601,516	0.61
1988	3,640	643,025	0.57
1989	4,244	1,090,924	0.39
1990	4,664	1,536,483	0.30
1991	4,181	1,827,167	0.23
1992	5,104	973,977	0.52
1993	4,494	904,292	0.50
1994	3,425	804,416	0.43
1995	2,523	720,461	0.35
1996	3,126	915,900	0.34
Total 1971-96	85,805	17,987,584	0.48

Sources: *Statistical Yearbook of the Immigration and Naturalization Service*, 1980, Table 13; *Statistical Yearbook of the Immigration and Naturalization Service*, Table 3; *Statistical Yearbook of the Immigration and Naturalization Service*, 1996, Table 3.

Resources

Internet Resources

American Jewish Congress (*http://www.ajcongress.org*) Web site for organization focused on Jewish life in America's democratic context and on Jewish life in Israel; provides information and action on issues of concern. (Address: Stephen Wise Congress House, 15 East 84th Street, New York, NY 10028; Phone: 212-879-4500; Fax: 212-249-3672)

American Jewish Historical Society (*http://www.ajhs.org*) Web site of the organization focused on the American-Jewish heritage, including information about its substantial archives and museum; offers genealogical reference service, bibiliographies, and links to American Jewish historical organizations and related Web links. (Address: American Jewish Historical Society, 2 Thornton Road, Waltham, MA 02453-7711; Phone: 781-891-8110; Fax: 781-899-9208; E-mail: ajhs@ajhs.org)

American Jewish Committee (*http://www.ajc.org*) Organization Web site offering information on activities, publications, and related links. (Address: Jacob Blaustein Building; 165 East 56th Street; New York, NY 10022; Fax: 212-319-0975)

JewishGen: The Official Home of Jewish Genealogy (*http://www.jewishgen.org*) Key Web site on Jewish genealogy worldwide, including "the JewishGen Family Finder (a database of over 100,000 surnames and towns), the comprehensive directory of InfoFiles, and a variety of databases such as the ShtetlSeeker." Offers a useful on-line guide to Jewish genealogy. It hosts Web sites for regional special interest groups and for the International Association of Jewish Genealogical Societies (IAJGS).

Sephardic and Sephardim Genealogy, Jewish Genealogy (*http://www.orthohelp.com/geneal/sefardim.htm*) Web site offering links to Sephardic Jewish Web sites, newslists, archival sources, and genealogy forms, and to information on Sephardic names.

Etsi—Sephardi Genealogical and Historical Society (*http://www.geocities.com/EnchantedForest/1321*) Web site in English and French on genealogy (*etsi* means "tree"), with special interest groups on topics such as Jews in the Ottoman Empire; offers index of books and articles reviewed in its publications. (Address: Etsi, c/o L. & P. Abensur, 77 bd Richard-Lenoir, 75011 Paris, France)

Cyndi's List—Jewish (*http://www.cyndislist.com/jewish.htm*) List of on-line genealogical resources for Jews, maintained by genealogical author Cyndi Howells.

Shtetl: Memorial (*http://metalab.unc.edu/yiddish/roots.html/*) Offers links to numerous Jewish genealogical sites around the world.

Louis Kessler's Jewish Genealogy Links (*http://www.lkessler.com/jglinks.shtml*) A personal list of the most useful Jewish genealogy Web sites.

JGL: Jewish Genealogy Links—Sephardic Resources (*http://www.pitt.edu/%7Emeisel/jewish/seph.htm*) Web site of links related to Sephardic Jews.

Dutch Jewish Genealogy Homepage (*http://web.inter.nl.net/users/DJGH/*) Web site of information and links related to Jews from the Netherlands.

Beyond the Pale: The History of Jews in Russia (*http://www.friends-partners.org/partners/beyond-the-pale*) On-line exhibit, with images and text, including emigration, plus related links.

Print Resources

General Works

Baum, Charlotte, et al. *The Jewish Woman in America*. New York: Dial, 1976.

Birmingham, Stephen. *"The Rest of Us": The Rise of America's Eastern European Jews*. Boston: Little, Brown, 1984.

Blau, Joseph L., and Salo W. Baron, eds. *The Jews of the United States, 1790–1840: A Documentary History*. New York: Columbia University Press, 1964.

Breitman, Richard, and Alan M. Kraut. *American Refugee Policy and European Jewry, 1933–1945*. Bloomington: Indiana University Press, 1987.

Brownstone, David M. *The Jewish-American Heritage*. New York: Facts on File, 1988.

Butwin, Frances. *The Jews in America*. Rev. ed. Minneapolis: Lerner, 1991.

Davidowicz, Lucy S. *On Equal Terms: Jews in America, 1881–1981*. New York: Holt, Rinehart and Winston, 1982.

Dimont, Max I. *The Jews in America: The Roots, History, and Destiny of American Jews*. New York: Simon and Schuster, 1978.

Diner, Hasia R. *Jews in America*. New York: Oxford University Press, 1999.

Dinnerstein, Leonard. *America and the Survivors of the Holocaust*. New York: Columbia University Press, 1982.

Feingold, Henry. *Zion in America*. New York: Hippocrene, 1981.

Feingold, Henry, ed. *The Jewish People in America*. 5 vols. Baltimore: Johns Hopkins University Press, for the American Jewish Historical Society, 1992. Faber, Eli. *A Time for Planting: The First Migration, 1654–1820*; Diner, Hasia R. *A Time for Gathering: The Second Migration, 1820–1880*; Sorin, Gerald. *A Time for Building: The Third Migration, 1880–1920*; Feingold, Henry L. *A Time for Searching: Entering the Mainstream, 1920–1945*; Shapiro, Edward S. *A Time for Healing: American Jewry Since World War II*.

Feldstein, Stanley. *The Land That I Show You: Three Centuries of Jewish Life in America*. Garden City, N.Y.: Anchor, 1978.

Gurock, Jeffrey S., ed. *American Jewish History: The Colonial and Early National Periods, 1654–1840*. New York: Routledge, 1998.

Gutstein, Linda. *History of the Jews in America*. Secaucus, N.J.: Chartwell, 1988.

Hertzberg, Arthur. *The Jews in America: Four Centuries of an Uneasy Encounter: A History*. New York: Simon and Schuster, 1989. New York: Columbia University Press, 1997.

Hoobler, Dorothy, and Thomas Hoobler. *The Jewish American Family Album*. New York: Oxford University Press, 1995.

Howe, Irving. *World of Our Fathers*. New York: Schocken, 1989.

Hyman, Paula E., and Deborah Dash Moore, eds. *Jewish Women in America: An Historical Encyclopedia*. 2 vols. New York: Routledge, for the American Jewish Historical Society, 1997.

Israel: A Country Study. 3d ed. Helen Chapin Metz, ed. Washington, D.C.: Federal Research Division, Library of Congress, 1990. (Available on-line at *http://lcweb2.loc.gov/frd/cs*)

Karp, Abraham J. *Haven and Home: A History of the Jews in America*. New York: Schocken, 1985.

Kenvin, Helene Schwartz. *This Land of Liberty: A History of America's Jews*. West Orange, N.J.: Behrman House, 1986.

Levitan, Tina. *First Facts in American Jewish History: From 1492 to the Present*. Northvale, N.J.: Jason Aronson, 1996.

Marcus, Jacob Rader. *The Colonial American Jew, 1492–1776*. 3 vols. Detroit: Wayne State University Press, 1970.

———. *The American Jewish Woman: A Documentary History*. New York: KTAV Publishing House, 1981.

———. *United States Jewry, 1776–1985*. Detroit: Wayne State University Press, 1989.

———. *The American Jew, 1585–1990: A History*. Brooklyn, N.Y.: Carlson, 1995.

Meltzer, Milton. *Taking Root: Jewish Immigrants in America.* New York: Farrar, Straus, and Giroux, 1976.

Muggamin, Howard. *The Jewish Americans.* Rev. ed. New York: Chelsea House, 1996.

Orleck, Annelise. *The Soviet Jewish Americans.* Westport, Conn.: Greenwood, 1999.

Raphael, Marc Lee, ed. *Jews and Judaism in the United States: A Documentary History.* New York: Behrman House, 1983.

Rosenberg, Roy A. *Everything You Need to Know About America's Jews and Their History.* New York: Plume, 1997.

Sachar, Howard Morley. *A History of the Jews in America.* New York: Knopf, 1992.

Sarna, Jonathan D., ed. *The American Jewish Experience.* New York: Holmes and Meier, 1986.

Schoener, Allon. *The American Jewish Album: 1654 to the Present.* New York: Rizzoli, 1983.

Shulman, Abraham. *The New Country.* New York: Scribner, 1976.

Sloan, Irving J., comp. *The Jews in America, 1621–1977: A Chronology and Fact Book.* 2d ed. Dobbs Ferry, N.Y.: Oceana, 1978.

Weinberg, Sydney Stahl. *The World of Our Mothers.* New York: Schocken Books, 1990.

Genealogical Works

Marlin, Robert W. *My Sixteen: A Self-Help Guide to Finding Your Sixteen Great-Great Grandparents.* Nashville: Land Yacht Press, 1996.

Sagan, Miriam. *Tracing Our Jewish Roots.* Santa Fe, N.M.: J. Muir, 1993.

Schleifer, Jay. *A Student's Guide to Jewish American Genealogy.* Phoenix: Oryx, 1996.

Stern, Malcolm H. *Americans of Jewish Descent: A Compendium of Genealogy.* New York: Ktav Publishing, 1971.

Stern, Malcolm H. *First American Jewish Families: 600 Genealogies, 1654–1988.* 3d ed. Baltimore: Ottenheimer, 1991.

For more resources, see "General European Immigration Resources" on p. 317 and "General Asian Immigration Resources" on p. 479.

General European Immigration Statistics

See Tables 7.1–7.5, p. 659–738, for annual immigration figures for Europe. For more information on immigration statistics from Europe, see "General Notes on Immigration Statistics" on p. 684, under "Immigration from Europe, 1820–1970."

Graph 2.68: Number of Immigrants from Europe by Decade, 1820–1996

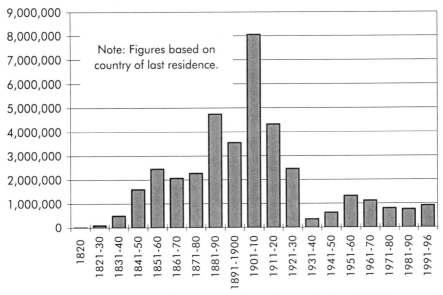

Note: Figures based on country of last residence.

Table 2.45: Number and Percentage of Immigrants from Europe in Total U.S. Immigration by Decade, 1820–1996

Decade	Number of Immigrants from Europe	Total U.S. Immigrants	Percentage of Immigrants from Europe in Total U.S. Immigration
1820	7,690	8,385	91.71
1821-30	98,797	143,439	68.88
1831-40	495,681	599,125	82.73
1841-50	1,597,442	1,713,251	93.24
1851-60	2,452,577	2,598,214	94.39
1861-70	2,065,141	2,314,824	89.21
1871-80	2,271,925	2,812,191	80.79
1881-90	4,735,484	5,246,613	90.26
1891-1900	3,555,352	3,687,564	96.41
1901-10	8,056,040	8,795,386	91.59
1911-20	4,321,887	5,735,811	75.35
1921-30	2,463,194	4,107,209	59.97
1931-40	347,566	528,431	65.77
1941-50	621,147	1,035,039	60.01
1951-60	1,325,727	2,515,479	52.70
1961-70	1,123,492	3,321,677	33.82
1971-80	800,368	4,493,314	17.81
1981-90	761,550	7,338,062	10.38
1991-96	916,733	6,146,213	14.92
Total 1820-1996	38,017,793	63,140,227	60.21

Source: Adapted from Table 2, Immigration by Region and Selected Country of Last Residence, Fiscal Years 1820–1996, from the *Statistical Yearbook of the Immigration and Naturalization Service*, 1996.

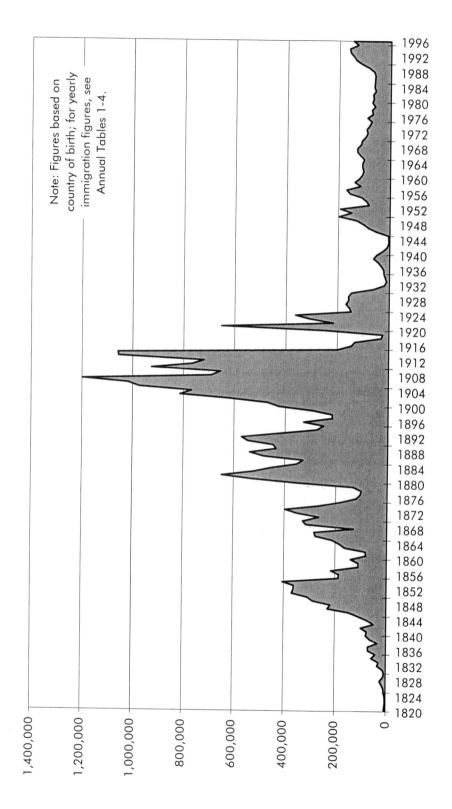

Graph 2.69: Number of Immigrants from Europe Annually, 1820–1996

Note: Figures based on country of birth; for yearly immigration figures, see Annual Tables 1-4.

Table 2.46: Number and Percentage of Foreign-Born Immigrants from Europe by Decade in Total U.S. Population at End of Decade, 1850–1990

Decade	Number of Foreign-Born Immigrants from Europe	Total U.S. Population	Percentage of Foreign-Born Immigrants from Europe in Total U.S. Population
1850	2,031,867	23,191,876	8.76
1860	3,805,701	31,443,321	12.10
1870	4,936,618	39,818,449	12.40
1880	5,744,311	50,155,783	11.45
1890	8,020,608	62,947,714	12.74
1900	8,871,780	75,994,575	11.67
1910	11,791,841	91,972,266	12.82
1920	11,882,053	105,710,620	11.24
1930	11,748,399	122,775,046	9.57
1940	(NA)	131,669,275	(NA)
1950	(NA)	150,697,361	(NA)
1960	7,233,725	179,323,175	4.03
1970	5,712,026	203,235,298	2.81
1980	6,745,550	227,726,000	2.96
1990	4,016,478	249,907,000	1.61

Source: Adapted from Series C 228–295, Foreign-Born Population, by Country of Birth: 1850–1970, in *Historical Statistics of the United States, Colonial Times to 1970, Bicentennial Edition*, and other updating tables from the U.S. Census Bureau.

Graph 2.70: Percentage of Immigrants from Europe in Total U.S. Immigration by Decade, 1820–1996

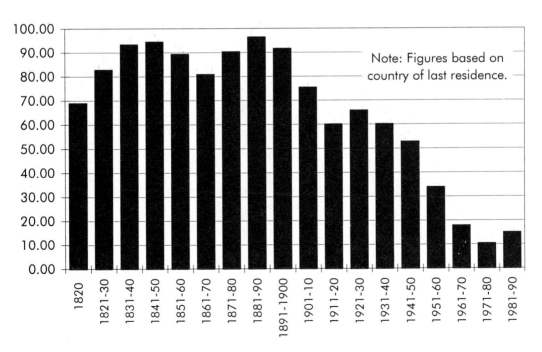

Note: Figures based on country of last residence.

Graph 2.71: Number of Foreign-Born Immigrants from Europe by Decade in Total U.S. Population at End of Decade, 1850–1990

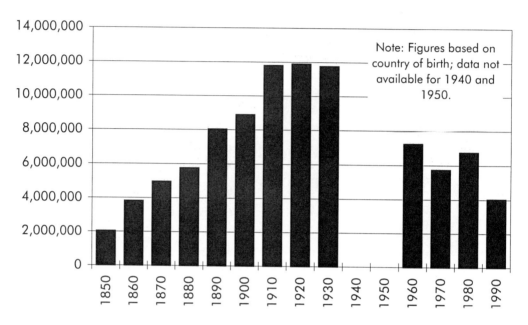

Note: Figures based on country of birth; data not available for 1940 and 1950.

Graph 2.72: Percentage of Foreign-Born Immigrants from Europe by Decade in Total U.S. Population at End of Decade, 1850–1990

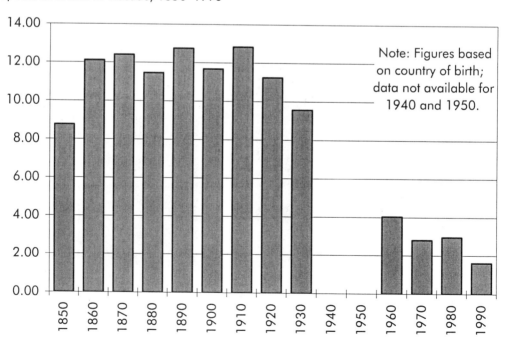

Note: Figures based on country of birth; data not available for 1940 and 1950.

General European Immigration Resources

Internet Resources

CenEuroGenWeb (*http://www.rootsweb.com/~ceneurgw/*) Part of the WorldGenWeb project, linking genealogical research sites around the world, by region, with resources by individual country and links to other parts of Europe.

EastEuropeGenWeb (*http://www.rootsweb.com/~easeurgw/*) Part of the WorldGenWeb project, linking genealogical research sites around the world, by region, with resources by individual country and links to other parts of Europe; also offers links to other general resources and mailing lists.

MediterraneanGenWeb (*http://www.mediterraneangenweb.org*) Part of the WorldGenWeb project, linking genealogical research sites around the world, by region, with resources by individual country and links to neighboring regions of the world.

Cyndi's List–Western Europe (*http://www.cyndislist.com/westeuro.htm*) and Cyndi's List—Eastern Europe (*http://www.cyndislist.com/easteuro.htm*) Lists of on-line genealogical resources for western and eastern Europe, maintained by genealogical author Cyndi Howells.

Federation of Eastern European Family History Societies (FEEFHS) (*http://www.feefhs.org*) Web site offers searchable index, resource guide, Internet journal, research notes, links to professional databases, map indexes, and specialist cross-indexes for individual ethnic groups. (Address: P.O. Box 510898, Salt Lake City, UT 84151-0898)

East European Genealogical Society (EEGS) (*http://www.eegsociety.org*) Web site offering information about the organization, answers to frequently asked questions (FAQs), and back issues of its publications. (Address: P.O. Box 2536, Winnipeg, MB, Canada R3C 4A7; Phone: 204-989-3292)

Print Resources

General Works

Berthoff, Rowland. *Republic of the Dispossessed: The Exceptional Old-European Consensus in America.* Columbia: University of Missouri Press, 1997.

Blumenthal, Shirley. *Coming to America: Immigrants from Eastern Europe.* New York: Delacorte, 1981.

Brown, Gene. *Discovery and Settlement: Europe Meets the New World, 1490–1700.* New York: Twenty-First Century Books, 1993.

Leonard, Henry Beardsell. *The Open Gates: The Protest Against the Movement to Restrict European Immigration, 1896–1924.* New York: Arno Press, 1980.

Lescott-Leszczynski, John. *The History of U.S. Ethnic Policy and its Impact on European Ethnics.* Boulder, Col.: Westview, 1984.

Luebke, Frederick C., ed. *European Immigrants in the American West: Community Histories.* Albuquerque: University of New Mexico Press, 1998.

Matulich, Loretta. *A Cross-Disciplinary Study of the European Immigrants of 1870 to 1925.* New York: Arno Press, 1980. Originally printed as the authors' thesis.

Mayberry, Jodine. *Eastern Europeans.* New York: Watts, 1991.

Overland, Orm, ed. *In the European Grain: American Studies from Central and Eastern Europe.* Amsterdam: Vu University Press, 1990.

Rips, Gladys Nadler. *Coming to America: Immigrants from Southern Europe.* New York: Delacorte, 1981.

Robbins, Albert. *Coming to America: Immigrants from Northern Europe.* New York: Delacorte, 1981.

Rollyson, Carl, comp. *Teenage Refugees from Eastern Europe Speak Out.* New York: Rosen, 1997.

Stave, Bruce M., et al. *From the Old Country: An Oral History of European Migration to America.* Hanover, N.H.: University Press of New England, 1999. Originally published: New York: Twayne, 1994.

Taylor, Philip A. M. *The Distant Magnet: European Emigration to the U.S.A.* London: Eyre & Spottiswoode, 1971.

Vecoli, Rudolph J., and Suzanne M. Sinke, eds. *A Century of European Migrations, 1830–1930.* Urbana: University of Illinois Press, 1991.

Walch, Timothy, ed. *Immigrant America: European Ethnicity in the United States.* New York: Garland, 1994.

Wyman, Mark. *Round-Trip to America: The Immigrants Return to Europe, 1880–1930.* Ithaca, N.Y.: Cornell University Press, 1993.

See Parts I and VII and the Appendixes of this book for more general information, statistics, and resources on immigration.

Part III

Immigration from

Africa

Introduction

Immigration to the United States from Africa was negligible until the 1965 Immigration Act opened the United States door wide to immigrants from the Eastern Hemisphere. Of the 532,123 recorded African immigrants who reached the United States from 1820 (when the United States began to keep official immigration statistics) to 1996, some 455,740, or 85.6 percent, arrived between 1971 and 1996. Only 14.4 percent had arrived in the previous 151 years.

Note that the figures above do not reflect the arrival of approximately 400,000 to 500,000 black African slaves from 1619 until the Civil War, for they were not counted as immigrants in the official figures (see "The Slave Trade" on p. 321). Most of the increase in the number of ethnic African Americans in the United States has been derived from these earlier involuntary immigrants. However, some of that increase was due to Afro-Caribbean immigration (see articles on immigration from various Caribbean islands).

Following are an article on the slave trade and country-by-country treatments of the main sources of immigration to the United States from Africa. These are followed by the overall recorded U.S. immigration statistics for Africa and general resources on African immigration.

The Slave Trade

The overwhelming majority of those who came from Africa to the United States before Lincoln's Emancipation Proclamation came as slaves, rather than as "immigrants," and were therefore not counted as immigrants by colonial and United States governments. However, these involuntary Americans, taken against their will, arriving in chains, and sold by slavers to slavers, became part of the American mosaic and are today revered as the ancestors of tens of millions of African Americans—those that survived, that is. Although estimates vary, it is probable that easily 15 to 20 percent did not survive the passage, and that many more did not survive the early months and years of slavery.

Background of African Slavery

In 1441, Portuguese ships exploring and trading south along Africa's west coast finally extended their range south of Muslim-held northern Africa, reaching west Africa. They returned to Portugal with ten black African women and men whom they enslaved, the first recorded victims of the Atlantic slave trade. So began the huge European expansion of the African slave trade, by then centuries old and primarily in Muslim hands.

Many historians use 1451 as the starting date for the Atlantic slave trade, for that was when substantial numbers of African slaves, perhaps 700 to 800 a year, began to reach Portugal. The Atlantic slave trade therefore is generally seen as running from 1451 to 1870, roughly the effective end of the slave trade to the Americas.

There is no single widely accepted estimate of the number of black Africans taken by slavers and transported in the Atlantic slave trade. Nor is there a single such estimate of the number of those who survived the voyage to become slaves in the Americas. The estimates that follow—for the whole Atlantic slave trade and for the numbers of black African slaves who reached the United States—should therefore be regarded as quite approximate.

From 1451 through 1870, an estimated 9.6 million to 11.5 million black Africans reached the Americas as slaves. Assuming a probable 20 percent death rate en route, the number of those shipped out of Africa would have been 11.4 million to 13.8 million slaves. Of these, a massive 3.5 million to 4 million went to Brazil; 1.7 million to 1.9 million to the British Caribbean; 1.6 million to 1.8 million to the French Caribbean; 1.55 million to 1.75 million to Spanish America; 500,000 to 600,000 to the Dutch Caribbean; 275,000 to 325,000 to Europe and the Atlantic islands; and 400,000 to 500,000 to the areas that became the United States.

Table 3.1: Estimated Number of Black Africans Transported to Various Destinations in the Transatlantic Slave Trade, 1451–1870

Destination	Moderately Low Estimate	Moderately High Estimate
Brazil	3,500,000	4,000,000
British Caribbean	1,700,000	1,900,000
French Caribbean	1,600,000	1,800,000
Spanish Americas	1,550,000	1,750,000
Dutch Caribbean	500,000	600,000
Europe and the Atlantic Islands	275,000	325,000
United States and Earlier Colonies	400,000	500,000
Other	75,000	625,000
Total	9,600,000	11,500,000

Note: Figures summarize estimates given in accompanying article.

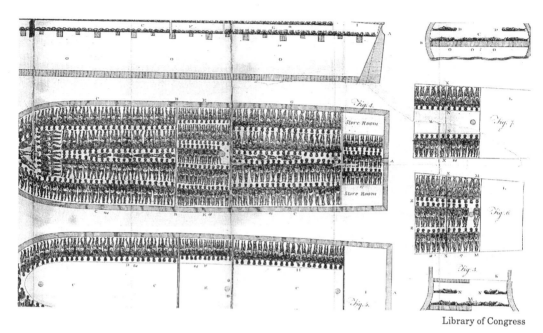

Library of Congress

This 1808 cross-section view shows how black Africans being transported as slaves were packed into every available space on the ship.

In cultural terms, to say "black African" is much like saying "European," rather than describing people by their country or ethnic origins. Over more than four centuries, at least 12 million people were taken from their homes and sold into slavery, in aggregate from most or all of the peoples of sub-Saharan Africa.

Nor were the ports from which they were shipped necessarily in their countries of origin. Large numbers of slaves were shipped from the west African coast, from Senegal, Gambia, Sierra Leone, the Windward Coast, the Gold Coast, the Bight of Biafra, and Guinea, with slavers' routes extending ever farther into the interior of northern and central Africa as the numbers of slaves taken increased. Huge numbers of slaves were also shipped out of Angola and other central African countries, again with several ever-lengthening slave routes into the interior. As the slave trade bit even deeper into the African peoples, substantial numbers of people were taken as slaves in southeastern Africa, to be shipped largely out of east coast ports in Mozambique and then transported across the Atlantic.

Slave Trade to North America

In what would become the United States, the slave trade began in 1619, when the first recorded black African slaves were sold at Jamestown, Virginia. Slaves continued to arrive, with a total of approximately 30,000 to 35,000 during the balance of the 17th century. These numbers would be eclipsed by the much larger numbers of the 18th century, caused largely by the increasing use of slaves in farming in the southern colonies, most notably at the start in tobacco and later even more notably in cotton. From 1701 to 1810, an estimated 350,000 to 400,000 black Africans were brought in as slaves, with the overwhelming majority shipped into southern ports, mainly in Virginia and the Carolinas.

The United States formally banned the slave trade in 1807. However, slaves continued to be imported into southern ports until the Civil War, with their numbers probably totaling an additional 50,000 to 60,000 in that period.

Historians' estimates indicate that probably half of the African slaves brought directly to the British North American mainland were shipped out of west African ports, although many of the victims had been captured in north central Africa. Approximately a quarter were shipped out of Biafra, with most of these coming out of central Africa. Angola was the main shipping point for the final quarter of the North American slaves, with very many of these coming out of eastern and southern Africa.

The African-American portion of the United States population grew far more quickly than did the numbers of black African American slaves. By 1770, the estimated population of the British North American colonies had reached 251,000, of whom 28,000, or 11 percent, were slaves. By 1780, the population of the colonies had soared to 2.78 million, of whom 575,000, or more than 20 percent, were slaves. Largely through normal population increase, the African-American population had risen almost twice as fast as the white population.

After the start of the American Revolution, the antislavery movement gained strength in the colonies and then the new United States. Vermont abolished slavery in 1777. Antislavery laws followed in Pennsylvania (1780), New Hampshire (1783), Connecticut (1784), Rhode Island (1784), New Jersey (1799), and New York (1804), though many of these provided only for the gradual end of slavery. Massachusetts abolished slavery by court decision in 1783. On the federal level, the Northwest Ordinance of 1787 banned slavery in what were then called the Northwest Territories, extending northwest of the Ohio River, in what would later become part of the American midwestern heartland. Although Lin-

coln's Emancipation Proclamation came in 1863, the end of slavery came only with Union victory in the Civil War.

In 1820, when the first reasonably reliable U.S. Census was taken, the slave population had grown to 1.538 million, and 333,000 free African Americans were counted; that gave a combined total of 1.871 million, with the number of African Americans having more than tripled in 40 years. The white population, then at 9.618 million, had also more than tripled, to 3.25 times its 1780 level. African Americans constituted 19.5 percent of the total population, not far from their percentage in 1780.

In 1860, on the eve of the Civil War, the slave population totaled 3.954 million, along with 488,000 free African Americans, for a total of 4.442 million. In those 40 years, African-American population growth had slowed somewhat, but had reached almost 2.4 times its 1820 level. In the same period, the white population, at 32.513 million, had grown even faster, to 3.38 times its 1820 level. African Americans were then 13.7 percent of the total population, much lower than the 1780 or 1820 levels.

For further information on United States immigration from Africa, see articles on some individual African nations that are substantial-to-modest sources of United States immigrants. See also "An Overview" on p. 2, and "The Journey" on p. 53. Note also that many immigrants from elsewhere in the Americas, especially from the Caribbean, are in the United States often defined as being African Americans (see articles on individual countries).

Graph 3.1: Estimated Number of Black Africans Transported to Various Destinations in the Transatlantic Slave Trade, 1451–1870

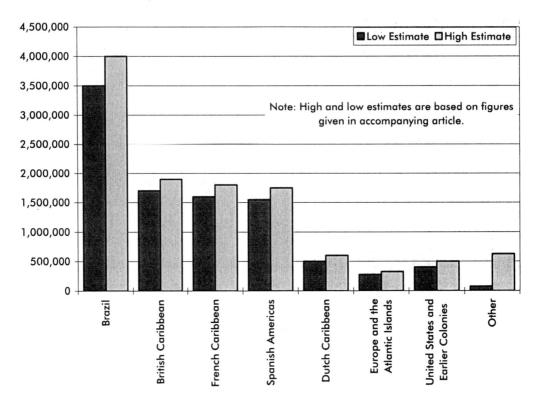

Note: High and low estimates are based on figures given in accompanying article.

Graph 3.2: Estimated Percentage of Black Africans Transported to Various Destinations in the Transatlantic Slave Trade, 1451–1870

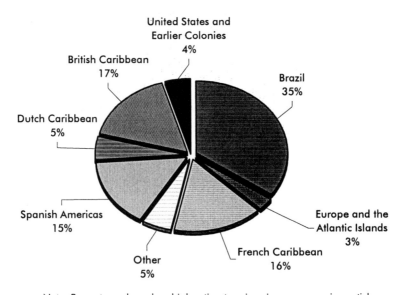

Note: Percentages based on high estimates given in accompanying article.

Resources

Internet Resources

African-American Census Schedules Online (*http://www.prairiebluff.com/aacensus/*) Web site containing downloadable census forms, links to on-line census records, including slave schedules and mortality schedules, and links to other African-American genealogical resources.

Christine's Genealogy Web site (*http://ccharity.com/*) Web site offering African-American genealogical materials, including a database of servitude and emancipation records (1722–1863), and links to many other sites.

Genealogy (*http://www.coax.net/people/lwf/genes.htm*) Web site provides links to state, family, and other sites related to African-American genealogy and history, including sources of records and other materials, newsletters, archives of discussion groups, and related organizations.

International Black Index Source Directory (*http://www.blackindex.com*) Searchable directory of resources and links relating to African genealogy.

Print Resources

Burnside, Madeleine. *Spirits of the Passage: The Transatlantic Slave Trade in the Seventeenth Century*. New York: Simon & Schuster, 1997.

Cramer, Clayton E. *Black Demographic Data, 1790–1860: A Sourcebook*. Westport, Conn.: Greenwood, 1997.

Eltis, David, and David Richardson, eds. *Routes to Slavery: Direction, Ethnicity, and Mortality in the Transatlantic Slave Trade*. London; Portland, Ore.: Frank Cass, 1997.

Frank, Andrew. *The Birth of Black America: The Age of Discovery and the Slave Trade*. New York: Chelsea House, 1996.

Haskins, James, and Kathleen Benson. *Bound for America: The Forced Migration of Africans to the New World*. New York: Lothrop, Lee & Shepard Books, 1999.

Klein, Herbert S. *The Middle Passage: Comparative Studies in the Atlantic Slave Trade*. Princeton, N.J.: Princeton University Press, 1978.

———. *The Atlantic Slave Trade*. New York: Cambridge University Press, 1999.

Palmer, Colin A. *The First Passage—Blacks in the Americas, 1502–1617*. New York: Oxford University Press, 1995.

Rawley, James A. *The Transatlantic Slave Trade: A History*. New York: Norton, 1981.

Reynolds, Edward. *Stand the Storm: A History of the Atlantic Slave Trade*. New York: Allison & Busby, 1985; Chicago: I. R. Dee, 1993.

Thomas, Hugh. *The Slave Trade: The Story of the Atlantic Slave Trade, 1440–1870*. New York: Simon & Schuster, 1997.

Thomas, Velma Maia. *Lest We Forget: The Passage from Africa to Slavery and Emancipation*. New York: Crown, 1997.

White, Anne Terry. *Human Cargo: The Story of the Atlantic Slave Trade*. Champaign, Il.: Garrard, 1972.

For more resources, see "General African Immigration Resources" on p. 361.

Immigrants from Egypt

With an estimated population of 62.7 million in 1997, Egypt is the most populous of the Arab countries. It also has one of the world's highest rates of population growth, during the 1990s in the range of 2.6 percent to 2.8 percent. The country's population has grown considerably beyond its resources, a basic problem greatly worsened by massive rural flight to the cities, coupled with a long Islamic guerrilla insurgency, still in progress.

From 1971 to 1996, a total of almost 85,000 Egyptians immigrated to the United States. The great majority of these were drawn from Egypt's most highly trained people, among them doctors and other medical professionals, teachers, scientists, and technicians, all of whom might have made major contributions to their own country had Egypt been able to hold them.

These U.S. immigrants were part of a much larger emigration out of Egypt, which in the 1980s saw an estimated 3 million Egyptians migrate to jobs in the oil countries of the Middle East. These emigrants were sending home as much money in aggregate as might have been generated by another Egyptian major industry. At least 1 million of these emigrants returned home to Egypt in the 1990s, as world oil prices declined and many jobs abroad evaporated.

Table 3.2: Number and Percentage of Immigrants from Egypt in Total U.S. Immigration Annually, 1971–1996

Year	Number of Immigrants from Egypt	Total U.S. Immigration	Percentage of Immigrants from Egypt in Total U.S. Immigration
1971	3,643	370,473	0.98
1972	2,512	384,685	0.65
1973	2,274	400,063	0.57
1974	1,831	394,861	0.46
1975	1,707	396,194	0.43
1976	2,290	502,289	0.46
1977	2,328	462,315	0.50
1978	2,836	601,442	0.47
1979	3,241	460,348	0.70
1980	2,833	530,639	0.53
1981	3,366	596,600	0.56
1982	2,800	594,131	0.47
1983	2,600	559,763	0.46
1984	2,642	543,903	0.49
1985	2,802	570,009	0.49
1986	2,989	601,708	0.50
1987	3,377	601,516	0.56
1988	3,016	643,025	0.47
1989	3,717	1,090,924	0.34
1990	4,117	1,536,483	0.27
1991	5,602	1,827,167	0.31
1992	3,576	973,977	0.37
1993	3,556	904,292	0.39
1994	3,392	804,416	0.42
1995	5,648	720,461	0.78
1996	6,186	915,900	0.68
Total 1971-96	84,881	17,987,584	0.47

Sources: *Statistical Yearbook of the Immigration and Naturalization Service,* 1980; Table 13; *Statistical Yearbook of the Immigration and Naturalization Service,* 1986, Table 3; *Statistical Yearbook of the Immigration and Naturalization Service,* 1996, Table 3.

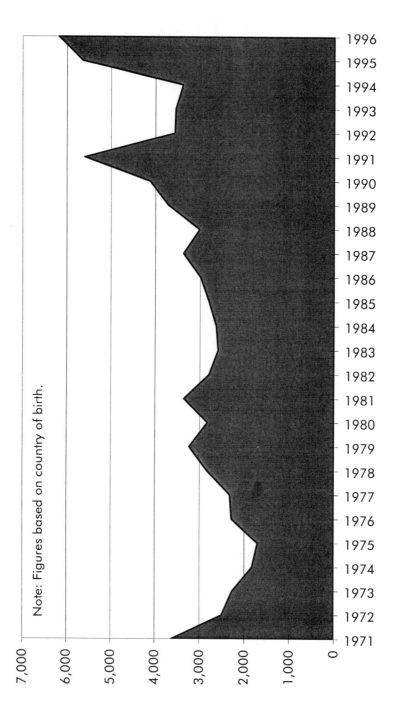

Graph 3.3: Number of Immigrants from Egypt Annually, 1971–1996

Note: Figures based on country of birth.

Resources

Internet Resources

AfricaGenWeb Project (*http://
www.rootsweb.com/~africagw/*) Part of
the WorldGenWeb project, linking
genealogical research sites around the
world, by region; includes resources by
individual country in Africa and links
to general resources.

Print Resources

Egypt: A Country Study. 5th ed. Helen
Chapin Metz, ed. Washington, D.C.:
Federal Research Division, Library of
Congress, 1991. (Available on-line at
http://lcweb2.loc.gov/frd/cs)

For more resources, see "General African Immigration Resources" on p. 361.

Immigrants from Ethiopia

Ethiopia is one of the world's poorest countries, with an average per capita income of less than $150 per year. Although infant mortality continues high and health care is poor, it is also a country with a birth rate high enough to ensure that it suffers from massive population growth, in the range of 3 percent per year in the late 1990s. Nor has it ever recovered from the long Eritrean-Ethiopian War (1962–1991) or from the dictatorship of Haile Mariam Mengistu (1977–1991), which was characterized by the mass murder of tens of thousands of political opponents, the forced internal migration of hundred of thousands of Ethiopians, and the accompanying major drought and famine (1984–1985). That period saw an estimated 2.5 million refugees from starvation and disease in the Horn of Africa, while Ethiopian and Eritrean combatants refused to let relief supplies from abroad reach them. An estimated 1 million people died during the war, most of them refugees.

One of the results of Ethiopia's time of great troubles was the flight of many of its most highly trained and educated people to other countries, among them the United States. Many of these were opponents of the dictatorship; others sought only a better life.

From 1971 to 1980, Ethiopian immigration into the United States was negligible, amounting to an average of only a few hundred immigrants per year. Immigration picked up in the 1980s into the range of 2,000 to 3,000 per year, and continued to grow in the 1990s, into the range of 4,000 to 5,000 per year. Although Ethiopia was no longer a military dictatorship involved in a long series of wars, none of the country's major problems had been solved and solutions did not seem close. In 1997, Ethiopia's estimated population was 60.3 million, up from an estimated 51 million in 1990, only 7 years earlier.

Table 3.3: Number and Percentage of Immigrants from Ethiopia in Total U.S. Immigration Annually, 1971–1996

Year	Number of Immigrants from Ethiopia	Total U.S. Immigration	Percentage of Immigrants from Ethiopia in Total U.S. Immigration
1971	130	370,473	0.04
1972	192	384,685	0.05
1973	149	400,063	0.04
1974	276	394,861	0.07
1975	206	396,194	0.05
1976	332	502,289	0.07
1977	354	462,315	0.08
1978	539	601,442	0.09
1979	726	460,348	0.16
1980	977	530,639	0.18
1981	1,749	596,600	0.29
1982	1,810	594,131	0.30
1983	2,643	559,763	0.47
1984	2,461	543,903	0.45
1985	3,362	570,009	0.59
1986	2,737	601,708	0.45
1987	2,156	601,516	0.36
1988	2,571	643,025	0.40
1989	3,389	1,090,924	0.31
1990	4,336	1,536,483	0.28
1991	5,127	1,827,167	0.28
1992	4,602	973,977	0.47
1993	5,191	904,292	0.57
1994	3,887	804,416	0.48
1995	5,960	720,461	0.83
1996	6,086	915,900	0.66
Total 1971-96	61,948	17,987,584	0.34

Sources: *Statistical Yearbook of the Immigration and Naturalization Service*, 1980, Table 13; *Statistical Yearbook of the Immigration and Naturalization Service*, 1986, Table 3; *Statistical Yearbook of the Immigration and Naturalization Service*, 1996, Table 3.

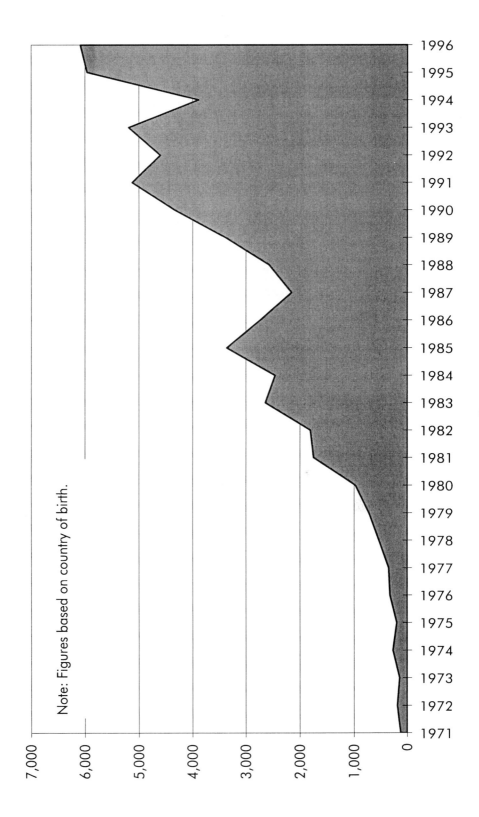

Graph 3.4: Number of Immigrants from Ethiopia Annually, 1971–1996

Note: Figures based on country of birth.

Resources

Internet Resources

AfricaGenWeb Project (*http://www.rootsweb.com/~africagw/*) Part of the WorldGenWeb project, linking genealogical research sites around the world, by region; includes resources by individual country in Africa and links to general resources, including African-American sites and Middle Eastern Arab sites.

Print Resources

Meshesha, Mekonnen. *Ethiopian Refugees: Beyond the Famine and the War.* Newton, Mass.: Newton International Press, 1994.

Schnapper, LaDena, ed. *Teenage Refugees from Ethiopia Speak Out.* New York: Rosen, 1997.

For more resources, see "General African Immigration Resources" on p. 361.

Other Immigrants from Africa

Following are immigration statistics relating to several other African countries. Some have sent few emigrants to the United States at any time, while others have become independent since World War II and have only very brief documented histories of immigration into the United States. However, all have some United States immigration history worthy of graphic presentation. Note that figures for the Cape Verde Islands are included under "Immigrants from Portugal" on p. 129.

See "General African Immigration Resources" on p. 361 for wider information and resources.

Immigrants from Ghana

Table 3.4: Number and Percentage of Immigrants from Ghana in Total U.S. Immigration Annually, 1971–1996

Year	Number of Immigrants from Ghana	Total U.S. Immigration	Percentage of Immigrants from Ghana in Total U.S. Immigration
1971	182	370,473	0.05
1972	326	384,685	0.08
1973	487	400,063	0.12
1974	369	394,861	0.09
1975	275	396,194	0.07
1976	404	502,289	0.08
1977	454	462,315	0.10
1978	711	601,442	0.12
1979	828	460,348	0.18
1980	1,159	530,639	0.22
1981	951	596,600	0.16
1982	824	594,131	0.14
1983	976	559,763	0.17
1984	1,050	543,903	0.19
1985	1,041	570,009	0.18
1986	1,164	601,708	0.19
1987	1,120	601,516	0.19
1988	1,239	643,025	0.19
1989	2,045	1,090,924	0.19
1990	4,466	1,536,483	0.29
1991	3,330	1,827,167	0.18
1992	1,867	973,977	0.19
1993	1,604	904,292	0.18
1994	1,458	804,416	0.18
1995	3,152	720,461	0.44
1996	6,606	915,900	0.72
Total 1971-96	38,088	17,987,584	0.21

Sources: *Statistical Yearbook of the Immigration and Naturalization Service*, 1980, Table 13; *Statistical Yearbook of the Immigration and Naturalization Service*, 1986, Table 3; *Statistical Yearbook of the Immigration and Naturalization Service*, 1996, Table 3.

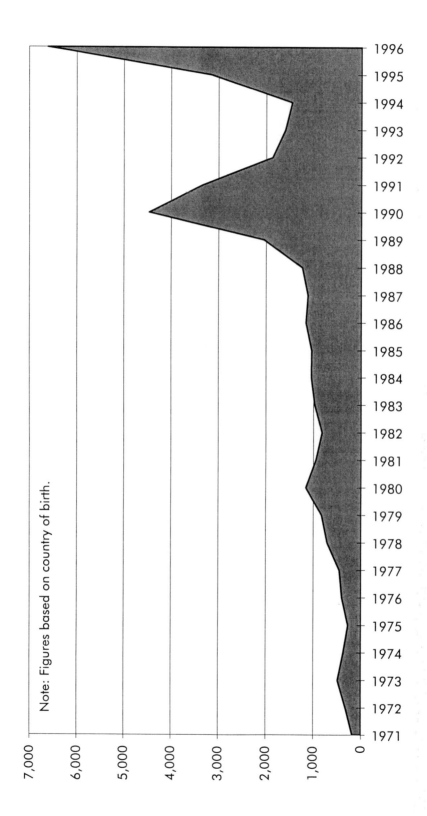

Graph 3.5: Number of Immigrants from Ghana Annually, 1971–1996

Note: Figures based on country of birth.

Resources

Attah-Poku, Agyemang. *The Socio-
Cultural Adjustment Question: The
Role of Ghanaian Immigrant Ethnic
Associations in America*. Brookfield,
Vt.: Avebury, 1996.

Ghana: A Country Study. 3d ed. LaVerle
Berry, ed. Washington, D.C.: U.S.
Government Printing Office, 1995.
(Available on-line at *http://
lcweb2.loc.gov/frd/cs*)

Onwonga, Billy M. N. *Welcome to America:
Foreigner's Life in America*. Freeman,
S.D.: Pine Hill Press, 1995.

Immigrants from Kenya

Table 3.5: Number and Percentage of Immigrants from Kenya in Total U.S. Immigration Annually, 1971–1996

Year	Number of Immigrants from Kenya	Total U.S. Immigration	Percentage of Immigrants from Kenya in Total U.S. Immigration
1971	331	370,473	0.09
1972	295	384,685	0.08
1973	300	400,063	0.07
1974	386	394,861	0.10
1975	446	396,194	0.11
1976	528	502,289	0.11
1977	493	462,315	0.11
1978	516	601,442	0.09
1979	618	460,348	0.13
1980	592	530,639	0.11
1981	657	596,600	0.11
1982	601	594,131	0.10
1983	710	559,763	0.13
1984	753	543,903	0.14
1985	735	570,009	0.13
1986	719	601,708	0.12
1987	698	601,516	0.12
1988	773	643,025	0.12
1989	910	1,090,924	0.08
1990	1,297	1,536,483	0.08
1991	1,185	1,827,167	0.06
1992	953	973,977	0.10
1993	1,065	904,292	0.12
1994	1,017	804,416	0.13
1995	1,419	720,461	0.20
1996	1,666	915,900	0.18
Total 1971-96	19,663	17,987,584	0.11

Sources: *Statistical Yearbook of the Immigration and Naturalization Service, 1980,* Table 13; *Statistical Yearbook of the Immigration and Naturalization Service, 1986,* Table 3; *Statistical Yearbook of the Immigration and Naturalization Service, 1996,* Tabe 3.

Resources

Kenya: A Country Study. 3d ed. Harold D. Nelson, ed. Washington, D.C.: Federal Research Division, Library of Congress, 1983.

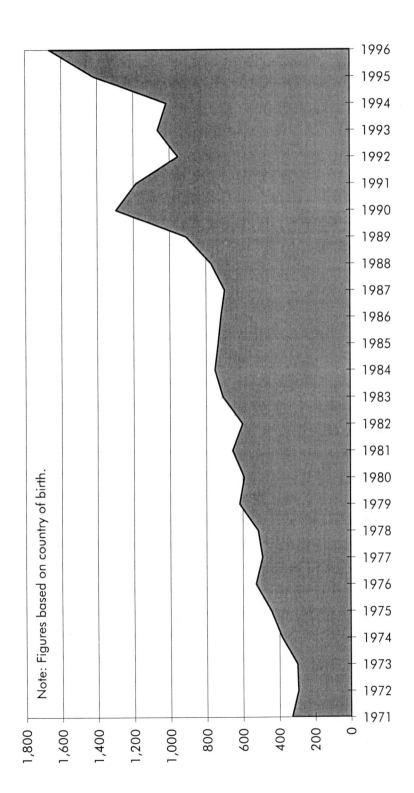

Graph 3.6: Number of Immigrants from Kenya Annually, 1971–1996

Note: Figures based on country of birth.

Immigrants from Liberia

Table 3.6: Number and Percentage of Immigrants from Liberia in Total U.S. Immigration Annually, 1971–1996

Year	Number of Immigrants from Liberia	Total U.S. Immigration	Percentage of Immigrants from Liberia in Total U.S. Immigration
1971	116	370,473	0.03
1972	134	384,685	0.03
1973	195	400,063	0.05
1974	191	394,861	0.05
1975	163	396,194	0.04
1976	300	502,289	0.06
1977	215	462,315	0.05
1978	333	601,442	0.06
1979	327	460,348	0.07
1980	426	530,639	0.08
1981	556	596,600	0.09
1982	593	594,131	0.10
1983	518	559,763	0.09
1984	585	543,903	0.11
1985	618	570,009	0.11
1986	618	601,708	0.10
1987	622	601,516	0.10
1988	769	643,025	0.12
1989	1,175	1,090,924	0.11
1990	2,004	1,536,483	0.13
1991	1,292	1,827,167	0.07
1992	999	973,977	0.10
1993	1,050	904,292	0.12
1994	1,762	804,416	0.22
1995	1,929	720,461	0.27
1996	2,206	915,900	0.24
Total 1971-96	19,696	17,987,584	0.11

Sources: *Statistical Yearbook of the Immigration and Naturalization Service*, 1980, Table 13; *Statistical Yearbook of the Immigration and Naturalization Service*, 1986, Table 3; *Statistical Yearbook of the Immigration and Naturalization Service*, 1996, Table 3.

Resources

Chicoine, Stephen. *A Liberian Family.* Minneapolis: Lerner, 1997.

Liberia: A Country Study. 3d ed. Harold D. Nelson, ed. Washington, D.C.: Federal Research Division, Library of Congress, 1984.

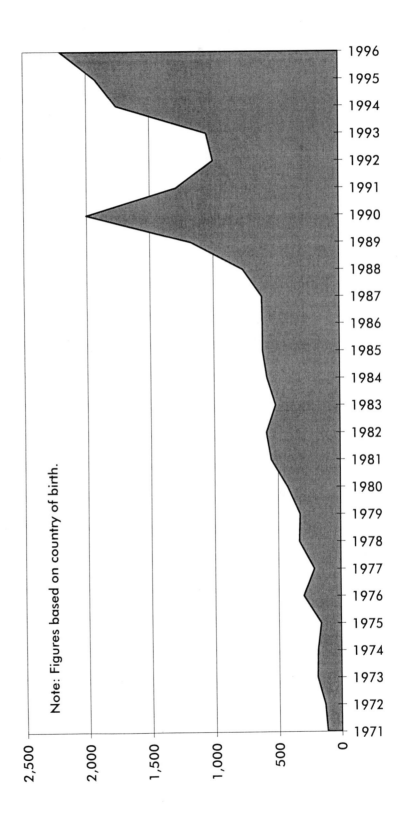

Graph 3.7: Number of Immigrants from Liberia Annually, 1971–1996

Note: Figures based on country of birth.

Immigrants from Morocco

Table 3.7: Number and Percentage of Immigrants from Morocco in Total U.S. Immigration Annually, 1971–1996

Year	Number of Immigrants from Morocco	Total U.S. Immigration	Percentage of Immigrants from Morocco in Total U.S. Immigration
1971	391	370,473	0.11
1972	421	384,685	0.11
1973	445	400,063	0.11
1974	455	394,861	0.12
1975	390	396,194	0.10
1976	516	502,289	0.10
1977	401	462,315	0.09
1978	461	601,442	0.08
1979	486	460,348	0.11
1980	465	530,639	0.09
1981	512	596,600	0.09
1982	445	594,131	0.07
1983	479	559,763	0.09
1984	506	543,903	0.09
1985	570	570,009	0.10
1986	646	601,708	0.11
1987	635	601,516	0.11
1988	715	643,025	0.11
1989	984	1,090,924	0.09
1990	1,200	1,536,483	0.08
1991	1,601	1,827,167	0.09
1992	1,316	973,977	0.14
1993	1,176	904,292	0.13
1994	1,074	804,416	0.13
1995	1,726	720,461	0.24
1996	1,783	915,900	0.19
Total 1971-96	19,799	17,987,584	0.11

Sources: *Statistical Yearbook of the Immigration and Naturalization Service*, 1980, Table 13; *Statistical Yearbook of the Immigration and Naturalization Service*, 1986, Table 3; *Statistical Yearbook of the Immigration and Naturalization Service*, 1996, Table 3.

Resources

Morocco: A Country Study. 5th ed. Harold D. Nelson, ed. Washington, D.C.: Federal Research Division, Library of Congress, 1985.

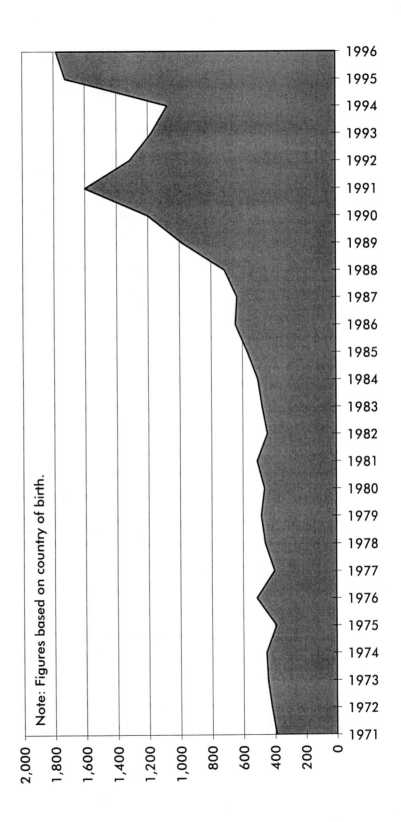

Graph 3.8: Number of Immigrants from Morocco Annually, 1971–1996

Note: Figures based on country of birth.

Immigrants from Nigeria

Table 3.8: Number and Percentage of Immigrants from Nigeria in Total U.S. Immigration Annually, 1971–1996

Year	Number of Immigrants from Nigeria	Total U.S. Immigration	Percentage of Immigrants from Nigeria in Total U.S. Immigration
1971	451	370,473	0.12
1972	738	384,685	0.19
1973	738	400,063	0.18
1974	670	394,861	0.17
1975	653	396,194	0.16
1976	907	502,289	0.18
1977	653	462,315	0.14
1978	1,007	601,442	0.17
1979	1,054	460,348	0.23
1980	1,896	530,639	0.36
1981	1,918	596,600	0.32
1982	2,257	594,131	0.38
1983	2,354	559,763	0.42
1984	2,337	543,903	0.43
1985	2,846	570,009	0.50
1986	2,976	601,708	0.49
1987	3,278	601,516	0.54
1988	3,343	643,025	0.52
1989	5,213	1,090,924	0.48
1990	8,843	1,536,483	0.58
1991	7,912	1,827,167	0.43
1992	4,551	973,977	0.47
1993	4,448	904,292	0.49
1994	3,950	804,416	0.49
1995	6,818	720,461	0.95
1996	10,221	915,900	1.12
Total 1971-96	82,032	17,987,584	0.46

Sources: *Statistical Yearbook of the Immigration and Naturalization Service*, 1980, Table 13; *Statistical Yearbook of the Immigration and Naturalization Service*, 1986, Table 3; *Statistical Yearbook of the Immigration and Naturalization Service*, 1996, Table 3.

Resources

Nigeria: A Country Study. 4th ed. Harold D. Nelson, ed. Washington, D.C.: Federal Research Division, Library of Congress, 1982. (Available on-line at *http://lcweb2.loc.gov/frd/cs*)

Udofia, Paul E. *Nigerians in the United States: Potentialities and Crises.* Boston: William Monroe Trotter Institute, 1996.

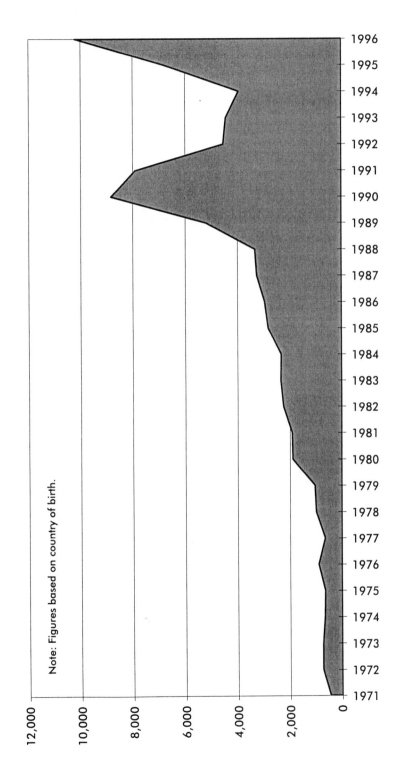

Graph 3.9: Number of Immigrants from Nigeria Annually, 1971–1996

Note: Figures based on country of birth.

Immigrants from Sierra Leone

Table 3.9: Number and Percentage of Immigrants from Sierra Leone in Total U.S. Immigration Annually, 1971–1996

Year	Number of Immigrants from Sierra Leone	Total U.S. Immigration	Percentage of Immigrants from Sierra Leone in Total U.S. Immigration
1971	35	370,473	0.01
1972	48	384,685	0.01
1973	65	400,063	0.02
1974	61	394,861	0.02
1975	66	396,194	0.02
1976	137	502,289	0.03
1977	157	462,315	0.03
1978	212	601,442	0.04
1979	217	460,348	0.05
1980	267	530,639	0.05
1981	277	596,600	0.05
1982	283	594,131	0.05
1983	319	559,763	0.06
1984	368	543,903	0.07
1985	371	570,009	0.07
1986	323	601,708	0.05
1987	453	601,516	0.08
1988	571	643,025	0.09
1989	939	1,090,924	0.09
1990	1,290	1,536,483	0.08
1991	951	1,827,167	0.05
1992	693	973,977	0.07
1993	690	904,292	0.08
1994	698	804,416	0.09
1995	919	720,461	0.13
1996	1,918	915,900	0.21
Total 1971-96	12,328	17,987,584	0.07

Sources: *Statistical Yearbook of the Immigration and Naturalization Service*, 1980, Table 13; *Statistical Yearbook of the Immigration and Naturalization Service*, 1986, Table 3; *Statistical Yearbook of the Immigration and Naturalization Service*, 1996, Table 3.

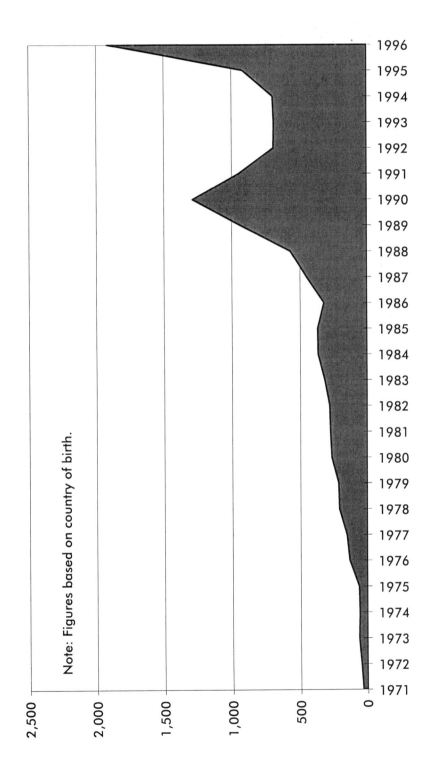

Graph 3.10: Number of Immigrants from Sierra Leone Annually, 1971–1996

Note: Figures based on country of birth.

Immigrants from South Africa

Table 3.10: Number and Percentage of Immigrants from South Africa in Total U.S. Immigration Annually, 1971–1996

Year	Number of Immigrants from South Africa	Total U.S. Immigration	Percentage of Immigrants from South Africa in Total U.S. Immigration
1971	375	370,473	0.10
1972	521	384,685	0.14
1973	503	400,063	0.13
1974	525	394,861	0.13
1975	586	396,194	0.15
1976	1,098	502,289	0.22
1977	1,988	462,315	0.43
1978	1,689	601,442	0.28
1979	2,214	460,348	0.48
1980	1,960	530,639	0.37
1981	1,559	596,600	0.26
1982	1,434	594,131	0.24
1983	1,261	559,763	0.23
1984	1,246	543,903	0.23
1985	1,210	570,009	0.21
1986	1,566	601,708	0.26
1987	1,741	601,516	0.29
1988	1,832	643,025	0.28
1989	1,899	1,090,924	0.17
1990	1,990	1,536,483	0.13
1991	1,854	1,827,167	0.10
1992	2,516	973,977	0.26
1993	2,197	904,292	0.24
1994	2,144	804,416	0.27
1995	2,560	720,461	0.36
1996	2,966	915,900	0.32
Total 1971-96	41,434	17,987,584	0.23

Sources: *Statistical Yearbook of the Immigration and Naturalization Service*, 1980, Table 13; *Statistical Yearbook of the Immigration and Naturalization Service*, 1986, Table 3; *Statistical Yearbook of the Immigration and Naturalization Service*, 1996, Table 3.

Resources

Major Genealogical Record Sources in South Africa. Salt Lake City, Utah: Genealogical Department of the Church of Jesus Christ of Latter-Day Saints, 1976.

South Africa: A Country Study. 3d ed. Rita M. Byrnes, ed. Washington, D.C.: Federal Research Division, Library of Congress, 1997.

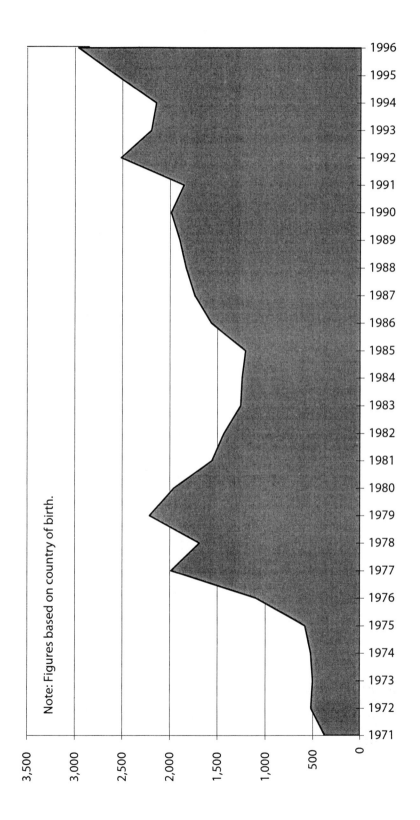

Graph 3.11: Number of Immigrants from South Africa Annually, 1971–1996

Note: Figures based on country of birth.

Immigrants from Tanzania

Table 3.11: Number and Percentage of Immigrants from Tanzania in Total U.S. Immigration Annually, 1971–1996

Year	Number of Immigrants from Tanzania	Total U.S. Immigration	Percentage of Immigrants from Tanzania in Total U.S. Immigration
1971	183	370,473	0.05
1972	271	384,685	0.07
1973	264	400,063	0.07
1974	243	394,861	0.06
1975	304	396,194	0.08
1976	381	502,289	0.08
1977	302	462,315	0.07
1978	301	601,442	0.05
1979	401	460,348	0.09
1980	339	530,639	0.06
1981	423	596,600	0.07
1982	304	594,131	0.05
1983	364	559,763	0.07
1984	418	543,903	0.08
1985	395	570,009	0.07
1986	370	601,708	0.06
1987	385	601,516	0.06
1988	388	643,025	0.06
1989	507	1,090,924	0.05
1990	635	1,536,483	0.04
1991	500	1,827,167	0.03
1992	352	973,977	0.04
1993	426	904,292	0.05
1994	357	804,416	0.04
1995	524	720,461	0.07
1996	553	915,900	0.06
Total 1971-96	9,890	17,987,584	0.05

Sources: *Statistical Yearbook of the Immigration and Naturalization Service*, 1980, Table 13; *Statistical Yearbook of the Immigration and Naturalization Service*, 1986, Table 3; *Statistical Yearbook of the Immigration and Naturalization Service*, 1996, Table 3.

Resources

Tanzania: A Country Study. 2d ed. Irving Kaplan, ed. Washington, D.C.: Federal Research Division, Library of Congress, 1978.

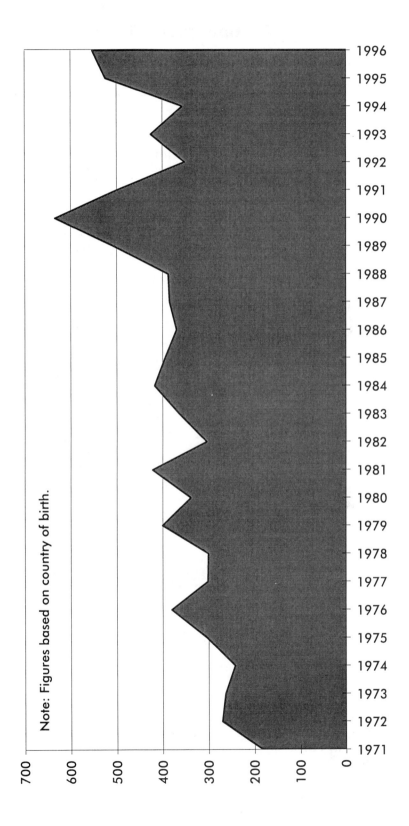

Graph 3.12: Number of Immigrants from Tanzania Annually, 1971–1996

Note: Figures based on country of birth.

Immigrants from Uganda

Table 3.12: Number and Percentage of Immigrants from Uganda in Total U.S. Immigration Annually, 1971–1996

Year	Number of Immigrants from Uganda	Total U.S. Immigration	Percentage of Immigrants from Uganda in Total U.S. Immigration
1971	97	370,473	0.03
1972	159	384,685	0.04
1973	339	400,063	0.08
1974	320	394,861	0.08
1975	859	396,194	0.22
1976	425	502,289	0.08
1977	241	462,315	0.05
1978	303	601,442	0.05
1979	284	460,348	0.06
1980	343	530,639	0.06
1981	410	596,600	0.07
1982	304	594,131	0.05
1983	332	559,763	0.06
1984	369	543,903	0.07
1985	301	570,009	0.05
1986	401	601,708	0.07
1987	357	601,516	0.06
1988	343	643,025	0.05
1989	393	1,090,924	0.04
1990	674	1,536,483	0.04
1991	538	1,827,167	0.03
1992	437	973,977	0.04
1993	415	904,292	0.05
1994	391	804,416	0.05
1995	383	720,461	0.05
1996	422	915,900	0.05
Total 1971-96	9,840	17,987,584	0.05

Sources: *Statistical Yearbook of the Immigration and Naturalization Service, 1980,* Table 13; *Statistical Yearbook of the Immigration and Naturalization Service, 1986,* Table 3; *Statistical Yearbook of the Immigration and Naturalization Service, 1996,* Table 3.

Resources

Uganda: A Country Study. 2d ed. Rita M. Byrnes, ed. Washington, D.C.: Federal Research Division, Library of Congress, 1992. (Available on-line at *http://lcweb2.loc.gov/frd/cs*)

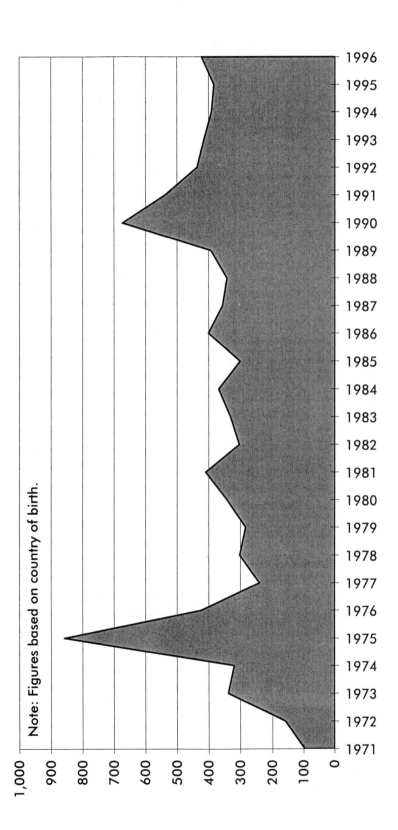

Graph 3.13: Number of Immigrants from Uganda Annually, 1971–1996

Note: Figures based on country of birth.

General African Immigration Statistics

Table 3.13: Number and Percentage of Immigrants from Africa in Total U.S. Immigration by Decade, 1820–1996

Decade	Immigrants from Africa	Total U.S. Immigrants	Percentage of Immigrants from Africa in Total U.S. Immigration
1820	1	8,385	0.00
1821-1830	16	143,439	0.01
1831-1840	54	599,125	0.01
1841-1850	55	1,713,251	0.00
1851-1860	210	2,598,214	0.01
1861-1870	312	2,314,824	0.01
1871-1880	358	2,812,191	0.01
1881-1890	857	5,246,613	0.02
1891-1900	350	3,687,564	0.01
1901-1910	7,368	8,795,386	0.08
1911-1920	8,443	5,735,811	0.15
1921-1930	6,286	4,107,209	0.15
1931-1940	1,750	528,431	0.33
1941-1950	7,367	1,035,039	0.71
1951-1960	14,092	2,515,479	0.56
1961-1970	28,954	3,321,677	0.87
1971-1980	80,779	4,493,314	1.80
1981-1990	176,893	7,338,062	2.41
1991-1996	198,068	6,146,213	3.22
Total 1820-1996	532,213	63,140,227	0.84

Note: Figures do not include Africans transported as slaves.

Source: Adapted from Table 2, Immigration by Region and Selected Country of Last Residence, Fiscal Years 1820–1996, from the *Statistical Yearbook of the Immigration and Naturalization Service*, 1996.

Table 3.14: Number and Percentage of Foreign-Born Immigrants from Africa by Decade in Total U.S. Population at End of Decade, 1850–1990

Decade	Number of Foreign-Born Immigrants from Africa	Total U.S. Population	Percentage of Foreign-Born Immigrants from Africa in Total U.S. Population
1850	551	23,191,876	0.00
1860	526	31,443,321	0.00
1870	2,657	39,818,449	0.01
1880	2,204	50,155,783	0.00
1890	2,207	62,947,714	0.00
1900	2,538	75,994,575	0.00
1910	3,992	91,972,266	0.00
1920	5,781	105,710,620	0.01
1930	8,859	122,775,046	0.01
1940	(NA)	131,669,275	(NA)
1950	(NA)	150,697,361	(NA)
1960	18,737	179,323,175	0.01
1970	61,463	203,235,298	0.03
1980	199,723	227,726,000	0.09
1990	363,819	249,907,000	0.15

NA = Not available

Source: Adapted from Series C 228–295, Foreign-Born Population, by Country of Birth: 1850–1970, in *Historical Statistics of the United States, Colonial Times to 1970, Bicentennial Edition*, and other updating tables from the U.S. Census Bureau.

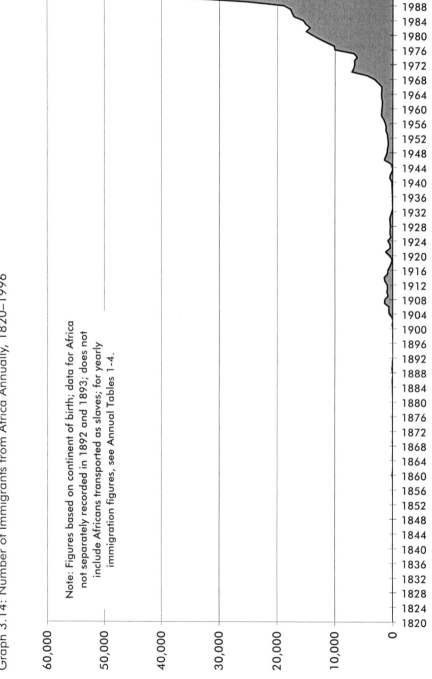

Graph 3.14: Number of Immigrants from Africa Annually, 1820–1996

Note: Figures based on continent of birth; data for Africa not separately recorded in 1892 and 1893; does not include Africans transported as slaves; for yearly immigration figures, see Annual Tables 1-4.

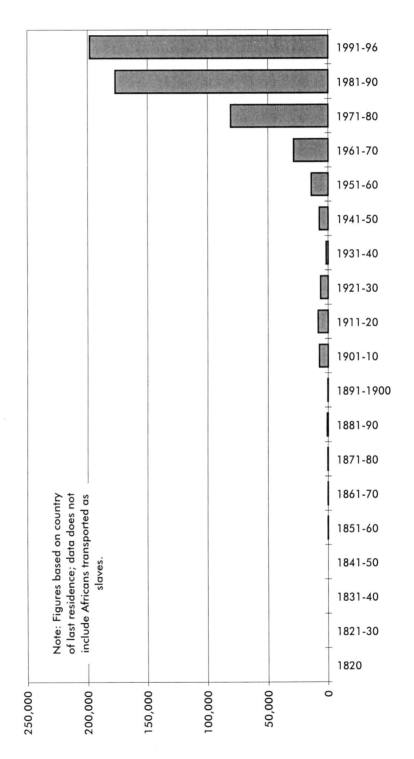

Graph 3.15: Number of Immigrants from Africa by Decade, 1820–1996

Note: Figures based on country of last residence; data does not include Africans transported as slaves.

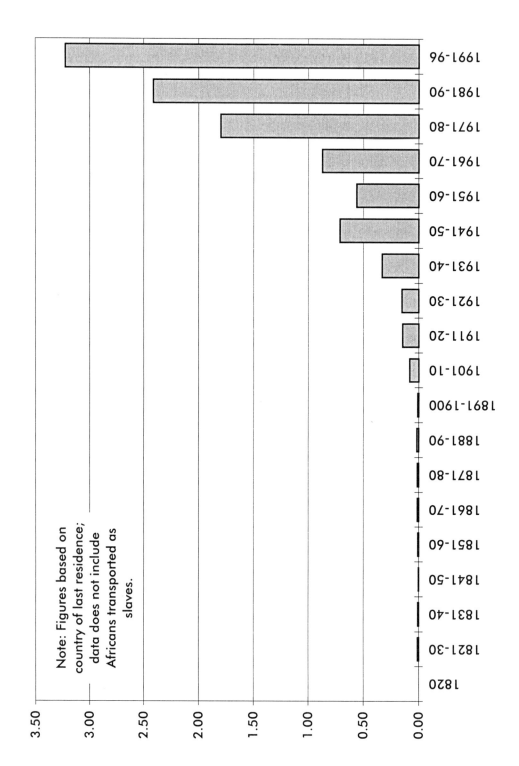

Graph 3.16: Percentage of Immigrants from Africa in Total U.S. Immigration by Decade, 1820–1996

Note: Figures based on country of last residence; data does not include Africans transported as slaves.

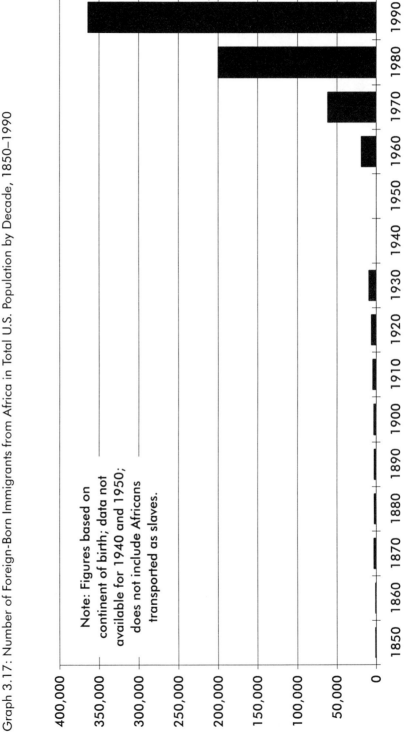

Graph 3.17: Number of Foreign-Born Immigrants from Africa in Total U.S. Population by Decade, 1850–1990

Note: Figures based on continent of birth; data not available for 1940 and 1950; does not include Africans transported as slaves.

Graph 3.18: Percentage Distribution of Americans of Black African Origin by Region of the United States, 1990

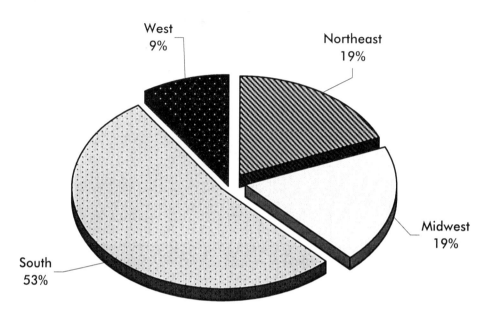

See Annual Tables 1–5, pp. 659–713, for annual immigration figures for Africa; note that these figures do not include Africans brought to the United States as slaves, who were not counted as immigrants.

For more information on immigration statistics from Africa, see "General African Immigration Statistics" on p. 355, under "Immigration from Africa, 1820–1970."

General African Immigration Resources

Internet Resources

AfricaGenWeb Project (*http://
www.rootsweb.com/~africagw/*) Part of
the WorldGenWeb project, linking
genealogical research sites around the
world, by region; includes resources by
individual country in Africa and links
to general resources, including African-
American sites and Middle Eastern
Arab sites.

Print Resources

General Works

Altman, Susan. *The Encyclopedia of
African American Heritage*. New York:
Facts on File, 1997.

Apraku, Kofi Konadu. *African Emigrés in
the United States: A Missing Link in
Africa's Social and Economic
Development*. New York: Praeger, 1991.

Black Diaspora Committee of Howard
University. *The Black Diaspora:
Africans and Their Descendants in the
Wider World, 1800 to the Present*. Rev.
ed. Needham Heights, Mass.: Ginn,
1990.

Chambers, Catherine. *The History of
Emigration from Africa*. New York:
Watts, 1997.

Garwood, Alfred N., ed. *Black Americans:
A Statistical Sourcebook*. Boulder, Col.:
Numbers & Concepts, 1990.

Harris, Joseph E., ed. *Global Dimensions
of the African Diaspora*. 2d ed.
Washington, D.C.: Howard University
Press, 1993.

Hart, Ayanna. *Africans in America*. Rev.
ed. Minneapolis: Lerner, 1995.
Originally published as *Negro in
America*.

Hornsby, Alton. *The Black Almanac*. 4th
ed. Woodbury, N.Y.: Barron's, 1977.

Reef, Catherine. *Africans in America: The
Spread of People and Culture*. New
York: Facts on File, 1999.

Segal, Ronald. *The Black Diaspora*.
Boston: Faber and Faber, 1995.

Smith, Carter, II, ed. *The African-
American Experience on File*. New
York: Facts on File, 1998.

Smith, Jessie Carney, and Carrell
Peterson Horton, comps. *Historical
Statistics of Black America*. 2 vols.
Detroit: Gale, 1995.

Woodtor, Dee Parmer. *Finding a Place
Called Home: A Guide to African-
American Genealogy and Historical
Identity*. New York: Random House,
1999.

Chronologies

Christian, Charles Melvin. *Black Saga:
The African American Experience: A
Chronology*. Boston: Houghton Mifflin,
1995.

Gates, Henry Louis, Jr. *The Amistad
Chronology of African-American
History, 1445–1990*. New York:
Amistad, 1993.

Harley, Sharon. *The Timetables of African-
American History: A Chronology of the
Most Important People and Events in
African-American History*. New York:
Simon & Schuster, 1995.

Hornsby, Alton, Jr. *Chronology of African
American History: From 1492 to the
Present*. 2d ed. Detroit: Gale, 1997.

Hornsby, Alton, Jr., and Deborah Gillan
Straub. *African American Chronology*.
Detroit: UXL, 1994.

Jenkins, Everett, Jr. *Pan-African
Chronology II: A Comprehensive
Reference to the Black Quest for*

Freedom in Africa, the Americas, Europe, and Asia, 1865-1915. Jefferson, N.C.: McFarland, 1998.

Jenkins, Everett, Jr. *Pan-African Chronology: A Comprehensive Reference to the Black Quest for Freedom in Africa, the Americas, Europe and Asia, 1400–1865.* Jefferson, N.C.: McFarland, 1996.

Sloan, Irving J. *Blacks in America, 1492–1970: A Chronology and Fact Book.* 4th ed. Dobbs Ferry, N.Y.: Oceana, 1977.

See Parts I and VII and the Appendixes of this volume for more general information, statistics, and resources on immigration.

Part IV

Immigration from Asia

Introduction

Immigration to the United States from Asia was very small until Chinese immigrants began to arrive following the California gold strike of 1848. Although substantial numbers of Chinese immigrants arrived from then until the 1882 Chinese Exclusion Act, Asian immigration was still very small as compared with the massive European immigration of the period. It reached a high of only 4.42 percent of total U.S. immigration in the 1870s.

Asian immigration to the United States, largely from Japan and Turkey, grew substantially again in the early decades of the 20th century. However, Japanese immigration was largely cut off by the 1907 "Gentlemen's Agreement."

Asian immigration during the early 20th century was far less than it seemed. This is because Turkish immigration, ostensibly from Asia, was in reality largely from the European portions of the Turkish empire. Even that was cut off by the restrictive immigration laws of the early 1920s.

Immigration to the United States from Asia remained small until passage of the 1965 Immigration Act. That opened the previously largely closed United States door to immigrants from the Eastern Hemisphere. Asian immigration moved up sharply in the late 1960s, and then skyrocketed in the 1970s. A major additional factor was the arrival of more than 1.2 million immigrants from Vietnam, Cambodia, and Laos between 1978 to 1996.

Overall a total of 7,894,571 immigrants arrived in the United States from Asia between 1820, when the United States began to keep official immigration statistics, and 1996. Of these, 6,210,726 arrived between 1971 and 1996, or 78.7 percent of the total immigration from Asia in the past 157 years. Previously prohibited, Asian arrivals had became a major factor in U.S. immigration by the late 20th century.

Following are country-by-country treatments of the main sources of immigration to the United States from Asia. These are followed by the overall recorded U.S. immigration statistics for Asia and general resources on Asian immigration.

Immigrants from China

Chinese immigration into the United States has come largely in two waves. The first began quite sharply in 1849 as part of the California Gold Rush, in direct response to the 1848 gold find at Sutter's Mill, near Sacramento, California. It ended just as sharply, with passage of the 1882 Chinese Exclusion Act, which with later anti-Chinese laws cut off most immigration to the United States from China until after World War II. The second great wave began in the middle of the 20th century and continues today.

Early Immigrants from China

The Great Chinese Encyclopedia, written in the early sixth century A.D., reported that in the late fifth century Chinese Buddhist priests had journeyed far to the east by sea, to a land they called *Fusang,* probably on what is now the United States west coast, and then traveled south to what is now Mexico. A whole body of research, speculation, and argument has built up around that and other possible later journeys. In the absence of verifiable evidence, we can only say that Chinese sailing ships in use then could have made such a journey, but that even if they did so, no trace of a lasting Chinese settlement has been found on the west coast of North or Central America.

What is quite verifiable is that Chinese visitors to the Americas came on Spanish galleons returning from the Philippines to Panama after 1564. That was when Spanish navigator Miguel López de Legazpi found a return route across the Pacific from Manila, in the Philippines, to Panama by sailing from Manila far to the north, to the latitude of Japan, and then riding the prevailing winds east. The route reached North America at the latitude of San Francisco, then led south along the coast against wind and current to Acapulco and Panama. After that Spanish galleons (also called "China ships") regularly criss-crossed the Pacific in the Manila trade, as Spain built a massive, extraordinarily lucrative trade with the Far East, using Manila harbor as its trading port. The

Spanish galleons would bring gold, silver, pearls, and European goods such as lace to Manila; there they met Chinese junks that had carried silk goods, porcelain, and a wide variety of other goods across the China Sea to Manila. Later, Indian and Indonesian ships carrying spices, tea, drugs, and many other kinds of valuable goods also reached Manila.

Many of the Spanish ships in the Manila trade were built in the Philippines, at least partly by highly skilled Chinese shipbuilders. Spanish crews returning to the Americas also reportedly included Chinese sailors, and may have included sailors from other parts of Asia. These Chinese sailors were the first reasonably verifiable Chinese visitors to the New World.

By the mid-1700s, there were certainly Chinese in Spanish-ruled California, some working as shipbuilders. Small numbers of Chinese continued to immigrate to California before Gold Rush days. In 1788, the British Meares expedition, which included many Chinese, sailed from Guangzhou (Canton), China, to Vancouver Island, where they established a fortified post; 75 more Chinese arrived there as settlers in 1789. Although the fort was soon attacked and taken by the Spanish, many Chinese are thought to have remained in California, with some going to Mexico.

In the late 1700s, a few Chinese also began to arrive in the United States, beginning with sailors visiting on American ships returning from the Far East. The first five Chinese students arrived at a Cornwall, Connecticut, religious mission school in 1818. A Chinese junk, the *Keying,* arrived in New York in 1847, but its crew returned to China.

The historic port city of Guangzhou (Canton), in south China's Guangdong (Kwangtung) province, was the main Chinese emigration port for the early Chinese headed for North America. The great majority of these were from the six counties of the Pearl River delta area around Guangzhou. Why this was so is still not entirely clear. One likely reason is that people from this area were the earliest Chinese to have extensive contacts with Europeans. It is also quite probable that the earliest immigrants from Guangdong set up the same kinds of "immigrant chains" seen in other immigrant groups, where the earliest immigrants send letters and money back home, stimulating many others to follow. Through such contacts, Chinese in Guangdong may have built up considerable knowledge of the west coast of the Americas, for there were Chinese in California and Mexico long before the first main wave of Chinese immigration.

The First Great Wave

Only a few things were needed to start large numbers of Chinese on their way to the New World: the ability to leave China, coupled with a push to leave; and a pull, in the form of opportunity.

The push, when it came, was powerful, and stemmed from several related developments. China had enjoyed a long period of economic and population growth before large-scale European penetration of the country began in the early 19th century. Chinese census figures reported that the country's population climbed from 200 million to 400 million people between 1762 and 1834. However, with European penetration came the opium trade, which would lead to the Opium War and the European invasion and partial conquest of China. Rural insurrections also began to increase, and by the mid-19th century would develop into full-scale civil war.

In 1815–1816, the British began large-scale shipments of opium into China; despite increasingly desperate Chinese government efforts to stop the trade, it grew enormously in the years that followed. By the late 1830s, the British were shipping more than 40,000 cases of opium per year into China. When the Chinese government banned the trade, the British began and quickly won the Opium War (1840), forcing China to accept opium, to open major Chinese ports to the Europeans, and to cede Hong Kong to Britain. Other European countries followed suit in the 70 years that followed, destroying China's ability to resist. Largely in response to the destabilization of the country, rural uprisings grew into the Taiping

Rebellion, an enormous civil war that between 1850 and 1866 cost 20 million to 40 million lives.

As a result of both sets of developments, much of China's economy was crushed. Millions of Chinese emigrated abroad. Most of these moved from the formerly prosperous and heavily populated south China to southeast Asia and Indonesia, but some went to the New World. From 1845 on, tens of thousands began to immigrate to Central and South America. Many Chinese emigrants went as contract laborers to literally killing jobs in the Americas, such as the Peruvian mines and Cuban sugarcane plantations. These were the immigrants called "coolies" (those who do "bitter work"), a term applied to most Chinese contract laborers. Many of these Chinese emigrants were deceived into thinking they were taking passage as free people. Very few of these early contract laborers made their way to the United States.

Starting in 1849, many others immigrated to the United States, drawn by the lure of gold. These were not contract laborers, but free people, although many arrived deeply in debt for their passage money.

Table 4.1: Number and Percentage of Immigrants from China in Total U.S. Immigration by Decade, 1820–1996

Decade	Number of Immigrants from China	Total U.S. Immigration	Percentage of Immigrants from China in Total U.S. Immigration
1820	1	8,385	0.01
1821-1830	2	143,439	0.00
1831-1840	8	599,125	0.00
1841-1850	35	1,713,251	0.00
1851-1860	41,397	2,598,214	1.59
1861-1870	64,301	2,314,824	2.78
1871-1880	123,201	2,812,191	4.38
1881-1890	61,711	5,246,613	1.18
1891-1900	14,799	3,687,564	0.40
1901-1910	20,605	8,795,386	0.23
1911-1920	21,278	5,735,811	0.37
1921-1930	29,907	4,107,209	0.73
1931-1940	4,928	528,431	0.93
1941-1950	16,709	1,035,039	1.61
1951-1960	9,657	2,515,479	0.38
1961-1970	34,764	3,321,677	1.05
1971-1980	124,326	4,493,314	2.77
1981-1990	346,747	7,338,062	4.73
1991-1996	208,735	6,146,213	3.40
Total 1820-1996	1,176,660	63,140,227	1.86

Note: Beginning in 1957, China included Taiwan. As of January 1, 1979, the United States recognized the People's Republic of China.

Source: Adapted from Table 2, Immigration by Region and Selected Country of Last Residence, Fiscal Years 1820–1996, from the *Statistical Yearbook of the Immigration and Naturalization Service*, 1996.

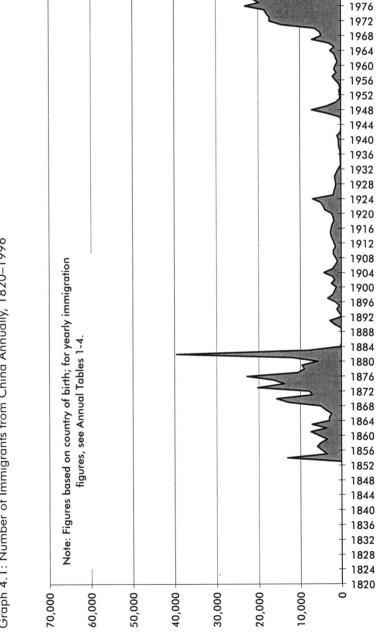

Graph 4.1: Number of Immigrants from China Annually, 1820–1996

Note: Figures based on country of birth; for yearly immigration figures, see Annual Tables 1-4.

Graph 4.2: Number of Immigrants from China by Decade, 1820–1996

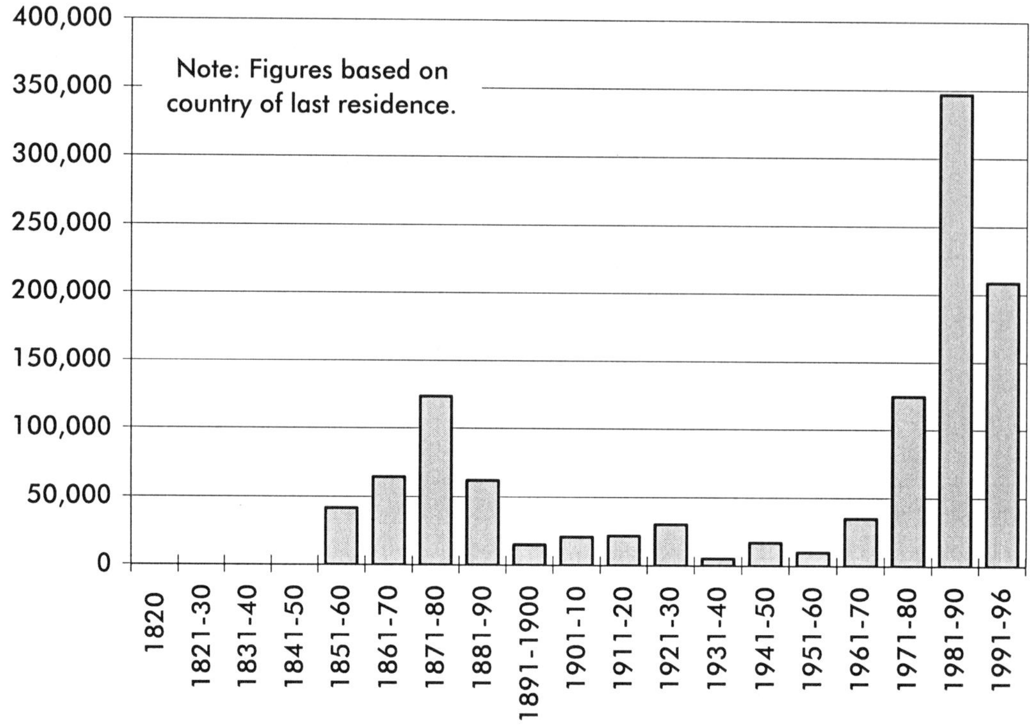

Note: Figures based on country of last residence.

From 1849 until Chinese immigration was sharply curtailed by the Chinese Exclusion Act of 1882, approximately 300,000 Chinese immigrated to the United States. This was the first main wave of Chinese-American immigration. U.S. Census Bureau figures show that close to 280,000 Chinese immigrants arrived in that period, with more than 50,000 of these arriving in 1881 and 1882 alone, just before the door was effectively closed. However, many arrivals in Gold Rush days were not counted. (Immigrants to West Coast ports were not regularly counted until 1850.) On the other hand, substantial numbers of Chinese returned to China during that period. Many more would do so in the decades that followed the Exclusion Act, as Chinese Americans were forced off the land and out of towns all over the Amercan West because of anti-Chinese bigotry.

The Crossing

The ability to leave China came with the decline of China's Manchu rulers, hard pressed by the European invasions and the huge Taiping civil war. The Manchus had previously forbidden emigration, with beheading the penalty for those trying to leave illegally, and for those who returned after leaving illegally. In the middle of the 19th century, those laws—though little enforced—were still officially in effect. That is why most Chinese emigrants sailed from British-held Hong Kong. Some left from Portuguese-held Macao; however, that was a much less safe place, for it was also a port used by the "coolie" trade.

There were two main sailing routes to the United States, both very long voyages around much of the world The main route, taken by most Chinese immigrants, took sailing ships directly across the Pacific, from South China to San Francisco. Those headed for the East Coast then took a further very long trip, south around Cape Horn and then north in the Atlantic to the

Authors' Archives

Chinese immigrants were subjected to attacks such as this throughout the West in the late 19th century, driving many of them into city ghettos.

Graph 4.3: Percentage of Immigrants from China in Total U.S. Immigration by Decade, 1820–1996

Note: Figures based on country of last residence.

This Chinese-American hose team won a fire-fighting competition in Deadwood, in the Dakota Territory, in 1888.

U.S. East Coast ports. Emigrants headed for the East Coast might also take passage from south China on ships that traveled southeast across the Indian Ocean around the Cape of Good Hope, and then across and north in the Atlantic to the U.S. East Coast.

In Gold Rush days, the trip under sail from China to San Francisco cost an expensive fifty to two hundred dollars, and might be in anything from a small, impossibly crowded, very dangerous ship to a large transpacific clipper ship in the China trade. Even at fifty dollars, it often took years for Chinese laborers who might make one to two dollars per week to pay back borrowed passage money. When steam replaced sail, however, ships quickly grew larger, the voyage became shorter, and fares came down a great deal. After 1866, when the Pacific Mail Steamship

Company began regular service to China, a one-way fare home to China from San Francisco might cost as little as thirteen to fifteen dollars.

Early Days

The first substantial Chinese community in the United States formed in the main entry port, San Francisco. The first Chinese merchants' association was founded there in 1849, and it was there that the closely knit body of district and clan associations formed, which would informally organize the Chinese-American communities throughout the West, with branches in other parts of the country. They would later become the "Six Companies," more formally the Chinese Consolidated Benevolent Associations, and in the 1880s the national Chinese Consolidated Benevolent Association. By then, they were also acting as defense organizations, for the Chinese were encountering the multiple bigotries that would soon drive them back into the "Chinatowns." These ethnic ghettos would keep most early Chinese immigrants out of the mainstream of American life, despite their attempts to join that mainstream.

An estimated 15,000 Chinese immigrants did become gold miners in California and elsewhere; many of them made their livings by taking the remaining gold out of "worked out" claims. Others played a major role in building the first transcontinental railroad, and other transportation links throughout the West. Many thousands of others worked in the developing California farming industry, as farmhands and as tenant farmers, although discriminatory California laws barred them from owning land. Thousands more worked in land reclamation, building dams and drainage to reclaim flooded lands throughout the state. Large numbers of Chinese, themselves from the south China coast, went to work in the fishing industry, along the whole length of the Pacific coast. Chinese businesspeople and skilled workers also built small businesses of many kinds in and near the Chinese communities that were soon scattered throughout the West.

Racism, however, would block and distort Chinese-American history. Even in the 1850s, there was anti-Chinese violence in the California goldfields, which would later spread to silver mining communities throughout the West. Often anti-Chinese violence was spread within the labor movement, with the Chinese being attacked as "strikebreakers" who were "taking American jobs." Above all, the Chinese were discriminated against by law, being treated as "colored" people in a society that until after the Civil War still tolerated slavery—and would take deep discrimination against African Americans, Native Americans, and Asian Americans into the late 20th century.

As anti-Chinese hysteria grew, there were anti-Chinese riots in many western towns and cities during the 1870s and 1880s, including the Los Angeles Chinatown massacre of 1871, in which 21 Chinese were murdered. Six years later, in 1877, came the massive San Francisco riots, a three-day-long attack involving tens of thousands of rioters, which had to be put down by the armed forces and San Francisco's 5,000-strong Vigilance Committee. Among the hundreds of other attacks, one of the worst was the mass murder of 28 Chinese during the 1885 riots in Rock Springs, Wyoming.

Exclusion

In the pervasive anti-Chinese atmosphere of the day, it became easy to limit and then to almost completely stop Chinese immigration. The U.S.–China Burlingame Treaty of 1868 had established unimpeded immigration both ways between the United States and China, although it prohibited Chinese and Americans from becoming citizens of each others' countries. Because of the treaty, the U.S. Supreme Court struck down many state anti-Chinese laws between 1868 and 1880.

In 1880, however, bowing to anti-Chinese pressure, the United States renegotiated—that is, forced—a new treaty with China. It allowed the United States to retain its privileges under the 1868 treaty, while establishing restrictions on Chinese immigration. In 1882, the U.S. Congress passed the Chinese Exclusion Act, effectively barring all but a few Chinese immigrants. In 1884, a second Chinese Exclusion Act was passed, and in 1888 the Scott Act barred 20,000 Chinese who had returned to China, many to visit their families, from coming back to the United States. A series of further exclusion acts effectively barred most Chinese immigration into the United States until the mid-20th century. These were extended to Hawaii in 1898 and the Philippines in 1902.

A small trickle of Chinese immigrants continued to reach the United States during the seven decades that followed the Chinese Exclusion Act. Most of these were Chinese claiming citizenship by birthright, often with false papers, a tactic that had unexpected success because the great San Francisco earthquake and fire of 1906 had destroyed most of the city's birth records. These immigrants falsely claiming descent from Chinese-American citizens were popularly called "paper sons and daughters."

Some, of course, were citizens by birthright. Some Chinese also came to the United States as illegal immigrants, across the Mexican and Canadian borders, along with a few who came directly by sea.

Although some thousands of Chinese immigrants came as "birthright" citizens and illegal aliens, U.S. Census Bureau figures indicate that in the six years from 1884 through 1889, a total of only 495 legal Chinese immigrants were recorded as having arrived in the United States. From 1882 through 1960, an average of less than 2,000 legal Chinese immigrants a year were admitted into the United States.

This was the time of the infamous "Shed," the dilapidated warehouse on a San Francisco wharf where for 28 years (1882–1910) Chinese immigrants were detained, often for months, on a host of pretexts. It was succeeded by the equally infamous Angel Island, the U.S. immigration station in San Francisco Bay, where from 1910 to 1940 Chinese immigrants were held, some of them for as long as two years.

Chinese Immigrants to Hawaii

Starting in the 1790s, small numbers of Chinese immigrated to Hawaii, most of them skilled workers and businesspeople from Guangdong. American missionaries and planters came a little later, starting to arrive in some numbers in the 1820s. With these immigrations came epidemic diseases, among them bubonic plague and cholera, which sharply reduced the numbers of Native Hawaiians. Of the estimated 225,000 Hawaiians in the island when Captain James Cook arrived in 1788, only about 50,000 remained in 1875.

By the 1850s, Hawaiian and American planters had created a need for plantation laborers that could no longer be met by Native Hawaiians. This, in turn, created a need for Chinese plantation contract laborers, which was met by Hakka-speaking Chinese from Fukien (Fujian). These early Chinese immigrants to Hawaii generally sailed out of Amoy (Xiamen), north of Guangdong on the China coast. Most later Chinese immigrants to Hawaii would come out of Guangdong. The Chinese did not remain plantation laborers very long, though. Most bought out their labor contracts early and went into farming on their own. They soon came to dominate the rice trade, while American planters grew sugarcane, coffee, and pineapples.

The course of Chinese immigration and integration into Hawaiian life was very different from that followed in the United States. Although the Chinese still faced discrimination, they did not face the kind of murderous hysteria encountered on the mainland. As a result, the Chinese in Hawaii were not forced into anything like Chinatowns. Instead, they opened businesses and farms, married Hawaiian wives, and entered the mainstream of Hawaiian life—at least until the American takeover of the islands in 1894. With that takeover, mainland-style discrimination came to Hawaii, but by then Chinese Hawaiian integration was well under way. Nor were the Chinese Hawaiians driven out of Hawaii's communities; by the 1930s, they had entered the skilled professions. There were also far more Chinese women in Hawaii than in mainland United States; many of them soon entered the world of work.

The Second Great Wave

In the mid-20th century, the Chinese immigration picture changed, as part of a major American effort to erase discrimina-

Graph 4.4: Percentage Distribution of Americans of Chinese Origin by Region of the United States, 1990

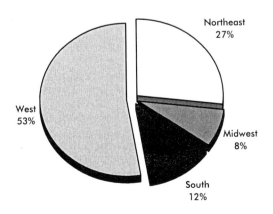

Northeast 27%

West 53%

Midwest 8%

South 12%

Table 4.2: Number and Percentage of Foreign-Born Immigrants from China by Decade in Total U.S. Population at End of Decade, 1850–1990

Decade	Number of Foreign-Born Immigrants from China	Total U.S. Population	Percentage of Foreign-Born Immigrants from China in Total U.S. Population
1850	758	23,191,876	0.00
1860	35,565	31,443,321	0.11
1870	63,042	39,818,449	0.16
1880	104,468	50,155,783	0.21
1890	106,701	62,947,714	0.17
1900	81,534	75,994,575	0.11
1910	56,756	91,972,266	0.06
1920	43,560	105,710,620	0.04
1930	46,129	122,775,046	0.04
1940	(NA)	131,669,275	(NA)
1950	(NA)	150,697,361	(NA)
1960	99,735	179,323,175	0.06
1970	172,132	203,235,298	0.08
1980	286,120	227,726,000	0.13
1990	529,837	249,907,000	0.21

NA = Not available

Source: Adapted from Series C 228–295, Foreign-Born Population, by Country of Birth: 1850–1970, in *Historical Statistics of the United States, Colonial Times to 1970, Bicentennial Edition,* and other updating tables from the U.S. Census Bureau.

tory restrictive immigration laws that was initiated by President John F. Kennedy. From 1962 to 1965, approximately 15,000 Chinese were admitted to the United States on a temporary basis. In 1965 came the first of a series of laws which, in aggregate, made it possible for approximately 20,000 Chinese a year to legally immigrate to the United States from what had in 1949 become the Communist People's Republic of China. The former nationalist government and many Chinese who opposed Communist rule had retreated to the island of Taiwan. From 1957 on, immigration from Taiwan, which was mostly Chinese, was counted in the overall immigration count for China. By the mid-1990s, emigration from China to the United States was averaging approximately 50,000 per year.

In the modern period, immigration to the United States from China was somewhat larger than the figures above indicate, because some immigrants recorded as having come from Hong Kong were actually from the People's Republic of China. Before 1952, immigrants from Hong Kong were included in mainland China totals. There are no reliable figures on how many of the 382,924 immigrants from Hong Kong from 1952 to 1996 were actually from mainland China. As a practical matter, however, the overwhelming majority of those emigrating from Hong Kong to the United States have been ethnic Chinese, and in the United States became Chinese Americans. Since the return of Hong Kong to China, there can be no further question; immigrants coming from Hong Kong are now coming from the People's Republic of China.

Because of the long decades of exclusion, the Chinese-born in the total U.S. population had "climbed" only to the same minuscule 0.21 percent figure in 1990 as it had been in 1880 (see Table 7.4., "Number of Immigrants to the United States by Region and Selected Country of Birth

Graph 4.5: Number of Foreign-Born Immigrants from China in Total U.S. Population by Decade, 1850–1990

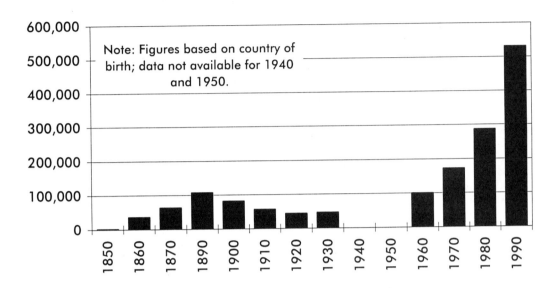

Graph 4.6: Number of Immigrants from Hong Kong Annually, 1971–1996

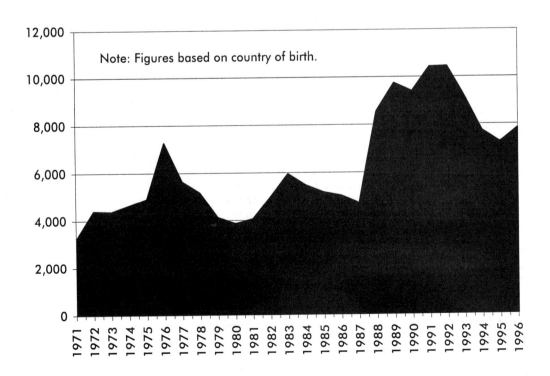

Annually, 1986–1996" on p. 702), while estimates of the number of those of Chinese-American heritage were in the 1 million to 1.5 million range in the mid-1990s.

The second wave of Chinese immigrants has been far more varied in origin and skills than the first wave, being composed of people from all over China. In the 1950s, many were Chinese students, stranded in the United States when the Communist victory made China impossible for them to return to, at least for a while. In the decades that followed, many immigrants were highly skilled and educated people who practiced their professions and turned their other skills to good use in the United States.

Among the later arrivals were also many unskilled people, however, with little in the way of material resources. They flocked to Chinese communities in San Francisco, New York, and other United States cities, taking the same kind of path that immigrants of many nationalities had taken for hundreds of years.

As East Asians, they continued to meet some of the same kind of bigotry and discrimination that Chinese Americans of the 19th century had experienced. But with antidiscrimination laws and to a large extent different attitudes in place in the United States, these new Chinese Americans were not literally driven back into Chinatowns.

Many Chinese Americans still faced discrimination, however, and beyond that several kinds of severe economic problems. Many of the elderly in central-city Chinese communities do not even receive Social Security payments, live on very little, and are dependent on social services to survive. Many young Chinese Americans are caught in a trap comprised of unemployment, lack of training and job opportunities, poverty, gang involvement, drugs, and resultant despair. Many new immigrants

Table 4.3: Number and Percentage of Immigrants from Hong Kong in Total U.S. Immigration Annually, 1971–1996

Year	Number of Immigrants from Hong Kong	Total U.S. Immigration	Percentage of Immigrants from Hong Kong in Total U.S. Immigration
1971	3,204	370,473	0.86
1972	4,391	384,685	1.14
1973	4,359	400,063	1.09
1974	4,629	394,861	1.17
1975	4,891	396,194	1.23
1976	7,259	502,289	1.45
1977	5,632	462,315	1.22
1978	5,158	601,442	0.86
1979	4,119	460,348	0.89
1980	3,860	530,639	0.73
1981	4,055	596,600	0.68
1982	4,971	594,131	0.84
1983	5,948	559,763	1.06
1984	5,465	543,903	1.00
1985	5,171	570,009	0.91
1986	5,021	601,708	0.83
1987	4,706	601,516	0.78
1988	8,546	643,025	1.33
1989	9,740	1,090,924	0.89
1990	9,393	1,536,483	0.61
1991	10,427	1,827,167	0.57
1992	10,452	973,977	1.07
1993	9,161	904,292	1.01
1994	7,731	804,416	0.96
1995	7,249	720,461	1.01
1996	7,834	915,900	0.86
Total 1971-96	163,372	17,987,584	0.91

Sources: *Statistical Yearbook of the Immigration and Naturalization Service*, 1986, Table 3; *Statistical Yearbook of the Immigration and Naturalization Service*, 1996, Table 3.

are working in illegal sweatshops, hampered by lack of English, substandard housing, and discrimination. In addition, some new arrivals are "illegals," who have made their long journey to the United States in the modern equivalents of the worst 19th-century cargo ships.

Resources

Internet Resources

People's Republic of ChinaGenWeb Project (*http://www.rootsweb.com/~chnwgw/*) Part of the WorldGenWeb project, linking genealogical research sites around the world, by region; a site in development, offered in English and Chinese; offers historical and genealogical material and links to related sites.

Republic of China (Taiwan) RocGenWeb (*http://www.rootsweb.com/~twnwgw*) Part of the WorldGenWeb project, linking genealogical research sites around the world, by region.

Organization of Chinese Americans (*http://www.ocanatl.org*) Organization Web site offering news, action alerts, and related Web sites. (Address: 1001 Connecticut Avenue, NW, Suite 707, Washington, D.C. 20036; Phone: 202-223-5500; Fax: 202-296-0540)

Print Resources

General Works

Bandon, Alexandra. *Chinese Americans.* New York: New Discovery, 1994.

Brownstone, David. *The Chinese-American Heritage.* New York: Facts on File, 1988.

Chan, Sucheng, ed. *Entry Denied: Exclusion and the Chinese Community in America, 1882–1943.* Philadelphia: Temple University Press, 1991.

Chen, Jack. *The Chinese of America.* San Francisco: Harper & Row, 1980.

China: A Country Study. 4th ed. Robert L. Worden, et al., eds. Washington, D.C.: Federal Research Division, Library of Congress, 1988. (Available on-line at *http://lcweb2.loc.gov/frd/cs*)

Daley, William. *The Chinese Americans.* New York: Chelsea House, 1996. Original ed. 1987.

Daniels, Roger. *Asian America: Chinese and Japanese in the United States Since 1850.* Seattle: University of Washington Press, 1988.

Gyory, Andrew. *Closing the Gate: Race, Politics, and the Chinese Exclusion Act.* Chapel Hill: University of North Carolina Press, 1998.

Hoexter, Corinne K. *From Canton to California: The Epic of Chinese Immigration.* New York: Four Winds Press, 1976.

Lai, H. Mark, et al. *Island: Poetry and History of Chinese Immigrants on Angel Island 1910–1940.* Seattle: University of Washington Press, 1991.

Ling, Huping. *Surviving on the Gold Mountain: A History of Chinese American Women and Their Lives.* Albany: State University of New York Press, 1998.

Mark, Diane Mei Lin. *A Place Called Chinese America.* Dubuque, Iowa: Kendall/Hunt, 1993.

Mayberry, Jodine. *Chinese.* New York: Watts, 1990.

McCunn, Ruthanne Lum. *An Illustrated History of the Chinese in America.* San Francisco: Design Enterprises of San Francisco, 1979.

Melendy, H. Brett. *Chinese and Japanese Americans.* New York: Hippocrene Books, 1984.

Meltzer, Milton. *The Chinese Americans.* New York: Crowell, 1980.

Moy, Tina. *Chinese Americans.* New York: Marshall Cavendish, 1995.

Ng, Franklin. *The Taiwanese Americans.* Westport, Conn.: Greenwood, 1998.

Stefoff, Rebecca. *Journey to Gold Mountain: The Chinese in 19th-Century America*. New York: Chelsea House, 1994. Adapted from work by Ronald Takaki.

Steiner, Stan. *Fusang, the Chinese Who Built America*. New York: Harper & Row, 1979.

Tsai, Shih-shan Henry. *The Chinese Experience in America*. Bloomington: Indiana University Press, 1986.

Wilson, John. *Chinese Americans*. Vero Beach, Fla.: Rourke, 1991.

Wu, Dana Ying-Hui, and Jeffrey Dao-Sheng Tung. *The Chinese-American Experience*. Brookfield, Col.: Millbrook, 1993.

Zo, Kil Young. *Chinese Emigration into the United States, 1850–1880*. New York: Arno Press, 1978. Reprint of 1971 thesis.

Genealogical Works

Lee, Kathleen. *Tracing Our Chinese Roots*. Santa Fe, NM: J. Muir, 1994.

Low, Jeanie W. Chooey. *China Connection: Finding Ancestral Roots for Chinese in America*. 2d ed. San Francisco: JWC Low, 1993.

She, Colleen. *A Student's Guide to Chinese American Genealogy*. Phoenix: Oryx, 1996.

For more resources, see "General Asian Immigration Resources" on p. 479.

Immigrants from Japan

Emigration of any kind from Japan was decisively affected by the history of Japanese-Western relations, stretching back to 1542, when the first known Europeans reached Japan. They were Portuguese sailors in a Chinese junk, who were blown off course and landed on Kyushu. The long European attack and conquest of much of Asia had begun almost half a century earlier, when Portuguese navigator Vasco da Gama had arrived at Calicut, India, in 1498, after sailing around the Cape of Good Hope and across the Indian Ocean.

Portuguese Jesuit missionary Francis Xavier reached Japan in 1549, beginning almost a century of often-successful Christian and Portuguese penetration of the country. Other Europeans followed, among them Dutch traders who reached Japan in 1609 and English traders in 1613. By that time, however, a powerful anti-Christian and anti-European reaction had developed in Japanese ruling circles. In 1597, 9 foreign priests and 17 Japanese Christians were crucified by order of Japanese ruler Toyotomi Hideyoshi.

Japan then moved toward full-scale repression of Christians and foreigners. Finally, in 1637, the forces of the Tokugawa shogunate smashed a major Japanese Christian rising, massacring tens of thousands of Christians who had surrendered after their failed defense of Hara Castle. The massacre ended Christian, Portuguese, and all major foreign influence in Japan for more than two centuries. The Portuguese were expelled from Japan, and the entire country was closed to all but a few outsiders, notably Chinese traders at Nagasaki and Dutch traders at Hirado. To even travel abroad required special status and government permission.

During the early 19th century, Japan remained closed to foreigners, even though the Western conquest of a great deal of south and east Asia was well under way, as Europeans had been expanding there for more than three centuries by then. From the 1840s, however, European naval and military power began to come very close to Japan. In the wake of the Opium War (1840), which began the dismemberment of China, the Western powers began to exert what would become full control of the entire Chinese Pacific coast, and it soon became clear that Japan's naval forces were no match for those of the West.

The Opening of Japan

On July 8, 1853, a four-ship U.S. flotilla commanded by Commodore Matthew Perry sailed into Tokyo Bay. Formal Japanese–United States trade relations were established by the Treaty of Kanagawa (March 31, 1854). Four months later, the Harris Treaty, forced on Japan by U.S. consul Townsend Harris, set up unequal trade relations between the two countries. A few weeks after that, Britain, France, Russia, and the Netherlands also forced unequal treaties on Japan.

Ultimately, this massive foreign invasion shook traditional Japan out of its isolation and into a highly competitive stance. Major forces within Japan's ruling elites moved toward establishing a powerful central government committed to modernization, and most notably toward the development of naval, military, and industrial power.

Resistance to foreign domination led to early defeats. In 1863, Tokugawa shogunate forces attacked foreign ships in the Straits of Shimonseki. Western naval forces responded by shelling Japanese coastal cities, a move the Japanese could not combat. This and other factors triggered a Japanese civil war, which was won by the modernizers. In what was called the Meiji Restoration, they placed a figurehead Meiji dynasty emperor on the Japanese throne, built a newly powerful, outward-looking central government, and proceeded with modernization. In 1868, the civil war ended with the defeat of the shogunate's forces at Fushima and Tobo, south of Kyoto, and the victors' subsequent unopposed occupation of Edo (Tokyo), which became the national capital. The last major campaign against the new government was the unsuccessful Satsuma Rebellion, which ended at Kogoshima in September 1877.

And so Japan opened to the world. Only a few decades later, it would emerge as a new world power, after it defeated the Russian Empire in the Russo-Japanese War (1904–1905).

After the Meiji Restoration, Japan also began to open outward, allowing students, some travelers, and some emigrants to leave the country. The new government also sent many delegations and students abroad, to study and help Japan catch up to Western industrial, financial, military, and naval technology and practices.

Early Immigration

The first substantial groups of Japanese immigrants to the United States went to Hawaii, later part of the United States, and to San Francisco, in 1868. They left Japan illegally, for the new government had not yet relaxed its emigration laws. One group, of 149 immigrants, went to Hawaii. The other, a group of 40 immigrants, went to San Francisco, where they established the Wakamatsu Tea and Silk Farm Colony at Gold Hill, California.

The Hawaii group was reportedly mal-treated. In any event, the Japanese government ultimately brought 40 of them back to Japan and restated its antiemigration policy.

The Main Wave

Immigration began in earnest in 1885, when the Japanese government made it possible to emigrate. From 1885 to 1994, approximately 30,000 Japanese immigrated to Hawaii as contract laborers on sugar plantations. The great majority of these were from a small area in southern Japan, on Honshu and Kyushu islands, including the Hiroshima Prefecture. This region of southern Japan continued to be the main source of Japanese immigration to Hawaii and the United States mainland until the early 1920s, during the entire early period of Japanese immigration.

From 1894 to 1908, approximately 140,000 more Japanese arrived in Hawaii. In all, some 200,000 Japanese, most of them farm laborers, immigrated to Hawaii from 1892 to 1924. Many of these were "sojourners," who returned to Japan, sometimes traveling back and forth several times before returning permanently. Many others later went on to settle in the United States. Although perhaps 200,000 Japanese had immigrated to Hawaii by 1924, its Japanese-American population numbered only 110,000 in 1920, including Japan-born and Hawaii-born Japanese Americans.

Japanese immigration into the United States was modest in the 19th century. In 1899, its peak year, it reached only a recorded 2,844. From 1900 on, however, it built up considerably, though it was never anything remotely like the massive European immigration of the time. In 1907, its peak year by far, recorded Japanese immigration totaled 30,229. That was also the peak year of European immigration when, by contrast, almost 1.2 million Europeans entered the United States, sometimes coming through Ellis Island at a rate of more than 10,000 a day.

Table 4.4: Number and Percentage of Immigrants from Japan in Total U.S. Immigration by Decade, 1861–1996

Decade	Number of Immigrants from Japan	Total U.S. Immigration	Percentage of Immigrants from Japan in Total U.S. Immigration
1861-1870	186	2,314,824	0.01
1871-1880	149	2,812,191	0.01
1881-1890	2,270	5,246,613	0.04
1891-1900	25,942	3,687,564	0.70
1901-1910	129,797	8,795,386	1.48
1911-1920	83,837	5,735,811	1.46
1921-1930	33,462	4,107,209	0.81
1931-1940	1,948	528,431	0.37
1941-1950	1,555	1,035,039	0.15
1951-1960	46,250	2,515,479	1.84
1961-1970	39,988	3,321,677	1.20
1971-1980	49,775	4,493,314	1.11
1981-1990	47,085	7,338,062	0.64
1991-1996	44,155	6,146,213	0.72
Total 1820-1996	**506,399**	**506,399**	**100.00**

Note: No data available for Japan until 1861.

Source: Adapted from Table 2, Immigration by Region and Selected Country of Last Residence, Fiscal Years 1820–1996, from the *Statistical Yearbook of the Immigration and Naturalization Service*, 1996.

Graph 4.7: Number of Immigrants from Japan Annually, 1861–1996

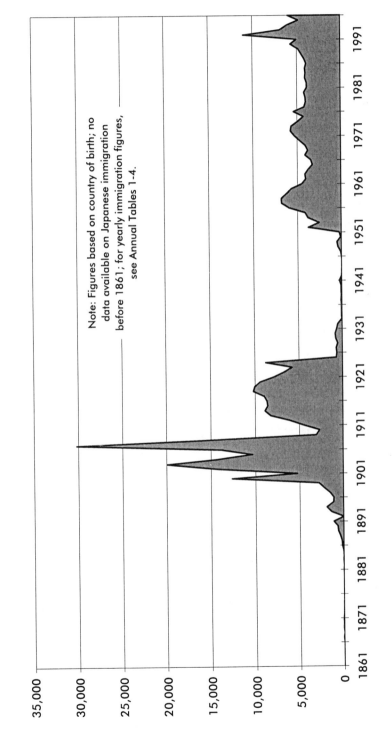

Note: Figures based on country of birth; no data available on Japanese immigration before 1861; for yearly immigration figures, see Annual Tables 1-4.

Graph 4.8: Number of Immigrants from Japan by Decade, 1861–1996

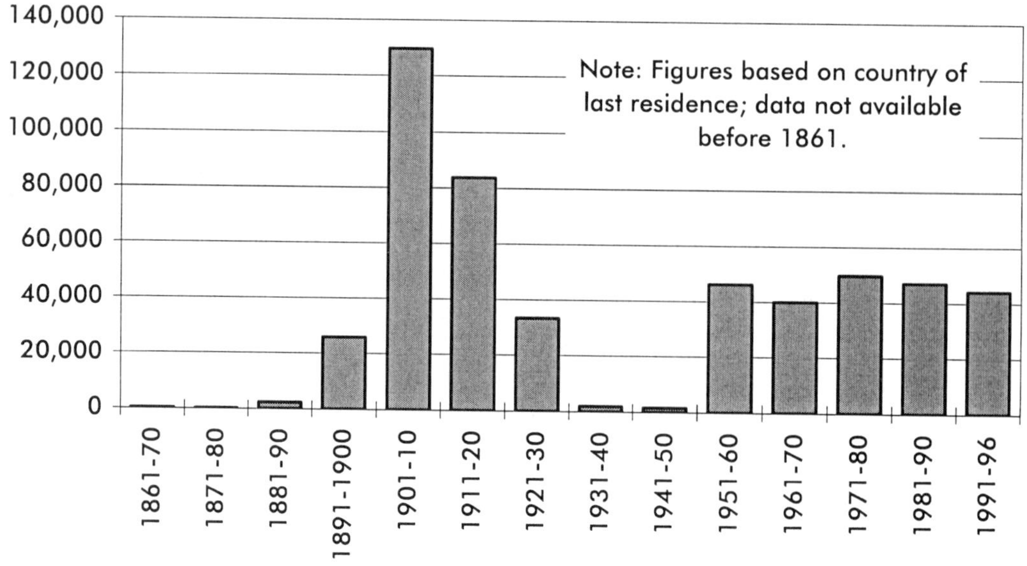

Note: Figures based on country of last residence; data not available before 1861.

Anti-Japanese Discrimination

From 1901 to 1924, approximately 240,000 Japanese immigrants entered the United States. That number would have been larger if the Japanese had not encountered powerful anti-Asian bigotry in California and other western states. In that period, Japanese immigrants began to encounter the same kind of bitter anti-Asian campaigns that had already resulted in the 1882 Chinese Exclusion Act and subsequent anti-Chinese laws.

The result was enormous pressure to pass anti-Japanese laws similar to those already barring Chinese immigration. In 1906, the San Francisco school board ordered all Japanese children to attend already-segregated Chinese schools. The Japanese government, by then an increasingly powerful Asian and world power, protested this as a violation of existing Japanese–United States treaties providing for equal treatment in both countries for their nationals. U.S. president Theodore Roosevelt and the Japanese government then negotiated a "Gentlemen's Agreement" providing that the Japanese would, in essence, limit Japanese immigra-

tion to the United States in return for protection against anti-Japanese U.S. legislation.

The agreement held. The Japanese did limit immigration to the United States, and the U.S. government did not pass Japanese exclusion and other anti-Japanese laws, although California did pass laws discriminating against Japanese ownership of land. The agreement, however, did not limit Japanese immigration nearly as much as the anti-Japanese had thought it would, because most of the Japanese already in the United States were single men. In large numbers, they sent back to Japan for the women who would become their wives; these women, who were chosen on the basis of photographs sent to their intended husbands, were popularly known as "picture brides." Bringing in brides from the homeland was a practice that had been and would be common to many immigrant groups. In the case of the Japanese, it meant that tens of thousands of women came to the United States to marry. In time, they righted the sexual and family balance in the emerging Japanese-American community.

President Theodore Roosevelt also secured from Congress the ability to block by executive order the entrance into the

United States of those with valid U.S. passports from U.S. possessions. This move was aimed mainly at the growing secondary immigration of Japanese to the mainland from Hawaii. Despite the entrance of many Japanese "picture brides," the net effect of the "Gentlemen's Agreement" and the blockage of entry from Hawaii was a sharp cut in Japanese immigration. Japanese immigration from 1900 to 1908, a period of nine years, totaled 135,000, but from 1909 to 1917 it totaled only 60,000. Nor did that reflect the influence of World War I, for the Pacific was little affected by the war, and Japanese immigration maintained a rather steady rate throughout the period, actually rising somewhat.

On the mainland, Japanese immigrants continued to cluster in the Pacific coast states throughout much of the century. The overwhelming majority of the young men who emigrated early in the century at first found jobs secured for them by labor contractors, building railroads, and working in canneries, lumber camps, and mines. However, most rather quickly found their way into farming, by far the main occupation favored by early Japanese Americans. Many also went into a wide range of their own small businesses and skilled trades, as well as into the hotel and restaurant industry.

Table 4.5: Number and Percentage of Foreign-Born Immigrants from Japan by Decade in Total U.S. Population at End of Decade, 1870–1990

Decade	Number of Foreign-Born Immigrants from Japan	Total U.S. Population	Percentage of Foreign-Born Immigrants from Japan in Total U.S. Population
1870	73	39,818,449	0.00
1880	401	50,155,783	0.00
1890	2,292	62,947,714	0.00
1900	24,788	75,994,575	0.03
1910	67,744	91,972,266	0.07
1920	81,502	105,710,620	0.08
1930	70,993	122,775,046	0.06
1940	(NA)	131,669,275	(NA)
1950	(NA)	150,697,361	(NA)
1960	109,175	179,323,175	0.06
1970	120,235	203,235,298	0.06
1980	221,794	227,726,000	0.10
1990	290,128	249,907,000	0.12

NA = Not available

Note: From 1970 figures include foreign-born Japanese-Americans from Hawaii and Alaska.

Source: Adapted from Series C 228–295, Foreign-Born Population, by Country of Birth: 1850–1970, in *Historical Statistics of the United States, Colonial Times to 1970, Bicentennial Edition*, and other updating tables from the U.S. Census Bureau.

In the bitterly anti-immigrant atmosphere of the early 1920s, Japanese immigrants were singled out for especially repressive legislation. Rather than being covered by the very low quotas of the 1924 Immigration Act, Japanese immigrants were defined as "ineligible for citizenship" because they were not "Caucasian," thereby effectively putting into place a Japanese exclusion act. The immigration figures indicate the result of this: Japanese immigration, which had been 8,801 in 1924, shrank to 723 in 1925, and did not reach 1,000 in any year after that until 1952.

World War II Internment Camps

A new low in the treatment of Japanese Americans was reached after the United States and Japan went to war in December 1941. Immediately after the Japanese attacked Pearl Harbor, 4,000 to 5,000 Japanese-born immigrants and Japanese Americans were arrested and held as potential threats to U.S. security. On February 9, 1942, President Franklin D.

Graph 4.9: Percentage Distribution of Americans of Japanese Origin by Region of the United States, 1990

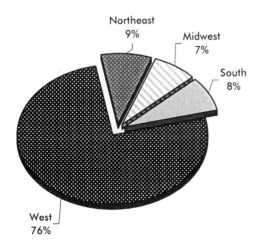

Northeast 9%

Midwest 7%

South 8%

West 76%

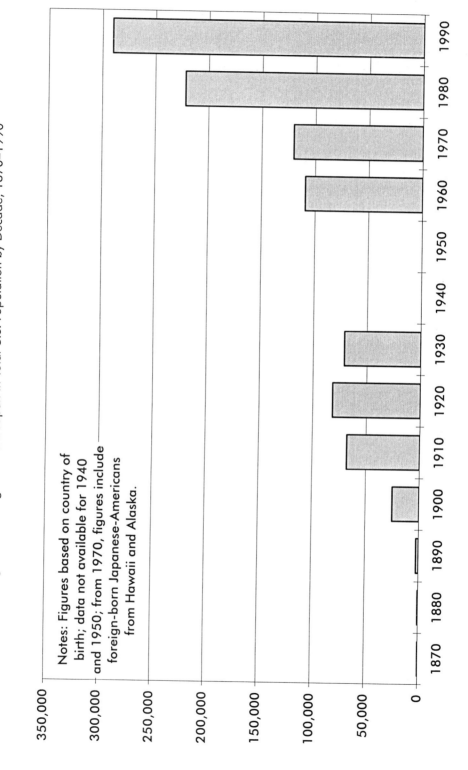

Graph 4.10: Number of Foreign-Born Immigrants from Japan in Total U.S. Population by Decade, 1870–1990

Notes: Figures based on country of birth; data not available for 1940 and 1950; from 1970, figures include foreign-born Japanese-Americans from Hawaii and Alaska.

Roosevelt issued Executive Order 9066, which effectively authorized the U.S. military to remove and hold in "relocation camps" all the Japanese and Japanese Americans on the West Coast. From then until late October 1942, some 110,000 of these were removed from their homes and put into 10 relocation camps.

Most of those removed were given no more than one week's notice, and were forced in that week to sell their homes, farms, and businesses at ruinous losses. Most were American-born, and many were of so-called mixed blood, defined by the U.S. Army as those of at least "one-sixteenth" Japanese ancestry. Many did not even know they had any Japanese ancestry. The entire sorry affair was clearly a combination of wartime panic and the most overt kind of racism, and was in no way recompensed by the very tardy apologies and modest reparations offered by the U.S. government in the 1970s.

The relocation camps were located in Utah, Arizona, Colorado, Wyoming, Arkansas, Idaho, and California. Approximately 35,000 of those interned were resettled in other parts of the United States later in the war. The rest of these exiled Japanese Americans were held in the camps until the January 1945 *Endo v. United States* U.S. Supreme Court decision forced their release. Ironically, almost 35,000 Japanese Americans, from Hawaii and the mainland, served in the U.S. armed forces during World War II, many with great distinction—even while their families were being held in the camps.

Later Japanese Immigration

The Immigration Act of 1952 abolished racial discrimination and set up a far more favorable quota system. That was followed by the door-opening 1965 Immigration Act. However, Japanese immigration into the United States remained low during the latter part of the 20th century. It topped 7,000 only once, in 1992, when 11,000 Japanese immigrants were recorded. In all probability, the low level of immigration reflected Japan's long period of prosperity, perhaps coupled with long, sober assessment of the persistence of anti-Asian racism in the United States.

These Japanese Americans are having their belongings examined en route to internment camps in 1942, having been forced to sell all their other property.

Resources

Internet Resources

National Japanese American Historical Society (*http://www.nikkeiheritage.org/*) Web site of organization focusing on Japanese-American history and culture. (Address: 1684 Post Street, San Francisco, CA 94115; Phone: 415-921-5007; Fax: 415-921-5087; E-mail: njahs@njahs.org)

Japanese American National Museum (*http://www.lausd.k12.ca.us/janm/main.htm*) Web site of the Los Angeles museum, including exhibits, information on national school projects, and links to resources. (Address: 369 East First Street, Los Angeles, CA 90012; Phone: 1-800-461-5266 or 213-625-0414; Fax: 213-625-1770)

Japanese American Citizens League (*http://www.jacl.org*) Web site of organization seeking to combat discrimination against Japanese Americans, with related links.

JapanGenWeb (*http://www.rootsweb.com/~jpnwgw/*) Part of the WorldGenWeb project, linking genealogical research sites around the world, by region, providing information and resources by region within Japan, including historical information and links to sites about Japan and genealogy.

Print Resources

Daniels, Roger. *Asian America: Chinese and Japanese in the United States Since 1850.* Seattle: University of Washington Press, 1988.

Japan: A Country Study. 5th ed. Ronald E. Dolan and Robert L. Worden, eds. Washington, D.C.: Federal Research Division, Library of Congress, 1992. (Available on-line at *http://lcweb2.loc.gov/frd/cs*)

Kawaguchi, Gary. *Tracing Our Japanese Roots.* Santa Fe, N.M.: John Muir, 1995.

Leathers, Noel L. *The Japanese in America.* Rev. ed. Minneapolis: Lerner, 1991.

Melendy, H. Brett. *Chinese and Japanese Americans.* New York: Hippocrene, 1984.

Montero, Darrel. *Japanese Americans.* Boulder, Col.: Westview, 1980.

Niiya, Brian, ed. *Japanese American History: An A-to-Z Reference from 1868 to the Present.* New York: Facts on File, 1993.

O'Brien, David J., and Stephen S. Fugita. *The Japanese American Experience.* Bloomington: Indiana University Press, 1991.

Spickard, Paul R. *Japanese Americans: The Formation and Transformations of an Ethnic Group.* New York: Twayne, 1996.

Stefoff, Rebecca. *Issei and Nisei: The Settling of Japanese America.* New York: Chelsea House, 1994. Adapted from work by Ronald Takaki.

Wilson, Robert A., and Bill Hosokawa. *East to America: A History of the Japanese in the United States.* New York: Morrow, 1980.

For more resources, see "General Asian Immigration Resources" on p. 479.

Immigrants from Korea

Korea had been part of the Chinese sphere of influence in the East Asia since the successful Manchu invasion of 1637. It successfully resisted a forced opening to the West in the 1860s and early 1870s, shelling foreign ships attempting to make landfall in Korea. However, the Japanese forced Korea to open in 1876, with the unequal Treaty of Kanghwa, which signaled the beginning of what would become the Japanese conquest of Korea. In 1882, Korea opened to the West as well, signing unequal treaties with the United States and other Western powers.

After Japan's defeat of a dramatically weakened China in the Sino-Japanese War (1894–1895), Korea became part of the Japanese sphere of influence in East Asia. It became a fully controlled Japanese protectorate after Japan decisively defeated Russia in the Russo-Japanese War (1904–1905), which saw Japan's emergence as a world power.

Early Immigration

Emigration from Korea to Hawaii and the Americas began in 1902, during a time when Japan and Russia contested for control of the country, with neither therefore in complete control of every aspect of Korean life and policy. In that year, U.S. consul Horace N. Allen secured the Korean government's permission for the Hawaiian Sugar Planters Association to recruit sugar plantation workers. Even with an active recruitment program, though, Korean immigration to Hawaii was small, consisting of approximately 7,000 immigrants from 1902 to 1907. Some 4,000 of these had previously converted to Christianity.

The overwhelming majority of those who emigrated from Korea in that early period did so for economic reasons, for by 1905 Korea had experienced two recent major wars, both fought largely on Korean soil. Some also had political reasons for emigrating, for the Japanese were increasingly exerting control. Japan did fully annex Korea in 1910, holding it until the end of World War II.

Korean immigration to the United States mainland was even smaller than that to Hawaii. Most of the approximately 1,000 Koreans who arrived on the United States mainland through 1910 had first lived in Hawaii. Only a few hundred, some of them undocumented political dissidents, had come directly from Korea. Their numbers remained small because after 1905 the Japanese government limited emigration from Korea, and after 1907 stopped it altogether, under the Japanese–United States "Gentlemen's Agreement" (see "Immigrants from Japan" on p. 381). In 1907, U.S. president Theodore Roosevelt also banned the U.S. immigration of Japanese and Korean laborers from Hawaii, Mexico, and Canada. Korean immigration into Hawaii was modest as well, totaling an estimated 15,000 to 20,000 from 1902 to 1920. Of these, more than 1,000 were "picture brides," women chosen by photographs who came to wed previous immigrants (see "The Journey" on p. 53).

The net effect of the whole body of immigration restrictions was to effectively exclude most Korean immigration into the United States. As late as 1940, fewer than 2,000 Koreans were recorded as living in the United States. Only in 1958 did the number of Korean immigrants into the mainland United States exceed 1,000. Nor did Korean immigration rise greatly then.

Table 4.6: Number and Percentage of Immigrants from Korea in Total U.S. Immigration by Decade, 1948–1996

Decade	Number of Immigrants from Korea	Total U.S. Immigration	Percentage of Immigrants from Korea in Total U.S. Immigration
1948-1950	107	1,035,039	0.01
1951-1960	6,231	2,515,479	0.25
1961-1970	34,526	3,321,677	1.04
1971-1980	267,638	4,493,314	5.96
1981-1990	333,746	7,338,062	4.55
1991-1996	109,334	6,146,213	1.78
Total 1948-1996	751,582	63,140,227	1.19

Note: Figures for Korean immigration not separately recorded until 1948.

Source: Adapted from Table 2, Immigration by Region and Selected Country of Last Residence, Fiscal Years 1820–1996, from the *Statistical Yearbook of the Immigration and Naturalization Service,* 1996.

Only after passage of the 1965 Immigration Act did substantial numbers of Koreans begin to reach the mainland. Most of these were from South Korea, the country having been divided after the Korean War (1950–1953); from then through the end of the century, North Korea's government made any substantial emigration to the West impossible.

The New Korean Immigration

In the 1970s, the number of Korean immigrants began to soar, and it is this very new immigration that created a substantial Korean-American community. From 1970 to 1996, more than 710,000 Korean immigrants reached the United States.

The new Korean immigrants have had largely economic reasons for coming to the United States, though some have also come because of recurring turbulent political conditions in their homeland. Korea has experienced explosive massive population growth in recent decades, along with major country-to-city migration of the sort that has helped destabilize so many of the world's developing countries.

Table 4.7: Number and Percentage of Foreign-Born Immigrants from Korea by Decade in Total U.S. Population at End of Decade, 1960–1990

Decade	Number of Foreign-Born Immigrants from Korea	Total U.S. Population	Percentage of Foreign-Born Immigrants from Korea in Total U.S. Population
1960	11,171	179,323,175	0.01
1970	38,711	203,235,298	0.02
1980	289,885	227,726,000	0.13
1990	568,397	249,907,000	0.23

Note: Figures for foreign-born Korean Americans not available for earlier periods.

Source: Adapted from Series C 228–295, Foreign-Born Population, by Country of Birth: 1850–1970, in *Historical Statistics of the United States, Colonial Times to 1970, Bicentennial Edition*, and other updating tables from the U.S. Census Bureau.

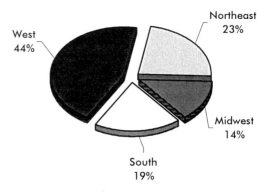

Graph 4.11: Percentage Distribution of Americans of Korean Origin by Region of the United States, 1990

West 44%

Northeast 23%

Midwest 14%

South 19%

South Korea has also successfully educated large numbers of people, notably in medicine and health care, teaching, and a wide range of white collar occupations. As a result, a high proportion of recent Korean immigrants have been trained in colleges and professional schools. Yet Koreans, like all Asian Americans, continue to suffer pervasive discrimination in precisely these kinds of occupations, forcing very many Korean Americans into a wide range of other occupations. Most notably, many who could not find the jobs they were trained to do instead became self-employed, running a wide range of small businesses. Korean business owners probably have been most visible as greengrocers in cities throughout the country.

Geographically, Koreans have tended to cluster in the largest cities, with major communities in Los Angeles, New York, and the whole length of the urban corridor stretching from Washington, D.C., to Boston.

Graph 4.12: Number of Immigrants from Korea by Decade, 1948–1996

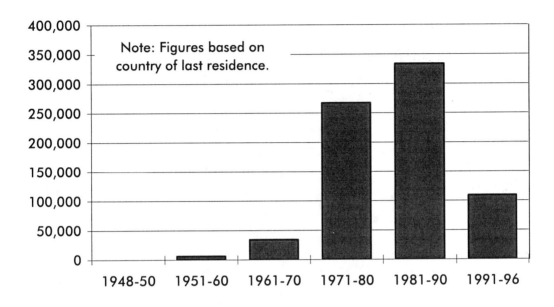

Graph 4.13: Percentage of Immigrants from Korea in Total U.S. Immigration by Decade, 1948–1996

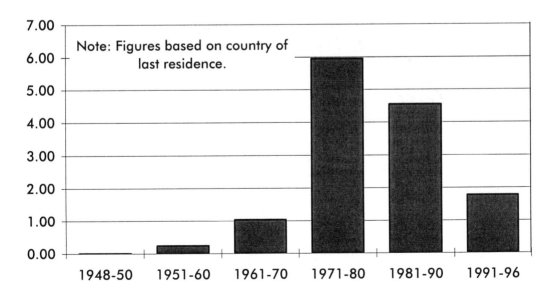

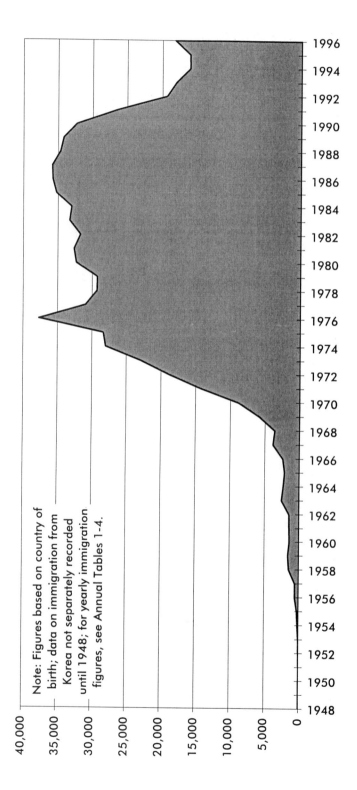

Graph 4.14: Number of Immigrants from Korea Annually, 1948–1996

Note: Figures based on country of birth; data on immigration from Korea not separately recorded until 1948; for yearly immigration figures, see Annual Tables 1-4.

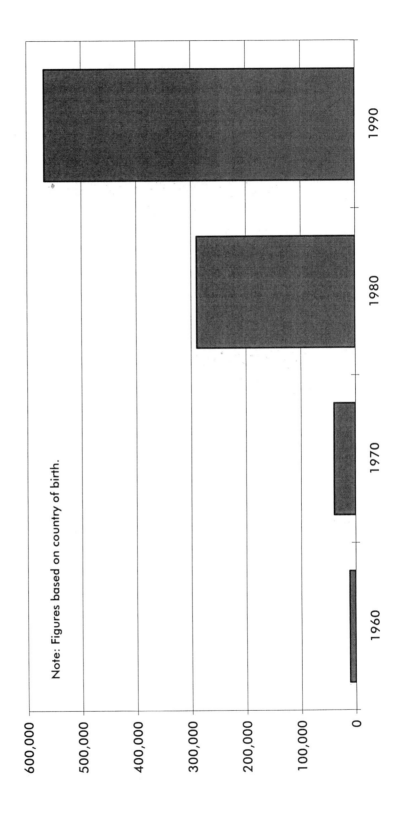

Graph 4.15: Number of Foreign-Born Immigrants from Korea in Total U.S. Population by Decade, 1960–1990

Note: Figures based on country of birth.

Resources

Internet Resources

Korean American Historical Society (*http://www.kahs.org*) Organization Web site offering information about its programs and publications, and related links. (Address: 10303 Meridian Avenue N., Suite 200, Seattle, WA 98133-9483; Phone: 206-528-5784; Fax: 206-523-4340; E-mail: kahs@arkay-intl.com)

The Korea Society (*http://www.koreasociety.org*) Web site of organization focusing on Korean studies. (Address: 950 Third Avenue, 8th Floor, New York, NY 10022; Phone: 212-759-7525)

Korean American Alliance (KAA) (*http://www.kaa.org*) Organization Web site offering information on programs, archives of KAA newsletters, and related links. (Address: P.O. Box 1412, Annandale, VA 22003-1412)

Korean American Coalition (KAC) (*http://www.kac83.org/flash4.html*) Web site of Korean American advocacy organization. (Address: 3421 W. 8th Street, 2nd Floor, Los Angeles, CA 90005; Phone: 213-365-5999; Citizenship Phone: 213-365-5990; Fax: 213-380-7990; E-mail: kacla1983@aol.com)

Print Resources

Choy, Bong Youn. *Koreans in America.* Chicago: Nelson-Hall, 1979.

Hurh, Won Moo. *The Korean Americans.* Westport, Conn.: Greenwood, 1998.

Mayberry, Jodine. *Koreans.* New York: Watts, 1991.

Melendy, H. Brett. *Asians in America: Filipinos, Koreans, and East Indians.* Boston: Twayne, 1977.

North Korea: A Country Study. 4th ed. Andrea Matles Savada, ed. Washington, D.C.: Federal Research Division, Library of Congress, 1994. (Available on-line at *http://lcweb2.loc.gov/frd/cs*)

Patterson, Wayne, and Hyung-Chan Kim. *Koreans in America.* Rev. ed. Minneapolis: Lerner, 1992.

South Korea: A Country Study. 4th ed. Andrea Matles Savada and William Shaw, eds. Washington, D.C.: Federal Research Division, Library of Congress, 1992. (Available on-line at *http://lcweb2.loc.gov/frd/cs*)

Takaki, Ronald T. *From the Land of Morning Calm: The Koreans in America.* New York: Chelsea House, 1994. Adapted by Rebecca Stefoff.

For more resources, see "General Asian Immigration Resources" on p. 479.

Immigrants from Vietnam,

Cambodia, and Laos

Substantial immigration from Vietnam, Cambodia, and Laos into the United States began after the Vietnam War and is intertwined with the recent history of southeast Asia.

In 1862, French colonial forces began the final phase of their attacks on the countries that would become French Indochina. These were Cambodia, Laos, and Vietnam, the latter including the regions of Tonkin in the north, Annam in the center, and Cochin-China in the south. Cambodia quickly fell, without resistance, becoming a French protectorate in 1863. In 1885, the French completed their conquest of Vietnam and much of Laos, compelling Chinese forces to withdraw. Two years later, in 1887, France established the Indochinese Union, naming their new colonial possession Indochina. The conquest of Laos was completed when the French attacked Siam (now Thailand) in 1893, forcing it to give up eastern Laos, which it had held until then.

The Wars

The first major challenge to French rule in the region came in 1940, when Japanese forces attacked and took Indochina, which would remain in Japanese hands until the end of World War II. In 1941, Communist leader Ho Chi Minh organized the League for the Independence of Vietnam, the Vietminh, which by 1945 held large portions of northern Vietnam.

The French returned after the war but did not again take effective control of Indochina. In 1946, Vietminh and French colonial forces began fighting each other in the Vietnamese War of Independence (Indochina War). That effectively ended in 1954, after the Vietminh victory at Dien Bien Phu, after which the French withdrew and the country was partitioned into North and South Vietnam. During 1950 and 1951, Laotian and Cambodian independence armies had also entered the war.

A North-South civil war immediately began in Vietnam, which expanded enormously with U.S. military intervention, in time becoming the Vietnam War (1965–1973). Ultimately, more than 700,000 foreign troops, among them 625,000 Americans, were engaged on the South Vietnamese side. For a complex of reasons, among them a huge United States antiwar movement, U.S. and other foreign forces withdrew in 1973. The Vietnamese Civil War ended with a victory by North Vietnam, after the surrender of Saigon in May 1975.

The parallel Laotian Civil War (1950–1975) ended with the Communist Pathet Lao occupation of Vientiane, also in May 1975.

The also parallel Cambodian Civil War (1969–1975) had ended a month earlier with Communist Khmer Rouge occupation of Phnom Penh in April 1975. This was followed by the enormous crime of the Cambodian Holocaust (1975–1978), in which an estimated 2 million to 3 million Cambodians died at the hands of the Khmer Rouge, many during a mass relocation of city populations to the countryside. That slaughter was ended in 1978 when the Vietnamese invaded and occupied Cambodia. That also triggered a long Vietnamese campaign

Table 4.8: Number and Percentage of Immigrants from Vietnam in Total U.S. Immigration by Decade, 1952–1996

Decade	Number of Immigrants from Vietnam	Total U.S. Immigration	Percentage of Immigrants from Vietnam in Total U.S. Immigration
1952-60	335	2,515,479	0.01
1961-70	4,340	3,321,677	0.13
1971-80	172,820	4,493,314	3.85
1981-90	280,782	7,338,062	3.83
1991-96	187,986	6,146,213	3.06
Total 1952-96	646,263	63,140,227	1.02

Note: Figures for Vietnamese immigration not separately recorded until 1952.

Source: Adapted from Table 2, Immigration by Region and Selected Country of Last Residence, Fiscal Years 1820–1996, from the *Statistical Yearbook of the Immigration and Naturalization Service*, 1996.

Graph 4.16: Number of Immigrants from Vietnam by Decade, 1952–1996

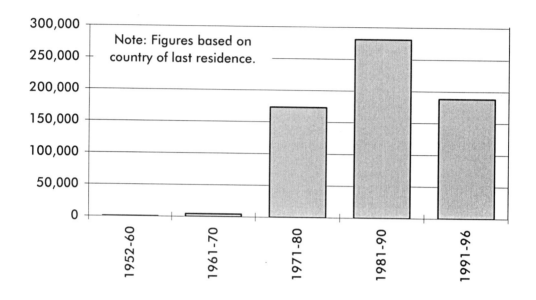

Graph 4.17: Percentage of Immigrants from Vietnam in Total U.S. Immigration by Decade, 1952–1996

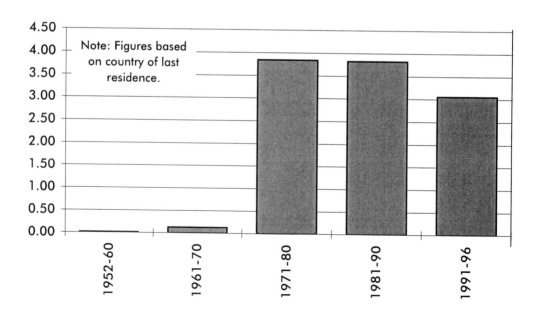

against the Khmer Rouge, followed by a new Cambodian civil war, which would not end until 1999.

The Emigration

During and after the later stages of this extraordinary sequence of wars and mass murders, millions of people tried to flee the three countries. Given the role played by the United States in all three sets of related wars, the United States took responsibility for accepting hundreds of thousands of refugees from all three countries. At the same time, the United States refused to accept hundreds of thousands of other southeast Asian refugees who fled in the years following the wars, describing them as "economic" rather than "political" refugees.

After the fall of Saigon, at least 200,000 South Vietnamese immediately fled the country, large numbers of them former military personnel and their families and other government-related people. Of these, approximately 130,000 went to the United States within a year, while the balance went to other countries and into southeast Asian refugee camps.

Table 4.9: Number and Percentage of Immigrants from Vietnam, Cambodia, and Laos in Total U.S. Population Annually, 1971–1996

Year	Immigrants from Cambodia	Immigrants from Laos	Immigrants from Vietnam	Total Number of Immigrants from Vietnam Cambodia, and Laos	Total U.S. Immigration	Immigrants from Vietnam Cambodia, and Laos in Total U.S. Immigration
1971	21	24	2,038	2,083	370,473	0.56
1972	39	35	3,412	3,486	384,685	0.91
1973	66	46	4,569	4,681	400,063	1.17
1974	40	61	3,192	3,293	394,861	0.83
1975	98	96	3,039	3,233	396,194	0.82
1976	126	163	4,230	4,519	502,289	0.90
1977	126	237	4,629	4,992	462,315	1.08
1978	3,677	4,369	88,543	96,589	601,442	16.06
1979	1,432	3,565	22,546	27,543	460,348	5.98
1980	2,801	13,970	43,483	60,254	530,639	11.35
1981	12,749	15,805	55,631	84,185	596,600	14.11
1982	13,438	36,528	72,553	122,519	594,131	20.62
1983	18,120	23,662	37,560	79,342	559,763	14.17
1984	11,856	12,279	37,236	61,371	543,903	11.28
1985	13,563	9,133	31,895	54,591	570,009	9.58
1986	13,501	7,842	29,993	51,336	601,708	8.53
1987	12,460	6,828	24,231	43,519	601,516	7.23
1988	9,629	10,667	25,789	46,085	643,025	7.17
1989	6,076	12,524	37,739	56,339	1,090,924	5.16
1990	5,179	10,446	48,792	64,417	1,536,483	4.19
1991	3,251	9,950	55,307	68,508	1,827,167	3.75
1992	2,573	8,696	77,735	89,004	973,977	9.14
1993	1,639	7,285	59,614	68,538	904,292	7.58
1994	1,404	5,089	41,345	47,838	804,416	5.95
1995	1,492	3,936	41,752	47,180	720,461	6.55
1996	1,568	2,847	42,067	46,482	915,900	5.08
Total 1971-96	136,924	206,083	898,920	1,241,927	17,987,584	6.90

Sources: *Statistical Yearbook of the Immigration and Naturalization Service*, 1980, Table 13; *Statistical Yearbook of the Immigration and Naturalization Service*, 1986, Table 3; *Statistical Yearbook of the Immigration and Naturalization Service*, 1996, Table 3.

Graph 4.18: Percentage Distribution of Americans of Vietnamese Origin by Region of the United States, 1990

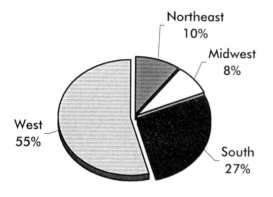

Northeast
10%

Midwest
8%

West
55%

South
27%

From 1978 to 1982, a second large wave of Vietnamese fled the country. These were mainly ethnic Chinese Vietnamese, fleeing the country after major Chinese-Vietnamese military clashes in 1979, coupled with the nationalization of many ethnic Chinese businesses in southern Vietnam. Chinese had been immigrating into the states that made up Vietnam for at least 400 years, and comprised a substantial ethnic community, much of it engaged in a wide range of businesses. This wave of emigrants fled largely by sea to neighboring countries, often in tiny, barely seaworthy craft; they were called the "boat people." Many ultimately found their way to the United States, although the United States and many other countries interposed substantial obstacles to their immigration starting in the late 1980s, as the flood of refugees grew.

After 1975, large numbers of refugees also fled Laos. Some of the earliest to leave were former government officials, soldiers, and their families, numbering some tens of thousands. A year later, an estimated 70,000 Hmong mountain people also fled, for they had sided with the Royal Lao government during the civil war, and now faced reprisals. In the same period, lowland Laotians, the main body of the population, began to leave in substantial numbers. In all, an estimated 300,000 fled Laos, a nation of 3 million people. Some fled by sea, most by land to neighboring

Thailand, where they were held in refugee camps, often for years, before they were allowed to emigrate elsewhere abroad.

The flight from Cambodia was most difficult of all during the Cambodian Holocaust years, and only a few tens of thousands are estimated to have escaped. Starting in 1979, however, the Vietnamese occupation government of Cambodia allowed hundreds of thousands to leave, most of them across the border into refugee camps in Thailand, although there they were harshly received and sometimes sent back by the Thai government. An estimated 600,000 Cambodian refugees had reached Thailand by early 1980, and many remained there into the mid-1990s.

Many southeast Asian refugees entered the United States under special laws, including the 1975 Indochina Migration and Refugee Assistance Act, the 1976 Laotian refugee act, the 1977 Indochina refugee act, the 1978 alien orphan children adoption act, and the 1980 Refugee Act. For more on these laws, see "Appendix B: Immigration and Naturalization Legislation" on p. 723.

Before the 1970s, only a few thousand immigrants from what was then called Indochina had entered the United States. That immigrant flow continued to be small through 1974, and then suddenly grew into a torrent. From 1971 to 1996, a recorded total of almost 1,242,000 Vietnamese, Laotians, and Cambodians made their way to

Graph 4.19: Percentage of Immigrants from Vietnam, Laos, and Cambodia in Total U.S. Immigrants from the Three Nations, 1971–1996

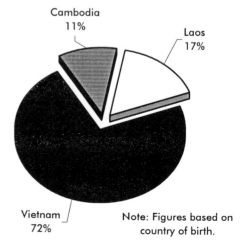

Cambodia
11%

Laos
17%

Vietnam
72%

Note: Figures based on country of birth.

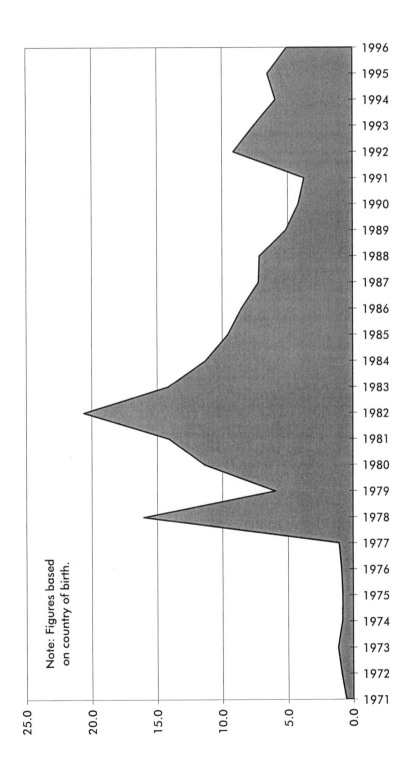

Graph 4.20: Percentage of Immigrants from Vietnam, Cambodia, and Laos in Total U.S. Immigration Annually, 1971–1996

Note: Figures based on country of birth.

the United States, in aggregate providing a substantial new southeast Asian component to American life. These were approximately half of the estimated 2.5 million southeast Asian refugees who fled the three countries in the decades following the end of their civil wars. Of those that entered the United States, 898,820 (72 percent), were born in Vietnam, 206,083 (17 percent) in Laos, and 136,924 (11 percent) in Cambodia.

Governmental and private assistance programs helped these substantial numbers of new Americans from southeast Asia to resettle, survive, and begin to build new lives after their arrival in the United States. Public assistance continued to help large numbers in the decades that followed, as many of the new arrivals were involuntary immigrants who arrived with little in the way of resources or skills. In addition, because they were often perceived as "colored" and Asians, many encountered pervasive discrimination,

Graph 4.22: Percentage Distribution of Americans of Cambodian Origin by Region of the United States, 1990

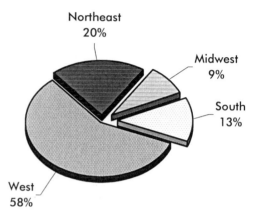

which further impeded the process of absorption into American life, economically, culturally, and educationally.

As so many other immigrant groups had done before them, many southeast Asian immigrants responded by building their own communities and industries, with major numbers settling in California, New York, Texas, and Louisiana. For those who entered the fishing industry in the Gulf of Mexico and the Pacific coast states, that meant a highly publicized series of confrontations with native-born workers during the 1980s; some of these conflicts dragged on right through the 1990s.

On the other hand, full participation in the United States education system meant that many in the second generation attained college educations, and the skills and credentials that then took them into the American professional and business worlds. Again, in this they were following the pattern for a wide range of groups from other parts of the world.

Graph 4.21: Percentage Distribution of Americans of Laotian Origin by Region of the United States, 1990

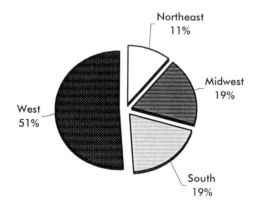

National Archives

This Vietnamese boy carries his entire belongings in his teeth, as he climbs up a cargo net to the American ship that rescued him and 28 other refugees from a 35-foot wooden boat in the South China Sea.

National Archives

This woman and her three children were among 28 refugees from a small wooden boat, rescued by a whaler in the South China Sea.

Resources

Print Resoures

General Works

Haines, David W., ed. *Refugees as Immigrants: Cambodians, Laotians, and Vietnamese in America*. Totowa, N.J.: Rowman & Littlefield, 1989.

McGuire, William. *Southeast Asians*. New York: Watts, 1991.

Nguyen-Hong-Nhiem, Lucy, and Joel Martin, eds. *The Far East Comes Near: Autobiographical Accounts of Southeast Asian Students in America*. Amherst: University of Massachusetts Press, 1989.

Takaki, Ronald T. *From Exiles to Immigrants: The Refugees from Southeast Asia*. New York: Chelsea House, 1995. Adapted by Rebecca Stefoff with Carol Takaki.

Tenhula, John. *Voices from Southeast Asia: The Refugee Experience in the United States*. New York: Holmes & Meier, 1991.

On Vietnamese

Caplan, Nathan S., et al. *The Boat People and Achievement in America: A Study of Economic and Educational Success*. Ann Arbor: University of Michigan Press, 1989.

Freeman, James M. *Changing Identities: Vietnamese Americans, 1975–1995*. Boston: Allyn and Bacon, 1995.

———. *Hearts of Sorrow*. Stanford, Calif.: Stanford University Press, 1989.

Haskins, James. *The New Americans: Vietnamese Boat People*. Hillside, N.J.: Enslow, 1980.

Henkin, Alan B., and Liem Thanh Nguyen. *Between Two Cultures: The Vietnamese in America*. Saratoga, Calif.: Century Twenty One, 1981.

Isaac, John. *Vietnam: The Boat People Search for a Home*. Woodbridge, Conn.: Blackbirch, 1997.

Kelly, Gail Paradise. *From Vietnam to America: A Chronicle of the Vietnamese Immigration to the United States*. Boulder, Col.: Westview, 1977.

Kent, Zachary. *The Story of the Saigon Airlift*. Chicago: Children's Press, 1991.

Liu, William Thomas, et al. *Transition to Nowhere: Vietnamese Refugees in America*. Nashville: Charter House, 1979.

Montero, Darrel. *Vietnamese Americans: Patterns of Resettlement and Socioeconomic Adaptation in the United States*. Boulder, Col.: Westview, 1979.

Rutledge, Paul. *The Vietnamese in America*. Minneapolis: Lerner, 1987.

Vietnam: A Country Study. Ronald J. Cima, ed. Washington, D.C.: Federal Research Division, Library of Congress, 1989. (Available on-line at *http://lcweb2.loc.gov/frd/cs*)

On Cambodians

Cambodia: A Country Study. 3d ed. Russell R. Ross, ed. Washington, D.C.: Federal Research Division, Library of Congress, 1990. (Available on-line at *http://lcweb2.loc.gov/frd/cs*)

Hopkins, Mary Carol. *Braving a New World: Cambodian (Khmer) Refugees in an American City*. Westport, Conn.: Bergin & Garvey, 1996.

Knight, Margy Burns. *Who Belongs Here? An American Story*. Gardiner, Maine: Tilbury House, 1993.

Lucas, Alice. *Cambodians in America: Courageous People from a Troubled Country*. San Francisco, Calif.: Many Cultures Publishing, 1993.

St. Pierre, Stephanie, comp. *Teenage Refugees from Cambodia Speak Out*. New York: Rosen, 1995.

On Laotians

Laos: A Country Study. 3d ed. Andrea Matles Savada, ed. Washington, D.C.: Federal Research Division, Library of Congress, 1995. (Available on-line at *http://lcweb2.loc.gov/frd/cs*)

Proudfoot, Robert. *Even the Birds Don't Sound the Same Here: The Laotian Refugees' Search for Heart in American Culture*. New York: P. Lang, 1990.

For more resources, see "General Asian Immigration Resources" on p. 479.

Immigrants from the Philippines

From 1564, when Miguel López de Legazpi found a west-to-east route across the Pacific, the Philippines had been a major colony of Spain. Manila was the center of their China trade with the whole of eastern and southern Asia. The Philippine War of Independence (1896–1898) was in progress when U.S. admiral George Dewey's cruiser squadron sank a Spanish squadron in Manila Bay, on May 1, 1898. United States and Philippine forces then quickly took the country. However, U.S. forces stayed on; Spain ceded the country to the United States in the Treaty of Paris (December 10, 1898), and the treaty was ratified by the U.S. Senate in February 1899.

Still seeking their independence, the Filipinos began a country-wide Philippine-American War, which was effectively ended by the capture of Philippine president Emilio Aguinaldo in 1901. An Islamic Moro insurrection continued until 1905, with guerrilla fighting until 1906.

With the seizure of their country, Filipinos gained the right to hold U.S. passports and to freely enter the United States (and so until 1935 were not recorded as immigrants). In 1906, Hawaiian sugar planters began efforts to recruit Filipino laborers, though with little early success. They intensified their efforts, and in 1909 began to bring substantial numbers of Filipino contract laborers to Hawaii. They became a major portion of the Hawaiian agricultural work force.

From 1905 to 1935, more than 120,000 Filipinos, most of them young single men, arrived in Hawaii, though the net number was somewhat less, for some traveled back and forth several times. Many ultimately went home to the Philippines, while many others went on to the U.S. mainland. In the 1920s, substantial numbers of Filipinos began immigrating to the mainland, both from Hawaii and directly from the Philippines.

By 1930, an estimated 40,000 Filipinos had immigrated to the mainland. However, in the early 1930s the Depression sharply limited the number of jobs available and equally sharply cut Filipino immigration. The mainland Filipino immigrants were largely young single men. Most of them went to work in California as migrant farm laborers, while smaller numbers worked in canneries and in a wide range of other service and industrial jobs.

Filipinos in the United States encountered a great deal of racism, being classified in practice, by legislation, and in the courts as not being "Caucasian." They were not allowed to become citizens and in many states, including California, were not allowed to marry white women. Like the Chinese in the previous century, they were from the first also seen as competitors for available jobs, who would work for less than whites. Pressure grew, especially in the job-starved 1930s, for passage of a Filipino exclusion law, like the 1882 Chinese Exclusion Act (see "Immigrants from China" on p. 365).

That law soon came. In 1934, the Tydings-McDuffie Independence Act granted the Philippines commonwealth status, making it possible to declare Filipinos aliens. The new law functioned as planned, setting up a quota of 50 Filipino admissions per year and effectively stopping immigration. A year later, in 1935, the U.S. Congress passed the Philippines Repatriation Act, which offered payments to those Filipinos who wanted to return to the Philippines, if they would give up their right of return to the United States. Although the Tydings-McDuffie Act did

Table 4.10: Number and Percentage of Immigrants from the Philippines in Total U.S. Immigration by Decade, 1935–1996

Decade	Number of Immigrants from the Philippines	Total U.S. Immigration	Percentage of Immigrants from the Philippines in Total U.S. Immigration
1935-1940	528	528,431	0.10
1941-1950	4,691	1,035,039	0.45
1951-1960	19,307	2,515,479	0.77
1961-1970	98,376	3,321,677	2.96
1971-1980	354,987	4,493,314	7.90
1981-1990	548,764	7,338,062	7.48
1991-1996	352,750	6,146,213	5.74
Total 1935-1996	1,379,403	63,140,227	2.18

Note: Figure for immigration from the Philippines not separately recorded before 1935.

Source: Adapted from Table 2, Immigration by Region and Selected Country of Last Residence, Fiscal Years 1820–1996, from the Statistical Yearbook of the Immigration and Naturalization Service, 1996.

Table 4.11: Number and Percentage of Foreign-Born Immigrants from the Philippines by Decade in Total U.S. Population at End of Decade, 1960–1990

Decade	Number of Foreign-Born Immigrants from the Philippines	Total U.S. Population	Percentage of Foreign-Born Immigrants from the Philippines in Total U.S. Population
1960	104,843	179,323,175	0.06
1970	184,842	203,235,298	0.09
1980	501,440	227,726,000	0.22
1990	912,674	249,907,000	0.37

Note: Figures for immigrants from the Philippines not available for earlier periods.

Source: Adapted from Series C 228–295, Foreign-Born Population, by Country of Birth: 1850–1970, in *Historical Statistics of the United States, Colonial Times to 1970, Bicentennial Edition*, and other updating tables from the U.S. Census Bureau.

From 1967 to 1996, more than 1.3 million Filipino immigrants entered the United States. Large numbers of these were highly trained people, including many health care professionals. Among them were tens of thousands of nurses, who found it relatively easy to achieve United States licensing, a far more difficult task for such professionals as doctors and dentists. Most were in their 20s and 30s, and many brought their young families with them, settling in major cities and suburban areas, where skilled jobs were to be found. Racism remained, as did unequal opportunity. However, legal discrimination had been curtailed by new civil rights laws, now firmly in place, providing a far more favorable situation for this second and much larger wave of immigrants from the Philippines.

effect exclusion, the Repatriation Act did not work, as few Filipinos chose to leave the United States.

When the Philippines became independent, in 1946, the immigration quota was raised to 100 per year, consonant with the quotas established by the restrictive 1924 Immigration Act. After 1934, Filipino immigration had virtually stopped and did not rise to 1,000 per year until 1948. It remained low, rising into the 3,000-per-year range only in the early 1960s.

The 1965 Immigration Act reopened the door for Filipinos, as it did for so many other immigrant groups. By 1970, Filipino immigration had climbed sharply, into the 30,000-per-year range. By the mid-1980s, it had climbed into the range of 50,000 to 60,000 per year.

Graph 4.23: Percentage Distribution of Americans of Filipino Origin by Region of the United States, 1990

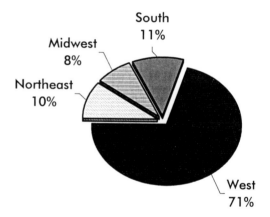

South 11%

Midwest 8%

Northeast 10%

West 71%

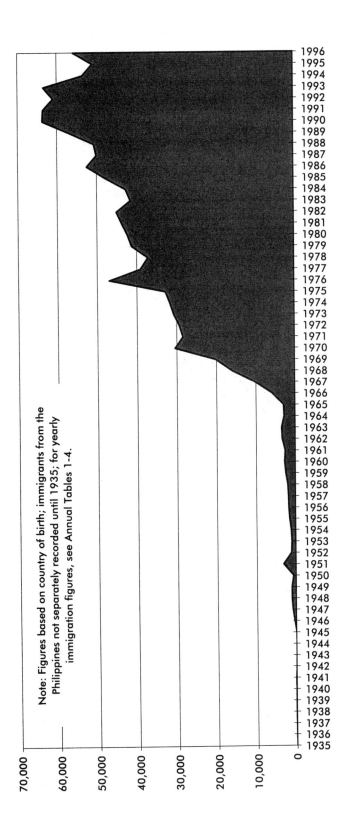

Graph 4.24: Number of Immigrants from the Philippines Annually, 1935–1996

Note: Figures based on country of birth; immigrants from the Philippines not separately recorded until 1935; for yearly immigration figures, see Annual Tables 1-4.

Graph 4.25: Number of Immigrants from the Philippines by Decade, 1935–1996

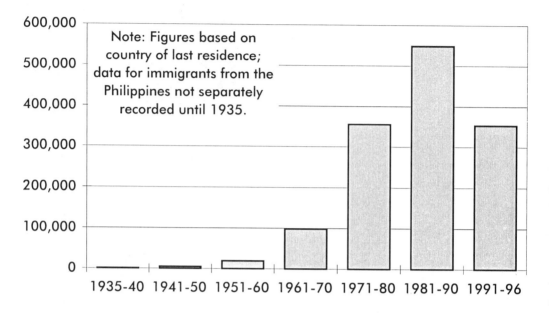

Note: Figures based on country of last residence; data for immigrants from the Philippines not separately recorded until 1935.

Graph 4.26: Number of Foreign-Born Immigrants from the Philippines in Total U.S. Population by Decade, 1960–1990

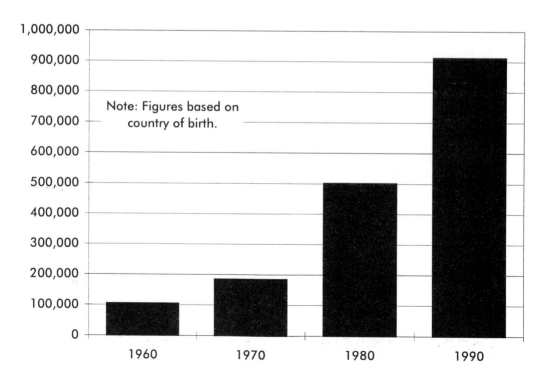

Note: Figures based on country of birth.

Resources

Internet Resources

Philippines—WorldGenWeb Project (*http://www.geocities.com/Heartland/Ranch/9121/*) Part of the WorldGenWeb project, linking genealogical research sites around the world, by region; includes maps, query boards, links to government and private resources and related sites.

Print Resources

Bandon, Alexandra. *Filipino Americans.* New York: New Discovery Books, 1993.

Bautista, Veltisezar B. *The Filipino Americans: From 1763 to the Present: Their History, Culture, and Traditions.* Farmington Hills, Mich.: Bookhaus, 1998.

Cordova, Fred. *Filipinos, Forgotten Asian Americans: A Pictorial Essay, 1763- Circa 1963.* Dubuque, Iowa: Kendall/Hunt, 1983.

Foronda, Marcelino A., Jr. *America Is in the Heart: Ilokano Immigration to the United States, 1906–1930.* Manila: De La Salle University, 1976.

Kim, Hyung-chan, and Cynthia C. Meija, eds. *The Filipinos in America, 1898– 1974: A Chronology and Fact Book.* Dobbs Ferry, N.Y.: Oceana, 1976.

Lasker, Bruno. *Filipino Immigration.* New York: Arno Press, 1969. Reprint of *Filipino Immigration to Continental United States and to Hawaii,* published in Chicago, 1931.

Mayberry, Jodine. *Filipinos.* New York: Watts, 1990.

Melendy, H. Brett. *Asians in America: Filipinos, Koreans, and East Indians.* Boston: Twayne, 1977.

Philippines: A Country Study. 4th ed. Ronald E. Dolan, ed. Washington, D.C.: Federal Research Division, Library of Congress, 1993. (Available on-line at *http://lcweb2.loc.gov/frd/cs*)

Root, Maria P. P., ed. *Filipino Americans: Transformation and Identity.* Thousand Oaks, Calif.: Sage Publications, 1997.

Stefoff, Rebecca. *In the Heart of Filipino America: Immigrants from the Pacific Isles.* New York: Chelsea House, 1994. Adapted from work by Ronald Takaki.

Winter, Frank H. *The Filipinos in America.* Minneapolis: Lerner, 1988.

For more resources, see "General Asian Immigration Resources" on p. 479.

Immigrants from Thailand

The roots of Thai immigration into the United States lie in Thailand's involvement with the American presence in southeast Asia, from the early 1950s through the wars in Vietnam, Cambodia, and Laos, and on into the late 1990s.

Before the Americans, there were the French, who attacked and defeated the Thais (then the Siamese) in 1893. The Thai monarchy was forced to cede eastern Laos, until then held by Thailand, to the French, pay indemnities, and then grant imperial concessions to the French and several other European powers.

During World War II, Thailand was occupied by the Japanese, and formally joined the Japanese side, although there was an anti-Japanese guerrilla movement throughout the war. After the war, Thailand became a Western ally in southeast Asia, and in the early 1950s began to serve as a major base for the growing U.S. presence in the region. The Americans would replace the French after 1954, when the French withdrew after being defeated by the Vietminh in the Indochina War.

From the early 1950s until the end of the southeast Asian war in the mid-1970s, Thailand received well over $1 billion in U.S. military assistance and probably a good deal more, counting covert funds. Thailand became a U.S. ally in the Vietnam War, hosting several major, acknowledged U.S. military bases, along with at least 50,000 U.S. troops. How many more U.S. troops were in Thailand is not clear.

There was little Thai interest in immigrating to the United States before the end of World War II. That changed with increasing and prolonged Thai-American

Table 4.12: Number and Percentage of Immigrants from Thailand in Total U.S. Immigration Annually, 1971–1996

Year	Number of Immigrants from Thailand	Total U.S. Immigration	Percentage of Immigrants from Thailand in Total U.S. Immigration
1971	2,915	370,473	0.57
1972	4,102	384,685	0.64
1973	4,941	400,063	1.24
1974	4,956	394,861	1.26
1975	4,217	396,194	1.06
1976	8,096	502,289	1.61
1977	3,945	462,315	0.85
1978	3,574	601,442	0.59
1979	3,194	460,348	0.69
1980	4,115	530,639	0.78
1981	4,799	596,600	0.80
1982	5,568	594,131	0.94
1983	5,875	559,763	1.05
1984	4,885	543,903	0.90
1985	5,239	570,009	0.92
1986	6,204	601,708	1.03
1987	6,733	601,516	1.12
1988	6,888	643,025	1.07
1989	9,332	1,090,924	0.86
1990	8,914	1,536,483	0.58
1991	7,397	1,827,167	0.40
1992	7,090	973,977	0.73
1993	6,654	904,292	0.74
1994	5,489	804,416	0.68
1995	5,136	720,461	0.71
1996	4,310	915,900	0.47
Total 1971-96	144,568	17,987,584	0.80

Sources: *Statistical Yearbook of the Immigration and Naturalization Service,* 1980, Table 13; *Statistical Yearbook of the Immigration and Naturalization Service,* 1986, Table 3; *Statistical Yearbook of the Immigration and Naturalization Service,* 1996, Table 3.

contact. First, there were many marriages and other liaisons between Americans and Thais. Thai spouses and children were among the first to become U.S. immigrants during the post-World War II period. In addition, many Thai soldiers worked closely with the Americans, developing an interest in immigration, largely for economic reasons. Nor was Thailand an especially stable country. It was a constitutional monarchy in form, but in fact was governed by a destabilizing series of military dictatorships, with coup after coup.

Graph 4.27: Percentage Distribution of Americans of Thai Origin by Region of the United States, 1990

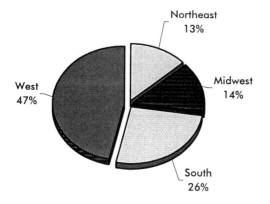

Northeast
13%

Midwest
14%

West
47%

South
26%

In the late 1960s, after the 1965 Immigration Law made large-scale immigration to the United States from Asia possible, Thai immigration began in earnest. Though never including large numbers of refugees, as did the Vietnamese, Cambodian, and Laotian immigrations, the Thai immigration came to total almost 145,000 from 1971 to 1996. It quickly moved beyond spouses and children, with many young professionals and businesspeople also immigrating to the United States, often with their families.

Relatively large numbers of Thai immigrants were health professionals, including a large number of nurses. Perhaps an even larger number of Thai immigrants went into the restaurant industry. By the 1980s Thai restaurants had become a very well-received feature of the American ethnic cuisine landscape.

Geographically, new Thai immigrants tended to concentrate in California and in the New York City area. However, closely knit Thai communities were soon to be found throughout the United States. As with so many other American immigrant groups, the first U.S.-born generation of Thai Americans tended to spread out into the wider American stream, ethnically and geographically.

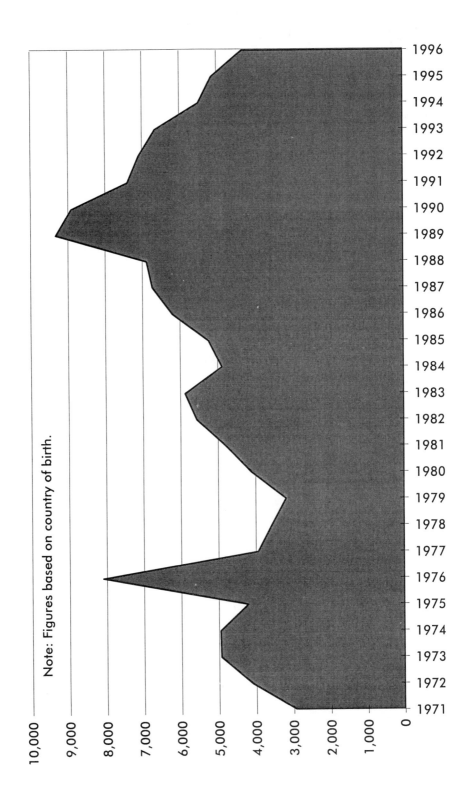

Graph 4.28: Number of Immigrants from Thailand Annually, 1971–1996

Note: Figures based on country of birth.

Resources

Internet Resources

Thai Genealogy (*http://
www.rootsweb.com/~thawgw/
thaindex.htm*) Part of the
WorldGenWeb Project, offering
information on history and genealogical
links and resources.

Print Resources

Larsen, Wanwadee. *Confessions of a Mail
Order Bride: American Life Through
Thai Eyes.* Far Hills, N.J.: New Horizon
Press, 1989.
Thailand: A Country Study. 6th ed.
Barbara Leitch LePoer, ed.
Washington, D.C.: Federal Research
Division, Library of Congress, 1989.
(Available on-line at *http://
lcweb2.loc.gov/frd/cs*)

For more resources, see "General Asian
Immigration Resources" on p. 479.

Immigrants from India

India has a long and rich history. When the Ottoman Turks cut Europe's trading routes to the East in 1453, European navigators sought new ocean routes to Asia, especially to India, China, and the Spice Islands (the East Indies). Columbus headed west across the Atlantic, arriving in the Caribbean in 1492. He and others originally thought that he had reached a part of Asia near India, so the Caribbean islands came to be known as the West Indies, and the native inhabitants of the Americas were called Indians. Other European navigators headed south and east around Africa; the first to cross the Indian Ocean to arrive at India itself was Vasco da Gama in 1498.

That was the beginning of the colonization of India, with various European nations fighting to control the then-rich region. At that time the whole subcontinent was called India, though in political terms it was made up of many small kingdoms and principalities. By the 19th century, India had fallen almost completely under the control of the British. It would not become independent until 1947, when what had been British India was partitioned into largely Hindu India and largely Muslim Pakistan. The transfer of power was accomplished without armed conflict between Britain and the two new nations. However, it was accompanied by a tremendous wave of communal rioting and mass murder in which 500,000 to 1 million died, as well as a huge internal migration of Muslims and Hindus between the two countries that involved 10 million to 18 million people.

U.S. immigration statistics from 1820 through 1946, before the creation of India and Pakistan, refer to immigration from British-ruled India, which included both nations. After independence, separate U.S. immigration figures were kept for each country, and also for Bangladesh (earlier called East Pakistan) after it became independent of Pakistan in 1971 (see "Immigrants from Pakistan" on p. 425, and "Immigrants from Bangladesh" on p. 429).

Table 4.13: Number and Percentage of Immigrants from India in Total U.S. Immigration by Decade, 1820–1996

Decade	Number of Immigrants from India	Total U.S. Immigration	Percentage of Immigrants from India in Total U.S. Immigration
1820	1	8,385	0.01
1821-1830	8	143,439	0.01
1831-1840	39	599,125	0.01
1841-1850	36	1,713,251	0.00
1851-1860	43	2,598,214	0.00
1861-1870	69	2,314,824	0.00
1871-1880	163	2,812,191	0.01
1881-1890	269	5,246,613	0.01
1891-1900	68	3,687,564	0.00
1901-1910	4,713	8,795,386	0.05
1911-1920	2,082	5,735,811	0.04
1921-1930	1,886	4,107,209	0.05
1931-1940	496	528,431	0.09
1941-1950	1,761	1,035,039	0.17
1951-1960	1,973	2,515,479	0.08
1961-1970	27,189	3,321,677	0.82
1971-1980	164,134	4,493,314	3.65
1981-1990	250,786	7,338,062	3.42
1991-1996	225,253	6,146,213	3.66
Total 1820-1996	680,969	63,140,227	1.08

Source: Adapted from Table 2, Immigration by Region and Selected Country of Last Residence, Fiscal Years 1820–1996, from the *Statistical Yearbook of the Immigration and Naturalization Service*, 1996.

Graph 4.29: Percentage Distribution of Americans of Asian Indian Origin by Region of the United States, 1990

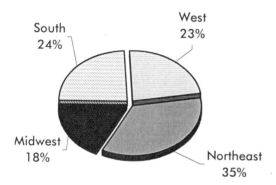

South 24%

West 23%

Midwest 18%

Northeast 35%

Only twice before 1966 did the annual number of immigrants from India top 1,000. That was during a minor spurt between 1907 and 1910, when more than 3,800 immigrants came in a four-year period. These were almost entirely single men, most of them of the Sikh religion, from the Indian state of Punjab. In the United States, they worked in agriculture and logging in California and the Pacific Northwest, as well as in western Canada.

That phase of Asian Indian immigration was short-lived, for the newcomers quickly encountered bitter discrimination, and the United States also instituted increasingly restrictive immigration policies. By 1912, emigration from India had slowed to a trickle, the annual figure reaching 500 only once in the half century between 1912 and 1962.

The situation changed dramatically with passage of the 1965 Immigration Act, which opened the door to a flood of new immigrants from many countries. Although increasing numbers of Asian Indian students had come to the United States in the 1950s, the discriminatory quotas set by the 1924 Immigration Act had until then remained in place. After

1965, however, emigration from India began to grow, slowly at first and then with a rush. From 1966 through 1970, Indian immigration averaged a little under 5,000 per year. But from 1971 to 1996, it averaged more than 24,600 per year, totaling 640,000 and adding a substantial Indian component to the United States ethnic mix. In addition, some immigrants of recent or older Indian ancestry came in this period from other parts of the world, such as the Caribbean and parts of Africa. Their numbers are unclear, for they were counted in the data from those other regions.

The new Asian Indian immigration was quite different from that of the early 20th century. India's new contribution to the United States consisted largely of hundreds of thousands of its best-educated, mostly highly trained young people. They established substantial communities in New York and California, while also spreading throughout the country. Some quickly settled into a considerable range of occupations, notably in academia, medicine, science, technology, and business. Others struggled to surmount pervasive racial and ethnic discrimination, and held low-grade jobs, though many later moved into a wide range of businesses.

In the late 1990s, Asian Indian immigration to the United States continued to grow, as it did to several other countries, constituting a sizable "brain drain" for India. On the other hand, money sent back home to relatives still in India had by then become a substantial source of capital in India, with these remittances equivalent to the stimulus produced by major foreign investment. As educated, highly productive Indian immigrants continued to flow into the United States and many other countries, the Indian government sought to stimulate investment and spending in India by emigrants abroad, by making travel to India less expensive for them and by making it easier for them to make investments and do business in India.

Graph 4.30: Number of Immigrants from India Annually, 1820–1996

Note: Figures based on country of birth; for yearly immigration figures, see Annual Tables 1-4.

Graph 4.31: Number of Immigrants from India by Decade, 1820–1996

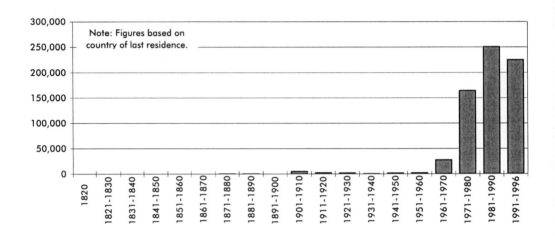

Graph 4.32: Percentage of Immigrants from India in Total U.S. Immigration by Decade, 1820–1996

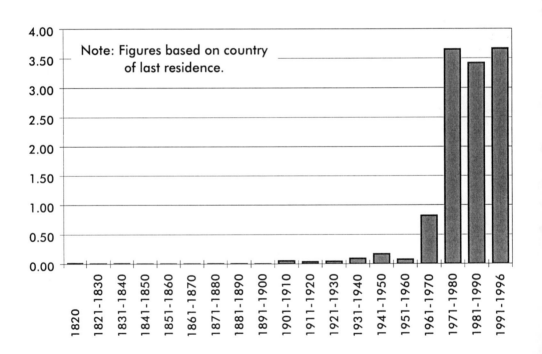

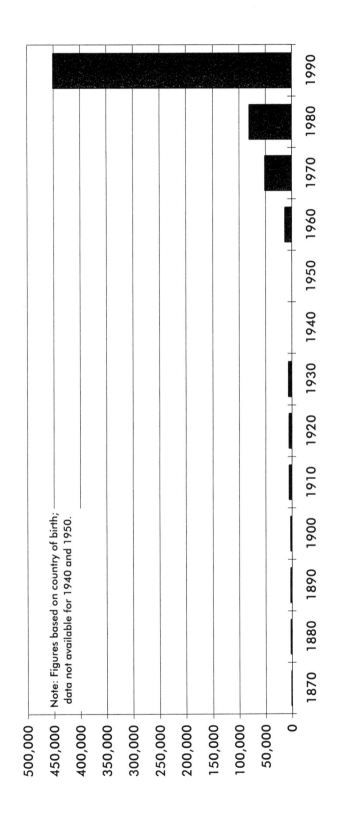

Graph 4.33: Number of Foreign-Born Immigrants from India in Total U.S. Population by Decade, 1870–1990

Note: Figures based on country of birth; data not available for 1940 and 1950.

Thumbu Sammy, aged 17, Hindoo
ex SS "Adriatic", April 14, 1911.

American Museum of Immigration, Statue of Liberty National Monument, National Park Service, U.S. Department of the Interior

This teenage Hindu immigrant, photographed at Ellis Island, arrived from India aboard the S. S. Adriatic in 1911.

Resources

Internet Resources

AsiaGenWeb Project (*http://www.rootsweb.com/~asiagw/*) Part of the WorldGenWeb project, linking genealogical research sites around the world, by region.

Family History in India (*http://www.ozemail.com.au/~clday/*) Web site "for people tracing their British, European and Anglo-Indian family history in India, Burma, Pakistan, Bangladesh and Sri Lanka"; part of the WorldGenWeb project, linking genealogical research sites around the world, by region.

Hindustan (*http://www.hindustan.org*) Web site for Indian communities worldwide, featuring discussion boards on current issues.

Print Resources

Bagai, Leona B. *The East Indians and the Pakistanis in America*. Rev. ed. Minneapolis: Lerner, 1972.

Banerjee, Kalyan Kumar. *Indian Freedom Movement Revolutionaries in America*. Calcutta: Jijnasa, 1969.

Chandrasekhar, S., ed. *From India to America: A Brief History of Immigration, Problems of Discrimination, Admission, and Assimilation*. La Jolla, Calif.: Population Review Publications, 1982.

Gordon, Susan. *Asian Indians*. New York: Watts, 1990.

Helweg, Arthur Wesley, and Usha M. Helweg. *An Immigrant Success Story: East Indians in America*. Philadelphia: University of Pennsylvania Press, 1990.

India: A Country Study. 5th ed. James Heitzman and Robert L. Worden, eds. Washington, D.C.: Federal Research Division, Library of Congress, 1996. (Available on-line at *http://lcweb2.loc.gov/frd/cs*)

Melendy, H. Brett. *Asians in America: Filipinos, Koreans, and East Indians*. Boston: Twayne, 1977.

Prior, Katherine. *The History of Emigration from the Indian Subcontinent*. New York: Watts, 1997.

Warner, Rachel. *Indian Migrations*. New York: Thomson Learning, 1995.

Williams, Raymond Brady. *Religions of Immigrants from India and Pakistan: New Threads in the American Tapestry*. New York: Cambridge University Press, 1988.

For more resources, see "General Asian Immigration Resources" on p. 479.

Immigrants from Pakistan

Until 1947, Pakistan was part of British-ruled India. It emerged as an independent Muslim nation in 1947, after the partition of India into what would become the highly antagonistic states of India and Pakistan. (For preindependence immigration to the United States, see "Immigrants from India" on p. 417)

Immigration to the United States from Pakistan was negligible after its 1947 independence, primarily due to the highly restrictive discriminatory quotas that had been established by the 1924 Immigration Act. With the 1965 Immigration Act, those quotas were abolished, opening the United States to a new flood of immigrants from many countries, among them Pakistan.

Despite the new immigration law, recorded or "legal" immigration into the United States from Pakistan—though far larger than before—was modest until the late 1980s. During the 1970s, it averaged less than 3,000 per year. Immigration picked up somewhat during the 1980s, into the range of 4,000 to 5,000 per year, then surged into the 10,000-per-year range during the 1990s. In all, more than 163,000 recorded Pakistani immigrants entered the United States from 1971 to 1996.

A substantial number of illegal Pakistani immigrants also entered the country. In 1996, U.S. government estimates indicated that approximately 41,000 undocumented "illegal" Pakistanis were living in the United States.

Graph 4.34: Percentage Distribution of Americans of Pakistani Origin by Region of the United States, 1990

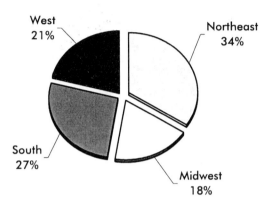

Like late-20th-century immigrants from India, the new Pakistani immigration was comprised mainly of tens of thousands of the country's best-educated and-trained people, among them substantial numbers of doctors, scientists, academics, and businesspeople. They often concentrated in New York and California, but also found jobs in other parts of the country. Like Indians and other Asian immigrants, many also suffered from continuing racial and ethnic discrimination in the United States, despite their education, training, and occupations.

Table 4.14: Number and Percentage of Immigrants from Pakistan in Total U.S. Immigration Annually, 1971–1996

Year	Number of Immigrants from Pakistan	Total U.S. Immigration	Percentage of Immigrants from Pakistan in Total U.S. Immigration
1971	2,125	370,473	0.57
1972	2,480	384,685	0.64
1973	2,525	400,063	0.63
1974	2,570	394,861	0.65
1975	2,620	396,194	0.66
1976	3,636	502,289	0.72
1977	3,183	462,315	0.69
1978	3,876	601,442	0.64
1979	3,967	460,348	0.86
1980	4,265	530,639	0.80
1981	5,288	596,600	0.89
1982	4,536	594,131	0.76
1983	4,807	559,763	0.86
1984	5,509	543,903	1.01
1985	5,744	570,009	1.01
1986	5,994	601,708	1.00
1987	6,319	601,516	1.05
1988	5,438	643,025	0.85
1989	8,000	1,090,924	0.73
1990	9,729	1,536,483	0.63
1991	20,355	1,827,167	1.11
1992	10,214	973,977	1.05
1993	8,927	904,292	0.99
1994	8,698	804,416	1.08
1995	9,774	720,461	1.36
1996	12,519	915,900	1.37
Total 1971-96	163,098	17,987,584	0.91

Sources: *Statistical Yearbook of the Immigration and Naturalization Service*, 1980, Table 13; *Statistical Yearbook of the Immigration and Naturalization Service*, 1986, Table 3; *Statistical Yearbook of the Immigration and Naturalization Service*, 1996, Table 3.

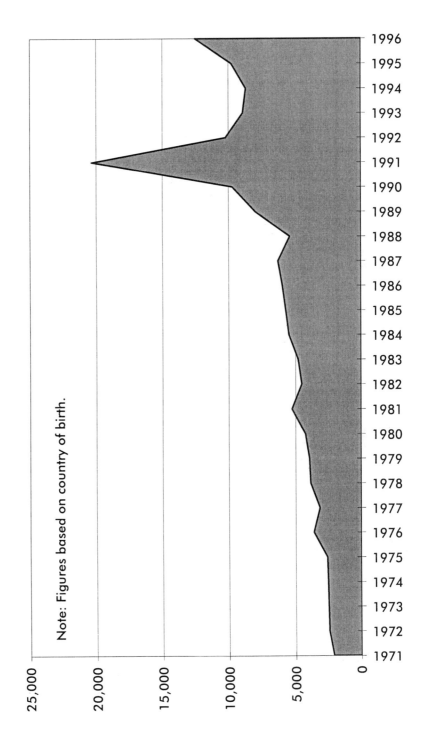

Graph 4.35: Number of Immigrants from Pakistan Annually, 1971–1996

Note: Figures based on country of birth.

Resources

Internet Resources

*Pakistan Link (http://
www.pakistanlink.com)* On-line
magazine for Pakistani Americans.

(10564 Progress Way, Suite D, Cypress,
CA 90630; Phone: 714-236-7910; Fax:
714-236-7911)

Print Resources

Bagai, Leona B. *The East Indians and the
Pakistanis in America.* Rev. ed.
Minneapolis: Lerner, 1972.
Pakistan: A Country Study. 6th ed. Peter
R. Blood, ed. Washington, D.C.: U.S.
Government Printing Office, 1995.
Warner, Rachel. *Indian Migrations.* New
York: Thomson Learning, 1995.

Williams, Raymond Brady. *Religions of
Immigrants from India and Pakistan:
New Threads in the American Tapestry.*
New York: Cambridge University
Press, 1988.

For more resources, see "General Asian
Immigration Resources" on p. 479

Immigrants from Bangladesh

Until 1947, largely Muslim Bangladesh was part of East Bengal, in British-ruled India. Then with the partition of India into independent India and Pakistan, East Bengal became part of Pakistan. In 1971, after the Bangladesh War of Independence and the related India-Pakistan War, Bangladesh won its own independence.

United States immigration statistics regarding Bangladesh have been available only since 1973. (See "Immigrants from India" on p. 417, and "Immigrants from Pakistan" on p. 425, for earlier statistics from the region.)

Despite the end of restrictive U.S. immigration quotas in 1965, immigration to the United States from Bangladesh was negligible in the 1970s and early 1980s, reaching 1,000 per year only in 1985. In all, it totaled less than 56,000 from 1972 to 1996, with most of that number coming during the 1990s.

Like late-20th-century immigrants from neighboring countries on the Indian subcontinent, the Bangladesh immigration to the United States was in the main drawn from the country's most highly trained people, many of them medical and scientific professionals, academics, and businesspeople. Most of them settled in California and New York, though they also followed available jobs throughout the United States. Also like their neighbors, many immigrants from Bangladesh met with continuing ethnic and racial discrimination in the United States, however highly trained and educated they were.

Table 4.15: Number and Percentage of Immigrants from Bangladesh in Total U.S. Immigration Annually, 1973–1996

Year	Number of Immigrants from Bangladesh	Total U.S. Immigration	Percentage of Immigrants from Bangladesh in Total U.S. Immigration
1973	154	400,063	0.04
1974	147	394,861	0.04
1975	404	396,194	0.10
1976	762	502,289	0.15
1977	590	462,315	0.13
1978	716	601,442	0.12
1979	549	460,348	0.12
1980	532	530,639	0.10
1981	756	596,600	0.13
1982	639	594,131	0.11
1983	787	559,763	0.14
1984	823	543,903	0.15
1985	1,146	570,009	0.20
1986	1,634	601,708	0.27
1987	1,649	601,516	0.27
1988	1,325	643,025	0.21
1989	2,180	1,090,924	0.20
1990	4,252	1,536,483	0.28
1991	10,676	1,827,167	0.58
1992	3,740	973,977	0.38
1993	3,291	904,292	0.36
1994	3,434	804,416	0.43
1995	6,072	720,461	0.84
1996	8,221	915,900	0.90
Total 1973-96	54,479	17,987,584	0.30

Sources: *Statistical Yearbook of the Immigration and Naturalization Service*, 1980, Table 13; *Statistical Yearbook of the Immigration and Naturalization Service*, 1996, Table 3.

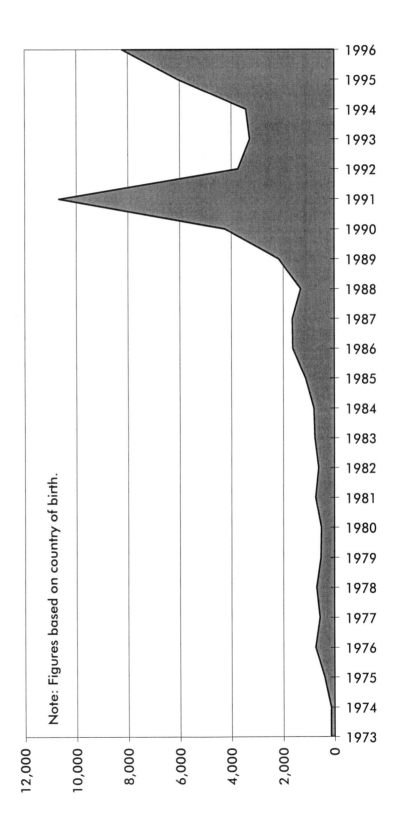

Graph 4.36: Number of Immigrants from Bangladesh Annually, 1973–1996

Note: Figures based on country of birth.

Resources

Internet Resources

Bangladesh Youth Federation (*http://www.byf.com*) Web site of organization of Bangladeshi North Americans, including information and news about Bangladesh and related Web links.

Bengal Online (*http://www.sitemarvel.com/bengalonline*) Web site for Bengali students around the world.

Print Resources

Bangladesh: A Country Study. 2d ed. James Heitzman and Robert L. Worden, eds. Washington, D.C.: Federal Research Division, Library of Congress, 1989. (Available on-line at *http://lcweb2.loc.gov/frd/cs*)

Warner, Rachel. *Indian Migrations*. New York: Thomson Learning, 1995.

For more resources, see "General Asian Immigration Resources" on p. 479.

Immigrants from Turkey

In terms of immigration to the United States, there were two vastly different Turkish nations. One was the pre–World War I remainder of the Ottoman Empire; the other was the much smaller modern Turkey that emerged after that war.

In the first decade of the 20th century, when Turkish immigration into the United States first became at all significant, the Ottoman Empire was in its final days. By then, the Ottoman Turks had lost all but a small portion of the once-huge European part of their empire, but until 1912 they continued to hold territories in the Balkans, including Albania, Macedonia, and parts of Greece and Bulgaria (see "Immigrants from the Yugoslav (South Slav) States" on p. 259, and "Immigrants from Greece" on p. 221). In addition to Anatolia (essentially modern Turkey), the Turks also still retained large territories in southwest Asia and northern Africa.

From that Turkey, a total of approximately 350,000 immigrants entered the United States from 1890 to 1924, though the total may be somewhat understated.

The immigrants in that period included an estimated 80,000 to 85,000 Armenians. Some 50,000 to 55,000 of these Armenians fled to the United States to escape Turkish massacres and discrimination from the early 1890s through the beginning of World War I in 1914. The remaining 30,000 to 35,000 Armenian immigrants to the United States came as refugees, from the end of World War I through 1924. The latter were mainly survivors of the Armenian Holocaust, in which an estimated 1 million to 1.5 million Armenians were killed by the Turkish government during World War I, most of them dying from famine and disease while in Turkish concentration camps in the Syrian desert.

Table 4.16: Number and Percentage of Immigrants from Turkey in Total U.S. Immigration by Decade, 1820–1996

Decade	Number of Immigrants from Turkey	Total U.S. Immigrants	Percentage of Immigrants from Turkey in Total U.S. Immigration
1820	1	8,385	0.01
1821-1830	20	143,439	0.01
1831-1840	7	599,125	0.00
1841-1850	59	1,713,251	0.00
1851-1860	83	2,598,214	0.00
1861-1870	131	2,314,824	0.01
1871-1880	404	2,812,191	0.01
1881-1890	3782	5,246,613	0.07
1891-1900	30,425	3,687,564	0.83
1901-1910	157369	8,795,386	1.79
1911-1920	134,066	5,735,811	2.34
1921-1930	33824	4,107,209	0.82
1931-1940	1,065	528,431	0.20
1941-1950	798	1,035,039	0.08
1951-1960	3,519	2,515,479	0.14
1961-1970	10142	3,321,677	0.31
1971-1980	13399	4,493,314	0.30
1981-1990	23233	7,338,062	0.32
1991-1996	24,415	6,146,213	0.40
Total 1820-1996	436,742	63,140,227	0.69

Source: Adapted from Table 2, Immigration by Region and Selected Country of Last Residence, Fiscal Years 1820–1996, from the *Statistical Yearbook of the Immigration and Naturalization Service,*1996.

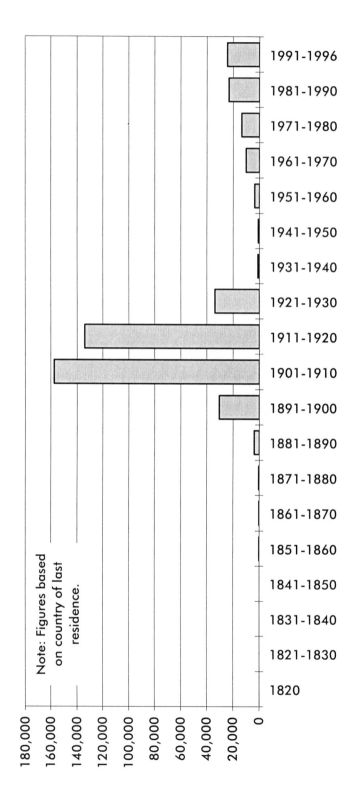

Graph 4.37: Number of Immigrants from Turkey by Decade, 1820–1996

Note: Figures based on country of last residence.

Immigration to the United States from the Ottoman Empire in this period also included a roughly estimated 100,000 Syrians, the great majority of these Maronite Christians from what would later become Lebanon (see "Immigrants from Syria" on p. 443, and "Immigrants from Lebanon" on p. 439). These immigrants were also in part fleeing Turkish oppression, though for many immigrating to the United States was primarily a matter of economic opportunity. From the 1890s, these Syrian immigrants formed tightly knit ethnic communities in several eastern metropolitan areas, most notably in New York and Boston.

Table 4.17: Number and Percentage of Foreign-Born Immigrants from Turkey by Decade in Total U.S. Population at End of Decade, 1850–1990

Decade	Number of Foreign-Born Immigrants from Turkey	Total U.S. Population	Percentage of Foreign-Born Immigrants from Turkey in Total U.S. Population
1850	106	23,191,876	0.00
1860	128	31,443,321	0.00
1870	302	39,818,449	0.00
1880	1,205	50,155,783	0.00
1890	1,839	62,947,714	0.00
1900	9,910	75,994,575	0.01
1910	32,230	91,972,266	0.04
1920	16,303	105,710,620	0.02
1930	48,911	122,775,046	0.04
1940	(NA)	131,669,275	(NA)
1950	(NA)	150,697,361	(NA)
1960	52,228	179,323,175	0.03
1970	48,085	203,235,298	0.02
1980	51,915	227,726,000	0.02
1990	55,087	249,907,000	0.02

NA = Not available

Source: Adapted from Series C 228–295, Foreign-Born Population by Country of Birth: 1850–1970, in *Historical Statistics of the United States, Colonial Times to 1970, Bicentennial Edition,* and other updating tables from the U.S. Census Bureau.

Much of the rest of the immigration to the United States from Turkey in that period came from what remained of the Turkish empire in the Balkans. Far fewer came from other parts of the empire, including Turkey itself.

After World War I, in which the Turks fought on the side of the Central Powers, their empire was dismembered. Refusing to accept the terms of the postwar Treaty of Sèvres (1920), the Turks, now led by Mustafa Kemal (later named Atatürk), defeated invading Greek forces. The Turks ultimately signed the Treaty of Lausanne (1923), which allowed them to keep their prewar holdings in Armenia and Kurdistan, as well as continuing to hold Anatolia (Turkey), though the rest of the prewar empire was gone. In the wake of these treaties came massive population shifts. Approximately 1.3 million ethnic Greeks left Turkey for Greece, while some 400,000 Turks immigrated to the new Turkey from Greece.

Between the loss of empire, the war with Greece, and the restrictive United States immigration laws of 1921 and 1924, Turkish immigration into the United States slowed to a crawl. From 1930 to 1960 a total of only a little over 5,000 Turks entered the United States. From 1961 to 1996, a little over 70,000 more came. Many of these were professionals migrating to the United States to seek better economic opportunity. It was a period in which millions of other Turks did emigrate, but they went largely to western Europe as "guest laborers" rather than to the United States.

American Museum of Immigration, Statue of Liberty National Monument, National Park Service, U.S. Department of the
Interior

*Many immigrants numbered with those from Turkey were from among the empire's many ethnic
minorities, such as these two Albanian soldiers photographed at Ellis Island.*

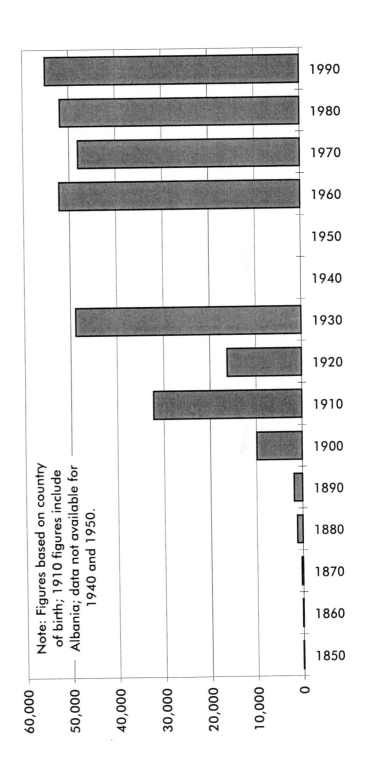

Graph 4.38: Number of Foreign-Born Immigrants from Turkey by Decade, 1850–1990

Note: Figures based on country of birth; 1910 figures include Albania; data not available for 1940 and 1950.

Resources

Internet Resources

TurkeyGenWeb Project (*http://
www.rootsweb.com/~turwgw/*) Web
site providing message boards, forums,
and other links; part of the wider
MediterraneanGenWeb (*http://
www.rootsweb.com/~sthamgw/
medgw.html*) Part of the WorldGenWeb
project, linking genealogical research
sites around the world, by region, with
resources by individual country and
links to neighboring regions of the
world.

Armenian Geneaology–WorldGenWeb
Project (*http://rootsweb.com/
~armwgw/links.html*) Part of the
WorldGenWeb project, with links to
various sites containing information
about Armenian genealogy.

Assembly of Turkish American
Associations (*http://www.ataa.org*)
Web site focusing on current issues,
including international links.

Armenian Assembly of America (*http://
www.aaainc.org*) Organization Web site
offering information on news and
issues. (Address: 122 C Street, NW,
Suite 350, Washington, DC 20001)

Armenian Network (*http://
www.armnet.org*) Web site of
organization of and for the Armenian
American community.

Print Resources

General Works

Turkey: A Country Study. 5th ed. Helen
Chapin Metz, ed. Washington, D.C.:
Federal Research Division, Library of
Congress, 1996. (Available on-line at
http://lcweb2.loc.gov/frd/cs)

On Armenians

Avakian, Arra S. *The Armenians in
America.* Minneapolis: Lerner, 1977.

Bakalian, Anny P. *Armenian-Americans:
From Being to Feeling Armenian.* New
Brunswick, N.J.: Transaction
Publishers, 1993.

Kezerian, Nephi K., and LaPreal J.
Kezerian. *Genealogy for Armenians: A
Book Project of the Armenian
Genealogical Society.* Provo, Utah: The
Society, 1995.

Kulhanjian, Gary A. *The Historical and
Sociological Aspects of Armenian
Immigration to the United States 1890–
1930.* San Francisco: R and E Research
Associates, 1975.

Mirak, Robert. *Torn Between Two Lands:
Armenians in America, 1890 to World
War I.* Cambridge, Mass.: Department
of Near Eastern Languages and
Civilizations, Harvard University,
1983.

Waldstreicher, David. *The Armenian
Americans.* New York: Chelsea House,
1989.

Wertsman, Vladimir, ed. *The Armenians in
America, 1618–1976: A Chronology and
Fact Book.* Dobbs Ferry, N.Y.: Oceana,
1978.

For more resources, see "General Asian
Immigration Resources" on p. 479.

Immigrants from Lebanon

Lebanon is a very small Middle Eastern country, with an estimated population of 3.2 million in 1997. It was part of the Ottoman Empire until after World War I. Like Syria, it was a French-administered League of Nations mandate territory from 1920 to 1941, when it formally became an independent nation. However, it did not in fact achieve independence until 1946, following withdrawal of French forces in 1945.

During the decade immediately following independence, Lebanon emerged as a regional banking and financial center, drawing substantial international investment funds. Its capital, Beirut, became a large, cosmopolitan city, and Lebanon was widely viewed as a living demonstration that many contending political and religious factions could live together successfully in the explosive Middle East, even though at least 1 million Palestinians were living in United Nations–administered refugee camps throughout the region, some hundreds of thousands of them in Lebanon. Lebanese peace had been assured by agreement among its main Christian and Muslim groups.

It was not to be. The pressures generated by the continuing Arab-Israeli conflict, coupled with the rise of Islamic militant movements, soon generated instability and conflict in Lebanon. From the late 1950s until at least the end of the 20th century, Lebanese history was to be dominated by a long series of enormously destructive armed conflicts.

In 1958, the first Lebanese Civil War—pitting its right-wing, pro-Western government against an Arab nationalist–Christian Left coalition—brought fighting to the streets of Beirut before a 14,000-strong U.S. force intervened, making international mediation possible. However, the compromises reached did not hold, and the destabilization had begun. In 1967, Palestine Liberation Organization (PLO) commandos intensified their cross-border raids against Israel from southern Lebanon, drawing greatly increased Israeli response. PLO forces and command centers were transferred to Lebanon after they were expelled from Jordan in 1971.

In 1975, the second Lebanon Civil War (1975–1976) began. Heavy fighting in Beirut between Christian militias and PLO forces soon spread throughout the country, drawing in many factions. Syria intervened to stop the fighting in 1976, but Syrian troops stayed on, and Lebanon ultimately became a Syrian protectorate, remaining so through the end of the century.

The long series of armed conflicts lasted into the early 1990s, and included a major invasion of Lebanon by Israeli forces (1982–1983). They took Beirut and drove PLO and Syrian forces into the Bekaa Valley before withdrawing, to be replaced by an international peacekeeping force. Though the Israelis largely withdrew from southern Lebanon in 1985, they maintained a buffer zone against guerrilla attacks from that region. In 1983, the Syrians expelled PLO forces from Lebanon, but rival militias continued the civil war, with Lebanon in a state of near-anarchy. In 1989, the Lebanese government made a failed attempt to expel Syrian forces.

The net effect of the long Lebanese wars was to leave the country a shambles, with tens of thousands dead and its once-promising economy wrecked, with runaway inflation, massive foreign debts, and unemployment running in the 40-percent range. By 1989, more than 1 million refugees had fled Beirut. Substantial Israeli-Arab clashes continued in southern Lebanon, with no end in sight. On the positive side, some signs of post–civil war recovery had appeared by the late 1990s, among them significant rebuilding in shattered Beirut.

As a direct result of the Lebanese wars, emigration out of the country became enormous. After 1975, hundreds of thousands of Lebanese emigrated abroad, with almost 100,000 of these coming to the United States. Lebanese immigration, which had averaged less than 2,000 per year until the mid-1970s, jumped to an average of 4,600 in the 21 years that followed, and in the 1990s rose to more than 5,000 a year. With war continuing in southern Lebanon, economic conditions very little improved, and Syrian occupation troops still not withdrawn, there seemed little likelihood that many Lebanese Americans would return to Lebanon permanently, and every probability that the now open chain of immigration from Lebanon would continue to draw substantial numbers of Lebanese immigrants into the United States.

Table 4.18: Number and Percentage of Immigrants from Lebanon in Total U.S. Immigration Annually, 1971–1996

Year	Number of Immigrants from Lebanon	Total U.S. Immigration	Percentage of Immigrants from Lebanon in Total U.S. Immigration
1971	1,867	370,473	0.50
1972	1,984	384,685	0.52
1973	1,977	400,063	0.49
1974	2,400	394,861	0.61
1975	2,075	396,194	0.52
1976	4,532	502,289	0.90
1977	5,685	462,315	1.23
1978	4,556	601,442	0.76
1979	4,634	460,348	1.01
1980	4,136	530,639	0.78
1981	3,955	596,600	0.66
1982	3,529	594,131	0.59
1983	2,941	559,763	0.53
1984	3,203	543,903	0.59
1985	3,385	570,009	0.59
1986	3,994	601,708	0.66
1987	4,367	601,516	0.73
1988	4,910	643,025	0.76
1989	5,716	1,090,924	0.52
1990	5,634	1,536,483	0.37
1991	6,009	1,827,167	0.33
1992	5,838	973,977	0.60
1993	5,465	904,292	0.60
1994	4,319	804,416	0.54
1995	3,884	720,461	0.54
1996	4,382	915,900	0.48
Total 1971-1996	105,377	17,987,584	0.59

Sources: *Statistical Yearbook of the Immigration and Naturalization Service*, 1980, Table 13; *Statistical Yearbook of the Immigration and Naturalization Service*, 1986, Table 3; *Statistical Yearbook of the Immigration and Naturalization Service*, 1996. Table 3

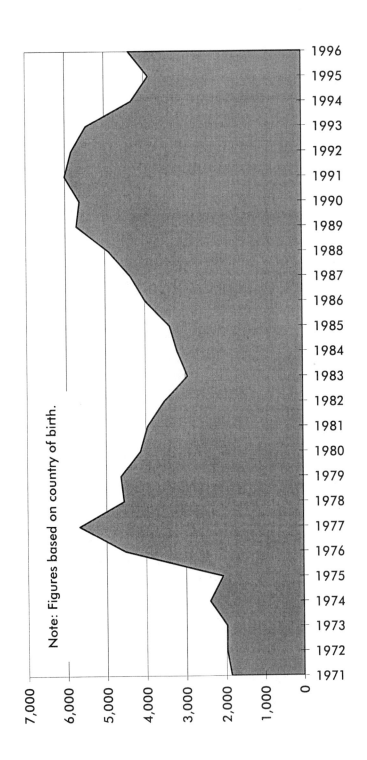

Graph 4.39: Number of Immigrants from Lebanon Annually, 1971–1996

Note: Figures based on country of birth.

Resources

Internet Resources

Lebanon GenWeb Project (*http://
www.rootsweb.com/~lbnwgw/*) Part of
the WorldGenWeb project, linking
genealogical research sites around the
world, by region.

Print Resources

Kayal, Philip M., and Joseph M. Kayal.
*The Syrian-Lebanese in America: A
Study in Religion and Assimilation.*
New York: Twayne, 1975.

*The Lebanese Texans and the Syrian
Texans.* Rev. ed. San Antonio:
University of Texas Institute of Texan
Cultures at San Antonio, 1988.

Lebanon: A Country Study. 3d ed. Thomas
Collelo, ed. Washington, D.C.: Federal
Research Division, Library of Congress,
1989. (Available on-line at *http://
lcweb2.loc.gov/frd/cs*)

Marston Harik, Elsa. *The Lebanese in
America.* Minneapolis: Lerner, 1987.

Moses, John G. *The Lebanese in America.*
Utica, N.Y.: J. G. Moses, 1987.

Whitehead, Sandra. *Lebanese Americans.*
Tarrytown, N.Y.: Benchmark Books,
1996.

For more resources, see "General Asian
Immigration Resources" on p. 479.

Immigrants from Syria

Syria was part of the Ottoman Empire until after World War I. It was a French-administered League of Nations mandate territory from 1920 to 1941, when it formally became an independent nation. However, it did not actually achieve independence until 1946, following the withdrawal of French forces in 1945. After the military coup of 1963, Syria became an Arab Islamic Socialist state, led by the Ba'ath Party. Since 1971, it has been solely ruled by Ba'ath Party leader Hafez al-Assad.

Syria's estimated 1997 population of almost 15 million has grown very quickly during the 1980s and 1990s, sometimes at rates exceeding 3.5 percent per year. Yet population pressure has not generated large-scale emigration, for the country has significant quantities of oil, a working agricultural economy, and a substantial social welfare system. On the other hand, its largely state-owned major industries and highly centralized top-down economic planning have produced little growth, forcing a 1990s move toward a market economy and attempts to attract international investment.

Late in the century, some emigration from Syria to the United States has developed. Much of it consists of skilled professional and technical people coming to the United States in search of economic opportunity. Also among the immigrants recorded from Syria are some Christian Armenians and some of the estimated 200,000 Palestinian refugees long resident in Syria. In all, a little more than 50,000 immigrants have entered the United States from Syria from 1971 to 1996, at a modest average of less than 2,000 per year.

Table 4.19: Number and Percentage of Foreign-Born Immigrants from Syria by Decade in Total U.S. Population at End of Decade, 1920–1990

Decade	Number of Foreign-Born Immigrants from Syria	Total U.S. Population	Percentage of Foreign-Born Immigrants from Syria in Total U.S. Population
1920	51,901	105,710,620	0.05
1930	57,227	122,775,046	0.05
1940	(NA)	131,669,275	(NA)
1950	(NA)	150,697,361	(NA)
1960	16,717	179,323,175	0.01
1970	14,962	203,235,298	0.01
1980	(NA)	227,726,000	(NA)
1990	36,782	249,907,000	0.01

NA = Not available

Source: Adapted from Series C 228–295, Foreign-Born Population, by Country of Birth: 1850–1970, in *Historical Statistics of the United States, Colonial Times to 1970, Bicentennial Edition*, and other updating tables from the U.S. Census Bureau.

Graph 4.40: Number of Immigrants from Syria, 1971–1996

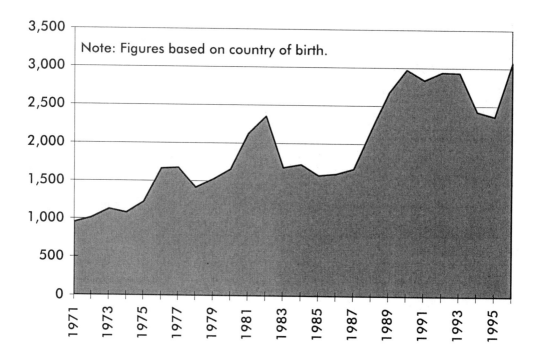

Graph 4.41: Number of Foreign-Born Immigrants from Syria in Total U.S. Population by Decade, 1920–1990

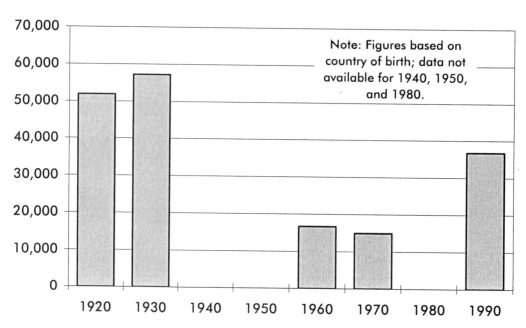

Table 4.20: Number and Percentage of Immigrants from Syria in Total U.S. Immigration Annually, 1971–1996

Year	Number of Immigrants from Syria	Total U.S. Immigration	Percentage of Immigrants from Syria in Total U.S. Immigration
1971	951	370,473	0.26
1972	1,012	384,685	0.26
1973	1,128	400,063	0.28
1974	1,082	394,861	0.27
1975	1,222	396,194	0.31
1976	1,666	502,289	0.33
1977	1,676	462,315	0.36
1978	1,416	601,442	0.24
1979	1,528	460,348	0.33
1980	1,658	530,639	0.31
1981	2,127	596,600	0.36
1982	2,354	594,131	0.40
1983	1,683	559,763	0.30
1984	1,724	543,903	0.32
1985	1,581	570,009	0.28
1986	1,604	601,708	0.27
1987	1,669	601,516	0.28
1988	2,183	643,025	0.34
1989	2,675	1,090,924	0.25
1990	2,972	1,536,483	0.19
1991	2,837	1,827,167	0.16
1992	2,940	973,977	0.30
1993	2,933	904,292	0.32
1994	2,426	804,416	0.30
1995	2,362	720,461	0.33
1996	3,072	915,900	0.34
Total 1971-96	50,481	17,987,584	0.28

Sources: *Statistical Yearbook of the Immigration and Naturalization Service*, 1980, Table 13; *Statistical Yearbook of the Immigration and Naturalization Service*, 1986, Table 3; *Statistical Yearbook of the Immigration and Naturalization Service*, 1996, Table 3.

Resources

Internet Resources

SyriaGenWeb Project (*http://
www.rootsweb.com/~syrwgw/*) Part of
the WorldGenWeb project, linking
genealogical research sites around the
world, by region.

Print Resources

Kayal, Philip M., and Joseph M. Kayal.
*The Syrian-Lebanese in America: A
Study in Religion and Assimilation.*
New York: Twayne, 1975.

Syria: A Country Study. 3d ed. Thomas
Collelo, ed. Federal Research Division,
Library of Congress, 1988. (Available
on-line at *http://lcweb2.loc.gov/frd/cs*)

For more resources, see "General Asian
Immigration Resources" on p. 479.

Immigrants from Jordan

The small Arab nation of Jordan occupies the east bank of the Jordan River. It was part of the Ottoman Empire until after World War I, and then became a British-administered League of Nations mandate territory. Jordan became a fully independent nation in 1946, and immediately became embroiled in the run-up to neighboring Israel's War of Independence (1948–1949), which was also the First Arab-Israeli War.

Jordan would be deeply involved in the conflicts between Israel and its neighbors throughout the rest of the century, always on the Arab side, although King Hussein of Jordan was for half a century one of the leading moderates and peacemakers in the Arab world. That conflict would also dominate the country's internal political history during that long period. Jordan served as the main guerrilla war base for the Palestine Liberation Organization (PLO) against Israel until 1971, when Jordanian forces expelled the PLO, which moved its headquarters to Lebanon. Even so, in the late 1990s an estimated 2 million of Jordan's population of 6 million were of Palestinian origin and profoundly anti-Israeli.

The Arab-Israeli wars and the refugee populations they brought generated massive instability in Jordan's economy. However, another major contributor to Jordan's problems was the enormous population pressure that developed in the four decades following independence. With a rate of population increase that in many years was a huge 3.5 percent, Jordan's population ballooned. The 4 million Jordanians and 2 million Palestinians in the small desert country greatly overstrained Jordan's moderate resources, which by the late 1990s depended a great deal on international aid.

Many Jordanians went abroad from the 1970s on, some permanently and most as guest workers planning to return home. During the 1970s and 1980s, high world oil prices and good jobs drew 350,000 Jordanians, many of them professionals and skilled workers, to the oil states of the Middle East. The money they sent home generated the kind of revenue another major industry would have produced. However, many of these guest workers returned home in the 1990s, as declining oil prices cut the numbers of available jobs.

Some Jordanians, including many of the country's most highly skilled technical and professional people, immigrated to the United States, in a flow that totaled more than 87,000 immigrants from 1971 to 1996. A good many of these did return home, for in 1990 the estimate of Jordan-born United States immigrants was only 32,000. Given Jordan's very difficult population pressure and Palestinian refugee problems, coupled with an unemployment rate in the 15 percent to 25 percent range, U.S. immigration from Jordan might reasonably be expected to grow, well into the 21st century.

Table 4.21: Number and Percentage of Immigrants from Jordan in Total U.S. Immigration Annually, 1971–1996

Year	Number of Immigrants from Jordan	Total U.S. Immigration	Percentage of Immigrants from Jordan in Total U.S. Immigration
1971	2,588	370,473	0.70
1972	2,756	384,685	0.72
1973	2,450	400,063	0.61
1974	2,838	394,861	0.72
1975	2,578	396,194	0.65
1976	3,328	502,289	0.66
1977	2,875	462,315	0.62
1978	3,483	601,442	0.58
1979	3,360	460,348	0.73
1980	3,322	530,639	0.63
1981	3,825	596,600	0.64
1982	2,923	594,131	0.49
1983	2,718	559,763	0.49
1984	2,438	543,903	0.45
1985	2,998	570,009	0.53
1986	3,081	601,708	0.51
1987	3,125	601,516	0.52
1988	3,232	643,025	0.50
1989	3,921	1,090,924	0.36
1990	4,449	1,536,483	0.29
1991	4,259	1,827,167	0.23
1992	4,036	973,977	0.41
1993	4,741	904,292	0.52
1994	3,990	804,416	0.50
1995	3,649	720,461	0.51
1996	4,445	915,900	0.49
Total 1971-96	87,408	17,987,584	0.49

Sources: *Statistical Yearbook of the Immigration and Naturalization Service,* 1980, Table 13; *Statistical Yearbook of the Immigration and Naturalization Service,* 1986, Table 3; *Statistical Yearbook of the Immigration and Naturalization Service,* 1996, Table 3.

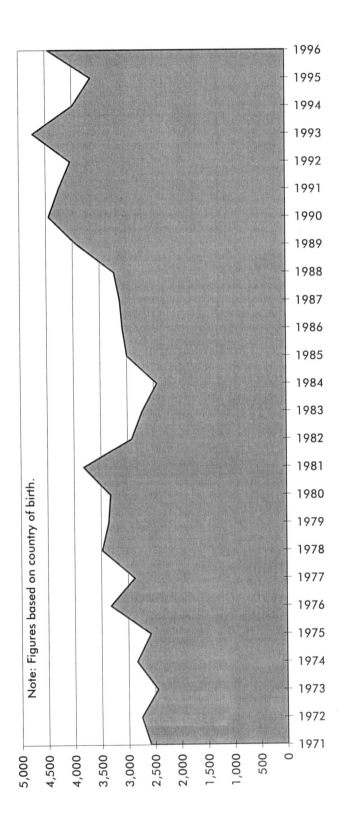

Graph 4.42: Number of Immigrants from Jordan Annually, 1971–1996

Note: Figures based on country of birth.

Resources

Internet Resources

MidEastGenWeb (*http://
www.rootsweb.com/~mdeastgw/*) Part
of the WorldGenWeb project, linking
genealogical research sites around the
world, by region, with resources by
individual country.

Print Resources

Jordan: A Country Study. 4th ed. Helen
Chapin Metz, ed. Washington, D.C.:
Federal Research Division, Library of
Congress, 1991. (Available on-line at
http://lcweb2.loc.gov/frd/cs)

For more resources, see "General Asian
Immigration Resources" on p. 479.

Immigrants from Iran

Immigration into the United States from Iran was modest until the 1978 run-up to the 1979 Iranian Revolution, which toppled the government of Shah Mohammad Reza Pahlavi and brought Islamic fundamentalists to power in Iran. By 1981, revolutionary leader Ayatollah Ruhollah Khomeini had turned Iran into a fully Islamic fundamentalist state.

Before and after 1978, the main body of immigrants from Iran to the United States were drawn from the country's elite, many

of whom came to the United States to study and stayed on to become Iranian Americans. There were not many Iranian immigrants; from 1925 to 1970, a total of only a little more than 15,000 Iranian immigrants entered the United States. Immigration picked up somewhat, but was still modest, from 1971 to 1978, totaling a little more than 21,000.

As the signs of impending revolution increased in Iran, many more Iranians began to leave the country, among them academics, health professionals, scientists, and moneyed businesspeople. At the same time, many of the tens of thousands of Iranian students in the United States elected to extend their stay in America rather than return to Iran. Large numbers of those who stayed later made the change permanent. As Islamic fundamentalism began to completely dominate Iranian life, more of those who had remained in Iran also left. Many of these emigrants came to the United States, often with large financial resources.

From 1979 to 1996, Iranian immigration to the United States totaled 259,000, an average of more than 14,000 per year. During the early 1990s, even though the Iranian regime liberalized somewhat, the high level of Iranian immigration did not slacken, averaging 15,000 per year from 1990 to 1996.

Table 4.22: Number and Percentage of Immigrants from Iran in Total U.S. Immigration by Decade, 1925–1996

Decade	Number of Immigrants from Iran	Total U.S. Immigrants	Percentage of Immigrants from Iran in Total U.S. Immigration
1925-1930	241	4,107,209	0.01
1931-1940	195	528,431	0.04
1941-1950	1,380	1,035,039	0.13
1951-1960	3,388	2,515,479	0.13
1961-1970	10,339	3,321,677	0.31
1971-1980	45,136	4,493,314	1.00
1981-1990	116,172	7,338,062	1.58
1991-1996	45,773	6,146,213	0.74
Total 1820-1996	222,624	63,140,227	0.35

Note: Data not separately reported until 1925.

Source: Adapted from Table 2, Immigration by Region and Selected Country of Last Residence, Fiscal Years 1820–1996, from the *Statistical Yearbook of the Immigration and Naturalization Service*, 1996.

Table 4.23: Number and Percentage of Immigrants from Iran in Total U.S. Immigration Annually, 1971–1996

Year	Number of Immigrants from Iran	Total U.S. Immigration	Percentage of Immigrants from Iran in Total U.S. Immigration
1971	2,411	370,473	0.65
1972	3,059	384,685	0.80
1973	2,998	400,063	0.75
1974	2,608	394,861	0.66
1975	2,337	396,194	0.59
1976	3,731	502,289	0.74
1977	4,261	462,315	0.92
1978	5,861	601,442	0.97
1979	8,476	460,348	1.84
1980	10,410	530,639	1.96
1981	11,105	596,600	1.86
1982	10,314	594,131	1.74
1983	11,163	559,763	1.99
1984	13,807	543,903	2.54
1985	16,071	570,009	2.82
1986	16,505	601,708	2.74
1987	14,426	601,516	2.40
1988	15,246	643,025	2.37
1989	21,243	1,090,924	1.95
1990	24,977	1,536,483	1.63
1991	19,569	1,827,167	1.07
1992	13,233	973,977	1.36
1993	14,841	904,292	1.64
1994	11,422	804,416	1.42
1995	9,201	720,461	1.28
1996	11,084	915,900	1.21
Total 1971-96	280,359	17,987,584	1.56

Sources: *Statistical Yearbook of the Immigration and Naturalization Service*, 1980, Table 13; *Statistical Yearbook of the Immigration and Naturalization Service*, 1986, Table 3; *Statistical Yearbook of the Immigration and Naturalization Service*, 1996, Table 3.

Graph 4.43: Number of Immigrants from Iran by Decade, 1925–1996

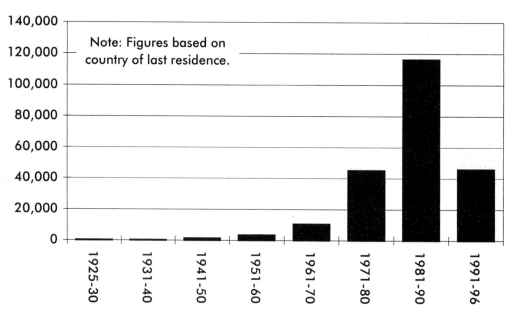

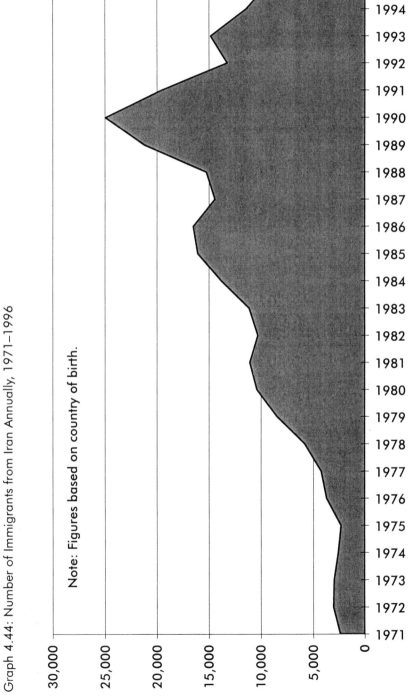

Graph 4.44: Number of Immigrants from Iran Annually, 1971–1996

Note: Figures based on country of birth.

Resources

Internet Resources

International Federation of Iranian Refugees (*http://www.hambastegi.org*) Organization of and for Iranian refugees abroad. (Address: IFIR Secretariat, G.P.O., P.O. Box 7051, New York, NY 10116; Phone: 212-747-1046; Fax: 212-425-7260; E-mail: ifiric@aol.com)

Print Resources

Ansari, Abdolmaboud. *The Making of the Iranian Community in America.* New York: Pardis Press, 1992.

Fathi, Asghar, ed. *Iranian Refugees and Exiles Since Khomeini.* Costa Mesa, Calif.: Mazda Publishers, 1991.

Iran: A Country Study. 4th ed. Helen Chapin Metz, ed. Washington, D.C.: Federal Research Division, Library of Congress, 1989. (Available on-line at *http://lcweb2.loc.gov/frd/cs*)

Kelley, Ron, et al., eds. *Irangeles: Iranians in Los Angeles.* Berkeley: University of California Press, 1993.

Strazzabosco, Gina, ed. *Teenage Refugees from Iran Speak Out.* New York: Rosen, 1995.

For more resources, see "General Asian Immigration Resources" on p. 479.

Immigrants from Iraq

Historically known as Mesopotamia and sometimes called the cradle of civilization, Iraq was part of the Ottoman Empire until after World War I. It was a British-administered League of Nations mandate territory from 1920 until 1932, when it formally became an independent state. However, it was a British protectorate through World War II until 1958, when it became a fully independent republic, after the nationalist coup headed by Abdul Karim Kassem. In 1971, Saddam Hussein took power in Iraq, formally becoming president in 1979.

During his decades in power, Saddam Hussein led Iraq into the long, tremendously costly, inconclusive Iran-Iraq War (1980–1988) and then into quick defeat in the Persian Gulf War (1990–1991). He emerged from the latter with damaging international sanctions and a partial blockade of Iraq in place throughout the 1990s. In that period, Iraq became as a practical matter a desperately poor country, unable to use its immense oil wealth. It was also a politically troubled one, with an insurgent Kurdish minority in its north, protected by international concern, and a restive Shia minority in its south, defeated but still supported by Iran and protected by Allied air power.

Iraqi immigration to the United States totaled almost 70,000 from 1971 to 1996, averaging approximately 2,500 per year during the 1970s and 1980s. It picked up somewhat in the 1990s, to an average of more than 5,000 per year from 1992 to 1996, as small numbers of Iraqis were able to make their way out of the country.

Table 4.24: Number and Percentage of Immigrants from Iraq in Total U.S. Immigration Annually, 1971–1996

Year	Number of Immigrants from Iraq	Total U.S. Immigration	Percentage of Immigrants from Iraq in U.S. Immigration
1971	1,231	370,473	0.33
1972	1,491	384,685	0.39
1973	1,039	400,063	0.26
1974	2,281	394,861	0.58
1975	2,796	396,194	0.71
1976	4,038	502,289	0.80
1977	2,811	462,315	0.61
1978	2,188	601,442	0.36
1979	2,871	460,348	0.62
1980	2,658	530,639	0.50
1981	2,535	596,600	0.42
1982	3,105	594,131	0.52
1983	2,343	559,763	0.42
1984	2,930	543,903	0.54
1985	1,951	570,009	0.34
1986	1,323	601,708	0.22
1987	1,072	601,516	0.18
1988	1,022	643,025	0.16
1989	1,516	1,090,924	0.14
1990	1,756	1,536,483	0.11
1991	1,494	1,827,167	0.08
1992	4,111	973,977	0.42
1993	4,072	904,292	0.45
1994	6,025	804,416	0.75
1995	5,596	720,461	0.78
1996	5,481	915,900	0.60
Total 1971-96	69,736	17,987,584	0.39

Sources: *Statistical Yearbook of the Immigration and Naturalization Service*, 1980, Table 13; *Statistical Yearbook of the Immigration and Naturalization Service*, 1986, Table 3; *Statistical Yearbook of the Immigration and Naturalization Service*, 1996, Table 3.

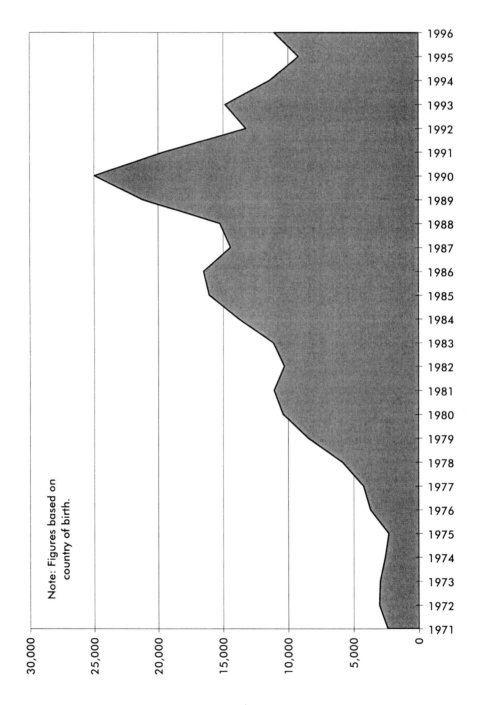

Graph 4.45: Number of Immigrants from Iraq Annually, 1971–1996

Note: Figures based on country of birth.

Resources

Iraq: A Country Study. 4th ed. Helen
Chapin Metz, ed. Washington, D.C.:
Federal Research Division, Library of
Congress, 1990. (Available on-line at
http://lcweb2.loc.gov/frd/cs)

For more resources, see "General Asian
Immigration Resources" on p. 479.

Other Immigrants from Asia

Following are immigration statistics on several other Asian countries that have generated modest United States immigration in the final decades of the 20th century.

See "General Asian Immigration Statistics" on p. 475 and "General Asian Immigration Resources" on p. 479 for wider information and resources.

Immigrants from Afghanistan

Table 4.25: Number and Percentage of Immigrants from Afghanistan in Total U.S. Immigration Annually, 1971–1996

Year	Number of Immigrants from Afghanistan	Total U.S. Immigration	Percentage of Immigrants from Afghanistan in Total U.S. Immigration
1971	69	370,473	0.02
1972	96	384,685	0.02
1973	137	400,063	0.03
1974	96	394,861	0.02
1975	116	396,194	0.03
1976	142	502,289	0.03
1977	138	462,315	0.03
1978	180	601,442	0.03
1979	353	460,348	0.08
1980	722	530,639	0.14
1981	1,881	596,600	0.32
1982	1,569	594,131	0.26
1983	2,566	559,763	0.46
1984	3,222	543,903	0.59
1985	2,794	570,009	0.49
1986	2,831	601,708	0.47
1987	2,424	601,516	0.40
1988	2,873	643,025	0.45
1989	3,232	1,090,924	0.30
1990	3,187	1,536,483	0.21
1991	2,879	1,827,167	0.16
1992	2,685	973,977	0.28
1993	2,964	904,292	0.33
1994	2,344	804,416	0.29
1995	1,424	720,461	0.20
1996	1,263	915,900	0.14
Total 1971-1996	42,187	17,987,584	0.23

Sources: *Statistical Yearbook of the Immigration and Naturalization Service, 1980*, Table 13; *Statistical Yearbook of the Immigration and Naturalization Service, 1986*, Table 3; *Statistical Yearbook of the Immigration and Naturalization Service, 1996*, Table 3.

Resources

Afghanistan: A Country Study. 5th ed. Richard F. Nyrop and Donald M. Seekins, eds. Washington, D.C.: Federal Research Division, Library of Congress, 1986.

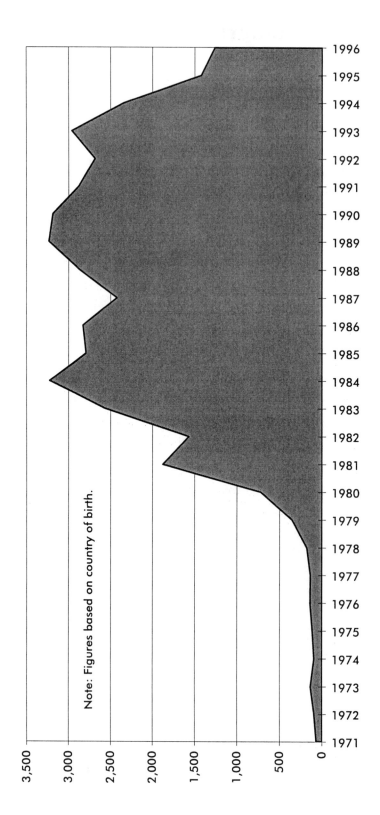

Graph 4.46: Number of Immigrants from Afghanistan Annually, 1971–1996

Note: Figures based on country of birth.

Immigrants from Burma

Table 4.26: Number and Percentage of Immigrants from Burma in Total U.S. Immigration Annually, 1971–1996

Year	Number of Immigrants from Burma	Total U.S. Immigration	Percentage of Immigrants from Burma in Total U.S. Immigration
1971	1,068	370,473	0.29
1972	785	384,685	0.20
1973	669	400,063	0.17
1974	558	394,861	0.14
1975	734	396,194	0.19
1976	1,001	502,289	0.20
1977	1,101	462,315	0.24
1978	1,188	601,442	0.20
1979	1,534	460,348	0.33
1980	1,211	530,639	0.23
1981	1,083	596,600	0.18
1982	820	594,131	0.14
1983	723	559,763	0.13
1984	719	543,903	0.13
1985	990	570,009	0.17
1986	863	601,708	0.14
1987	941	601,516	0.16
1988	803	643,025	0.12
1989	1,170	1,090,924	0.11
1990	1,120	1,536,483	0.07
1991	946	1,827,167	0.05
1992	816	973,977	0.08
1993	849	904,292	0.09
1994	938	804,416	0.12
1995	1,233	720,461	0.17
1996	1,320	915,900	0.14
Total 1971-96	25,183	17,987,584	0.14

Resources

Burma: A Country Study. 3d ed. Frederica
  M. Bunge, ed. Washington, D.C.:
  Federal Research Division, Library of
  Congress, 1983.

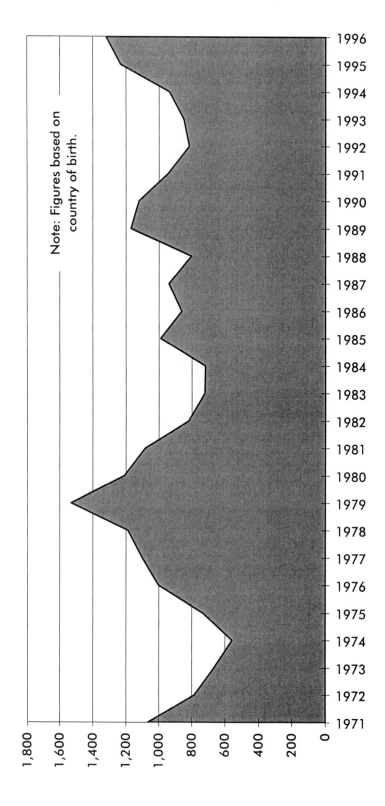

Graph 4.47: Number of Immigrants from Burma Annually, 1971–1996

Immigrants from Cyprus

Table 4.27: Number and Percentage of Immigrants from Cyprus in Total U.S. Immigration Annually, 1971–1996

Year	Number of Immigrants from Cyprus	Total U.S. Immigration	Percentage of Immigrants from Cyprus in Total U.S. Immigration
1971	382	370,473	0.10
1972	315	384,685	0.08
1973	294	400,063	0.07
1974	267	394,861	0.07
1975	554	396,194	0.14
1976	971	502,289	0.19
1977	478	462,315	0.10
1978	408	601,442	0.07
1979	323	460,348	0.07
1980	279	530,639	0.05
1981	326	596,600	0.05
1982	276	594,131	0.05
1983	265	559,763	0.05
1984	291	543,903	0.05
1985	294	570,009	0.05
1986	307	601,708	0.05
1987	331	601,516	0.06
1988	286	643,025	0.04
1989	284	1,090,924	0.03
1990	316	1,536,483	0.02
1991	243	1,827,167	0.01
1992	262	973,977	0.03
1993	229	904,292	0.03
1994	204	804,416	0.03
1995	188	720,461	0.03
1996	187	915,900	0.02
Total 1971-96	8,560	17,987,584	0.05

Sources: *Statistical Yearbook of the Immigration and Naturalization Service,* 1980, Table 13; *Statistical Yearbook of the Immigration and Naturalization Service,* 1986, Table 3; *Statistical Yearbook of the Immigration and Naturalization Service,* 1996, Table 3.

Resources

Cyprus: A Country Study. 4th ed. Eric Solsten, ed. Washington, D.C.: Federal Research Division, Library of Congress, 1993. (Available on-line at *http://lcweb2.loc.gov/frd/cs*)

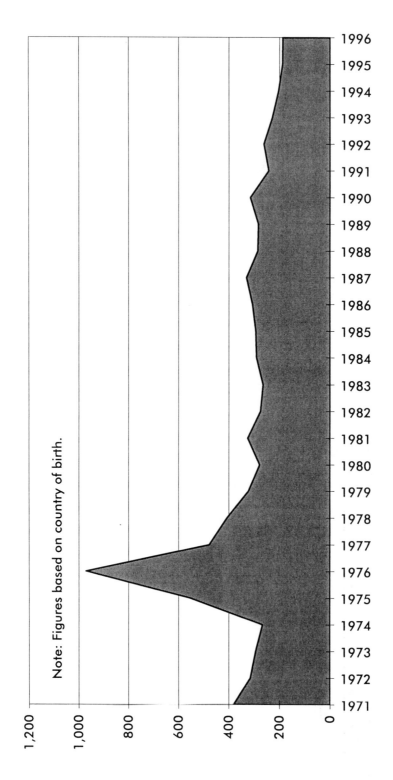

Graph 4.48: Number of Immigrants from Cyprus Annually, 1971–1996

Note: Figures based on country of birth.

Immigrants from Indonesia

Table 4.28: Number and Percentage of Immigrants from Indonesia in Total U.S. Immigration Annually, 1971–1996

Year	Number of Immigrants from Indonesia	Total U.S. Immigration	Percentage of Immigrants from Indonesia in Total U.S. Immigration
1971	680	370,473	0.18
1972	508	384,685	0.13
1973	450	400,063	0.11
1974	447	394,861	0.11
1975	458	396,194	0.12
1976	676	502,289	0.13
1977	778	462,315	0.17
1978	694	601,442	0.12
1979	820	460,348	0.18
1980	977	530,639	0.18
1981	1,006	596,600	0.17
1982	1,194	594,131	0.20
1983	952	559,763	0.17
1984	1,113	543,903	0.20
1985	1,269	570,009	0.22
1986	1,183	601,708	0.20
1987	1,254	601,516	0.21
1988	1,342	643,025	0.21
1989	1,513	1,090,924	0.14
1990	3,498	1,536,483	0.23
1991	2,223	1,827,167	0.12
1992	2,916	973,977	0.30
1993	1,767	904,292	0.20
1994	1,367	804,416	0.17
1995	1,020	720,461	0.14
1996	1,084	915,900	0.12
Total 1971-96	31,189	17,987,584	0.17

Sources: *Statistical Yearbook of the Immigration and Naturalization Service*, 1980, Table 13; *Statistical Yearbook of the Immigration and Naturalization Service*, 1986, Table 3; *Statistical Yearbook of the Immigration and Naturalization Service*, 1996, Table 3.

Resources

Indonesia: A Country Study. 5th ed. William H. Frederick and Robert L. Worden, eds. Washington, D.C.: Federal Research Division, Library of Congress, 1993. (Available on-line at *http://lcweb2.loc.gov/frd/cs*)

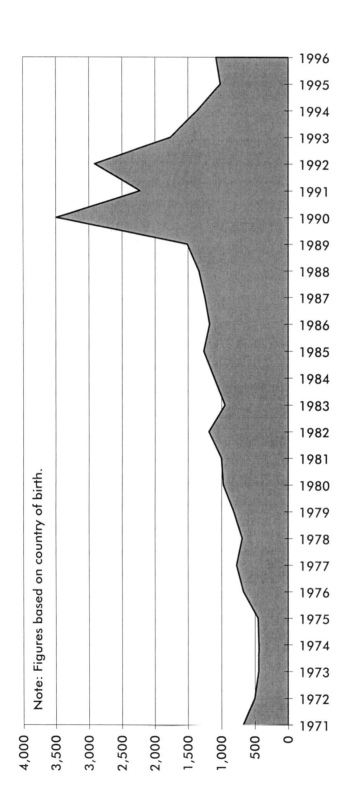

Graph 4.49: Number of Immigrants from Indonesia Annually, 1971–1996

Note: Figures based on country of birth.

Immigrants from Kuwait

Table 4.29: Number and Percentage of Immigrants from Kuwait in Total U.S. Immigration Annually, 1971–1996

Year	Number of Immigrants from Kuwait	Total U.S. Immigration	Percentage of Immigrants from Kuwait in Total U.S. Immigration
1971	112	370,473	0.03
1972	94	384,685	0.02
1973	87	400,063	0.02
1974	143	394,861	0.04
1975	146	396,194	0.04
1976	133	502,289	0.03
1977	160	462,315	0.03
1978	168	601,442	0.03
1979	303	460,348	0.07
1980	257	530,639	0.05
1981	317	596,600	0.05
1982	286	594,131	0.05
1983	344	559,763	0.06
1984	437	543,903	0.08
1985	503	570,009	0.09
1986	496	601,708	0.08
1987	507	601,516	0.08
1988	599	643,025	0.09
1989	710	1,090,924	0.07
1990	691	1,536,483	0.04
1991	861	1,827,167	0.05
1992	989	973,977	0.10
1993	1,129	904,292	0.12
1994	1,065	804,416	0.13
1995	961	720,461	0.13
1996	1,202	915,900	0.13
Total 1971-96	12,700	17,987,584	0.07

Sources: *Statistical Yearbook of the Immigration and Naturalization Service*, 1980, Table 13; *Statistical Yearbook of the Immigration and Naturalization Service*, 1986, Table 3; *Statistical Yearbook of the Immigration and Naturalization Service*, 1996, Table 3.

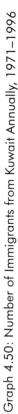

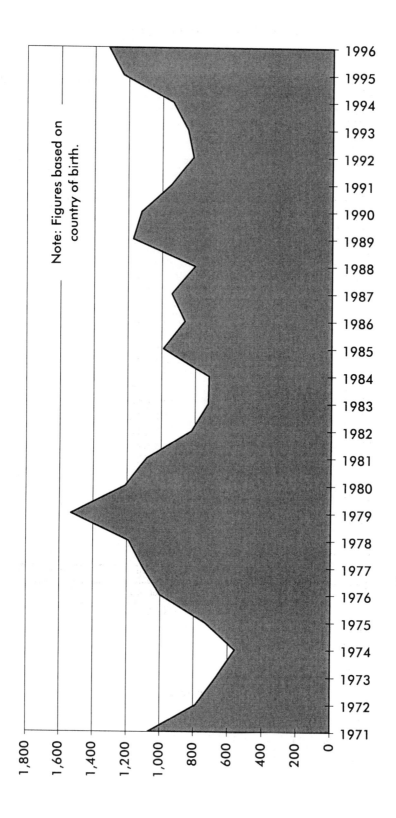

Graph 4.50: Number of Immigrants from Kuwait Annually, 1971–1996

Note: Figures based on country of birth.

Immigrants from Malaysia

Table 4.30: Number and Percentage of Immigrants from Malaysia in Total U.S. Immigration Annually, 1971–1996

Year	Number of Immigrants from Malaysia	Total U.S. Immigration	Percentage of Immigrants from Malaysia in Total U.S. Immigration
1971	284	370,473	0.08
1972	365	384,685	0.09
1973	347	400,063	0.09
1974	311	394,861	0.08
1975	332	396,194	0.08
1976	484	502,289	0.10
1977	455	462,315	0.10
1978	577	601,442	0.10
1979	623	460,348	0.14
1980	795	530,639	0.15
1981	1,033	596,600	0.17
1982	1,046	594,131	0.18
1983	852	559,763	0.15
1984	879	543,903	0.16
1985	939	570,009	0.16
1986	886	601,708	0.15
1987	1,016	601,516	0.17
1988	1,250	643,025	0.19
1989	1,506	1,090,924	0.14
1990	1,867	1,536,483	0.12
1991	1,860	1,827,167	0.10
1992	2,235	973,977	0.23
1993	2,026	904,292	0.22
1994	1,480	804,416	0.18
1995	1,223	720,461	0.17
1996	1,414	915,900	0.15
Total 1971-96	26,085	17,987,584	0.15

Sources: *Statistical Yearbook of the Immigration and Naturalization Service, 1980*, Table 13; *Statistical Yearbook of the Immigration and Naturalization Service, 1986*, Table 3; *Statistical Yearbook of the Immigration and Naturalization Service, 1996*, Table 3.

Resources

Malaysia: A Country Study. 4th ed. Frederica M. Bunge, ed. Washington, D.C.: Federal Research Division, Library of Congress, 1985.

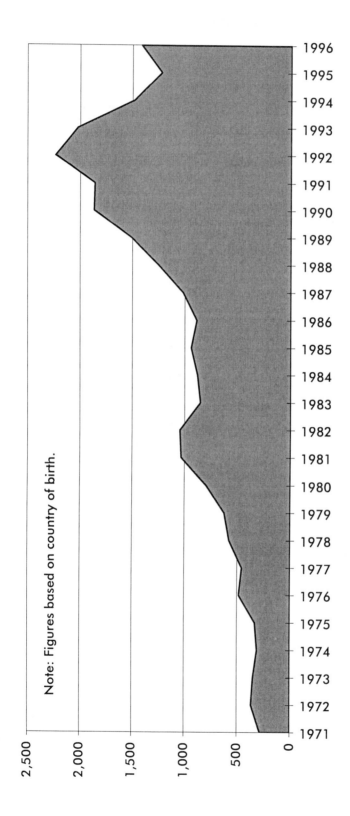

Graph 4.51: Number of Immigrants from Malaysia Annually, 1971–1996

Note: Figures based on country of birth.

Immigrants from Singapore

Table 4.31: Number and Percentage of Immigrants from Singapore in Total U.S. Immigration Annually, 1971–1996

Year	Number of Immigrants from Singapore	Total U.S. Immigration	Percentage of Immigrants from Singapore in Total U.S. Immigration
1971	130	370,473	0.04
1972	143	384,685	0.04
1973	186	400,063	0.05
1974	176	394,861	0.04
1975	203	396,194	0.05
1976	307	502,289	0.06
1977	308	462,315	0.07
1978	320	601,442	0.05
1979	321	460,348	0.07
1980	322	530,639	0.06
1981	408	596,600	0.07
1982	390	594,131	0.07
1983	362	559,763	0.06
1984	377	543,903	0.07
1985	460	570,009	0.08
1986	480	601,708	0.08
1987	469	601,516	0.08
1988	492	643,025	0.08
1989	566	1,090,924	0.05
1990	620	1,536,483	0.04
1991	535	1,827,167	0.03
1992	774	973,977	0.08
1993	798	904,292	0.09
1994	542	804,416	0.07
1995	399	720,461	0.06
1996	561	915,900	0.06
Total 1971-96	10,649	17,987,584	0.06

Sources: *Statistical Yearbook of the Immigration and Naturalization Service, 1980,* Table 13; *Statistical Yearbook of the Immigration and Naturalization Service, 1986,* Table 3; *Statistical Yearbook of the Immigration and Naturalization Service, 1996,* Table 3.

Resources

Singapore: A Country Study. 2d ed. Barbara Leitch LePoer, ed. Washington, D.C.: Federal Research Division, Library of Congress, 1991. (Available on-line at *http://lcweb2.loc.gov/frd/cs)*

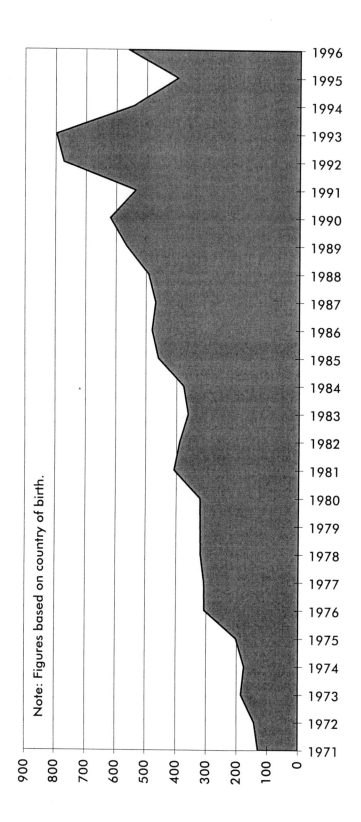

Graph 4.52: Number of Immigrants from Singapore Annually, 1971–1996

Note: Figures based on country of birth.

Immigrants from Sri Lanka

Table 4.32: Number and Percentage of Immigrants from Sri Lanka in Total U.S. Immigration Annually, 1971–1996

Year	Number of Immigrants from Sri Lanka	Total U.S. Immigration	Percentage of Immigrants from Sri Lanka in Total U.S. Immigration
1971	180	370,473	0.05
1972	306	384,685	0.08
1973	455	400,063	0.11
1974	379	394,861	0.10
1975	432	396,194	0.11
1976	510	502,289	0.10
1977	376	462,315	0.08
1978	375	601,442	0.06
1979	397	460,348	0.09
1980	397	530,639	0.07
1981	448	596,600	0.08
1982	505	594,131	0.08
1983	472	559,763	0.08
1984	554	543,903	0.10
1985	553	570,009	0.10
1986	596	601,708	0.10
1987	630	601,516	0.10
1988	634	643,025	0.10
1989	757	1,090,924	0.07
1990	976	1,536,483	0.06
1991	1,377	1,827,167	0.08
1992	1,081	973,977	0.11
1993	1,109	904,292	0.12
1994	989	804,416	0.12
1995	960	720,461	0.13
1996	1,277	915,900	0.14
Total 1971-96	16,725	17,987,584	0.09

Sources: *Statistical Yearbook of the Immigration and Naturalization Service*, 1980, Table 13; *Statistical Yearbook of the Immigration and Naturalization Service*, 1986, Table 3; *Statistical Yearbook of the Immigration and Naturalization Service*, 1996, Table 3.

Resources

Sri Lanka: A Country Study. 2d ed. Russell R. Ross and Andrea Matles Savada, eds. Washington, D.C.: Federal Research Division, Library of Congress, 1990. (Available on-line at *http://lcweb2.loc.gov/frd/cs*)

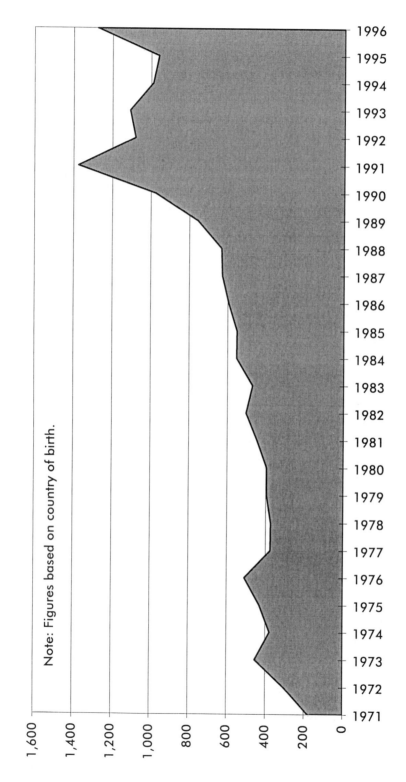

Graph 4.53: Number of Immigrants from Sri Lanka Annually, 1971–1996

Note: Figures based on country of birth.

General Asian Immigration Statistics

See Annual Tables 1–5 on pp. 659–738 for annual immigration figures for Asia. For more information on immigration statistics from Asia, see "General Notes on Immigration Statistics" on p. 684 under "Immigration from Asia, 1820–1970."

Graph 4.54: Number of Immigrants from Asia by Decade, 1820–1996

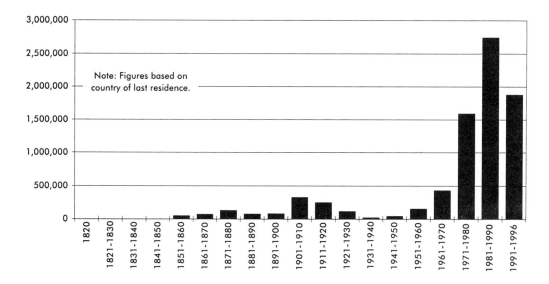

Graph 4.55: Percentage of Immigrants from Asia in Total U.S. Immigration by Decade, 1820–1996

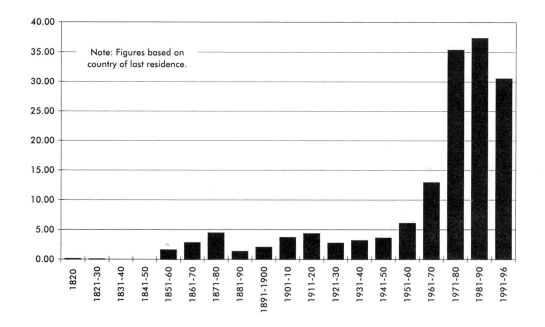

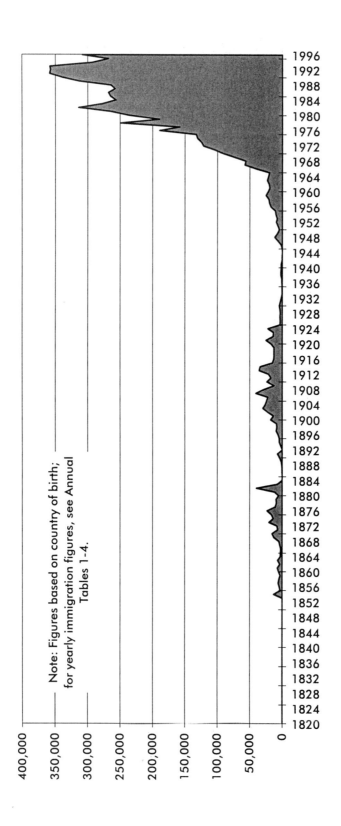

Graph 4.56: Number of Immigrants from Asia Annually, 1820–1996

Note: Figures based on country of birth; for yearly immigration figures, see Annual Tables 1-4.

Table 4.33: Number and Percentage of Immigrants from Asia in Total U.S. Immigration by Decade, 1820–1996

Decade	Number of Immigrants from Asia	Total U.S. Immigrants	Percentage Immigrants from Asia in Total U.S. Immigration
1820	6	8,385	0.07
1821-1830	30	143,439	0.02
1831-1840	55	599,125	0.01
1841-1850	141	1,713,251	0.01
1851-1860	41,538	2,598,214	1.60
1861-1870	64,759	2,314,824	2.80
1871-1880	124,160	2,812,191	4.42
1881-1890	69,942	5,246,613	1.33
1891-1900	74,862	3,687,564	2.03
1901-1910	323,543	8,795,386	3.68
1911-1920	247,236	5,735,811	4.31
1921-1930	112,059	4,107,209	2.73
1931-1940	16,595	528,431	3.14
1941-1950	37,028	1,035,039	3.58
1951-1960	153,249	2,515,479	6.09
1961-1970	427,642	3,321,677	12.87
1971-1980	1,588,178	4,493,314	35.35
1981-1990	2,738,157	7,338,062	37.31
1991-1996	1,875,391	6,146,213	30.51
Total 1820-1996	7,894,571	63,140,227	12.50

Source: Adapted from Table 2, Immigration by Region and Selected Country of Last Residence, Fiscal Years 1820–1996, from the *Statistical Yearbook of the Immigration and Naturalization Service*, 1996.

Table 4.34: Number and Percentage of Foreign-Born Immigrants from Asia by Decade in Total U.S. Population at End of Decade, 1850–1996

Decade	Number of Foreign-Born Immigrants from Asia	Total U.S. Population	Percentage of Foreign-Born Immigrants from Asia in Total U.S. Population
1850	1,135	23,191,876	0.0049
1860	36,796	31,443,321	0.1170
1870	64,565	39,818,449	0.1621
1880	107,630	50,155,783	0.2146
1890	113,396	62,947,714	0.1801
1900	120,248	75,994,575	0.1582
1910	191,484	91,972,266	0.2082
1920	237,950	105,710,620	0.2251
1930	275,665	122,775,046	0.2245
1940	(NA)	131,669,275	(NA)
1950	275,990	150,697,361	0.1831
1960	499,312	179,323,175	0.2784
1970	824,887	203,235,298	0.4059
1980	2,539,777	227,726,000	1.1153
1990	4,979,037	249,907,000	1.9924

NA = Not available

Note: Asian portions of Turkey not included before 1900. European territories of Turkey included from 1950.

Source: Adapted from Series C 228–295, 1850–1970, in *Historical Statistics of the United States, Colonial Times to 1970, Bicentennial Edition*, and other updating tables from the U.S. Census Bureau.

Graph 4.57: Number of Foreign-Born Immigrants from Asia by Decade, 1850–1990

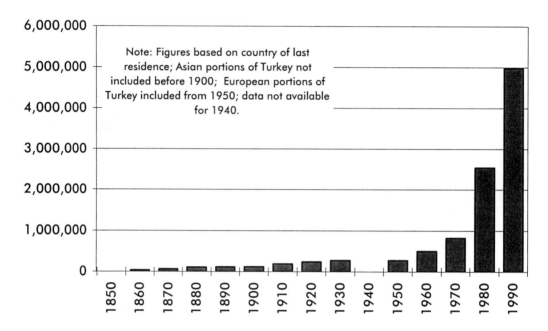

Graph 4.58: Percentage Distribution of Americans of Asian and Pacific Islander Origin by Region of the United States, 1990

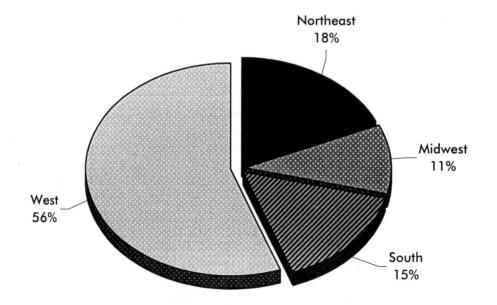

General Asian Immigration Resources

Internet Resources

AsiaGenWeb Project (*http://www.rootsweb.com/~asiagw/*) Part of the WorldGenWeb project, linking genealogical research sites around the world, by region, with resources by individual country in Asia.

MidEastGenWeb (*http://www.rootsweb.com/~mdeastgw/*) Part of the WorldGenWeb project, linking genealogical research sites around the world, by region, with resources by individual country.

Cyndi's List—Asia & the Pacific (*http://www.cyndislist.com/asia.htm*) List of online genealogical resources for the region, maintained by genealogical author Cyndi Howells.

Asian-American Village (*http://www.imdiversity.com/villages/asian/village_asian_american.asp*) Web site magazine and resources for Asian Pacific Americans, including history and current news; part of IMdiversity.com.

Print Resources

Baron, Deborah G., and Susan B. Gall, eds. *Asian American Chronology.* New York: U.X.L., 1996.

Cao, Lan, and Himilce Novas. *Everything You Need to Know About Asian American History.* New York: Plume, 1996.

Chan, Sucheng. *Asian Americans: An Interpretive History.* Boston: Twayne, 1991.

Daniels, Roger. *Asian America: Chinese and Japanese in the United States Since 1850.* Seattle: University of Washington Press, 1988.

Gall, Susan B., and Timothy L. Gall, eds. *Statistical Record of Asian Americans.* Detroit: Gale, 1993.

Hamamoto, Darrell Y., and Rodolfo D. Torres, eds. *New American Destinies: A Reader in Contemporary Asian and Latino Immigration.* New York: Routledge, 1997.

Hing, Bill Ong. *Making and Remaking Asian America Through Immigration Policy, 1850–1990.* Stanford, Calif.: Stanford University Press, 1993.

Hundley, Norris, Jr., ed. *The Asian American: The Historical Experience: Essays.* Santa Barbara, Calif.: Clio Books, 1976.

Kim, Hyung-chan, ed. *Dictionary of Asian American History.* New York: Greenwood Press, 1986.

Leonard, Karen Isaksen. *The South Asian Americans.* Westport, Conn.: Greenwood, 1997.

McGuire, William. *Southeast Asians.* New York: Watts, 1991.

Ng, Franklin, ed. *The History and Immigration of Asian Americans.* New York: Garland, 1998.

Perrin, Linda. *Coming to America: Immigrants from the Far East.* New York: Delacorte Press, 1980.

Rustomji-Kerns, Roshni, et al., eds. *Encounters: People of Asian Descent in the Americas.* Lanham, Md.: Rowman & Littlefield, 1999.

Sotoohi, Maureen Devine, ed. *Perspectives: Authentic Voices of Asian Americans.* North Billerica, Mass.: Curriculum Associates, 1996.

Takaki, Ronald T. *Strangers from a Different Shore: A History of Asian Americans.* Rev. ed. Boston: Little, Brown, 1998.

Wong, James I., et al., eds. *Historical Highlights of the Asians in America: A Chronological Summary.* Stockton, Calif.: Koinonia Productions, 1984.

See Parts I and VII and the Appendixes
of this volume for more general information, statistics, and resources on immigration.

Part V

Immigration from

the Americas

Introduction

The total number of immigrants into the United States from elsewhere in the Americas has historically been difficult to ascertain, even though immigration to the United States from most of the individual countries in the hemisphere is well documented. This is so for several reasons. In the first place, land crossings from Canada and Mexico have only been counted with any degree of completeness since 1908, before then being either not tabulated at all or tabulated only in part. In addition, immigration to the United States from Mexico has long been undercounted, especially during the second half of the 20th century, when at least several million undocumented illegal immigrants arrived from Mexico or from neighboring countries via Mexico.

On the other hand, immigration to the United States from Mexico (and to a much lesser extent from Canada) has also often been overcounted. That is because some immigrants may enter and leave the United States repeatedly, as often as several times a year, being counted each time on arrival but frequently not upon departure. (See "Appendix C: Estimates of Emigration and Illegals" on p. 749.)

Recorded immigration to the United States from the Americas picked up enormously from the 1960s through the mid-1990s, as population pressures, civil wars, economic crises, and social instability in Latin America all contributed to a massive flight to the cities and to international migration. From 1961 to 1996, some 10,433,840 recorded immigrants entered the United States from the Americas. That is 64 percent of the total of 16,187,054 immigrants from the Americas recorded as entering the United States between 1820 (when the United States began to keep continuous official immigration statistics) and 1996. In addition, several million "illegals" entered from 1960 to 1996.

Following are country-by-country treatments of the main sources of immigration to the United States from the Americas. These are followed by the overall recorded U.S. immigration statistics for the Americas and a list of general resources on immigration to the United States from the area.

Immigrants from Canada

The history of immigration into the United States from Canada began long before either country was born, during the long French-British contest for North America, which was ultimately settled on the Plains of Abraham in 1759. (For the early settlement of the region, see "An Overview" on p. 2.)

Early Emigrations

The first substantial emigration out of Canada to what would become the United States occurred in 1755, when the British, who had taken Acadia (Nova Scotia) from the French in 1713, forcibly expelled 6,000 French Canadians from Acadia, shipping them south to the British east coast colonies and then resettling their lands with British colonists. Most of these involuntary emigrants later found their way back home to French Canada, to the French-speaking West Indies, to Louisiana, or to France.

A second involuntary immigration of people with French–North American ancestry occurred in 1803, with the United States purchase of the Louisiana Territory from France. This included French settlements in the Mississippi basin from the Canadian border to New Orleans. With the Louisiana Purchase came an estimated 8,000 to 10,000 settlers of French ancestry, most of whom remained in the United States.

For settlers of British ancestry, most of the migration up to that point had been north to Canada, rather than south into the United States. This included large numbers of British-American Loyalists fleeing to Canada during and after the American Revolution.

Diversion to Canada

Then, in the early 1800s, the British government began making systematic attempts to limit British immigration into the new United States. Its main tools for doing so were the British Passenger Acts of 1803, 1816, 1817, 1823, and 1825. These were all ostensibly passed to relieve what were indeed terrible conditions on British North Atlantic immigrant ships, but were in truth primarily aimed at encouraging immigration to Canada, rather than the United States. They did so by making the price of passage to Canada half or even less than half the passage to New York and other U.S. East Coast cities. From the 1820s on, a large timber trade developed between Canada and Britain; timber ships that would otherwise be returning empty from Britain to Canada were then used to carry large numbers of immigrants to Canada. The British aim was thwarted, however, for many of these immigrants then proceeded from Canada south to the United States, often overland into New England.

That emigration of recent European immigrants out of Canada was the genesis of much of the large Irish population of New England. It was a pattern that would continue until the advent of steamships and their much lower transatlantic fares later in the century (see "The Journey" on p. 53).

Problems with Immigration Figures

The passage of these Europeans through Canada into the United States was also the beginning of major miscounting of Canadian immigration into the United States. From 1820, the U.S. government counted immigrants arriving by sea and began to accumulate detailed immigration statistics. However, early U.S. immigration acts did not require that people arriving by land be counted, resulting in wholly unreliable reporting of the numbers of such arrivals over the Canadian and Mexican borders. Even when people crossing the border were counted, there was no attempt to distinguish between immigrants just passing through Canada en route to the United States and Canadians moving south across the border. From 1855 to 1861, complete counting of those coming across the Canadian border was attempted, with little success, but even this was discontinued during the Civil War. Those coming across the Canadian border were not counted at all from 1885 to 1894, except for immigrants arriving in Canada by sea who intended to go on to the United States. Partial land entry counting resumed in 1904, but reasonably full counting was not achieved until 1908.

The net effect of all this was that U.S. immigration statistics regarding Canadian immigrants were wholly unreliable until 1908. We do supply those figures in this book, as part of data which is useful in some periods; however, for the period before 1908, we find Canadian estimates of immigration totals and U.S. estimates of the numbers of Canadian-born in the U.S. population to be more useful, especially in pointing to immigration trends. To the Canadian-born must be added some estimate of the numbers of people born elsewhere who immigrated to Canada and only later emigrated to the United States, rather than passing through Canada essentially as transients.

Mid-19th-Century Immigration

French-Canadian migration to New England and to the northern Midwest of the United States was spurred after a low-level insurrection that broke out briefly in Quebec in 1837. Intertwined with the effects of the rebellion was the Panic of 1837, which ushered in a protracted recession, despite Canada's westward expansion. In that recession, Canadian farm prices declined sharply, most notably in Quebec, where rising population was already creating economic pressure, especially among small farmers with large families.

In the late 1830s and the 1840s, some thousands of Quebec's farmers migrated to the United States, though many returned a few years later, when the Canadian government declared an amnesty and hard times in Canada had eased somewhat. However, Quebec agriculture did not fully recover, and hard times on the land became semi-permanent in the province. That would provide some of the basis for the much larger French-Canadian migrations late in the 19th century.

A basis for French-Canadian immigration had been laid in a different way as well. The thousands of Québecois who remained in the United States formed "immigrant chains" like those developed by most immigrant groups, telling stories of a new life and also providing help and a starting point for other immigrants, often friends and family, who followed them to the new country. By the early 1850s, at least 40,000 and possibly as many as 100,000 French Canadians had spread out

Authors' Archives

In 1755, the British expelled some 6,000 people of French ancestry from Acadia (now Nova Scotia).

Graph 5.1: Number of Immigrants from Canada Annually, 1820–1996

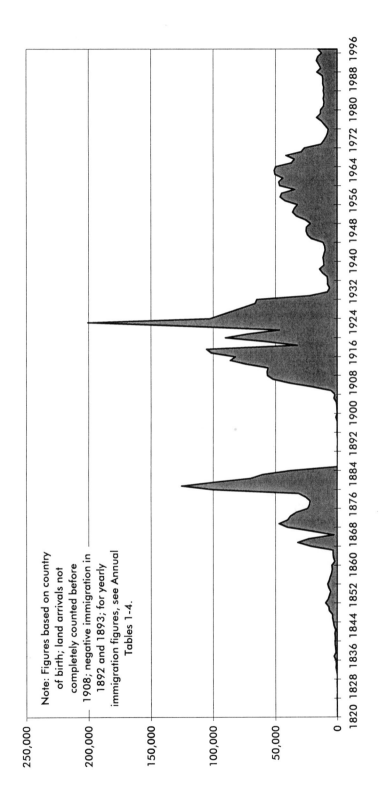

Note: Figures based on country of birth; land arrivals not completely counted before 1908; negative immigration in 1892 and 1893; for yearly immigration figures, see Annual Tables 1-4.

Graph 5.2: Percentage of Immigrants from Canada in Total U.S. Immigration, 1820–1996

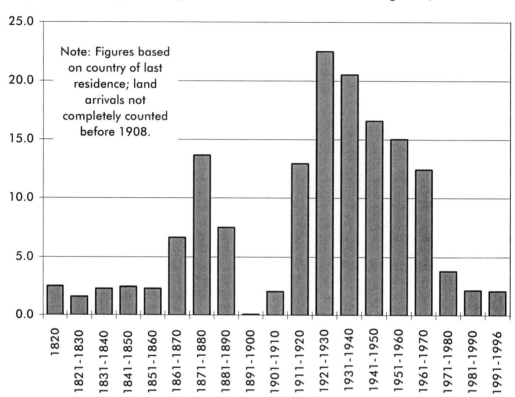

Note: Figures based on country of last residence; land arrivals not completely counted before 1908.

throughout New England and the northern Midwest. Many of them worked in New England's textile and other industries and in farflung timber and mining enterprises.

Before the U.S. Civil War, substantial numbers of British Canadians also came south across the border, especially from the depressed Maritime provinces into New England. In 1850, an estimated 148,000 Canadian-born immigrants, plus an undetermined number of foreign-born Canadians, were living in the United States. In 1860, the estimated number of Canadian-born in the United States had climbed to 250,000, and in 1890 to 981,000. It stood at 1.2 million by the end of the 19th century, and peaked at 1.3 million in 1930. In some periods, as at the end of the massive immigration of the 1880s, the actual number of Canadian-born in the United States was probably much higher than the estimate.

During the U.S. Civil War, many young Canadians came south across the border to serve in the Union Army, some out of con-

viction and some responding to U.S. government recruiting efforts, which included substantial bonuses for joining up. Among these were tens of thousands of young French-Canadian recruits. Antislavery sentiment was strong throughout Canada, which was historically the terminus of the "Underground Railroad" and a refuge for thousands of escaped slaves, some of whom went back to the United States to fight for the Union.

After the Civil War, the United States began its long surge to the Pacific and its simultaneous emergence as a major industrial country, which would in the next century become a world power. There were interruptions, certainly, as in the hard times of the late 1870s and early 1890s. Despite these, the United States became the world's greatest magnet for immigrants. In contrast, Canada did not develop into a major world economy; some areas, as in Quebec and the Maritime provinces, found the nearby United States a powerful and sometimes stifling competitor.

From 1870 to 1930, at least 4 million Canadians immigrated to the United States, the majority of them before World War I, with a second major wave immigrating during the 1920s. The flow of Canadian immigrants slowed to a comparative trickle during the 1930s. It later rebounded, with 1.3 million more Canadian immigrants entering the United States from the end of World War II to 1996.

Like most immigrant groups, French Canadians tended to form close-knit, at first rather isolated, United States communities, buttressed by their shared Catholicism. That was especially so where French Canadians were most numerous throughout the 19th century, as in northern New

Table 5.2: Number and Percentage of Immigrants from Canada in Total U.S. Immigration by Decade, 1820–1996

Decade	Number of Immigrants from Canada	Total U.S. Immigration	Percentage of Immigrants from Canada in Total U.S. Immigration
1820	209	8,385	2.49
1821-1830	2,277	143,439	1.59
1831-1840	13,624	599,125	2.27
1841-1850	41,723	1,713,251	2.44
18511-60	59,309	2,598,214	2.28
1861-1870	153,878	2,314,824	6.65
1871-1880	383,640	2,812,191	13.64
1881-1890	393,304	5,246,613	7.50
1891-1900	3,311	3,687,564	0.09
1901-1910	179,226	8,795,386	2.04
1911-1920	742,185	5,735,811	12.94
1921-1930	924,515	4,107,209	22.51
1931-1940	108,527	528,431	20.54
1941-1950	171,718	1,035,039	16.59
1951-1960	377,952	2,515,479	15.03
1961-1970	413,310	3,321,677	12.44
1971-1980	169,939	4,493,314	3.78
1981-1990	156,938	7,338,062	2.14
1991-1996	127,481	6,146,213	2.07
Total 1820-1996	4,423,066	63,140,227	7.01

Note: Land arrival not completely counted before 1908.

Source: Adapted from Table 2, Immigration by Region and Selected Country of Last Residence, Fiscal Years 1820–1996, from the *Statistical Yearbook of the Immigration and Naturalization Service*, 1996.

Table 5.1: Number and Percentage of Foreign-Born Immigrants from Canada by Decade in Total U.S. Population at End of Decade, 1850–1990

Decade	Number of Foreign-Born Immigrants from Canada	Total U.S. Population	Percentage of Foreign-Born Immigrants from Canada in Total U.S. Population
1850	147,711	23,191,876	0.64
1860	249,970	31,443,321	0.79
1870	493,464	39,818,449	1.24
1880	717,157	50,155,783	1.43
1890	980,938	62,947,714	1.56
1900	1,179,922	75,994,575	1.55
1910	1,209,717	91,972,266	1.32
1920	1,138,174	105,710,620	1.08
1930	1,310,369	122,775,046	1.07
1940	(NA)	131,669,275	(NA)
1950	1,003,038	150,697,361	0.67
1960	952,500	179,323,175	0.53
1970	812,421	203,235,298	0.40
1980	842,859	227,726,000	0.37
1990	744,830	249,907,000	0.30

NA = Not available

Source: Adapted from Series C 228–295, Foreign-Born Population, by Country of Birth: 1850–1970, in *Historical Statistics of the United States, Colonial Times to 1970, Bicentennial Edition*, and other updating tables from the U.S. Census Bureau.

England, northern Michigan, and northern Illinois. These communities were refreshed by the arrival of large numbers of Québecois through the early years of the 20th century. During most of the 20th century, however, the old ethnic ties loosened, following the common pattern of gradually integrating immigrant groups in the United States and elsewhere.

British Canadians, on the other hand, tended to integrate readily into the mainstream of English-speaking United States life. Indeed, they integrated so seamlessly that they were rarely perceived as "immigrants." Their numbers include many well-known figures, such as broadcasters Peter Jennings and Robert MacNeil, actor William Shatner, and composer-singer Joni Mitchell.

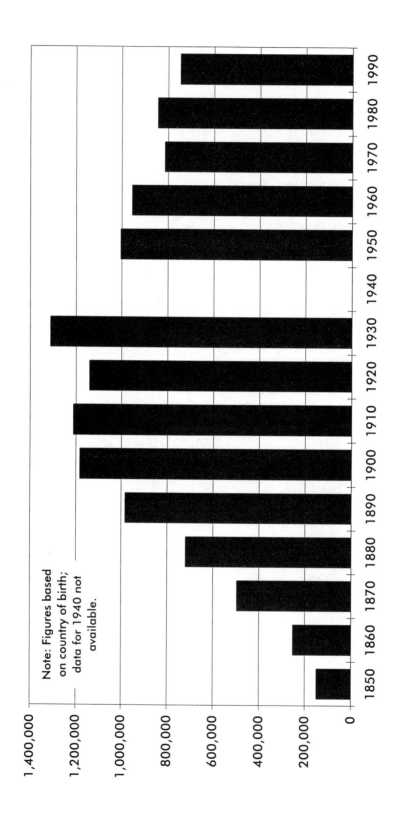

Graph 5.3: Number of Foreign-Born Immigrants from Canada in Total U.S. Population by Decade, 1850–1990

Note: Figures based on country of birth; data for 1940 not available.

Graph 5.4: Number of Immigrants from Canada by Decade, 1820–1996

Note: Figures based on country of last residence; land arrivals not completely counted before 1908.

Resources

Internet Resources

National Archives of Canada—Archives nationales du Canada (*http://www.archives.ca*) Official Web site in English and French, including news, information on publications, tips on genealogy research, and ArchiviaNet research tools.

Canada GenWeb Project (*http://www.rootsweb.com/~canwgw*) Web site in English and French offering information and resources on Canadian ancestry, including resources by province, downloadable archives, query boards, lists of volunteers for help, and related links.

Cyndi's List—Canada Index (*http://www.cyndislist.com/canada.htm*) List of on-line genealogical resources for Canada, maintained by genealogical author Cyndi Howells.

Canadian Genealogy and History Links (*http://www.islandnet.com/~jveinot/cghl/cghl.html*) Web site offering wide range of Web links.

Acadian Genealogy Homepage (*http://www.acadian.org/*) Web site offering information about and from the Acadian/French-Canadian Genealogy CD-ROM "In Search of Our Acadian Roots," plus numerous genealogy links.

Acadian-Cajun.com (*http://www.acadian-cajun.com/*) Web site offering information on Acadian and Cajun history and genealogy, with links to related sites.

The Habitant's Home Page (*http://habitant.org/*) Privately maintained Web site focusing on Acadian and French-Canadian genealogy; provides information on French-Canadian research projects, bibliographic guides, and links to related sites.

Genealogy—Acadian and French Canadian Style (*http://ourworld.compuserve.com/homepages/lwjones/*) Privately maintained Web site offering information and links on Acadian and French Canadian genealogy.

Print Resources

Castro, Max J., ed. *Free Markets, Open Societies, Closed Borders? Trends in International Migration and Immigration Policy in the Americas.* Coral Gables, Fla.: North-South Center Press, 1999.

Ducharme, Jacques. *The Shadows of the Trees: The Story of French-Canadians in New England.* New York/London: Harper & Brothers, 1943.

Hansen, Marcus Lee. *The Mingling of the Canadian and American Peoples.* New York: Arno Press, 1970. Reprint of 1940 ed.

Immigration Profiles: Canada. Washington, D.C.: U.S. Dept. of Justice, Immigration and Naturalization Service, 1991.

Truesdell, Leon Edgar. *The Canadian Born in the United States.* New Haven, Conn.: Yale University Press, 1943.

For more resources, see "Introduction" on p. 482.

Immigrants from Mexico

The first Mexican War of Independence (1810–1822) proclaimed Mexico independent of Spain in 1810 and established the first Mexican Republic in 1822. Its capital was the old Aztec capital at Tenochtitlán, renamed Mexico City by the Spanish conquerors. (See "An Overview" on p. 2, for treatment of the Spanish conquest of Mexico as part of the European invasion and conquest of the Americas.) In this period, Mexico was much larger than it is today, including much of what is now the American Southwest as well as Texas and California.

Mexican immigration into the United States was negligible during the three decades that followed independence. In fact, it was the United States that penetrated northern Mexico in those decades, laying the basis for the wars and annexations that would follow. In the 1820s, substantial numbers of United States settlers began entering the northern Mexican province of Texas, with and without Mexican approval, largely as cotton growers and ranchers. In the same period, encouraged by the new Mexican government, United States traders out of Missouri opened up the Santa Fe Trail, inaugurating travel and trade between Missouri and New Mexico. The result was that by 1834 a major southwestern trade route, the Santa Fe Trail, had developed. Also in the same period, New England seaborne traders in the China trade also traded with and sometimes settled in California, while small numbers of Americans began to arrive in California by land.

By the mid-1830s, the newly arrived Americans in Texas, by then numbering an estimated 25,000, greatly outnumbered the Mexican population, estimated at only 4,000. In 1835, the Americans declared Texas an independent state under their control and defeated the Mexican army in the brief war that followed. They then sought annexation by the United States. That was delayed for nine years, while pro-slavery and anti-slavery forces argued the question of whether Texas was to be slave or free, with the United States finally annexing it as a slave state in 1845. Mexico, which had never recognized Texas independence, threatened war over the annexation.

Involuntary Immigrants

In 1846, Mexico and the United States did go to war, which resulted in a complete Mexican defeat. On September 14, 1847, the Americans occupied Mexico City, completing the conquest of Mexico. By the terms of the Treaty of Guadalupe-Hidalgo (February 2, 1848), Mexico ceded to the United States an area of 1 million square miles, approximately half of Mexico. These territories would become the U.S. states of Texas, California, Nevada, and Utah, most of Arizona and New Mexico, and parts of Colorado and Wyoming.

The people of the conquered area, numbering an estimated 80,000, became involuntary Americans, the first substantial Spanish-speaking ethnic group in United States territory. The vast majority of them also became victims of American racism and discrimination. They were reviled and enormously disadvantaged as a "colored" minority, for a great many Mexicans, then as now, were *mestizos*, whose heritage included both Native American and Spanish roots. The circumstances of the conquest, the widespread racism that followed, and the continuing troubled relations between Mexico and the United States were to affect Mexican Americans deeply and adversely from that time forward.

Immigrants by Choice

Even so, some people crossed the border from what was left of Mexico into the greatly expanded United States. The main body of Mexican immigrants came by land, as they would continue to do throughout the 20th century. However, that immigration by land was not recorded at all until 1904, and only very lightly until 1908, when full land-arrival recording began. Therefore, official United States immigration and emigration figures are unreliable before 1908 and should be recognized merely as low estimates for that period.

The first three decades following the United States annexation saw a good deal of population movement across what was essentially an open border between Mexico and the United States. Some of those arriving from Mexico were political refugees, though in this period their numbers were small. More political refugees began to arrive after Porfirio Díaz took power in 1876.

The main reasons for Mexican immigration in the late 19th and early 20th centuries were both economic and political. During the long Díaz regime (1876–1911), the Mexican government became increasingly corrupt and repressive. Díaz directed government resources and attention toward his policy of modernization, hoping thereby to bring a unified Mexico into the developing industrial world. However, corruption, repression, banditry, and high taxation were scarcely a recipe for success. Nor did it help that some of the success achieved was on the medical front; new

knowledge contributed to the increased survival of babies and mothers, thus fueling what would soon become an explosive population increase.

On the "pull" side, Texas, the Southwest, and California were changing greatly, becoming an integral part of a unified, highly industrialized United States, which was quickly emerging as a world power. After the American Civil War, a continent-wide rail network was quickly established across the United States, and populations and commercial life began to flourish in the extensive lands that had been taken from Mexico. Throughout these areas, the use of irrigation expanded enormously, spurred by federal and state legislation. In east and central Texas, cotton cultivation boomed; in Colorado, a sugarbeet industry took hold; and equally largescale produce farming spread throughout the Southwest and California. Such farming was hugely labor-intensive. Mexicans filled the need for cheap labor, even more so after the Chinese Exclusion Acts went into effect in 1882 and Japanese immigration was restricted in 1907.

Table 5.3: Number and Percentage of Immigrants from Mexico in Total U.S. Immigration by Decade, 1820–1996

Decade	Number of Immigrants from Mexico	Total U.S. Immigrants	Immigrants from Mexico in Total U.S. Immigration
1820	1	8,385	0.01
1821-1830	4,817	143,439	3.36
1831-1840	6,599	599,125	1.10
1841-1850	3,271	1,713,251	0.19
1851-1860	3,078	2,598,214	0.12
1861-1870	2,191	2,314,824	0.09
1871-1880	5,162	2,812,191	0.18
1881-1890	1,913	5,246,613	0.04
1891-1900	971	3,687,564	0.03
1901-1910	49,642	8,795,386	0.56
1911-1920	219,004	5,735,811	3.82
1921-1930	459,287	4,107,209	11.18
1931-1940	22,319	528,431	4.22
1941-1950	60,589	1,035,039	5.85
1951-1960	299,811	2,515,479	11.92
1961-1970	453,937	3,321,677	13.67
1971-1980	640,294	4,493,314	14.25
1981-1990	1,655,943	7,338,062	22.57
1991-1996	1,653,896	6,146,213	26.91
Total 1820-1996	5,542,625	63,140,227	8.78

Notes: Data not available for 1886–1894. Land arrivals not completely recorded before 1908.

Source: Adapted from Table 2, Immigration by Region and Selected Country of Last Residence, Fiscal Years 1820–1996, from the Statistical Yearbook of the Immigration and Naturalization Service, 1996.

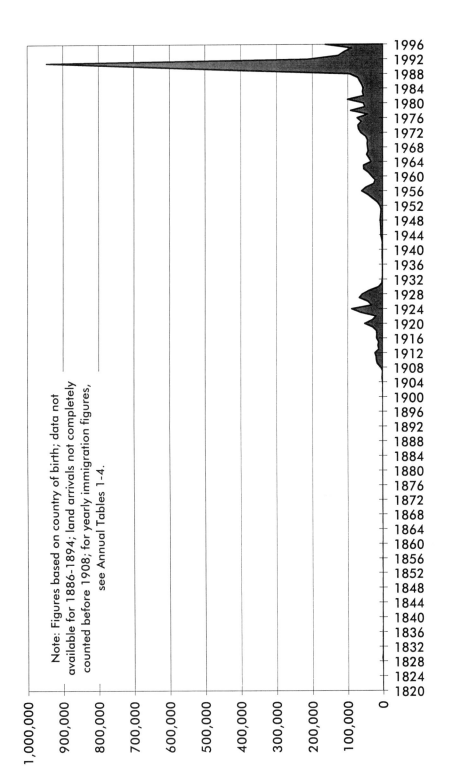

Graph 5.5: Number of Immigrants from Mexico Annually, 1820–1996

Note: Figures based on country of birth; data not available for 1886-1894; land arrivals not completely counted before 1908; for yearly immigration figures, see Annual Tables 1-4.

With "push" and "pull" both very much in place, Mexican immigration into the United States began to grow. Although immigration figures are inadequate, estimates of the numbers of foreign-born Mexican Americans in the United States grew sharply, more than doubling in the first decade of the 20th century, from 103,000 to 222,000.

By 1920, those numbers indicated more than another doubling, going from 222,000 foreign-born Mexican-Americans in 1910 to 486,000 in 1920. In the same period, U.S. immigration figures indicated that 219,000 Mexicans had immigrated to the United States. Although better kept than before, those U.S. figures were still suspect; many land arrivals were still not recorded, while at the same time many immigrants who went back and forth across the border frequently were recorded as new arrivals every time they entered the United States but never subtracted when they left. However, Mexican population pressures and all the United States "pull" factors remained the same in this period, so that, in sum, Mexican immigration was very probably understated rather than overstated.

One factor pushing Mexicans into the United States was unique to its time: the Mexican Revolution (1910–1920). For Mexico, the revolution was a catastrophe that

cost the lives of an estimated 1 million people, out of a prior population of 15 million. The revolution also sent perhaps a million Mexican refugees to the United States. They worked throughout the growing American economy wherever jobs were available. During World War I (1914–1918), when immigration to the United States from Europe was virtually stopped by the submarine war in the Atlantic, Mexican workers filled many war industry jobs in the Midwest and West.

In the 1920s, the numbers of Mexicans recorded as entering the United States continued to grow very sharply. From 1921 to 1930, some 459,000 Mexicans are recorded as immigrating into the United States. That reflected the booming U.S. economy's huge appetite for more workers, along with the continuously growing Mexican population pressures. It also reflected the impact of the new and extraordinarily restrictive 1921 and 1924 U.S. immigration laws (see "Immigration Restrictions" on p. 47). These cut the previous flood of emigration from southern and eastern Europe to the United States to a trickle, while allowing immigration to the United States from the Western Hemisphere to swell almost unchecked. By 1930, there were an estimated 641,000 Mexican-born Americans.

Graph 5.6: Percentage of Immigrants from Mexico in Total U.S. Immigration by Decade, 1820–1996

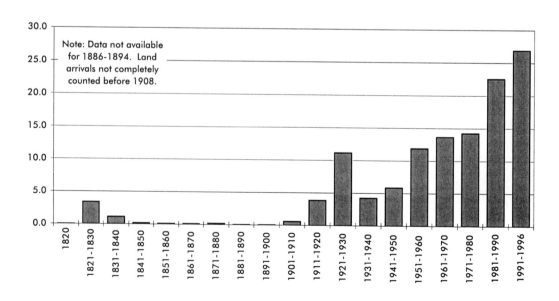

Note: Data not available for 1886-1894. Land arrivals not completely counted before 1908.

Immigration to the United States from Mexico slowed greatly during the Great Depression of the 1930s, while at the same time substantial numbers of recently arrived immigrants returned to Mexico. Those who remained in the United States as aliens, no matter how long established, found themselves facing continuing pervasive racism, now coupled with specific anti-alien state legislation, especially in the West and Southwest. Even minimal state and federal home relief and job programs were often denied to Mexican residents. The net effect was a sharp drop in the number of foreign-born Mexicans, which fell to around 350,000 by 1940. As late as 1950, that number stood at 454,000, still only 70 percent of what it had been in 1930. From 1942 on, however, there were far more Mexican workers in the United States than showed up in statistical data about Mexican immigration and the foreign-born.

Braceros

In August 1942, the first *bracero* program went into effect, under an agreement between the Mexican and United States governments. Braceros were Mexican contract workers imported into the United States, largely as harvest hands in the Southwest but also as workers to fill many other kinds of jobs, all with agreed-upon guarantees as to wages, transportation, living conditions, and working conditions. Part of their costs were paid by their employers and part by the U.S. government. During the first bracero program, from 1942 to 1948, the number of braceros averaged approximately 35,000 per year, for a total of 200,000. At the same time, increasingly large numbers of undocumented Mexican workers were crossing the border, many traveling back and forth several times during the year.

Throughout 1949 and 1950, the number of undocumented Mexican workers in the United States continued to grow, as did the widespread abuse of these defenseless aliens by many United States employers. A new bracero agreement in August 1949 reflected the Mexican government's attempt to curb such abuse and the U.S. government's attempt to control the numbers of illegal immigrants, while at the same time still guaranteeing the major source of very low-cost farm labor in California and the Southwest. This second

Graph 5.7: Number of Immigrants from Mexico by Decade, 1820–1996

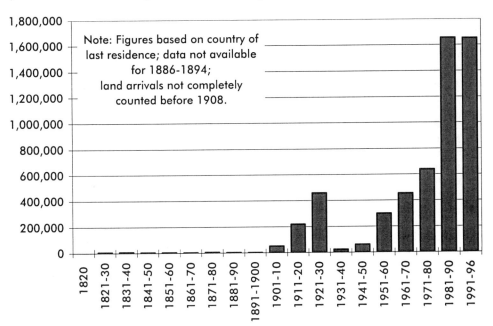

Graph 5.8: Number of Foreign-Born Immigrants from Mexico in Total U.S. Immigration by Decade, 1850–1990

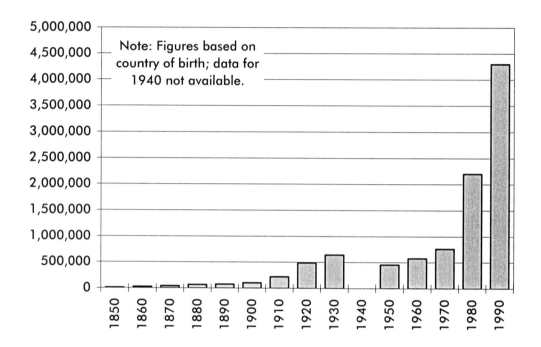

bracero agreeement was largely a matter of declaring "legal" approximately 150,000 undocumented Mexican workers already in the United States, coupled with an agreement to curb illegal cross-border human traffic—a plan that never worked.

During the Korean War, a third bracero agreement was negotiated between the two countries. This one lasted from 1951 to 1965, bringing a total of 4.5 million Mexican workers into the United States, an average of 300,000 per year. It brought no significantly better conditions for Mexican agricultural or other workers, nor did it slow the growing tide of Mexican "illegals," who in that period also entered the United States at an estimated rate of 300,000 per year.

Underneath all the agreements, Mexico's population growth continued to accelerate, and the condition and prospects of Mexico's poor and dispossessed continued to worsen. Simultaneously, southwestern United States agriculture continued to expand, providing large numbers of low-

paying jobs. These jobs were often performed under inhumane conditions, but they were jobs, often better-paying than those available in Mexico.

Attempts at Control

Given the combination of factors that pushed working people out of Mexico and pulled them into the United States, it is not surprising that migration north across the border continued to accelerate throughout the latter part of the 20th century. Sporadic, ineffectual United States efforts to cut the numbers of undocumented Mexican immigrants had no long-lasting effects; nor did periodic attempts to legalize those who had already entered the United States illegally and then sharply cut the flow of further "illegals." Although the 1965 Immigration Act opened the door to much larger numbers of legal immigrants from all over the world, including Mexico, the flow of illegal immigrants continued to rise. Strong attempts, led by Cesar Chavez and his colleagues, were made to unionize agricultural workers and win them better pay and working conditions. However, these campaigns were only partly successful, for the flood of new, poor immigrants made it possible for growers to resist union demands and maintain substandard pay and conditions.

One major failed attempt to cut the flow of illegal immigrants was "Operation Wetback," in 1954, which capped five years of increasingly harsh U.S. government attempts to deport and keep out illegal immigrants. From 1950 to 1955, an estimated 3 million to 4 million Mexicans were deported, approximately 1.1 million of them without hearings or appeals, during Operation Wetback. The flow of illegal immigrants was affected for a few years but then picked up again, for conditions in Mexico changed only for the worse, and United States growers continued to provide seasonal jobs for those who made it across the border.

Another major failed attempt to curb the numbers of "illegals" came in the mid-1980s, with passage of the 1986 Immigra-

Graph 5.9: Percentage Distribution of Americans of Mexican Origin by Region of the United States, 1990

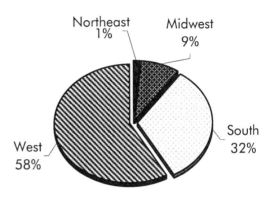

tion Act. This attempted to make employers responsible for not hiring undocumented aliens, while at the same time legalizing many undocumented aliens already in the United States. The program did legalize approximately 1 million undocumented Mexican Americans, but did not work at all to cut the continuing and growing flow of undocumented workers across the border.

A third failed attempt to curb "illegals" was generated by the Mexican government. In the 1960s it began to establish special business districts on the Mexican side of the border, with tax and other advantages for foreign employers who would locate factories there and employ large numbers of Mexican workers. By the mid-1990s, more than 2,000 factories employing an estimated three-quarters of a million Mexican workers were in place. Often owned by United States companies, these factories produced low-priced goods sold in United States markets at competitive prices. They tended to be highly profitable for their corporate owners, although United States labor unions sharply criticized them as unfair competition and environmentalists on both sides of the borders pointed out that they were unchecked industrial polluters. Whatever their merits, their existence in no way checked the flow of undocumented aliens across the Mexican border.

Table 5.4: Number and Percentage of Foreign-Born Immigrants from Mexico by Decade in Total U.S. Population at End of Decade, 1850–1990

Decade	Number of Foreign-Born Immigrants from Mexico	Total U.S. Population	Percentage of Foreign-Born Immigrants from Mexico in Total U.S. Population
1850	13,317	23,191,876	0.06
1860	27,466	31,443,321	0.09
1870	42,435	39,818,449	0.11
1880	68,399	50,155,783	0.14
1890	77,853	62,947,714	0.12
1900	103,393	75,994,575	0.14
1910	221,915	91,972,266	0.24
1920	486,418	105,710,620	0.46
1930	641,462	122,775,046	0.52
1940	(NA)	131,669,275	(NA)
1950	454,417	150,697,361	0.30
1960	575,902	179,323,175	0.32
1970	759,711	203,235,298	0.37
1980	2,199,221	227,726,000	0.97
1990	4,298,014	249,907,000	1.72

NA = Not available

Source: Adapted from Series C 228–295, Foreign-Born Population, by Country of Birth: 1850–1970, in *Historical Statistics of the United States, Colonial Times to 1970, Bicentennial Edition*, and other updating tables from the U.S. Census Bureau.

Recent Immigration

Legal immigration into the United States from Mexico grew to a total of more than 640,000 from 1971 to 1980, with an even larger rise in the flow of "illegals" from Mexico. In the following decade, from 1981 to 1990, legal immigration jumped to nearly 1,656,000. This figure reflected both the legalization of hundreds of thousands of Mexican Americans by the 1986 Immigration Act and a sharp increase in actual new immigration. Immigration jumped even higher from 1990 to 1996, totaling 1,654,000 in only six years, again reflecting both the impact of the 1986 law and more actual immigration.

The numbers of undocumented Mexican immigrants also continued to grow. By October 1996, the U.S. Immigration and Naturalization Service was estimating that there were 5 million undocumented aliens in the United States, 2.7 million of them from Mexico. The 2.7 million figure was widely viewed as considerably overstated, for reasons that included the U.S. authorities' failure to distinguish in their counting between Mexicans who regularly traveled back and forth across the border and those who had entered the United States to work and then settled there. Needless to say, it was also very difficult to count "illegals" who were in essence hiding from the U.S. authorities. The net result is probably that the numbers of Mexican "illegals" were and continue to be substantially overestimated, but a true count is not really available (see "Appendix C: Estimates of Emigration and Illegals" on p. 749).

In the late 1990s, millions of increasingly impoverished Mexicans continued to enter the United States, both as "legals" and "illegals." There is every likelihood that they will continue to do so until the United States economy slows and provides far fewer jobs, or until the Mexican economy provides more jobs. Taking a longer view, Mexican population pressure continues to be a massive, underlying adverse factor. Mexico's population was estimated at 13.6 million in 1900. In 1998, its estimated population had risen to more than 100 million, an increase of 735 percent in the course of the 20th century.

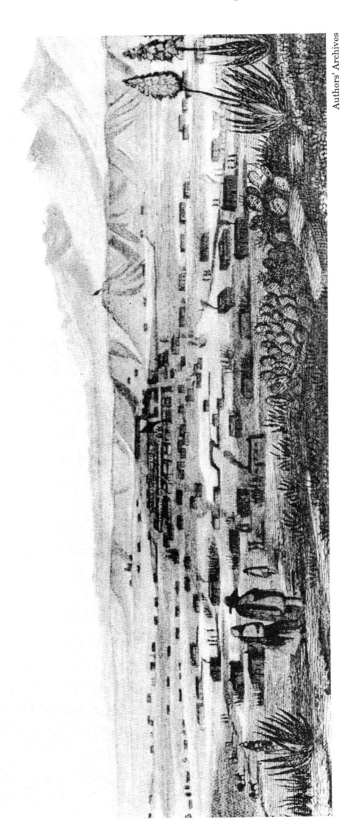

Authors' Archives

This is an image of Santa Fe in 1846, two years before it was taken by the United States from Mexico as part of what became the state of New Mexico.

Resources

Internet Resources

Azteca Web Page (*http://www.mexica.net*) Los Angeles–based Web site of interest to "Mexicans, Chicanos, and Mexican-Americans," in English and Spanish; includes historical information, mailing lists, and articles and links on issues of current concern.

MexicoGenWeb Project (*http://www.rootsweb.com/~mexwgw*) Part of the WorldGenWeb project, linking genealogical research sites around the world, by region; provides resources by state within Mexico; offered in English and Spanish.

Print Resources

Acuna, Rodolfo. *Occupied America: A History of Chicanos.* 3d ed. New York: Harper & Row, 1988.

Bandon, Alexandra. *Mexican Americans.* New York: New Discovery, 1993.

Bean, Frank D., et al, eds. *Mexican and Central American Population and U.S. Immigration Policy.* Austin: Center for Mexican American Studies, University of Texas at Austin, 1989.

Cardoso, Lawrence A. *Mexican Emigration to the United States, 1897–1931: Socio-Economic Patterns.* Tucson: University of Arizona Press, 1980.

Catalano, Julie. *The Mexican Americans.* New York: Chelsea House, 1996.

Davis, Marilyn P. *Mexican Voices/American Dreams: An Oral History of Mexican Immigration to the United States.* New York: Holt, 1990.

Diaz-Briquets, Sergio, and Sidney Weintraub, eds. *Determinants of Emigration from Mexico, Central America, and the Caribbean.* Boulder, Col.: Westview, 1991.

Garcia, Richard A., ed. *The Chicanos in America, 1540–1974: A Chronology and Fact Book.* Dobbs Ferry, N.Y.: Oceana, 1977.

Garver, Susan, and Paula McGuire. *Coming to North America: from Mexico, Cuba, and Puerto Rico.* New York: Delacorte, 1981.

Griswold del Castillo, Richard, and Arnoldo de Leon. *North to Aztlan: A History of Mexican Americans in the United States.* New York: Twayne, 1996.

Gutierrez, David. *Walls and Mirrors: Mexican Americans, Mexican Immigrants, and the Politics of Ethnicity.* Berkeley: University of California Press, 1995.

Hoobler, Dorothy, and Thomas Hoobler. *The Mexican American Family Album.* New York: Oxford University Press, 1994.

Jimenez, Carlos M. *The Mexican American Heritage.* 2d ed. Berkeley, Calif.: TQS Publications, 1994.

Machado, Manuel A. *Listen Chicano: An Informal History of the Mexican-American.* Chicago: Nelson-Hall, 1978.

Maciel, David R., and Maria Herrera-Sobek, eds. *Culture Across Borders: Mexican Immigration and Popular Culture.* Tucson: University of Arizona Press, 1998.

Martinez, Elizabeth Coonrod. *The Mexican-American Experience.* Brookfield, Conn.: Millbrook Press, 1995.

Mayberry, Jodine. *Mexicans.* New York: Watts, 1990.

Meier, Matt S., and Feliciano Ribera. *Mexican Americans, American Mexicans: From Conquistadors to Chicanos.* Rev. ed. New York: Hill and Wang, 1993.

Mexico: A Country Study. 4th ed. Tim L. Merrill and Ramon Miro, eds. Washington, D.C.: Federal Research Division, Library of Congress, 1997.

Moquin, Wayne, comp. *A Documentary History of the Mexican Americans.* New York: Praeger, 1971.

Pinchot, Jane. *The Mexicans in America.* Minneapolis: Lerner, 1989.

Prago, Albert. *Strangers in Their Own Land: A History of Mexican-Americans.* New York: Four Winds Press, 1973.

Raat, W. Dirk. *Revoltosos: Mexico's Rebels in the United States, 1903–1923.* College Station: Texas A&M University Press, 1981.

Reisler, Mark. *By the Sweat of Their Brow: Mexican Immigrant Labor in the United States, 1900–1940.* Westport, Conn.: Greenwood, 1976.

Rosaldo, Renato, et al. *Chicano: The Evolution of a People.* 2d ed. Malabar, Fla.: Krieger, 1982.

Ryskamp, George R., and Peggy Ryskamp. *A Student's Guide to Mexican American Genealogy.* Phoenix: Oryx, 1996.

Samora, Julian, et al. *A History of the Mexican-American People.* Rev. ed. Notre Dame, Ind.: University of Notre Dame Press, 1993.

Weber, David J., ed. *Foreigners in Their Native Land: Historical Roots of the Mexican Americans.* Albuquerque: University of New Mexico Press, 1973.

For more resources, see "Introduction" on p. 482.

Immigrants from Cuba

Cuba was a Spanish colony from the early 16th century, but by the late 19th century the Cubans were fighting hard for their independence. They were defeated in the Ten Years War (1868–1878) but tried again 17 years later, in the Cuban War of Independence. The revolution's leader, José Martí, was killed in battle in the first year of the war, in 1895, but his movement continued and grew. By early 1898, a Cuban guerrilla army estimated at 30,000 had engaged Spanish regular army forces numbering 100,000, and fighting raged throughout the country, with neither side winning victory.

Then, on February 15, 1898, the American battleship *Maine* exploded and sank in Havana harbor, with a loss of 260 lives. American newspaper attacks blaming Spain quickly led to a U.S. declaration of war against Spain, on April 25. By July 3, an attacking American army and blockading naval forces had defeated Spanish forces and sunk the Spanish fleet, forcing a Spanish surrender. In the same period, U.S. forces also defeated Spain in the Philippines and Puerto Rico.

The Cuban War of Independence did not then go over into a Cuban-American war, as did the failed Philippine War of Independence. U.S. forces occupied Cuba until 1902, leaving after the Republic of Cuba was formally established. The U.S. base at Guantánamo was established in this period.

Those were the formalities. In fact, U.S. forces again occupied Cuba from 1906 to 1909, preventing a new revolution and holding Cuba as a protectorate. In 1917, U.S. troops came in once more, to defeat a revolution in progress. Then in 1934, under U.S. president Franklin D. Roosevelt's "Good Neighbor Policy," Cuba was freed.

In the newly independent Cuba, general Fulgencio Batista y Zalvidar gradually came to power. He became army chief of staff in 1934, was formally president from 1940 to 1944, and openly became dictator from 1952 until he was unseated by a new Cuban Revolution in 1959.

Early Immigrants

Until 1898, the United States was far less a country where Cuban-American immigrants sought to build new lives than a place from which Cuban political refugees could organize a revolution against Spain. Thousands of such Cuban political exiles returned home from the United States to make a revolution in 1868 and again in 1895. Meanwhile, a modest Cuban-American immigrant community developed, largely because of unsettled conditions in the home country, only 90 miles off the Florida coast.

There had been some Cuban cigar-makers in Key West, Florida, from the late 1830s; more came in 1869, after the outbreak of the Ten Years War. In the mid-1880s, the Cuban-American cigar industry expanded to Tampa, Florida, while in the late 19th and early 20th centuries other Cuban communities began to grow in Ocala and Miami, both in Florida, as well as in New York and other United States cities. Cuban immigration continued to be small, however. In 1870 there were only a little more than 5,000 foreign-born Cuban Americans, and in 1930 there were still only 18,500.

Table 5.5: Number and Percentage of Immigrants from Cuba in Total U.S. Immigration by Decade, 1925–1996

Decade	Number of Immigrants from Cuba	Total U.S. Immigrants	Percentage of Immigrants from Cuba in Total U.S. Immigration
1925-30	15,901	4,107,209	0.39
1931-40	9,571	528,431	1.81
1941-50	26,313	1,035,039	2.54
1951-60	78,948	2,515,479	3.14
1961-70	208,536	3,321,677	6.28
1971-80	264,863	4,493,314	5.89
1981-90	144,578	7,338,062	1.97
1991-96	91,383	6,146,213	1.49
Total 1820-1996	840,093	63,140,227	1.33

Note: Data not recorded separately until 1925.

Source: Adapted from Table 2, Immigration by Region and Selected Country of Last Residence, Fiscal Years 1820–1996, from the *Statistical Yearbook of the Immigration and Naturalization Service*, 1996.

Graph 5.10: Percentage of Immigrants from Cuba in Total U.S. Immigration, 1925–1996

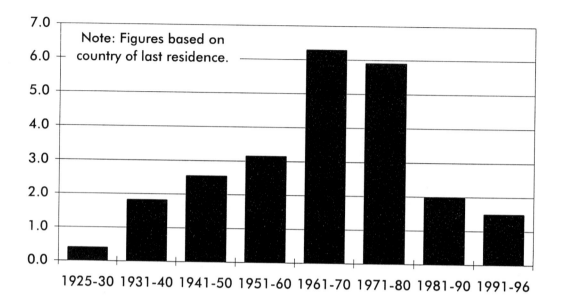

Graph 5.11: Number of Immigrants from Cuba by Decade, 1925–1996

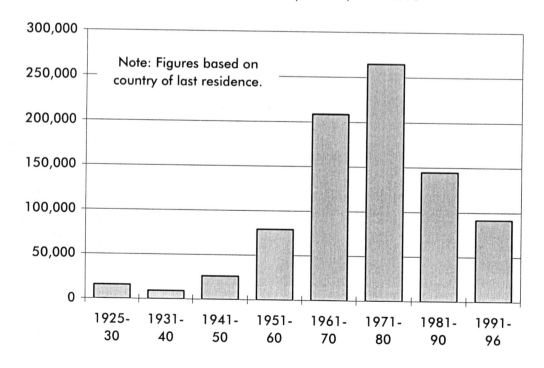

Table 5.6: Number and Percentage of Immigrants from Cuba in Total U.S. Immigration Annually, 1971–1996

Year	Number of Immigrants from Cuba	Total U.S. Immigration	Percentage of Immigrants from Cuba in Total U.S. Immigration
1971	21,615	370,473	5.83
1972	20,045	384,685	5.21
1973	24,147	400,063	6.04
1974	18,929	394,861	4.79
1975	25,955	396,194	6.55
1976	35,996	502,289	7.17
1977	69,708	462,315	15.08
1978	29,754	601,442	4.95
1979	15,585	460,348	3.39
1980	15,054	530,639	2.84
1981	10,858	596,600	1.82
1982	8,209	594,131	1.38
1983	8,978	559,763	1.60
1984	10,599	543,903	1.95
1985	20,334	570,009	3.57
1986	33,114	601,708	5.50
1987	28,916	601,516	4.81
1988	17,558	643,025	2.73
1989	10,046	1,090,924	0.92
1990	10,645	1,536,483	0.69
1991	10,349	1,827,167	0.57
1992	11,791	973,977	1.21
1993	13,666	904,292	1.51
1994	14,727	804,416	1.83
1995	17,937	720,461	2.49
1996	26,466	915,900	2.89
Total 1971-96	530,981	17,987,584	2.95

Sources: *Statistical Yearbook of the Immigration and Naturalization Service*, 1980, Table 13; *Statistical Yearbook of the Immigration and Naturalization Service*, 1986, Table 3; *Statistical Yearbook of the Immigration and Naturalization Service*, 1996, Table 3.

Since Castro

That all changed with a new revolution in 1959. The revolution had begun in 1953, when Fidel Castro Ruz led the failed "26th of July" insurrection against the Batista government. He was imprisoned for two years, went into United States exile (as had so many Cuban revolutionaries before him), and returned to Cuba in December 1956 to lead a guerrilla insurgency. In October 1958, his forces came down out of the Sierra Maestra to quickly overrun Cuba, against very light government opposition. Castro took Havana—and with it took power—on January 8, 1959. Turning Cuban society upside down, he built a Soviet-allied Communist state, and in the process triggered a set of mass migrations out of Cuba, mainly to the United States.

The first wave of United States–bound Cuban refugees began to arrive in 1959. Numbering approximately 150,000, these were the "golden exiles," comprised largely of many of Cuba's most highly educated and skilled professionals and businesspeople. Despite language difficulties, and with U.S. government immigration and resettlement aid, these immigrants quickly established close-knit, generally prosperous communities in southern Florida.

These and later refugee migrations would take place against a background of bitterly antagonistic relations between the United States and Cuba. On April 17,

1961, some 1,200 to 1,500 U.S.-backed Cuban exiles landed in Cuba in the failed Bay of Pigs invasion. From October 22 to December 2, 1962, in the Cuban Missile Crisis, the United States and the Soviet Union came very, very close to precipitating a nuclear war, until the Soviet Union agreed to unconditional withdrawal of its bombers and the dismantling of its missile sites in Cuba.

After the 1962 Cuban Missile Crisis, all flights between Cuba and the United States were banned by the United States. Largely because of that, only about 30,000 Cubans managed to reach the United States from 1962 to 1965. Then in October 1965 the Cuban government loosened its emigration policies, announcing that those Cubans with families in the United States would be allowed to leave from the port city of Camarioca if their families came for them. Their families did so, quickly evacuating 5,000 refugees in hundreds of small boats. The Cuban and U.S. governments then agreed to institute a U.S.-financed airlift, which in an orderly fashion ultimately brought more than 250,000 Cubans to the United States from 1965 to 1972. After that, Cuban immigration sagged, with only 38,000 arriving from 1973 to 1979, among them several thousand political prisoners released in the late 1970s.

The third large wave of Cuban immigrants arrived in a far from orderly fashion, between April and September 1980.

These were the "Mariel boat people," who ultimately numbered 125,000. Their permission to emigrate from Cuba came after mounting pressure to allow them to leave resulted in an armed clash at Peru's embassy in Havana. Cuba then announced that anyone who reached the grounds of the embassy could leave the country. After more than 10,000 Cubans did so, the government opened the port city of Mariel to anyone who would come to take refugees out of Cuba.

Thousands of exile boats rushed to Mariel in the months that followed, taking out an estimated 125,000 more Cuban refugees. This wave also included a substantial body of formerly imprisoned criminals and political prisoners, sent out by the Cuban government. Some of the Cubans in this wave were held in detention camps and jails by the U.S. government for years, among them a substantial number of Cubans who had not been previously imprisoned or presented other entry problems.

In all, a total of at least 700,000 Cuban immigrants reached the United States from 1959 to 1996, with some estimates reaching into the 900,000 to 1,000,000 range. By 1996, there were large, stable Cuban-American communities in southern Florida and many other areas, reflecting the resettlement of Cuban refugees throughout the country.

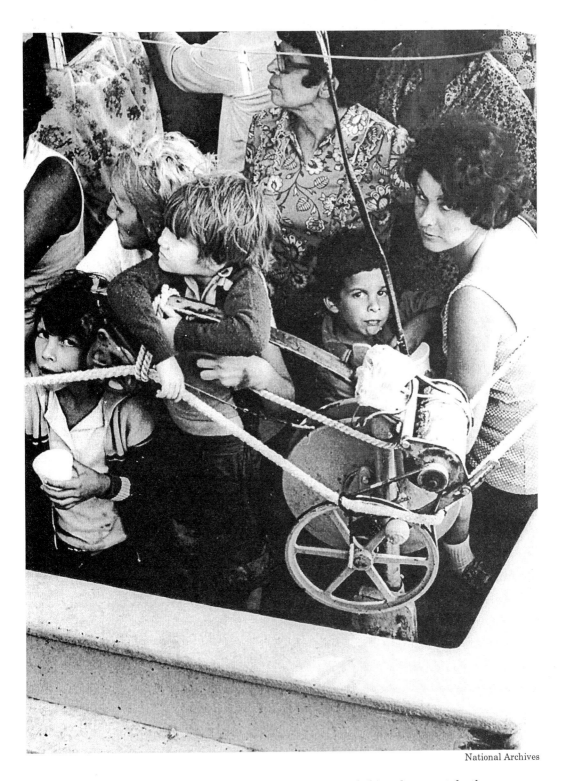

National Archives

After Castro took over in Cuba, many Cubans like these crowded into boats to take them across 90 miles of water to refuge in the United States.

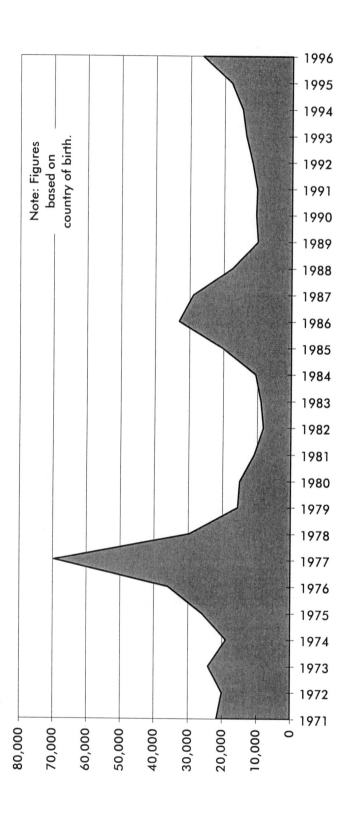

Graph 5.12: Number of Immigrants from Cuba Annually, 1971–1996

Note: Figures based on country of birth.

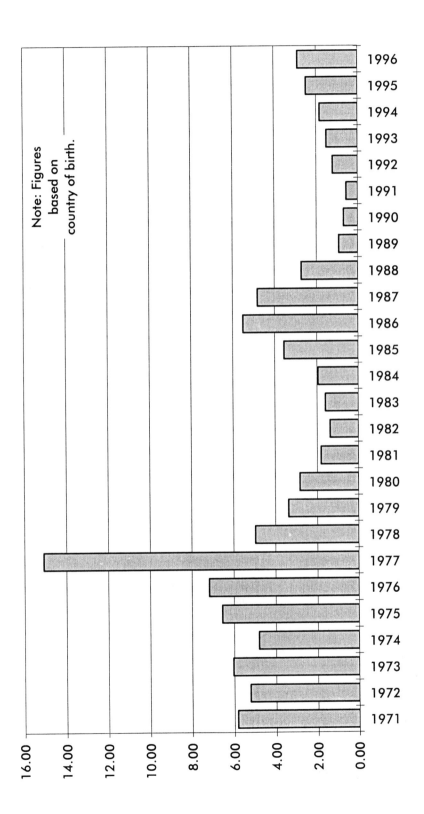

Graph 5.13: Percentage of Immigrants from Cuba in Total U.S. Immigration Annually, 1971–1996

Note: Figures based on country of birth.

Graph 5.14: Number of Foreign-Born Immigrants from Cuba in Total U.S. Population by Decade, 1870–1990

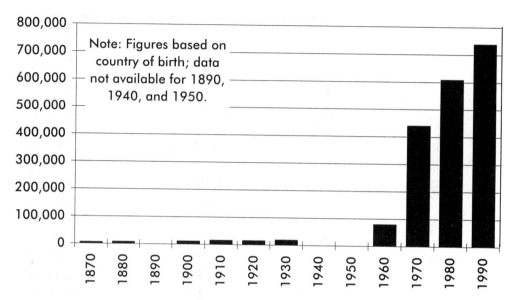

Graph 5.15: Percentage Distribution of Americans of Cuban Origin by Region of the United States, 1990

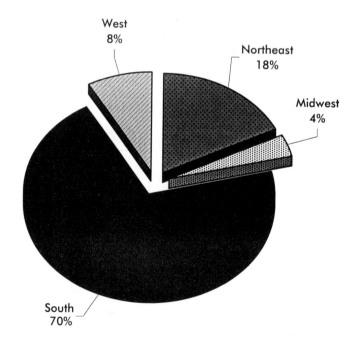

Table 5.7: Number and Percentage of Foreign-Born Immigrants from Cuba in Total U.S. Population by Decade, 1870–1990

Decade	Total Foreign-Born Immigrants from Cuba	Total U.S. Population	Percentage of Foreign-Born Immigrants from Cuba in Total U.S. Population
1870	5,319	39,818,449	0.01
1880	6,917	50,155,783	0.01
1890	(NA)	62,947,714	(NA)
1900	11,081	75,994,575	0.01
1910	15,133	91,972,266	0.02
1920	14,872	105,710,620	0.01
1930	18,493	122,775,046	0.02
1940	(NA)	131,669,275	(NA)
1950	(NA)	150,697,361	(NA)
1960	79,150	179,323,175	0.04
1970	439,048	203,235,298	0.22
1980	607,814	227,726,000	0.27
1990	736,971	249,907,000	0.29

NA = Not available

Note: Figures not separately recorded before 1870.

Source: Adapted from Series C 228–295, Foreign-Born Population, by Country of Birth: 1850–1970, in *Historical Statistics of the the United States, Colonial Times to 1970, Bicentennial Edition*, and other updating tables from the U.S. Census Bureau.

Resources

Internet Resources

CubaGenWeb (*http://
www.cubagenweb.org/*) Part of the
WorldGenWeb project, linking
genealogical research sites around the
world, by region; in English and
Spanish; includes advice, resources,
and links to related sites.

Print Resources

Clark, Juan M., et al. *The 1980 Mariel
Exodus: An Assessment and Prospect.*
Washington, D.C.: Council for Inter-
American Security, 1981.

Cortes, Carlos E., ed. *Cuban Exiles in the
United States.* New York: Arno Press,
1980.

Cortes, Carlos E., ed. *Cuban Experience in
the United States.* New York: Arno
Press, 1980.

Cuba: A Country Study. 3d ed. James D.
Rudolph, ed. Washington, D.C.: Federal
Research Division, Library of Congress,
1985.

Galvan, Raul. *Cuban Americans.* New
York: Marshall Cavendish, 1994.

Garver, Susan, and Paula McGuire.
*Coming to North America: From
Mexico, Cuba, and Puerto Rico.* New
York: Delacorte, 1981.

Gernand, Renee. *The Cuban Americans.*
New York: Chelsea House, 1988.

Gonzalez-Pando, Miguel. *The Cuban
Americans.* Westport, CT: Greenwood,
1998.

Grenquist, Barbara. *Cubans.* New York:
Watts, 1991.

Haskins, James. *The New Americans:
Cuban Boat People.* Hillside, N.J.:
Enslow, 1982.

Hoobler, Dorothy, and Thomas Hoobler.
The Cuban American Family Album.
New York: Oxford University Press,
1996.

Larzelere, Alex. *The 1980 Cuban Boatlift.*
Washington, D.C.: National Defense
University Press, 1988.

Llanes, Jose. *Cuban Americans: Masters of
Survival.* Cambridge, Mass.: Abt Books,
1982.

Masud-Piloto, Felix Roberto. *With Open
Arms: Cuban Migration to the United
States.* Totowa, N.J.: Rowman &
Littlefield, 1988.

Masud-Piloto, Felix Roberto. *From
Welcomed Exiles to Illegal Immigrants:
Cuban Migration to the U.S., 1959–
1995.* Lanham, Md.: Rowman &
Littlefield, 1996.

Mendez Rodenas, Adriana. *Cubans in
America.* Minneapolis: Lerner, 1994.

Olson, James Stuart, and Judith E. Olson.
*Cuban Americans: From Trauma to
Triumph.* New York: Twayne, 1995.

Ripoll, Carlos. *Cubans in the United
States.* New York: E. Torres, Americas
Pub. Co., 1987.

Rivera, Mario Antonio. *Decision and
Structure: U.S. Refugee Policy in the
Mariel Crisis.* Lanham, Md.: University
Press of America, 1991.

For more resources, see "Introduction"
on p. 482.

Immigrants from Haiti

From 1957 to 1996, an estimated 1 million people emigrated from Haiti. Approximately half of those Haitian emigrants ultimately reached the United States. More than 300,000 of these were legal immigrants, while at least 200,000 and possibly more were "illegals," many of them arriving in small boats. These were the Haitian "boat people," some of whom perished en route, and whose plight provided one of the most poignant of the world's multitude of 20th-century refugee stories.

They were not the first Haitian refugees to reach the United States, however; the first wave had come 150 years earlier.

Haitian Background

Haiti comprises approximately one third of the Caribbean island of Hispaniola, which was one of the islands visited by Christopher Columbus in 1492. Spain established its first New World colonial base on Hispaniola in 1496 with the founding of the city of Santo Domingo, which later gave its name to the Spanish portion of Hispaniola.

In 1501, the first black African slaves to reach the New World were brought to Hispaniola by the Spanish. By that time, the virtual extinction of the island's Native Americans—estimated to have originally numbered several hundred thousand—was well under way. By 1550, only about 150 Native Americans were left, the rest having been killed, worked to death, or struck down by the epidemic diseases brought by the Europeans. The Spanish were by then importing hundreds of thousands of black African slaves to the island.

The island fell to France in 1697, and under French rule became a major slave-holding society, with masses of black African slaves. The population also included a much smaller number of free black Africans, some of them of mixed African and European ancestry, called mulattoes, along with slaveholding white European colonists.

By 1791, the island held an estimated 500,000 black African slaves. Some thousands of them, called Maroons, had fled into the interior, forming armed independent guerrilla groups. That year a major slave rebellion began, in alliance with French Republican forces, against the largely royalist slaveholding elite of the island. In 1793, the French island government abolished slavery on the island, an act confirmed by the French National Assembly in 1794. Black leader Toussaint-Louverture emerged as leader of the revolution and by 1800 had won control of Hispaniola, then quickly taking full power from the French. However, a new French army sent by Napoléon Bonaparte in 1802 during a lull in Europe's Napoleonic Wars, defeated the forces of Toussaint, who died in a French prison a year later.

In 1803, with the European wars again taking Napoleon's full attention, France sold the Louisiana Territory to the United States and also withdrew its forces from Hispaniola. On January 1, 1804, the independent nation of Haiti was proclaimed on the western third of the island, with the other two-thirds becoming Santo Domingo (see "Immigrants from the Dominican Republic" on p. 521).

Independence

The new nation was led by Jean-Jacques Dessalines, whose forces then embarked on a reign of terror against Haiti's remaining white colonists, some of whom were able to flee abroad. Approximately 95 percent of the Haiti that emerged was of fully black African descent, and the remaining 5 percent of mixed black African and European, or mulatto, descent. The new country's colonial economy had been shattered, the main mass of its people were bare-bones subsistence farmers with no appreciable resources, and the legacy of its bitter colonial past would include a century and a half of instability and ever-shifting dictatorships.

The civil war and its bloody aftermath produced Haiti's first substantial refugee population. More than 150 years later, still-poor and still-unstable Haiti would produce a far greater body of refugees.

Graph 5.16: Number of Immigrants from Haiti by Decade, 1932–1996

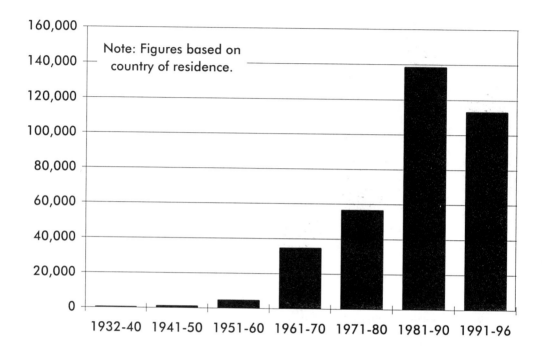

Note: Figures based on country of residence.

Table 5.8: Number and Percentage of Immigrants from Haiti in Total U.S. Immigration by Decade, 1932–1996

Decade	Number of Immigrants from Haiti	Total U.S. Immigrants	Percentage of Immigrants from Haiti in Total U.S. Immigration
1932-40	191	528,431	0.04
1941-50	911	1,035,039	0.09
1951-60	4,442	2,515,479	0.18
1961-70	34,499	3,321,677	1.04
1971-80	56,335	4,493,314	1.25
1981-90	138,379	7,338,062	1.89
1991-96	112,924	6,146,213	1.84
Total 1932-1996	347,681	63,140,227	0.55

Note: Data not recorded separately until 1932.

Source: Adapted from Table 2, Immigration by Region and Selected Country of Last Residence, Fiscal Years 1820–1996, from the *Statistical Yearbook of the Immigration and Naturalization Service*, 1996.

Early Refugees

From the early 1790s through 1810, an estimated 50,000 white colonists fled Haiti, along with some mulatto and black African allies. Approximately 10,000 to 20,000 of those went to the United States, though some estimates are higher, into the 30,000 to 40,000 range.

Some of the Haitian refugees went to French-speaking Louisiana, while others scattered into the United States coastal cities, among them Philadelphia, New York, and Boston. Most were not really immigrants, but rather refugees, sojourners who did not stay in the United States but ultimately returned to France or went on to other French-speaking areas.

Early Immigration

Immigration to the United States from Haiti was very small until the second half of the 20th century. It remained so even after U.S. forces occupied Haiti in 1915. Intent on safeguarding U.S. investments in Haiti and on maintaining U.S. imperial control of the Caribbean, U.S. forces would remain in Haiti until 1934.

Haitian immigration was not recorded separately until 1932 and then remained very small. From 1932 to 1950, only 1,110 immigrants were recorded from Haiti. In the decade that followed, only 4,400 more were recorded, most of them political refugees from the dictatorship of François "Papa Doc" Duvalier (1957–1971). Immigration began in earnest during Duvalier's regime, accelerated during the reign of his son Jean-Claude "Baby Doc" Duvalier (1971–1986), and continued high during the unstable years that followed.

Haiti was the poorest country in the Western Hemisphere, with a 470-percent population growth in the 20th century, from an estimated 1.6 million in 1900 to an estimated 7.5 million in 1998. For Haitians, poverty, population pressure, and decades of brutal dictatorship combined to create an enormous push out of the country. In the United States, there were jobs— not often good jobs for most unskilled, des-

titute Haitian immigrants, but jobs that enabled Haitian Americans to feed their families and educate their children.

Many middle-class Haitians came early, soon after Duvalier took power in 1957, for they were political dissidents, whose opposition to the dictatorship put their lives in danger. Poorer Haitians also began to leave in substantial numbers. The 1965 Immigration Act, which opened the door to greatly increased immigration to the United States from many countries, made it somewhat more difficult for immigrants from some Western Hemisphere countries, including Haiti. As a result, increasing numbers of Haitians from the late 1960s on simply overstayed their visas, while waiting on lengthening lists to become legal immigrants.

In the late 1970s, increasing numbers of Haitians became "boat people," with most making the 700-mile sea journey in small boats that openly landed on the south Florida coast, with the Haitians then becoming illegal immigrants (see "Appendix C: Estimates of Emigration and Illegals" on p. 749). Meanwhile, a major legal battle began between the U.S. government, which called these Haitians "economic refugees" and therefore illegal, and refugee advocates, who called them "political refugees" and therefore legally entitled to enter the United States. An estimated total of 40,000 boat people arrived in 1980 and 1981, although only 13,000 legal Haitian immigrants were recorded.

Although Jean-Claude Duvalier's rule ended in 1986 with his resignation, it was followed by a succession of short-lived military dictatorships, punctuated by the seven-month-long administration of Jean-Bertrand Aristide in 1991. Finally, in September 1994, United States pressure forced the end of military rule and Aristide's return to power.

Through it all, Haiti remained poor, with an unemployment rate in the 50-percent range and increasing population pressure. Haitians continued to immigrate to the United States in large numbers. Although immigration to the United States from Haiti slowed somewhat in the mid-1990s, there was every reason to believe

that it would accelerate again, as Haiti's
economic and population growth problems
remained unsolved.

Table 5.9: Number and Percentage of Immigrants from Haiti in Total U.S. Immigration
Annually, 1971–1996

Year	Number of Immigrants from Haiti	Total U.S. Immigration	Percentage of Immigrants from Haiti in Total U.S. Immigration
1971	7,444	370,473	2.01
1972	5,809	384,685	1.51
1973	4,786	400,063	1.20
1974	3,946	394,861	1.00
1975	5,145	396,194	1.30
1976	6,691	502,289	1.33
1977	5,441	462,315	1.18
1978	6,470	601,442	1.08
1979	6,433	460,348	1.40
1980	6,540	530,639	1.23
1981	6,683	596,600	1.12
1982	8,779	594,131	1.48
1983	8,424	559,763	1.50
1984	9,839	543,903	1.81
1985	10,165	570,009	1.78
1986	12,666	601,708	2.11
1987	14,819	601,516	2.46
1988	34,806	643,025	5.41
1989	13,658	1,090,924	1.25
1990	20,324	1,536,483	1.32
1991	47,527	1,827,167	2.60
1992	11,002	973,977	1.13
1993	10,094	904,292	1.12
1994	13,333	804,416	1.66
1995	14,021	720,461	1.95
1996	18,386	915,900	2.01
Total 1971-96	313,231	17,987,584	1.74

Sources: *Statistical Yearbook of the Immigration and Naturalization Service*, 1980, Table 13; *Statistical Yearbook of the Immigration and Naturalization Service*, 1986, Table 3; *Statistical Yearbook of the Immigration and Naturalization Service*, 1996, Table 3.

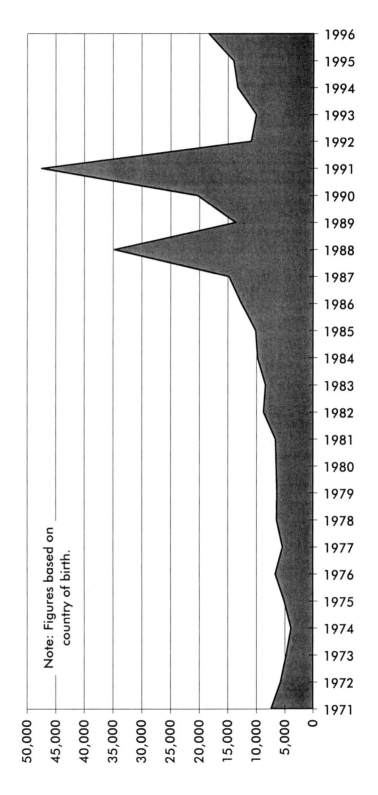

Graph 5.17: Number of Immigrants from Haiti Annually, 1971–1996

Note: Figures based on country of birth.

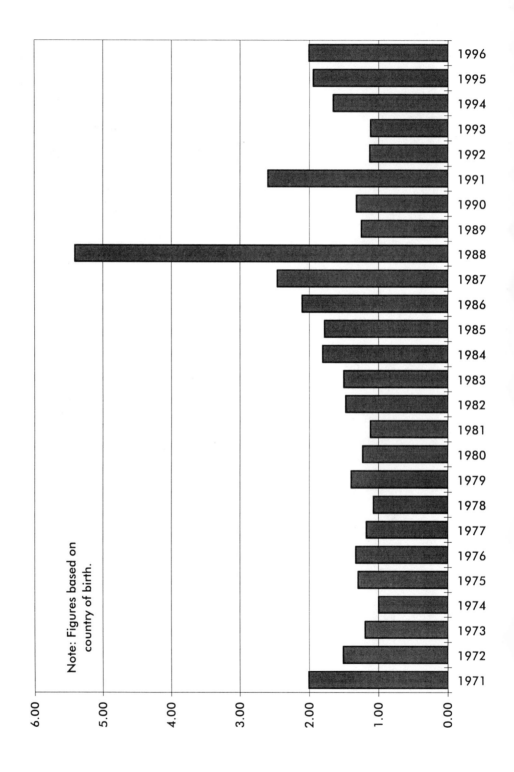

Graph 5.18: Percentage of Immigrants from Haiti in Total U.S. Immigration Annually, 1971–1996

Note: Figures based on country of birth.

Resources

Chierici, Rose-Marie Cassagnol. *Demele, "Making It": Migration and Adaptation Among Haitian Boat People in the United States*. New York: AMS Press, 1991.

Dominican Republic and Haiti: Country Studies. 2d ed. Richard A. Haggerty, ed. Washington, D.C.: Federal Research Division, Library of Congress, 1991. (Available as separate countries on-line at *http://lcweb2.loc.gov/frd/cs*)

Greenberg, Keith Elliot. *A Haitian Family*. Minneapolis: Lerner, 1998.

Stepick, Alex. *Haitian Refugees in the U.S.* London: Expedite Graphic, 1986. Originally published London: Minority Rights Group, 1982.

———. *Pride Against Prejudice: Haitians in the United States*. Boston: Allyn and Bacon, 1998.

Zephir, Flore. *Haitian Immigrants in Black America: A Sociological and Sociolinguistic Portrait*. Westport, Conn.: Bergin & Garvey, 1996.

For more resources, see "Introduction" on p. 482.

Immigrants from the Dominican Republic

The Dominican Republic shares the Caribbean island of Hispaniola with Haiti. It occupies approximately two-thirds of the island, on which Christopher Columbus made landfall during his first voyage in 1492. The Spanish portion of the island was long known as Santo Domingo, after its capital city, established in 1496 by Bartholomew Columbus, brother of Christopher. Probably the oldest continuously occupied European settlement in the New World, Santo Domingo became Spain's first New World colony and was its major base during the early decades of the Spanish conquest of substantial portions of the Americas.

In 1503, Santo Domingo was also the site of the first importation of black African slaves into the Americas. By 1520, these slaves were the island's main workforce, for a combination of bitterly repressive Spanish colonial policies and European-borne epidemics had largely destroyed the Tainos, who were the original Native American population of the island. By 1550, only an estimated 500 to 1,000 Tainos were left, of a pre-Conquest population estimated variously at from 300,000 to 1 million.

After the Spanish conquests of Mexico and Peru during the first half of the 16th century, Santo Domingo was no longer a major Spanish base. Its modest resources mainly exhausted, it became for Spain only a minor Caribbean colony, with small resources to appropriate and only modest income to extract from its slave laborers. As French and English penetration of the New World developed, it was repeatedly attacked. In 1697, Spain ceded the western third of the island to France; this became Haiti.

Under French control, Haitian agriculture became a tremendous profit source, with France importing an estimated 500,000 slaves by the time of the Haitian Revolution, in 1791. Santo Domingo, on the other hand, with twice as much land, had only an estimated 60,000 slaves, along with an estimated 40,000 whites and 20,000 to 25,000 free blacks.

The resulting history of the two nations was very different. Haiti, with an enormous and bitterly oppressed black African slave population, many thousands of black guerillas (Maroons) in the back country, and a French government beset by revolution and war at home, embarked on a long and bloody series of revolutions. Haitian and French forces took control of all of Hispaniola in 1796, but in 1809 Spanish forces again took control of Spain's former two-thirds of the island. In 1821, Santo Domingo won independence from Spain, but was then quickly retaken by Haitian forces, which occupied it until Dominican independence was won again in 1844.

The Dominican-Haitian war ended in 1850. What followed in the Dominican Republic was more than a century of instability, with rival factions conducting coup after coup, and a series of dictatorships in control of the country. The Dominican Republic was retaken by Spain from 1861 to 1865, but after Union victory in the American Civil War Spain withdrew under U.S. pressure.

In 1905, the Dominican Republic became a de facto U.S. protectorate and remained so for much of the rest of the 20th century. From 1916 to 1924, the United States openly occupied the country.

Table 5.10: Number and Percentage of Immigrants from the Dominican Republic in Total U.S. Immigration by Decade, 1932–1996

Decade	Number of Immigrants from the Dominican Republic	Total U.S. Immigrants	Percentage of Immigrants from the Dominican Republic in Total U.S. Immigration
1932-1940	1,150	528,431	0.22
1941-1950	5,627	1,035,039	0.54
1951-1960	9,897	2,515,479	0.39
1961-1970	93,292	3,321,677	2.81
1971-1980	148,135	4,493,314	3.30
1981-1990	252,035	7,338,062	3.43
1991-1996	254,832	6,146,213	4.15
Total 1820-1996	764,968	63,140,227	1.21

Note: Data not recorded separately until 1932.

Source: Adapted from Table 2, Immigration by Region and Selected Country of Last Residence, Fiscal Years 1820–1996, from the *Statistical Yearbook of the Immigration and Naturalization Service*, 1996.

The last of the Dominican dictators was Rafael Leonidas Trujillo Molina, who ruled from 1930 to 1961. U.S. forces occupied the country again in 1965, settling a civil war in favor of the country's military government.

Social Problems

Until the early 1950s, the Dominican Republic remained a modestly productive, mainly agricultural country, as it had been since Spanish colonial times. However, the country then experienced the same combination of enormous population growth, country-to-city migration, and consequent destabilization that has plagued so many of the world's other developing countries during the second half of the 20th century.

By the early 1980s, it also had to deal with huge foreign debts, soaring inflation, austerity budgets imposed at times by international lending agencies, fluctuating world commodity prices, and massive unemployment, always averaging more than 20 percent. By the late 1990s, pressures had multiplied, while the estimated Dominican population had topped 8.2 million in 1997, up 1,640 percent from the 500,000 estimated in 1900.

Modern Emigration

The result of all these pressures was a very large emigration out of the Dominican Republic into whatever other countries might supply jobs and money, both to support those still at home and to help bring

Table 5.11: Number and Percentage of Immigrants from the Dominican Republic in Total U.S. Immigration Annually, 1971–1996

Year	Number of Immigrants from the Dominican Republic	Total U.S. Immigration	Percentage of Immigrants from the Dominican Republic in Total U.S. Immigration
1971	12,624	370,473	3.41
1972	10,760	384,685	2.80
1973	13,921	400,063	3.48
1974	15,680	394,861	3.97
1975	14,066	396,194	3.55
1976	15,088	502,289	3.00
1977	11,655	462,315	2.52
1978	19,458	601,442	3.24
1979	17,519	460,348	3.81
1980	17,245	530,639	3.25
1981	18,220	596,600	3.05
1982	17,451	594,131	2.94
1983	22,058	559,763	3.94
1984	23,147	543,903	4.26
1985	23,787	570,009	4.17
1986	26,175	601,708	4.35
1987	24,858	601,516	4.13
1988	27,189	643,025	4.23
1989	26,723	1,090,924	2.45
1990	42,195	1,536,483	2.75
1991	41,405	1,827,167	2.27
1992	41,969	973,977	4.31
1993	45,420	904,292	5.02
1994	51,189	804,416	6.36
1995	38,512	720,461	5.35
1996	39,604	915,900	4.32
Total 1971-96	657,918	17,987,584	3.66

Sources: *Statistical Yearbook of the Immigration and Naturalization Service, 1980*, Table 13; *Statistical Yearbook of the Immigration and Naturalization Service, 1986*, Table 3; *Statistical Yearbook of the Immigration and Naturalization Service, 1996*, Table 3.

others out. The United States became by far the most favored destination, and after the 1965 Immigration Act opened the door, large numbers of Dominicans poured into the United States.

From 1932 until 1960, fewer than 18,000 Dominican immigrants were recorded as entering the United States. However, that number shot up to more than 93,000 from 1960 to 1970. Then from 1971 to 1996, almost 658,000 recorded Dominican immigrants entered the United States. In late 1996, the U.S. government estimated that an additional 75,000 undocumented Dominicans were also in the United States (see "Appendix C: Estimates of Emigration and Illegals" on p. 749). From 1991 to 1996, arriving Dominican immigrants averaged 43,000 per year.

The main body of Dominican immigrants have settled in the metropolitan New York area, though late in the century many have also settled in southern Florida, with its very fast-growing Hispanic-American population. Dominicans have also settled in several other major East Coast cities.

Originally entering the United States labor force in low-paying industrial and service occupations, Dominicans have also moved into a wide range of businesses and office jobs. With baseball widely popular in their home country, Dominicans have also entered United States professional baseball, some emerging as major stars.

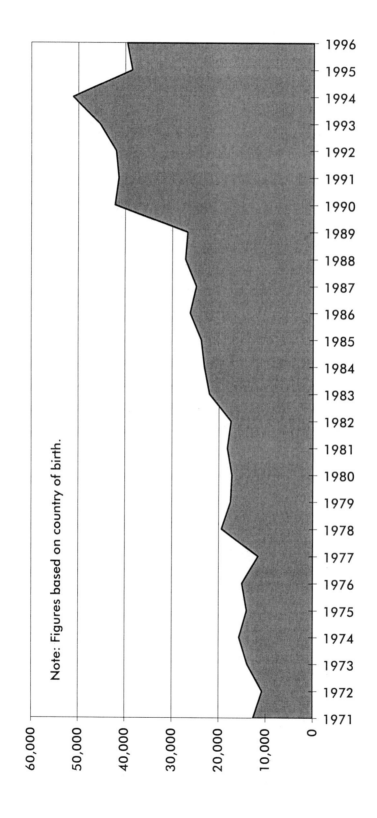

Graph 5.19: Number of Immigrants From the Dominican Republic Annually, 1971–1996

Note: Figures based on country of birth.

Graph 5.20: Number of Immigrants from the Dominican Republic by Decade, 1932–1996

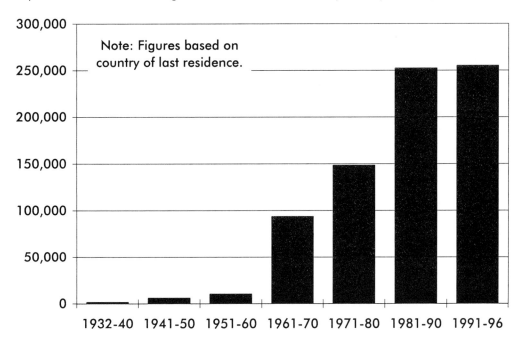

Graph 5.21: Percentage of Immigrants from the Dominican Republic in Total U.S. Immigration, 1932–1996

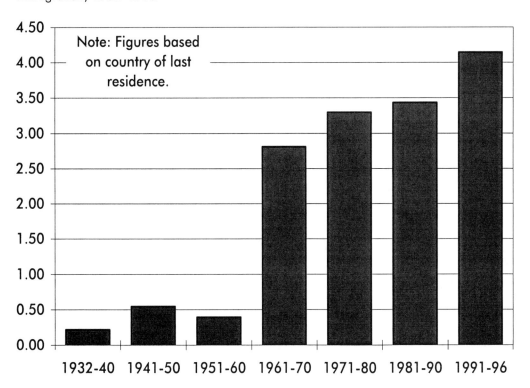

Resources

Bandon, Alexandra. *Dominican Americans.* Parsippany, N.J.: New Discovery, 1995.

Dominican Republic and Haiti: Country Studies. 2d ed. Richard A. Haggerty, ed. Washington, D.C.: Federal Research Division, Library of Congress, 1991. (Available as separate countries on-line at *http://lcweb2.loc.gov/frd/cs*)

Dwyer, Christopher. *The Dominican Americans.* New York: Chelsea House, 1991.

Torres-Saillant, Silvio, and Ramona Hernandez. *The Dominican Americans.* Westport, Conn.: Greenwood, 1999.

For more resources, see "Introduction" on p. 482.

Immigrants from Jamaica

Well over half a million Jamaican immigrants entered the United States from 1953 to 1996, in addition to at least 100,000 undocumented or illegal immigrants. In 1996, the U.S. government estimated that there were still 50,000 undocumented Jamaicans living in the United States (see "Appendix C: Estimates of Emigration and Illegals" on p. 749).

Jamaican immigration data was not recorded until 1953, but Jamaican immigrants began entering the United States long before then, with substantial numbers of Jamaicans (and others from what were then the British West Indies) entering under the British quota. The 1952 U.S. McCarran Act ended that, establishing small quotas for Jamaica and other British West Indian states.

Jamaica became an independent nation in 1962, the same year that Britain established its own restrictive Commonwealth Immigrants Act, building pressure for Jamaicans to immigrate to the United States instead. After the 1965 Immigration Act opened the way, Jamaican and other West Indian immigrants joined the new flood of immigrants to the United States.

Jamaica had been taken by England from Spain in the late 1660s, formally coming under British rule in 1670. Although there were some increases in the small European population from then until the early 1800s, the main population increase

Table 5.13: Number and Percentage of Immigrants from Jamaica in Total U.S. Immigration Annually, 1971–1996

Year	Number of Immigrants from Jamaica	Total U.S. Immigration	Percentage of Immigrants from Jamaica in Total U.S. Immigration
1971	14,571	370,473	3.93
1972	13,427	384,685	3.49
1973	9,963	400,063	2.49
1974	12,408	394,861	3.14
1975	11,076	396,194	2.80
1976	11,100	502,289	2.21
1977	11,501	462,315	2.49
1978	19,265	601,442	3.20
1979	19,714	460,348	4.28
1980	18,970	530,639	3.57
1981	23,569	596,600	3.95
1982	18,711	594,131	3.15
1983	19,535	559,763	3.49
1984	19,822	543,903	3.64
1985	18,923	570,009	3.32
1986	19,595	601,708	3.26
1987	23,148	601,516	3.85
1988	20,966	643,025	3.26
1989	24,523	1,090,924	2.25
1990	25,013	1,536,483	1.63
1991	23,828	1,827,167	1.30
1992	18,915	973,977	1.94
1993	17,241	904,292	1.91
1994	14,349	804,416	1.78
1995	16,398	720,461	2.28
1996	19,089	915,900	2.08
Total 1971-96	465,620	17,987,584	2.59

Sources: *Statistical Yearbook of the Immigration and Naturalization Service*, 1980, Table 13; *Statistical Yearbook of the Immigration and Naturalization Service*, 1986, Table 3; *Statistical Yearbook of the Immigration and Naturalization Service*, 1996, Table 3.

Table 5.12: Number and Percentage of Immigrants from Jamaica in Total U.S. Immigration by Decade, 1953–1996

Decade	Number of Immigrants from Jamaica	Total U.S. Immigrants	Percentage of Immigrants from Jamaica in Total U.S. Immigration
1953-60	8,869	2,515,479	0.35
1961-70	74,906	3,321,677	2.26
1971-80	137,577	4,493,314	3.06
1981-90	208,148	7,338,062	2.84
1991-96	106,720	6,146,213	1.74
Total 1953-96	536,220	63,140,227	0.85

Note: Data not recorded separately until 1953.

Source: Adapted from Table 2, Immigration by Region and Selected Country of Last Residence, Fiscal Years 1820–1996, from the *Statistical Yearbook of the Immigration and Naturalization Service*, 1996.

by far came from the importation of hundreds of thousands of black African slaves. By 1800, the estimated slave population of the island was 300,000, as Jamaica became a plantation-based sugar producer. That remained so even after Britain abolished slavery in 1838. Jamaica's one-crop economy made the country highly vulnerable to swings in world demand and prices for sugar throughout its colonial period. In the 20th century, bauxite mining and tourism developed as major Jamaican industries.

Jamaican immigration to Britain, the United States, Canada, and other English-speaking countries became substantial in the late 19th century. Many who emigrated were young, highly literate, skilled members of Jamaica's developing middle class. They were seeking greater opportunities abroad than were available in their home country's class-conscious society,

Graph 5.22: Number of Immigrants from Jamaica by Decade, 1953–1996

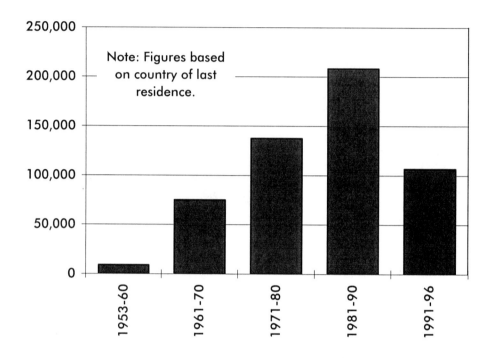

Graph 5.23: Percentage of Immigrants from Jamaica in Total U.S. Immigration, 1953–1996

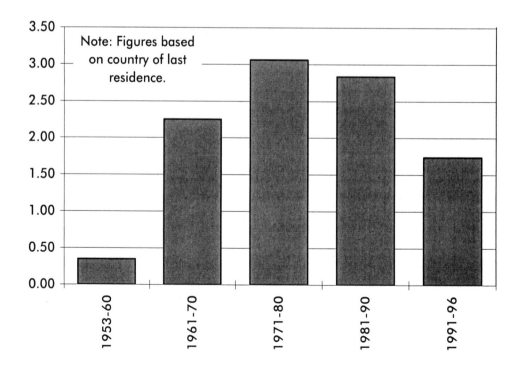

where the main properties and institutions were firmly in the hands of British colonials.

From the early 1880s until the onset of the Great Depression of the 1930s, at least 50,000 Jamaicans immigrated into the United States, filling a wide range of jobs, many of them in professional, administrative, and other white-collar occupations. Approximately two thirds of these immigrants settled in the New York area, though substantial numbers also settled in Florida, other southern states, and some of the larger East Coast cities. Jamaican migration accelerated during the second and third decades of the 20th century, as the island's lands and businesses came to be even more tightly held by whites, now including many absentee owners. Immigration then slowed as U.S. jobs became all but unavailable during the Great Depression.

Immigration to the United States from Jamaica picked up dramatically again only in the 1970s, as Jamaica's economy slid into a deepening depression. Sugar and bauxite both encountered sharply lower world prices, even as the island's new government borrowed large sums of money to finance public expenditures. The net results included massive and continuing unemployment; ruinous inflation; and huge, unmanageable foreign debts. In the early 1980s, the economy suffered a further blow as international lending agencies forced acceptance of austerity programs that sharply increased unemployment and lowered living standards.

A major Jamaican response was to leave, to emigrate, to seek a better life elsewhere. With continuing British restriction on West Indian immigration, Jamaicans in great numbers flocked to the United States, where the doors were open. In 1999, there was no slowdown in sight.

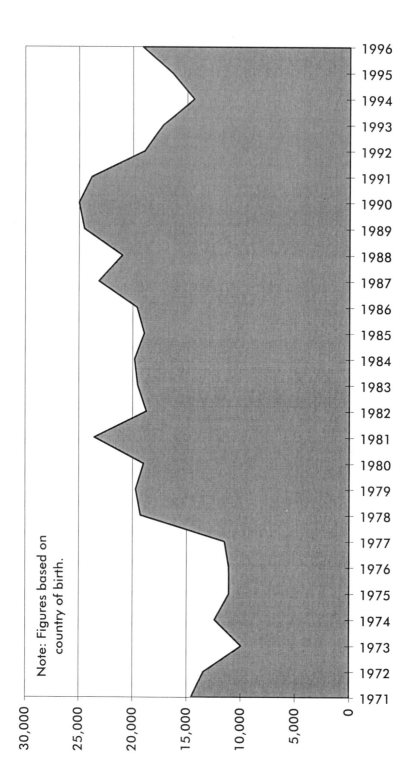

Graph 5.24: Number of Immigrants From Jamaica Annually, 1971–1996

Note: Figures based on country of birth.

Resources

Genealogy of Jamaica, West Indies (*http://users.pullman.com/mitchelm/jamaica.htm*) Privately maintained Web site offering information and links relating to Jamaican genealogy.

For more resources, see "General Immigration Statistics for the Americas" on p. 619.

Immigrants from the Bahamas

The Bahamas archipelago, a set of 700 islands in the northern Caribbean, was a small Spanish colony during the 15th and early 16th centuries. English colonists arrived in 1649, and in 1666 a settlement was founded on New Providence, the country's largest island. The chief early English immigration to the Bahamas came in the 1780s, when Loyalists from the American South fled from the new United States. They arrived with their slaves and established a cotton-based plantation system on New Providence and other islands. The modern population of the island reflects its history of slavery: more than 85 percent of the current population is Afro-Bahamian.

Largely a British backwater during most of its colonial period, the Bahamas began to develop as a United States tourist destination in the post–World War II period, with tourism soon supplying the country's main source of income and employment. In the 1980s and 1990s, the country also became a major banking and financial center, successfully developed its oil refining industry, and also sought, though without much success, to diversify into manufacturing and agriculture.

On the whole, despite recurring unemployment, the country prospered and absorbed most of the new workers generated by its considerable rate of population growth, so that there was little pressure to immigrate to the nearby United States. The immigration figures reflected this, remaining low throughout the postwar period. Although the country had an estimated population of 288,000 in 1997, an average of only a little over 700 immigrants a year arrived from 1991 to 1996, and a total of a little under 16,000 from 1971 to 1996.

For resources, see "General Immigration Resources for the Americas" on p. 632.

Table 5.14: Number and Percentage of Immigrants from the Bahamas in Total U.S. Immigration Annually, 1971–1996

Year	Number of Immigrants from the Bahamas	Total U.S. Immigration	Percentage of Immigrants from the Bahamas in Total U.S. Immigration
1971	204	370,473	0.06
1972	255	384,685	0.07
1973	365	400,063	0.09
1974	529	394,861	0.13
1975	256	396,194	0.06
1976	406	502,289	0.08
1977	400	462,315	0.09
1978	585	601,442	0.10
1979	651	460,348	0.14
1980	547	530,639	0.10
1981	546	596,600	0.09
1982	577	594,131	0.10
1983	505	559,763	0.09
1984	499	543,903	0.09
1985	533	570,009	0.09
1986	570	601,708	0.09
1987	556	601,516	0.09
1988	1,283	643,025	0.20
1989	861	1,090,924	0.08
1990	1,378	1,536,483	0.09
1991	1,062	1,827,167	0.06
1992	641	973,977	0.07
1993	686	904,292	0.08
1994	589	804,416	0.07
1995	585	720,461	0.08
1996	768	915,900	0.08
Total 1971-96	15,837	17,987,584	0.09

Sources: *Statistical Yearbook of the Immigration and Naturalization Service*, 1980, Table 13; *Statistical Yearbook of the Immigration and Naturalization Service*, 1986, Table 3; *Statistical Yearbook of the Immigration and Naturalization Service*, 1996, Table 3.

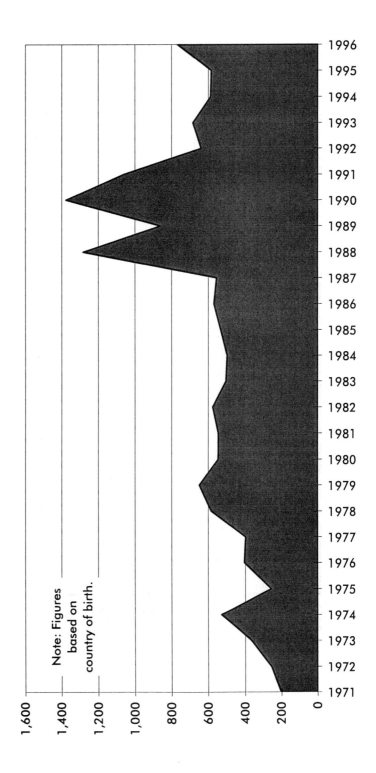

Graph 5.25: Number of Immigrants from the Bahamas Annually, 1971–1996

Note: Figures
based on
country of birth.

Immigrants from Barbados

Compared to many other Caribbean nations, the small, democratic, English-speaking island nation of Barbados has been for decades an oasis of stability, without skyrocketing inflation, huge unemployment rates, or massive foreign debt. It has high life expectancy, a long-standing 95 percent literacy rate, and a relatively high per capita income. Its economy is reasonably well-balanced, with tourism, manufacturing, some agriculture, and some oil and gas reserves. On the negative side, the very small country (166 square miles) supported an estimated 267,000 people in 1997, making it the most densely populated country in the Caribbean. It is also very dependent on its international trade revenues, making it prone to suffer from economic reverses in neighboring countries.

A major net result of all of the above is that Barbados does have some recurring unemployment, even though it also has some immigration from other countries in the region. Barbados was a British colony from the 17th century until 1966, when it became independent. Historically, therefore, unemployed Barbadians, or simply those seeking a different life, generally emigrated to Britain. However, after passage of Britain's restrictive Commonwealth Immigrants Act in 1962, they more often emigrated to the United States. From 1971 to 1996, a total of almost 45,000 recorded immigrants from Barbados entered the United States, at rates that averaged 2,000 to 3,000 per year in the late 1970s and approximately 1,000 in the 1990s.

For resources, "General Immigration Resources for the Americas" on p. 632.

This is a portrait of Bridgetown, the capital of Barbados, as it appeared in 1695.

Table 5.15: Number and Percentage of Immigrants from Barbados in Total U.S. Immigration Annually, 1971–1996.

Year	Number of Immigrants from Barbados	Total U.S. Immigration	Percentage of Immigrants from Barbados in Total U.S. Immigration
1971	1,731	370,473	0.47
1972	1,620	384,685	0.42
1973	1,448	400,063	0.36
1974	1,461	394,861	0.37
1975	1,618	396,194	0.41
1976	2,210	502,289	0.44
1977	2,763	462,315	0.60
1978	2,969	601,442	0.49
1979	2,461	460,348	0.53
1980	2,667	530,639	0.50
1981	2,394	596,600	0.40
1982	1,961	594,131	0.33
1983	1,849	559,763	0.33
1984	1,577	543,903	0.29
1985	1,625	570,009	0.29
1986	1,595	601,708	0.27
1987	1,665	601,516	0.28
1988	1,455	643,025	0.23
1989	1,616	1,090,924	0.15
1990	1,745	1,536,483	0.11
1991	1,460	1,827,167	0.08
1992	1,091	973,977	0.11
1993	1,184	904,292	0.13
1994	897	804,416	0.11
1995	734	720,461	0.10
1996	1,043	915,900	0.11
Total 1971-96	44,839	17,987,584	0.25

Sources: *Statistical Yearbook of the Immigration and Naturalization Service*, 1980, Table 13; *Statistical Yearbook of the Immigration and Naturalization Service*, 1986, Table 3; *Statistical Yearbook of the Immigration and Naturalization Service*, 1996, Table 3.

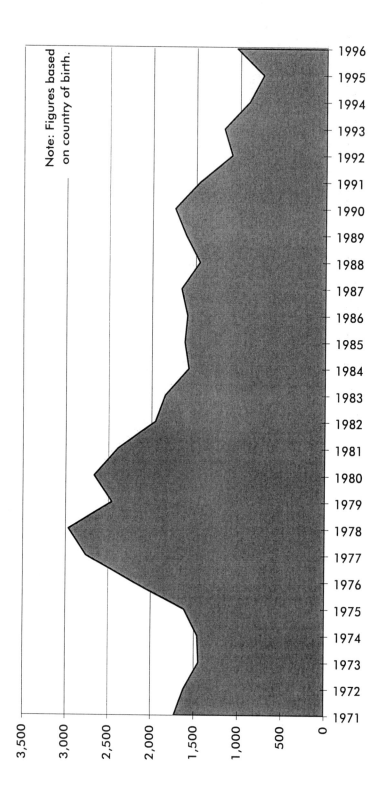

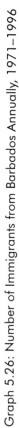

Graph 5.26: Number of Immigrants from Barbados Annually, 1971–1996

Note: Figures based on country of birth.

Immigrants from the Leeward Islands

The Leeward Islands include two small Caribbean nations: Antigua and Barbuda, and the Federation of St. Kitts and Nevis, as well as several much smaller islands that continue to be British-ruled, among them the British Virgin Islands, Anguilla, and Montserrat. Here we discuss the two independent island nations.

Antigua and Barbuda

Though the island of Antigua was "discovered" by Christopher Columbus in 1493, neither the Spanish nor the French successfully colonized it. The first permanent European settlement there was established in 1632 by the British. They quickly turned it into a sugar-producing possession, with tens of thousands of black African slaves imported to work on the sugar plantations. After the abolition of slavery, in 1838, the Antiguan plantations and their Afro-Antiguan workers continued to be the mainstay of the island's labor force.

In the late 20th century, although changes in world sugar markets forced the economy away from sugar and toward tourism in the 1960s, the descendants of those black African slaves continue to constitute the main body of the population, estimated to be 65,000 in 1997. The much smaller island of Barbuda, an area of 66 square miles, holds fewer than 2,000 people. Antigua and Barbuda became an independent nation in 1981.

Although the move toward tourism considerably eased the nation's loss of sugar markets, which was further eased by the development of government-funded public works projects, Antigua and Barbuda encountered major problems in the 1980s, including recession, relatively large international debts, and rising unemployment. One result was an increase in the outflow of migrants, many of them to the United States.

U.S. immigration figures show a temporary bulge in Antiguan immigration, from under 1,000 a year throughout the 1970s to a total of more than 5,000 in 1982 and 1983. Migration then subsided to earlier levels and declined further in the 1990s. In all, a total of more than 21,000 documented immigrants from Antigua and Barbuda entered the United States from 1971 to 1996. That is a very substantial migration, given the country's small population.

St. Kitts and Nevis

The even smaller neighboring island nation of St. Kitts and Nevis had an estimated population of almost 46,000 in 1997. Yet from 1971 to 1997, St. Kitts and Nevis sent a total of more than 20,000 emigrants to the United States, while also sending emigrants to other countries in the Caribbean and to other English-speaking nations around the world.

St. Kitts (until 1983 formally known as St. Christopher) was the first English colony in the Caribbean, its settlement dating back to 1623. From 1624, there were also competing French settlers on the island. Between them, the French and the English destroyed the island's earlier Carib Native American inhabitants during the balance of the 17th century.

In 1713, Britain completed its conquest of the island. British planters then proceeded to build a society based on sugar cultivation and the importation of large numbers of black African slaves to work the sugar plantations. The descendants of these black African slaves constitute more than 90 percent of the current population of the islands. St. Kitts and Nevis became an independent nation in 1983.

St. Kitts remained largely a one-crop economy well into the 20th century. As in many other countries in the region, it became apparent by the late 20th century that sugar alone, even in good times, would not do as well as the development of a balanced modern economy. By the early 1980s, the country had begun a major move to diversify into tourism, manufacturing, and other agricultural products, which proved modestly successful in the 1990s. However, sugar produced by St. Kitts was no longer competitive in world markets, and jobs were scarce. With unemployment high, relatively large numbers still emigrated abroad.

By the 1990s, so many people had emigrated from St. Kitts and Nevis that the country's population was growing only very slightly, at just a small fraction of 1 percent per year. At the same time, money sent home from abroad had become a large source of national income, equivalent to the development of another major industry.

For resources, "General Immigration Resources for the Americas" on p. 632

Table 5.16: Number and Percentage of Immigrants from Antigua and Barbuda in Total U.S. Immigration Annually, 1971–1996

Year	Number of Immigrants from Antigua and Barbuda	Total U.S. Immigration	Percentage of Immigrants from Antigua and Barbuda in Total U.S. Immigration
1971	325	370,473	0.09
1972	344	384,685	0.09
1973	404	400,063	0.10
1974	461	394,861	0.12
1975	435	396,194	0.11
1976	646	502,289	0.13
1977	835	462,315	0.18
1978	908	601,442	0.15
1979	770	460,348	0.17
1980	972	530,639	0.18
1981	929	596,600	0.16
1982	3,234	594,131	0.54
1983	2,008	559,763	0.36
1984	953	543,903	0.18
1985	957	570,009	0.17
1986	812	601,708	0.13
1987	874	601,516	0.15
1988	837	643,025	0.13
1989	979	1,090,924	0.09
1990	1,319	1,536,483	0.09
1991	944	1,827,167	0.05
1992	619	973,977	0.06
1993	554	904,292	0.06
1994	438	804,416	0.05
1995	374	720,461	0.05
1996	406	915,900	0.04
Total 1971-96	22,337	17,987,584	0.12

Sources: *Statistical Yearbook of the Immigration and Naturalization Service*, 1980, Table 13; *Statistical Yearbook of the Immigration and Naturalization Service*, 1986, Table 3; *Statistical Yearbook of the Immigration and Naturalization Service*, 1996, Table 3.

Table 5.17: Number and Percentage of Immigrants from St. Kitts and Nevis in Total U.S. Immigration Annually, 1971–1996

Year	Number of Immigrants from St. Kitts and Nevis	Total U.S. Immigration	Percentage of Immigrants from St. Kitts and Nevis in Total U.S. Immigration
1971	331	370,473	0.09
1972	383	384,685	0.10
1973	402	400,063	0.10
1974	425	394,861	0.11
1975	419	396,194	0.11
1976	904	502,289	0.18
1977	896	462,315	0.19
1978	1,014	601,442	0.17
1979	786	460,348	0.17
1980	874	530,639	0.16
1981	867	596,600	0.15
1982	1,039	594,131	0.17
1983	2,773	559,763	0.50
1984	1,648	543,903	0.30
1985	769	570,009	0.13
1986	573	601,708	0.10
1987	589	601,516	0.10
1988	660	643,025	0.10
1989	795	1,090,924	0.07
1990	896	1,536,483	0.06
1991	830	1,827,167	0.05
1992	626	973,977	0.06
1993	544	904,292	0.06
1994	370	804,416	0.05
1995	360	720,461	0.05
1996	357	915,900	0.04
Total 1971-96	20,130	17,987,584	0.11

Sources: *Statistical Yearbook of the Immigration and Naturalization Service*, 1980, Table 13; *Statistical Yearbook of the Immigration and Naturalization Service*, 1986, Table 3; *Statistical Yearbook of the Immigration and Naturalization Service*, 1996, Table 3.

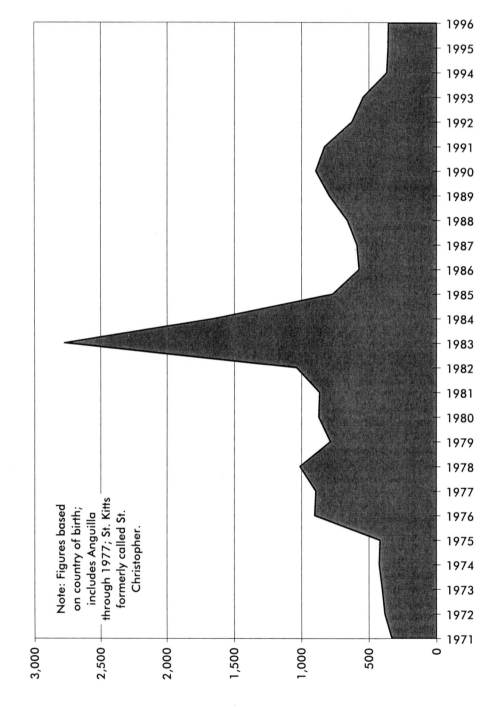

Graph 5.27: Number of Immigrants from St. Kitts and Nevis Annually, 1971–1996

Note: Figures based on country of birth; includes Anguilla through 1977; St. Kitts formerly called St. Christopher.

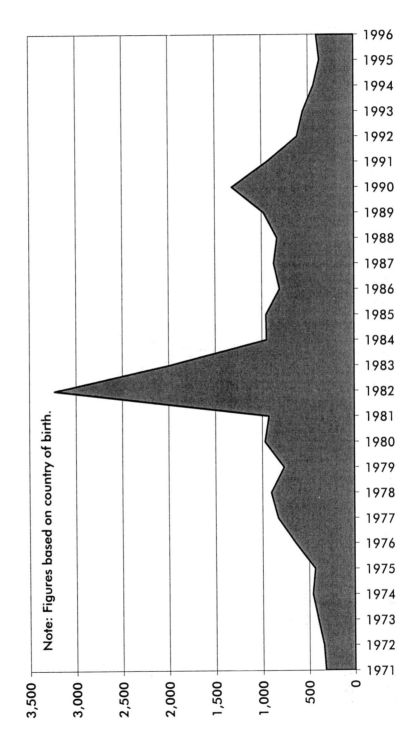

Graph 5.28: Number of Immigrants from Antigua and Barbuda Annually, 1971–1996

Note: Figures based on country of birth.

Immigrants from Trinidad and Tobago

Although an oil-rich, high-income country when compared to other Caribbean countries, Trinidad and Tobago encountered major economic problems in the 1970s. That together with population pressure brought substantial immigration to the United States. From 1971 to 1996, some 142,000 legal immigrants entered the United States from Trinidad and Tobago, along with tens of thousands of undocumented "illegals." In 1996, the U.S. government estimated that 50,000 "illegals" from Trinidad and Tobago were living in the United States (see "Appendix C: Estimates of Emigration and Illegals" on p. 749).

A Spanish colony for 300 years, the southern Caribbean islands of Trinidad and Tobago were taken by England in 1797, formally becoming English possessions in 1802. Trinidad is by far the larger of the two, with 95 percent of the population and territory. The country became independent in 1962.

During the 18th and 19th centuries, the English developed the islands as a one-crop economy, importing tens of thousands of black Africans to work as slaves on sugar plantations. After slavery was abolished by the British in 1838, many former slaves left the plantations. The British planters responded by importing tens of thousands of indentured laborers from India. The ultimate result was that the islands today have an ethnically mixed population, with 40 percent each being of black African and Asian Indian descent.

Late in the 18th century, the colony's economy encountered prolonged, systemic depression because of its inability to compete in the world sugar market. However, substantial oil deposits were discovered in 1907, and gas later; oil production and petrochemical products became the mainstay of the country's 20th-century economy.

In the early 1970s, an enormous rise in world oil prices brought a major boom to Trinidad. However, oil required few workers, and already-existing problems of unemployment were not solved. In the 1980s and 1990s, with oil prices sharply lower, continuing high unemployment, and increasing population pressure, many were impelled to emigrate in search of jobs. Although the combined legal and illegal immigration to the United States from Trinidad and Tobago probably totaled no more than 250,000 in the period, it was proportionately very high, for it came from a small country that had an estimated population of only 1.3 million in 1997.

For resources, see "General Immigration Resources for the Americas" on p. 632.

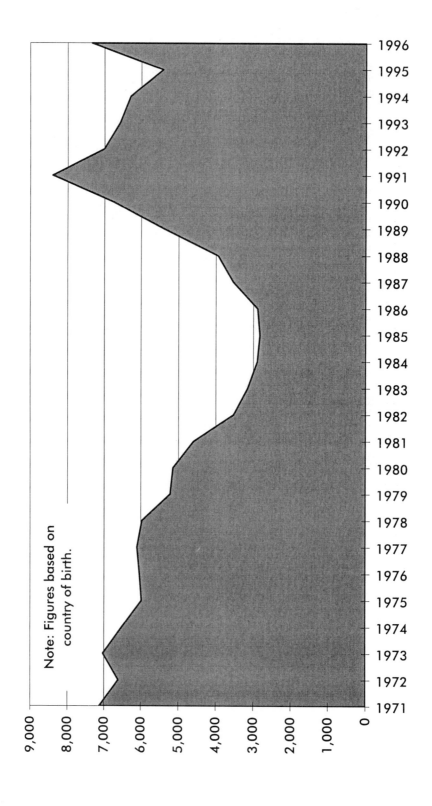

Graph 5.29: Number of Immigrants from Trinidad and Tobago Annually, 1971–1996

Note: Figures based on country of birth.

Immigrants from the Windward Islands

The Windward Islands consist of the four Caribbean countries of Dominica, St. Lucia, St. Vincent and the Grenadines, and Grenada. All four were conquered by the French during the European invasion of the Americas, after long opposition by their Native American inhabitants, the Caribs, who mounted an effective resistance on Dominica until the 1730s. All four were fought over by France and Britain during their centuries-long worldwide imperial contest, with the last island, St. Lucia, falling to Britain in 1815. Their historical similarities abound, but they are quite different countries.

Dominica

After long Carib resistance, which was eventually defeated more through disease than by military action, Dominica fell to the French in the early 1730s. They did not hold it very long, although the country continues to reflect French influences. Dominica fell to Britain in 1763, at the end of the worldwide Seven Years War. It became an independent nation in 1978.

During the colonial period, the British developed large sugar plantations, often held by absentee owners and worked by the tens of thousands of black African slaves they imported. These slaves became

Table 5.18: Number and Percentage of Immigrants from Dominica in Total U.S. Immigration Annually, 1971–1996

Year	Number of Immigrants from Dominica	Total U.S. Immigration	Percentage of Immigrants from Dominica in Total U.S. Immigration
1971	216	370,473	0.06
1972	198	384,685	0.05
1973	258	400,063	0.06
1974	236	394,861	0.06
1975	274	396,194	0.07
1976	377	502,289	0.08
1977	572	462,315	0.12
1978	595	601,442	0.10
1979	1,009	460,348	0.22
1980	846	530,639	0.16
1981	721	596,600	0.12
1982	569	594,131	0.10
1983	546	559,763	0.10
1984	442	543,903	0.08
1985	540	570,009	0.09
1986	564	601,708	0.09
1987	740	601,516	0.12
1988	611	643,025	0.10
1989	748	1,090,924	0.07
1990	963	1,536,483	0.06
1991	982	1,827,167	0.05
1992	809	973,977	0.08
1993	683	904,292	0.08
1994	507	804,416	0.06
1995	591	720,461	0.08
1996	797	915,900	0.09
Total 1971-96	15,394	17,987,584	0.09

Sources: *Statistical Yearbook of the Immigration and Naturalization Service*, 1980, Table 13; *Statistical Yearbook of the Immigration and Naturalization Service*, 1986, Table 3; *Statistical Yearbook of the Immigration and Naturalization Service*, 1996, Table 3.

by far the largest part of the population, remaining so after emancipation in 1838 and into the 20th century. In 1997, Dominica's estimated population of 70,000 was largely composed of their descendants.

Dominica is one of the Western Hemisphere's poorest countries, with an estimated average per capita income of a little more than $1,000 per year. Unemployment is high, health care is poor, and foreign debt and debt service have increased in recent years. Population, however, is not increasing, in part because emigrant outflow is relatively quite high. In absolute terms, immigration to the United States from Dominica is small, at a total of a little over 15,000 from 1971 to 1996. However, that 15,000 is a substantial proportion of the country's small population.

St. Lucia

In contrast to Dominica, the neighboring island nation of St. Lucia has experienced considerable population pressure in the past three decades. Its annual growth rate in some years has been as high as 2 percent and its infant mortality rate has been falling, factors which together guarantee sharp increases in population. In addition, St. Lucia's unemployment rate has for long periods topped 20 percent—despite substantial progress in turning its declining sugar-based agriculture toward far more successful banana and coconut production, plus declining inflation rates, a growing tourist industry, and considerable building of infrastructure.

One major result has been immigration to other countries in the region and to the United States. Almost 15,000 documented immigrants from St. Lucia arrived in the United States from 1971 to 1996. That is a very substantial outflow of emigrants for a country that had an estimated population of only 150,000 in 1997.

St. Lucia was settled by the French in 1660, after earlier French and English invasion attempts had been fought off by the island's Native American inhabitants, the Caribs. It then became part of the worldwide British-French imperial contest of the time, finally falling to the British in 1815. During the colonial period, it became a sugar and banana producer, as did most

of the Caribbean island nations, importing black African slaves whose descendants today constitute more than 90 percent of the country's population. It is one of the poorest countries in the Western Hemisphere, with a per capita annual income of only a little more than $1,000. It became an independent nation in 1979.

St. Vincent and the Grenadines

The small Caribbean nation of St. Vincent and the Grenadines consists of the main island of St. Vincent and a series of small islands stretching south toward Grenada. The part of the small island chain closest to St. Vincent is named the Grenadines; the rest are part of Grenada.

The country is situated in a highly volcanic area, and major damage was done by several earthquakes in the 1970s. In economic and migration terms, however, the main factor has been a high birth rate. The very modest agricultural economy of the islands has been unable to support the rapidly rising population, even though its staples—bananas, arrowroot, and coconuts—have been fairly stable during the late 20th century. However, the island continues to be one of the poorest countries in the Western Hemisphere, with an average per capita income of less than $1,000 per year. Although tourism has grown considerably in recent decades, it has not been enough to offset population pressure and international pressure on exports.

The net result has been a relatively high rate of emigration. Most emigrants went to Britain until that country passed its restrictive immigration law in 1962. From then on most emigrated to the United States. From 1971 to 1996, a total of almost 16,000 immigrants arrived from St. Vincent and the Grenadines, a substantial number considering that the country's estimated population was only 116,000 in 1997.

St. Vincent was settled by the English in the 1660s. Until then, the Native American inhabitants, the Caribs, had successfully resisted European invasion. The island immediately became part of the long French-British contest in the region, itself

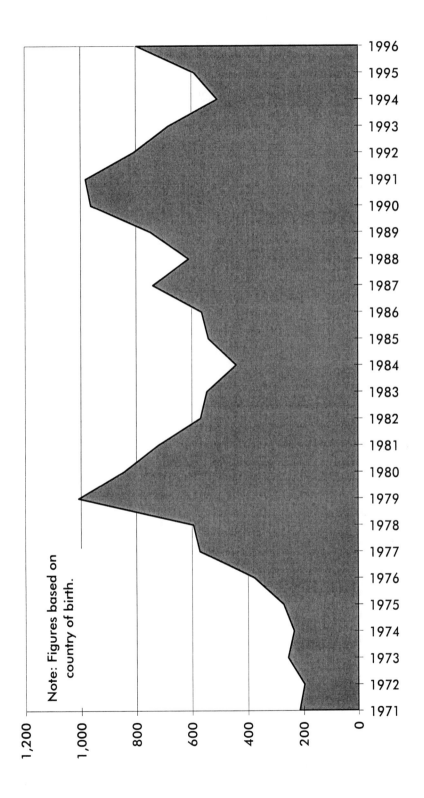

Graph 5.30: Number of Immigrants from Dominica Annually, 1971–1996

Note: Figures based on country of birth.

Table 5.19: Number and Percentage of Immigrants from St. Lucia in Total U.S. Immigration Annually, 1971–1996

Year	Number of Immigrants from St. Lucia	Total U.S. Immigration	Percentage of Immigrants from St. Lucia in Total U.S. Immigration
1971	242	370,473	0.07
1972	238	384,685	0.06
1973	264	400,063	0.07
1974	283	394,861	0.07
1975	278	396,194	0.07
1976	379	502,289	0.08
1977	545	462,315	0.12
1978	572	601,442	0.10
1979	953	460,348	0.21
1980	1,193	530,639	0.22
1981	733	596,600	0.12
1982	586	594,131	0.10
1983	662	559,763	0.12
1984	484	543,903	0.09
1985	499	570,009	0.09
1986	502	601,708	0.08
1987	496	601,516	0.08
1988	606	643,025	0.09
1989	709	1,090,924	0.06
1990	833	1,536,483	0.05
1991	766	1,827,167	0.04
1992	654	973,977	0.07
1993	634	904,292	0.07
1994	449	804,416	0.06
1995	403	720,461	0.06
1996	582	915,900	0.06
Total 1971-96	14,545	17,987,584	0.08

Sources: *Statistical Yearbook of the Immigration and Naturalization Service,* 1980, Table 13; *Statistical Yearbook of the Immigration and Naturalization Service,* 1986, Table 3; *Statistical Yearbook of the Immigration and Naturalization Service,* 1996, Table 3.

part of the worldwide European imperial wars of the period. St. Vincent finally fell to Britain in 1783. During the colonial period, it became one of several sugar plantation-based Caribbean economies, importing tens of thousands of black African slaves. Their descendants constitute the main population of the island. St. Vincent and the Grenadines became an independent nation in 1979.

Grenada

Grenada is the southernmost of the four Windward Island nations. The island was taken by the French in the early 1650s, ending the resistance of the Native American Caribs to the invading Europeans. It then became part of the long worldwide European imperial contests of the period, ultimately falling to Britain in 1783. During the colonial period, its economy was based largely on sugar production and its plantations worked by tens of thousands of imported black African slaves. Their descendants today constitute the overwhelming majority of the island nation's population. Although the Grenadian economy moved away from its dependence on sugar during the late 20th century, and toward other agricultural products and tourism, Grenada remains a very poor country, its per capita annual income in the $1,100 range.

Grenada became an independent country in 1974. In 1983, it was the scene of a major international incident, when invad-

Table 5.20: Number and Percentage of Immigrants from St. Vincent and Grenadines in Total U.S. Immigration Annually, 1971–1996

Year	Number of Immigrants from St. Vincent and Grenadines	Total U.S. Immigration	Percentage of Immigrants from St. Vincent and Grenadines in Total U.S. Immigration
1971	294	370,473	0.08
1972	294	384,685	0.08
1973	347	400,063	0.09
1974	332	394,861	0.08
1975	346	396,194	0.09
1976	456	502,289	0.09
1977	585	462,315	0.13
1978	679	601,442	0.11
1979	639	460,348	0.14
1980	763	530,639	0.14
1981	799	596,600	0.13
1982	719	594,131	0.12
1983	767	559,763	0.14
1984	695	543,903	0.13
1985	693	570,009	0.12
1986	635	601,708	0.11
1987	746	601,516	0.12
1988	634	643,025	0.10
1989	892	1,090,924	0.08
1990	973	1,536,483	0.06
1991	808	1,827,167	0.04
1992	687	973,977	0.07
1993	657	904,292	0.07
1994	524	804,416	0.07
1995	349	720,461	0.05
1996	606	915,900	0.07
Total 1971-96	15,919	17,987,584	0.09

Sources: *Statistical Yearbook of the Immigration and Naturalization Service*, 1980, Table 13; *Statistical Yearbook of the Immigration and Naturalization Service*, 1986, Table 3; *Statistical Yearbook of the Immigration and Naturalization Service*, 1996, Table 3.

Table 5.21: Number and Percentage of Immigrants from Grenada in Total U.S. Immigration Annually, 1971–1996

Year	Number of Immigrants from Grenada	Total U.S. Immigration	Percentage of Immigrants from Grenada in Total U.S. Immigration
1971	361	370,473	0.10
1972	332	384,685	0.09
1973	420	400,063	0.10
1974	707	394,861	0.18
1975	568	396,194	0.14
1976	787	502,289	0.16
1977	1,240	462,315	0.27
1978	1,206	601,442	0.20
1979	946	460,348	0.21
1980	1,198	530,639	0.23
1981	1,120	596,600	0.19
1982	1,066	594,131	0.18
1983	1,154	559,763	0.21
1984	980	543,903	0.18
1985	934	570,009	0.16
1986	1,045	601,708	0.17
1987	1,098	601,516	0.18
1988	842	643,025	0.13
1989	1,046	1,090,924	0.10
1990	1,294	1,536,483	0.08
1991	979	1,827,167	0.05
1992	848	973,977	0.09
1993	827	904,292	0.09
1994	595	804,416	0.07
1995	583	720,461	0.08
1996	787	915,900	0.09
Total 1971-96	22,963	17,987,584	0.13

Sources: *Statistical Yearbook of the Immigration and Naturalization Service*, 1980, Table 13; *Statistical Yearbook of the Immigration and Naturalization Service*, 1986, Table 3; *Statistical Yearbook of the Immigration and Naturalization Service*, 1996, Table 3.

ing U.S. forces quickly took the island, halting construction of a Cuban base and toppling the government.

The estimated population of Grenada in 1997 was 99,000, and that population would have been rising fast if not for the country's emigrant outflow. Grenada's high birth rate, falling infant mortality rate, weak economy, and widespread unemployment (sometimes in the 40-percent range) have for decades constituted a recipe for heavy emigration. Until Britain's restrictive 1962 immigration law, most emigrants from Grenada went to Britain, with some going to other Commonwealth countries and some to the United States.

After 1962, the United States became the most common destination. From 1971 to 1996, almost 23,000 documented Grenadian immigrants entered the United States. The steady flow of immigrants was small in comparison to that from many other countries, but very large as a proportion of Grenada's population.

For resources, see "General Immigration Resources for the Americas" on p. 632.

National Park Service, Augustus F. Sherman Collection

Many of the modern immigrants from the Caribbean are descendants of people brought from Africa as slaves, such as these women from the islands at Ellis Island in 1911.

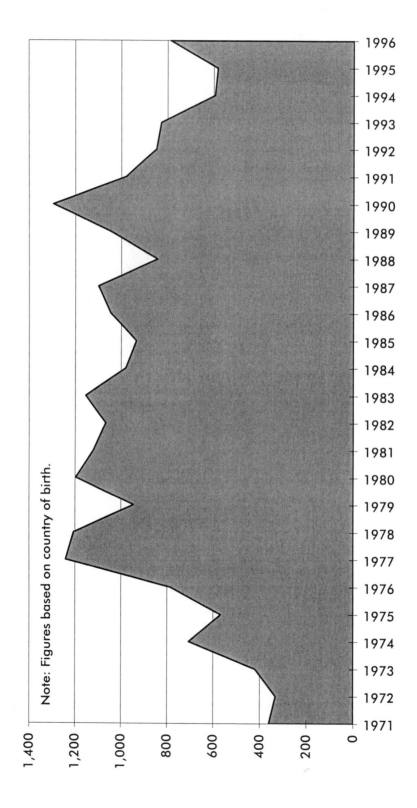

Graph 5.31: Number of Immigrants from Grenada Annually, 1971–1996

Note: Figures based on country of birth.

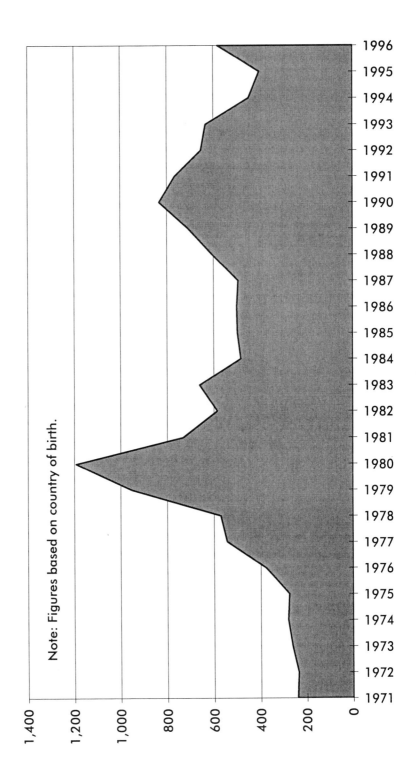

Graph 5.32: Number of Immigrants from St. Lucia Annually, 1971–1996

Note: Figures based on country of birth.

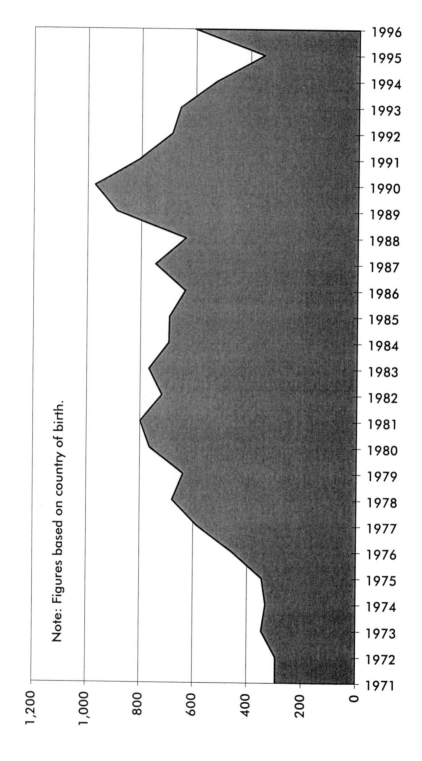

Graph 5.33: Number of Immigrants from St. Vincent and Grenadines Annually, 1971–1996

Note: Figures based on country of birth.

Immigrants from El Salvador

El Salvador is a small, poor Central American country that has experienced great population pressure because of a high rate of population growth. It is also a country that from 1979 to 1992 experienced an extraordinarily damaging civil war, from which it has by no means yet recovered.

El Salvador's estimated population in 1950 was 1,859,000; by 1998, it had grown to 5,752,000, an increase of 309 percent in only 38 years. Forward estimates indicate that the country's population should double every 25 years. However, El Salvador's resources are severely limited. The country's mainly agricultural economy is organized in favor of large landholders, who cultivate coffee, cotton, and sugar, all profitable export crops, on their acreage. The great mass of El Salvador's people own no land and work as seasonal agricultural laborers for those who do. The cash crops are very sensitive to swings in world commodity prices, which can turn profit to loss at any time and are far beyond the control of either El Salvador's landholders or its government. In any such downturn, the poor suffer greatly.

Even before the civil war, hundreds of thousands of Salvadorans had emigrated to neighboring countries. However, large numbers were not yet going to the United States. Salvadoran immigration to the United States was in the 2,000-per-year range from 1971 to 1975, building into the 5,000-per-year range at the end of the decade.

Then in 1979 the long-simmering left-right civil war in El Salvador erupted. During the 1980s it grew into a protracted guerrilla insurgency, with the guerrillas receiving some military aid from Nicaragua and the Salvadoran army receiving massive military assistance from the United States. It soon became an exceedingly "dirty" war, with army-supported death squads developing a reign of terror throughout the country, in which they murdered tens of thousands of Salvadorans and triggered the flight of an estimated 600,000 to 750,000 people to other countries. That flight continued after the war, as Salvadorans unable to find work in

Table 5.22: Number and Percentage of Immigrants from El Salvador in Total U.S. Immigration by Decade, 1932–1996

Decade	Number of Immigrants from El Salvador	Total U.S. Immigrants	Percentage of Immigrants from El Salvador in Total U.S. Immigration
1932-40	673	528,431	0.13
1941-50	5,132	1,035,039	0.50
1951-60	5,895	2,515,479	0.23
1961-70	14,992	3,321,677	0.45
1971-80	34,436	4,493,314	0.77
1981-90	213,539	7,338,062	2.91
1991-96	146,980	6,146,213	2.39
Total 1932-1996	421,647	63,140,227	0.67

Note: Data not recorded separately until 1932.

Source: Adapted from Table 2, Immigration by Region and Selected Country of Last Residence, Fiscal Year 1820–1996, from the *Statistical Yearbook of the Immigration and Naturalization Service*, 1996.

their largely destroyed economy emigrated to other countries, most notably to the United States.

The mass flight of refugees out of El Salvador was stimulated by the knowledge that the death squads were not in the early years stopped or slowed by the Salvadoran army or government. Any deterrence came only much later, after widespread international protests had developed. Some of those murdered were highly visible religious figures, attracting much attention in this largely Catholic country. Early death squad victims included Catholic archbishop Oscar Arnulfo Romero and seven Americans, including three nuns. Among the tens of thousands of later victims were six Jesuit priests, murdered by a uniformed death squad.

An estimated 500,000 Salvadorans entered the United States during and immediately after the civil war, most of them as undocumented illegal immigrants who made their way north through Mexico and then across the United States border. Along with the Guatemalan and Nicaraguan refugees of that time, they were clas-

sified by the U.S. government as "economic," rather than "political" refugees, and were not granted asylum.

Their classification was disputed by substantial numbers of Americans, who responded by organizing the "asylum movement," sheltering and protecting the refugees in what amounted to a latter-day version of the Underground Railroad that had brought southern black slaves to freedom before and during the American Civil War. A 1986 immigration amnesty act gave relief to a limited number of Central American refugees, while a 1990 federal court decision forced the U.S. government to adopt a somewhat less rigid standard for those seeking asylum. A 1991 federal law also allowed some refugees to live and work in the United States for several years. However, most of the Salvadoran "illegals" continued to be illegal immigrants under U.S. law (see "Appendix C: Estimates of Emigration and Illegals" on p. 749).

U.S. immigration figures show that more than 396,000 Salvadoran immigrants entered the United States from 1971 to 1996. In 1980, estimates indicated that

Graph 5.34: Percentage of Immigrants from El Salvador in Total U.S. Immigration by Decade, 1932–1996

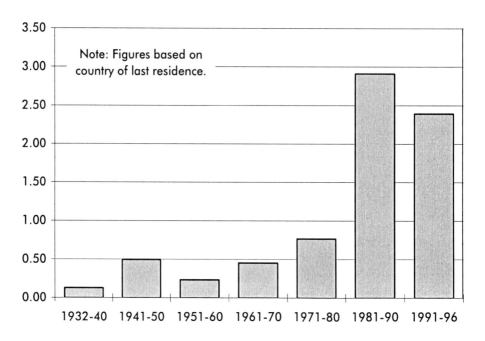

Note: Figures based on country of last residence.

more than 94,000 Salvadorans were living in the United States. That number had grown to 465,000 in 1990. The number of undocumented Salvadorans estimated to be living illegally in the United States in 1996 was still a very high 335,000. Taken together, the statistics indicated that a huge immigration to the United States had taken place and was still occurring, spurred by the size of El Salvador's population.

After their arrival in the United States, Salvadorans tended to develop tightly knit, largely closed communities, mainly in and around major cities, most notably Los Angeles and New York. That is the normal tendency in most new immigrant groups, but for Salvadorans it has also been a matter of safety, because so many are either themselves "illegals" or feel that they must protect family members, friends, and others in the community who are "illegals."

On the employment side, most Salvadorans of the first U.S. generation work in low-paying jobs, requiring little previous training. Those who are "illegals" try to find jobs in which their lack of essential documents will not expose them. All too often, that has also meant accepting very low-paying, substandard jobs in which they have been exploited by unscrupulous employers.

Graph 5.35: Number of Immigrants from El Salvador by Decade, 1932–1996

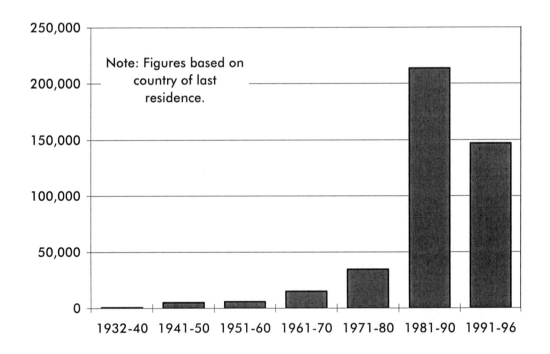

Note: Figures based on country of last residence.

Table 5.23: Number and Percentage of Immigrants from El Salvador in Total U.S. Immigration Annually, 1971–1996

Year	Number of Immigrants from El Salvador	Immigration	Percentage of Immigrants from El Salvador in Total U.S. Immigration
1971	1,776	370,473	0.48
1972	2,001	384,685	0.52
1973	2,042	400,063	0.51
1974	2,278	394,861	0.58
1975	2,416	396,194	0.61
1976	3,022	502,289	0.60
1977	4,426	462,315	0.96
1978	5,826	601,442	0.97
1979	4,479	460,348	0.97
1980	6,101	530,639	1.15
1981	8,210	596,600	1.38
1982	7,107	594,131	1.20
1983	8,596	559,763	1.54
1984	8,787	543,903	1.62
1985	10,156	570,009	1.78
1986	10,929	601,708	1.82
1987	10,693	601,516	1.78
1988	12,045	643,025	1.87
1989	57,878	1,090,924	5.31
1990	80,173	1,536,483	5.22
1991	47,351	1,827,167	2.59
1992	26,191	973,977	2.69
1993	26,818	904,292	2.97
1994	17,644	804,416	2.19
1995	11,744	720,461	1.63
1996	17,903	915,900	1.95
Total 1971-96	396,592	17,987,584	2.20

Sources: *Statistical Yearbook of the Immigration and Naturalization Service*, 1980, Table 13; *Statistical Yearbook of the Immigration and Naturalization Service*, 1986, Table 3; *Statistical Yearbook of the Immigration and Naturalization Service*, 1996, Table 3.

Resources

El Salvador: A Country Study. 2d ed. Richard A. Haggerty, ed. Washington, D.C.: Federal Research Division, Library of Congress, 1990. (Available on-line at *http://lcweb2.loc.gov/frd/cs*)

For more resources, see "Introduction" on p. 482.

Immigrants from Guatemala

Guatemala was a Spanish colony from 1523 until 1821, when Mexico and most of Central America broke away from Spain. It became an independent country in 1839, when it left the dissolving United Provinces of Central America. Independent Guatemala, a largely agricultural country through the century and a half that followed, then developed under a long succession of military-backed governments.

As European and United States commercial interests penetrated the country late in the 19th century, ownership of its producing land became concentrated in the hands of large landowners working with foreign companies to create export crops. Coffee cultivated largely by exploited Mayan laborers became the country's main cash crop. Dominated by United States companies and a de facto U.S. protectorate, Guatemala also encouraged British, French, and German commercial interests. However, at the outbreak of World War II the United States forced the Germans out and strengthened its own hold on the country.

Political Changes

A major shift occurred after World War II. From 1945 to 1950, liberal president Juan José Arévalo, a social democrat elected with an 85 percent majority, introduced substantial changes that in sum created a Guatemalan equivalent of the New Deal. This was a compound of social reform, moves toward equality for the Mayans, and resistance to United States commercial domination. In 1950, he was succeeded by the far more Marxist-oriented Jacobo Arbenz Guzmán, who won 65 percent of the vote and then proceeded to introduce a major land reform law that, in net effect, confiscated the estates of Guatemala's large landowners and redistributed the land to the rural poor. Arbenz also sharply attacked foreign commercial interests, legalized the Communist Party, and removed several Supreme Court judges.

In 1954, the United States responded by backing a right-wing military takeover of the Guatemalan government, which installed Carlos Castillo Armas as the head of a military-controlled government. Guatemala's increasingly difficult problems have been greatly intensified during the final half of the 20th century by the 41-year-long guerrilla insurrection that began after the overthrow of the Arbenz government.

Castillo's new government instituted harshly repressive military rule (1954–1995), which destroyed much of the nation's economy and brought massive internal migration, runaway inflation, and unemployment that ran as high as 50 to 60 percent in the 1990s. Hundreds of thousands fled to neighboring countries and north through Mexico to the United States, many as undocumented, illegal immigrants. Although peace finally came in 1995, it was a very fragile peace, for none of Guatemala's underlying problems had been solved, and most had not yet even been seriously addressed.

Beneath Guatemala's worsening economic problems, the population continued to grow at a rate estimated to bring about a doubling of the country's already unsustainable population every 24 to 25 years. The estimated population of Guatemala in 1950 was 2.8 million. In 1998, the country's estimated population had grown to 10.8 million, an increase in only 48 years of 386 percent. Much of that enormous increase has come from a reduction in infant mortality and other improvements in public health, accompanied by continuing high birth rates.

Modern Immigration

Substantial Guatemalan immigration into the United States unfolded during the 1970s, partly as a result of the continuing guerrilla war at home. That was accompanied by a government-sponsored reign of terror, especially in the rural highlands where most of the country's Mayan population lived. Many of these Guatemalan immigrants walked over the Mexican border and later came across the U.S. border as undocumented "illegals." Recorded Guatemalan immigration, however, continued to be modest, reaching 4,000 a year only in 1983. The real picture was best expressed by U.S. government estimates of the numbers of Guatemalan-born immigrants living in the United States, which had reached 63,000 in 1980, including "legals" and "illegals."

The 1980s presented a far different picture, for by 1990 the U.S. estimate of the Guatemalan-born population living in the United States was 226,000, reflecting the real size of the combined legal and illegal Guatamalan immigration, which continued to be high. By 1996, an estimated 165,000 Guatemalan "illegals" were living in the United States, although legal immigration figures were down (see "Appendix C: Estimates of Emigration and Illegals" on p. 749).

Large numbers of "illegal" Guatemalans and Salvadorans fleeing civil wars in their homelands to the United States were not accorded political refugee status by the U.S. government, and therefore were not granted legal asylum. A loose coalition of church and other social justice organiza-tions in the United States responded during the 1970s and 1980s by forming the Sanctuary movement, which provided (literally) sanctuary to many who might otherwise have been found and deported, often to death or imprisonment.

Whether legal or illegal, Guatemalans in the United States tended to form the same kinds of close-knit immigrant communities that have characterized scores of other immigrant groups. Most occupied low-paying jobs; that was particularly so for undocumented immigrants, who were often exploited. They also could not get insurance, legally own cars, or do many other things taken for granted by most Americans. Many were able to become "legal" by the terms of 1980s and 1990s immigration legislation, though many arrived too late to benefit from the legalization acts, their status still awaiting normalization. The largest number of Guatemalans settled in California and the Southwest, although substantial Guatemalan communities also developed in New York and other East Coast cities.

Table 5.24: Number and Percentage of Immigrants from Guatemala in Total U.S. Immigration Annually, 1971–1996

Year	Number of Immigrants from Guatemala	Total U.S. Immigration	Percentage of Immigrants from Guatemala in Total U.S. Immigration
1971	2,194	370,473	0.59
1972	1,640	384,685	0.43
1973	1,759	400,063	0.44
1974	1,638	394,861	0.41
1975	1,859	396,194	0.47
1976	2,555	502,289	0.51
1977	3,599	462,315	0.78
1978	3,996	601,442	0.66
1979	2,583	460,348	0.56
1980	3,751	530,639	0.71
1981	3,928	596,600	0.66
1982	3,633	594,131	0.61
1983	4,090	559,763	0.73
1984	3,937	543,903	0.72
1985	4,389	570,009	0.77
1986	5,158	601,708	0.86
1987	5,729	601,516	0.95
1988	5,723	643,025	0.89
1989	19,049	1,090,924	1.75
1990	32,303	1,536,483	2.10
1991	25,527	1,827,167	1.40
1992	10,521	973,977	1.08
1993	11,870	904,292	1.31
1994	7,389	804,416	0.92
1995	6,213	720,461	0.86
1996	8,763	915,900	0.96
Total 1971-1996	183,796	17,987,584	1.02

Sources: *Statistical Yearbook of the Immigration and Naturalization Service*, 1980, Table 13; *Statistical Yearbook of the Immigration and Naturalization Service*, 1986, Table 3; *Statistical Yearbook of the Immigration and Naturalization Service*, 1996, Table 3.

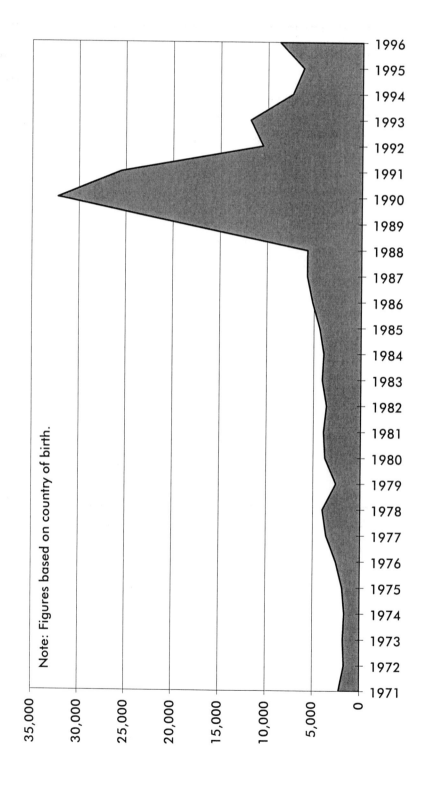

Graph 5.36: Number of Immigrants from Guatemala Annually, 1971–1996

Note: Figures based on country of birth.

Resources

Guatemala: A Country Study. 2d ed. Richard R. Nyrop, ed. Washington, D.C.: Federal Research Division, Library of Congress, 1984.

Hadden, Gerry, comp. *Teenage Refugees from Guatemala Speak Out*. New York: Rosen, 1997.

Kohpahl, Gabriele. *Voices of Guatemalan Women in Los Angeles: Understanding Their Immigration*. New York: Garland, 1998.

Malone, Michael. *A Guatemalan Family*. Minneapolis: Lerner, 1996.

For more resources, see "Introduction" on p. 482.

Immigrants from Guyana

Until 1966 the colony of British Guiana, Guyana is a small country on the northeast coast of South America, with a population estimated at 853,000 in 1997. Its population is highly literate, in the 95 percent to 97 percent range, and its people unusually diverse in ethnic terms, reflecting its rather complex history. It is not a country suffering from massive, uncontrollable population pressure, or from a huge and unstoppable country-to-city internal migration. Even so, it is a country with a relatively enormous emigrant outflow, perhaps half of it to the United States and the rest largely to other English-speaking countries.

The first Europeans to invade Guyana were the Dutch, in 1616, who then proceeded to develop a largely agricultural colony based on the exploitation of black African slaves. As in the North American New Netherlands colony, few Dutch settlers came, and by the mid-1700s the Dutch were welcoming British settlers. Ultimately, in 1796, Britain took the several Dutch colonies in the area, which formally became British territories in 1814 and were then joined to become British Guiana.

A major change came in 1838, when slavery was abolished by Britain. The Afro-Guyanese former slaves left the British-owned sugarcane plantations that had until then been the basis of Guyanese economic life. To take their places, the British imported Portuguese and then Chinese indentured plantation laborers. The effort had little long-term success, as both groups tended to work off their indentures and then leave the plantations to pursue other occupations. The major source of indentured sugar plantation laborers then became India, from which the British imported an estimated 240,000 laborers between the late 1830s and the early 1920s. The resulting Guyanese ethnic mix had by the late 20th century created a multiethnic, multireligious community that included Afro-Guyanese and Indo-Guyanese totaling approximately 92 percent to 94 percent of the population, with the Indo-Guyanese outnumbering the Afro-Guyanese, along with much smaller numbers of Portuguese, Chinese, and Native American–Guyanese.

Unfortunately, Guyana's economy did not develop well after it achieved independence in 1966. High commodity prices buoyed its largely agricultural economy in the late 1960s, but worldwide declines in commodity prices during the 1970s hit Guyana hard. Even more important, Guyana's new Socialist government introduced a top-down, highly centralized planned economy, rather than a market economy. As in many other Socialist countries, this did not work very well, resulting in the development of a large illegal market, coupled with hefty foreign debts, very high real inflation rates, and widespread unemployment.

Despite what might have been very favorable population and literacy factors, Guyana in the 1970s sank into a seemingly permanent economic depression. As a direct result, very large numbers of Guyanese emigrated, most of them to the United States. That migration was continuing in the mid-1990s, with no solutions yet in sight, although moves toward a market economy had started in the mid-1980s.

From 1971 to 1996, almost 197,000 Guyanese immigrants entered the United States, their numbers rising steadily during the 1970s and then leveling off into the range of 9,000 to 10,000 per year during the 1980s and 1990s. Many were highly skilled professionals, managers, civil servants, and white-collar workers, whose absence was a great loss to Guyana. On the other hand, the money they sent home to Guyana became a major positive factor in the country's economic life.

For resources, see "Introduction" on p. 482.

Table 5.25: Number and Percentage of Immigrants from Guyana in Total U.S. Immigration Annually, 1971–1996

Year	Number of Immigrants from Guatemala	Total U.S. Immigration	Percentage of Immigrants from Guatemala in Total U.S. Immigration
1971	2,194	370,473	0.59
1972	1,640	384,685	0.43
1973	1,759	400,063	0.44
1974	1,638	394,861	0.41
1975	1,859	396,194	0.47
1976	2,555	502,289	0.51
1977	3,599	462,315	0.78
1978	3,996	601,442	0.66
1979	2,583	460,348	0.56
1980	3,751	530,639	0.71
1981	3,928	596,600	0.66
1982	3,633	594,131	0.61
1983	4,090	559,763	0.73
1984	3,937	543,903	0.72
1985	4,389	570,009	0.77
1986	5,158	601,708	0.86
1987	5,729	601,516	0.95
1988	5,723	643,025	0.89
1989	19,049	1,090,924	1.75
1990	32,303	1,536,483	2.10
1991	25,527	1,827,167	1.40
1992	10,521	973,977	1.08
1993	11,870	904,292	1.31
1994	7,389	804,416	0.92
1995	6,213	720,461	0.86
1996	8,763	915,900	0.96
Total 1971-1996	183,796	17,987,584	1.02

Sources: *Statistical Yearbook of the Immigration and Naturalization Service*, 1980, Table 13; *Statistical Yearbook of the Immigration and Naturalization Service*, 1986, Table 3; *Statistical Yearbook of the Immigration and Naturalization Service*, 1996, Table 3.

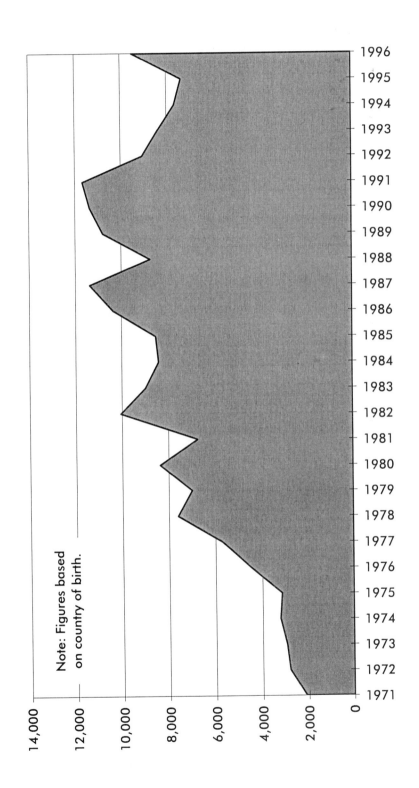

Graph 5.37: Number of Immigrants from Guyana Annually, 1971–1996

Note: Figures based on country of birth.

Immigrants from Nicaragua

Nicaragua became a Spanish colony in 1522, and for almost three centuries developed largely as a backwater area within Spain's American colonial empire. In most periods, it was in fact governed out of Guatemala, itself a none-too-important Spanish Central American colony. In 1821, Nicaragua declared itself independent of Spain. There followed a period in which Mexico attempted to control Central America and several Central American states joined together to assert their full independence as the United Provinces of Central America.

In 1838, Nicaragua emerged as a fully independent nation, entering upon its own turbulent, unstable history. This was punctuated by civil wars and continuing armed intervention by competing great powers, who long saw the country as the

logical site for an Atlantic-to-Pacific canal, a dream finally realized elsewhere with the building of the Panama Canal.

From 1855 to 1857, Nicaragua was seized by the forces of United States adventurer William Walker, who was ultimately defeated and expelled. Thirty years of peace and some growth followed, with booms in coffee and banana exports fueling growth—although the benefits of that growth were reaped largely by foreign commercial interests and their local representatives.

Nicaragua remained a poor and rural country, the largest and least populated of the Central American states. Peace ended with the accession to power of General José Santos Zelaya, who ruled from 1893 to 1910. He publicly resisted but at the same time cooperated with the United States commercial interests that were turning the

Table 5.26: Number and Percentage of Immigrants from Nicaragua in Total U.S. Immigration Annually, 1971–1996

Year	Number of Immigrants from Nicaragua	Total U.S. Immigration	Percentage of Immigrants from Nicaragua in Total U.S. Immigration
1971	566	370,473	0.15
1972	606	384,685	0.16
1973	670	400,063	0.17
1974	942	394,861	0.24
1975	947	396,194	0.24
1976	1,260	502,289	0.25
1977	1,850	462,315	0.40
1978	1,888	601,442	0.31
1979	1,938	460,348	0.42
1980	2,337	530,639	0.44
1981	2,752	596,600	0.46
1982	3,077	594,131	0.52
1983	2,983	559,763	0.53
1984	2,718	543,903	0.50
1985	2,786	570,009	0.49
1986	2,826	601,708	0.47
1987	3,294	601,516	0.55
1988	3,311	643,025	0.51
1989	8,830	1,090,924	0.81
1990	11,562	1,536,483	0.75
1991	17,842	1,827,167	0.98
1992	8,949	973,977	0.92
1993	7,086	904,292	0.78
1994	5,255	804,416	0.65
1995	4,408	720,461	0.61
1996	6,903	915,900	0.75
Total 1971-96	107,586	17,987,584	0.60

Sources: *Statistical Yearbook of the Immigration and Naturalization Service*, 1980, Table 13; *Statistical Yearbook of the Immigration and Naturalization Service*, 1986, Table 3; *Statistical Yearbook of the Immigration and Naturalization Service*, 1996, Table 3.

country into a de facto U.S. protectorate. Civil war broke out in 1903 and again in 1909.

In 1909, the United States intervened, sending troops to Nicaragua and forcing Zelaya from power. Nicaragua became more openly a U.S. protectorate, with U.S. forces stationed in the country from 1912 to 1938. During the latter years of this period, U.S.-backed general Anastasio Somoza García took power as dictator, ruling until he was assassinated in 1956. Other members of his family succeeded him, the last Somoza dictator being his son, U.S.-backed Anastasio Somoza Debayle. He ruled until 1979, when he was forced to flee the country, after he lost United States backing and his corrupt government and army proved unable to withstand pressure from his revolutionary opponents, the Sandinistas. Originally a small Cuba-backed guerrilla group, the Sandinistas had started their armed insurrection in 1961.

The Sandinistas took power in 1979, but themselves quickly became embroiled in a long civil war (1980–1988). The Marxist-oriented and increasingly dictatorial Sandinista government, which was backed by Cuba and the Soviet Union, was opposed by United States–backed rebels, many of them former Sandinistas, known as the Contras. U.S. aid to the Contras was largely covert, because of domestic American sentiment against the war. Finally, the explosive Iran-Contra scandal (1986–1988) ended U.S. involvement, and the war itself. Peace was followed by the free elections of 1989, and the emergence of a free Nicaragua, initially led by former Sandinista leader Violeta Barrios de Chamorro.

Until the second half of the 20th century, Nicaragua had survived all. Its largely agricultural economy was based on the export earnings generated by coffee, by far its largest commodity, and by cotton and other agricultural products. In the 1950s, however, its population growth began to accelerate, as birth rates continued high while infant mortality and other causes of death dropped, a set of factors common to many developing nations. In addition, and again as in so many other nations, internal migration from country to city accelerated, with its almost inevitable social and practical costs.

On top of all this, Somoza government corruption, declining commodity prices, and high rates of inflation put additional pressures on the Nicaraguan economy. Despite all that, as well as the devastating effects of the long civil war, the Nicaraguan population increased by an estimate of more than 370 percent between 1965 and 1997, a period of only 37 years.

Inevitably, immigration to the United States grew, some of it legal, but most of it illegal. Recorded immigration to the United States from Nicaragua averaged approximately 2,000 a year from 1971 to 1988. It jumped to 9,000 a year in the three years following the civil war (1988–1991), and then dropped to fewer than 5,000 a year into the mid-1990s. However, tens of thousands of undocumented Nicaraguans also arrived. In 1996, the U.S. government estimated that 70,000 undocumented Nicaraguans were in the United States (see "Appendix C: Estimates of Emigration and Illegals" on p. 749). Not all of these were in response to the civil war; Nicaragua's economy had not greatly improved since the end of the war, while its problems and population had multiplied.

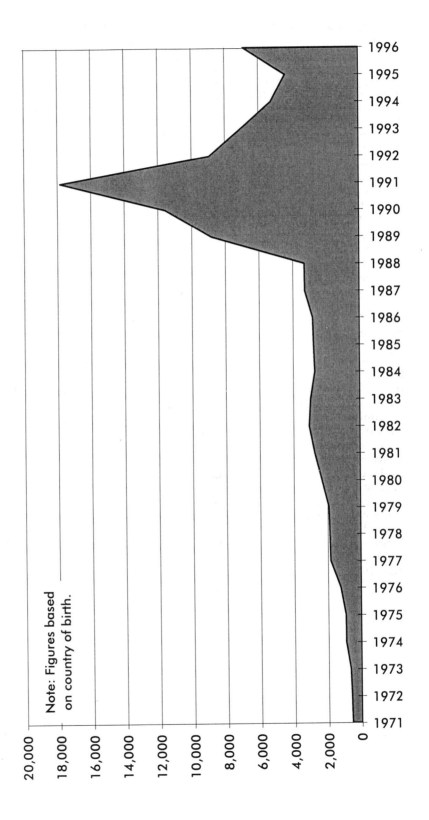

Graph 5.38: Number of Immigrants from Nicaragua Annually, 1971–1996

Note: Figures based on country of birth.

Resources

Nicaragua: A Country Study. 2d ed. James D. Rudolph, ed. Washington, D.C.: Federal Research Division, Library of Congress, 1982.

For more resources, see "Introduction" on p. 482.

Immigrants from Honduras

A Spanish colony from 1524, Honduras declared itself an independent country in 1821, when Mexico and several Central American states jointly declared themselves independent of Spain. Full working independence came in 1838, when Honduras left the United Provinces of Central America. Honduran political history then became a record of literally hundreds of armed conflicts, as rival factions fought to dominate what was then a lightly populated, very backward agricultural country, for long periods dominated by foreign commercial interests and governments. In the late 1990s, Honduras remained one of the poorest countries in the Western Hemisphere, with a very young, fast-growing, largely illiterate population and a host of major problems, old and new.

Foreign mining companies extracted much of Honduras's small silver and gold resources during the 19th century. United States interests largely achieved dominance late in the century, as Honduras began to become a de facto U.S. protectorate. By the second decade of the 20th century, that protectorate status was fully established, with United States banana companies and the U.S. military turning the country into a classic "banana republic," as such countries were disparagingly called. From 1912 to 1924, the U.S. government often threatened intervention, landing armed forces on several occasions. In 1924, U.S. forces ended a civil war, then essentially installed a new government.

From 1932 until the restoration of civilian rule in 1982, Honduras was dominated by a series of military-controlled governments, beginning with the long rule of General Tiburcio Carías Andino from 1933 to 1949. From the mid-1950s, Honduras was also drawn into a series of Central American wars. It became a U.S. base in the action that in 1954 toppled the government of Jacobo Arbenz in Guatemala, and then played a similar role during the civil wars in neighboring Nicaragua (1978–1988) and El Salvador (1979–1992).

Underneath all the wars, insurrections, and changes of government, the Honduran population grew. In 1926, the estimated population of the country was 700,000. In 1997, its estimated population was 6 million. That is an increase of 857 percent in only 71 years, and simply unsustainable. Nor was the enormous population increase uniform; as was so all over the world, it was accompanied by a flight of many of the rural poor to the increasingly nonworking cities. In Honduras, the population increase was somewhat accentuated by the immigration of as many as 400,000 refugees from neighboring countries because of civil wars as well as economic distress. Other continuing Honduran problems were commodity price declines, starting in the early 1970s, and a persistently high rate of inflation. Even foreign aid diminished sharply in the late 20th century, as international lending agencies imposed austerity budgets on impoverished debtor countries, worsening the plight of the poor in those countries.

One substantial result was a huge emigration out of Honduras to any country that might provide jobs, with money to live on and send back home. Essentially, that meant the United States. From 1971 to 1996, a total of almost 109,000 legally documented Honduran immigrants came to the United States. At least that number of undocumented immigrants, or "illegals," also came (see "Appendix C: Estimates of Emigration and Illegals" on p. 749). The U.S. government estimated that 90,000 undocumented Hondurans were living in the United States in 1996.

Table 5.27: Number and Percentage of Immigrants from Honduras in Total U.S. Immigration Annually, 1971–1996

Year	Number of Immigrants from Honduras	Total U.S. Immigration	Percentage of Immigrants from Honduras in Total U.S. Immigration
1971	1,146	370,473	0.31
1972	964	384,685	0.25
1973	1,330	400,063	0.33
1974	1,390	394,861	0.35
1975	1,357	396,194	0.34
1976	1,598	502,289	0.32
1977	1,626	462,315	0.35
1978	2,727	601,442	0.45
1979	2,545	460,348	0.55
1980	2,552	530,639	0.48
1981	2,358	596,600	0.40
1982	3,186	594,131	0.54
1983	3,619	559,763	0.65
1984	3,405	543,903	0.63
1985	3,726	570,009	0.65
1986	4,532	601,708	0.75
1987	4,751	601,516	0.79
1988	4,302	643,025	0.67
1989	7,593	1,090,924	0.70
1990	12,024	1,536,483	0.78
1991	11,451	1,827,167	0.63
1992	6,552	973,977	0.67
1993	7,306	904,292	0.81
1994	5,265	804,416	0.65
1995	5,496	720,461	0.76
1996	5,870	915,900	0.64
Total 1971-96	108,671	17,987,584	0.60

Sources: *Statistical Yearbook of the Immigration and Naturalization Service,* 1980, Table 13; *Statistical Yearbook of the Immigration and Naturalization Service,* 1986, Table 3; *Statistical Yearbook of the Immigration and Naturalization Service,* 1996, Table 3.

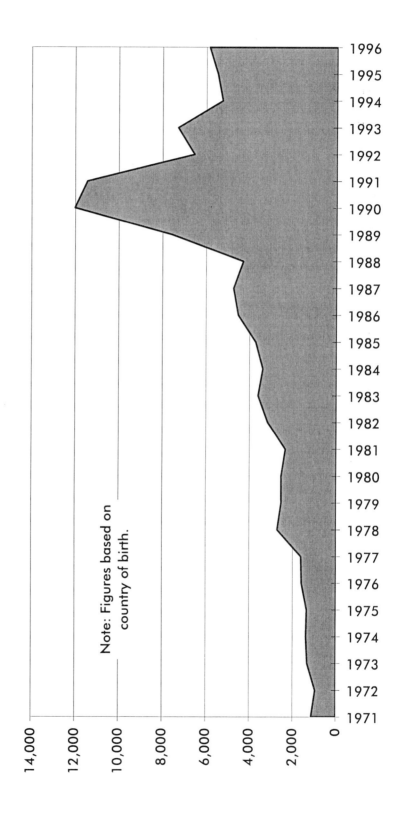

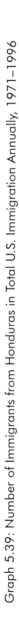

Graph 5.39: Number of Immigrants from Honduras in Total U.S. Immigration Annually, 1971–1996

Note: Figures based on country of birth.

Resources

Honduras: A Country Study. 3d ed. Tim L. Merrill, ed. Washington, D.C.: Federal Research Division, Library of Congress, 1995. (Available on-line at *http://lcweb2.loc.gov/frd/cs*)

For more resources, see "Introduction" on p. 482.

Immigrants from Belize

Formerly the colony of British Honduras, Belize became an independent nation and a member of the Commonwealth in 1981. It continued to have strong and formal ties to Britain, including a Belizean-born British governor-general and British defense guarantees.

Belize is a small nation on the Caribbean coast of the Yucatan peninsula, with a 1997 estimated population of only 229,000. First penetrated by Spanish invaders in the early 16th century, it was contested by England and Spain in the two centuries that followed, ultimately falling to England in the mid-1790s. It formally became a British colony in 1862.

For much of its early history, the country's economy was dependent on wood harvesting and export, most notably of mahogany and other high-quality woods, though its sugarcane plantations had become central by the mid-20th century. Therein lay a great problem, for sharply declining world sugar prices in the early 1980s brought depression to Belize's largely one-crop economy. As a result, relatively large numbers of emigrants left the country for the United States. Only 32,000 documented immigrants from Belize entered the United States from 1971 to 1996, but estimates indicate that at least an equal number of undocumented "illegals" also entered. Some estimates place the number of "illegals" as high as 60,000, though the reality is more likely a total 1971–1996 immigration of approximately 60,000 to 70,000, with more than half "illegals."

Graph 5.40: Number of Immigrants from Belize Annually, 1971–1996

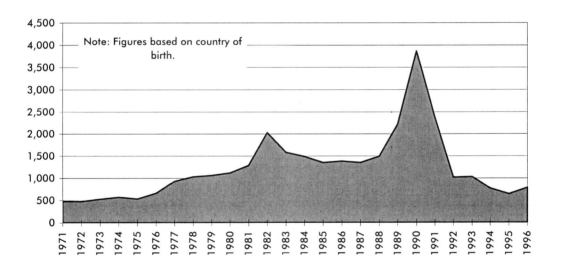

Table 5.28: Number and Percentage of Immigrants from Belize in Total U.S. Immigration Annually, 1971–1996

Year	Number of Immigrants from Belize	Total U.S. Immigration	Percentage of Immigrants from Belize in Total U.S. Immigration
1971	481	370,473	0.13
1972	475	384,685	0.12
1973	528	400,063	0.13
1974	573	394,861	0.15
1975	534	396,194	0.13
1976	661	502,289	0.13
1977	930	462,315	0.20
1978	1,033	601,442	0.17
1979	1,063	460,348	0.23
1980	1,120	530,639	0.21
1981	1,289	596,600	0.22
1982	2,031	594,131	0.34
1983	1,585	559,763	0.28
1984	1,492	543,903	0.27
1985	1,353	570,009	0.24
1986	1,385	601,708	0.23
1987	1,354	601,516	0.23
1988	1,497	643,025	0.23
1989	2,217	1,090,924	0.20
1990	3,867	1,536,483	0.25
1991	2,377	1,827,167	0.13
1992	1,020	973,977	0.10
1993	1,035	904,292	0.11
1994	772	804,416	0.10
1995	644	720,461	0.09
1996	786	915,900	0.09
Total 1971-1996	32,102	17,987,584	0.18

Sources: *Statistical Yearbook of the Immigration and Naturalization Service,* 1980, Table 13; *Statistical Yearbook of the Immigration and Naturalization Service,* 1986, Table 3; *Statistical Yearbook of the Immigration and Naturalization Service,* 1996, Table 3.

Resources

Guyana and Belize: Country Studies. 2d ed. Tim Merrill, ed. Washington, D.C.: Federal Research Division, Library of Congress, 1993. (Available online as single-country studies at *http://lcweb2.loc.gov/frd/cs*)

For more resources, see "Introduction" on p. 482.

Immigrants from Argentina

Argentina is the second-largest country in South America, with an estimated population of 36.1 million in 1998. Its birth rate is low, health care and life expectancy high, and rate of population growth a modest 1.5 percent in the mid-1990s. The country's economy is well able to sustain its people, and Argentina suffers from none of the massive population and economic pressures that plague so many other Central and South American countries. Therefore, no great population outflow has developed in the 20th century. Quite the opposite has been so: Argentina has been one of the leading destinations for immigrants from around the world.

On the other hand, the county has suffered from severe political instability since the fall of dictator Juan Domingo Perón (ruled 1946–1955), with a series of military takeovers of the government and a con-

tinuing low-level guerrilla insurgency. Perón returned to power from 1973 to 1974, died in office, and was succeeded by his wife, Isabel Perón, who ruled until overthrown by military coup in 1976. The Argentine military then embarked on a severely repressive course, the "dirty war" (1976–1982), in which tens of thousands of people were murdered by paramilitary "death squads." Some estimates of the numbers murdered ran as high as 40,000. Tens and perhaps hundreds of thousands of other Argentinians were forced to flee the country. Most went to neighboring countries, but some thousands went as far away as the United States.

The military government collapsed after Argentina's defeat by Britain in the Falklands War in 1982 and was replaced in 1983 by an elected civilian government, which proceeded to restore Argentinian democracy. During the 1980s and early 1990s, however, Argentina encountered substantial fiscal problems, among them runaway inflation and ballooning foreign debts. Those problems subsided after the introduction of rigorous austerity programs, but they cost a large number of jobs and brought major cuts in social programs.

Argentinian immigration to the United States has totaled 150,000 since 1932, when it first began to be separately tabulated. It has to a limited extent followed the swings in Argentina's political and economic stability. In the 1990s, it again became very small, averaging only a little over 3,000 per year, the lowest level since the 1950s.

Table 5.29: Number and Percentage of Immigrants from Argentina in Total U.S. Immigration by Decade, 1932–1996

Decade	Number of Immigrants from Argentina	Total U.S. Immigrants	Percentage of Immigrants from Argentina in Total U.S. Immigration
1932-1940	1,349	528,431	0.26
1941-1950	3,338	1,035,039	0.32
1951-1960	19,486	2,515,479	0.77
1961-1970	49,721	3,321,677	1.50
1971-1980	29,897	4,493,314	0.67
1981-1990	27,327	7,338,062	0.37
1991-1996	18,877	6,146,213	0.31
Total 1820-1996	149,995	63,140,227	0.24

Source: Adapted from Table 2, Immigration by Region and Selected Country of Last Residence, Fiscal Years 1820–1996, from the *Statistical Yearbook of the Immigration and Naturalization Service*, 1996.

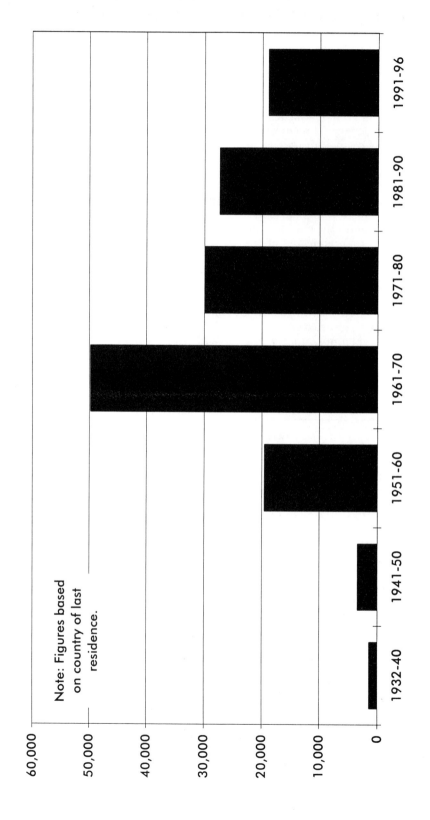

Graph 5.41: Number of Immigrants from Argentina by Decade, 1932–1996

Note: Figures based on country of last residence.

Table 5.30: Number and Percentage of Immigrants from Argentina in Total U.S. Immigration Annually, 1971–1996

Year	Number of Immigrants from Argentina	Total U.S. Immigration	Percentage of Immigrants from Argentina in Total U.S. Immigration
1971	1,992	370,473	0.54
1972	1,819	384,685	0.47
1973	2,034	400,063	0.51
1974	2,077	394,861	0.53
1975	2,227	396,194	0.56
1976	2,789	502,289	0.56
1977	2,787	462,315	0.60
1978	3,732	601,442	0.62
1979	2,856	460,348	0.62
1980	2,815	530,639	0.53
1981	2,236	596,600	0.37
1982	2,065	594,131	0.35
1983	2,029	559,763	0.36
1984	2,141	543,903	0.39
1985	1,844	570,009	0.32
1986	2,187	601,708	0.36
1987	2,106	601,516	0.35
1988	2,371	643,025	0.37
1989	3,301	1,090,924	0.30
1990	5,437	1,536,483	0.35
1991	3,889	1,827,167	0.21
1992	3,877	973,977	0.40
1993	2,824	904,292	0.31
1994	2,318	804,416	0.29
1995	1,762	720,461	0.24
1996	2,456	915,900	0.27
Total 1971-96	67,971	17,987,584	0.38

Sources: *Statistical Yearbook of the Immigration and Naturalization Service,* 1980, Table 13; *Statistical Yearbook of the Immigration and Naturalization Service,* 1986, Table 3; *Statistical Yearbook of the Immigration and Naturalization Service,* 1996, Table 3.

Resources

Internet Resources

SouthAmGenWeb (*http://www.rootsweb.com/~sthamgw/*) Part of the WorldGenWeb project, linking genealogical research sites around the world, by region, with resources by individual nation.

Print Resources

Argentina: A Country Study. 3d ed. James D. Rudolph, ed. Washington, D.C.: Federal Research Division, Library of Congress, 1985.

For more resources, see "Introduction" on p. 482.

Immigrants from Brazil

A colony of Portugal from the 1530s until its independence in the 1820s, Brazil is the largest and most populous country in South America, with more than half the continent's territory and an estimated population of 161 million in 1998. It is also a major world economy, with substantial agricultural industries and significant industrial concentrations.

During the second half of the 20th century, Brazil has experienced enormous population growth, more than tripling since 1950, from 52 million to 161 million. It has also experienced a very large country-to-city flight, periodic deep recessions, and, late in the century, a recurring fiscal crisis that left the nation with an unmanageable foreign debt in excess of $100 billion.

Brazil has traditionally been a major immigrant destination for people from around the world. However, in the course of the economic crisis that began in the 1980s, the number of people emigrating from Brazil exceeded the number of new arrivals, for the first time in the nation's history. One result was an increase in recorded Brazilian immigration into the United States, which grew from an average of fewer than 1,500 people per year in the 1970s and early 1980s to an average of more than 5,000 per year in the 1990s. There has been some undocumented immigration as well, but how much is difficult to quantify. U.S. estimates indicate more than 82,000 Brazilian immigrants were living in the United States in 1990, which would suggest the presence of at least some thousands of "illegals" (see "Appendix C: Estimates of Emigration and Illegals" on p. 749).

Table 5.31: Number and Percentage of Immigrants from Brazil in Total U.S. Immigration Annually, 1971–1996

Year	Number of Immigrants from Canada	Total U.S. Immigration	Percentage of Immigrants from Canada in Total U.S. Immigration
1820	209	8,385	2.49
1821-1830	2,277	143,439	1.59
1831-1840	13,624	599,125	2.27
1841-1850	41,723	1,713,251	2.44
185118-60	59,309	2,598,214	2.28
1861-1870	153,878	2,314,824	6.65
1871-1880	383,640	2,812,191	13.64
1881-1890	393,304	5,246,613	7.50
1891-1900	3,311	3,687,564	0.09
1901-1910	179,226	8,795,386	2.04
1911-1920	742,185	5,735,811	12.94
1921-1930	924,515	4,107,209	22.51
1931-1940	108,527	528,431	20.54
1941-1950	171,718	1,035,039	16.59
1951-1960	377,952	2,515,479	15.03
1961-1970	413,310	3,321,677	12.44
1971-1980	169,939	4,493,314	3.78
1981-1990	156,938	7,338,062	2.14
1991-1996	127,481	6,146,213	2.07
Total 1820-1996	4,423,066	63,140,227	7.01

Sources: Statistical Yearbook of the Immigration and Naturalization Service, 1980, Table 13; Statistical Yearbook of the Immigration and Naturalization Service, 1986, Table 3; Statistical Yearbook of the Immigration and Naturalization Service, 1996, Table 3.

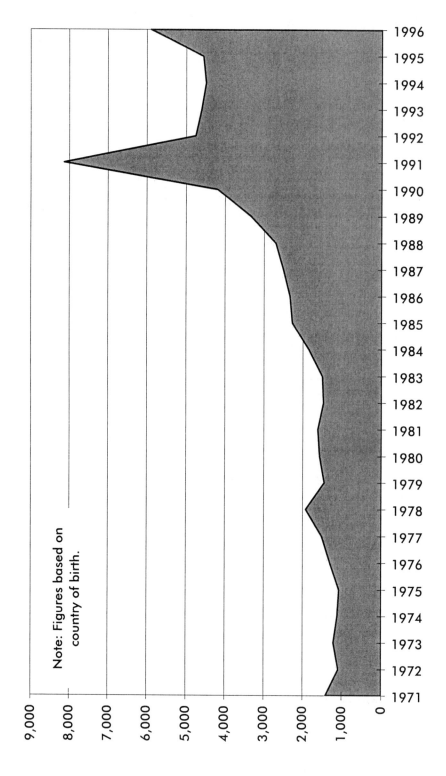

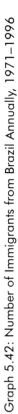

Graph 5.42: Number of Immigrants from Brazil Annually, 1971–1996

Note: Figures based on country of birth.

Resources

Brazil: A Country Study. 5th ed. Rex A. Hudson, ed. Washington, D.C.: Federal Research Division, Library of Congress, 1998.

Clague, Yelone. *The American Way: More Than Skin Deep.* Kansas City, MO: Midgard Press, 1993.

Margolis, Maxine L. *Little Brazil: An Ethnography of Brazilian Immigrants in New York City.* Princeton, N.J.: Princeton University Press, 1994.

———. *An Invisible Minority: Brazilians in New York City.* Boston: Allyn and Bacon, 1998.

For more resources, see "Introduction" on p. 482.

Immigrants from Colombia

Colombia was a Spanish colony until 1819 and then part of the independent nation of Gran Colombia until 1830. At that point the nation broke up into three separate countries: Colombia, Venezuela, and Ecuador.

From the start, Colombia was split between a very conservative faction that stressed the primacy of the Catholic Church, land ownership by a few powerful families, and central authority; and a liberal faction that stressed the development of democracy, including widespread landholding, the separation of church and state, and representative political institutions. The conservatives lost their attempt to maintain slavery in 1850, when it was abolished by a liberal government led by José Hilario López. In that same year, the split in the country's politics was institutionalized by the formation of the Liberal and Conservative parties, which would carry their multifold quarrel through to at least the end of the 20th century.

Politically, Colombia would develop rather differently from most Latin American states, with civilian governments dominating. Unlike many Latin American countries, it has had only three military governments, none of them lasting long enough to smash Colombia's democratic political system. The parties did engage in a massive, destabilizing rural guerrilla war from 1947 to 1958, called *La Violencia*, in which an estimated 200,000 to 300,000 people died.

In economic terms, Colombia during the mid-19th century developed a diversified, largely agricultural economy. Late in the century, as world export markets for coffee and tobacco grew, these became the country's main cash crops. During the first decade of the 20th century, the country turned decisively toward coffee, responding to a worldwide coffee boom in which prices soared as consumption rose. With its focus on this single crop, the Colombian economy then also became far more vulnerable to swings in commodity prices and world economic conditions.

In the 20th century, Colombia's population began to soar, as would happen wherever modern medical technology brought decreased infant mortality and longer life spans while birth rates continued high. In 1905, the estimated Colombian population was 5.3 million. By 1997, the estimated population was 42.2 million, an increase to 796 percent of the 1905 estimate, in only 92 years.

Apart from Colombia's other late-20th-century problems, which were considerable, that massive population increase, much of it occurring from mid-century on, goes far to explain the country's major internal migration and its large export of emigrants to the United States. This continued despite some improvements in the country's economy: the development, in the late 20th century, of a significant, revenue-producing oil industry within Colombia itself, substantial remittances home from Colombians who were working abroad, and a large amount of hidden income from the drug trade, which had become another major domestic industry. On the other hand, unstable conditions cost the country much of its once-sizable tourist industry, and the income gap between rich and poor Colombians was growing steadily wider.

Unstable domestic conditions contributed to all the country's problems. The large guerrilla civil war that was *La Violencia* did not fully end in 1958. A low-level guerrilla insurgency continued, and by the 1980s had again grown into a substantial civil war that wracked the rural regions of the country. In addition, the government's war against the drug cartels had caused the drug cartels and the guerrillas to join forces, with the very rich cartels supplying much-needed money for arms to the poor but highly effective guerrillas.

With the countryside in ferment, the flight to the cities in full swing, and few jobs available in either city or country, it was quite logical for large numbers of Colombians to emigrate abroad. A job in the United States might provide enough money to live on and some to send home, to support spouses, children, and other relatives who stayed behind or help them emigrate too.

During the 1970s, legal—that is, documented—Colombian immigration picked up substantially, averaging more than

10,000 a year by the early 1980s. So, too, did illegal immigration. By 1980, an estimated 143,000 Colombian-born people were living in the United States. Legal and illegal immigration soared in the 1980s, averaging 15,000 legal immigrants per year from 1985 to 1990 and at least the same number of "illegals." By 1990, an estimated 286,000 Colombian-born people were living in the United States. Legal Colombian immigration continued high during the 1990s, while the number of Colombian illegals was estimated at 65,000 in 1996.

The first Colombian immigrant communities formed in New York City. These were followed by communities in other major cities, as Colombians moved into a wide range of jobs and then into small businesses. By the mid-1980s, a substantial Colombian community had formed in Miami. In the late 1990s, as new Colombian immigrants continued to arrive, earlier Colombian Americans were following well-established immigrant patterns, building businesses and careers, moving from city to suburb and watching their United States–educated children, many of them also United States–born, move into a far wider range of occupations and locations.

Table 5.32: Number and Percentage of Immigrants from Colombia in Total U.S. Immigration Annually, 1971–1996

Year	Number of Immigrants from Colombia	Total U.S. Immigration	Percentage of Immigrants from Colombia in U.S. Immigration
1971	6,440	370,473	1.74
1972	5,173	384,685	1.34
1973	5,230	400,063	1.31
1974	5,837	394,861	1.48
1975	6,434	396,194	1.62
1976	7,212	502,289	1.44
1977	8,272	462,315	1.79
1978	11,032	601,442	1.83
1979	10,637	460,348	2.31
1980	11,289	530,639	2.13
1981	10,335	596,600	1.73
1982	8,608	594,131	1.45
1983	9,658	559,763	1.73
1984	11,020	543,903	2.03
1985	11,982	570,009	2.10
1986	11,408	601,708	1.90
1987	11,700	601,516	1.95
1988	10,322	643,025	1.61
1989	15,214	1,090,924	1.39
1990	24,189	1,536,483	1.57
1991	19,702	1,827,167	1.08
1992	13,201	973,977	1.36
1993	12,819	904,292	1.42
1994	10,847	804,416	1.35
1995	10,838	720,461	1.50
1996	14,283	915,900	1.56
Total 1971-1996	283,682	17,987,584	1.58

Sources: *Statistical Yearbook of the Immigration and Naturalization Service*, 1980, Table 13; *Statistical Yearbook of the Immigration and Naturalization Service*, 1986, Table 3; *Statistical Yearbook of the Immigration and Naturalization Service*, 1996, Table 3.

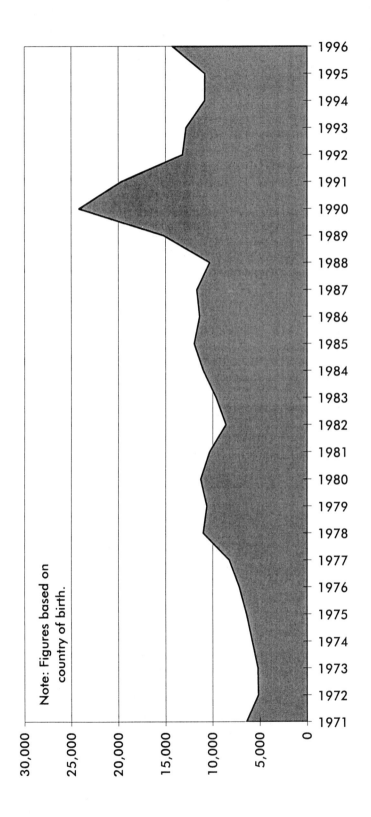

Graph 5.43: Number of Immigrants from Colombia Annually, 1971–1996

Note: Figures based on country of birth.

Resources

Colombia: A Country Study. 4th ed. Dennis M. Hanratty and Sandra W. Meditz, eds. Washington, D.C.: Federal Research Division, Library of Congress, 1990. (Available on-line at *http://lcweb2.loc.gov/frd/cs*)

Cornelius, Wayne A., et al. *The Dynamics of Migration, International Migration.* Washington, D.C.: Interdisciplinary Communications Program, Smithsonian Institution, 1976.

Eusse Hoyos, Gerardo. *The Outflow of Professional Manpower from Colombia.* Bogotá: United Nations Institute for Training and Research, 1969.

Redden, Charlotte Ann. *A Comparative Study of Colombian and Costa Rican Emigrants to the United States.* New York: Arno Press, 1976.

For more resources, see "Introduction" on p. 482.

Immigrants from Ecuador

A former Spanish colony that has been independent since 1830, Ecuador began to develop some very substantial problems in the mid-20th century, which became highly visible in the early 1950s.

In the early 1950s, world market prices for bananas declined sharply. Ecuador had by then become one of the world's leading banana exporters, and bananas had become the largely agricultural country's chief export cash crop. This much-needed export income had helped to sustain Ecuador's fast-growing population, which was accelerating as the birth rate continued high and infant mortality dropped sharply. With depression in the banana market, unemployment grew sharply in Ecuador.

In the early 1960s, Ecuador also faced the first of a long series of political crises, as its democratic, populist government resisted United States pressure to break relations with Cuba after Fidel Castro came to power. Even as Cuban-American relations worsened—with the aborted 1961 Bay of Pigs invasion and the 1962 Cuban missile crisis, which came very close to triggering U.S.-Soviet nuclear war—Ecuador's president, José María Velasco Ibarra, refused to break relations with Cuba.

Velasco was removed from office by the Ecuadorian military in 1961 and replaced by his vice president, Carlos Julio Arosemena Monroy, then supported by the military. Arosemena Monroy—who had also publicly supported Castro and had made a highly publicized trip to the Soviet Union—in turn refused to break with Castro, until confronted with a military rebellion in late 1962. Then he did break with Castro and the Soviet Union, but too late to placate the military and the United States. He was overthrown by a military coup in 1963, and Ecuador began 16 years of ineffectual and corrupt military dominance, which included the repression and imprisonment of the opposition.

On the economic side, banana and other commodity prices continued low, even as the military attempted to secure popularity by greatly increasing spending on public works and thereby creating unproductive public-sector jobs. The government also heavily subsidized food prices and other necessities and attempted a land reform program, which failed. Even large new oil income was not enough; successive military and military-dominated governments went very heavily into debt to foreign creditors. Debt service and newly incurred debts would hamper the Ecuadorian economy for decades, as would continuing high rates of unemployment.

Through all this, the Ecuadorian population continued to grow, in some periods at rates of 3 percent per year or even more, which produced a doubling of population within 25 years. Ecuador's population explosion was still going on in the late 1990s, for although by then the birth rate had declined somewhat, infant mortality had also declined and other health factors had continued to improve, bringing longer life expectancies.

Although immigration to the United States from Ecuador was modest until the mid-1960s, the worsening situation at home, coupled with the advent of less restrictive U.S. immigration laws in 1965, began to bring substantial numbers of immigrants to the United States from Ecuador. By the early 1970s, many were arriving as documented legal immigrants, but some undocumented illegal immigrants came as well. In all, recorded immigrants from Ecuador totaled more than 151,000 from 1971 to 1996, while tens of thousands more arrived as "illegals." The U.S. government estimated that 55,000 undocumented Ecuadorians were living in the United States in 1996 (see "Appendix C: Estimates of Emigration and Illegals" on p. 749).

Most Ecuadorian immigrants initially settled in the New York City area, though they had by the mid-1990s spread to several other major urban areas as well, including Miami and Los Angeles. Coming as they did from several sectors of Ecuadorian society, Ecuadorian Americans worked at the whole range of occupations, from low-paying service and industrial jobs to highly skilled and well-paid professions. Many also went into their own small businesses.

Table 5.33: Number and Percentage of Immigrants from Ecuador in Total U.S. Immigration Annually, 1971–1996

Year	Number of Immigrants from Ecuador	Total U.S. Immigration	Percentage of Immigrants from Ecuador in Total U.S. Immigration
1971	4,981	370,473	1.34
1972	4,337	384,685	1.13
1973	4,139	400,063	1.03
1974	4,795	394,861	1.21
1975	4,727	396,194	1.19
1976	5,632	502,289	1.12
1977	5,302	462,315	1.15
1978	5,732	601,442	0.95
1979	4,383	460,348	0.95
1980	6,133	530,639	1.16
1981	5,129	596,600	0.86
1982	4,127	594,131	0.69
1983	4,243	559,763	0.76
1984	4,164	543,903	0.77
1985	4,482	570,009	0.79
1986	4,516	601,708	0.75
1987	4,641	601,516	0.77
1988	4,716	643,025	0.73
1989	7,532	1,090,924	0.69
1990	12,476	1,536,483	0.81
1991	9,958	1,827,167	0.54
1992	7,286	973,977	0.75
1993	7,324	904,292	0.81
1994	5,906	804,416	0.73
1995	6,397	720,461	0.89
1996	8,321	915,900	0.91
Total 1971-96	151,379	17,987,584	0.84

Sources: *Statistical Yearbook of the Immigration and Naturalization Service*, 1980, Table 13; *Statistical Yearbook of the Immigration and Naturalization Service*, 1986, Table 3; *Statistical Yearbook of the Immigration and Naturalization Service*, 1996, Table 3.

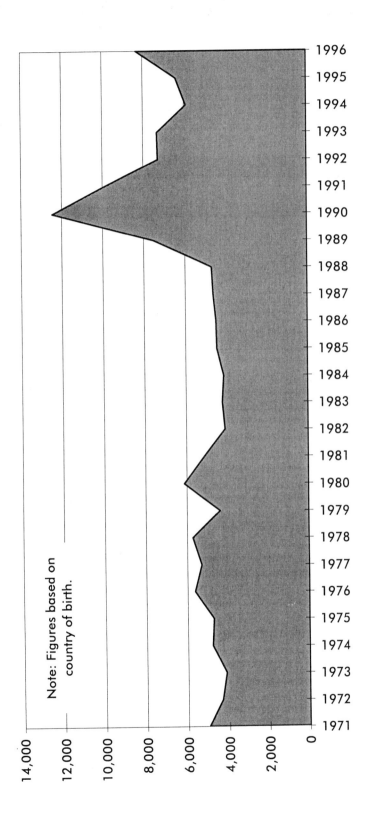

Graph 5.44: Number of Immigrants from Ecuador Annually, 1971–1996

Note: Figures based on country of birth.

Resources

Ecuador: A Country Study. 3d ed. Dennis M. Hanratty, ed. Washington, D.C.: Federal Research Division, Library of Congress, 1991. (Available on-line at *http://lcweb2.loc.gov/frd/cs*)

For more resources, see "Introduction" on p. 482.

Immigrants from Peru

Until the late 1980s, emigration from Peru to the United States was small, especially as compared to emigration from many other countries south of the Rio Grande. In the early 1970s, fewer than 2,000 Peruvians a year were entering the United States as immigrants, and from then until 1989, still less than 6,000 annually.

Peru had developed major political and economic problems by the late 1980s, among them the Sendero Luminoso (Shining Path) insurgency, deepening recession, huge international debts, high inflation rates, persistent unemployment, and a massive country-to-city internal migration. Yet until mid-1987, the country's problems had not yet become critical.

Financial crisis came in 1988 and 1989, as inflation soared and became uncontrollable, remaining high despite repeated major currency devaluations and the doubling and tripling of food prices. For most Peruvians, it suddenly became far harder to make ends meet.

Right-wing candidate Alberto Fujimori won the 1990 Peruvian presidential elections, and quickly introduced an even more severe austerity program, also taking action against the resurgent Sendero Luminoso insurgency. During 1991, he began to rule by decree, using emergency powers granted by the Peruvian Congress. In 1992, he took power by coup, dissolving the Congress, while his army instituted a reign of terror in the countryside. His eco-

Table 5.34: Number and Percentage of Immigrants from Peru in Total U.S. Immigration Annually, 1971–1996

Year	Number of Immigrants from Peru	Total U.S. Immigration	Percentage of Immigrants from Peru in Total U.S. Immigration
1971	1,086	370,473	0.29
1972	1,443	384,685	0.38
1973	1,713	400,063	0.43
1974	1,942	394,861	0.49
1975	2,256	396,194	0.57
1976	3,356	502,289	0.67
1977	3,903	462,315	0.84
1978	5,243	601,442	0.87
1979	4,135	460,348	0.90
1980	4,021	530,639	0.76
1981	4,664	596,600	0.78
1982	4,151	594,131	0.70
1983	4,384	559,763	0.78
1984	4,368	543,903	0.80
1985	4,181	570,009	0.73
1986	4,895	601,708	0.81
1987	5,901	601,516	0.98
1988	5,936	643,025	0.92
1989	10,175	1,090,924	0.93
1990	15,726	1,536,483	1.02
1991	16,237	1,827,167	0.89
1992	9,868	973,977	1.01
1993	10,447	904,292	1.16
1994	9,177	804,416	1.14
1995	8,066	720,461	1.12
1996	12,871	915,900	1.41
Total 1971-96	160,145	17,987,584	0.89

Sources: *Statistical Yearbook of the Immigration and Naturalization Service,* 1980, Table 13; *Statistical Yearbook of the Immigration and Naturalization Service,* 1986, Table 3; *Statistical Yearbook of the Immigration and Naturalization Service,* 1996, Table 3.

nomic measures met with considerable success, and his dictatorship survived. In 1995, he held new presidential elections, winning two-thirds of the votes cast.

In that period, Peru produced a substantial flow of emigrants, both to neighboring countries and to the United States. From 1989 to 1996, Peruvian immigration to the United States totaled more than 92,000, an average of more than 11,000 per year. In addition, tens of thousands of Peruvian "illegals" began to arrive. By 1996, an estimated 30,000 undocumented Peruvians were living in the United States (see "Appendix C: Estimates of Emigration and Illegals" on p. 749).

Resources

Peru: A Country Study. 4th ed. Rex A. Hudson, ed. Washington, D.C.: Federal Research Division, Library of Congress, 1993. (Available on-line at *http://lcweb2.loc.gov/frd/cs*)

For more resources, see "Introduction" on p. 482.

Immigrants from Bolivia

Immigration into the United States from Bolivia averaged only a little more than 1,000 per year from 1971 to 1996, with no substantial increase in the 1990s. Although a poor country, with substantial country-to-city internal migration and rising population, Bolivia's international migration was largely to other South American countries, much of it consisting of seasonal agricultural workers. Even when sharp austerity programs in the 1980s and 1990s managed to stop runaway inflation at the cost of creating 25 percent to 40 percent unemployment rates, no significant increase in immigration to the United States from Bolivia was recorded.

By far Bolivia's most lucrative single kind of business in recent decades has been coca cultivation, which during the 1990s engaged hundreds of thousands of Bolivians. Although outlawed and the object of highly publicized joint Bolivian–United States antidrug operations, huge quantities of cocaine continued to be refined from Bolivian coca, to be sold in worldwide drug markets. Should Bolivia ever turn decisively away from coca cultivation, or coca become a less lucrative commodity, a mass flight from Bolivia might indeed develop.

Table 5.35: Number and Percentage of Immigrants from Bolivia in Total U.S. Immigration Annually, 1971–1996

Year	Number of Immigrants from Bolivia	Total U.S. Immigration	Percentage of Immigrants from Bolivia in Total U.S. Immigration
1971	441	370,473	0.12
1972	551	384,685	0.14
1973	449	400,063	0.11
1974	479	394,861	0.12
1975	451	396,194	0.11
1976	652	502,289	0.13
1977	699	462,315	0.15
1978	1,030	601,442	0.17
1979	751	460,348	0.16
1980	730	530,639	0.14
1981	820	596,600	0.14
1982	750	594,131	0.13
1983	823	559,763	0.15
1984	918	543,903	0.17
1985	1,006	570,009	0.18
1986	1,079	601,708	0.18
1987	1,170	601,516	0.19
1988	1,038	643,025	0.16
1989	1,805	1,090,924	0.17
1990	2,843	1,536,483	0.19
1991	3,006	1,827,167	0.16
1992	1,510	973,977	0.16
1993	1,545	904,292	0.17
1994	1,404	804,416	0.17
1995	1,332	720,461	0.18
1996	1,913	915,900	0.21
Total 1971-96	29,195	17,987,584	0.16

Sources: *Statistical Yearbook of the Immigration and Naturalization Service*, 1980, Table 13; *Statistical Yearbook of the Immigration and Naturalization Service*, 1986, Table 3; *Statistical Yearbook of the Immigration and Naturalization Service*, 1996, Table 3.

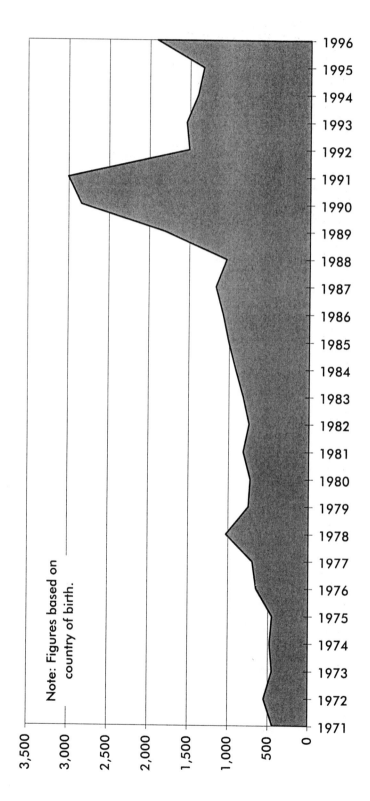

Graph 5.45: Number of Immigrants from Bolivia Annually, 1971–1996

Note: Figures based on country of birth.

Resources

Bolivia: A Country Study. 3d ed. Rex A. Hudson and Dennis M. Hanratty, eds. Washington, D.C.: Federal Research Division, Library of Congress, 1991. (Available on-line at *http://lcweb2.loc.gov/frd/cs*)

For more resources, see "Introduction" on p. 482.

Immigrants from Chile

Immigration to the United States from Chile has been modest throughout the country's history. The first Chileans to arrive in any significant numbers emigrated at the time of the 1849 California Gold Rush, and most stayed relatively briefly, trying to make their fortunes as prospectors. Estimates of the number of Chilean arrivals run as high as several thousand. However, no reliable record exists as to the numbers of Chileans who arrived during that period or the numbers who subsequently returned home. The relative few who stayed on in the United States did not form tightly-knit immigrant communities but instead merged into the general population.

Until the mid-1970s, immigration to the United States from Chile was negligible. It topped 1,000 in 1973 for the first time in the modern era, exceeding 2,000 for the first time in 1977. From 1971 to 1996, Chilean immigration totaled somewhat more than 52,000, averaging 2,000 per year.

Chile's population was estimated at 14.6 million in 1997. With a declining birth rate, inflation under control, and an unemployment rate ranging from 4 to 6 percent, Chile in the 1990s was not generating the kind of large-scale international migration that was characteristic of many Central and South American countries. There were certainly problems, however, perhaps most notably a growing gap between Chile's rich and poor.

From 1973 to 1988, Chileans were afflicted by a repressive right-wing military dictatorship, led from 1974 by General Augusto Pinochet Duarte. In that period, tens of thousands of Chileans were murdered by government forces, while far more were imprisoned, tortured, and driven into exile. Many of those who escaped fled to neighboring countries, though Chilean refugees in those years were to be found all over the world. In the United States, some refugees stayed on as immigrants, while small numbers of others were transients, who returned home after the dictatorship collapsed.

Table 5.36: Number and Percentage of Immigrants from Chile in Total U.S. Immigration Annually, 1971–1996

Year	Number of Immigrants from Chile	Total U.S. Immigration	Percentage of Immigrants from Chile in U.S. Immigration
1971	956	370,473	0.26
1972	857	384,685	0.22
1973	1,139	400,063	0.28
1974	1,285	394,861	0.33
1975	1,111	396,194	0.28
1976	1,681	502,289	0.33
1977	2,596	462,315	0.56
1978	3,122	601,442	0.52
1979	2,289	460,348	0.50
1980	2,569	530,639	0.48
1981	2,048	596,600	0.34
1982	1,911	594,131	0.32
1983	1,970	559,763	0.35
1984	1,912	543,903	0.35
1985	1,992	570,009	0.35
1986	2,243	601,708	0.37
1987	2,140	601,516	0.36
1988	2,137	643,025	0.33
1989	3,037	1,090,924	0.28
1990	4,049	1,536,483	0.26
1991	2,842	1,827,167	0.16
1992	1,937	973,977	0.20
1993	1,778	904,292	0.20
1994	1,640	804,416	0.20
1995	1,534	720,461	0.21
1996	1,706	915,900	0.19
Total 1971-96	52,481	17,987,584	0.29

Sources: *Statistical Yearbook of the Immigration and Naturalization Service*, 1980, Table 13; *Statistical Yearbook of the Immigration and Naturalization Service*, 1986, Table 3; *Statistical Yearbook of the Immigration and Naturalization Service*, 1996, Table 3.

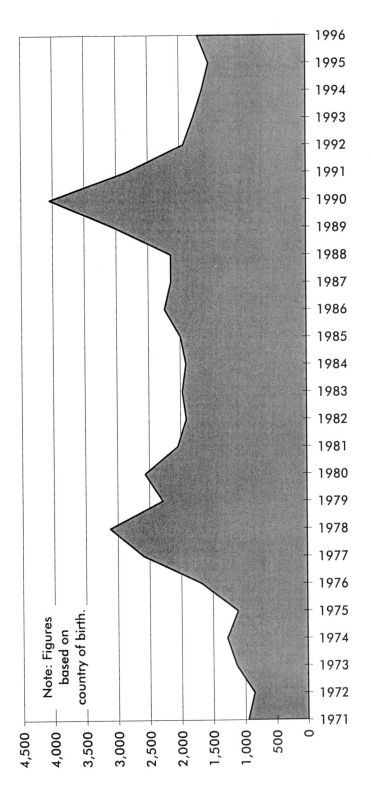

Graph 5.46: Number of Immigrants from Chile Annually, 1971–1996

Note: Figures based on country of birth.

Resources

Chile: A Country Study. 3d ed. Rex A. Hudson, ed. Washington, D.C.: Federal Research Division, Library of Congress, 1994. (Available on-line at *http://lcweb2.loc.gov/frd/cs*)

For more resources, see "Introduction" on p. 482.

Immigrants from Venezuela

Venezuela is South America's most richly endowed country, with its own oil, natural gas, and hydroelectric resources and a wide range of minerals. During the 20th century, it has been a destination for millions of immigrants from other countries. Its own migrations have been largely internal, in the form of massive country-to-city population movements.

Venezuela is also a country with a very high rate of population growth, which, combined with medical advances, has resulted in a doubling of its population every 20 years since 1950. Its growth rate slowed somewhat late in the 20th century, but was still at a very high 2.5 percent per year in the mid-1990s. At the same time, the income gap between rich and poor grew wider.

Although only 41,000 Venezuelans immigrated to the United States from 1971 to 1996, the rate of migration to the United States rose somewhat in the mid-1990s. Should threatened political instability develop, it may increase more sharply.

Table 5.37: Number and Percentage of Immigrants from Venezuela in Total U.S. Immigration Annually, 1971–1996

Year	Number of Immigrants from Venezuela	Total U.S. Immigration	Percentage of Immigrants from Venezuela in Total U.S. Immigration
1971	507	370,473	0.14
1972	485	384,685	0.13
1973	640	400,063	0.16
1974	604	394,861	0.15
1975	527	396,194	0.13
1976	721	502,289	0.14
1977	736	462,315	0.16
1978	990	601,442	0.16
1979	841	460,348	0.18
1980	1,010	530,639	0.19
1981	1,104	596,600	0.19
1982	1,336	594,131	0.22
1983	1,508	559,763	0.27
1984	1,721	543,903	0.32
1985	1,714	570,009	0.30
1986	1,854	601,708	0.31
1987	1,694	601,516	0.28
1988	1,791	643,025	0.28
1989	2,099	1,090,924	0.19
1990	3,142	1,536,483	0.20
1991	2,622	1,827,167	0.14
1992	2,340	973,977	0.24
1993	2,743	904,292	0.30
1994	2,427	804,416	0.30
1995	2,627	720,461	0.36
1996	3,468	915,900	0.38
Total 1971-96	41,251	17,987,584	0.23

Sources: *Statistical Yearbook of the Immigration and Naturalization Service*, 1980, Table 13; *Statistical Yearbook of the Immigration and Naturalization Service*, 1986, Table 3; *Statistical Yearbook of the Immigration and Naturalization Service*, 1996, Table 3.

Resources

Venezuela: A Country Study. 4th ed. Richard A. Haggerty, ed. Washington, D.C.: Federal Research Division, Library of Congress, 1993. (Available on-line at *http://lcweb2.loc.gov/frd/cs)*

For more resources, see "Introduction" on p. 482.

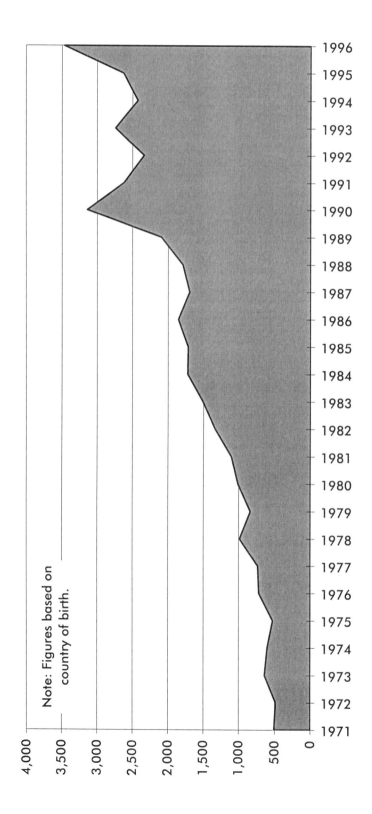

Graph 5.47: Number of Immigrants from Venezuela Annually, 1971–1996

Other Immigrants from the Americas

Following are immigration statistics relating to several other Central and South American countries. They have sent relatively few emigrants to the United States historically, but have generated modest United States immigration in the final decades of the 20th century and so have some U.S. immigration history worthy of graphic presentation.

Immigrants from Costa Rica

Table 5.38: Number and Percentage of Immigrants from Costa Rica in Total U.S. Immigration Annually, 1971–1996

Year	Number of Immigrants from Costa Rica	Total U.S. Immigration	Percentage of Immigrants from Costa Rica in Total U.S. Immigration
1971	968	370,473	0.26
1972	907	384,685	0.24
1973	901	400,063	0.23
1974	752	394,861	0.19
1975	889	396,194	0.22
1976	1,452	502,289	0.29
1977	1,664	462,315	0.36
1978	1,575	601,442	0.26
1979	1,467	460,348	0.32
1980	1,535	530,639	0.29
1981	1,359	596,600	0.23
1982	1,272	594,131	0.21
1983	1,182	559,763	0.21
1984	1,473	543,903	0.27
1985	1,281	570,009	0.22
1986	1,356	601,708	0.23
1987	1,391	601,516	0.23
1988	1,351	643,025	0.21
1989	1,985	1,090,924	0.18
1990	2,840	1,536,483	0.18
1991	2,341	1,827,167	0.13
1992	1,480	973,977	0.15
1993	1,368	904,292	0.15
1994	1,205	804,416	0.15
1995	1,062	720,461	0.15
1996	1,504	915,900	0.16
Total 1971-96	36,560	17,987,584	0.20

Sources: *Statistical Yearbook of the Immigration and Naturalization Service, 1980,* Table 13; *Statistical Yearbook of the Immigration and Naturalization Service, 1986,* Table 3; *Statistical Yearbook of the Immigration and Naturalization Service, 1996,* Table 3.

Resources

Costa Rica: A Country Study. 2d ed. Harold D. Nelson, ed. Washington, D.C.: Federal Research Division, Library of Congress, 1984.

Redden, Charlotte Ann. *A Comparative Study of Colombian and Costa Rican Emigrants to the United States.* New York: Arno Press, 1980.

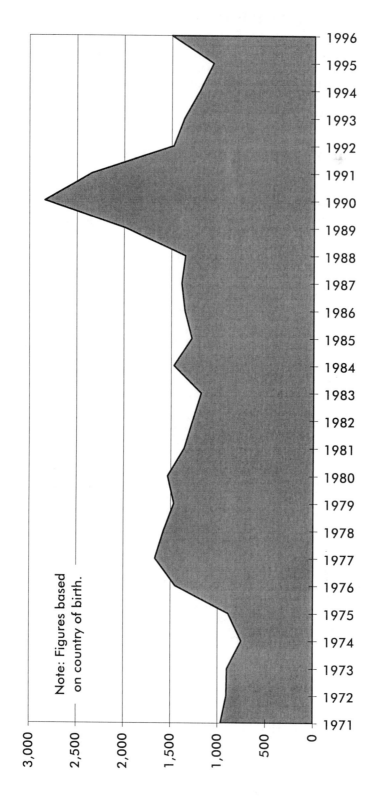

Graph 5.48: Number of Immigrants from Costa Rica Annually, 1971–1996

Note: Figures based on country of birth.

Immigrants from Panama

Table 5.39: Number and Percentage of Immigrants from Panama in Total U.S. Immigration Annually, 1971–1996

Year	Number of Immigrants from Panama	Total U.S. Immigration	Percentage of Immigrants from Panama in Total U.S. Immigration
1971	1,497	370,473	0.40
1972	1,517	384,685	0.39
1973	1,612	400,063	0.40
1974	1,664	394,861	0.42
1975	1,694	396,194	0.43
1976	2,162	502,289	0.43
1977	2,390	462,315	0.52
1978	3,108	601,442	0.52
1979	3,472	460,348	0.75
1980	3,572	530,639	0.67
1981	4,613	596,600	0.77
1982	3,320	594,131	0.56
1983	2,546	559,763	0.45
1984	2,276	543,903	0.42
1985	2,611	570,009	0.46
1986	2,194	601,708	0.36
1987	2,084	601,516	0.35
1988	2,486	643,025	0.39
1989	3,482	1,090,924	0.32
1990	3,433	1,536,483	0.22
1991	4,204	1,827,167	0.23
1992	2,845	973,977	0.29
1993	2,679	904,292	0.30
1994	2,378	804,416	0.30
1995	2,247	720,461	0.31
1996	2,560	915,900	0.28
Total 1971-96	68,646	17,987,584	0.38

Sources: *Statistical Yearbook of the Immigration and Naturalization Service, 1980,* Table 13; *Statistical Yearbook of the Immigration and Naturalization Service, 1986,* Table 3; *Statistical Yearbook of the Immigration and Naturalization Service, 1996,* Table 3.

Resources

Panama: A Country Study. 4th ed. Sandra W. Meditz and Dennis M. Hanratty, eds. Washington, D.C.: Federal Research Division, Library of Congress, 1989.

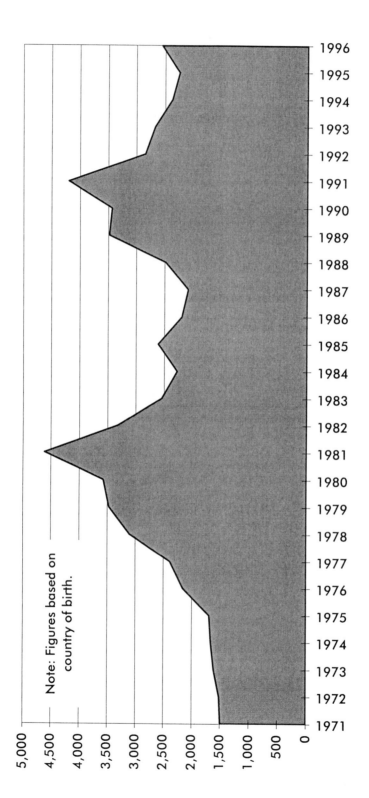

Graph 5.49: Number of Immigrants from Panama Annually, 1971–1996

Note: Figures based on country of birth.

Immigrants from Uruguay

Table 5.40: Number and Percentage of Immigrants from Uruguay in Total U.S. Immigration Annually, 1971–1996

Year	Number of Immigrants from Uruguay	Total U.S. Immigration	Percentage of Immigrants from Uruguay in Total U.S. Immigration
1971	601	370,473	0.16
1972	591	384,685	0.15
1973	617	400,063	0.15
1974	705	394,861	0.18
1975	781	396,194	0.20
1976	831	502,289	0.17
1977	1,156	462,315	0.25
1978	1,052	601,442	0.17
1979	754	460,348	0.16
1980	887	530,639	0.17
1981	972	596,600	0.16
1982	707	594,131	0.12
1983	681	559,763	0.12
1984	712	543,903	0.13
1985	790	570,009	0.14
1986	699	601,708	0.12
1987	709	601,516	0.12
1988	612	643,025	0.10
1989	948	1,090,924	0.09
1990	1,457	1,536,483	0.09
1991	1,161	1,827,167	0.06
1992	716	973,977	0.07
1993	568	904,292	0.06
1994	516	804,416	0.06
1995	414	720,461	0.06
1996	540	915,900	0.06
Total 1971-96	20,177	17,987,584	0.11

Sources: *Statistical Yearbook of the Immigration and Naturalization Service,* 1980, Table 13; *Statistical Yearbook of the Immigration and Naturalization Service,* 1986, Table 3; *Statistical Yearbook of the Immigration and Naturalization Service,* 1996, Table 3.

Resources

Uruguay: A Country Study. 2d ed. Rex A. Hudson and Sandra W. Meditz, eds. Washington, D.C.: Federal Research Division, Library of Congress, 1992. (Available on-line at *http://lcweb2.loc.gov/frd/cs*)

See "General Immigration Statistics for the Americas" on p. 619, and "General Immigration Resources for the Americas" on p. 632, for further information and resources.

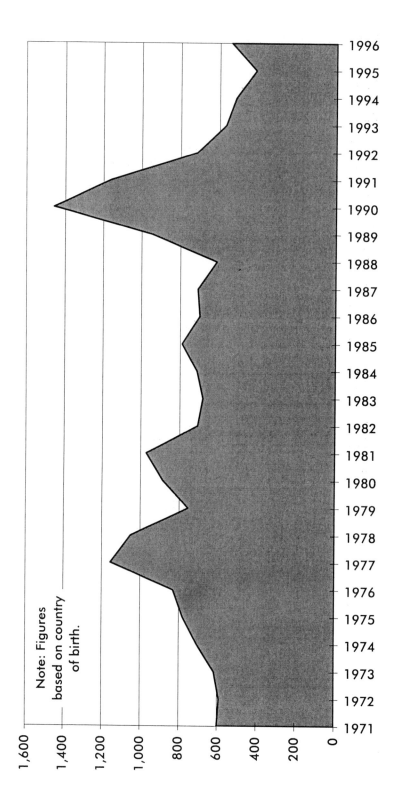

Graph 5.50: Number of Immigrants from Uruguay Annually, 1971–1996

Note: Figures based on country of birth.

General Immigration Statistics

for the Americas

Table 5.41: Number and Percentage of Immigrants from the Americas in Total U.S. Immigration by Decade, 1820–1996

Decade	Number of Immigrants from the Americas	Total U.S. Immigrants	Percentage of Immigrants from the Americas in Total U.S. Immigration
1820	387	8,385	4.62
1821-30	11,564	143,439	8.06
1831-40	33,424	599,125	5.58
1841-50	62,469	1,713,251	3.65
1851-60	74,720	2,598,214	2.88
1861-70	166,607	2,314,824	7.20
1871-80	404,044	2,812,191	14.37
1881-90	426,967	5,246,613	8.14
1891-1900	38,972	3,687,564	1.06
1901-10	361,888	8,795,386	4.11
1911-20	1,143,671	5,735,811	19.94
1921-30	1,516,716	4,107,209	36.93
1931-40	160,037	528,431	30.29
1941-50	354,804	1,035,039	34.28
1951-60	996,944	2,515,479	39.63
1961-70	1,716,374	3,321,677	51.67
1971-80	1,982,735	4,493,314	44.13
1981-90	3,615,225	7,338,062	49.27
1991-96	3,119,506	6,146,213	50.75
Total 1820-1996	16,187,054	63,140,227	25.64

Source: Adapted from Table 2, Immigration by Region and Selected Country of Last Residence, Fiscal Years 1820–1996, from the *Statistical Yearbook of the Immigration and Naturalization Service*, 1996.

Table 5.42: Number and Percentage of Immigrants from Central America in Total U.S. Immigration by Decade, 1820–1996

Year	Number of Immigrants from Central America	Total U.S. Immigrants	Percentage of Immigrants from Central America in Total U.S. Immigration
1820	2	8,385	0.02
1821-30	105	143,439	0.07
1831-40	44	599,125	0.01
1841-50	368	1,713,251	0.02
1851-60	449	2,598,214	0.02
1861-70	95	2,314,824	0.00
1871-80	157	2,812,191	0.01
1881-90	404	5,246,613	0.01
1891-1900	549	3,687,564	0.01
1901-10	8,192	8,795,386	0.09
1911-20	17,159	5,735,811	0.30
1921-30	15,769	4,107,209	0.38
1931-40	5,861	528,431	1.11
1941-50	21,665	1,035,039	2.09
1951-60	44,751	2,515,479	1.78
1961-70	101,330	3,321,677	3.05
1971-80	134,640	4,493,314	3.00
1981-90	468,088	7,338,062	6.38
1991-96	343,947	6,146,213	5.60
Total 1820-1996	1,163,575	63,140,227	1.84

Source: Adapted from Table 2, Immigration by Region and Selected Country of Last Residence, Fiscal Years 1820–1996, from the *Statistical Yearbook of the Immigration and Naturalization Service*, 1996.

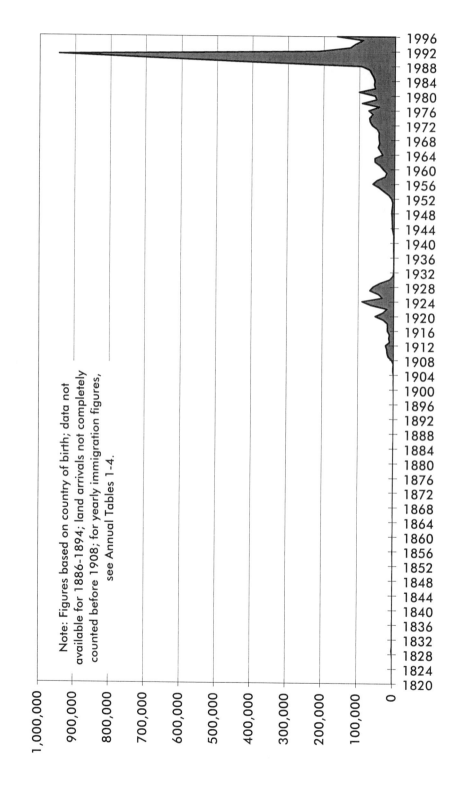

Graph 5.51: Number of Immigrants from North and South America Annually, 1820–1996

Note: Figures based on country of birth; data not available for 1886-1894; land arrivals not completely counted before 1908; for yearly immigration figures, see Annual Tables 1-4.

Graph 5.52: Number of Immigrants from the Americas by Decade, 1820–1996

Note: Figures based on country of last residence.

Graph 5.53: Percentage of Immigrants from the Americas in Total U.S. Immigration by Decade, 1820–1996

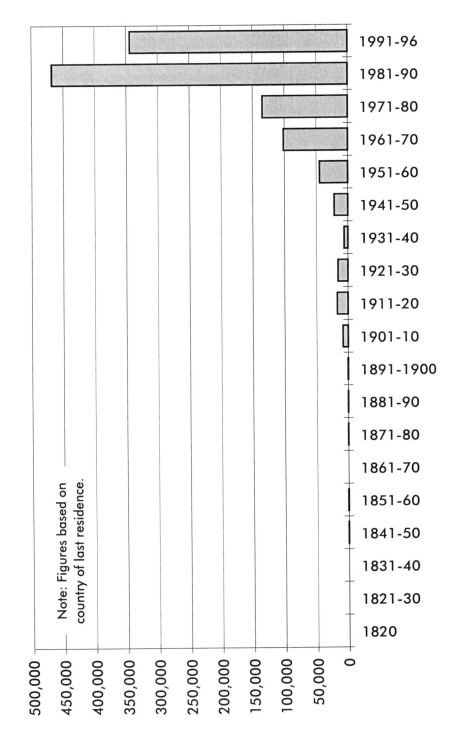

Graph 5.54: Number of Immigrants from Central America by Decade, 1820–1996

Note: Figures based on country of last residence.

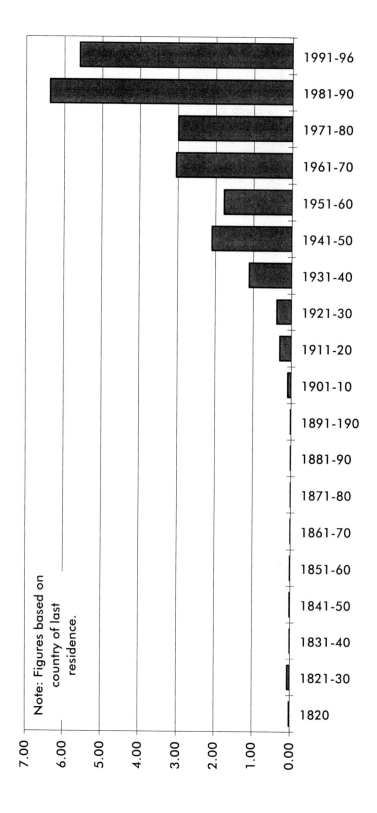

Graph 5.55: Percentage of Immigrants from Central America in Total U.S. Immigration by Decade, 1820–1996

Table 5.43: Number and Percentage of Immigrants from the Caribbean in Total U.S. Immigration by Decade, 1820–1996

Decade	Number of Immigrants from the Caribbean	Total U.S. Immigrants	Percentage of Immigrants from the Caribbean in Total U.S. Immigration
1820	164	8,385	1.96
1821-30	3,834	143,439	2.67
1831-40	12,301	599,125	2.05
1841-50	13,528	1,713,251	0.79
1851-60	10,660	2,598,214	0.41
1861-70	9,046	2,314,824	0.39
1871-80	13,957	2,812,191	0.50
1881-90	29,042	5,246,613	0.55
1891-1900	33,066	3,687,564	0.90
1901-10	107,548	8,795,386	1.22
1911-20	123,424	5,735,811	2.15
1921-30	74,899	4,107,209	1.82
1931-40	15,502	528,431	2.93
1941-50	49,725	1,035,039	4.80
1951-60	123,091	2,515,479	4.89
1961-70	470,213	3,321,677	14.16
1971-80	741,126	4,493,314	16.49
1981-90	872,051	7,338,062	11.88
1991-96	648,483	6,146,213	10.55
Total 1820-1996	3,351,660	63,140,227	5.31

Source: Adapted from Table 2, Immigration by Region and Selected Country of Last Residence, Fiscal Year 1820–1996, from the *Statistical Yearbook of the Immigration and Naturalization Service*, 1996.

Table 5.44: Number and Percentage of Immigrants from South America in Total U.S. Immigration by Decade, 1820–1996

Decade	Number of Immigrants from South America	Total U.S. Immigrants	Percentage of Immigrants from South America in Total U.S. Immigration
1820	11	8,385	0.13
1821-1830	531	143,439	0.37
1831-1840	856	599,125	0.14
1841-1850	3,579	1,713,251	0.21
1851-1860	1,224	2,598,214	0.05
1861-1870	1,397	2,314,824	0.06
1871-1880	1,128	2,812,191	0.04
1881-1890	2,304	5,246,613	0.04
1891-1900	1,075	3,687,564	0.03
1901-1910	17,280	8,795,386	0.20
1911-1920	41,899	5,735,811	0.73
1921-1930	42,215	4,107,209	1.03
1931-1940	7,803	528,431	1.48
1941-1950	21,831	1,035,039	2.11
1951-1960	91,628	2,515,479	3.64
1961-1970	257,940	3,321,677	7.77
1971-1980	295,741	4,493,314	6.58
1981-1990	461,847	7,338,062	6.29
1991-1996	345,668	6,146,213	5.62
Total 1820-1996	1,595,971	63,140,227	2.53

Source: Adapted from Table 2, Immigration by Region and Selected Country of Last Residence, Fiscal Year 1820–1996, from the *Statistical Yearbook of the Immigration and Naturalization Service*, 1996.

Graph 5.56: Number of Immigrants from the Caribbean by Decade, 1820–1996

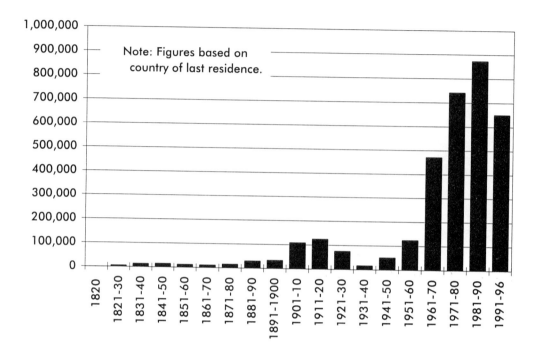

Graph 5.57: Percentage of Immigrants from the Caribbean in Total U.S. Immigration by Decade, 1820–1996

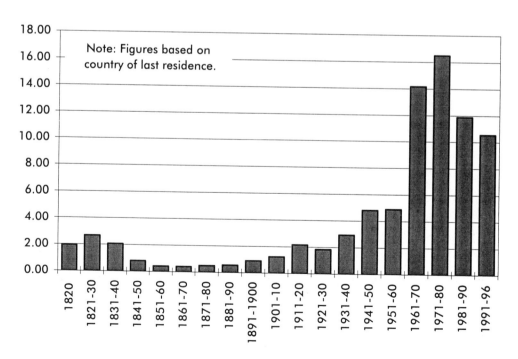

Graph 5.58: Number of Immigrants from South America by Decade, 1820–1996

Note: Figures based on country of last residence.

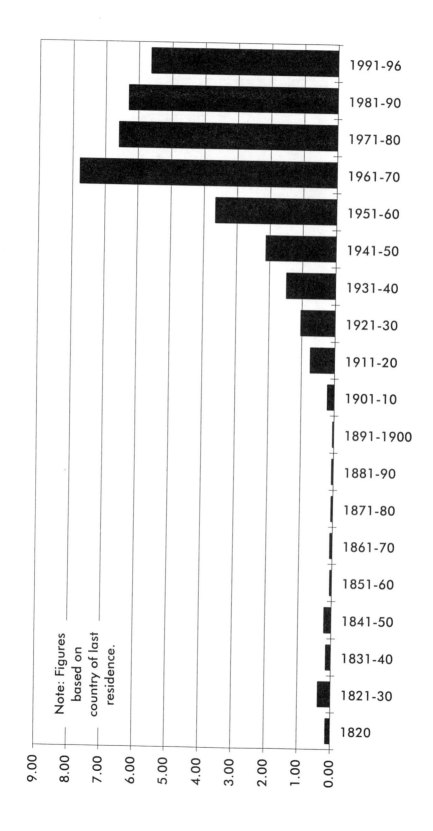

Graph 5.59: Percentage of Immigrants from South America in Total U.S. Immigration by Decade, 1820–1996

Note: Figures based on country of last residence.

Table 5.45: Number and Percentage of Foreign-Born Immigrants from North and South America by Decade in Total U.S. Population at End of Decade, 1850–1990

Decade	Number of Foreign-Born Immigrants from North and South America	Total U.S. Population	Percentage of Foreign-Born Immigrants from North and South America in Total U.S. Population
1850	168,484	23,191,876	0.73
1860	288,285	31,443,321	0.92
1870	551,335	39,818,449	1.38
1880	807,230	50,155,783	1.61
1890	1,088,245	62,947,714	1.73
1900	1,317,380	75,994,575	1.73
1910	1,489,231	91,972,266	1.62
1920	1,727,017	105,710,620	1.63
1930	2,102,209	122,775,046	1.71
1940	(NA)	131,669,275	(NA)
1950	1,655,324	150,697,361	1.10
1960	1,860,809	179,323,175	1.04
1970	2,616,391	203,235,298	1.29
1980	5,225,914	227,726,000	2.29
1990	9,161,754	249,907,000	3.67

NA = Not available

Source: Adapted from Series C 228–295, Foreign-Born Population, by Country of Birth: 1850–1970, in *Historical Statistics of the United States, Colonial Times to 1970, Bincentennial Edition,* and other updating tables from the U.S. Census Bureau.

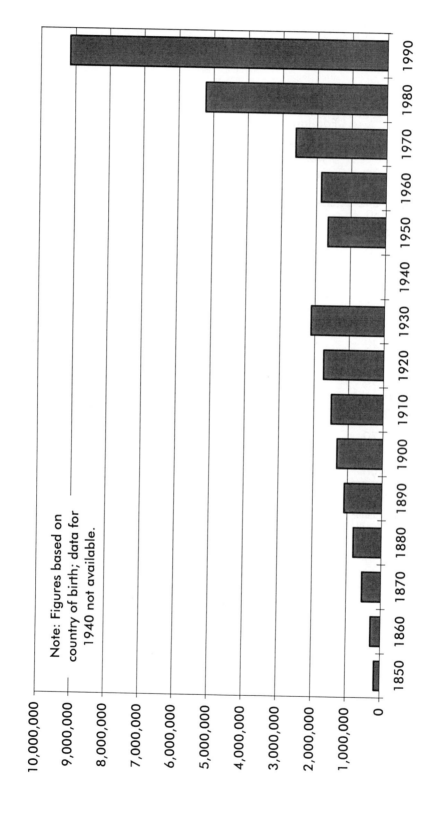

Graph 5.60: Number of Foreign-Born Immigrants from North and South America by Decade, 1850–1990

Note: Figures based on country of birth; data for 1940 not available.

Graph 5.61: Percentage of Foreign-Born Immigrants from North and South America by Decade in Total U.S. Population at End of Decade, 1850–1990

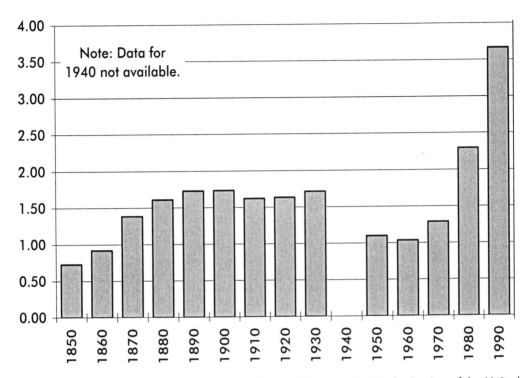

Graph 5.62: Percentage Distribution of Americans of Hispanic Origin by Region of the United States, 1990

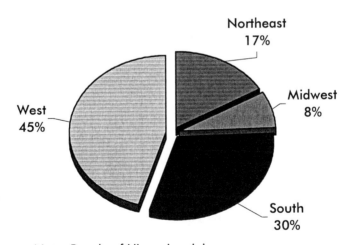

Note: People of Hispanic origin
may be of any race.

General Immigration Resources

for the Americas

Internet Resources

SouthAmGenWeb (*http://www.rootsweb.com/~sthamgw/*) Part of the WorldGenWeb project, linking genealogical research sites around the world, by region, with resources by individual nation.

CentralAmGenWeb (*http://www.rootsweb.com/~nrthamgw/*) Originally separate, but now part of NorthAmGenWeb, itself part of the WorldGenWeb project, linking genealogical research sites around the world, by region, with resources by individual country.

CaribbeanGenWeb (*http://www.rootsweb.com/~caribgw/*) Part of the WorldGenWeb project, linking genealogical research sites around the world, by region, with resources by individual country in the Caribbean and West Indies; offers archives, discussion groups, mailing lists, and ability to post queries and genealogical information.

Hispanic Genealogical Society of New York (*http://www.hispanicgenealogy.com*) Web site of organization, offering publications in Spanish and English. (Address: 1230 Fifth Avenue, Suite 458, New York, NY 10029)

Print Resources

General Works

Aguayo, Sergio, and Patricia Weiss Fagen. *Central Americans in Mexico and the United States: Unilateral, Bilateral, and Regional Perspectives*. Washington, D.C.: Hemispheric Migration Project, Center for Immigration Policy and Refugee Assistance, Georgetown University, 1988.

Bachelis, Faren Maree. *The Central Americans*. New York: Chelsea House, 1990.

Bean, Frank D., et al, eds. *Mexican and Central American Population and U.S. Immigration Policy*. Austin: Center for Mexican American Studies, University of Texas at Austin, 1989.

Castro, Max J., ed. *Free Markets, Open Societies, Closed Borders?: Trends in International Migration and Immigration Policy in the Americas*. Coral Gables, Fla.: North-South Center Press, 1999.

Cockcroft, James D. *Latinos in the Making of the United States*. New York: Watts, 1995.

Cortes, Carlos E., ed. *Nineteenth-Century Latin Americans in the United States*. New York: Arno Press, 1980.

de Varona, Frank, ed. *Hispanic Presence in the United States: Historical Beginnings*. Miami: National Hispanic Quincentennial Commission: Mnemosyne, 1993.

de Varona, Frank. *Latino Literacy: The Complete Guide to Our Hispanic History and Culture*. New York: Henry Holt, 1996.

Diaz-Briquets, Sergio, and Sidney Weintraub, eds. *Determinants of Emigration from Mexico, Central America, and the Caribbean*. Boulder, CO: Westview, 1991.

Duignan, Peter, and L. H. Gann. *The Spanish Speakers in the United States: A History*. Lanham, Md.: University Press of America, 1998.

Eastmond, Marita. *The Dilemmas of Exile: Chilean Refugees in the U.S.A.* Gothenburg, Sweden: Department of Social Anthropology, Gothenburg University, 1989.

Fernandez-Shaw, Carlos M. *The Hispanic Presence in North America from 1492 to Today*. Updated ed. New York: Facts on File, 1999. Original publication 1991.

Ferris, Elizabeth G. *The Central American Refugees*. New York : Praeger, 1987.

Gann, Lewis H., and Peter J. Duignan. *The Hispanics in the United States: A History*. Boulder, Col.: Westview, 1986.

Garver, Susan, and Paula McGuire. *Coming to North America: From Mexico, Cuba, and Puerto Rico*. New York: Delacorte, 1981.

Hamamoto, Darrell Y., and Rodolfo D. Torres, eds. *New American Destinies: A Reader in Contemporary Asian and Latino Immigration*. New York: Routledge, 1997.

Hernandez, José. *Conquered Peoples in America*. 5th ed. Dubuque, Iowa: Kendall/Hunt, 1994.

The Hispanic Almanac. New York: Hispanic Policy Development Project, 1984.

Jaffe, Abram J., et al. *Spanish Americans in the United States: Changing Demographic Characteristics*. New York: Research Institute for the Study of Man, 1976.

Kanellos, Nicolás. *Chronology of Hispanic American History: From Pre-Columbian Times to the Present*. New York: Gale, 1995.

———. *Hispanic Firsts: 500 Years of Extraordinary Achievement*. Detroit: Gale, 1997.

———. *Thirty Million Strong: Reclaiming the Hispanic Image in American Culture*. Golden, Col.: Fulcrum, 1998.

Kanellos, Nicolás, and Bryan Ryan, eds. *Hispanic American Chronology*. New York: U X L, 1996.

Novas, Himilce. *Everything You Need to Know About Latino History*. Rev. ed. New York: Plume, 1998.

Ochoa, George. *The New York Public Library Amazing Hispanic American History: A Book of Answers for Kids*. New York: John Wiley, 1998.

Pannier, Wendy S., and Joan Thatcher. *With a Spanish Heritage*. Valley Forge, Pa.: Fund of Renewal, 1975.

Peterson, Linda S. *Central American Migration: Past and Present*. Washington, D.C.: Center for International Research, U.S. Bureau of the Census, 1986.

Redden, Charlotte Ann. *A Comparative Study of Colombian and Costa Rican Emigrants to the United States*. New York: Arno Press, 1976.

Sanchez, Richard. *Building a New World*. Edina, Minn.: Abdo & Daughters, 1994.

Schick, Frank L., and Renee Schick, eds. *Statistical Handbook on U.S. Hispanics*. Phoenix: Oryx, 1991.

Shorris, Earl. *Latinos: A Biography of the People*. New York: Norton, 1992.

Smith, Carter, III, and David Lindroth, eds. *Hispanic-American Experience on File*. New York: Facts on File, 1999.

Suro, Roberto. *Strangers Among Us: How Latino Immigration Is Transforming America*. New York: Knopf, 1998.

On the Caribbean

Chamberlain, Mary, ed. *Caribbean Migration: Globalised Identities*. New York: Routledge, 1998.

Dominguez, Virginia R. *From Neighbor to Stranger: The Dilemma of Caribbean Peoples in the United States*. New Haven: Antilles Research Program, Yale University, 1975.

Larsen, Ronald J. *The Puerto Ricans in America*. Minneapolis: Lerner, 1989.

Levine, Barry B., ed. *The Caribbean Exodus*. New York: Praeger, 1987.

Loescher, Gil, and John Scanlan. *Human Rights, Power Politics, and the International Refugee Regime: The Case of U.S. Treatment of Caribbean Basin Refugees*. Princeton, N.J.: Center of International Studies, Woodrow Wilson School of Public and International Affairs, Princeton University, 1985.

Meditz, Sandra W., and Dennis M. Hanratty, eds. *Islands of the Commonwealth Caribbean, A Regional Study*. Washington, D.C.: U.S. Government Printing Office, 1989.

Palmer, Ransford W., ed. *In Search of a Better Life: Perspectives on Migration from the Caribbean*. New York: Praeger, 1990.

Pastor, Robert A. *Migration and Development in the Caribbean: The Unexplored Connection*. Boulder, Col.: Westview Press, 1985.

Stinner, William F., et al, eds. *Return Migration and Remittances: Developing a Caribbean Perspective*. Washington, D.C.: Research Institute on Immigration and Ethnic Studies, Smithsonian Institution, 1982.

Genealogical Works

Byers, Paula K., ed. *Hispanic American Genealogical Sourcebook*. New York: Gale, 1995.

Flores, Norma P., and Patsy Ludwig. *A Beginner's Guide to Hispanic Genealogy = Introducción a la Investigación Genealogical Latino*. San Mateo, Calif.: Western Book/Journal Press, 1993.

Herrera Saucedo, George E. *An Introduction to Hispanic Genealogical Research: A Manual*. Los Angeles: G. E. Herrera, 1995.

Platt, Lyman De. *Genealogical Historical Guide to Latin America*. Detroit: Gale Research, 1978.

———. *Hispanic Surnames and Family History*. Baltimore: Genealogical Publishing, 1996.

Ryskamp, George R. *Tracing Your Hispanic Heritage*. Riverside, Calif.: Hispanic Family History Research, 1984.

See Parts I and VII and the Appendixes of this volume for more general information, statistics, and resources on immigration.

Part VI
Immigration from
Oceania

Introduction

Oceania consists of Australia, New Zealand, and the Pacific islands, which include the regions of Melanesia, Micronesia, and Polynesia. Among the most heavily populated of the Pacific island nations are Papua New Guinea, Fiji, Tonga, and Western Samoa.

Following is a chapter on Australia and New Zealand. They are presented together because they have in most periods been tabulated together by U.S. immigration authorities. Immigration to the United States from New Zealand has been small throughout history and continues to be so. The Australian immigration figures, though modest, are by far the larger of the two.

Following the chapter are immigration statistics on two of the Pacific islands, Fiji and Tonga, then general immigration statistics and resources for Oceania as a whole.

Immigrants from Australia and New Zealand

The first sizable body of Australian immigrants came to the United States as part of the California Gold Rush (1849–1850). In that period, an estimated 6,000 to 8,000 Australians reached California, most of them via San Francisco. Among them were small numbers of ex-convicts, part of Australia's original European population, and these were seized upon by some people in California to set off a substantial anti-alien scare. Nicknamed the "Sydney Ducks" by the local press, they were—with little basis in fact—blamed for setting off a wave of organized crime in San Francisco and the goldfields. The great majority of these Australians were transients, rather than permanent settlers; most of them returned to Australia after the first flush of gold fever wore off.

Aside from the Gold Rush years, immigration to the United States from Australia and New Zealand has been small, averaging less than 1,000 per year right through 1944. From 1945 to 1947, Australian and New Zealand immigration surged somewhat, with a total of more than 10,000 new arrivals. These were mainly World War II Australian and New Zealander "war brides" joining their American husbands after the war. After that, Australian and New Zealand immigration grew slowly into the 2,000 to 3,000 yearly range, staying at that level through 1996. In all, Australian and New Zealand immigrants totaled a little less than 157,000 between 1870 and 1996.

Table 6.1: Number and Percentage of Immigrants from Australia in Total U.S. Immigration Annually, 1971–1996

Year	Number of Immigrants from Australia	Total U.S. Immigration	Percentage of Immigrants from Australia in Total U.S. Immigration
1971	1,400	370,473	0.38
1972	1,551	384,685	0.40
1973	1,400	400,063	0.35
1974	1,236	394,861	0.31
1975	1,116	396,194	0.28
1976	1,760	502,289	0.35
1977	1,389	462,315	0.30
1978	1,565	601,442	0.26
1979	1,400	460,348	0.30
1980	1,480	530,639	0.28
1981	1,281	596,600	0.21
1982	1,367	594,131	0.23
1983	1,273	559,763	0.23
1984	1,308	543,903	0.24
1985	1,362	570,009	0.24
1986	1,354	601,708	0.23
1987	1,253	601,516	0.21
1988	1,356	643,025	0.21
1989	1,546	1,090,924	0.14
1990	1,754	1,536,483	0.11
1991	1,678	1,827,167	0.09
1992	2,238	973,977	0.23
1993	2,320	904,292	0.26
1994	2,049	804,416	0.25
1995	1,751	720,461	0.24
1996	1,950	915,900	0.21
Total 1971-1996	40,137	17,987,584	0.22

Sources: *Statistical Yearbook of the Immigration and Naturalization Service,* 1980, Table 13; *Statistical Yearbook of the Immigration and Naturalization Service,* 1986, Table 3; *Statistical Yearbook of the Immigration and Naturalization Service,* 1996, Table 3.

Table 6.2: Number and Percentage of Immigrants from Australia and New Zealand in Total U.S. Immigration Annually, 1870–1996

Year	Number of Immigrants from Australia and New Zealand	Total U.S. Immigrants	Percentage of Immigrants from Australia and New Zealand in Total U.S. Immigration
1870	36	387,203	0.01
1871	18	321,350	0.01
1872	2,180	404,806	0.54
1873	1,135	459,803	0.25
1874	960	313,339	0.31
1875	1,104	227,498	0.49
1876	1,205	169,986	0.71
1877	912	141,857	0.64
1878	606	138,469	0.44
1879	813	177,826	0.46
1880	953	457,257	0.21
1881	1,188	669,431	0.18
1882	878	788,992	0.11
1883	554	603,322	0.09
1884	502	518,592	0.10
1885	449	395,346	0.11
1886	522	334,203	0.16
1887	528	490,109	0.11
1888	697	546,889	0.13
1889	1,000	444,427	0.23
1890	699	455,302	0.15
1891	777	560,319	0.14
1892	267	579,663	0.05
1893	248	439,730	0.06
1894	244	285,631	0.09
1895	155	258,536	0.06
1896	87	343,267	0.03
1897	139	230,832	0.06
1898	153	229,299	0.07
1899	456	311,715	0.15
1900	214	448,572	0.05
1901	325	487,918	0.07
1902	384	648,743	0.06
1903	1,150	857,046	0.13
1904	1,461	812,870	0.18
1905	2,091	1,026,499	0.20
1906	1,682	1,100,735	0.15
1907	1,947	1,285,349	0.15
1908	1,098	782,870	0.14
1909	839	751,786	0.11
1910	998	1,041,570	0.10
1911	984	878,587	0.11
1912	794	838,172	0.09
1913	1,229	1,197,892	0.10
1914	1,336	1,218,480	0.11

Year	Number of Immigrants from Australia and New Zealand	Total U.S. Immigrants	Percentage of Immigrants from Australia and New Zealand in Total U.S. Immigration
1915	1,282	326,700	0.39
1916	1,484	298,826	0.50
1917	1,014	295,403	0.34
1918	925	110,618	0.84
1919	1,234	141,132	0.87
1920	2,066	430,001	0.48
1921	2,191	805,228	0.27
1922	855	309,556	0.28
1923	711	522,919	0.14
1924	635	706,896	0.09
1925	416	294,314	0.14
1926	556	304,488	0.18
1927	712	335,175	0.21
1928	578	307,255	0.19
1929	619	279,678	0.22
1930	1,026	241,700	0.42
1931	616	97,139	0.63
1932	291	35,576	0.82
1933	122	23,068	0.53
1934	130	29,470	0.44
1935	132	34,956	0.38
1936	147	36,329	0.40
1937	145	50,244	0.29
1938	228	67,895	0.34
1939	213	82,998	0.26
1940	207	70,756	0.29
1941	194	51,776	0.37
1942	120	28,781	0.42
1943	120	23,725	0.51
1944	577	28,551	2.02
1945	1,625	38,119	4.26
1946	6,009	108,721	5.53
1947	2,821	147,292	1.92
1948	1,218	170,570	0.71
1949	661	188,317	0.35
1950	460	249,187	0.18
1951	490	205,717	0.24
1952	545	265,520	0.21
1953	742	170,434	0.44
1954	845	208,177	0.41
1955	932	237,790	0.39
1956	1,171	321,625	0.36
1957	1,228	326,867	0.38
1958	1,783	253,265	0.70
1959	1,878	260,686	0.72

Table 6.2 Continued

Year	Number of Immigrants from Australia and New Zealand	Total U.S. Immigrants	Percentage of Immigrants from Australia and New Zealand in Total U.S. Immigration
1960	1,892	265,398	0.71
1961	1,556	271,344	0.57
1962	1,427	283,763	0.50
1963	1,642	306,260	0.54
1964	1,767	292,248	0.60
1965	1,803	296,697	0.61
1966	1,894	323,040	0.59
1967	2,128	361,972	0.59
1968	2,374	454,448	0.52
1969	2,278	358,579	0.64
1970	2,693	373,326	0.72
1971	1,870	370,478	0.50
1972	2,048	384,685	0.53
1973	1,890	400,063	0.47
1974	1,645	394,861	0.42
1975	1,500	386,194	0.39
1976	2,313	502,289	0.46
1977	1,986	462,315	0.43
1978	2,184	601,442	0.36
1979	1,999	460,348	0.43
1980	2,209	530,639	0.42
1981	1,947	596,600	0.33
1982	2,009	594,131	0.34
1983	1,879	559,763	0.34
1984	1,903	543,903	0.35
1985	2,041	570,009	0.36
1986	1,964	601,708	0.33
1987	1,844	601,516	0.31
1988	2,024	643,025	0.31
1989	2,335	1,090,924	0.21
1990	2,583	1,536,483	0.17
1991	2,471	1,827,167	0.14
1992	3,205	973,977	0.33
1993	3,372	904,292	0.37
1994	2,967	804,416	0.37
1995	2,478	720,461	0.34
1996	2,750	915,900	0.30
Total 1870-1996	156,821	56,150,192	0.28

Sources notes for 1820–1970: 1820–1932, U.S. Immigration and Naturalization Service, unpublished data, and U.S. Bureau of Immigration, Annual Reports of the Commissioner General of Immigration, as follows: 1820–1926, Report for 1926, pp. 170–178; 1927–1931, Report for 1931, pp. 222–223; Report for 1932, pp. 120–125; 1933–1957, U.S. Immigration and Naturalization Service, unpublished data; 1958–1970, Annual Report of the Immigration and Naturalization Service, annual issues; Statistical Yearbook 13.

Sources: Figures for 1820–1970 adapted from Historical Yearbook of the United States, Bicentennial Edition, U.S. Bureau of the Census, 1975, Chapter C 89–119. Figures for 1971–1997 adapted from Statistical Yearbook of the Immigration and Naturalization Service, 1980, Table 13; Statistical Yearbook of the Immigration and Naturalization Service, 1986, Table 3; Statistical Yearbook of the Immigration and Naturalization Service, 1996, Table 3.

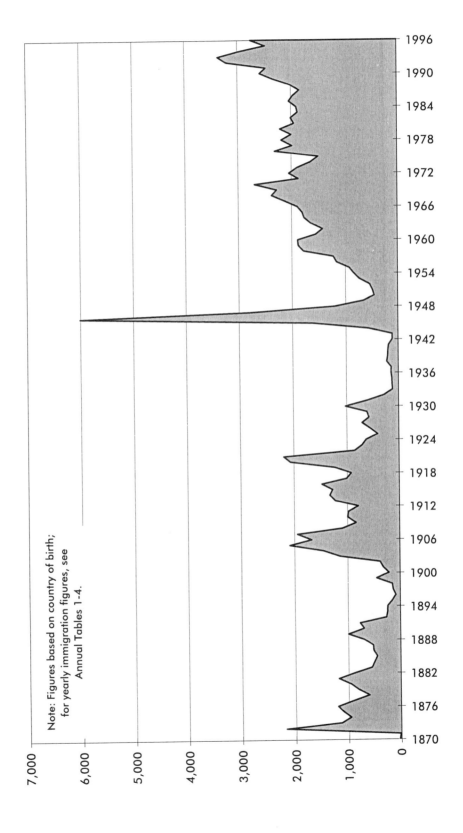

Graph 6.1: Number of Immigrants from Australia and New Zealand Annually, 1870–1996

Note: Figures based on country of birth; for yearly immigration figures, see Annual Tables 1-4.

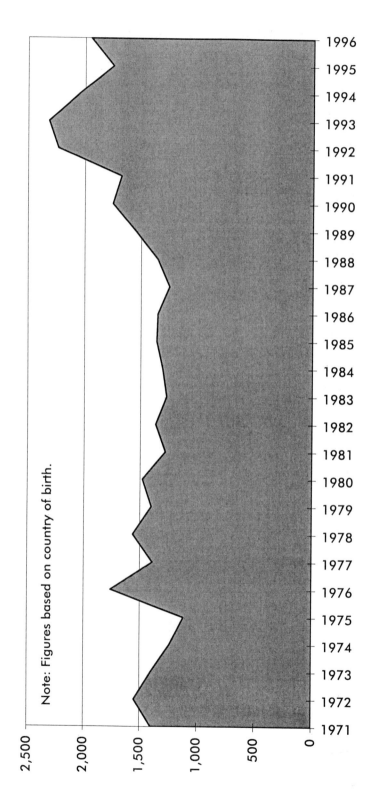

Graph 6.2: Number of Immigrants from Australia Annually, 1971–1996

Note: Figures based on country of birth.

Table 6.3: Number and Percentage of Foreign-Born Immigrants from Australia by Decade in Total U.S. Immigration at End of Decade, 1860–1990

Decade	Number of Foreign-Born Immigrants from Australia	Total U.S. Population	Percentage of Foreign-Born Immigrants from Australia in Total U.S. Population
1860	1,419	31,443,321	0.00
1870	3,118	39,818,449	0.01
1880	4,906	50,155,783	0.01
1890	5,984	62,947,714	0.01
1900	6,807	75,994,575	0.01
1910	9,035	91,972,266	0.01
1920	10,914	105,710,620	0.01
1930	12,816	122,775,046	0.01
1940	(NA)	131,669,275	(NA)
1950	(NA)	150,697,361	(NA)
1960	22,209	179,323,175	0.01
1970	24,271	203,235,298	0.01
1980	(NA)	227,726,000	(NA)
1990	42,267	249,907,000	0.02

NA = Not available

Source: Adapted from Series C 228–295, Foreign-Born Population, by Country of Birth: 1850–1970, in *Historical Yearbook of the Immigration of the United States, Colonial Times to 1970, Bicentennial Edition,* and other updating tables from the U.S. Census Bureau.

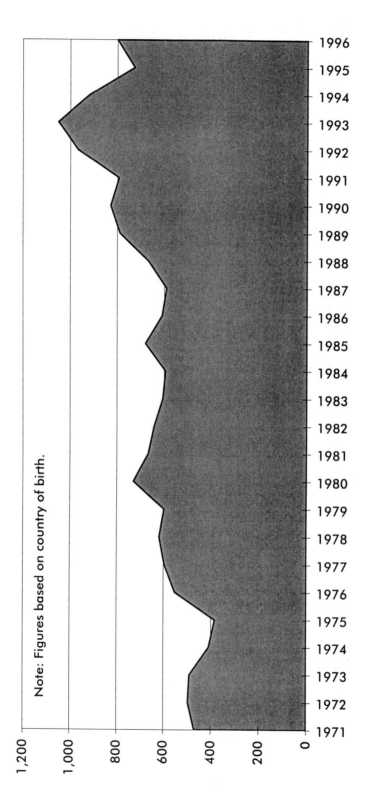

Graph 6.3: Number of Immigrants from New Zealand Annually, 1971–1996

Note: Figures based on country of birth.

Table 6.4: Number and Percentage of Immigrants from New Zealand in Total U.S. Immigration Annually, 1971–1996

Year	Number of Immigrants from New Zealand	Total U.S. Immigration	Percentage of Immigrants from New Zealand in Total U.S. Immigration
1971	470	370,473	0.13
1972	497	384,685	0.13
1973	490	400,063	0.12
1974	409	394,861	0.10
1975	384	396,194	0.10
1976	553	502,289	0.11
1977	597	462,315	0.13
1978	619	601,442	0.10
1979	599	460,348	0.13
1980	729	530,639	0.14
1981	666	596,600	0.11
1982	642	594,131	0.11
1983	606	559,763	0.11
1984	595	543,903	0.11
1985	679	570,009	0.12
1986	610	601,708	0.10
1987	591	601,516	0.10
1988	668	643,025	0.10
1989	789	1,090,924	0.07
1990	829	1,536,483	0.05
1991	793	1,827,167	0.04
1992	967	973,977	0.10
1993	1,052	904,292	0.12
1994	918	804,416	0.11
1995	727	720,461	0.10
1996	800	915,900	0.09
Total 1971-1996	17,279	17,987,584	0.10

Sources: *Statistical Yearbook of the Immigration and Naturalization Service*, 1980; Table 13; *Statistical Yearbook of the Immigration and Naturalization Service*, 1986, Table 3; *Statistical Yearbook of the Immigration and Naturalization Service*, 1996, Table 3.

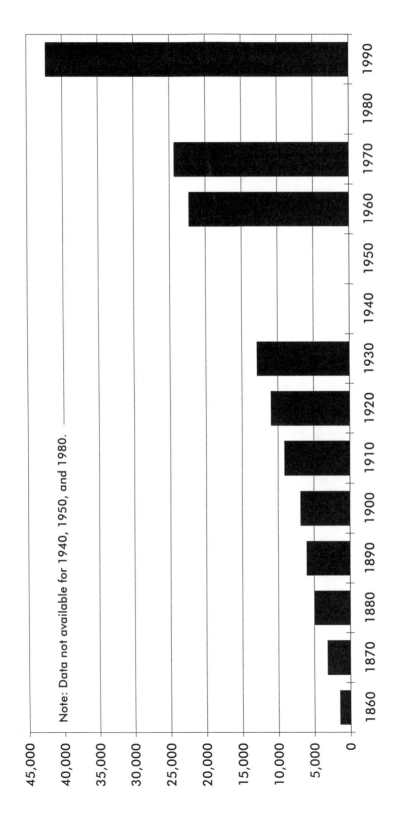

Graph 6.4: Number of Foreign-Born Immigrants from Australia in Total U.S. Population by Decade, 1860–1990

Note: Data not available for 1940, 1950, and 1980.

Resources

Internet Resources

Cyndi's List—Australia & New Zealand (*http://www.cyndislist.com/austnz.htm*) Web site of genealogical resources maintained by genealogical author Cyndi Howells.

Australasia Genealogy Web (*http://home.vicnet.net.au/~AGWeb/agweb.htm*) Web site of genealogical resources with searchable name index and related links.

Australian and New Zealand Genealogy Pages (*http://opax.swin.edu.au/andrew/aust_genealogy.html*) Privately maintained set of links.

Australian and New Zealand Genealogical Links Galore (*http://www.benet.net.au/~brandis/links/genlinks.html*) Privately maintained Web site of links.

New Zealand Genealogy Internet Guide (*http://www.geocities.com/Heartland/Pointe/8355*) Web site offering resources and links for Australia and New Zealand, and also Germany and the Netherlands.

Print Resources

Moore, John Hammon, ed. *Australians in America, 1876–1976*. St. Lucia, Queensland, Australia: University of Queensland Press, 1977.

Other Immigrants from Oceania

Following are immigration statistics relating to two of the nations from Oceania. None of the Pacific island nations has ever sent many emigrants to the United States , but these two have some United States immigration history worthy of graphic presentation.

See "General Immigration Statistics for Oceania" on p. 652, and "General Immigration Resources for Oceania" on p. 655, for wider information and resources.

For more information on immigration statistics from Oceania, see "General Notes on Immigration Statistics" on p. 684, under "Immigration from Australasia, 1870–1970."

Immigrants from Fiji

Table 6.5: Number and Percentage of Immigrants from Fiji Annually, 1971–1996

Year	Number of Immigrants from Fiji	Total U.S. Immigration	Percentage of Immigrants from Fiji in Total U.S. Immigration
1971	323	370,473	0.09
1972	302	384,685	0.08
1973	388	400,063	0.10
1974	431	394,861	0.11
1975	684	396,194	0.17
1976	831	502,289	0.17
1977	854	462,315	0.18
1978	809	601,442	0.13
1979	1,000	460,348	0.22
1980	724	530,639	0.14
1981	1,060	596,600	0.18
1982	659	594,131	0.11
1983	712	559,763	0.13
1984	901	543,903	0.17
1985	980	570,009	0.17
1986	972	601,708	0.16
1987	1,205	601,516	0.20
1988	1,028	643,025	0.16
1989	968	1,090,924	0.09
1990	1,353	1,536,483	0.09
1991	1,349	1,827,167	0.07
1992	807	973,977	0.08
1993	854	904,292	0.09
1994	1,007	804,416	0.13
1995	1,491	720,461	0.21
1996	1,847	915,900	0.20
Total 1971-96	23,539	17,987,584	0.13

Sources: *Statistical Yearbook of the Immigration and Naturalization Service,* 1980, Table 13; *Statistical Yearbook of the Immigration and Naturalization Service,* 1986, Table 3; *Statistical Yearbook of the Immigration and Naturalization Service,* 1996, Table 3.

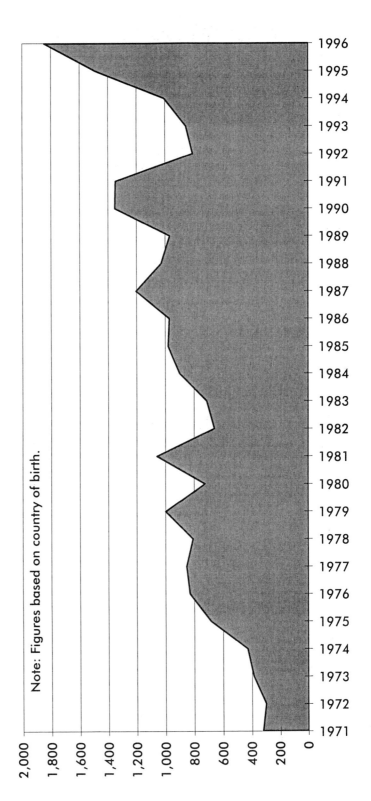

Graph 6.5: Number of Immigrants from Fiji Annually, 1971–1996

Note: Figures based on country of birth.

Immigrants from Tonga

Table 6.6: Number and Percentage of Immigrants from Tonga Annually, 1971–1996

Year	Number of Immigrants from Tonga	Total U.S. Immigration	Percentage of Immigrants from Tonga in Total U.S. Immigration
1971	226	370,473	0.06
1972	355	384,685	0.09
1973	391	400,063	0.10
1974	447	394,861	0.11
1975	527	396,194	0.13
1976	647	502,289	0.13
1977	489	462,315	0.11
1978	706	601,442	0.12
1979	809	460,348	0.18
1980	453	530,639	0.09
1981	588	596,600	0.10
1982	561	594,131	0.09
1983	481	559,763	0.09
1984	555	543,903	0.10
1985	669	570,009	0.12
1986	510	601,708	0.08
1987	545	601,516	0.09
1988	434	643,025	0.07
1989	646	1,090,924	0.06
1990	1,375	1,536,483	0.09
1991	1,685	1,827,167	0.09
1992	703	973,977	0.07
1993	348	904,292	0.04
1994	293	804,416	0.04
1995	403	720,461	0.06
1996	416	915,900	0.05
Total 1971-96	15,262	17,987,584	0.08

Sources: *Statistical Yearbook of the Immigration and Naturalization Service*, 1980, Table 13; *Statistical Yearbook of the Immigration and Naturalization Service*, 1986, Table 3; *Statistical Yearbook of the Immigration and Naturalization Service*, 1996, Table 3.

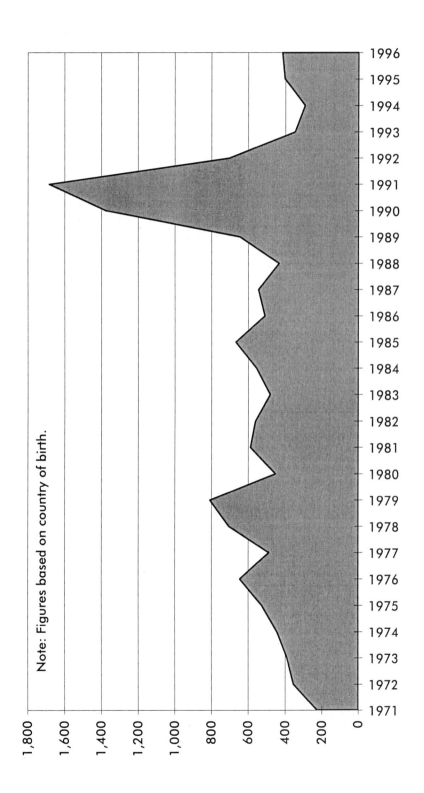

Graph 6.6: Number of Immigrants from Tonga Annually, 1971–1996

Note: Figures based on country of birth.

General Immigration Statistics for Oceania

Table 6.7: Number and Percentage of Immigrants from Oceania in Total U.S. Immigration Annually, 1820–1996

Decade	Number of Immigrants from Oceania	Total U.S. Immigrants	Percentage of Immigrants from Oceania in Total U.S. Immigration
1820	1	8,385	0.01
1821-30	2	143,439	0.00
1831-40	9	599,125	0.00
1841-50	29	1,713,251	0.00
1851-60	158	2,598,214	0.01
1861-70	214	2,314,824	0.01
1871-80	10,914	2,812,191	0.39
1881-90	12,574	5,246,613	0.24
1891-1900	3,965	3,687,564	0.11
1901-10	13,024	8,795,386	0.15
1911-20	13,427	5,735,811	0.23
1921-30	8,726	4,107,209	0.21
1931-40	2,483	528,431	0.47
1941-50	14,551	1,035,039	1.41
1951-60	12,976	2,515,479	0.52
1961-70	25,122	3,321,677	0.76
1971-80	41,242	4,493,314	0.92
1981-90	45,205	7,338,062	0.62
1991-96	36,326	6,146,213	0.59
Total 1820-1996	240,948	63,140,227	0.38

Source: Adapted from Table 2, Immigration by Region and Selected Country of Last Residence, Fiscal Years 1820–1996, from the *Statistical Yearbook of the Immigration and Naturalization Service*, 1996.

Table 6.8: Number and Percentage of Foreign-Born Immigrants from the Pacific Islands by Decade in Total U.S. Population at End of Decade, 1850–1990

Decade	Number of Foreign-Born Immigrants from the Pacific Islands	Total U.S. Population	Foreign-Born Immigrants from the Pacific Islands in Total U.S. Population
1850	588	23,191,876	0.00
1860	721	31,443,321	0.00
1870	910	39,818,449	0.00
1880	1,953	50,155,783	0.00
1890	3,369	62,947,714	0.01
1900	2,013	75,994,575	0.00
1910	2,415	91,972,266	0.00
1920	3,712	105,710,620	0.00
1930	4,527	122,775,046	0.00
1940	(NA)	131,669,275	(NA)
1950	(NA)	150,697,361	(NA)
1960	12,521	179,323,175	0.01
1970	8,870	203,235,298	0.00
1980	(NA)	227,726,000	(NA)
1990	58,878	249,907,000	0.02

NA = Not available

Note: 1960, 1970, and 1990 figures include New Zealand and Trust Territories. 1960 and 1970 figures exclude U.S. territories.

Source: Adapted from Series C 228–295, Foreign-Born Population, by Country of Birth: 1850–1970, in *Historical Statistics of the United States, Colonial Times to 1970, Bicentennial Edition*, and other updating tables from the U.S. Census Bureau.

Graph 6.7: Number of Immigrants from Oceania Annually, 1820–1996

Note: Figures based on country of last residence; for yearly immigration figures, see Annual Tables 1-4.

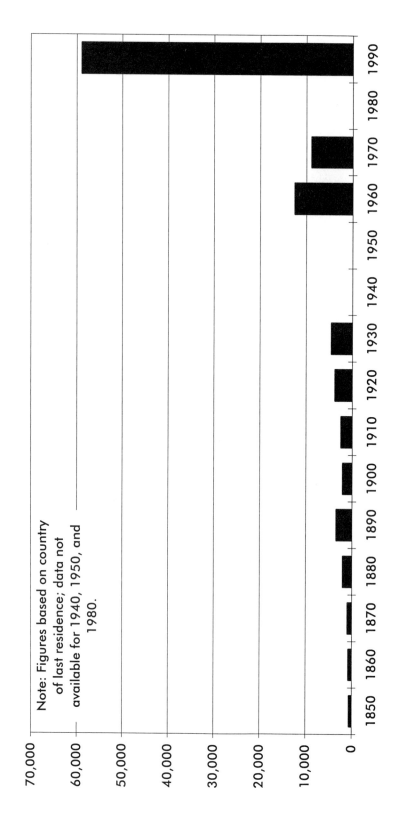

Graph 6.8: Number of Foreign-Born Immigrants from the Pacific Islands in Total U.S. Population by Decade, 1850–1990

Note: Figures based on country of last residence; data not available for 1940, 1950, and 1980.

General Immigration Resources for Oceania

Internet Resources

PacificGenWeb (*http://www.rootsweb.com/~pacifgw/*) Part of the WorldGenWeb project, linking genealogical research sites around the world, by region, with resources by individual country.

Asian Community Online Network (*http://www.igc.org/acon*) Web site offering news, publications, and links for Asian Pacific Americans; a project of the Institute for Global Communications (*http://www.igc.org/igc*)

Print Resources

Ahlburg, Dennis A., and Michael J. Levin. *The North East Passage: A Study of Pacific Islander Migration to American Samoa and the United States.* Canberra: National Centre for Development Studies, Research School of Pacific Studies, the Australian National University, 1990.

Barkan, Elliott Robert. *Asian and Pacific Islander Migration to the United States: A Model of New Global Patterns.* Westport, Conn.: Greenwood, 1992.

Barringer, Herbert R., et al. *Asians and Pacific Islanders in the United States.* New York: Russell Sage Foundation, 1993.

Ford, Douglas. *The Pacific Islanders.* New York: Chelsea House, 1989.

Hune, Shirley. *Pacific Migration to the United States: Trends and Themes in Historical and Sociological Literature.* Prepared for the Research Institute on Immigration and Ethnic Studies, Smithsonian Institution, Washington, D.C. Washington, D.C.: The Institute, 1977.

Oceania, A Regional Study. 2d ed. Frederica M. Bunge and Melinda W. Cooke, eds. Washington, D.C.: Federal Research Division, Library of Congress, 1985.

Revilla, Linda A., et al., eds. *Bearing Dreams, Shaping Visions: Asian Pacific American Perspectives.* Pullman: Washington State University Press, 1993.

See Parts I and VII and the Appendixes of this volume for more general information, statistics, and resources on immigration.

Part VII
Annual Immigration
Statistics

Annual Immigration Statistics Introduction

The tables in this section of the book are the basic annual immigration tables generated from official records kept by the U.S. government since 1820. These contain the basic data on immigration, which is the basis for most of the tables and graphs in this book and for any study of immigration to the United States.

The nature and detail of the immigration data has differed greatly over the nearly two centuries. The names and boundaries of many countries have changed around the world. The U.S. government has also changed they way it has collected and organized its data. As a result the tables vary considerably in format and level of detail. Most notably, statistics for many individual countries are broken out individually in tables for recent decades, where previously they were sometimes grouped under regional designations, such as "Other Asia."

The largest table, and the most basic one for historical purposes, is Table 7.1: Number of Immigrants to the United States by Region and Selected Country of Birth Annually, 1820–1970. This table is followed by an extensive set of notes describing how the data was collected over the decades from various portions of the world. (The tables in this section also contain specific notes at the end of each table.)

Note that Table 7.1 is quite extensive, running dozens of pages. To help you find precisely what you are looking for in the table, note that:

- Overall figures and data for European countries begin on p. 659.

- Data for Asian countries begin on p. 671.

- Data on American, African, and Australasian countries begin on p. 677.

Following this main table are more recent and often more detailed tables, which carry U.S. immigration data up through the late 1990s. These tables are:

- Table 7.2: Number of Immigrants to the United States by Region and Selected Country of Birth Annually, 1971–1980

- Table 7.3: Number of Immigrants to the United States by Region and Selected Country of Birth Annually, 1981–1985

- Table 7.4: Number of Immigrants to the United States by Region and Selected Country of Birth Annually, 1986–1996

- Table 7.5: Number of Immigrants to the United States by Region and Selected Country of Birth Annually, 1997–1998

Note that the latter table was generated while this book was in production and represents the most current official immigration statistics available as of mid-2001. Although the data in Table 7.5 arrived too late to be incorporated into the body of the book, this table will give readers the most recent immigration data available on any country or region of interest. Updates are published annually by the Immigration and Naturalization Service, but (as the above indicates) the volumes are often two or even three years behind.

Table 7.1: Number of Immigrants to the United States by Region and Selected Country of Birth Annually, 1820–1970

Year	World Immigration All Countries (1)	Total Europe	Northwestern Europe Great Britain	Ireland (2)	Scandinavia (3)	Other (4)
1820	8,385	7,691	2,410	3,614	23	452
1821	9,127	5,936	3,210	1,518	24	521
1822	6,911	4,418	1,221	2,267	28	522
1823	6,354	4,016	1,100	1,908	7	528
1824	7,912	4,965	1,264	2,345	20	671
1825	10,199	8,543	2,095	4,888	18	719
1826	10,837	9,751	2,319	5,408	26	968
1827	18,875	16,719	4,186	9,766	28	1,829
1828	27,382	24,729	5,352	12,488	60	4,700
1829	22,520	12,523	3,179	7,415	30	1,065
1830	23,322	7,217	1,153	2,721	19	1,305
1831	22,633	13,039	2,475	5,772	36	2,277
1832	60,482	34,193	5,331	12,436	334	5,695
1833	58,640	29,111	4,916	8,648	189	5,355
1834	65,365	57,510	10,490	24,474	66	4,468
1835	45,374	41,987	8,970	20,927	68	3,369
1836	76,242	70,465	13,106	30,578	473	5,189
1837	79,340	71,039	12,218	28,508	399	5,769
1838	38,914	34,070	5,420	12,645	112	3,839
1839	68,069	64,148	10,271	23,963	380	7,891
1840	84,066	80,126	2,613	39,430	207	7,978
1841	80,289	76,216	16,188	37,772	226	6,077
1842	104,565	99,945	22,005	51,342	588	5,361
1843	52,496	49,013	8,430	19,670	1,777	4,364
1844	78,615	74,745	14,353	33,490	1,336	4,343
1845	114,371	109,301	19,210	44,821	982	9,466

Table 7.1 Continued

Year	World Immigration All Countries (1)	Total Europe	Northwestern Europe			
			Great Britain	Ireland (2)	Scandinavia (3)	Other (4)
1846	154,416	146,315	22,180	51,752	2,030	12,303
1847	234,968	229,117	23,302	105,536	1,320	24,336
1848	226,527	218,025	35,159	112,934	1,113	9,877
1849	297,024	286,501	55,132	159,398	3,481	7,634
1850	369,980	308,323	51,085	164,004	1,589	11,470
1851	379,466	369,510	51,487	221,253	2,438	20,905
1852	371,603	362,484	40,699	159,548	4,106	11,278
1853	368,645	361,576	37,576	162,649	3,396	14,205
1854	427,833	405,542	58,647	101,606	4,222	23,070
1855	200,877	187,729	47,572	49,627	1,349	14,571
1856	200,436	186,083	44,658	54,349	1,330	12,403
1857	251,306	216,224	58,479	54,361	2,747	6,879
1858	123,126	111,354	28,956	26,873	2,662	4,580
1859	121,282	110,949	26,163	35,216	1,590	3,727
1860	153,640	141,209	29,737	48,637	840	5,278
1861	91,918	81,200	19,675	23,797	850	3,769
1862	91,985	83,710	24,639	23,351	2,550	4,386
1863	176,282	163,733	66,882	55,916	3,119	3,245
1864	193,418	185,233	53,428	63,523	2,961	5,621
1865	248,120	214,048	82,465	29,772	7,258	7,992
1866	318,568	278,916	94,924	36,690	14,495	13,648
1867	315,722	283,751	52,641	72,879	8,491	12,417
1868	138,840	130,090	24,127	32,068	11,985	4,293
1869	352,768	315,963	84,438	40,786	43,941	10,585
1870	387,203	328,626	103,677	56,996	30,742	9,152
1871	321,350	265,145	85,455	57,439	22,132	7,174

Year	World Immigration All Countries (1)	Total Europe	Northwestern Europe Great Britain	Ireland (2)	Scandinavia (3)	Other (4)
1872	404,806	352,155	84,912	68,732	28,575	15,614
1873	459,803	397,541	89,500	77,344	35,481	22,892
1874	313,339	262,783	62,021	53,707	19,178	15,998
1875	227,498	182,961	47,905	37,957	14,322	11987
1876	169,986	120,920	29,291	19,575	12,323	10923
1877	141,857	106,195	23,581	14,569	11,274	8621
1878	138,469	101,612	22,150	15,932	12,254	6929
1879	177,826	134,259	29,955	20,013	21,820	9081
1880	457,257	348,691	73,273	71,603	65,657	15042
1881	669,431	528,545	81,376	72,342	81,582	26883
1882	788,992	648,186	102,991	76,432	105,326	27,796
1883	603,322	522,587	76,606	81,486	71,994	24,271
1884	518,592	453,686	65,950	63,344	52,728	18,768
1885	395,346	353,083	57,713	51,795	40,704	13,732
1886	334,203	329,529	62,929	49,619	46,735	11,737
1887	490,109	482,829	93,378	68,370	67,629	17,307
1888	546,889	538,131	108,692	73,513	81,924	23,251
1889	444,427	434,790	87,992	65,557	57,504	22,010
1890	455,302	445,680	69,730	53,024	50,368	20,575
1891	560,319	546,085	66,605	55,706	60,107	21,824
1892	579,663	570,876	42,215	51,383	66,295	21,731
1893	439,730	429,324	35,189	43,578	58,945	17,888
1894	285,631	277,052	22,520	30,231	32,400	9,514
1895	258,536	250,342	28,833	46,304	26,852	7,313
1896	343,267	329,067	24,565	40,262	33,199	7,611
1897	230,832	216,397	12,752	28,421	21,089	5,323

Table 7.1 Continued

Year	World Immigration All Countries (1)	Total Europe	Northwestern Europe			
			Great Britain	Ireland (2)	Scandinavia (3)	Other (4)
1898	229,299	217,786	12,894	25,128	19,282	4,698
1899	311,715	297,349	13,456	31,673	22,192	5,150
1900	448,572	424,700	12,509	35,730	31,151	5,822
1901	487,918	469,237	14,985	30,561	39,234	9,279
1902	648,743	619,068	16,898	29,138	54,038	10,322
1903	857,046	814,507	33,637	35,310	77,647	17,009
1904	812,870	767,933	51,448	36,142	60,096	23,321
1905	1,026,499	974,273	84,189	52,945	60,625	24693
1906	1,100,735	1,018,365	67,198	34,995	52,781	23277
1907	1,285,349	1,199,566	79,037	34,530	49,965	26512
1908	782,870	691,901	62,824	30,556	30,175	22177
1909	751,786	654,875	46,793	25,033	32,496	17756
1910	1,041,570	926,291	68,941	29,855	48,267	23852
1911	878,587	764,757	73,384	29,112	42,285	25549
1912	838,172	718,875	57,148	25,879	27,554	22,921
1913	1,197,892	1,055,855	60,328	27,876	32,267	28,086
1914	1,218,480	1,058,391	48,729	24,688	29,391	25,591
1915	326,700	197,919	27,237	14,185	17,883	12,096
1916	298,826	145,699	16,063	8,639	14,761	8,715
1917	295,403	133,083	10,735	5,406	13,771	6,731
1918	110,618	31,063	2,516	331	6,506	3,146
1919	141,132	24,627	6,797	474	5,590	5,126
1920	430,001	246,295	38,471	9,591	13,444	24,491
1921	805,228	652,364	51,142	28,435	22,854	29,317
1922	309,556	216,385	25,153	10,579	14,625	11,149
1923	522,919	307,920	45,759	15,740	34,184	12,469

Year	World Immigration — All Countries (1)	Total Europe	Northwestern Europe			
			Great Britain	Ireland (2)	Scandinavia (3)	Other (4)
1924	706,896	364,339	59,490	17,111	35,577	16,077
1925	294,314	148,366	27,172	26,650	16,810	8,548
1926	304,488	155,562	25,528	24,897	16,818	8,773
1927	335,175	168,368	23,669	28,545	16,860	9,134
1928	307,255	158,513	19,958	25,268	16,184	9,079
1929	279,678	158,598	21,327	19,921	17,379	9,091
1930	241,700	147,438	31,015	23,445	6,919	9,170
1931	97,139	61,909	9,110	7,305	3,144	4,420
1932	35,576	20,579	2,057	539	938	1,558
1933	23,068	12,383	979	338	511	1,045
1934	29,470	17,210	1,305	443	557	1,270
1935	34,956	22,778	1,413	454	688	1808
1936	36,329	23,480	1,310	444	646	1745
1937	50,244	31,863	1,726	531	971	2512
1938	67,895	44,495	2,262	1,085	1,393	3352
1939	82,998	63,138	3,058	1,189	1,178	5214
1940	70,756	50,454	6,158	839	1,260	7743
1941	51,776	26,541	7,714	272	1,137	9009
1942	28,781	11,153	907	83	371	5,622
1943	23,725	4,920	974	165	239	1,531
1944	28,551	4,509	1,321	112	281	619
1945	38,119	5,943	3,029	427	224	365
1946	108,721	52,852	33,552	1,816	1,278	8,651
1947	147,292	83,535	23,788	2,574	4,918	14,562
1948	170,570	103,544	26,403	7,534	6,127	13,721
1949	188,317	129,592	21,149	8,678	6,665	12,288

Table 7.1 Continued

Year	World Immigration All Countries (1)	Total Europe	Northwestern Europe Great Britain	Ireland (2)	Scandinavia (3)	Other (4)
1950	249,187	199,115	12,755	5,842	5,661	10,857
1951	205,717	149,545	14,898	3,144	5,502	10,973
1952	265,520	193,626	22,177	3,526	5,416	12,476
1953	170,434	82,352	16,639	4,304	5,537	11,145
1954	208,177	92,121	16,672	4,655	5,459	11,853
1955	237,790	110,591	15,761	5,222	5,159	10,707
1956	321,625	156,866	19,008	5,607	5,681	15,254
1957	326,867	169,625	24,020	8,227	6,189	25,109
1958	253,265	115,198	24,147	9,134	5,873	11,364
1959	260,686	138,191	18,325	6,595	6,100	14,217
1960	265,398	120,178	19,967	6,918	6,185	17,234
1961	271,344	108,532	18,719	5,738	4,943	14,635
1962	283,763	103,989	18,066	5,118	4,716	13,117
1963	306,260	109,066	22,708	5,746	5,208	11,938
1964	292,248	108,215	25,758	6,055	5,497	11,120
1965	296,697	101,468	24,135	5,187	5,853	11526
1966	323,040	115,898	18,777	3,267	4,549	9,049
1967	361,972	128,775	23,004	2,765	4,230	9,881
1968	454,448	129,022	26,025	2,995	4,203	9,873
1969	358,579	114,052	15,072	1,981	2,149	5,944
1970	373,326	110,653	14,089	1,583	2,110	6,961

	Central Europe			Eastern Europe		Southern Europe	
Year	Germany (5)	Poland	Other (6)	U.S.S.R. and Baltic States (7)	Other (8)	Italy	Other (9)
1820	968	5		14	1	30	174
1821	383	1		7	–	63	209
1822	148	3		10	4	35	180
1823	183	3		7	2	33	245
1824	230	4		7	2	45	377
1825	450	1		10	–	75	287
1826	511	–		4	2	57	456
1827	432	1		19	1	35	422
1828	1,851	1		7	6	34	230
1829	597	–		1	1	23	212
1830	1,976	2		3	2	9	27
1831	2,413	–		1	–	28	37
1832	10,194	34		52	–	3	114
1833	6,988	1		159	1	1,699	1,155
1834	17,686	54		15	1	105	151
1835	8,311	54		9	–	60	219
1836	20,707	53		2	3	115	239
1837	23,740	81		19	–	36	269
1838	11,683	41		13	–	86	231
1839	21,028	46		7	–	84	477
1840	29,704	5		–	1	37	151
1841	15,291	15		174	6	179	288
1842	20,370	10		28	2	100	139
1843	14,441	17		6	5	117	186
1844	20,731	36		13	10	141	292
1845	34,355	6		1	3	137	320

Table 7.1 Continued

| Year | Central Europe | | | Eastern Europe | | Southern Europe | |
	Germany (5)	Poland	Other (6)	U.S.S.R. and Baltic States (7)	Other (8)	Italy	Other (9)
1846	57,561	4		248	4	151	82
1847	74,281	8		5	2	164	163
1848	58,465	-		1	3	241	232
1849	60,235	4		44	9	209	355
1850	78,896	5		31	15	431	797
1851	72,482	10		1	2	447	485
1852	145,918	110		2	3	351	469
1853	141,946	33		3	15	555	1,198
1854	215,009	208		2	7	1,263	1,508
1855	71,918	462		13	9	1,052	1,156
1856	71,028	20		9	5	1,365	916
1857	91,781	124		25	11	1,007	810
1858	45,310	9		246	17	1,240	1,461
1859	41,784	106		91	10	932	1,330
1860	54,491	82		65	4	1,019	1,056
1861	31,661	48	51	34	5	811	499
1862	27,529	63	111	79	11	566	425
1863	33,162	94	85	77	16	547	590
1864	57,276	165	230	256	11	600	1,162
1865	83,424	528	422	183	14	924	1,066
1866	115,892	412	93	287	18	1,382	1,075
1867	133,426	310	692	205	26	1,624	1,040
1868	55,831	-	192	141	4	891	558
1869	131,042	184	1,499	343	18	1,489	1,638
1870	118,225	223	4,425	907	6	2,891	1,382
1871	82,554	535	4,887	673	23	2,816	1,457

Year	Central Europe			Eastern Europe		Southern Europe	
	Germany (5)	Poland	Other (6)	U.S.S.R. and Baltic States (7)	Other (8)	Italy	Other (9)
1872	141,109	1,647	4,410	1,018	20	4,190	1,928
1873	149,671	3,338	7,112	1,634	53	8,757	1,759
1874	87,291	1,795	8,850	4,073	62	7,666	2,142
1875	47,769	984	7,658	7,997	27	3631	2724
1876	31,937	925	6,276	4,775	38	3015	1842
1877	29,298	533	5,396	6,599	32	3195	3097
1878	29,313	547	5,150	3,048	29	4344	1916
1879	34,602	489	5,963	4,453	29	5791	2063
1880	84,638	2,177	17,267	5,014	35	12354	1631
1881	210,485	5,614	27,935	5,041	102	15401	1784
1882	250,630	4,672	29,150	16,918	134	32,159	1,978
1883	194,786	2,011	27,625	9,909	163	31,792	1,944
1884	179,676	4,536	36,571	12,689	388	16,510	2,526
1885	124,443	3,085	27,309	17,158	941	13,642	2,561
1886	84,403	3,939	28,680	17,800	670	21,315	1,702
1887	106,865	6,128	40,265	30,766	2251	47,622	2,248
1888	109,717	5,826	45,811	33,487	1393	51,558	2,959
1889	99,538	4,922	34,174	33,916	1145	25,307	2,725
1890	92,427	11,073	56,199	35,598	723	52,003	3,960
1891	113,554	27,497	71,042	47,426	1222	76,055	5,047
1892	119,168	40,536	76,937	81,511	1331	61,631	8,138
1893	78,756	16,374	57,420	42,310	625	72,145	6,094
1894	53,989	1,941	38,638	39,278	1027	42,977	4,537
1895	32,173	790	33,401	35,907	768	35,427	2,574
1896	31,885	691	65,103	51,445	954	68,060	5,292
1897	22,533	4,165	33,031	25,816	943	59,431	2,893

Table 7.1 Continued

Year	Central Europe			Eastern Europe		Southern Europe	
	Germany (5)	Poland	Other (6)	U.S.S.R. and Baltic States (7)	Other (8)	Italy	Other (9)
1898	17,111	4,726	39,797	29,828	1,076	58,613	4,633
1899	17,476	(10)	62,491	60,982	1,738	77,419	4,772
1900	18,507	(10)	114,847	90,787	6852	100,135	8,360
1901	21,651	(10)	113,390	85,257	8199	135,996	10,685
1902	28,304	(10)	171,989	107,347	8234	178,375	14,423
1903	40,086	(10)	206,011	136,093	12600	230,622	25,492
1904	46,380	(10)	177,156	145,141	12,756	193,296	22,197
1905	40,574	(10)	275,693	184,897	11,022	221,479	18,156
1906	37,564	(10)	265,138	215,665	18,652	273,120	29,975
1907	37,807	(10)	338,452	258,943	36,510	285,731	52,079
1908	32,309	(10)	168,509	156,711	27,345	128,503	32,792
1909	25,540	(10)	170,191	120,460	11,659	183,218	21,729
1910	31,283	(10)	258,737	186,792	25,287	215,537	37,740
1911	32,061	(10)	159,057	158,721	21,655	182,882	40,051
1912	27,788	(10)	178,882	162,395	20,925	157,134	38,249
1913	34,329	(10)	254,825	291,040	18,036	265,542	43,526
1914	35,734	(10)	278,152	255,660	21,420	283,738	55,288
1915	7,799	(10)	18,511	26,187	2,892	49,688	21,441
1916	2,877	(10)	5,191	7,842	1,167	33,665	46,779
1917	1,857	(10)	1,258	12,716	369	34,596	45,644
1918	447	(10)	61	4,242	93	5,250	8,471
1919	52	(10)	53	1,403	51	1,884	3,197
1920	1,001	4,813	5,666	1,751	3,913	95,145	48,009
1921	6,803	95,089	77,069	10,193	32,793	222,260	76,409
1922	17,931	28,635	29,363	19,910	12,244	40,319	6,477
1923	48,277	26,538	34,038	21,151	16,082	46,674	7,008

Year	Central Europe			Eastern Europe		Southern Europe	
	Germany (5)	Poland	Other (6)	U.S.S.R. and Baltic States (7)	Other (8)	Italy	Other (9)
1924	75,091	28,806	32,700	20,918	13,173	56,246	9,150
1925	46,068	5,341	4,701	3,121	1,566	6,203	2,186
1926	50,421	7,126	6,020	3,323	1,596	8,253	2,807
1927	48,513	9,211	6,559	2,933	1,708	17,297	3,939
1928	45,778	8,755	7,091	2,652	1,776	17,728	4,244
1929	46,751	9,002	8,081	2,450	2,153	18,008	4,435
1930	26,569	9,231	9,184	2,772	2,159	22,327	4,647
1931	10,401	3,604	4,500	1,396	1,192	13,399	3,438
1932	2,670	1,296	1,749	636	592	6,662	1,882
1933	1,919	1,332	981	458	352	3,477	991
1934	4,392	1,032	1,422	607	347	4,374	1,461
1935	5,201	1,504	2,357	418	453	6,566	1,916
1936	6,346	869	2,723	378	424	6,774	1,821
1937	10,895	1,212	3,763	629	533	7,192	1,899
1938	17,199	2,403	5,195	960	542	7,712	2,392
1939	33,515	3,072	5,334	1,021	620	6,570	2,367
1940	21,520	702	3,628	898	491	5,302	1,913
1941	4,028	451	786	665	299	450	1,730
1942	2,150	343	396	197	117	103	864
1943	248	394	206	159	54	49	901
1944	238	292	316	157	109	120	944
1945	172	195	206	98	97	213	917
1946	2,598	335	511	153	98	2,636	1,224
1947	13,900	745	4,622	761	249	13,866	3,550
1948	19,368	2,447	6,006	897	485	16,075	4,481
1949	55,284	1,673	7,411	694	246	11,695	3,809

Table 7.1 Continued

Year	Central Europe			Eastern Europe		Southern Europe	
	Germany (5)	Poland	Other (6)	U.S.S.R. and Baltic States (7)	Other (8)	Italy	Other (9)
1950	128,592	696	17,792	526	277	12,454	3,663
1951	87,755	98	10,365	555	223	8,958	7,074
1952	104,236	235	23,529	548	137	11,342	10,004
1953	27,329	136	2,885	609	86	8,432	5,250
1954	33,098	67	2,873	475	104	13,145	3,720
1955	29,596	129	4,133	523	134	30,272	8,955
1956	44,409	263	10,284	643	394	40,430	14,893
1957	60,353	571	15,498	663	558	19,624	8,813
1958	29,498	1,470	3,508	641	673	23,115	5,775
1959	32,039	2,800	30,738	775	726	16,804	9,072
1960	29,452	4,216	9,073	856	761	13,369	12,147
1961	25,815	6,254	2,911	996	620	18,956	8,945
1962	21,477	5,660	2,533	753	753	20,119	11,677
1963	24,727	6,785	3,244	591	996	16,175	10,948
1964	24,494	7,097	3,248	763	1,054	12,769	10,360
1965	22,432	7,093	3,693	632	859	10,874	9,184
1966	17,654	8,490	3,972	768	878	26,447	22,047
1967	16,595	4,356	5,116	876	899	28,487	32,566
1968	16,590	3,676	5,659	974	883	25,882	32,262
1969	10,380	2,115	8,889	574	1,158	27,033	38,757
1970	10,632	2,013	10,411	836	1,357	27,369	33,292

Asia

Year	Total	Turkey in Asia	China (11)	India	Japan	Korea	Philippines	Other
1820	5		1	1				3
1821	1		–	–				–
1822	1		–	1				–
1823	–	No record of immigration from Turkey in Asia until 1869.	–	–	No record of immigration from Japan until 1861.	No record of immigration from Korea prior to 1948.	Philippines included in "All other countries" prior to 1936.	–
1824	1		–	1				–
1825	1		1	–				–
1826	1		–	1				–
1827	1		–	1				–
1828	3		–	3				–
1829	2		1	1				–
1830	1		–	–				–
1831	1		–	1				–
1832	4		–	4				–
1833	3		–	3				–
1834	6		–	6				–
1835	17		8	8				1
1836	4		–	4				–
1837	11		–	11				–
1838	1		–	1				–
1839	1		–	–				–
1840	1		–	1				–
1841	3		2	1				–
1842	7		4	2				1
1843	11		3	2				6
1844	6		3	1				2
1845	6		6	–				–

Table 7.1 Continued

Year	Total	Turkey in Asia	China (11)	India	Japan	Korea	Philippines	Other
1846	11		7	4				-
1847	12		4	8				-
1848	8		-	6				2
1849	11		3	8				-
1850	7		3	4				-
1851	2		-	2				-
1852	4		-	4				-
1853	47		42	5				-
1854	13,100		13,100	-				-
1855	3,540		3,526	6				8
1856	4,747		4,733	13				1
1857	5,945		5,944	1				-
1858	5,133		5,128	5				-
1859	3,461		3,457	2				2
1860	5,476		5,467	5				4
1861	7,528		7,518	6	1			3
1862	3,640		3,633	5	-			2
1863	7,216		7,214	1	-			1
1864	2,982		2,975	6	-			1
1865	2,947		2,942	5	-			-
1866	2,411		2,385	17	7			2
1867	3,961		3,863	2	67			29
1868	5,171		5,157	-	-			14
1869	12,949	2	12,874	3	63			7
1870	15,825	-	15,740	24	48			13
1871	7,240	4	7,135	14	78			9

Asia

No record of immigration from Turkey in Asia until 1869.

No record of immigration from Japan until 1861.

No record of immigration from Korea prior to 1948.

Philippines included in "All other countries" prior to 1936.

Asia

Year	Total	Turkey in Asia	China (11)	India	Japan	Korea	Philippines	Other
1872	7,825	-	7,788	12	17			5
1873	20,325	3	20,292	15	9			6
1874	13,838	6	13,776	17	21			18
1875	16,499	1	16,437	19	3			39
1876	22,943	8	22,781	25	4			125
1877	10,640	3	10,594	17	7	No record of		19
1878	9,014	7	8,992	8	2	immigration from		5
1879	9,660	31	9,604	15	4	Korea prior to 1948.		6
1880	5,839	4	5,802	21	4			8
1881	11,982	5	11,890	33	11	Philippines included		43
1882	39,629		39,579	10	5	in "All other		35
1883	8,113		8,031	9	27	countries" prior to		46
1884	510		279	12	20	1936.		199
1885	198		22	34	49			93
1886	317	15	40	17	194			51
1887	615	208	10	32	229			136
1888	843	273	26	20	404			120
1889	1,725	593	118	59	640			315
1890	4,448	1,126	1,716	43	691			872
1891	7,678	2,488	2,836	42	1136			1,176
1892	(13)							
1893	2,392	-	472	-	1380			540
1894	4,690	-	1,170	-	1931			1,589
1895	4,495	2,767	539	-	1150			39
1896	6,764	4,139	1,441	-	1110			74
1897	9,662	4,732	3,363	-	1526			41

Table 7.1 Continued

Asia

Year	Total	Turkey in Asia	China (11)	India	Japan	Korea	Philippines	Other
1898	8,637	4,275	2,071	-	2,230			61
1899	8,972	4,436	1,660	17	2,844			15
1900	17,946	3,962	1,247	9	12,635			93
1901	13,593	5,782	2,459	22	5,269			61
1902	22,271	6,223	1,649	93	14,270			36
1903	29,966	7,118	2,209	94	19,968	No record of immigration from Korea prior to 1948.	Philippines included in "All other countries" prior to 1936.	577
1904	26,186	5,235	4,309	261	14,264			2,117
1905	23,925	6,157	2,166	190	10,331			5,081
1906	22,300	6,354	1,544	216	13,835			351
1907	40,524	8,053	961	898	30,226			386
1908	28,365	9,753	1,397	1,040	15,803			372
1909	12,904	7,506	1,943	203	3,111			141
1910	23,533	15,212	1,968	1,696	2,720			1,937
1911	17,428	10,229	1,460	524	4,520			695
1912	21,449	12,788	1,765	175	6,114			607
1913	35,358	23,955	2,105	179	8,281			838
1914	34,273	21,716	2,502	221	8,929			905
1915	15,211	3,543	2,660	161	8,613			234
1916	13,204	1,670	2,460	112	8,680			282
1917	12,756	393	2,237	109	8,991			1,026
1918	12,701	43	1,795	130	10,213			520
1919	12,674	19	1,964	171	10,064			456
1920	17,505	5,033	2,330	300	9,432			410
1921	25,034	11,735	4,009	511	7,878			901
1922	14,263	1,998	4,406	360	6,716			783
1923	13,705	2,183	4,986	257	5,809			470

Asia

Year	Total	Turkey in Asia	China (11)	India	Japan	Korea	Philippines	Other
1924	22,065	2,820	6,992	183	8,801			3,269
1925	3,578	51	1,937	65	723			802
1926	3,413	37	1,751	93	654			878
1927	3,669	73	1,471	102	723	No record of immigration from Korea prior to 1948.		1,300
1928	3,380	80	1,320	102	550			1,328
1929	3,758	70	1,446	103	771		Philippines included in "All other countries" prior to 1936.	1,368
1930	4,535	118	1,589	110	837			1,881
1931	3,345	139	1,150	123	653			1,280
1932	1,931	43	750	87	526			525
1933	552	27	148	44	75			258
1934	597	22	187	28	86			274
1935	682	31	229	32	88		(16)	302
1936	793	20	273	13	91		72	324
1937	1,149	13	293	47	132		84	580
1938	2,492	11	613	34	93		116	1,625
1939	2,281	15	642	36	102		119	1,367
1940	2,050	7	643	52	102		137	1,109
1941	1,971	16	1,003	94	289		170	399
1942	615	31	179	36	44		51	274
1943	342	36	65	71	20		8	142
1944	231	15	50	41	4		4	117
1945	461	13	71	103	1		19	254
1946	2,108	16	252	425	14		475	926
1947	6,733	22	3,191	432	131		910	2,047
1948	11,907	16	7,203	263	423	44	1,168	2,790
1949	7,595	40	3,415	175	529	39	1,157	2,240

Table 7.1 Continued

Asia

Year	Total	Turkey in Asia	China (11)	India	Japan	Korea	Philippines	Other
1950	4,508	13	1,280	121	100	24	729	2,241
1951	7,149	3	335	109	271	21	3,228	3,182
1952	9,328	12	263	123	3,814	47	1,179	3,890
1953	8,231	13	528	104	2,579	75	1,074	3,858
1954	9,970	33	254	144	3,846	175	1,234	4,284
1955	10,935	54	568	194	4,150	263	1,598	4,108
1956	17,327	48	1,386	185	5,967	579	1,792	7,370
1957	20,008	77	2,098	196	6,829	577	1,874	8,357
1958	20,870	197	1,143	323	6,847	1,470	2,034	8,856
1959	25,259	229	1,702	351	6,248	1,614	2,503	12,612
1960	21,604	200	1,380	244	5,699	1,410	2,791	9,880
1961	19,495	296	900	292	4,490	1,442	2,628	9,447
1962	20,249	304	1,356	390	4,054	1,463	3,354	9,328
1963	23,242	307	1,605	965	4,147	2,560	3,483	10,175
1964	21,279	331	2,684	488	3,774	2,329	2,862	8,811
1965	20,040	365	1,611	467	3,294	2,139	2,963	9,201
1966	40,113	365	2,948	2,293	3,468	2,414	5,894	22,731
1967	57,574	491	7,118	4,129	4,125	3,845	10,336	27,530
1968	56,298	325	4,851	4,165	3,810	3,592	16,086	23,469
1969	72,959	556	5,264	5,205	4,095	5,854	20,263	31,722
1970	90,215	495	6,427	8,795	4,731	8,888	30,507	30,372

Year	Americas					Africa	Australasia		Other	
	Total	Canada and Newfound-land (12)	Mexico	West Indies	Other	Total	Total	Australia and New Zealand	Other Pacific Islands	All other countries
1820	387	209	1	164	13	1				-
1821	303	184	4	107	8	2				301
1822	378	204	5	159	10					2,886
1823	382	167	35	160	20					2,114
1824	559	155	110	259	35					1,956
1825	846	314	68	389	75	1	No record of immigration from Australasia, nor Australia and New Zealand specifically, until 1870.		No record of immigration from other Pacific Islands until 1871.	2,387
1826	831	223	106	427	75					808
1827	580	165	127	227	61	4				254
1828	2,090	267	1,089	652	82	6				1,571
1829	3,299	409	2,290	517	83	1				554
1830	2,296	189	983	937	187	2				6,695
1831	2,194	176	692	1,281	45	2				13,807
1832	2,871	608	827	1,256	180	2				7,397
1833	3,282	1,194	779	1,264	45	1				23,412
1834	2,779	1,020	885	791	83	1				26,243
1835	3,312	1,193	1,032	938	149	14				5,069
1836	4,936	2,814	798	1,178	146	6				44
1837	3,628	1,279	627	1,627	95	2				831
1838	2,990	1,476	211	1,231	72	10				4,660
1839	3,617	1,926	353	1,289	49	10				1,843
1840	3,815	1,938	395	1,446	36	6				294
1841	3,429	1,816	352	1,042	219	14				118
1842	3,994	2,078	403	1,410	103	3				627
1843	2,854	1,502	398	880	74	6				616
1844	3,740	2,711	197	771	61	14				612
1845	5,035	3,855	222	1,351	97	1				110

Table 7.1 Continued

Year	Total	Americas				Africa	Australasia		Other	
		Canada and Newfound-land (12)	Mexico	West Indies	Other	Total	Total	Australia and New Zealand	Other Pacific Islands	All other countries
1846	5,525	3,827	62	1,251	91	10				25
1847	5,231	6,473	24	1,338	154	3				2,564
1848	7,989	6,890	518	1,073	423					608
1849	8,904	9,376	597	3,171	2,624					495
1850	15,768	7,438	181	1,929	155	3	No record of immigration from Australasia, nor Australia and New Zealand specifically, until 1870.			1,605
1851	9,703	6,352	72	1,232	39					45,882
1852	7,695	5,424	162	406	38	8				248
1853	6,030	6,891	446	1,036	160					1,420
1854	8,533	7,761	420	887	192	14				984
1855	9,260	6,493	741	1,337	487	6				658
1856	9,058	5,670	133	923	85	25				334
1857	6,811	4,603	429	647	142	17				542
1858	5,821	4,163	265	879	159	11	No record of immigration from other Pacific Islands until 1871.			22,301
1859	5,466	4,514	229	1,384	216	126				801
1860	6,343	2,069	218	358	118	47				1,395
1861	2,763	3,275	142	585	173	12				486
1862	4,175	3,464	96	491	96	3				380
1863	4,147	3,636	99	718	154	37				448
1864	4,607	21,586	193	851	148	49				1,183
1865	22,778	32,150	239	895	298	33				559
1866	33,582	23,379	292	817	227	25				8,298
1867	24,715	2,785	129	419	82	3				3,626
1868	3,415	21,120	320	2,233	94	72				3,270
1869	23,767	40,414	463	1,679	102	31	36	36		161
1870	42,658	47,164	402	1,169	100	24	21	18	3	17
1871	48,835	40,204	569	1,322	110	41	2,416	2,180	236	27

Year	Americas Total	Canada and Newfoundland (12)	Mexico	West Indies	Other	Africa Total	Australasia Total	Australia and New Zealand	Other Pacific Islands	All other countries
1872	42,205	37,891	606	1,634	204	28	1,414	1,135	279	85
1873	40,335	33,020	386	1,777	156	58	1,193	960	233	164
1874	35,339									160
1875	26,640	24,097	610	1,790	143	54	1,268	1,104	164	128
1876	24,686	22,505	631	1,382	168	89	1,312	1,205	107	76
1877	24,065	22,137	445	1,390	93	16	914	912	2	36
1878	27,204	25,592	465	1,019	128	18	606	606		27
1879	33,043	31,286	556	1,123	78	12	816	813	3	15
1880	101,692	99,744	492	1,351	105	18	954	953	1	36
1881	127,577	125,450	325	1,680	122	33	1,191	1,188	3	63
1882	100,129	98,366	366	1,291	106	60	889	878	11	103
1883	71,729	70,274	469	903	83	67	747	554	193	99
1884	63,339	60,626	430	2,208	75	59	900	502	398	79
1885	41,203	38,336	323	2,477	67	112	679	449	230	98
1886	3,026	17	(14)	2,734	275	122	1,136	522	614	71
1887	5,270	9	(14)	4,876	385	40	1,282	528	754	73
1888	5,402	15	(14)	4,880	507	65	2,387	697	1,690	73
1889	5,459	28	(14)	4,923	508	187	2,196	1,000	1,196	61
1890	3,833	183	(14)	3,070	580	112	1,167	699	468	70
1891	5,082	234	(14)	3,906	942	103	1,301	777	524	62
1892	(13)	(13)	(14)	(13)	(13)	(13)	267	267	(13)	70
1893	2,593	(13)	(14)	2,593	-	(13)	248	248	(13)	8,520
1894	3,551	194	109	3,177	71	24	244	244		5,173
1895	3,508	244	116	3,096	52	36	155	155		70
1896	7,303	278	150	6,828	47	21	112	87	25	
1897	4,537	291	91	4,101	54	37	199	139	60	

Table 7.1 Continued

Year	Total	Americas Canada and Newfoundland (12)	Americas Mexico	Americas West Indies	Americas Other	Africa Total	Australasia Total	Australasia Australia and New Zealand	Other Other Pacific Islands	Other All other countries
1898	2,627	352	107	2,124	44	48	201	153	48	
1899	4,316	1,322	161		248	51	810	456	354	
1900	5,455	396	237	4,656	166	30	428	214	214	217
1901	4,416	540	347	3,176	353	173	498	325	173	13
1902	6,698	636	709	4,711	642	37	566	384	182	1
1903	11,023	1,058	528	8,170	1,267	176	1,349	1,150	199	103
1904	16,420	2,837	1,009	10,193	2,381	686	1,555	1,461	94	25
1905	25,217	2,168	2,637	16,641	3,771	757	2,166	2,091	75	90
1906	24,613	5,063	1,997	13,656	3,897	712	1,733	1,682	51	161
1907	41,762	19,918	1,406	16,689	3,749	1,486	1,989	1,947	42	33,012 (15)
1908	59,997	38,510	6,067	11,888	3,532	1,411	1,179	1,098	81	22
1909	82,208	51,941	16,251	11,180	2,836	858	892	839	53	17
1910	89,534	56,555	18,691	11,244	3,044	1,072	1,097	998	99	49
1911	94,364	56,830	19,889	13,403	4,242	956	1,043	984	59	43
1912	95,926	55,990	23,238	12,467	4,231	1,009	898	794	104	39
1913	103,907	73,802	11,926	12,458	5,721	1,409	1,340	1,229	111	15
1914	122,695	86,139	14,614	14,451	7,491	1,539	1,446	1,336	110	23
1915	111,206	82,215	12,340	11,598	5,053	934	1,399	1,282	117	136
1916	137,424	101,551	18,425	12,027	5,421	894	1,574	1,484	90	31
1917	147,779	105,399	17,869	15,507	9,004	566	1,142	1,014	128	31
1918	65,418	32,452	18,524	8,879	5,563	299	1,090	925	165	77
1919	102,286	57,782	29,818	8,826	5,860	189	1,310	1,234	76	47
1920	162,666	90,025	52,361	13,808	6,472	648	2,185	2,066	119	46
1921	124,118	72,317	30,758	13,774	7,269	1,301	2,281	2,191	90	702
1922	77,448	46,810	19,551	7,449	3,638	520	915	855	60	130
1923	199,972	117,011	63,768	13,181	6,012	548	759	711	48	25

| | Americas | | | | | Africa | Australasia | | Other | |
| | Total | Canada and Newfoundland (12) | Mexico | West Indies | Other | Total | Total | Australia and New Zealand | Other Pacific Islands | All other countries |
Year										
1924	318,855	200,690	89,336	17,559	11,270	900	679	635	44	15
1925	141,496	102,753	32,964	2,106	3,673	412	462	416	46	58
1926	144,393	93,368	43,316	3,222	4,487	529	591	556	35	
1927	161,872	84,580	67,721	4,019	5,552	520	746	712	34	
1928	144,281	75,281	59,016	4,058	5,926	475	606	578	28	
1929	116,177	66,451	40,154	4,306	5,266	509	636	619	17	
1930	88,104	65,254	12,703	5,225	4,922	572	1,051	1,026	25	
1931	30,816	22,183	3,333	2,496	2,804	417	652	616	36	
1932	12,577	8,003	2,171	1,029	1,374	186	303	291	12	
1933	9,925	6,187	1,936	862	940	71	137	122	15	
1934	11,409	7,945	1,801	861	802	104	147	130	17	
1935	11,174	7,782	1,560	931	901	118	141	132	9	3
1936	11,786	8,121	1,716	985	964	105	165	147	18	63
1937	16,903	12,011	2,347	1,322	1,223	155	174	145	29	
1938	20,486	14,404	2,502	2,110	1,470	174	248	228	20	
1939	17,139	10,813	2,640	2,231	1,455	218	222	213	9	
1940	17,822	11,078	2,313	2,675	1,756	202	228	207	21	
1941	22,445	11,473	2,824	4,687	3,461	564	255	194	61	
1942	16,377	10,599	2,378	1,599	1,801	473	163	120	43	
1943	18,162	9,761	4,172	2,312	1,917	141	160	120	40	
1944	23,084	10,143	6,598	3,198	3,145	112	615	577	38	
1945	29,646	11,530	6,702	5,452	5,962	406	1,663	1,625	38	
1946	46,066	21,344	7,146	5,878	11,698	1,516	6,106	6,009	97	
1947	52,753	24,342	7,558	6,728	14,125	1,284	2,960	2,821	139	73
1948	52,746	25,485	8,384	6,932	11,945	1,027	1,336	1,218	118	27
1949	49,334	25,156	8,083	6,733	9,362	995	776	661	115	10

Table 7.1 Continued.

Year	Total	Americas Canada and Newfoundland (12)	Mexico	West Indies	Other	Africa Total	Australasia Total	Australia and New Zealand	Other Other Pacific Islands	All other countries
1950	44,191	21,885	6,744	6,206	9,356	849	517	460	57	25
1951	47,631	25,880	6,153	5,902	9,696	845	527	490	37	7
1952	61,049	33,354	9,079	6,672	11,944	931	578	545	33	20
1953	77,650	36,283	17,183	8,628	15,556	989	782	742	40	8
1954	95,587	34,873	30,645	8,411	21,658	1,248	910	845	65	430
1955	110,436	32,435	43,702	12,876	21,423	1,203	1,028	932	96	8,341
1956	144,713	42,363	61,320	19,512	21,518	1,351	1,346	1,171	175	3,597
1957	134,160	46,354	49,321	18,362	20,123	1,600	1,458	1,228	230	22
1958	113,132	45,143	26,791	16,983	24,215	2,008	2,045	1,783	262	16
1959	93,061	34,599	22,909	12,109	23,444	1,992	2,162	1,878	284	12
1960	119,525	46,668	32,708	13,636	26,513	1,925	2,140	1,892	248	21
1961	139,580	47,470	41,476	20,520	30,114	1,851	1,881	1,556	325	26
1962	155,871	44,272	55,805	20,917	34,877	1,834	1,819	1,427	392	5
1963	169,966	50,509	55,986	22,951	40,520	1,982	1,977	1,642	335	1
1964	158,644	51,114	34,448	24,067	49,015	2,015	2,070	1,767	303	27
1965	171,019	50,035	40,686	31,141	49,157	1,949	2,199	1,803	396	25
1966	162,551	37,273	47,217	37,999	40,062	1,967	2,500	1,894	606	22
1967	170,235	34,768	43,034	61,987	30,446	2,577	2,811	2,128	683	22
1968	262,736	41,716	44,716	140,827	35,477	3,220	3,172	2,374	798	11
1969	164,045	29,303	45,748	53,190	35,804	4,460	3,061	2,278	783	
1970	161,727	26,850	44,821	56,614	33,442	7,099	3,632	2,693	939	2

(-) Represents zero.

(1) For 1820–1867, excludes returning citizens; therefore, for those years; does not agree with series C 120 and C 139.
(2) Comprises Eire and Northern Ireland.
(3) Comprises Norway, Sweden, Denmark, and Iceland.
(4) Comprises Netherlands, Belgium, Luxemburg, Switzerland, and France.

(5) Includes Austria, 1938–1945.
(6) Comprises Czechoslovakia (since 1920), Yugoslavia (since 1920), Hungary (since 1861), and Austria (since 1861), except for the years 1938–1945, when Austria was included with Germany.
(7) Comprises U.S.S.R., excluding Asian U.S.S.R. between 1931 and 1963, Latvia, Estonia, Lithuania, and Finland.
(8) Comprises Romania, Bulgaria, and Turkey in Europe.
(9) Comprises Spain, Portugal, Greece, and other Europe, not elsewhere classified.
(10) Between 1899 and 1919, included with Austria-Hungary, Germany, and Russia.
(11) Beginning 1957, includes Taiwan.
(12) Prior to 1920, Canada and Newfoundland were recorded as British North America.
(13) Included in "All other countries."
(14) No record of immigration from Mexico for 1886 to 1893.
(15) Included 32,897 persons returning to their homes in the United States.

Note: For years ending June 30, except: 1820–1831 and 1844–1849, years ending Sept. 30; 1833–1842 and 1851–1867 years ending Dec. 31; 1832 covers 15 months ending Dec. 31; 1843, 9 months ending Sept. 30; 1850, 15 months ending Dec. 31; 1868, 6 months ending June 30.

Source: Adapted from Historical Statistics of the United States Bicentennial Edition, U.S. Bureau of the Census, 1975, Chapter C 89–119.

Source notes: 1820–1932, U.S. Immigration and Naturalization Service, unpublished data, and U.S. Bureau of Immigration, Annual Report of the Commissioner General of Immigration, as follows: 1820–1926, Report for 1926, pp. 170–178; 1927–1931, Report for 1931, pp. 222–223; 1932, Report for 1932, pp. 120–125; for 1933–1957, U.S. Immigration and Naturalization Service, unpublished data; 1958–1970, Annual Report of Immigration, unpublished data; 1958–1970, Annual Report of the Immigration and Naturalization Service, annual issues.

General Notes on Immigration Statistics

Authors' Note: The following are the actual notes accompanying the general immigration statistics summarized by the U.S. Census Bureau. The notes were written to accompany the general immigration figures from 1820 to 1970 (in this book Annual Table 7.1, starting on p. 659), but apply more widely to most of the immigration figures in this book.

The continuous record of immigration to the United States began in 1819, under the Act of 1819, which required the captain or master of a vessel arriving from abroad to deliver to the local collector of customs a list or manifest of all passengers taken on board. This list was to designate the age, sex, and occupation of each passenger, "the country to which they severally belonged," and the number that had died on the voyage. Copies of these manifests were to be transmitted to the Secretary of State, who reported the information periodically to Congress. Subsequently, the Act of 1855 prescribed quarterly reports to the Secretary of State and annual reports to Congress. Later acts have continued to require the collection of such information.

Although the reporting of alien arrivals was required by the Act of 1798, which expired two years later, the number arriving before 1819 is not known. William J. Bromwell, in his *History of Immigration to the United States,* 1856 (pp. 18–19), estimated the number of passengers of foreign birth arriving here from the close of the Revolutionary War to 1819, at 250,000. This estimate was used by the Bureau of Statistics, which later compiled the official statistics of immigration.

Immigration statistics were compiled by the Department of State for 1820–1870; by the Treasury Department, Bureau of Statistics, for 1867–1895; and since 1892, by a separate Office or Bureau of Immigration, now a part of the Immigration and Naturalization Service. For 1892–1932, the Bureau of Immigration issued annual reports. For 1933–1940, the data were summarized in the *Annual Report of the Secretary of Labor;* for 1941, they were issued in the *Annual Report of the Attorney General;* for 1942, no report was published;

and for subsequent years, the statistics appeared in the *Annual Report of the Immigration and Naturalization Service.*

Since 1820 the official immigration data have undergone many changes in the reporting area covered. During the first decades only arrivals by vessel at Atlantic and Gulf ports were reported. Arrivals at Pacific ports were first included in 1850. During the Civil War the only Southern ports that reported were those controlled by the Federal Government. Later the reporting area was expanded to include arrivals at outlying possessions. Arrivals in Alaska were first reported in 1871, but only irregularly thereafter until 1904, after which Alaska was regularly included among the places of entry. Arrivals in Hawaii were first included in 1901, Puerto Rico in 1902, and the Virgin Islands in 1942.

Counting arrivals at the land borders was not required by the early immigration acts, and the counting of such arrivals did not approach completeness until after 1904. For 1820–1823, a few arrivals by land borders were included. Complete reporting was attempted in 1855 with only partial success, was interrupted for several years by the Civil War, and was discontinued in 1885. Beginning in 1894, European immigrants who arrived at Canadian ports with the declared intention of proceeding to the United States were included in the immigration statistics. Some immigration was reported at land border stations established in 1904. More stations were opened in the following years, but reporting of land border arrivals was not fully established until 1908.

The statistical treatment of Canadian and Mexican immigrants has differed at times from that of other immigrants. When reporting of arrivals by land borders was discontinued in 1885, regular reporting of Canadian and Mexican arrivals by vessel was also discontinued; however, a few Canadian and Mexican immigrants were reported in most of the following years. Arrivals of Canadians and Mexicans by land borders began to be reported in 1906, and reporting was fully established in 1908 under authority of the Act of 1907, which provided for the inspection of Canadians and Mexicans at the land borders.

Not all aliens entering via the Canadian and Mexican borders are counted for inclusion in the immigration statistics. Before 1930, no count was made of residents of a year or longer of Canada, Newfoundland, or Mexico who planned to remain in the United States less than 6 months. For 1930–1945 the following classes of aliens entering via the land borders were counted and included in the statistics of immigration:

1) Those who have not been in the United States within 6 months, who come to stay more than 6 months;

2) those for whom straight head tax is a prerequisite to admission, or for whom head tax is specially deposited and subsequently converted to straight head tax account;

3) those required by law or regulation to present an immigration visa or re-entry permit, and those who surrender either, regardless of whether they are required by law or regulation to do so;

4) those announcing an intention to depart via a seaport of the United States for Hawaii or insular possessions of the United States, or for foreign countries, except arrivals from Canada intending to return thereto by water; and

5) those announcing an intention to depart across the other land boundary.

These classes were revised in 1945 so that the statistics of arriving aliens at land border ports of entry for 1945–1952 included (1) arriving aliens who came into the United States for 30 days or more; and (2) returning alien residents who had been out of the United States more than 6 months. Arriving aliens who came into the United States for 29 days or less were not counted, except for those certified by public health officials, those held for a board of special inquiry, those excluded and deported, and those in transit who announced an intention to depart across another land boundary or by sea.

Since 1953, all arriving aliens at land border ports of entry have been counted and included, except for Canadian citizens and British subjects resident in Canada who were admitted for 6 months or less, and Mexican citizens who were admitted for 72 hours or less.

Persons who cross the land borders for brief periods (border crossers) are not included in the immigration and emigration statistics. The Immigration and Naturalization Service publishes statistics on alien and citizen border crossers in the *Annual Report*, however.

Arrivals in and departures from the Philippines were recorded in the port tables for 1910–1924 but were not included in the total immigration data. For 1925–1931, such arrivals and departures were obtained annually from the Bureau of Insular Affairs, War Department, and published in separate tables. The Immigration Service has no records since 1932 of arrivals in, or departures from, the Philippines to foreign countries.

Data on aliens admitted to conterminous United States from insular possessions were compiled from 1908 through 1964. Aliens admitted from the Virgin Islands were first recorded in 1917. The departure of aliens from the mainland to Puerto Rico was first recorded in 1918. Data on aliens from Guam began in 1929; Samoa, in 1932.

Definition of Terms

For 1820–1867, immigration totals (compiled by the Department of State) were shown as alien passenger arrivals, but may have included alien passengers who died before arrival, and did include, for 1856–1867, temporary visitors among arriving alien passengers. For the 12-year period, the temporary visitors constituted about 1 1/2 percent of the alien passenger arrivals.

For 1868–1891, the Bureau of Statistics immigrant arrival figures (excluding temporary visitors) were reported. Since 1892, official immigration data have been compiled by the Office of Immigration (and its successors) and for 1892–1895 its totals were 7 to 8 percent lower than those for the Bureau of Statistics for that period. The difference is largely attributable to the limitation of the Office of Immigration figures to alien steerage passengers; cabin-class passengers were not again included as immigrants until 1904. A further difference was that the Bureau of Statistics figures were for arrivals, while those of the Office of Immigration were for admissions.

For 1895–1897, the Office of Immigration switched to recording arrivals, and its figures for those years include the 2,419 aliens debarred in 1895, the 2,799 in 1896, and 1,880 in 1897. In later years, the immigration data were further refined to exclude aliens in transit through the United States (1904) and resident aliens returning from a visit abroad (1906).

In 1906, arriving aliens were divided into two classes: Immigrants, or those who intended to settle in the United States, and nonimmigrants, or admitted aliens who declared an intention not to settle in the United States, or were returning from abroad to resume domiciles formerly acquired in the United States.

The official record of emigration began in 1907 and ended in 1957. It was made possible by the Immigration Act of 1907, which required all steamship companies carrying departing aliens to furnish manifests similar to those required for arriving aliens.

For 1908–1932, aliens arriving in or departing from the United States were classified as follows: Arriving aliens with permanent domicile outside the United States who intended to reside permanently in the United States were classed as immigrants; departing aliens with permanent residence in the United States who intended to reside permanently abroad were classed as emigrants; all alien residents making a temporary trip abroad and all aliens residing abroad making a temporary trip to the United States were classed as nonimmigrants on the inward journey and nonemigrants on the outward. Permanent residence was defined as residence of 1 year or longer. (*Annual Report of the Commissioner General of Immigration,* 1908, p. 6.)

Since 1933, aliens arriving in the United States have been classified as immigrants or nonimmigrants. Immigrants are nonresident aliens admitted to the United States for permanent residence. Until July 1, 1968, they were further classified as quota and nonquota immigrants. Quota immigrants were those subject to the established quotas of Eastern Hemisphere countries and their dependencies.

Nonquota immigrants included natives of the Western Hemisphere and their spouses and children, immediate relatives of U.S. citizens, and certain groups of special immigrants. Beginning July 1, 1968, immigrants have been classified as those subject to the numerical limitations of the Eastern Hemisphere, those subject to the numerical limitations of the Western Hemisphere, and those exempt from numerical limitations. Those exempt include the immediate relatives (parents, spouses, and children) of U.S. citizens and various classes of special immigrants.

Nonimmigrants are nonresident aliens admitted to the United States for a temporary period. Included in this group are visitors for business and pleasure, students and their spouses and children, temporary workers and trainees and their spouses and children, foreign government officials, exchange visitors and their spouses and children, international representatives, treaty traders and investors, representatives of foreign information media, fiancés(ées) of U.S. citizens and their children, intracompany transferees and their spouses and children, NATO officials, aliens in transit, and, for statistical purposes, permanent resident aliens returning after short trips abroad. Excluded are border crossers, crewmen, and insular travelers.

Data on emigrants have not been kept since 1957. Emigrants were aliens who resided in the United States for a year or longer and who left for a permanent residence abroad. Nonemigrants were resident aliens of the United States who left the United States for a temporary period abroad, or nonresident aliens of the United States who had been in the United States for less than a year and were returning to their permanent residence abroad. Since 1957 data have been kept only on aliens departing. These figures include all aliens departing by sea or air, except for direct departures to Canada.

The old definitions of *immigrant, emigrant, nonimmigrant,* and *nonemigrant* somewhat impaired the reliability of net immigration figures. While immigrants were admitted for permanent residence, they could depart prior to residence of 1 year, in which case they were counted as immigrants on arrival and nonemigrants on departure. Persons coming in temporarily, however, as nonimmigrants who then failed to leave within a year would have been counted as emigrants on departure.

Immigrants, by Country, 1820–1970

Source: 1820–1932, U.S. Immigration and Naturalization Service, unpublished data, and U.S. Bureau of Immigration, *Annual Report of the Commissioner General of Immigration*, as follows: 1820–1926, *Report for 1926,* pp. 170–178; 1927–1931, *Report for 1931,* pp. 222–223; 1932, *Report for 1932,* pp. 120–125; 1933–1957, U.S. Immigration and Naturalization Service, unpublished data; 1958–1970, *Annual Report of the Immigration and Naturalization Service,* annual issues.

Prior to 1906, data cover countries from which the aliens came; thereafter, countries of last permanent residence. Owing to changes in the list of countries separately reported and to changes in boundaries, data for certain countries are not comparable throughout. Under the provisions of the Immigration and Nationality Act, subquotas of 100 each were established for colonies or dependencies, to be charged against the quota of the mother country. Because of these provisions, statistics were compiled, between January 1953 and July 1968, for each colony or dependency having a subquota. Under the Act of October 3, 1965, colonies and dependencies of foreign states are allotted 200 visa numbers each, chargeable to the mother country.

The principal changes in reporting immigrants by country since 1820 are shown in the detailed listing below.

See also "Authors' Note" on p. 684.

Immigration from Europe, 1820–1970

Source: See source for "Immigrants, by Country, 1820–1970" on this page.

Since 1820, territorial transfers in Europe have, to a certain extent, impaired the comparability of immigration statistics from that continent. Data for Austria-Hungary were not reported until 1861. Austria and Hungary have been reported separately since 1905. For 1938–1945, Austria is included with Germany. Bulgaria, Serbia, and Montenegro were first reported in 1899. In 1920, Bulgaria was reported separately, as was the Kingdom of Serbs, Croats, and Slovenes (identified as Yugoslavia since 1922). Prior to 1925, Northern Ireland was included with Ireland (Eire). The figures for Norway and Sweden were combined for 1820–1868; since 1869, each country has been reported separately. Poland was recorded as a separate country for 1820–1898 and again from 1920. During 1899–1919, Poland was included with Austria-Hungary, Germany, and Russia. There is no record of immigration from Romania prior to 1880.

International transfers in territory following World War I resulted in the establishment of several nations. In 1920, Czechoslovakia, Finland, Poland, and the Kingdom of Serbs, Croats, and Slovenes (designated as Yugoslavia in 1922) were added to the immigration lists; in 1924, Albania, Estonia, Latvia, and Lithuania were added; in 1925, the Free City of Danzig and Luxembourg were added. The Immigration Act of 1924, which established quotas for all independent countries in Europe, Asia, Africa, and the Pacific, effected a further change in the immigration lists of countries. This change, however, was not fully felt until 1931. In that year, Andorra, Iceland, Liechtenstein, Monaco, and San Marino were added to the European countries, and the Russian Empire was classified into European Russia (designated as U.S.S.R. in Europe from 1947 through 1963) and Siberia, or Asiatic Russia. Since 1964, all the U.S.S.R. has been included in Europe. The principal effect of the 1924 Act, however, was in the extension of the lists of Asian, African, and Western Hemisphere countries.

In 1950, Bessarabia and the northern portion of Bukovina were included in the U.S.S.R. instead of in Romania. The Dodecanese Islands were included in Greece instead of Italy. The Free Territory of Trieste, formerly a part of Italy and Yugoslavia, was established as an independent country until 1959, when it again became part of Italy and Yugoslavia in immigration statistics.

Immigration from Asia, 1820–1970

Source: See source for "Immigrants, by Country, 1820–1970" on p. 687.

China and India are the only countries in Asia for which the records of immigration to the United States date back to 1820. A few immigrants from Japan were recorded in 1861, 1866, and 1867, but complete records for Japan begin with 1869. Figures for Turkey in Asia are available since 1869. Data on some immigration from Arabia are recorded for 1876–1895; from Armenia for 1874–1895; and from Persia for 1871–1895. For 1896–1923, immigration from Asia included only China, India, Japan, Turkey in Asia, and "other Asia." In 1924, Syria was added, and in 1925, Armenia, Palestine, and Persia (Iran) were added to the lists of Asian countries. Since 1934, Armenia has been included in Russia. In 1931, Siberia, or Asiatic Russia, was separated from European Russia, and Iraq and Siam (Thailand) were added to the lists. Since 1964, all the U.S.S.R. has been included in Europe.

In 1945, the classification of country in the country-of-birth statistics (on which the Quota Law was based) was adopted for the immigration statistics. This change resulted in the addition to the immigration lists of Afghanistan, Arabian Peninsula, Bhutan, Muscat, Nepal, Saudi Arabia, and Asiatic colonies, dependencies, and protectorates of European countries. Since 1948, the following countries have been added to the immigration lists: (1948) Burma, Ceylon, Jordan, Korea, and Pakistan; (1949) Israel (formerly included with Palestine), Lebanon (formerly included with Syria), and Yemen; (1950) Indonesia; (1952) Bonin Volcano Islands, Ryukyu Islands, Cambodia, Laos, and Vietnam; (1957) Formosa; (1961) Cyprus; (1963) Kuwait; (1964) Malaysia; (1967) Singapore.

Immigration from the Americas, 1820–1970

Source: See source for "Immigrants, by Country, 1820–1970" on p. 687.

Prior to 1920, Canada and Newfoundland were recorded under country of last permanent residence as British North America. For 1920–1924, combined figures are available for Canada and Newfoundland; for 1925–1948, each was reported separately. Since 1950, Newfoundland has been included in Canada. Inspection of Canadians and Mexicans was first authorized by the Act of 1907. The first complete year for which all immigration via the land borders was recorded is, therefore, 1908.

Immigration from Mexico has been recorded for 1820–1885 and for 1894 to the present. Immigration statistics for the West Indies have been available since 1820. Between 1820 and 1860, there was no classification of West Indian immigrants by country. For 1861–1898, some immigration was recorded from Antigua (1873–1895), Bahamas (1871–1895), Barbados (1869–1895), Bermuda (1861–1895), Cuba (1869–1898), Curaçao (1873–1895), Haiti (1869–1895), Jamaica (1869–1895), Puerto Rico (1869–1895), Saint Croix (1871–1895), Saint Thomas (1872–1895), and Trinidad (1874–1895). For 1899–1924, there again was no classification by country of immigration from the West Indies. Immigration from Cuba has been separately recorded since 1925; from the British West Indies, Dominican Republic, Dutch West Indies, French West Indies, and Haiti since 1931; and from Bermuda since 1945. For detailed data, see *Annual Report of Commissioner General of Immigration* for each year, 1892–1932. Since January 1953, all countries in the West Indies have been reported.

Immigration from Central America has been recorded since 1820, but not by country during most of that period. Separate statistics are available for 1895–1898 for Guatemala, Honduras, Nicaragua, and El Salvador; and for 1895–1897 for Costa Rica. British Honduras was also enumerated separately for 1874–1910. With the above exceptions, only figures for total immigration from Central America were available until 1925. Immigration has been reported separately from British Honduras since 1925, and from the Canal Zone, Costa Rica, Guatemala, Honduras, Nicaragua, Panama, and El Salvador since 1931.

Immigration from South America has also been reported in total since 1820 but, with the following exceptions, not by country until 1925. For 1869–1895, separate enumerations were made for Brazil, Chile, Colombia, Ecuador, Guiana, Peru, and Venezuela; and for 1871–1895 for the Argentine Republic. Separate figures for Brazil have been again available since 1925; and since 1931 for Argentina, Bolivia, British Guiana (since 1967, Guyana), Dutch Guiana (Surinam), French Guiana, Chile, Colombia, Ecuador, Paraguay, Peru, Uruguay, and Venezuela.

Immigration from Africa, 1820–1970

Source: See source for "Immigrants, by Country, 1820–1970" on p. 687.

Immigration from Africa has been recorded since 1820 but, with few exceptions, was not classified by country until 1931. There is record of some immigration from Liberia in 1829, 1839, 1844, and 1857–1893; from Algeria in 1872–1894; from Egypt in 1869–1895; and from South Africa in 1869–1895. For 1890–1924, only immigration for continental Africa was reported. Immigration from Ethiopia (Abyssinia), Liberia, Morocco, and Union of South Africa has been recorded since 1931. In 1945, "other Africa" was classified into Cameroons (British Mandate), Cameroons (French Mandate), Ruanda and Urundi (trust territory, Belgium), South-West Africa (Mandate of the Union of South Africa), Tanganyika (trust territory, United Kingdom), Togoland (British Mandate), Togoland (trust territory, France), and colonies, dependencies, or protectorates of Belgium, France, Great Britain, Italy, Portugal, and Spain. Many of these countries have since gained their independence.

Since 1945, the following countries have been added at the following dates. 1953: Libya and Somaliland (Italian administration), and Southern Rhodesia. Eritrea, which was federated with Ethiopia, was included with Ethiopia. 1957: Ghana (composed of British territories, Gold Coast and British Togoland), Sudan, and Tunisia. 1961: Congo, Republic of the Congo, Dahomey, Gabon, Ivory Coast, Malagasy Republic, Republic of Mali, Niger,

Nigeria, Republic of Senegal, Somali Republic, and Upper Volta. 1963: Burundi and Rwanda, formerly Ruanda-Urundi. 1967: Botswana and Lesotho.

Immigration from Australasia, 1820–1970

Source: See source for "Immigrants, by Country, 1820–1970" on p. 687.

Immigration from Australia was recorded separately in 1822, 1839–1840, and for most of the years 1854–1898. For 1899–1924, a combined total was recorded for Australia, Tasmania, and New Zealand, but since 1925 Australia has again been reported separately. Separate figures for New Zealand are available for 1870–1890. For 1891–1893, New Zealand was included in "all other countries"; for 1894–1898, in "Pacific Islands, not specified"; and for 1899–1924, with Australia and Tasmania. After that, separate figures for New Zealand became available again, starting in 1925.

The following countries were added to the immigration lists of the Pacific in 1945: Nauru (British Mandate); Territory of New Guinea including appertaining islands (Australian Mandate); Western Samoa (New Zealand Mandate); Yap and other Pacific Islands under Japanese Mandate; and colonies, dependencies, or protectorates of France, Great Britain, Japan, Netherlands, and Portugal. In 1952, the Pacific Islands (trust territory, U.S. administration) were added. In 1962, Western Samoa gained its independence and, since 1968, Nauru has also been an independent nation. Yap and several of the other islands once under the mandate of Japan are now included in Japan.

Foreign-born Population, by Country of Birth, 1850–1970

Source: U.S. Bureau of the Census. 1850–1930, total foreign-born, Fifteenth Census Reports, *Population,* vol. II, p. 233; 1910–1940, foreign-born white, Sixteenth Census Reports, *Population,* vol. II, part 1, p. 43; 1950, *U.S. Census of Population: 1950,* vol. IV, *Special Reports, Nativity and Parentage,* p. 3A-71 and vol. IV, *Special Reports, Nonwhite Population by Race,* p.

3B-82, and unpublished data; 1960, *U.S. Census of Population: 1960,* vol. I, part 1; 1970, *U.S. Census of Population: 1970,* vol. II, *Subject Reports.*

The foreign-born population comprises all persons born outside the United States, Puerto Rico, or an outlying area of the United States, except those persons with at least one American parent. Persons born in any of the outlying areas, and American citizens born abroad or at sea, are regarded as native.

The statistics on country of birth are generally based on the political boundaries of foreign nations existing at the date of the specified decennial census. Because of boundary changes following World War I and World War II, accurate comparisons over the entire period, 1850–1950, can be made for relatively few countries. These countries include England, Scotland, Wales, Norway, Sweden, Netherlands, Switzerland, Spain, Portugal, Canada (total of Canada-French, Canada-other, and Newfoundland), and Mexico. For several other countries (for example, Italy, France, and Belgium), the figures are slightly affected by boundary changes, but these changes have not been so great as to destroy entirely the value of comparative figures. However, the boundaries of numerous other countries (for example, U.S.S.R., Austria, Hungary, Romania, and Greece) have been so changed that comparisons over time are subject to a large margin of error.

Statistics on country of birth of the foreign-born have generally been restricted to those countries which had at the time of the census a separate political entity. For 1860–1900, however, an exception was made in the case of Poland. Although Poland was not restored to its original status as an independent country until the end of World War I, its historical position was such that Polish immigrants generally regarded Poland as their country of birth regardless of the political sovereignty over their birthplace. For 1860–1890, persons reported as born in Poland were so tabulated without qualification. In the census of 1900, an attempt was made to distin-

guish Austrian, German, and Russian Poland, and separate statistics for each were presented. In the census of 1910, persons reported as born in Poland were assigned either to Russia, Germany, or Austria. The figures for 1910, however, have been adjusted on the basis of mother-tongue data, to conform as nearly as possible to the conditions in 1930.

Since World War I, the greatest difficulties encountered in the country-of-birth statistics have been the classification of persons born in the former Austro-Hungarian Empire. Many persons born within the prewar boundaries of this Empire could not or did not give the census enumerator the information needed for the determination of their country of birth on the basis of postwar geography. It is therefore quite possible that some persons were assigned to Austria who were really born within the present areas of either Czechoslovakia or Yugoslavia, and that persons were assigned to Hungary who were born within the present areas of Romania or Yugoslavia. Similarly, it is possible that some persons born in Latvia, Estonia, or Lithuania were assigned to Russia. Persons for whom Austria-Hungary was reported in the 1950 census were allocated on the basis of surname to the various countries created out of the territory of the old empire after World War I. Even with this procedure, however, there appears to be some indication that Austria and Hungary are overreported at the expense of Yugoslavia and Czechoslovakia. In 1950 the situation was further complicated by the fact that, although there were extensive de facto boundary changes as a result of World War II, only a small number of those changes were officially recognized by the United States at the time.

Since 1950, persons have been allocated to a specific country based on mother-tongue data. [See also other information on general population statistics in original source, under series A 91-104 and A 105-118.]

Source: *Historical Statistics of the United States, Bicentennial Edition,* U.S. Bureau of the Census, 1975.

Table 7.2: Number of Immigrants to the United States by Region and Selected Country of Birth Annually, 1971–1980

Country or region of birth	1971	1972	1973	1974	1975	1976
All countries	370,473	384,685	400,063	394,861	396,194	398,613
Europe	96,498	89,993	92,870	81,212	73,996	72,411
Albania	132	95	320	97	39	45
Andorra	-	-	1	-	-	2
Austria	628	601	528	416	402	344
Belgium	447	426	325	355	329	386
Bulgaria	283	302	350	213	145	205
Czechoslovakia	1,799	1,783	1,552	683	525	551
Denmark	502	504	428	440	353	408
Estonia	21	27	23	28	17	25
Finland	396	412	347	307	254	291
France	2,001	1,966	1,845	1,634	1,364	1,478
Germany	7,519	6,848	6,600	6,320	5,154	5836
Gibraltar	11	5	8	7	7	8
Greece	15,939	11,021	10,751	10,824	9,984	8,417
Hungary	1,549	1,698	1,624	1,288	882	861
Iceland	161	195	108	94	115	132
Ireland	1,614	1,780	2,000	1,572	1,285	1,171
Italy	22,137	21,427	22,151	15,884	11552	8,380
Latvia	77	84	43	61	48	51
Liechtenstein	1	2	4	5	-	4
Lithuania	62	84	74	63	48	51
Luxembourg	46	31	23	36	21	24
Malta	227	245	254	308	279	180
Monaco	16	10	8	12	6	5
Netherlands	1,159	998	1,016	1,024	816	943
Norway	435	387	415	433	387	286
Poland (1)	2,897	4,797	4,927	4,046	3,947	3,808
Portugal	11,692	10,343	10,751	11,302	11,845	10,511
Romania	1,643	1,329	1,623	1,552	1,161	2,179
San Marino	28	17	19	19	13	2
Spain	4,121	4,386	4,134	3,390	2,549	2,254
Sweden	601	603	573	587	482	544
Switzerland	786	695	577	534	538	597
U.S.S.R.	718	902	1,248	1,161	5,118	8,220
United Kingdom	10,787	10,078	10,638	10,710	10,807	11,392
Yugoslavia	6,063	5,922	7,582	5,817	3,524	2,820
Asia	103,459	121,058	124,160	130,662	132,469	149,881
Afghanistan	69	96	137	96	116	109
Bahrain (2)	19	27	29	9	21	8
Bangladesh	-	-	154	147	404	590
Bhutan	5	1	1	2	-	7
Brunei	3	10	3	9	22	20
Burma	1,068	785	669	558	734	726
China (3)	14,417	17,339	17,297	18,056	18,536	18,824
Christmas Island	2	1	-	2	-	1
Cocos Islands	-	1	-	-	-	2
Cyprus	382	315	294	267	554	829
Hong Kong	3,204	4,391	4,359	4,629	4,891	5,766
India (4)	14,317	16,929	13,128	12,795	15,785	17,500
Indonesia (5)	680	508	450	447	458	529
Iran	2,411	3,059	2,998	2,608	2,337	2,700
Iraq	1,231	1,491	1,039	2,281	2,796	3,432
Israel	1,739	2,099	1,917	1,998	2,125	2,982
Japan (6)	5,326	5,777	5,676	4,917	4,293	4275
Jordan (7)	2,588	2,756	2,450	2,838	2,578	2,566
Kampuchea	21	39	66	40	98	103
Korea	14,297	18,876	22,930	28,028	28,362	30,803
Kuwait	112	94	87	143	146	98
Laos	24	35	46	61	96	137
Lebanon	1,867	1,984	1,977	2,400	2,075	2,840
Macau	143	149	148	155	192	208
Malaysia	284	365	347	311	332	378
Maldives	-	1	-	-	-	1
Nepal	40	39	46	43	56	59
Oman	2	5	2	7	-	7
Pakistan	2,125	2,480	2,525	2,570	2,620	2,888
Philippines	28,471	29,376	30,799	31,751	32,857	37,281
Qatar (2)	-	-	-	11	8	19
Saudia Arabia	48	55	50	48	51	42
Singapore	130	143	186	176	203	220
Sri Lanka	180	306	455	379	432	411
Syria	951	1,012	1,128	1,082	1,222	1,271
Thailand	2,915	4,102	4,941	4,956	4,217	6,923
Turkey	1,748	1,986	1,899	1,867	1,592	1,676
United Arab Emirates (2)	-	-	-	3	3	6
Vietnam	2,038	3,412	4,569	3,192	3,039	3,048
Yemen (Aden)	38	94	139	113	97	48
Yemen (Sanaa)	564	920	1,219	561	227	549

Table 7.2 Continued

Country or region of birth	1971	1972	1973	1974	1975	1976
Africa	**6,772**	**6,612**	**6,655**	**6,182**	**6,729**	**7,723**
Algeria	102	102	96	92	72	80
Angola	14	26	14	30	71	270
Benin	3	6	8	6	6	9
Botswana	2	1	-	4	7	3
Burundi	3	2	4	7	2	10
Cameroon	3	7	11	13	16	12
Cape Verde	183	248	214	122	196	866
Central African Republic	-	1	2	2	2	-
Chad	3	5	2	2	1	1
Comoros	-	-	1	1	-	
Congo	28	45	5	8	7	4
Djibouti	-	3	1	1	1	3
Egypt	3,643	2,512	2,274	1,831	1,707	1,824
Equatorial Guinea	3	3	-	1	2	-
Ethiopia	130	192	149	276	206	226
French So. & Antarctic Lands	-	-	-	-	-	2
Gabon	-	-	2	-	2	-
Gambia, The	2	5	8	-	5	8
Ghana	182	326	487	369	275	304
Guinea	5	10	7	10	7	13
Guinea-Bissau	5	1	2	2	3	4
Ivory Coast	6	6	5	7	11	2
Kenya	331	295	300	386	446	427
Lesotho	3	3	3	2	-	2
Liberia	116	134	195	191	163	231
Libya	94	68	64	66	42	58
Madagascar	11	10	5	14	10	21
Malawi	22	13	7	19	20	23
Mali	1	3	2	1	4	7
Mauritania	2	3	5	2	4	-
Mauritius	24	23	22	15	23	36
Morocco	391	421	445	455	390	395
Mozambique	20	10	13	24	88	124
Namibia	17	15	10	32	19	10
Niger	2	3	-	-	3	8
Nigeria	451	738	738	670	653	714
Reunion	1	-	-	1	-	2
Rwanda	1	-	1	4	3	3
St. Helena	-	-	1	2	3	1
Sao Tome & Principe	-	2	1	-	-	-
Senegal	21	40	40	42	26	55
Seychelles	11	27	22	20	21	19
Sierra Leone	35	48	65	61	66	110
Somalia	3	16	11	10	17	22
South Africa	375	521	503	525	586	790
Sudan	51	41	65	43	38	40
Swaziland	5	4	3	5	7	6
Tanzania	183	271	264	243	304	304
Togo	1	5	7	17	7	9
Tunisia	80	112	84	67	93	61
Uganda	97	159	339	320	859	359
Upper Volta	1	2	2	-	2	3
Western Sahara	2	-	5	2	2	-
Zaire	30	18	35	32	43	51
Zambia	26	38	59	62	94	108
Zimbabwe	47	68	47	65	94	83
Oceania	**2,919**	**3,284**	**3,255**	**3,051**	**3,346**	**3,591**
American Samoa (8)	2	1	1	2	-	2
Australia	1,400	1,551	1,400	1,236	1,116	1,366
Cook Islands	1	1	4	7	3	2
Fiji	323	302	388	431	684	699
French Polynesia	30	31	20	26	47	25
Guam	3	3	-	-	1	-
Kiribati (9)	1	2	2	2	5	-
Nauru	-	2	-	-	1	-
New Caledonia	4	2	5	5	2	-
New Zealand	470	497	490	409	384	430
Pacific Is. Trust Territory	178	254	217	181	209	188
Papua New Guinea	12	8	5	2	4	6
Pitcairn Islands	2	2	1	4	1	5
Solomon Islands	1	1	2	5	6	12
Tonga	226	355	391	447	527	514
Tuvalu (9)	-	-	-	-	-	-
Vanuatu (10)	-	2		4	2	6
Western Samoa	266	270	329	290	354	336

Country or region of birth	1971	1972	1973	1974	1975	1976
North America	**140,126**	**144,377**	**152,788**	**151,445**	**146,669**	**142,307**
Canada	13,128	10,776	8,951	7,654	7,308	7,638
Greenland	1	-	-	1	1	-
Mexico	50,105	64,040	70,141	71,586	62,205	57,863
St Pierre & Miquelon	1	2	1	6	3	1
United States (11)	74	76	84	2	26	53
Caribbean	**68,189**	**61,373**	**64,769**	**62,959**	**67,430**	**66,839**
Anguilla (12)	-	-	-	-	-	-
Antigua	325	344	404	461	435	529
Bahamas, The	204	255	365	529	256	315
Barbados	1,731	1,620	1,448	1,461	1,618	1,743
Bermuda	142	156	148	156	162	195
British Virgin Islands	235	221	223	242	235	246
Cayman Islands	62	51	56	55	91	41
Cuba	21,615	20,045	24,147	18,929	25,955	29,233
Dominica	216	198	258	236	274	272
Dominican Republic	12,624	10,760	13,921	15,680	14,066	12,526
Grenada	361	332	420	707	568	592
Guadeloupe	82	79	64	51	47	77
Haiti	7,444	5,809	4,786	3,946	5,145	5,410
Jamaica	14,571	13,427	9,963	12,408	11,076	9,026
Martinique	32	42	21	32	36	26
Montserrat	188	190	197	184	173	203
Netherlands Antilles	345	304	280	305	257	224
Puerto Rico	6	1	2	-	-	-
St. Christopher-Nevis (12)	331	383	402	425	419	650
St. Lucia	242	238	264	283	278	297
St. Vincent & Grenadines	294	294	347	332	346	374
Trinidad & Tobago	7,130	6,615	7,035	6,516	5,982	4,839
Turks & Caicos Islands	7	9	16	21	11	21
US Virgin Islands	2	-	2	-	-	-
Central America	**8,628**	**8,110**	**8,842**	**9,237**	**9,696**	**9,913**
Belize	481	475	528	573	534	500
Costa Rica	968	907	901	752	889	1,137
El Salvador	1,776	2,001	2,042	2,278	2,416	2,363
Guatemala	2,194	1,640	1,759	1,638	1,859	1,970
Honduras	1,146	964	1,330	1,390	1,357	1,310
Nicaragua	566	606	670	942	947	934
Panama (13)	1,497	1,517	1,612	1,664	1,694	1,699
South America	**20,702**	**19,359**	**20,335**	**22,307**	**22,984**	**22,699**
Argentina	1,992	1,819	2,034	2,077	2,227	2,267
Bolivia	441	551	449	479	451	522
Brazil	1,413	1,089	1,213	1,114	1,070	1,038
Chile	956	857	1,139	1,285	1,111	1,266
Colombia	6,440	5,173	5,230	5,837	6,434	5,742
Ecuador	4,981	4,337	4,139	4,795	4,727	4,504
Falkland Islands	-	-	-	-	-	-
French Guiana	4	6	9	6	6	-
Guyana	2,115	2,826	2,969	3,241	3,169	3,326
Paraguay	120	109	108	135	119	110
Peru	1,086	1,443	1,713	1,942	2,256	2,640
Suriname	46	73	75	87	106	78
Uruguay	601	591	617	705	781	676
Venezuela	507	485	640	604	527	530
Born On Board Ship/Plane	**2**	**2**	**-**	**2**	**1**	**1**

Table 7.2 Continued

Country or region of birth	TQ 1976	1977	1978	1979	1980
All countries	103,676	462,315	601,442	460,348	530,639
Europe	18,166	70,010	73,198	60,845	72,121
Albania	10	78	68	39	30
Andorra	1	-	1	2	2
Austria	108	400	467	369	401
Belgium	101	377	439	395	426
Bulgaria	43	206	202	188	188
Czechoslovakia	128	575	744	763	1,051
Denmark	120	433	409	414	504
Estonia	6	17	17	23	20
Finland	65	277	358	327	356
France	397	1,618	1,844	1,705	1,905
Germany	1,695	6,372	6,739	6,314	6,595
Gibraltar	1	14	16	15	8
Greece	2,144	7,838	7,035	5,090	4,699
Hungary	205	853	941	861	819
Iceland	51	137	131	140	196
Ireland	302	1,238	1,190	982	1,006
Italy	2,035	7,510	7,415	6,174	5,467
Latvia	14	54	52	62	54
Liechtenstein	1	6	5	6	5
Lithuania	23	64	73	63	61
Luxembourg	2	31	21	20	23
Malta	33	193	245	273	192
Monaco	3	9	13	12	11
Netherlands	286	1,014	1,153	1,145	1,169
Norway	79	334	423	431	403
Poland (1)	961	4,010	5,050	4,418	4,725
Portugal	2,455	9,657	10,445	7,085	8,408
Romania	474	2,015	2,037	1,554	1,913
San Marino	1	2	7	6	7
Spain	532	2,487	2,297	1,933	1,879
Sweden	166	571	638	750	768
Switzerland	144	610	706	665	713
U.S.S.R.	1,856	5,742	5,161	2,543	10,543
United Kingdom	3,020	12,477	14,245	13,907	15,485
Yugoslavia	704	2,791	2,621	2,171	2,099
Asia	39,184	157,759	249,776	189,293	236,097
Afghanistan	33	138	180	353	722
Bahrain (2)	5	8	14	22	39
Bangladesh	172	590	716	549	532
Bhutan	1	12	4	12	13
Brunei	3	11	17	11	13
Burma	275	1,101	1,188	1,534	1,211
China (3)	5,034	19,765	21,331	24,272	27,651
Christmas Island	-	1	1	1	3
Cocos Islands	-	3	-	3	7
Cyprus	143	478	408	323	279
Hong Kong	1,493	5,632	5,158	4,119	3,860
India (4)	4,572	18,636	20,772	19,717	22,607
Indonesia (5)	147	778	694	820	977
Iran	1,031	4,261	5,861	8,476	10,410
Iraq	606	2,811	2,188	2,871	2,658
Israel	845	3,008	3,276	3,093	3,517
Japan (6)	1,142	4,192	4,028	4,063	4,225
Jordan (7)	762	2,875	3,483	3,360	3,322
Kampuchea	23	126	3,677	1,432	2,801
Korea	6,887	30,917	29,288	29,248	32,320
Kuwait	35	160	168	303	257
Laos	26	237	4,369	3,565	13,970
Lebanon	1,692	5,685	4,556	4,634	4,136
Macau	73	297	326	262	261
Malaysia	106	455	577	623	795
Maldives	1	2		2	2
Nepal	9	80	68	79	98
Oman	1	9	15	24	20
Pakistan	748	3,183	3,876	3,967	4,265
Philippines	9,738	39,111	37,216	41,300	42,316
Qatar (2)	4	13	11	5	16
Saudia Arabia	16	55	109	93	133
Singapore	87	308	320	321	322
Sri Lanka	99	376	375	397	397
Syria	395	1,676	1,416	1,528	1,658
Thailand	1,173	3,945	3,574	3,194	4,115
Turkey	479	1,758	1,578	1,764	2,233
United Arab Emirates (2)	1	13	11	30	32
Vietnam	1,182	4,629	88,543	22,546	43,483
Yemen (Aden)	12	48	126	174	261
Yemen (Sanaa)	133	376	258	203	160

Country or region of birth	TQ 1976	1977	1978	1979	1980
Africa	**2,322**	**10,155**	**11,524**	**12,838**	**13,981**
Algeria	30	89	145	140	175
Angola	120	294	241	163	194
Benin	4	5	13	14	32
Botswana	1	4	5	4	10
Burundi	0	9	6	15	8
Cameroon	4	21	39	29	65
Cape Verde	244	964	941	765	788
Central African Republic	-	1	2	2	3
Chad	-	3	6	5	6
Comoros	-	-	-	-	3
Congo	-	5	10	9	18
Djibouti	-	3	5	2	2
Egypt	466	2,328	2,836	3,241	2,833
Equatorial Guinea	2	8	5	2	15
Ethiopia	106	354	539	726	977
French So. & Antarctic Lands	-	6	7	6	5
Gabon	-	7	6	2	2
Gambia, The	2	10	18	13	27
Ghana	100	454	711	828	1,159
Guinea	-	11	9	17	18
Guinea-Bissau	4	14	7	9	11
Ivory Coast	4	10	21	12	28
Kenya	101	493	516	618	592
Lesotho	-	4	3	9	5
Liberia	69	215	333	327	426
Libya	18	65	86	111	163
Madagascar	6	21	16	18	19
Malawi	13	54	34	40	30
Mali	1	9	11	10	13
Mauritania	-	2	2	-	4
Mauritius	9	38	58	45	38
Morocco	121	401	461	486	465
Mozambique	34	145	78	69	81
Namibia	3	12	20	18	23
Niger	-	2	7	12	14
Nigeria	193	653	1,007	1,054	1,896
Reunion	-	1	1	5	-
Rwanda	1	6	11	14	7
St. Helena	1	3	2	3	6
Sao Tome & Principe	-	-	1	1	6
Senegal	15	80	75	63	106
Seychelles	1	31	29	59	56
Sierra Leone	27	157	212	217	267
Somalia	3	21	32	34	43
South Africa	308	1,988	1,689	2,214	1,960
Sudan	20	48	71	77	83
Swaziland	-	7	9	8	18
Tanzania	77	302	301	401	339
Togo	1	5	11	14	9
Tunisia	21	78	86	90	92
Uganda	66	241	303	284	343
Upper Volta	-	1	6	6	4
Western Sahara	-	-	-	-	-
Zaire	22	58	72	27	70
Zambia	70	253	211	232	178
Zimbabwe	34	161	198	268	246
Oceania	**988**	**4,091**	**4,396**	**4,449**	**3,951**
American Samoa (8)	1	2	3	7	3
Australia	394	1,389	1,565	1,400	1,480
Cook Islands	-	6	-	6	3
Fiji	132	854	809	1,000	724
French Polynesia	10	34	37	39	41
Guam	-	-	3	1	-
Kiribati (9)	-	5	6	4	8
Nauru	-	6	-	6	2
New Caledonia	1	5	1	2	4
New Zealand	123	597	619	599	729
Pacific Is. Trust Territory	58	193	137	114	149
Papua New Guinea	3	6	9	12	5
Pitcairn Islands	-	2	2	-	3
Solomon Islands	-	14	22	5	21
Tonga	133	489	706	809	453
Tuvalu (9)	-	-	-	-	-
Vanuatu (10)	1	6	13	6	4
Western Samoa	132	483	464	439	322

Table 7.2 Continued

Country or region of birth	TQ 1976	1977	1978	1979	1980
North America	**36,807**	**187,346**	**220,784**	**157,579**	**164,772**
Canada	2,458	12,688	16,863	13,772	13,609
Greenland	1	-	5	2	7
Mexico	16,001	44,079	92,367	52,096	56,680
St Pierre & Miquelon	-	4	9	2	6
United States (11)	22	79	26	86	206
Caribbean	**15,528**	**114,011**	**91,361**	**74,074**	**73,296**
Anguilla (12)	-	458	408	179	148
Antigua	117	835	908	770	972
Bahamas, The	91	400	585	651	547
Barbados	467	2,763	2,969	2,461	2,667
Bermuda	50	194	249	286	195
British Virgin Islands	45	580	449	320	255
Cayman Islands	17	47	103	90	95
Cuba	6,763	69,708	29,754	15,585	15,054
Dominica	105	572	595	1,009	846
Dominican Republic	2,562	11,655	19,458	17,519	17,245
Grenada	195	1,240	1,206	946	1,198
Guadeloupe	17	44	32	47	51
Haiti	1,281	5,441	6,470	6,433	6,540
Jamaica	2,074	11,501	19,265	19,714	18,970
Martinique	8	26	46	27	40
Montserrat	48	168	259	153	176
Netherlands Antilles	59	222	319	232	273
Puerto Rico	-	-	-	-	-
St. Christopher-Nevis (12)	254	896	1,014	786	874
St. Lucia	82	545	572	953	1,193
St. Vincent & Grenadines	82	585	679	639	763
Trinidad & Tobago	1,201	6,106	5,973	5,225	5,154
Turks & Caicos Islands	10	25	48	49	40
US Virgin Islands	-	-	-	-	-
Central America	**2,797**	**16,485**	**20,153**	**17,547**	**20,968**
Belize	161	930	1,033	1,063	1,120
Costa Rica	315	1,664	1,575	1,467	1,535
El Salvador	659	4,426	5,826	4,479	6,101
Guatemala	585	3,599	3,996	2,583	3,751
Honduras	288	1,626	2,727	2,545	2,552
Nicaragua	326	1,850	1,888	1,938	2,337
Panama (13)	463	2,390	3,108	3,472	3,572
South America	**6,209**	**32,954**	**41,764**	**35,344**	**39,717**
Argentina	522	2,787	3,732	2,856	2,815
Bolivia	130	699	1,030	751	730
Brazil	265	1,513	1,923	1,450	1,570
Chile	415	2,596	3,122	2,289	2,569
Colombia	1,470	8,272	11,032	10,637	11,289
Ecuador	1,128	5,302	5,732	4,383	6,133
Falkland Islands	-	2	2	3	3
French Guiana	1	6	16	4	14
Guyana	1,171	5,718	7,614	7,001	8,381
Paraguay	32	216	202	175	181
Peru	716	3,903	5,243	4,135	4,021
Suriname	13	48	74	65	114
Uruguay	155	1,156	1,052	754	887
Venezuela	191	736	990	841	1,010
Born On Board Ship/Plane	-	-	-	-	-

(1) Historical data for Danzia are included in Poland.
(2) Data for Bahrain, Qatar, and United Arab Emirates for 1971–1973 are included under Bahrain.
(3) Historical data for Outer Mongolia and Taiwan are included in China.
(4) Historical data for Portuguese India are included in India.
(5) Historical data for Irian Barat are included in Indonesia.
(6) Historical data for Bonin Islands, Okinawa, and Ryukyu Islands are included in Japan.
(7) Historical data for Palestine are included in Jordan.
(8) Historical data for Swains Island are included in American Samoa.
(9) Historical data for Gilbert (now Kiribati) and Ellice (now Tuvalu) Islands are included in Kiribati.
(10) Historical data for New Hebrides, both British and French, are included in Vanuatu.
(11) Historical data for Wake and Midway Islands are included in the United States.
(12) Prior to fiscal year 1977, historical data for Anguilla were included in St. Christopher-Nevis.
(13) Historical data for the Canal Zone are included in Panama.

Note: TQ 1976 is a transitional quarter added when the beginning of the fiscal year was shifted from July 1 to October 1.

Source: *Statistical Yearbook of the Immigration and Naturalization Service, 1980, Table 13.*

Table 7.3: Number of Immigrants to the United States by Region and Selected Country of Birth Annually, 1981–1985

Region and country of birth	1981	1982	1983	1984	1985
All countries	**596,600**	**594,131**	**559,763**	**543,903**	**570,009**
Europe	**66,695**	**69,174**	**58,867**	**64,076**	**63,043**
Austria	367	339	433	442	419
Belgium	467	559	538	537	538
Czechoslovakia	793	960	946	1,218	1,222
Denmark	506	463	513	512	478
Finland	317	346	311	264	290
France	1,745	1,994	2,061	2,135	2,187
Germany	6,552	(1)	(1)	(1)	(1)
Germany, Fed. Rep.	(1)	6,467	6,725	6,747	7,109
Greece	4,361	3,472	2,997	2,865	2,579
Hungary	581	642	632	825	1,009
Ireland	902	949	1,101	1,223	1,397
Italy	4,662	3,644	3,225	3,130	3,214
Netherlands	999	1,053	1,152	1,242	1,217
Norway	331	342	409	375	361
Poland	5,014	5,874	6,427	9,466	9,464
Portugal	7,049	3,510	3,231	3,779	3,781
Romania	1,974	3,124	2,543	4,004	5,188
Spain	1,711	1,586	1,507	1,393	1,413
Sweden	832	874	870	974	1,076
Switzerland	601	626	680	620	729
U.S.S.R.	9,223	15,462	5,214	6,088	3,521
United Kingdom	14,997	14,539	14,830	13,949	13,408
Yugoslavia	2,048	1,418	1,382	1,569	1,662
Other Europe	663	931	1,140	719	781

Table 7.3 Continued

Region and country of birth	1981	1982	1983	1984	1985
Asia	**264,343**	**313,291**	**277,701**	**256,273**	**264,691**
Afghanistan	1,881	1,569	2,566	3,222	2,794
Bangladesh	756	639	787	823	1,146
Burma	1,083	820	723	719	990
Cambodia	12,749	13,438	18,120	11,856	13,563
China	25,803	(2)	(2)	(2)	(2)
China, Mainland	(2)	27,100	25,777	23,363	24,787
Cyprus	326	276	265	291	294
Hong Kong	4,055	4,971	5,948	5,465	5,171
India	21,522	21,738	25,451	24,964	26,026
Indonesia	1,006	1,194	952	1,113	1,269
Iran	11,105	10,314	11,163	13,807	16,071
Iraq	2,535	3,105	2,343	2,930	1,951
Israel	3,542	3,356	3,239	3,066	3,113
Japan	3,896	3,903	4,092	4,043	4,086
Jordan	3,825	2,923	2,718	2,438	2,998
Korea	32,663	31,724	33,339	33,042	35,253
Kuwait	317	286	344	437	503
Laos	15,805	36,528	23,662	12,279	9,133
Lebanon	3,955	3,529	2,941	3,203	3,385
Malaysia	1,033	1,046	852	879	939
Pakistan	5,288	4,536	4,807	5,509	5,744
Philippines	43,772	45,102	41,546	42,768	47,978
Singapore	408	390	362	377	460
Sri Lanka	448	505	472	554	553
Syria	2,127	2,354	1,683	1,724	1,581
Taiwan	(3)	9,884	16,698	12,478	14,895
Thailand	4,799	5,568	5,875	4,885	5,239
Turkey	2,766	2,864	2,263	1,793	1,691
Vietnam	55,631	72,553	37,560	37,236	31,895
Yemen (Sanaa)	230	305	268	324	432

Region and country of birth	1981	1982	1983	1984	1985
Other Asia	1,017	771	885	685	751
Africa	**15,029**	**14,314**	**15,084**	**15,540**	**17,117**
Cape Verde	849	852	594	591	627
Egypt	3,366	2,800	2,600	2,642	2,802
Ethiopia	1,749	1,810	2,643	2,461	3,362
Ghana	951	824	976	1050	1041
Kenya	657	601	710	753	735
Liberia	556	593	518	585	618
Morocco	512	445	479	506	570
Nigeria	1,918	2,257	2,354	2,337	2,846
Sierra Leone	277	283	319	368	371
South Africa	1,559	1,434	1,261	1,246	1,210
Tanzania	423	304	364	418	395
Uganda	410	304	332	369	301
Other Africa	1,802	1,807	1,934	2,214	2,239
Oceania	**4,187**	**3,833**	**3,511**	**3,817**	**4,054**
Australia	1,281	1,367	1,273	1,308	1,362
Fiji	1,060	659	712	901	980
New Zealand	(3) 666	642	606	595	679
Tonga	588	561	481	555	669
Other Oceania	592	604	439	458	364
North America	**210,427**	**158,057**	**168,487**	**166,706**	**182,045**
Canada	11,191	10,786	11,390	10,791	11,385
Mexico	101,268	56,106	59,079	57,557	61,077
Caribbean	**73,301**	**67,379**	**73,306**	**74,265**	**83,281**
Antigua-Barbuda	929	3,234	2,008	953	957
Bahamas, The	546	577	505	499	533
Barbados	2,394	1,961	1,849	1,577	1,625

Table 7.3 Continued

Region and country of birth (Caribbean continued)	1981	1982	1983	1984	1985
Cuba	10,858	8,209	8,978	10,599	20,334
Dominica	721	569	546	442	540
Dominican Republic	18,220	17,451	22,058	23,147	23,787
Grenada	1,120	1,066	1,154	980	934
Haiti	6,683	8,779	8,424	9,839	10,165
Jamaica	23,569	18,711	19,535	19,822	18,923
St Kitts-Nevis	867	1,039	2,773	1,648	769
St. Lucia	733	586	662	484	499
St. Vincent & Grenadines	799	719	767	695	693
Trinidad & Tobago	4,599	3,532	3,156	2,900	2,831
Other Caribbean	1,263	946	891	680	691
Central America	**24,509**	**23,626**	**24,601**	**24,088**	**26,302**
Belize	1,289	2,031	1,585	1,492	1,353
Costa Rica	1,359	1,272	1,182	1,473	1,281
El Salvador	8,210	7,107	8,596	8,787	10,156
Guatemala	3,928	3,633	4,090	3,937	4,389
Honduras	2,358	3,186	3,619	3,405	3,726
Nicaragua	2,752	3,077	2,983	2,718	2,786
Panama	4,613	3,320	2,546	2,276	2,611
Other North America	158	160	111	5	-

Region and country of birth	1981	1982	1983	1984	1985
South America	35,913	35,448	36,087	37,460	39,058
Argentina	2,236	2,065	2,029	2141	1,844
Bolivia	820	750	823	918	1,006
Brazil	1,616	1,475	1,503	1,847	2,272
Chile	2,048	1,911	1,970	1,912	1,992
Colombia	10,335	8,608	9,658	11,020	11,982
Ecuador	5,129	4,127	4,243	4,164	4,482
Guyana	6,743	10,059	8,980	8,412	8,531
Peru	4,664	4,151	4,384	4,368	4,181
Uruguay	972	707	681	712	790
Venezuela	1,104	1,336	1,508	1,721	1,714
Other South America	246	259	308	245	264
Born on board ship	6	4	-	-	-
Unknown or not reported		10	26	31	1

(1) Prior to fiscal year 1982, data for Federal Republic of Germany and German Democratic Republic are consolidated under Germany.
(2) Prior to fiscal year 1982, data for Mainland China and Taiwan are consolidated under China.
(3) Includes Niue.

(-) Represents zero.

Source: Adapted from *Statistical Yearbook of the Immigration and Naturalization Service,* 1985, Table 3.

Table 7.4: Number of Immigrants to the United States by Region and Selected Country of Birth Annually, 1986–1996

Region and country of birth	1986	1987	1988	1989	1990
All Countries	601,708	601,516	643,025	1,090,924	1,536,483
Europe	62,512	61,174	64,797	82,891	112,401
Albania	53	62	82	71	78
Andorra	1	-	-	4	5
Austria	463	483	514	501	675
Belgium	620	636	581	548	682
Bulgaria	221	205	217	265	428
Czechoslovakia, former	1,118	1,357	1,482	992	1,412
Czech Republic	x	x	x	x	x
Slovak Republic	x	x	x	x	x
Unknown republic	x	x	x	x	x
Denmark	554	537	558	593	666
Estonia	6	15	11	14	20
Finland	322	331	390	325	369
France	2,518	2,513	2,524	2,598	2,849
Germany	x	x	x	x	x
East	136	108	110	137	105
West	6,991	7,210	6,645	6,708	7,388
Gibraltar	2	4	1	2	1
Greece	2,512	2,653	2,458	2,491	2,742
Hungary	1,006	994	1,227	1,193	1,655
Iceland	133	88	92	124	107
Ireland	1,839	3,060	5,058	6,961	10,333
Italy	3,089	2,784	2,949	2,910	3,287
Latvia	26	23	31	57	45
Liechtenstein	2	4	1	4	3
Lithuania	49	37	47	63	67
Luxembourg	24	26	28	16	31
Malta	135	113	112	74	77
Monaco	9	4	4	3	2
Netherlands	1,261	1,230	1,187	1,193	1,424
Norway	354	326	397	482	524
Poland	8,481	7,519	9,507	15,101	20,537
Portugal	3,766	3,912	3,199	3,758	4,035
Romania	5,198	3,837	3,875	4,573	4,647
San Marino	1	1	2	-	-
Soviet Union, former	2,588	2,384	2,949	11,128	25,524
Armenia	x	x	x	x	x
Azerbaijan	x	x	x	x	x
Belarus	x	x	x	x	x
Georgia	x	x	x	x	x
Kazakhstan	x	x	x	x	x
Kyrgyzstan	x	x	x	x	x
Moldova	x	x	x	x	x
Russia	x	x	x	x	x
Tajikistan	x	x	x	x	x
Turkmenistan	x	x	x	x	x
Ukraine	x	x	x	x	x
Uzbekistan	x	x	x	x	x
Unknown republic	x	x	x	x	x
Spain	1,591	1,578	1,483	1,550	1,886
Sweden	1,098	1,057	1,156	1,078	1,196
Switzerland	677	759	751	788	845
United Kingdom	13,657	13,497	13,228	14,090	15,928
Yugoslavia, former	2,011	1,827	1,941	2,496	2,828
Bosnia-Herzegovina	x	x	x	x	x
Croatia	x	x	x	x	x
Macedonia	x	x	x	x	x
Slovenia	x	x	x	x	x
Unknown	x	x	x	x	x

Region and country of birth	1986	1987	1988	1989	1990
Asia	**268,248**	**257,684**	**264,465**	**312,149**	**338,581**
Afghanistan	2,831	2,424	2,873	3,232	3,187
Bahrain	1	30	1	46	1
Bangladesh	1,634	1,649	1,325	2,180	4,252
Bhutan	1	-	2	1	1
Brunei	29	12	12	16	16
Burma	863	941	803	1,170	1,120
Cambodia	13,501	12,460	9,629	6,076	5,179
China, People's Republic	25,106	25,841	28,717	32,272	31,815
Cyprus	307	331	286	284	316
Hong Kong	5,021	4,706	8,546	9,740	9,393
India	26,227	27,803	26,268	31,175	30,667
Indonesia	1,183	1,254	1,342	1,513	3,498
Iran	16,505	14,426	15,246	21,243	24,977
Iraq	1,323	1,072	1,022	1,516	1,756
Israel	3,790	3,699	3,640	4,244	4,664
Japan	3,959	4,174	4,512	4,849	5,734
Jordan	3,081	3,125	3,232	3,921	4,449
Korea	35,776	35,849	34,703	34,222	32,301
Kuwait	496	507	599	710	691
Laos	7,842	6,828	10,667	12,524	10,446
Lebanon	3,994	4,367	4,910	5,716	5,634
Macau	243	254	183	246	301
Malaysia	886	1,016	1,250	1,506	1,867
Maldives	-	-	-	-	-
Mongolia	-	-	-	-	-
Nepal	86	78	106	134	184
Oman	11	11	7	18	9
Pakistan	5,994	6,319	5,438	8,000	9,729
Philippines	52,558	50,060	50,697	57,034	63,756
Qatar	41	30	39	49	33
Saudi Arabia	275	294	338	381	518
Singapore	480	469	492	566	620
Sri Lanka	596	630	634	757	976
Syria	1,604	1,669	2,183	2,675	2,972
Taiwan	13,424	11,931	9,670	13,974	15,151
Thailand	6,204	6,733	6,888	9,332	8,914
Turkey	1,753	1,596	1,642	2,007	2,468
United Arab Emirates	121	122	111	114	192
Vietnam	29,993	24,231	25,789	37,739	48,792
Yemen	x	x	x	x	x
Aden	60	150	259	135	218
Sanaa	420	577	360	831	1,727
Africa	**17,463**	**17,724**	**18,882**	**25,166**	**35,893**
Algeria	183	172	199	230	302
Angola	116	146	110	143	141
Benin	8	9	15	16	27
Botswana	30	15	24	10	21
Burkina Faso	3	4	6	11	8
Burundi	2	1	9	9	5
Cameroon	130	132	157	187	380
Cape Verde	760	657	921	1,118	907
Central African Republic	2	3	1	1	14
Chad	4	1	2	4	8
Comoros	-	-	1	-	-
Congo	6	12	4	10	9
Cote d'Ivoire	55	63	78	98	184
Djibouti	9	7	8	8	22
Egypt	2,989	3,377	3,016	3,717	4,117
Equatorial Guinea	1	-	1	2	5
Eritrea	x	x	x	x	x

Table 7.4 Continued

Region and country of birth	1986	1987	1988	1989	1990
(Africa, continued)					
Ethiopia	2,737	2,156	2,571	3,389	4,336
French Southern & Antarctic Lands	-	4	4	34	-
Gabon	8	5	3	7	11
Gambia	33	37	55	71	170
Ghana	1,164	1,120	1,239	2,045	4,466
Guinea	21	26	33	45	67
Guinea-Bissau	-	-	2	9	8
Kenya	719	698	773	910	1,297
Lesotho	16	7	7	8	16
Liberia	618	622	769	1,175	2,004
Libya	195	183	198	210	268
Madagascar	16	21	24	23	37
Malawi	32	49	53	84	48
Mali	11	13	20	18	34
Mauritania	2	7	2	9	3
Mauritius	60	36	47	56	67
Morocco	646	635	715	984	1,200
Mozambique	53	74	68	81	100
Namibia	17	10	25	26	23
Niger	5	15	3	7	3
Nigeria	2,976	3,278	3,343	5,213	8,843
Reunion	-	-	-	1	-
Rwanda	8	3	5	7	6
Sao Tome & Principe	-	3	2	7	1
Senegal	91	92	130	141	537
Seychelles	33	28	38	13	21
Sierra Leone	323	453	571	939	1,290
Somalia	139	197	183	228	277
South Africa	1,566	1,741	1,832	1,899	1,990
St. Helena	1	6	3	1	1
Sudan	230	198	217	272	306
Swaziland	7	12	6	7	11
Tanzania	370	385	388	507	635
Togo	22	19	22	29	30
Tunisia	121	120	98	125	226
Uganda	401	357	343	393	674
Western Sahara	-	-	1	-	-
Zaire	135	102	139	140	256
Zambia	168	161	182	259	209
Zimbabwe	221	252	216	230	272
Oceania	**3,894**	**3,993**	**3,839**	**4,360**	**6,182**
American Samoa	-	1	-	1	2
Australia	1,354	1,253	1,356	1,546	1,754
Christmas Island	-	-	-	-	-
Cook Islands	2	-	1	7	5
Fiji	972	1,205	1,028	968	1,353
French Polynesia	19	34	32	22	29
Kiribati	3	6	3	4	5
Marshall Islands	-	-	-	5	3
Micronesia, Federated States	-	-	-	8	7
Nauru	2	4	-	7	6
New Caledonia	2	11	4	7	8
New Zealand	610	591	668	789	829
Niue	-	-	1	-	-
Northern Mariana Islands	-	-	-	2	5
Pacific Islands, Trust Territories	141	120	66	2	22
Palau	-	-	-	34	62
Papua New Guinea	16	15	18	9	14
Solomon Islands	5	2	3	4	7

Region and country of birth	1986	1987	1988	1989	1990
(Oceania, continued)					
Tonga	510	545	434	646	1,375
Tuvalu	1	2	2	2	4
Vanuatu	4	2	2	2	2
Wallis & Futuna Islands	-	-	-	-	-
Western Samoa	253	202	221	295	690
North America	**207,714**	**216,550**	**250,009**	**607,398**	**957,558**
Canada	11,039	11,876	11,783	12,151	16,812
Greenland	1	1	1	1	3
Mexico	66,533	72,351	95,039	405,172	679,068
St. Pierre & Miguelon	-	-	-	-	-
Unknown	129	127	114	108	122
Caribbean	**101,632**	**102,899**	**112,357**	**88,932**	**115,351**
Anguilla	64	21	36	43	41
Antigua-Barbuda	812	874	837	979	1,319
Aruba	2	75	47	73	83
Bahamas, The	570	556	1,283	861	1,378
Barbados	1,595	1,665	1,455	1,616	1,745
Bermuda	172	154	166	182	203
British Virgin Islands	270	296	395	258	105
Cayman Islands	39	25	26	48	53
Cuba	33,114	28,916	17,558	10,046	10,645
Dominica	564	740	611	748	963
Dominican Republic	26,175	24,858	27,189	26,723	42,195
Grenada	1,045	1,098	842	1,046	1,294
Guadeloupe	38	37	54	38	54
Haiti	12,666	14,819	34,806	13,658	20,324
Jamaica	19,595	23,148	20,966	24,523	25,013
Martinique	18	34	25	30	32
Montserrat	147	104	104	124	172
Netherlands Antilles	116	81	62	65	80
St. Kitts-Nevis	573	589	660	795	896
St. Lucia	502	496	606	709	833
St. Vincent & the Grenadines	635	746	634	892	973
Trinidad & Tobago	2,891	3,543	3,947	5,394	6,740
Turks & Caicos Islands	26	21	47	78	206
Unknown	3	3	1	3	4
Central America	**28,380**	**29,296**	**30,715**	**101,034**	**146,202**
Belize	1,385	1,354	1,497	2,217	3,867
Costa Rica	1,356	1,391	1,351	1,985	2,840
El Salvador	10,929	10,693	12,045	57,878	80,173
Guatemala	5,158	5,729	5,723	19,049	32,303
Honduras	4,532	4,751	4,302	7,593	12,024
Nicaragua	2,826	3,294	3,311	8,830	11,562
Panama	2,194	2,084	2,486	3,482	3,433
South America	**41,874**	**44,385**	**41,007**	**58,926**	**85,819**
Argentina	2,187	2,106	2,371	3,301	5,437
Bolivia	1,079	1,170	1,038	1,805	2,843
Brazil	2,332	2,505	2,699	3,332	4,191
Chile	2,243	2,140	2,137	3,037	4,049
Colombia	11,408	11,700	10,322	15,214	24,189
Ecuador	4,516	4,641	4,716	7,532	12,476
Falkland Islands	-	-	1	-	1
French Guiana	1	-	3	2	2
Guyana	10,367	11,384	8,747	10,789	11,362
Paraguay	190	291	483	529	704
Peru	4,895	5,901	5,936	10,175	15,726
Suriname	103	144	151	163	240
Uruguay	699	709	612	948	1,457
Venezuela	1,854	1,694	1,791	2,099	3,142
Born on board ship	-	-	3	-	-
Unknown or not reported	**3**	**6**	**23**	**34**	**49**

Table 7.4 Continued

Region and country of birth	1991	1992	1993	1994	1995	1996
All Countries	**1,827,167**	**973,977**	**904,292**	**804,416**	**720,461**	**915,900**
Europe	**135,234**	**145,392**	**158,254**	**160,916**	**128,185**	**147,581**
Albania	142	682	1,400	1,489	1,420	4,007
Andorra	1	2	2	2	-	5
Austria	589	701	549	499	518	554
Belgium	525	780	657	516	569	651
Bulgaria	623	1,049	1,029	981	1,797	2,066
Czechoslovakia, former	1,156	1,181	1,000	874	1,174	1,389
Czech Republic	x	x	-	11	72	165
Slovak Republic	x	x	10	221	503	663
Unknown republic	x	x	990	642	599	561
Denmark	601	764	735	606	551	608
Estonia	23	194	191	272	205	280
Finland	333	525	544	471	476	602
France	2,450	3,288	2,864	2,715	2,505	3,079
Germany	6,509	9,888	7,312	6,992	6,237	6,748
East	x	x	x	x	x	x
West	x	x	x	x	x	x
Gibraltar	1	4	5	6	7	6
Greece	2,079	1,858	1,884	1,440	1,309	1,452
Hungary	1,534	1,304	1,091	880	900	1,183
Iceland	117	156	164	140	125	182
Ireland	4,767	12,226	13,590	17,256	5,315	1,731
Italy	2,619	2,592	2,487	2,305	2,231	2,501
Latvia	86	419	668	762	651	736
Liechtenstein	3	1	3	-	2	1
Lithuania	157	353	529	663	767	1,080
Luxembourg	21	25	14	24	15	32
Malta	83	85	52	75	72	52
Monaco	5	4	-	3	5	4
Netherlands	1,283	1,586	1,430	1,239	1,196	1,423
Norway	486	665	608	459	420	478
Poland	19,199	25,504	27,846	28,048	13,824	15,772
Portugal	4,524	2,748	2,081	2,169	2,615	2,984
Romania	8,096	6,500	5,601	3,444	4,871	5,801
San Marino	1	-	2	-	2	3
Soviet Union, former	56,980	43,614	58,571	63,420	54,494	62,777
Armenia	x	6,145	6,287	3,984	1,992	2,441
Azerbaijan	x	1,640	2,943	2,844	1,885	1,991
Belarus	x	3,233	4,702	5,420	3,791	4,268
Georgia	x	426	429	652	710	1,157
Kazakhstan	x	506	628	750	840	1,089
Kyrgyzstan	x	134	124	226	209	280
Moldova	x	1,705	2,646	2,260	1,856	1,849
Russia	x	8,857	12,079	15,249	14,560	19,668
Tajikistan	x	186	336	568	706	634
Turkmenistan	x	34	48	68	84	121
Ukraine	x	14,383	18,316	21,010	17,432	21,079
Uzbekistan	x	1,712	2,664	3,435	3,645	4,687
Unknown republic	x	4,653	7,369	6,954	6,784	3,513
Spain	1,849	1,631	1,388	1,418	1,321	1,659
Sweden	1,080	1,463	1,393	1,140	976	1,251
Switzerland	696	1,023	972	877	881	1,006
United Kingdom	13,903	19,973	18,783	16,326	12,427	13,624
Yugoslavia, former	2,713	2,604	2,809	3,405	8,307	11,854
Bosnia-Herzegovina	x	15	159	521	4,061	6,499
Croatia	x	77	370	412	608	810
Macedonia	x	-	-	367	666	863
Slovenia	x	8	50	67	65	77
Unknown	x	2,504	2,230	2,038	2,907	3,605

Region and country of birth	1991	1992	1993	1994	1995	1996
Asia	**358,533**	**356,955**	**358,047**	**292,589**	**267,931**	**307,807**
Afghanistan	2,879	2,685	2,964	2,344	1,424	1,263
Bahrain	45	1	471	581	581	81
Bangladesh	10,676	3,740	3,291	3,434	6,072	8,221
Bhutan	2	1	2	2	2	8
Brunei	15	17	26	14	14	20
Burma	946	816	849	938	1,233	1,320
Cambodia	3,251	2,573	1,639	1,404	1,492	1,568
China, People's Republic	33,025	38,907	65,578	53,985	35,463	41,728
Cyprus	243	262	229	204	188	187
Hong Kong	10,427	10,452	9,161	7,731	7,249	7,834
India	45,064	36,755	40,121	34,921	34,748	44,859
Indonesia	2,223	2,916	1,767	1,367	1,020	1,084
Iran	19,569	13,233	14,841	11,422	9,201	11,084
Iraq	1,494	4,111	4,072	6,025	5,596	5,481
Israel	4,181	5,104	4,494	3,425	2,523	3,126
Japan	5,049	11,028	6,908	6,093	4,837	6,011
Jordan	4,259	4,036	4,741	3,990	3,649	4,445
Korea	26,518	19,359	18,026	16,011	16,047	18,185
Kuwait	861	989	1,129	1,065	961	1,202
Laos	9,950	8,696	7,285	5,089	3,936	2,847
Lebanon	6,009	5,838	5,465	4,319	3,884	4,382
Macau	267	320	334	287	373	453
Malaysia	1,860	2,235	2,026	1,480	1,223	1,414
Maldives	1	-	2	-	1	1
Mongolia	2	6	8	21	17	17
Nepal	174	212	257	257	312	431
Oman	5	24	21	32	31	25
Pakistan	20,355	10,214	8,927	8,698	9,774	12,519
Philippines	63,596	61,022	63,457	53,535	50,984	55,876
Qatar	56	59	88	51	60	79
Saudi Arabia	552	584	616	668	788	1,164
Singapore	535	774	798	542	399	561
Sri Lanka	1,377	1,081	1,109	989	960	1,277
Syria	2,837	2,940	2,933	2,426	2,362	3,072
Taiwan	13,274	16,344	14,329	10,032	9,377	13,401
Thailand	7,397	7,090	6,654	5,489	5,136	4,310
Turkey	2,528	2,488	2,204	1,840	2,947	3,657
United Arab Emirates	164	172	196	286	317	343
Vietnam	55,307	77,735	59,614	41,345	41,752	42,067
Yemen	1,547	2,056	1,793	741	1,501	2,209
Aden	X	X	X	X	X	X
Sanaa	X	X	X	X	X	X
Africa	**36,179**	**27,086**	**27,783**	**26,712**	**42,456**	**52,889**
Algeria	269	407	360	364	650	1,059
Angola	132	107	92	75	81	125
Benin	24	10	21	18	23	38
Botswana	3	19	13	13	16	21
Burkina Faso	8	16	11	16	17	17
Burundi	16	11	13	14	26	36
Cameroon	452	236	262	305	506	803
Cape Verde	973	757	936	810	968	1,012
Central African Republic	0	8	15	7	2	27
Chad	9	4	-	9	11	13
Comoros	-	2	3	1	2	3
Congo	22	9	10	11	11	23
Cote d'Ivoire	347	259	250	268	289	432
Djibouti	21	14	14	10	25	19
Egypt	5,602	3,576	3,556	3,392	5,648	6,186
Equatorial Guinea	5	2	1	1	1	1
Eritrea	x	x	85	468	992	828

Table 7.4 Continued

Region and country of birth	1991	1992	1993	1994	1995	1996
(Africa, continued)						
Ethiopia	5,127	4,602	5,191	3,887	5,960	6,086
French Southern & Antarctic Lands	-	-	-	-	-	-
Gabon	11	9	5	11	13	29
Gambia	159	93	76	93	153	207
Ghana	3,330	1,867	1,604	1,458	3,152	6,606
Guinea	84	104	102	97	152	220
Guinea-Bissau	14	8	1	-	2	3
Kenya	1,185	953	1,065	1,017	1,419	1,666
Lesotho	4	15	5	8	10	11
Liberia	1,292	999	1,050	1,762	1,929	2,206
Libya	314	286	343	166	216	250
Madagascar	23	41	32	27	42	43
Malawi	68	72	53	55	56	58
Mali	63	55	51	55	94	124
Mauritania	9	2	9	10	22	26
Mauritius	64	61	83	65	67	84
Morocco	1,601	1,316	1,176	1,074	1,726	1,783
Mozambique	74	54	56	44	50	59
Namibia	14	29	37	24	35	30
Niger	1	2	4	8	10	102
Nigeria	7,912	4,551	4,448	3,950	6,818	10,221
Reunion	-	1	3	-	2	3
Rwanda	12	10	25	16	41	118
Sao Tome & Principe	4	7	-	1	6	4
Senegal	869	337	178	213	506	641
Seychelles	32	30	23	22	18	16
Sierra Leone	951	693	690	698	919	1,918
Somalia	458	500	1,088	1,737	3,487	2,170
South Africa	1,854	2,516	2,197	2,144	2,560	2,966
St. Helena	2	1	4	-	3	1
Sudan	679	675	714	651	1,645	2,172
Swaziland	5	8	10	7	20	16
Tanzania	500	352	426	357	524	553
Togo	33	45	41	52	83	157
Tunisia	275	216	167	149	189	228
Uganda	538	437	415	391	383	422
Western Sahara	-	-	-	-	-	3
Zaire	238	196	233	237	355	433
Zambia	228	210	225	198	222	226
Zimbabwe	261	296	308	246	299	385
Oceania	**6,236**	**5,169**	**4,902**	**4,592**	**4,695**	**5,309**
American Samoa	2	-	1	-	1	2
Australia	1,678	2,238	2,320	2,049	1,751	1,950
Christmas Island	-	-	2	-	-	-
Cook Islands	8	6	4	2	2	5
Fiji	1,349	807	854	1,007	1,491	1,847
French Polynesia	31	24	28	19	25	15
Kiribati	13	15	4	4	5	6
Marshall Islands	2	4	2	1	5	3
Micronesia, Federated States	6	11	11	7	7	5
New Caledonia	3	8	2	7	3	11
New Zealand	793	967	1,052	918	727	800
Niue	1	-	1	2	1	-
Northern Mariana Islands	6	3	3	-	4	4
Pacific Islands, Trust Territories	-	-	-	-	-	-
Palau	70	47	42	21	9	9
Papua New Guinea	20	17	15	22	13	17
Solomon Islands	2	1	3	5	2	2

Region and country of birth	1991	1992	1993	1994	1995	1996
(Oceania, continued)						
Tonga	1,685	703	348	293	403	416
Tuvalu	-	-	3	-	2	-
Vanuatu	5	1	-	-	1	-
Wallis & Futuna Islands	-	1	6	5	4	-
Western Samoa	561	314	200	227	237	215
North America	**1,210,981**	**384,047**	**301,380**	**272,226**	**231,526**	**340,540**
Canada	13,504	15,205	17,156	16,068	12,932	15,825
Greenland	8	2	3	1	2	2
Mexico	946,167	213,802	126,561	111,398	89,932	163,572
St. Pierre & Miquelon	-	1	-	-	1	-
Unknown	70	66	60	47	57	51
Caribbean	**140,139**	**97,413**	**99,438**	**104,804**	**96,788**	**116,801**
Anguilla	56	46	23	31	26	36
Antigua-Barbuda	944	619	554	438	374	406
Aruba	56	62	36	24	27	28
Bahamas, The	1,062	641	686	589	585	768
Barbados	1,460	1,091	1,184	897	734	1,043
Bermuda	146	153	156	118	111	103
British Virgin Islands	137	174	166	137	98	87
Cayman Islands	23	40	16	30	26	24
Cuba	10,349	11,791	13,666	14,727	17,937	26,466
Dominica	982	809	683	507	591	797
Dominican Republic	41,405	41,969	45,420	51,189	38,512	39,604
Grenada	979	848	827	595	583	787
Guadeloupe	34	50	49	41	48	52
Haiti	47,527	11,002	10,094	13,333	14,021	18,386
Jamaica	23,828	18,915	17,241	14,349	16,398	19,089
Martinique	25	25	17	20	11	23
Montserrat	143	104	102	69	83	99
Netherlands Antilles	40	37	65	48	58	76
St. Kitts-Nevis	830	626	544	370	360	357
St. Lucia	766	654	634	449	403	582
St. Vincent & the Grenadines	808	687	657	524	349	606
Trinidad & Tobago	8,407	7,008	6,577	6,292	5,424	7,344
Turks & Caicos Islands	121	59	39	26	27	35
Unknown	11	3	2	1	2	3
Central America	**111,093**	**57,558**	**58,162**	**39,908**	**31,814**	**44,289**
Belize	2,377	1,020	1,035	772	644	786
Costa Rica	2,341	1,480	1,368	1,205	1,062	1,504
El Salvador	47,351	26,191	26,818	17,644	11,744	17,903
Guatemala	25,527	10,521	11,870	7,389	6,213	8,763
Honduras	11,451	6,552	7,306	5,265	5,496	5,870
Nicaragua	17,842	8,949	7,086	5,255	4,408	6,903
Panama	4,204	2,845	2,679	2,378	2,247	2,560
South America	**79,934**	**55,308**	**53,921**	**47,377**	**45,666**	**61,769**
Argentina	3,889	3,877	2,824	2,318	1,762	2,456
Bolivia	3,006	1,510	1,545	1,404	1,332	1,913
Brazil	8,133	4,755	4,604	4,491	4,558	5,891
Chile	2,842	1,937	1,778	1,640	1,534	1,706
Colombia	19,702	13,201	12,819	10,847	10,838	14,283
Ecuador	9,958	7,286	7,324	5,906	6,397	8,321
Falkland Islands	-	-	-	-	-	-
French Guiana	2	2	6	10	4	5
Guyana	11,666	9,064	8,384	7,662	7,362	9,489
Paraguay	538	514	668	789	559	615
Peru	16,237	9,868	10,447	9,177	8,066	12,871
Suriname	178	238	211	190	213	211
Uruguay	1,161	716	568	516	414	540
Venezuela	2,622	2,340	2,743	2,427	2,627	3,468
Born on board ship	**-**	**2**	**-**	**-**	**-**	**-**
Unknown or not reported	**70**	**18**	**5**	**4**	**2**	**5**

(-) Represents zero.   X = Not applicable.

Source: *Statistical Yearbook of the Immigration and Naturalization Service*, 1996, Table 3.

Table 7.5: Immigrants to the United States by Region and Selected Country of Birth Annually, 1997–1998

Region and country of birth	1997	1998
All Countries	**798,378**	**660,477**
Europe	**119,871**	**90,793**
Albania	4,375	4,221
Andorra	3	-
Austria	487	291
Belgium	554	421
Bulgaria	2,774	3,735
Czechoslovakia, former	1,210	977
Czech Republic	186	144
Slovak Republic	629	491
Unknown republic	395	342
Denmark	429	457
Estonia	285	128
Finland	376	314
France	2,568	2,352
Germany	5,723	5,472
Germany, East	x	x
Germany, West	x	x
Gibraltar	3	1
Greece	1,049	863
Hungary	949	809
Iceland	119	111
Ireland	1,001	944
Italy	1,982	1,831
Latvia	615	370
Liechtenstein	1	1
Lithuania	812	1,191
Luxembourg	28	21
Malta	54	59
Monaco	4	6
Netherlands	1,059	917
Norway	372	298
Poland	12,038	8,469
Portugal	1,665	1,536
Romania	5,545	5,112
San Marino	-	-
Soviet Union, former	49,071	30,163
Armenia	2,094	1,146
Azerbaijan	1,450	504
Belarus	3,062	981
Georgia	812	295
Kazakhstan	1,025	540
Kyrgyzstan	287	111
Moldova	1,347	562
Russia	16,632	11,529
Tajikistan	311	66
Turkmenistan	99	44
Ukraine	15,696	7,448
Uzbekistan	3,312	601
Unknown republic	2,944	6,336
Spain	1,241	1,043
Sweden	958	823
Switzerland	1,063	828
United Kingdom	10,708	9,018
Yugoslavia, former	10,750	8,011
Bosnia-Herzegovina	6,392	4,212
Croatia	720	549
Macedonia	783	785
Slovenia	62	57
Unknown	2,793	2,408

Region and country of birth	1997	1998
Asia	**265,810**	**219,696**
Afghanistan	1,129	831
Bahrain	80	53
Bangladesh	8,681	8,621
Bhutan	6	6
Brunei	6	19
Burma	1,085	1,371
Cambodia	1,638	1,439
China, People's Republic	41,147	36,884
Cyprus	148	119
Hong Kong	5,577	5,275
India	38,071	36,482
Indonesia	906	1,020
Iran	9,642	7,883
Iraq	3,244	2,220
Israel	2,448	1,991
Japan	5,097	5,138
Jordan	4,171	3,255
Korea	14,239	14,268
Kuwait	837	749
Laos	1,935	1,612
Lebanon	3,568	3,290
Macau	277	276
Malaysia	1,051	1,011
Maldives	1	1
Mongolia	22	26
Nepal	447	476
Oman	36	25
Pakistan	12,967	13,094
Philippines	49,117	34,466
Qatar	70	60
Saudi Arabia	815	703
Singapore	460	389
Sri Lanka	1,128	1,085
Syria	2,269	2,840
Taiwan	6,745	7,097
Thailand	3,094	3,102
Turkey	3,145	2,682
United Arab Emirates	329	329
Vietnam	38,519	17,649
Yemen	1,663	1,859
Yemen (Aden)	X	X
Yemen (Sanaa)	X	X
Africa	**47,791**	**40,660**
Algeria	717	804
Angola	75	66
Benin	48	47
Botswana	18	12
Burkina Faso	13	14
Burundi	59	51
Cameroon	898	691
Cape Verde	920	814
Central African Republic	10	6
Chad	18	8
Comoros	3	-
Congo, Democratic Republic (1)	31	155
Congo, Republic (1)	414	118
Cote d'Ivoire	430	364
Djibouti	18	15
Egypt	5,031	4,831
Equatorial Guinea	2	7
Eritrea	948	641

Table 7.5 Continued

Region and country of birth	1997	1998
Ethiopia	5,904	4,205
French Southern & Antarctic Lands	-	-
Gabon	24	21
Gambia	176	227
Ghana	5,105	4,458
Guinea	158	46
Guinea-Bissau	24	165
Kenya	1,387	1,696
Lesotho	6	4
Liberia	2,216	1,617
Libya	171	166
Madagascar	33	42
Malawi	72	39
Mali	97	83
Mauritania	51	78
Mauritius	44	37
Morocco	2,359	2,410
Mozambique	48	39
Namibia	22	24
Niger	837	283
Nigeria	7,038	7,746
Reunion	1	-
Rwanda	170	52
Sao Tome & Principe	2	3
Senegal	435	373
Seychelles	15	5
Sierra Leone	1,884	955
Somalia	4,005	2,629
South Africa	2,093	1,904
St. Helena	-	-
Sudan	2,030	1,161
Swaziland	11	8
Tanzania	399	339
Togo	222	246
Tunisia	163	200
Uganda	400	355
Western Sahara	-	1
Zambia	262	213
Zimbabwe	274	186
Oceania	**4,344**	**3,935**
American Samoa	-	4
Australia	1,630	1,147
Christmas Island	1	-
Cook Islands	4	1
Fiji	1,549	1,717
French Polynesia	21	14
Kiribati	5	4
Marshall Islands	3	6
Micronesia, Federated States	2	4
Nauru	-	-
New Caledonia	-	4
New Zealand	655	628
Niue	3	1
Northern Mariana Islands	3	3
Pacific Islands, Trust Territories	x	x
Palau	8	6
Papua New Guinea	15	10
Samoa(2)	138	147
Solomon Islands	1	5
Tonga	303	230
Tuvalu	-	1
Vanuatu	1	2
Wallis & Futuna Is.	1	1

Region and country of birth	1997	1998
North America	**307,488**	**252,996**
Canada	11,609	10,190
Greenland	1	-
Mexico	146,865	131,575
St. Pierre & Miguelon	-	-
United States	38	31
Caribbean	**105,299**	**75,521**
Anguilla	19	26
Antigua-Barbuda	393	297
Aruba	26	23
Bahamas, The	641	602
Barbados	829	726
Bermuda	75	63
British Virgin Islands	93	55
Cayman Islands	35	28
Cuba	33,587	17,375
Dominica	746	283
Dominican Rep.	27,053	20,387
Grenada	755	655
Guadeloupe	52	30
Haiti	15,057	13,449
Jamaica	17,840	15,146
Martinique	20	20
Montserrat	99	65
Netherlands Antilles	43	61
Puerto Rico	1	2
St. Kitts-Nevis	377	405
St. Lucia	531	509
St. Vincent & Grenadines	581	414
Trinidad & Tobago	6,409	4,852
Turks & Caicos Is.	37	46
U.S. Virgin Islands	-	2
Central America	**43,676**	**35,679**
Belize	664	496
Costa Rica	1,330	1,204
El Salvador	17,969	14,590
Guatemala	7,785	7,759
Honduras	7,616	6,463
Nicaragua	6,331	3,521
Panama	1,981	1,646
South America	**52,877**	**45,394**
Argentina	1,964	1,511
Bolivia	1,734	1,513
Brazil	4,583	4,401
Chile	1,443	1,240
Colombia	13,004	11,836
Ecuador	7,780	6,852
Falkland Islands	1	1
French Guiana	6	1
Guyana	7,257	3, 963
Paraguay	304	275
Peru	10,853	10,154
Suriname	191	143
Uruguay	429	368
Venezuela	3,328	3,136
Born on board ship	**-**	**-**
Unknown or not reported	**197**	**7,003**

(-) Represents zero.

X = Not applicable.

Source: *Statistical Handbook of the Immigration and Naturalization Service,* 1998, Table 3.

(1) In May 1997 Zaire was formally recognized as the Dominican Republic of the Congo; the Congo is referred to by its conventional name, the Republic of the Congo.

Appendixes

Appendix A: General Immigration Resources

Internet Resources

General Sites

Center for Migration Studies (*http://cmsny.org*) Web site of a key institute studying migration and refugee movements; provides information on its project, publications, and library and archives, with searchable on-line catalog; also includes links to other international centers in the Federation of Centers of Migration Studies and to other links of interest, such as the Immigrant Ship Transcribers Guild. (Address: 209 Flagg Place, Staten Island, NY 10304-1199; Phone: 718-351-8800; Fax: 718-667-4598)

Immigration History Research Center (*http://www1.umn.edu/ihrc/*) Official Web site for this international resource on American immigration and ethnic history, based at the University of Minnesota, which "maintains archival and library collections, sponsors academic and public programs, and publishes bibliographic and scholarly works." Web site describes the collections, posts news and current events, lists publications, and provides information about visiting the IHRC. (Address: Immigration History Research Center, University of Minnesota, 826 Berry Street, St. Paul, MN 55114; Phone: 612-627-4208; Fax: 612-627-4190; E-mail: ihrc@gold.tc.umn.edu)

Balch Institute for Ethnic Studies (*http://www.libertynet.org/balch*) Web site for the museum, library, and archive, which houses the Temple-Balch Institute for Immigration Research; offers on-line newsletter, information on programs, and links of related interest. (Address: Center for Immigration Research, 18 South Seventh Street, Philadelphia, PA 19106; Phone: 215-925-8090)

European Research Centre on Migration and Ethnic Relations (ERCOMER) (*http://www.ercomer.org*) Web site of organization focusing on the "scientific study of migration (including asylum seekers), racism, and ethnicity"; provides information about publications, research projects, and events; offers on-line newsletter, statistics, a searchable on-line "virtual library on migration and ethnic relations," consisting of worldwide migration-related Web links. (Address: Utrecht University, Heidelberglaan 2, 3584 CS Utrecht, The Netherlands; Phone: +31-30-253 90 54; Fax: +31-30 253 92 80; E-mail: ERCOMERsecr@fss.uu.nl)

National Immigration Forum (*http://www.immigrationforum.org*) Searchable Web site offering information about current immigration issues, citizenship, race and ethnic relations, and its publications, plus newsletter archives and other resources. (Address: 220 I Street, NE, #220, Washington, DC 20002-4362; Phone: 202-544-0004; Fax: 202-544-1905)

U.S. Committee for Refugees (USCR) (*http://www.refugees.org*) Web site of organization focusing on problems of current refugees, offering news, international reports, issues, resources, and publications. (Address: 1717 Massachusetts Ave. NW, Suite 200, Washington, DC 20036; Phone: 202-347-3507; Fax: 202-347-3418; E-mail: uscr@irsa-uscr.org)

Ellis Island Sites

Ellis Island (*http://www.ellisislandrecords.org*) Official Web site for Ellis Island immigration records, which attracted enormous public interest and attention when it opened in 2001. It allows computer users (or individuals who visit Ellis Island) to search U.S. government immigration archives to find information about specific immigrants, including where they came from, how old they were when they arrived, the ship they traveled on and when it arrived, and a copy of the ship's manifest containing the immigrant's name. Users are able to narrow or expand their search, as by looking only at arrivals during particular years, on certain ships, and using alternate name spellings. Users who join the Statue of Liberty–Ellis Island Foundation are also able to create and maintain family scrapbooks online and to make annotations to passenger records. The still-developing Web site also includes a section on the immigrant experience, including stories of immigrant families and a timeline of immigration history, information about visiting Ellis Island and its associated museum, and a gift shop selling immigration-related items, such as books and photographs of immigrant ships and ship's manifests. It also offers links to the American Immigrant Wall of Honor (*www.wallofhonor.com*), on a searchable online database of names inscribed on the wall, with a form for adding names to the wall. This Web site replaced an earlier more limited one (*www.ellisisland.org*).

Ellis Island Virtual Tour (*http://www.capital.net/~alta/index.html*) Web site for teachers and students, offering a guided tour following immigrants of different nationalities, teaching resources, and related links.

Angel Island Sites

Angel Island Home Page (*http://www.angelisland.org*) Web site of the organization and the California Department of Parks and Recreation; includes historical information, information on events, and links. (Address: P.O. Box 866, Tiburon, CA 94920; Phone: 415-435-3522; Fax: 415-435-2950; Park information: 415-435-1915)

Angel Island Immigration Station Foundation (*http://www.a-better.com/angel/island.htm*) Organization Web site offering information about and images of Angel Island.

The UNOFFICIAL Angel Island Immigration Station Resource Page (*http://www.geocities.com/Tokyo/1940*) Web site offering a variety of Angel Island–related resources.

Print Resources

General Works

Archdeacon, Thomas J. *Becoming American: An Ethnic History*. New York: Free Press, 1983.

Barkan, Elliott Robert. *And Still They Come: Immigrants and American Society, 1920 to the 1990s*. Wheeling, Il.: H. Davidson, 1996.

Baseler, Marilyn C. *"Asylum for Mankind": America, 1607–1800*. Ithaca, N.Y.: Cornell University Press, 1998.

Bodnar, John E. *The Transplanted: A History of Immigrants in Urban America*. Bloomington: Indiana University Press, 1985.

Bouvier, Leon F. *Peaceful Invasions: Immigration and Changing America*. Washington, D.C.: Center for Immigration Studies, 1991; Lanham, Md.: University Press of America, 1992.

Coppa, Frank J., and Thomas J. Curran, eds. *The Immigrant Experience in America*. Boston: Twayne, 1976.

Cose, Ellis. *A Nation of Strangers: Prejudice, Politics, and the Populating of America*. New York: Morrow, 1992.

Daniels, Roger. *Coming to America: A History of Immigration and Ethnicity in American Life*. New York: HarperCollins, 1990.

Dinnerstein, Leonard, et al. *Natives and Strangers: A Multicultural History of Americans*. New York: Oxford University Press, 1996.

————. *Natives and Strangers: Blacks, Indians, and Immigrants in America*. 2d ed. New York: Oxford University Press, 1990.

————. *Natives and Strangers: Ethnic Groups and the Building of America*. New York: Oxford University Press, 1979.

Dislocation and Emigration: The Social Background of American Immigration. Cambridge, Mass.: Charles Warren Center for Studies in American History, Harvard University, 1973.

Emsden, Katharine, ed. *Coming to America: A New Life in a New Land*. Lowell, Mass.: Discovery Enterprises, 1993.

Evitts, William J. *Early Immigration in the United States*. New York: Watts, 1989.

Golab, Caroline. *Immigrant Destinations*. Philadelphia: Temple University Press, 1977.

Greene, Victor R. *American Immigrant Leaders, 1800–1910: Marginality and Identity*. Baltimore: Johns Hopkins University Press, 1987.

Haines, David W., ed. *Refugees in the United States: A Reference Handbook*. Westport, Conn.: Greenwood, 1985.

————. *Refugees in America in the 1990s: A Reference Handbook*. Westport, Conn.: Greenwood, 1996.

Handlin, Oscar. *The Uprooted*. 2d ed. Boston: Little, Brown, 1990.

Hauser, Pierre. *Illegal Aliens*. New York: Chelsea House, 1990.

Hoerder, Dirk, and Horst Rossler, eds. *Distant Magnets: Expectations and Realities in the Immigrant Experience, 1840–1930*. New York: Holmes & Meier, 1993.

Jones, Maldwyn Allen. *American Immigration*. 2d ed. Chicago: University of Chicago Press, 1992.

Kessner, Thomas, and Betty Boyd Caroli. *Today's Immigrants, Their Stories: A New Look at the Newest Americans*. New York: Oxford University Press, 1981.

Kraus, Michael. *Immigration, the American Mosaic: From Pilgrims to Modern Refugees*. Huntington, N.Y.: Krieger, 1979. Reprint of 1955, Van Nostrand, ed.

Kroes, Rob, ed. *American Immigration: Its Variety and Lasting Imprint*. Amsterdam: Amerika Instituut, Universiteit van Amsterdam, 1979.

Mark, Gregory Yee, et al., eds. *Our History, Our Way: An Ethnic Studies Anthology*. Dubuque, Iowa: Kendall/ Hunt, 1996.

Miller, E. Willard, and Ruby M. Miller. *United States Immigration: A Reference Handbook*. Santa Barbara, Calif.: ABC-CLIO, 1996.

Namias, June, ed. *First Generation: In the Words of Twentieth-Century American Immigrants*. Boston: Beacon Press, 1978.

Olson, James Stuart. *The Ethnic Dimension in American History*. 2d ed. New York: St. Martin's Press, 1994.

Parrillo, Vincent N. *Strangers to These Shores: Race and Ethnic Relations in the United States*. 3d ed. New York: Macmillan, 1990.

Portes, Alejandro, and Ruben G. Rumbaut. *Immigrant America: A Portrait*. 2d ed. Berkeley: University of California Press, 1996.

Pozzetta, George E., ed. *Assimilation, Acculturation, and Social Mobility*. New York: Garland, 1991.

————. *Emigration and Immigration: The Old World Confronts the New*. New York: Garland, 1991.

————. *Immigrant Institutions: The Organization of Immigrant Life*. New York: Garland, 1991.

Themes in Immigration History. New York: Garland, 1991.

Purcell, L. Edward. *Immigration*. Phoenix: Oryx, 1995.

Reimers, David M. *Still the Golden Door: The Third World Comes to America*. 2d ed. New York: Columbia University Press, 1992.

Rischin, Moses, ed. *Immigration and the American Tradition*. Indianapolis: Bobbs-Merrill, 1976.

Scott, Franklin Daniel. *The Peopling of America: Perspectives on Immigration*. Washington, D.C.: American Historical Association, 1984.

Seller, Maxine. *To Seek America: A History of Ethnic Life in the United States*. Rev. ed. Englewood, N.J.: J. S. Ozer, 1988.

Shenton, James P., ed. *Ethnic Groups in American Life*. New York: Arno Press, 1978.

Sowell, Thomas. *Ethnic America: A History*. New York: Basic Books, 1981.

Takaki, Ronald T. *A Different Mirror: A History of Multicultural America*. Boston: Little, Brown, 1993.

Thernstrom, Stephan, ed. *Harvard Encyclopedia of American Ethnic Groups*. Cambridge, Mass.: Belknap Press of Harvard University, 1980.

Ueda, Reed. *Postwar Immigrant America: A Social History*. Boston: Bedford Books of St. Martin's Press, 1994.

Unger, Sanford J. *Fresh Blood: The New American Immigrants*. New York: Simon & Schuster, 1995.

Walch, Timothy, ed. *Immigrant America: European Ethnicity in the United States*. New York: Garland, 1994.

Williamson, Chilton, Jr. *The Immigration Mystique: America's False Conscience*. New York: Basic Books, 1996.

World Book of America's Heritage: The Peoples, Traditions, and Aspirations That Shaped North America. Chicago: World Book, 1991.

General Sourcebooks and Chronologies

Appel, John J. *Immigrant Historical Societies in the United States, 1880–1950*. New York: Arno Press, 1980.

Center for Migration Studies, Olha Della Cava, ed. *A Guide to the Archives*. 4 vols. Staten Island: Center for Migration Studies of New York, 1974–1981.

Haley, Frances, ed. *Guide to Selected Ethnic Heritage Materials, 1974–1980*. Boulder, Col.: Social Science Education Consortium: ERIC Clearinghouse for Social Studies/Social Science Education, 1982.

Hecker, Melvin. *Ethnic America, 1970–1977: Updating the Ethnic Chronology Series*. Dobbs Ferry, N.Y.: Oceana, 1979.

Lankevich, George J. *Ethnic America, 1978–1980: Updating the Ethnic Chronology Series*. New York: Oceana, 1981.

Mendoza, Alejandro G. *The United States Immigration History Timeline*. New York: Terra Firma Press, 1990.

Multicultural Milestones in U.S. History. Upper Saddle River, N.J.: Globe Fearon, 1995.

University of Minnesota, Immigration History Research Center. *IHRC Ethnic Collections Series*. 9 vols. St. Paul: Immigration History Research Center, University of Minnesota, 1976– .

University of Minnesota, Immigration History Research Center, Suzanna Moody and Joel Wurl, eds. *The Immigration History Research Center: A Guide to Collections*. New York: Greenwood Press, 1991.

On Government Policy

Beck, Roy Howard. *Re-Charting America's Future: Responses to Arguments Against Stabilizing U.S. Population and Limiting Immigration*. Petoskey, Mich.: Social Contract Press, 1994.

The Case Against Immigration: The Moral, Economic, Social, and Environmental Reasons for Reducing U.S. Immigration Back to Traditional Levels. New York: W. W. Norton, 1996.

Booth, Alan, et al., eds. *Immigration and the Family: Research and Policy on U.S. Immigrants*. Mahwah, N.J.: Lawrence Erlbaum, 1997.

Bouvier, Leon F., and Lindsey Grant. *How Many Americans?: Population, Immigration and the Environment*. San Francisco: Sierra Club Books, 1994.

Daniels, Roger. *Not Like Us: Immigrants and Minorities in America, 1890–1924*. Chicago: Ivan R. Dee, 1997.

Fitzgerald, Keith A. *The Face of the Nation: Immigration, the State, and the National Identity*. Stanford, Calif.: Stanford University Press, 1996.

Gjerde, Jon, ed. *Major Problems in American Immigration and Ethnic History: Documents and Essays.* Boston: Houghton Mifflin, 1998.

Heer, David M. *Immigration in America's Future: Social Science Findings and the Policy Debate.* Boulder, Col.: Westview, 1996.

Jonas, Susanne, and Suzanne Dod Thomas, eds. *Immigration: A Civil Rights Issue for the Americas.* Wilmington, Del.: Scholarly Resources, 1999.

Keely, Charles B. *U.S. Immigration: A Policy Analysis.* New York: Population Council, 1979.

Kennedy, John F. *A Nation of Immigrants.* Rev. ed. New York: Harper & Row, 1986.

Morrow, Robert. *Immigration: Blessing or Burden?* Minneapolis: Lerner, 1997.

Musalo, Karen, et al. *Refugee Law and Policy: Cases and Materials.* Durham, N.C.: Carolina Academic Press, 1997.

Nanda, Ved P., ed. *Refugee Law and Policy: International and U.S. Responses.* New York: Greenwood, 1989.

Norwood, Frederick Abbott. *Strangers and Exiles: A History of Religious Refugees.* Nashville: Abingdon, 1969.

O'Neill, Teresa, ed. *Immigration: Opposing Viewpoints.* San Diego: Greenhaven Press, 1992.

Simmons, Patrick A., and Isaac F. Megbolugbe. *Catching the New Wave: Recent Immigration to the United States.* Washington, D.C.: Fannie Mae Office of Housing Research, 1995.

Wang, Peter H. *Legislating Normalcy: The Immigration Act of 1924.* San Francisco: R & E Research Associates, 1975.

Williamson, Chilton, Jr. *The Immigration Mystique: America's False Conscience.* New York: Basic Books, 1996.

Wokeck, Marianne Sophia. *Trade in Strangers: The Beginnings of Mass Migration to North America.* University Park: Pennsylvania State University Press, 1999.

Yans-McLaughlin, Virginia, ed. *Immigration Reconsidered: History, Sociology, and Politics.* New York: Oxford University Press, 1990.

On Ellis Island

Bearss, Edwin C. *The Ferryboat Ellis Island, Transport to Hope.* Washington, D.C.: Division of History, Office of Archeology and Historic Preservation, National Park Service, 1969.

Bell, James B., and Richard I. Abrams. *In Search of Liberty: The Story of the Statue of Liberty and Ellis Island.* Garden City, N.Y.: Doubleday, 1984.

Benton, Barbara. *Ellis Island: A Pictorial History.* New York: Facts on File, 1985.

Bolino, August C. *The Ellis Island Source Book.* 2d ed. Washington, D.C.: Kensington Historical Press, 1990.

Brownstone, David M., Irene M. Franck, and Douglass Brownstone. *Island of Hope, Island of Tears.* New York: Rawson, Wade, 1979. Barnes and Noble reprint, 2000.

Coan, Peter M. *Ellis Island Interviews: In Their Own Words.* New York: Facts on File, 1997.

Ellis Island: An Illustrated History of the Immigrant Experience. New York: Macmillan, 1991.

Fisher, Leonard Everett. *Ellis Island: Gateway to the New World.* New York: Holiday House, 1986.

Kilian, Pamela. *Ellis Island: Gateway to the American Dream.* New York: Crescent Books, 1991.

Kinney, Paul. *Ellis Island: The First Experience with Liberty.* Washington, D.C.: Portfolio Project, 1986.

Perec, Georges, with Robert Bober. *Ellis Island.* New York: New Press, 1995. Translated from the French by Harry Mathews.

Shapiro, Mary J. *Gateway to Liberty: The Story of the Statue of Liberty and Ellis Island.* New York: Vintage Books, 1986.

Visiting Ellis Island: A Souvenir of the Ellis Island Immigration Museum. New York: Collier Books, 1992.

Spencer, Sharon, and Dennis Toner. *Ellis Island, Then and Now.* Franklin Lakes, N.J.: Lincoln Springs Press, 1988.

Tifft, Wilton S. *Ellis Island.* Chicago: Contemporary, 1990.

Unrau, Harlan D. *Ellis Island: Historical Data, Statue of Liberty National Monument, New York/New Jersey.*

Denver: U.S. Dept. of the Interior, National Park Service, Denver Service Center, 1981.

Yans-McLaughlin, Virginia, et al. *Ellis Island and the Peopling of America: The Official Guide*. New York: New Press, 1997.

On Angel Island

Lai, H. Mark, et al. *Island: Poetry and History of Chinese Immigrants on Angel Island 1910–1940*. Seattle: University of Washington Press, 1991.

Firsthand Accounts

Dublin, Thomas, ed. *Immigrant Voices: New Lives in America, 1773–1986*. Urbana: University of Illinois Press, 1993.

Morrison, Joan, and Charlotte Fox Zabusky, comps. *American Mosaic: The Immigrant Experience in the Words of Those Who Lived It*. Pittsburgh: University of Pittsburgh Press, 1992. Originally published New York: Dutton, 1980.

Stave, Bruce M., et al. *From the Old Country: An Oral History of the European Migration to America*. New York: Twayne, 1994.

General Works for Young Readers

American Immigration. 10 vols. Danbury, Conn.: Grolier Educational, 1999.

Anderson, Kelly C. *Immigration*. San Diego: Lucent Books, 1993.

Anderson, Lydia. *Immigration*. New York: Watts, 1981.

Andryszewski, Tricia. *Immigration: Newcomers and Their Impact on the United States*. Brookfield, Conn.: Milbrook Press, 1995.

Ashabranner, Brent K. *The New Americans: Changing Patterns in U.S. Immigration*. New York: Dodd, Mead, 1983.

Our Beckoning Borders: Illegal Immigration to America. New York: Cobblehill Books, 1993.

Ashabranner, Brent K. *Still a Nation of Immigrants*. New York: Cobblehill Books/Dutton, 1993.

Berger, Melvin, and Gilda Berger. *Where Did Your Family Come From? A Book About Immigrants*. Nashville: Ideals Children's Books, 1993.

Where Did Your Family Come From? Philadelphia: Chelsea House, 1998.

Bouvier, Leon F. *Think About Immigration: Social Diversity in the U.S.* New York: Walker, 1988.

Bratman, Fred. *Becoming a Citizen: Adopting a New Home*. Austin, Tex: Raintree Steck-Vaughn, 1993.

Day, Carol Olsen, and Edmund Day. *The New Immigrants*. New York: Watts, 1985.

Fassler, David, and Kimberly Danforth. *Coming to America: The Kids' Book About Immigration*. Burlington, Vt.: Waterfront, 1993.

Greenberg, Judith E. *Newcomers to America: Stories of Today's Young Immigrants*. New York: Watts, 1996.

Hartmann, Edward George. *American Immigration*. Minneapolis: Lerner, 1979.

Katz, William Loren. *The Great Migrations, 1880s–1912*. Austin, Tex.: Raintree Steck-Vaughn, 1993.

Koral, April. *An Album of the Great Wave of Immigration*. New York: Watts, 1992.

Levine, Herbert M. *Immigration*. Austin, Tex.: Raintree Steck-Vaughn, 1998.

May, Charles Paul. *The Uprooted*. Philadelphia: Westminster Press, 1976.

Press, Petra. *A Multicultural Portrait of Immigration*. Tarrytown, N.Y.: Benchmark Books, 1996.

Reiff, Tana. *Stories of the Immigration Experience*, 10 vols. Belmont, Calif.: Fearon Education, 1989.

Reimers, David M. *A Land of Immigrants*. New York: Chelsea House Publishers, 1996.

Sandler, Martin W. *Immigrants*. New York, NY: HarperCollins, 1995.

Strom, Yale. *Quilted Landscapes*. New York: Simon & Schuster, 1996.

Thompson, Gare. *Immigrants: Coming to America*. New York: Children's Press, 1997.

On Government Policy for Young Readers

Goldish, Meish. *Immigration: How Should It Be Controlled?* New York: Twenty-First Century Books, 1994.

Knight, Margy Burns. *Who Belongs Here? An American Story*. Gardiner, Maine: Tilbury House, 1993.

On Ellis Island for Young Readers

Hargrove, Jim. *Gateway to Freedom: The Story of the Statue of Liberty and Ellis Island*. Chicago: Children's Press, 1986.

Jacobs, William Jay. *Ellis Island: New Hope in a New Land*. New York: Scribner's, 1990.

Kroll, Steven. *Ellis Island: Doorway to Freedom*. New York: Holiday House, 1995.

Levine, Ellen. *If Your Name Was Changed at Ellis Island*. New York: Scholastic, 1993.

Maestro, Betsy. *Coming to America: The Story of Immigration*. New York: Scholastic, 1996.

Owens, Tom. *Ellis Island*. New York: PowerKids Press, 1997.

Quiri, Patricia Ryon. *Ellis Island: A True Book*. New York: Children's Press, 1998.

Reef, Catherine. *Ellis Island*. New York: Dillon Press, 1991.

Severn, Bill. *Ellis Island: The Immigrant Years*. New York: J. Messner, 1971.

Siegel, Beatrice. *Sam Ellis's Island*. New York: Four Winds Press, 1985.

Stein, R. Conrad. *Ellis Island*. 2d ed. Chicago: Children's Press, 1992.

Firsthand Accounts for Young Readers

Bales, Carol Ann. *Tales of the Elders: A Memory Book of Men and Women Who Came to America as Immigrants, 1900-1930*. Morristown, N.J.: Silver Burdett Press, 1993. Originally published Chicago: Follett, 1977.

Greenberg, Judith E. *Newcomers to America: Stories of Today's Young Immigrants*. New York: Watts, 1996.

I Was Dreaming to Come to America: Memories from the Ellis Island Oral History Project. New York: Viking, 1995. Selected and illustrated by Veronica Lawlor.

Appendix B: Immigration and

Naturalization Legislation

The following compilation of federal immigration and naturalization statutes in the United States provides an overview of the legislative history of immigration to the United States. It is not exhaustive, either for the number of bills enacted or for the specific points of law within each bill. This review of the federal legislative process fosters a general understanding of the major issues as they developed in the area of immigration and naturalization in the United States. The dates of enactment and *Statutes-at-Large* reference numbers are presented in chronological order; they provide a basis for further inquiry for more detailed information.

1. ACT OF MARCH 26, 1790 *(1 Statutes-at-Large 103)*

The first federal activity in an area previously under the control of the individual states, this act established a uniform rule for naturalization by setting the residence requirement at two years.

2. ACT OF JANUARY 29, 1795 *(1 Statutes-at-Large 414)*

Repealed the 1790 act, raised the residence requirement to five years, and required a declaration of intention to seek citizenship at least three years before naturalization.

3. NATURALIZATION ACT OF JUNE 18, 1798 *(1 Statutes-at-Large 566)*

Provisions:

a. Clerks of court must furnish information about each record of naturalization to the Secretary of State.

b. Registry of each alien residing in the United States at that time, as well as those arriving thereafter.

c. Raised the residence requirement for naturalization to fourteen years.

4. ALIENS ACT OF JUNE 25, 1798 *(1 Statutes-at-Large 570)*

Represented the first Federal law pertinent to immigration rather than naturalization.
Provisions:

a. Authorized the President to arrest and/or deport any alien whom he deemed dangerous to the United States.

b. Required the captain of any vessel to report the arrival of aliens on board such vessel to the Collector, or other chief officer, of the Customs of the Port.

This law expired two years after its enactment.

5. ALIEN ENEMY ACT OF JULY 6, 1798 *(1 Statutes-at-Large 577)*

6. NATURALIZATION ACT OF APRIL 14, 1802 *(2 Statutes-at-Large 153)*

Provided that in the case of declared war or invasion the President shall have the power to restrain or remove alien enemy males of fourteen years and upwards, but with due protection of their property rights as stipulated by treaty.
Provisions:

a. Reduced the residence period for naturalization from fourteen to five years.

b. Established basic requirements for naturalization, including good moral character, allegiance to the Constitution, a formal declaration of intention, and witnesses.

7. STEERAGE ACT OF MARCH 2, 1819 *(3 Statutes-at-Large 488)*

First significant Federal law relating to immigration. Provisions:

a. Established the continuing reporting of immigration to the United States by requiring that passenger lists or manifests of all arriving vessels be delivered to the local Collector of Customs, copies transmitted to the Secretary of State, and the information reported to Congress.

b. Set specific sustenance rules for passengers of ships leaving U.S. ports for Europe.

c. Somewhat restricted the number of passengers on all vessels either coming to or leaving the United States.

8. ACT OF MAY 26, 1824 (4 Statutes-at-Large 36)

Facilitated the naturalization of certain aliens who had entered the United States as minors, by setting a two-year instead of a three-year interval between declaration of intention and admission to citizenship.

9. ACT OF FEBRUARY 22, 1847 (9 Statutes-at-Large 127)

"Passenger Acts," provided specific regulations to safeguard passengers on merchant vessels. Subsequently amended by the Act of March 2, 1847, expanding the allowance of passenger space.

10. PASSENGER ACT OF MARCH 3, 1855 (10 Statutes-at-Large 715)

Provisions:

a. Repealed the Passenger Acts (see the 1847 act) and combined their provisions in a codified form.

b. Reaffirmed the duty of the captain of any vessel to report the arrival of alien passengers.

c. Established separate reporting to the Secretary of State distinguishing permanent and temporary immigration.

11. ACT OF FEBRUARY 19, 1862 (12 Statutes-at-Large 340)

Prohibited the transportation of Chinese "coolies" on American vessels.

12. ACT OF JULY 4, 1864 (13 Statutes-at-Large 385)

First Congressional attempt to centralize control of immigration.
Provisions:

a. A Commissioner of Immigration was appointed by the President to serve

under the authority of the Secretary of State.

b. Authorized immigrant labor contracts, whereby would-be immigrants would pledge their wages to pay for transportation.

On March 30, 1868, the Act of July 4, 1864, was repealed.

13. NATURALIZATION ACT OF JULY 14, 1870 (16 Statutes-at-Large 254)

Provisions:

a. Established a system of controls on the naturalization process and penalties for fraudulent practices.

b. Extended the naturalization laws to aliens of African nativity and to persons of African descent.

14. ACT OF MARCH 3, 1875 (18 Statutes-at-Large 477)

Established the policy of direct federal regulation of immigration by prohibiting for the first time entry to undesirable immigrants.
Provisions:

a. Excluded criminals and prostitutes from admission.

b. Prohibited the bringing of any Oriental persons without their free and voluntary consent; declared the contracting to supply "coolie" labor a felony.

c. Entrusted the inspection of immigrants to collectors of the ports.

15. CHINESE EXCLUSION ACT OF MAY 6, 1882 (22 Statutes-at-Large 58)

Provisions:

a. Suspended immigration of Chinese laborers to the United States for ten years.

b. Permitted Chinese laborers already in the United States to remain in the country after a temporary absence.

c. Provided for deportation of Chinese illegally in the United States.

d. Barred Chinese from naturalization.

Permitted the entry of Chinese students, teachers, merchants, or those "proceeding to the United States . . . from curiosity."

On December 17, 1943, the Chinese exclusion laws were repealed.

16. IMMIGRATION ACT OF AUGUST 3, 1882 *(22 Statutes-at-Large 214)*

First general immigration law, established a system of central control of immigration through State Boards under the Secretary of the Treasury. Provisions:

a. Broadened restrictions on immigration by adding to the classes of inadmissible aliens, including persons likely to become a public charge.

b. Introduced a tax of 50 cents on each passenger brought to the United States.

17. ACT OF FEBRUARY 26, 1885 *(23 Statutes-at-Large 332)*

The first "Contract Labor Law," made it unlawful to import aliens into the United States under contract for the performance of labor or services of any kind. Exceptions were for aliens temporarily in the United States engaging other foreigners as secretaries, servants, or domestics; actors, artists, lecturers, and domestic servants; and skilled aliens working in an industry not yet established in the United States.

18. ACT OF FEBRUARY 23, 1887 *(24 Statutes-at-Large 414)*

Amended the Contract Labor Law to render it enforceable by charging the Secretary of the Treasury with enforcement of the act and providing that prohibited persons be sent back on arrival.

19. ACT OF MARCH 3, 1887 *(24 Statutes-at-Large 476)*

Restricted the ownership of real estate in the United States to American citizens and those who have lawfully declared their intentions to become citizens, with certain specific exceptions.

20. ACT OF OCTOBER 19, 1888 *(25 Statutes-at-Large 566)*

First measure since the Aliens Act of 1798 to provide for expulsion of aliens—directed the return within one year after entry of any immigrant who had landed in violation of the contract labor laws (see acts of February 26, 1885, and February 23, 1887).

21. IMMIGRATION ACT OF MARCH 3, 1891 *(26 Statutes-at-Large 1084)*

The first comprehensive law for national control of immigration.

Provisions:

a. Established the Bureau of Immigration under the Treasury Department to administer all immigration laws (except the Chinese Exclusion Act).

b. Further restricted immigration by adding to the inadmissible classes persons likely to become public charges, persons suffering from certain contagious diseases, felons, persons convicted of other crimes or misdemeanors, polygamists, and aliens assisted by others by payment of passage, and forbade the encouragement of immigration by means of advertisement.

c. Allowed the Secretary of the Treasury to prescribe rules for inspection along the borders of Canada, British Columbia, and Mexico so as not to obstruct or unnecessarily delay, impede, or annoy passengers in ordinary travel between these countries and the United States.

d. Directed the deportation of any alien who entered the United States unlawfully.

22. ACT OF MARCH 3, 1893 *(27 Statutes-at-Large 570)*

Provisions:

a. Added to the reporting requirements regarding alien arrivals to the United States such new information as occupation, marital status, ability to read or write, amount of money in possession, and facts regarding physical and mental health. This information was needed to determine admissibility according to the expanding list of grounds for exclusion.

b. Established boards of special inquiry to decide the admissibility of alien arrivals.

23. ACT OF APRIL 29, 1902 *(32 Statutes-at-Large 176)*

Extended the existing Chinese exclusion acts until such time as a new treaty with China was negotiated, and extended the application of the exclusion acts to insular territories of the United States, including the requirement of a certificate of residence, except in Hawaii.

24. ACT OF FEBRUARY 14, 1903 *(32 Statutes-at-Large 825)*

Transferred the Bureau of Immigration to the newly created Department of Commerce and Labor, and expanded the authority of the Commissioner-General of Immigration in the areas of rulemaking and enforcement of immigration laws.

25. IMMIGRATION ACT OF MARCH 3, 1903 *(32 Statutes-at-Large 1213)*

An extensive codification of existing immigration law.
Provisions:
a. Added to the list of inadmissible immigrants.
b. First measure to provide for the exclusion of aliens on the grounds of proscribed opinions by excluding "anarchists, or persons who believe in, or advocate, the overthrow by force or violence the government of the United States, or of all government, or of all forms of law, or the assassination of public officials."
c. Extended to three years after entry the period during which an alien who was inadmissible at the time of entry could be deported.
d. Provided for the deportation of aliens who became public charges within two years after entry from causes existing prior to their landing.
e. Reaffirmed the contract labor law (see the 1885 act).

26. ACT OF APRIL 27, 1904 *(33 Statutes-at-Large 428)*

Reaffirmed and made permanent the Chinese exclusion laws. In addition, clarified the territories from which Chinese were to be excluded.

27. NATURALIZATION ACT OF JUNE 29, 1906 *(34 Statutes-at-Large 596)*

Provisions:
a. Combined the immigration and naturalization functions of the federal government, changing the Bureau of Immigration to the Bureau of Immigration and Naturalization.
b. Established fundamental procedural safeguards regarding naturalization, such as fixed fees and uniform naturalization forms.
c. Made knowledge of the English language a requirement for naturalization.

28. IMMIGRATION ACT OF FEBRUARY 20, 1907 *(34 Statutes-at-Large 898)*

A major codifying act that incorporated and consolidated earlier legislation:
a. Required aliens to declare intention of permanent or temporary stay in the United States and officially classified arriving aliens as immigrants and non-immigrants, respectively.
b. Increased the head tax to $4.00 (established by the Act of August 3, 1882, and raised subsequently).
c. Added to the excludable classes imbeciles, feeble-minded persons, persons with physical or mental defects which may affect their ability to earn a living, persons afflicted with tuberculosis, children unaccompanied by their parents, persons who admitted the commission of a crime involving moral turpitude, and women coming to the United States for immoral purposes.
d. Exempted from the provisions of the contract labor law professional actors, artists, singers, ministers, professors, and domestic servants.
e. Extended from two to three years after entry authority to deport an alien who had become a public charge from causes which existed before the alien's entry.
f. Authorized the President to refuse admission to certain persons when he was satisfied that their immigration was detrimental to labor conditions in the United States. This was aimed mainly at Japanese laborers.

g. Created a Joint Commission on Immigration to make an investigation of the immigration system in the United States. The findings of this Commission were the basis for the comprehensive Immigration Act of 1917.

h. Reaffirmed the requirement for manifesting of aliens arriving by water and added a like requirement with regard to departing aliens.

29. WHITE SLAVE TRAFFIC ACT OF JUNE 25, 1910 *(36 Statutes-at-Large 825)*

The Mann Act, prohibited the importation or interstate transportation of women for immoral purposes.

30. ACT OF MARCH 4, 1913 *(37 Statutes-at-Large 737)*

Divided the Department of Commerce and Labor into separate departments and transferred the Bureau of Immigration and Naturalization to the Department of Labor. It further divided the Bureau of Immigration and Naturalization into a separate Bureau of Immigration and Bureau of Naturalization, each headed by its own Commissioner.

31. IMMIGRATION ACT OF FEBRUARY 5, 1917 *(39 Statutes-at-Large 874)*

Codified all previously enacted exclusion provisions. In addition:

a. Excluded illiterate aliens from entry.

b. Expanded the list of aliens excluded for mental health and other reasons.

c. Further restricted the immigration of Asian persons, creating the "barred zone" (known as the Asia-Pacific triangle), natives of which were declared inadmissible.

d. Considerably broadened the classes of aliens deportable from the United States and introduced the requirement of deportation without statute of limitation in certain more serious cases.

32. ACT OF MAY 22, 1918 *(40 Statutes-at-Large 559)*

"Entry and Departure Controls Act," authorized the President to control the departure and entry in times of war or national emergency of any alien whose presence was deemed contrary to public safety.

33. QUOTA LAW OF MAY 19, 1921 *(42 Statutes-at-Large 5)*

The first quantitative immigration law. Provisions:

a. Limited the number of aliens of any nationality entering the United States to 3 percent of the foreign-born persons of that nationality who lived in the United States in 1910. Approximately 350,000 such aliens were permitted to enter each year as quota immigrants, mostly from Northern and Western Europe.

b. Exempted from this limitation aliens who had resided continuously for at least one year immediately preceding their application in one of the independent countries of the Western Hemisphere; nonimmigrant aliens such as government officials and their households, aliens in transit through the United States, and temporary visitors for business and pleasure; and aliens whose immigration is regulated by immigration treaty.

c. Actors, artists, lecturers, singers, nurses, ministers, professors, aliens belonging to any recognized learned profession, and aliens employed as domestic servants were placed on a nonquota basis.

34. ACT OF MAY 11, 1922 *(42 Statutes-at-Large 540)*

a. Extended the Act of May 19, 1921, for two years, with amendments: Changed from one year to five years the residency requirement in a Western Hemisphere country.

b. Authorized fines of transportation companies for transporting an inadmissible alien unless it was deemed that inadmissibility was not known to the company and could not have been discovered with reasonable diligence.

35. IMMIGRATION ACT OF MAY 26, 1924 *(43 Statutes-at-Large 153)*

The first permanent limitation on immigration, established the "national origins quota system." In conjunction with the Immigration Act of 1917, governed American immigration policy until 1952 (see the Immigration and Nationality Act of 1952). Provisions:

a. Contained two quota provisions:
   1. In effect until June 30, 1927—set the annual quota of any quota nationality at 2 percent of the number of foreign-born persons of such nationality resident in the continental United States in 1890 (total quota—164,667).
   2. From July 1, 1927 (later postponed to July 1, 1929), to December 31, 1952—used the national origins quota system: the annual quota for any country or nationality had the same relation to 150,000 as the number of inhabitants in the continental United States in 1920 having that national origin had to the total number of inhabitants in the continental United States in 1920.

      Preference quota status was established for: unmarried children under 21; parents; spouses of U.S. citizens aged 21 and over; and for quota immigrants aged 21 and over who are skilled in agriculture, together with their wives and dependent children under age 16.

b. Nonquota status was accorded to: wives and unmarried children under 18 of U.S. citizens; natives of Western Hemisphere countries, with their families; nonimmigrants; and certain others. Subsequent amendments eliminated certain elements of this law's inherent discrimination against women, but comprehensive elimination was not achieved until 1952 (see the Immigration and Nationality Act of 1952).

c. Established the "consular control system" of immigration by mandating that no alien may be permitted entrance to the United States without an unexpired immigration visa issued by an American consular officer abroad. Thus, the State Department and the Immigration and Naturalization Service shared control of immigration.

d. Introduced the provision that, as a rule, no alien ineligible to become a citizen shall be admitted to the United States as an immigrant. This was aimed primarily at Japanese aliens.

e. Imposed fines on transportation companies who landed aliens in violation of U.S. Immigration laws.

f. Defined the term "immigrant" and designated all other alien entries into the United States as "nonimmigrant" (temporary visitor). Established classes of admission for nonimmigrant entries.

36. ACT OF MAY 28, 1924 *(43 Statutes-at-Large 240)*

An appropriations law, provided for the establishment of the U.S. Border Patrol.

37. ACT OF MARCH 31, 1928 *(45 Statutes-at-Large 400)*

Provided more time to work out computation of the quotas established by the Immigration Act of 1924 by postponing introduction of the quotas until July 1, 1929.

38. ACT OF APRIL 2, 1928 *(45 Statutes-at-Large 401)*

Provided that the Immigration Act of 1924 was not to be construed to limit the right of American Indians to cross the border, but with the proviso that the right does not extend to members of Indian tribes by adoption.

39. REGISTRY ACT OF MARCH 2, 1929 *(45 Statutes-at-Large 1512)*

Amended existing immigration law authorizing the establishment of a record of lawful admission for certain aliens not ineligible for citizenship when no record of admission for permanent residence could be found and the alien could prove entrance to the United States before July 1, 1924 (subsequently amended to June 3, 1921, by the Act of August 7, 1939—*53*

Statutes-at-Large 1243). Later incorporated into the Alien Registration Act of 1940.

40. ACT OF MARCH 4, 1929
(45 Statutes-at-Large 1551)

Provisions:

a. Added two deportable classes, consisting of aliens convicted of carrying any weapon or bomb and sentenced to any term of six months or more, and aliens convicted of violation of the prohibition law for which a sentence of one year or more is received.

b. Made reentry of a previously deported alien a felony punishable by fine or imprisonment or both.

c. Made entry by an alien at other than at a designated place or by fraud to be a misdemeanor punishable by fine or imprisonment or both.

d. Deferred the deportation of an alien sentenced to imprisonment until the termination of the imprisonment.

41. ACT OF FEBRUARY 18, 1931
(46 Statutes-at-Large 1171)

Provided for the deportation of any alien convicted of violation of U.S. laws concerning the importation, exportation, manufacture, or sale of heroin, opium, or coca leaves.

42. ACT OF MARCH 17, 1932
(47 Statutes-at-Large 67)

Provisions:

a. The contract labor laws were applicable to alien instrumental musicians, whether coming for permanent residence or temporarily.

b. Such aliens shall not be considered artists or professional actors under the terms of the Immigration Act of 1917, and thereby exempt from the contract labor laws, unless they are recognized to be of distinguished ability and are coming to fulfill professional engagements corresponding to such ability.

c. If the alien qualifies for exemption under the above proviso, the Secretary of Labor later may prescribe such conditions, including bonding, as will insure the alien's departure at the end of his engagement.

43. ACT OF MAY 2, 1932 *(47 Statutes-at-Large 145)*

Amended the Immigration Act of 1917, doubling the allocation for enforcement of the contract labor laws.

44. ACT OF JULY 1, 1932 *(47 Statutes-at-Large 524)*

Amended the Immigration Act of 1924, providing that the specified classes of nonimmigrant aliens be admitted for a prescribed period of time and under such conditions, including bonding where deemed necessary, as would ensure departure at the expiration of the prescribed time or upon failure to maintain the status under which admitted.

45. ACT OF JULY 11, 1932 *(47 Statutes-at-Large 656)*

Provided exemption from quota limits (i.e., gave nonquota status) to the husbands of American citizens, provided that the marriage occurred prior to issuance of the visa and prior to July 1, 1932. Wives of citizens were accorded nonquota status regardless of the time of marriage.

46. ACT OF JUNE 15, 1935 *(49 Statutes-at-Large 376)*

Designated as a protection for American seamen, repealed the laws giving privileges of citizenship regarding service on and protection by American vessels to aliens having their first papers (i.e., having made declaration of intent to become American citizens).

47. ACT OF MAY 14, 1937 *(50 Statutes-at-Large 164)*

Made deportable any alien who at any time after entering the United States

a. was found to have secured a visa through fraud by contracting a marriage which subsequent to entry into the United States had been judicially annulled retroactively to the date of the marriage; or

b. failed or refused to fulfill his promises for a marital agreement made to procure his entry as an immigrant.

48. ACT OF JUNE 14, 1940 (54 Statutes-at-Large 230)

Presidential Reorganization Plan, transferred the Immigration and Naturalization Service from the Department of Labor to the Department of Justice as a national security measure.

49. ALIEN REGISTRATION ACT OF JUNE 28, 1940 (54 Statutes-at-Large 670)

Provisions:

a. Required registration of all aliens and fingerprinting those over 14 years of age.
b. Established additional deportable classes, including aliens convicted of smuggling, or assisting in the illegal entry of, other aliens.
c. Amended the Act of October 16, 1919, making past membership—in addition to present membership—in proscribed organizations and subversive classes of aliens grounds for exclusion and deportation.
d. Amended the Immigration Act of 1917, authorizing, in certain meritorious cases, voluntary departure in lieu of deportation, and suspension of deportation.

50. ACT OF JULY 1, 1940 (54 Statutes-at-Large 711)

Amended the Immigration Act of 1924, requiring aliens admitted as officials of foreign governments to maintain their status or depart.

51. NATIONALITY ACT OF OCTOBER 14, 1940 (Effective January 13, 1941, as 54 Statutes-at-Large 1137)

Codified and revised the naturalization, citizenship, and expatriation laws to strengthen the national defense. The naturalization and nationality regulations were rewritten and the forms used in naturalization proceedings were revised.

52. PUBLIC SAFETY ACT OF JUNE 20, 1941 (55 Statutes-at-Large 252)

Directed a consular officer to refuse a visa to any alien seeking to enter the United States for the purpose of engaging in activities which would endanger the safety of the United States.

53. ACT OF JUNE 21, 1941 (55 Statutes-at-Large 252)

Extended the Act of May 22, 1918—gave the President power, during a time of national emergency or war, to prevent departure from or entry into the United States.

54. ACT OF DECEMBER 8, 1942 (56 Statutes-at-Large 1044)

Amended the Immigration Act of 1917, altering the reporting procedure in suspension of deportation cases to require the Attorney General to report such suspensions to Congress on the first and fifteenth of each month that Congress is in session.

55. ACT OF APRIL 29, 1943 (57 Statutes-at-Large 70)

Provided for the importation of temporary agricultural laborers to the United States from North, South, and Central America to aid agriculture during World War II. This program was later extended through 1947, then served as the legal basis of the Mexican "Bracero Program," which lasted through 1964.

56. ACT OF DECEMBER 17, 1943 (57 Statutes-at-Large 600)

Amended the Alien Registration Act of 1940, adding to the classes eligible for naturalization Chinese persons or persons of Chinese descent. A quota of 105 per year was established (effectively repealing the Chinese Exclusion laws—see the Act of May 6, 1882).

57. ACT OF FEBRUARY 14, 1944 (58 Statutes-at-Large 11)

Provided for the importation of temporary workers from countries in the Western Hemisphere pursuant to agreements with such countries for employment in industries and services essential to the war efforts. Agreements were subsequently made with British Honduras, Jamaica, Barbados, and the British West Indies.

58. WAR BRIDES ACT OF DECEMBER 28, 1945 *(59 Statutes-at-Large 659)*

Waived visa requirements and provisions of immigration law excluding physical and mental defectives when they concerned members of the American armed forces who, during World War II, had married nationals of foreign countries.

59. G.I. FIANCÉES ACT OF JUNE 29, 1946 *(60 Statutes-at-Large 339)*

Facilitated the admission to the United States of fiancé(e)s of members of the American armed forces.

60. ACT OF JULY 2, 1946 *(60 Statutes-at-Large 416)*

Amended the Immigration Act of 1917, granting the privilege of admission to the United States as quota immigrants and eligibility for naturalization to races indigenous to India and persons of Filipino descent.

61. ACT OF AUGUST 9, 1946 *(60 Statutes-at-Large 975)*

Gave nonquota status to Chinese wives of American citizens.

62. ACT OF JUNE 28, 1947 *(61 Statutes-at-Large 190)*

Extended by six months the Attorney General's authority to admit alien fiancé(e)s of veterans as temporary visitors pending marriage.

63. ACT OF MAY 25, 1948 *(62 Statutes-at-Large 268)*

Amended the Act of October 16, 1918, providing for the expulsion and exclusion of anarchists and similar classes, and gave the Attorney General similar powers to exclude as the Secretary of State had through the refusal of immigration visas.

64. DISPLACED PERSONS ACT OF JUNE 25, 1948 *(62 Statutes-at-Large 1009)*

First expression of U.S. policy for admitting persons fleeing persecution. Permitted the admission of up to 205,000 displaced persons during the two-year period beginning July 1, 1948 (chargeable against future year's quotas). Aimed at reducing the problem created by the presence in Germany, Austria, and Italy of more than one million displaced persons.

65. ACT OF JULY 1, 1948 *(62 Statutes-at-Large 1206)*

Amended the Immigration Act of 1917. Provisions:

a. Made available suspension of deportation to aliens even though they were ineligible for naturalization by reason of race.

b. Set condition for suspension of deportation that an alien shall have proved good moral character for the preceding five years, and that the Attorney General finds that deportation would result in serious economic detriment to a citizen or legal resident and closely related alien, or the alien has resided continuously in the United States for seven years or more.

66. CENTRAL INTELLIGENCE AGENCY ACT OF JUNE 20, 1949 *(63 Statutes-at-Large 208)*

Authorized the admission of a limited number of aliens in the interest of national security. Provided that whenever the Director of the Central Intelligence Agency, the Attorney General, and the Commissioner of Immigration determine that the entry of a particular alien into the United States for permanent residence is in the [interest of] national security or essential to the furtherance of the national intelligence mission, such alien and his immediate family may be given entry into the United States for permanent residence without regard to their admissibility under any laws and regulations or to their failure to comply with such laws and regulations pertaining to admissibility. The number was not to exceed 100 persons per year.

67. AGRICULTURAL ACT OF OCTOBER 31, 1949 (63 Statutes-at-Large 1051)

Facilitated the entry of seasonal farm workers to meet labor shortages in the United States. Further extension of the Mexican Bracero Program.

68. ACT OF JUNE 16, 1950 (64 Statutes-at-Large 219)

Amended the Displaced Persons Act of 1948. Provisions:

a. Extended the act to June 30, 1951, and its application to war orphans and German expellees; and refugees to July 1, 1952.
b. Increased the total of persons who could be admitted under the act to 415,744.

69. ACT OF JUNE 30, 1950 (64 Statutes-at-Large 306)

Provided relief to the sheepherding industry by authorizing that, during a one-year period, 250 special quota immigration visas be issued to skilled sheepherders chargeable to oversubscribed quotas.

70. ACT OF AUGUST 19, 1950 (64 Statutes-at-Large 464)

Made spouses and minor children of members of the American armed forces, regardless of the alien's race, eligible for immigration and nonquota status if marriage occurred before March 19, 1952.

71. INTERNAL SECURITY ACT OF SEPTEMBER 22, 1950 (64 Statutes-at-Large 987)

Amended various immigration laws with a view toward strengthening security screening in cases of aliens in the United States or applying for entry.
Provisions:

a. Present and former membership in the Communist Party or any other totalitarian party or its affiliates was specifically made a ground for inadmissibility.
b. Aliens in the United States who, at the time of their entry or by reason of subsequent actions, would have been inadmissible under the provisions of the Internal Security Act, were made deportable regardless of the length of their residence in the United States.
c. The discretion of the Attorney General in admitting otherwise inadmissible aliens temporarily, and in some instances permanently, was curtailed or eliminated.
d. The Attorney General was given authority to exclude and deport without a hearing an alien whose admission would be prejudicial to the public interest if the Attorney General's finding was based on confidential information the disclosure of which would have been prejudicial to the public interest of the United States.
e. The Attorney General was given authority to supervise deportable aliens pending their deportation and also was given greater latitude in selecting the country of deportation. However, deportation of an alien was prohibited to any country in which the alien would be subject to physical persecution.
f. Any alien deportable as a subversive criminal, or member of the immoral classes, who willfully failed to depart from the United States within six months after the issuance of the deportation order was made liable to criminal prosecution and could be imprisoned for up to ten years.
g. Every alien residing in the United States subject to alien registration was required to notify the Commissioner of Immigration and Naturalization of his address within 10 days of each January 1st in which he resided in the United States.

72. ACT OF MARCH 28, 1951 (65 Statutes-at-Large 28)

Provisions:

a. Gave the Attorney General authority to amend the record of certain aliens who were admitted only temporarily because of affiliations other than Communist.
b. Interpreted the Act of October 16, 1918, regarding exclusion and expulsion of aliens to include only voluntary membership or affiliation with a Communist organization and to exclude cases where the person in question was under 16

years of age, or where it was for the purpose of obtaining employment, food rations, or other necessities.

73. ACT OF JULY 12, 1951 *(65 Statutes-at-Large 119)*

Amended the Agricultural Act of 1949, serving as the basic framework under which the Mexican Bracero Program operated until 1962. Provided that

a. The U.S. government establish and operate reception centers at or near the Mexican border; provide transportation, subsistence, and medical care from the Mexican recruiting centers to the U.S. reception centers; and guarantee performance by employers in matters relating to transportation and wages, including all forms of remuneration.

b. U.S. employers pay the prevailing wages in the area; guarantee the workers employment for three-fourths of the contract period; and provide workers with free housing and adequate meals at a reasonable cost.

74. ACT OF MARCH 20, 1952 *(66 Statutes-at-Large 26)*

Provisions:

a. Amended the Immigration Act of 1917, making it a felony to bring in or willfully induce an alien unlawfully to enter or reside in the United States. However, the usual and normal practices incident to employment were not deemed to constitute harboring.

b. Defined further the powers of the Border Patrol, giving officers of the Immigration and Naturalization Service authority to have access to private lands, but not dwellings, within 25 miles of an external boundary for the purpose of patrolling the border to prevent the illegal entry of aliens.

75. ACT OF APRIL 9, 1952 *(66 Statutes-at-Large 50)*

Added the issuance of 500 immigration visas to sheepherders.

76. IMMIGRATION AND NATIONALITY ACT OF JUNE 27, 1952 (INA) *(66 Statutes-at-Large 163)*

Brought into one comprehensive statute the multiple laws which, before its enactment, governed immigration and naturalization in the United States. In general, perpetuated the immigration policies from earlier statutes with the following significant modifications:

a. Made all races eligible for naturalization, thus eliminating race as a bar to immigration.

b. Eliminated discrimination between sexes with respect to immigration.

c. Revised the national origins quota system of the Immigration Act of 1924 by changing the national origins quota formula: set the annual quota for an area at one-sixth of 1 percent of the number of inhabitants in the continental United States in 1920 whose ancestry or national origin was attributable to that area. All countries were allowed a minimum quota of 100, with a ceiling of 2,000 on most natives of countries in the Asia-Pacific triangle, which broadly encompassed the Asian countries.

d. Introduced a system of selected immigration by giving a quota preference to skilled aliens whose services are urgently needed in the United States and to relatives of U.S. citizens and aliens.

e. Placed a limit on the use of the governing country's quota by natives of colonies and dependent areas.

f. Provided an "escape clause" permitting the immigration of certain former voluntary members of proscribed organizations.

g. Broadened the grounds for exclusion and deportation of aliens.

h. Provided procedures for the adjustment of status of nonimmigrant aliens to that of permanent resident aliens.

i. Modified and added significantly to the existing classes of nonimmigrant admission.

j. Afforded greater procedural safeguards to aliens subject to deportation.

k. Introduced the alien address report system whereby all aliens in the United

States (including most temporary visitors) were required annually to report their current address to the INS.

l. Established a central index of all aliens in the United States for use by security and enforcement agencies.

m. Repealed the ban on contract labor (see Act of March 30, 1868) but added other qualitative exclusions.

77. REFUGEE RELIEF ACT OF AUGUST 7, 1953 *(67 Statutes-at-Large 400)*

Authorized the issuance of special nonquota visas allowing 214,000 aliens to become permanent residents of the United States, in addition to those whose admission was authorized by the Immigration and Nationality Act of 1952.

78. ACT OF SEPTEMBER 3, 1954 *(68 Statutes-at-Large 1145)*

Provisions:

a. Made special nonquota immigrant visas available to certain skilled sheepherders for a period of up to one year.

b. Exempted from inadmissibility to the United States aliens who had committed no more than one petty offense.

79. ACT OF SEPTEMBER 3, 1954 *(68 Statutes-at-Large 1146)*

Provided for the expatriation of persons convicted of engaging in a conspiracy to overthrow or levy war against the U.S. government.

80. ACT OF JULY 24, 1957 *(71 Statutes-at-Large 311)*

Permitted enlistment of aliens into the regular Army.

81. ACT OF AUGUST 30, 1957 *(71 Statutes-at-Large 518)*

Exempted aliens who were survivors of certain deceased members of the U.S. armed forces from provisions of the Social Security Act which prohibited the payment of benefits to aliens outside the United States.

82. REFUGEE-ESCAPEE ACT OF SEPTEMBER 11, 1957 *(71 Statutes-at-Large 639)*

Provisions:

a. Addressed the problem of quota oversubscription by removing the "mortgaging" of immigrant quotas imposed under the Displaced Persons Act of 1948 and other subsequent acts.

b. Provided for the granting of nonquota status to aliens qualifying under the first three preference groups on whose behalf petitions had been filed by a specified date.

c. Facilitated the admission into the United States of stepchildren, illegitimate children, and adopted children.

d. Conferred first preference status on spouse and children of first preference immigrants if following to join the immigrant.

e. Set an age limit of 14 for the adoption of orphans to qualify for nonquota status and further defined which orphans were eligible under the act.

f. Gave the Attorney General authority to admit certain aliens formerly excludable from the United States.

83. ACT OF JULY 25, 1958 *(72 Statutes-at-Large 419)*

Granted admission for permanent residence to Hungarian parolees of at least two years' residence in the United States, on condition that the alien was admissible at time of entry and still admissible.

84. ACT OF AUGUST 21, 1958 *(72 Statutes-at-Large 699)*

Authorized the Attorney General to adjust nonimmigrant aliens from temporary to permanent resident status subject to visa availability.

85. ACT OF SEPTEMBER 22, 1959 *(73 Statutes-at-Large 644)*

Facilitated the entry of fiancé(e)s and relatives of alien residents and citizens of the United States by reclassifying certain categories of relatives into preference portions of the immigration quotas. This was designed to assist in reuniting families both on a permanent basis, through the amendments to the Immigration and Nationality Act of 1952, and through temporary programs.

86. ACT OF JULY 14, 1960 *(74 Statutes-at-Large 504)*

"Fair Share Refugee Act"
Provisions:

a. Authorized the Attorney General to parole up to 500 alien refugee-escapees and make them eligible for permanent residence.
b. Amended the Act of September 2, 1958, to extend it to June 30, 1962.
c. Amended the Act of September 11, 1957, which provided special nonquota immigrant visas for adopted or to-be-adopted orphans under 14 years of age, extending it to June 30, 1961.
d. Amended the Immigration and Nationality Act of 1952, adding possession of marijuana to the sections concerning excludable and deportable offenses.
e. Made alien seamen ineligible for adjustment from temporary to permanent resident status.

87. ACT OF AUGUST 17, 1961 *(75 Statutes-at-Large 364)*

Provided that, in peacetime, no volunteer is to be accepted into the Army or Air Force unless the person is a citizen or an alien admitted for permanent residence.

88. ACT OF SEPTEMBER 26, 1961 *(75 Statutes-at-Large 650)*

Liberalized the quota provisions of the Immigration and Nationality Act of 1952:

a. Eliminated the ceiling of 2,000 on the aggregate quota of the Asia-Pacific triangle.
b. Provided that whenever one or more quota areas have a change of boundaries which might lessen their aggregate quota, they were to maintain the quotas they had before the change took place.
a. Codified and made permanent the law for admission of adopted children.
b. Established a single statutory form of judicial review of orders of deportation.

c. Insured a minimum quota of 100 for newly independent nations.
d. Called for the omission of information on race and ethnic origin from the visa application.
e. Strengthened the law against the fraudulent gaining of nonquota status by marriage.
f. Authorized the Public Health Service to determine which diseases are dangerous and contagious in constituting grounds for exclusion.

89. ACT OF OCTOBER 24, 1962 *(76 Statutes-at-Large 1247)*

Provisions:

a. Granted nonquota immigrant visas for certain aliens eligible for fourth preference (i.e., brothers, sisters, and children of citizens) and for first preference (i.e., aliens with special occupational skills).
b. Called for a semimonthly report to Congress from the Attorney General of first preference petitions approved.
c. Created a record of lawful entry and provided for suspension of deportation for aliens who have been physically present in the United States for at least seven years in some cases and ten years in others.

90. ACT OF DECEMBER 13, 1963 *(77 Statutes-at-Large 363)*

Extended the Mexican Bracero Program one additional year to December 31, 1964.

91. IMMIGRATION AND NATIONALITY ACT AMENDMENTS OF OCTOBER 3, 1965 *(79 Statutes-at-Large 911)*

Provisions:

a. Abolished the national origins quota system (see the Immigration Act of 1924 and the Immigration and Nationality Act of 1952), eliminating national origin, race, or ancestry as a basis for immigration to the United States.
b. Established allocation of immigrant visas on a first come, first served basis, subject to a seven-category preference system for relatives of U.S. citizens and permanent resident aliens (for the

reunification of families) and for persons with special occupational skills, abilities, or training (needed in the United States).

c. Established two categories of immigrants not subject to numerical restrictions:

1. Immediate relatives (spouses, children, parents) of U.S. citizens, and

2. Special immigrants: certain ministers of religion; certain former employees of the U.S. government abroad; certain persons who lost citizenship (e.g., by marriage or by service in foreign armed forces); and certain foreign medical graduates.

d. Maintained the principle of numerical restriction, expanding limits to world coverage by limiting Eastern Hemisphere immigration to 170,000 and placing a ceiling on Western Hemisphere immigration (120,000) for the first time. However, neither the preference categories nor the 20,000 per-country limit were applied to the Western Hemisphere.

e. Introduced a prerequisite for the issuance of a visa of an affirmative finding by the Secretary of Labor that an alien seeking to enter as a worker will not replace a worker in the United States nor adversely affect the wages and working conditions of similarly employed individuals in the United States.

92. FREEDOM OF INFORMATION ACT OF JULY 4, 1966 *(80 Statutes-at-Large 250)*

Provisions:

a. Established that the record of every proceeding before the INS in an individual's case be made available to the alien or his attorney of record.

b. Required that public reading rooms be established in each Central and District office of the INS, where copies of INS decisions could be made available to the public.

Effective July 4, 1967.

93. ACT OF NOVEMBER 2, 1966 *(80 Statutes-at-Large 1161)*

Authorized the Attorney General to adjust the status of Cuban refugees to that of permanent resident alien, chargeable to the 120,000 annual limit for the Western Hemisphere.

94. ACT OF NOVEMBER 6, 1966 *(80 Statutes-at-Large 1322)*

Provisions:

a. Extended derivative citizenship to children born on or after December 24, 1952, of civilian U.S. citizens serving abroad.

b. Provided that time spent abroad by U.S. citizens (or their dependent children) in the employ of the U.S. Government or certain international organizations could be treated as physical presence in the United States for the purpose of transmitting U.S. citizenship to children born abroad.

95. ACT OF DECEMBER 18, 1967 *(81 Statutes-at-Large 661)*

Facilitated the expeditious naturalization of certain noncitizen employees of U.S. nonprofit organizations.

96. ACT OF JUNE 19, 1968 *(82 Statutes-at-Large 197)*

Omnibus crimes control and safe streets legislation, declared it illegal for aliens who are illegally in the country and for former citizens who have renounced their citizenship to receive, possess, or transport a firearm.

97. ACT OF OCTOBER 24, 1968 *(82 Statutes-at-Large 1343)*

Amended the Immigration and Nationality Act of 1952, providing for expeditious naturalization of noncitizens who have rendered honorable services in the U.S. armed forces during the Vietnam conflict, or in other periods of military hostilities.

98. ACT OF APRIL 7, 1970 *(84 Statutes-at-Large 116)*

Provisions:

a. Created two new classes of nonimmigrant admission—fiancé(e)s of U.S. citizens and intracompany transferees.

b. Modified the H1 I temporary worker class of nonimmigrant admission (workers of distinguished merit and ability).

c. Altered the provisions of the law regarding the two-year residence requirement, making it easier for nonimmigrants who have been in the United States as exchange visitors to adjust to a different nonimmigrant status or to permanent resident status.

99. ACT OF AUGUST 10, 1971
(85 Statutes-at-Large 302)

Amended the Communications Act of 1934, providing that lawful permanent resident aliens be permitted to operate amateur radio stations in the United States and hold licenses for their stations.

100. ACT OF SEPTEMBER 28, 1971
(85 Statutes-at-Large 348)

Amended the Selective Service Act of 1967. Provided that:

a. Registration for the selective service shall not be applicable to any alien admitted to the United States as a nonimmigrant as long as he continues to maintain a lawful nonimmigrant status in the United States.

b. No alien residing in the United States for less than one year shall be inducted for training and service into the U.S. armed forces.

101. ACT OF OCTOBER 27, 1972
(86 Statutes-at-Large 1289)

Reduced restrictions concerning residence requirements for retention of U.S. citizenship acquired by birth abroad through a U.S. citizen parent and an alien parent.

102. SOCIAL SECURITY ACT AMENDMENTS OF OCTOBER 30, 1972 *(86 Statutes-at-Large 1329)*

Amended the Social Security Act, providing that Social Security numbers be assigned to aliens at the time of their lawful admission to the United States for permanent residence or temporarily to engage in lawful employment.

103. ACT OF OCTOBER 20, 1974
(88 Statutes-at-Large 1387)

Repealed the "Coolie Trade" legislation of 1862. Such legislation, passed to protect Chinese and Japanese aliens from exploitation caused by discriminatory treatment from immigration laws then in effect, had become virtually inoperative because most of the laws singling out Oriental peoples had been repealed or modified.

104. INDOCHINA MIGRATION AND REFUGEE ASSISTANCE ACT OF MAY 23, 1975 *(89 Statutes-at-Large 87)*

Established a program of domestic resettlement assistance for refugees who have fled from Cambodia and Vietnam.

105. ACT OF JUNE 21, 1976
(90 Statutes-at-Large 691)

Made Laotians eligible for programs established by the Indochina Migration and Refugee Assistance Act of 1975.

106. ACT OF OCTOBER 12, 1976
(90 Statutes-at-Large 2243)

Placed restrictions on foreign medical school graduates (both immigrants and nonimmigrants) coming to the United States for practice or training in the medical profession. Effective January 10, 1977.

107. IMMIGRATION AND NATIONALITY ACT AMENDMENTS OF OCTOBER 20, 1976 *(90 Statutes-at-Large 2703)*

Provisions:

a. Applied the same 20,000 per-country limit to the Western Hemisphere as applied to the Eastern Hemisphere.

b. Slightly modified the seven-category preference system and applied it to the Western Hemisphere.

c. Amended the 1966 act, providing that Cuban refugees who are adjusted to permanent resident status will not be charged to any numerical limitation, provided they were physically present in the United States on or before the effective date of these amendments.

108. ACT OF OCTOBER 20, 1976, Effective January 1, 1978 *(90 Statutes-at-Large 2706)*

Denied unemployment compensation to aliens not lawfully admitted for permanent residence or otherwise permanently residing in the United States under color of law.

109. ACT OF AUGUST 1, 1977 *(91 Statutes-at-Large 394)*

Eased restrictions on foreign medical school graduates, e.g., exempted aliens who are of national or international renown in the field of medicine, and exempted certain alien physicians already in the United States from the examination requirement. (See Act of October 12, 1976.)

110. ACT OF OCTOBER 28, 1977 *(91 Statutes-at-Large 1223)*

Provisions:

a. Permitted adjustment to permanent resident status for Indochinese refugees who are natives or citizens of Vietnam, Laos, or Cambodia, were physically present in the United States for at least two years, and were admitted or paroled into the United States during specified periods of time.

b. Extended the time limit during which refugee assistance may be provided to such refugees.

111. ACT OF OCTOBER 5, 1978 *(92 Statutes-at-Large 907)*

Combined the separate ceilings for Eastern and Western Hemisphere immigration into one worldwide limit of 290,000.

112. ACT OF OCTOBER 5, 1978 *(92 Statutes-at-Large 917)*

Provisions:

a. Made several changes pertaining to the adoption of alien children, including permission for U.S. citizens to petition for the classification of more than two alien orphans as immediate relatives.

b. Eliminated the requirement of continuous residence in the United States for two years prior to filing for naturalization.

113. ACT OF OCTOBER 7, 1978 *(92 Statutes-at-Large 963)*

Made permanent the President's authority to regulate the entry of aliens and to require U.S. citizens to bear valid passports when entering or leaving the United States:

a. Called for unrestricted use of passports to and in any country other than a country with which the United States is at war, where armed hostilities are in progress, or where there is imminent danger to the public health or the physical safety of U.S. travelers.

b. Declared it the general policy of the United States to impose restrictions on travel within the United States by citizens of another country only when the government of that country imposes restrictions on travel of U.S. citizens within that country.

114. ACT OF OCTOBER 14, 1978 *(92 Statutes-at-Large 1263)*

Required any alien who acquires or transfers any interest in agricultural land to submit a report to the Secretary of Agriculture within 90 days after acquisition or transfer.

115. ACT OF OCTOBER 30, 1978 *(92 Statutes-at-Large 2065)*

Provided for the exclusion and expulsion of aliens who persecuted others on the basis of race, religion, national origin, or political opinion under the direction of the Nazi government of Germany or its allies.

116. ACT OF NOVEMBER 2, 1978 *(92 Statutes-at-Large 2479)*

Provided for the seizure and forfeiture of vessels, vehicles, and aircraft used in smuggling aliens or knowingly transporting aliens to the United States illegally. An exception was made where the owner or person in control did not consent to the illegal act.

117. PANAMA CANAL ACT OF SEPTEMBER 27, 1979 (93 Statutes-at-Large 452)

Allowed admission as permanent residents to certain aliens with employment on or before 1977 with the Panama Canal Company, the Canal Zone government, or the U.S. government in the Canal Zone, and their families.

118. REFUGEE ACT OF MARCH 17, 1980 (94 Statutes-at-Large 102)

Provided the first permanent and systematic procedure for the admission and effective resettlement of refugees of special humanitarian concern to the United States:

a. Eliminated refugees as a category of the preference system.

b. Set the worldwide ceiling of immigration to the United States at 270,000, exclusive of refugees.

c. Established procedures for annual consultation with Congress on numbers and allocations of refugees to be admitted in each fiscal year, as well as procedures for responding to emergency refugee situations.

d. Defined the term "refugee" (to conform to the 1967 United Nations Protocol on Refugees) and made clear the distinction between refugee and asylee status.

e. Established a comprehensive program for domestic resettlement of refugees.

f. Provided for adjustment to permanent resident status of refugees who have been physically present in the United States for at least one year and of asylees one year after asylum is granted.

119. REFUGEE EDUCATION ASSISTANCE ACT OF OCTOBER 10, 1980 (94 Statutes-at-Large 1799)

Established a program of formula grants to State education agencies for basic education of refugee children. Also provided for services to Cuban and Haitian entrants identical to those for refugees under the Refugee Act of 1980.

120. ACT OF JUNE 5, 1981 (95 Statutes-at-Large 14)

Supplemental appropriations and rescissions bill, reduced previously appropriated funds for migration and refugee assistance, including funds provided for reception and processing of Cuban and Haitian entrants.

121. ACT OF AUGUST 13, 1981 (95 Statutes-at-Large 357)

Federal appropriations bill for fiscal year 1982, also contained items restricting the access of aliens to various publicly funded benefits. Immigration-related provisions:

a. Precluded the Secretary of HUD from making financial assistance available to any alien unless that alien is a resident of the United States by virtue of admission or adjustment as a permanent resident alien, refugee or asylee, parolee, conditional entrant, or pursuant to withholding of deportation. Alien visitors, tourists, diplomats, and students were specifically excluded.

b. Severely restricted eligibility of aliens to Aid to Families with Dependent Children.

122. IMMIGRATION AND NATIONALITY ACT AMENDMENTS OF DECEMBER 20, 1981 (95 Statutes-at-Large 1611)

"INS Efficiency Bill," amended the Immigration and Nationality Act of 1952 and the Act of November 2, 1978:

a. Authorized INS to seize vehicles without having to establish whether the owner was involved in the illegal activity in question.

b. Eliminated the requirement that the government bear administrative and incidental expenses where an innocent owner is involved.

c. Eliminated the requirement that the INS satisfy any valid lien or other third party interest in a vehicle without expense to the interest holder.

d. Eliminated the required annual notification by aliens of their current address.

123. ACT OF SEPTEMBER 30, 1982
(96 Statutes-at-Large 1157)

Allowed admission as permanent residents to certain nonimmigrant aliens residing in the Virgin Islands.

124. ACT OF OCTOBER 2, 1982
(96 Statutes-at-Large 1186)

Greatly limited the categories of aliens to whom the Legal Services Corporation may provide legal assistance.

125. ACT OF OCTOBER 22, 1982
(96 Statutes-at-Large 1716)

Provided that children born of U.S. citizen fathers in Korea, Vietnam, Laos, Kampuchea, or Thailand after 1950 and before enactment, may come to the United States as immediate relatives or as first or fourth preference immigrants.

126. IMMIGRATION REFORM AND CONTROL ACT OF NOVEMBER 6, 1986 (IRCA) *(100 Statutes-at-Large 3359)*

Comprehensive immigration legislation:

a. Authorized legalization (i.e., temporary and then permanent resident status) for aliens who had resided in the United States in an unlawful status since January 1, 1982 (entering illegally or as temporary visitors with authorized stay expiring before that date or with the Government's knowledge of their unlawful status before that date) and are not excludable.

b. Created sanctions prohibiting employers from knowingly hiring, recruiting, or referring for a fee aliens not authorized to work in the United States.

c. Increased enforcement at U.S. borders.

d. Created a new classification of seasonal agricultural worker and provisions for the legalization of certain such workers.

e. Extended the registry date (i.e., the date from which an alien has resided illegally and continuously in the United States and thus qualifies for adjustment to permanent resident status) from June 30, 1948, to January 1, 1972.

f. Authorized adjustment to permanent resident status for Cubans and Haitians who entered the United States without inspection and had continuously resided in country since January 1, 1982.

g. Increased the numerical limitation for immigrants admitted under the preference system for dependent areas from 600 to 5,000 beginning in fiscal year 1988.

h. Created a new special immigrant category for certain retired employees of international organizations and their families and a new nonimmigrant status for parents and children of such immigrants.

i. Created a nonimmigrant Visa Waiver Pilot program allowing certain aliens to visit the United States without applying for a nonimmigrant visa.

j. Allocated 5,000 nonpreference visas in each of fiscal years 1987 and 1988 for aliens born in countries from which immigration was adversely affected by the 1965 act.

127. IMMIGRATION MARRIAGE FRAUD AMENDMENTS OF NOVEMBER 10, 1986 *(100 Statutes-at-Large 3537)*

Provisions:

a. Stipulated that aliens deriving their immigrant status based on a marriage of less than two years are conditional immigrants. To remove conditional status, the aliens must apply within 90 days after their second-year anniversary of receiving conditional status.

b. Required alien fiancé(e)s of U.S. citizens to have met their citizen petitioner in person within two years of the date the petition was filed.

128. AMERASIAN HOMECOMING ACT OF DECEMBER 22, 1987 *(101 Statutes-at-Large 1329)*

An appropriations law providing for admission of children born in Vietnam between specified dates to Vietnamese mothers and American fathers, together with their immediate relatives. They are admitted as nonquota immigrants but receive refugee program benefits.

129. ACT OF SEPTEMBER 28, 1988 *(102 Statutes-at-Large 1876)*

United States–Canada Free-Trade Agreement Implementation Act:

a. Facilitated temporary entry on a reciprocal basis between the United States and Canada.

b. Established procedures for the temporary entry into the United States of Canadian citizen professional business persons to render services for remuneration.

c. No nonimmigrant visa, prior petition, labor certification, or prior approval required, but appropriate documentation must be presented to the inspecting officer establishing Canadian citizenship and professional engagement in one of the occupations listed in the qualifying occupation schedule.

130. ACT OF NOVEMBER 15, 1988 *(102 Statutes-at-Large 3908)*

Provided for the extension of stay for certain nonimmigrant H-1 nurses.

131. FOREIGN OPERATIONS ACT OF NOVEMBER 21, 1989 *(103 Statutes-at-Large 1195)*

An appropriations law, provided for adjustment to permanent resident status for Soviet and Indochinese nationals who were paroled into the United States between certain dates after denial of refugee status.

132. ACT OF DECEMBER 18, 1989 *(103 Statutes-at-Large 2099)*

The "Immigration Nursing Relief Act of 1989"
Provisions:

a. Adjustment from temporary to permanent resident status, without regard to numerical limitation, of certain nonimmigrants who were employed in the United States as registered nurses for at least three years and meet established certification standards.

b. Establishment of a new nonimmigrant category for the temporary admission of qualified registered nurses.

133. IMMIGRATION ACT OF NOVEMBER 29, 1990 *(104 Statutes-at-Large 4978)*

A major overhaul of immigration law:

a. Increased total immigration under an overall flexible cap of 675,000 immigrants beginning in fiscal year 1995, preceded by a 700,000 level during fiscal years 1992 through 1994. The 675,000 level to consist of: 480,000 family-sponsored; 140,000 employment-based; and 55,000 "diversity immigrants."

b. Revised all grounds for exclusion and deportation, significantly rewriting the political and ideological grounds. For example, repealed the bar against the admission of communists as nonimmigrants and limited the exclusion of aliens on foreign policy grounds.

c. Authorized the Attorney General to grant temporary protected status to undocumented alien nationals of designated countries subject to armed conflict or natural disasters.

d. Revised and established new nonimmigrant admission categories:

1. Redefined the H-1(b) temporary worker category and limited number of aliens who may be issued visas or otherwise provided nonimmigrant status under this category to 65,000 annually.

2. Limited number of H-2(b) temporary worker category aliens who may be issued visas or otherwise provided nonimmigrant status to 66,000 annually.

3. Created new temporary worker admission categories (O, P, Q, and R), some with annual caps on number of aliens who may be issued visas or otherwise provided nonimmigrant status.

e. Revised and extended the Visa Waiver Pilot Program through fiscal year 1994.

f. Revised naturalization authority and requirements:

1. Transferred the exclusive jurisdiction to naturalize aliens from the Federal and State courts to the Attorney General.

2. Amended the substantive requirements or naturalization: State resi-

dency requirements revised and reduced to 3 months; added another ground for waiving the English language requirement; lifted the permanent bar to naturalization for aliens who applied to be relieved from U.S. military service on grounds of alienage who previously served in the service of the country of the alien's nationality.

g. Revised enforcement activities. For example:

 1. Broadened the definition of "aggravated felony" and imposed new legal restrictions on aliens convicted of such crimes.
 2. Revised employer sanctions provisions of the Immigration Reform and Control Act of 1986.
 3. Authorized funds to increase Border Patrol personnel by 1,000.
 4. Revised criminal and deportation provisions.

h. Recodified the 32 grounds for exclusion into nine categories, including revising and repealing some of the grounds (especially health grounds).

134. ARMED FORCES IMMIGRATION ADJUSTMENT ACT OF OCTOBER 1, 1991 *(105 Statutes-at-Large 555)*

Provisions:

a. Granted special immigrant status to certain types of aliens who honorably served in the Armed Forces of the United States for at least 12 years.

b. Delayed until April 1, 1992, the implementation of provisions relating to O and P nonimmigrant visas. (See Act of November 29, 1990.)

135. ACT OF DECEMBER 12, 1991 *(105 Statutes-at-Large 1733)*

Miscellaneous and Technical Immigration and Naturalization Amendments Act, amended certain elements of the Immigration Act of 1990. Revised provisions regarding the entrance of O and P nonimmigrants, including the repeal of numerical limits of visas for the P categories of admission, and made other technical corrections. (See Act of November 29, 1990.)

136. CHINESE STUDENT PROTECTION ACT OF OCTOBER 9, 1992 *(106 Statutes-at-Large 1969)*

Provided for adjustment to permanent resident status (as employment-based immigrants) by nationals of the People's Republic of China who were in the United States after June 4, 1989, and before April 11, 1990.

137. SOVIET SCIENTISTS IMMIGRATION ACT OF OCTOBER 10, 1992 *(106 Statutes-at-Large 3316)*

Provisions:

a. Conferred permanent resident status (as employment-based immigrants) on a maximum of 750 scientists from the independent states of the former Soviet Union and the Baltic states. The limit does not include spouses and children.

b. Stipulated that employment must be in the biological, chemical, or nuclear technical field or work in conjunction with a high technology defense project.

c. Waived the requirement that workers with expertise in these fields were needed by an employer in the United States.

138. NORTH AMERICAN FREE-TRADE AGREEMENT IMPLEMENTATION ACT OF DECEMBER 8, 1993 *(107 Statutes-at-Large 2057)*

Supersedes the United States–Canada Free-Trade Agreement Act of September 28, 1988. Provisions:

a. Facilitated temporary entry on a reciprocal basis between the United States and Canada and Mexico.

b. Established procedures for the temporary entry into the United States of Canadian and Mexican citizen professional business persons to render services for remuneration:

 1. For Canadians, no nonimmigrant visa, prior petition, labor certification, or prior approval required, but appropriate documentation must be presented to the inspecting officer establishing Canadian citizenship and professional engagement in one

of the occupations listed in the qualifying occupation schedule;

2. For Mexicans, nonimmigrant visa, prior petition by employer, and Department of Labor attestation are required in addition to proof of Mexican citizenship and professional engagement in one of the occupations listed in the qualifying occupation schedule;

3. For Canadians, nonimmigrant visas are not required of spouses and minor children who possess Canadian citizenship;

4. For Mexicans, nonimmigrant visas are required of spouses and minor children who possess Mexican citizenship;

5. For Canadians, no limit to number of admissions;

6. For Mexicans, a limit was set for a transition period for up to ten years at 5,500 initial petition approvals per year.

139. VIOLENT CRIME CONTROL AND LAW ENFORCEMENT ACT OF SEPTEMBER 13, 1994 (108 Statutes-at-Large 1796)

Provisions:

a. Authorized establishment of a criminal alien tracking center.

b. Established a new nonimmigrant classification for alien witness cooperation and counterterrorism information.

c. Revised deportation procedures for certain criminal aliens who are not permanent residents and expanded special deportation proceedings.

d. Provided for expeditious deportation for denied asylum applicants.

e. Provided for improved border management through increased resources.

f. Strengthened penalties for passport and visa offenses.

140. ANTITERRORISM AND EFFECTIVE DEATH PENALTY ACT OF APRIL 24, 1996 (110 Statutes-at-Large 1214)

Provisions:

a. Expedited procedures for the removal of alien terrorists.

b. Established specific measures to exclude members and representatives of terrorist organizations:

1. Provided for the exclusion of alien terrorists;

2. Waived authority concerning notice of denial application for visas;

3. Denied other forms of relief for alien terrorists;

4. Excluded from process aliens who have not been inspected and admitted.

c. Modified asylum procedures to improve identification and processing of alien terrorists:

1. Established mechanisms for denial of asylum to alien terrorists;

2. Granted authority to inspection officers to both inspect and exclude asylee applicants;

3. Improved judicial review process to expedite hearings and removal (if necessary) of alien terrorists.

d. Provided for criminal alien procedural improvements:

1. Provided access to certain confidential immigration and naturalization files through court order;

2. Established a criminal alien identification system;

3. Established certain alien smuggling–related crimes as RICO-predicate offenses;

4. Granted authority for alien smuggling investigations;

5. Expanded criteria for deportation for crimes of moral turpitude;

6. Established an interior repatriation program;

7. Allowed for deportation of nonviolent offenders prior to completion of sentence of imprisonment;

8. Authorized State and Local law enforcement officials to arrest and detain certain illegal aliens;

9. Expedited process of criminal alien removal;

10. Limited collateral attacks on underlying deportation order;

11. Established deportation procedures for certain criminal aliens who are not permanent residents.

141. PERSONAL RESPONSIBILITY AND WORK OPPORTUNITY RECONCILIATION ACT OF AUGUST 22, 1996 *(110 Statutes-at-Large 2105)*

Provisions:

a. Established restrictions on the eligibility of legal immigrants for means-tested public assistance:

1. Barred legal immigrants (with certain exceptions) from obtaining food stamps and Supplemental Security Income (SSI) and established screening procedures for current recipients of these programs;

2. Barred legal immigrants (with certain exceptions) entering the U.S. after date of enactment from most federal means-tested programs for 5 years;

3. Provided states with broad flexibility in setting public benefit eligibility rules for legal immigrants by allowing states to bar current legal immigrants from both major federal programs and state programs;

4. Increased the responsibility of the immigrants' sponsors by making the affidavit of support legally enforceable, imposing new requirements on sponsors, and expanding sponsor-deeming requirements to more programs and by lengthening the deeming period.

b. Broadened the restrictions on public benefits for illegal aliens and nonimmigrants:

1. Barred illegal, or "not qualified," aliens from most federal, state, and local public benefits;

2. Required INS to verify immigration status in order for aliens to receive most federal public benefits.

142. ILLEGAL IMMIGRATION REFORM AND IMMIGRANT RESPONSIBILITY ACT OF SEPTEMBER 30, 1996 *(110 Statutes-at-Large 3009)*

Division C of the Omnibus Consolidated Appropriations Act, 1997. Provisions:

a. Established measures to control U.S. borders, protect legal workers through worksite enforcement, and remove criminal and other deportable aliens:

1. Increased border personnel, equipment, and technology, as well as enforcement personnel at land and air ports of entry;

2. Authorized improvements in barriers along the Southwest border;

3. Increased anti-smuggling authority and penalties for alien smuggling;

4. Increased penalties for illegal entry, passport and visa fraud, and failure to depart;

5. Increased INS investigators for worksite enforcement, alien smuggling, and visa overstayers;

6. Established three voluntary pilot programs to confirm the employment eligibility of workers and reduced the number and types of documents that may be presented to employers for identity and eligibility to work;

7. Broadly reformed exclusion and deportation procedures, including consolidation into a single removal process, as well as the institution of expedited removal to speed deportation and alien exclusion through more stringent grounds of admissibility;

8. Increased detention space for criminal and other deportable aliens;

9. Instituted 3- and 10-year bars to admissibility for aliens seeking to reenter after having been unlawfully present in the United States;

10. Barred re-entry of individuals who renounced their U.S. citizenship in order to avoid U.S. tax obligations.

b. Placed added restrictions on benefits for aliens:

1. Provided for a pilot program on limiting issuance of driver's licenses to illegal aliens;

2. Declared ineligibility of aliens not lawfully present for Social Security benefits;

3. Established procedures for requiring proof of citizenship for Federal public benefits;

4. Established limitations on eligibility for preferential treatment of aliens not lawfully present on the basis of residence for higher education benefits;

5. Provided for verification of immigration status for purposes of Social Security and higher educational assistance;

6. Tightened the requirements for an affidavit of support for sponsored immigrants, making the affidavit a legally binding contract to provide financial support;

7. Provided authority of States and political subdivisions of States to limit assistance to aliens in providing general cash public assistance;

8. Increased maximum criminal penalties for forging or counterfeiting the seal of a Federal department or agency to facilitate benefit fraud by an unlawful alien.

c. Miscellaneous provisions:

1. Recodified existing INS regulations regarding asylum;

2. Provided that the Attorney General's parole authority may be exercised only on a case-by-case basis for urgent humanitarian reasons or significant public benefit.

3. Created new limits on the ability of F-I students to attend public schools without reimbursing those institutions;

4. Established new mandates for educational institutions to collect information on foreign students' status and nationality and provide it to INS;

5. Tightened restrictions regarding foreign physicians' ability to work in the United States;

6. Added new consular processing provisions and revised the visa waiver program.

Source: *Statistical Yearbook of the Immigration and Naturalization Service*, 1996

143. BALANCED BUDGET ACT OF AUGUST 5, 1997 (*111 Statutes-at-Large 270*)

Continued or partially restored to legal aliens eligibility benefits that had been restricted by the Personal Responsibility and Work Opportunity Reconciliation Act of 1996. Such restrictions do not apply to "qualified aliens" (legal permanent residents, refugees, aliens granted asylum or similar relief, aliens paroled into the United States for at least one year, and certain battered family members; plus Cuban/Haitian entrants added by the Balanced Budget Act) who meet 10-year work requirements; or are veterans or certain active duty personnel, and close family. The alienage restrictions do not apply to aliens who become citizens through naturalization. Provisions:

a. Continued eligibility both for aged and for disabled "qualified aliens" receiving Supplemental Security Income (SSI) benefits as of August 26, 1996, as well as those disabled after August 22, 1996. SSI recipients remain eligible for Medicaid; for others, Medicaid is a state option.

b. Exempted for 7 years the bar against SSI and Medicaid for refugees and asylees (including Cuban/Haitian entrants and Amerasians).

c. Exempted members of Indian Tribes and certain Native Americans born in Canada from the SSI and Medicaid bar on "qualified aliens."

144. NICARAGUAN ADJUSTMENT AND CENTRAL AMERICAN RELIEF ACT (NACARA) OF NOVEMBER 19,1997 (*111 Statutes-at-Large 2193*)

Pertains to certain Central American and other aliens who were long-term illegal residents in the United States when hardship relief rules were made more stringent by the Illegal Immigration Reform and Immigrant Responsibility Act (IIRIRA). Provisions:

a. Allowed approximately 150,000 Nicaraguans and 5,000 Cubans adjustment to permanent resident status without having to make any hardship showing.

b. Allowed approximately 200,000 Salvadorans and 50,000 Guatemalans as well as certain aliens from the former Soviet Union to seek hardship relief under more lenient hardship rules than existed prior to IIRIRA amendments.

145. AGRICULTURAL RESEARCH REFORM ACT OF FEBRUARY 11, 1998 (*112 Statutes-at-Large 575*)

Continued or partially restored eligibility to legal aliens benefits that had been restricted by the Personal Responsibility and Work Opportunity Reconciliation Act of 1996. Such restrictions do not apply to "qualified aliens" (legal permanent residents, refugees, aliens granted asylum or similar relief, aliens paroled into the United States for at least one year, and certain battered family members; plus Cuban/Haitian entrants added by the Balanced Budget Act) who meet 10-year work requirements; or are veterans or certain active duty personnel, and close family. The alienage restrictions do not apply to aliens who become citizens through naturalization. Provisions:

a. Continued eligibility to receive Food Stamps for "qualified aliens" 65 or over by August 22, 1996, subsequently disabled, and/or while under 18.

b. Exempted for 7 years the bar against Food Stamps for refugees and asylees (including Cuban/Haitian entrants and Amerasians).

c. Exempted members of Indian Tribes and certain Native Americans born in Canada from the Food Stamps bar on "qualified aliens."

146. VISA WAIVER PILOT PROGRAM REAUTHORIZATION ACT OF APRIL 27, 1998 (*112 Statutes-at-Large 56*)

Extended the Visa Waiver Pilot program through fiscal year 2000, modified the qualifications for designation as a Pilot program country, and expanded the data reporting requirements.

147. AMERICAN COMPETITIVENESS AND WORKFORCE IMPROVEMENT ACT OF OCTOBER 21, 1998 (*112 Statutes-at-Large 2681*)

Part of the Omnibus Appropriations Act, 1999. Provisions:

a. Raised the ceiling for the number of aliens who may be issued visas under the H-1(b) temporary worker category by 142,500 over 3 years. The ceiling is 115,000 in both fiscal years 1999 and 2000, 107,500 in 2001, and reverts back to 65,000 in 2002.

b. Added new attestation requirements for recruitment and lay-off protections, requiring them only of firms that are "H-1(b) dependent" (generally at least 15 percent of workforce are H-1(b) workers).

c. All firms must offer H-1(b) workers benefits as well as wages comparable to their U.S. workers.

d. Education and training for U.S. workers will be funded by a $500 fee paid by the employer for each H-1(b) worker hired.

148. NON-CITIZEN BENEFIT CLARIFICATION ACT OF OCTOBER 28, 1998 (*112 Statutes-at-Large 2926*)

Continued or partially restored eligibility to legal aliens benefits that had been restricted by the Personal Responsibility and Work Opportunity Reconciliation Act of 1996. Such restrictions do not apply to "qualified aliens" (legal permanent residents, refugees, aliens granted asylum or similar relief, aliens paroled into the United States for at least one year, and certain battered family members; plus Cuban/Haitian entrants added by the Balanced Budget Act) who meet 10-year work requirements; or are veterans or certain active duty personnel, and close family.

The alienage restrictions do not apply to aliens who become citizens through naturalization. Provisions:

a. Continued eligibility both for aged and for disabled non–"qualified aliens" receiving Supplemental Security Income (SSI) benefits as of August 26, 1996. SSI recipients remain eligible for Medicaid; others ineligible.

b. Non–"qualified aliens" are ineligible for Food Stamps.

149. IRISH PEACE PROCESS CULTURAL AND TRAINING PROGRAM ACT OF OCTOBER 30, 1998 (*112 Statutes-at-Large 3013*)

Amended the INA to establish new nonimmigrant classes (Q2 and Q3) to allow temporary admission to young people (and their spouses and minor children) of disadvantaged areas in Northern Ireland and certain counties of the Republic of Ireland for the purpose of developing job skills and conflict resolution abilities, so that those young people can return to their homes better able to contribute toward economic regeneration and the Irish peace process. Period of temporary admission not to exceed 36 months; program repealed, effective October 1, 2005.

150. AGRICULTURE, RURAL DEVELOPMENT, FOOD AND DRUG ADMINISTRATION, AND RELATED AGENCIES APPROPRIATIONS ACT OF OCTOBER 22, 1999 (*113 Statutes-at-Large 1135*)

Amended the INA to reduce from 60 to 45 days the minimum period of time prior to need that employers must file H-2A labor certifications; and to increase from 20 to 30 days the minimum days in advance of need before the Secretary of Labor must act on H-2A certification requests.

151. NURSING RELIEF FOR DISADVANTAGED AREAS ACT OF NOVEMBER 12, 1999 (*113 Statutes-at-Large 1312*)

Provisions:

a. Short-term solution for nursing shortages in a limited number of medically underserved areas. Established a new H-1C nonimmigrant class of admission for 500 nurses annually for 4 years in health professional shortage areas. Set forth admission requirements, including a maximum 3-year stay. Petitioning hospitals would have to be in shortage areas defined by the Department of Health and Human Services, have at least 190 acute care beds, and have specified percentages of Medicare and Medicaid patients. Subject to fewer restrictions than the previous, expired H-1A provisions.

b. Amended the L nonimmigrant class of admission (intracompany transferees) to provide that international management consulting firms that break off from other international accounting firms may continue to use L visas for foreign nationals who work for them, provided they maintain the qualifying worldwide organization structure.

152. ACT OF NOVEMBER 13, 1999 (*113 Statutes-at-Large 1483*)

Amended the INA to extend for an additional 2 years the S nonimmigrant class of admission for alien witnesses and informants, and to authorize appropriations for the Health and Human Services Refugee Resettlement Assistance program for fiscal year 2000–02.

153. CONSOLIDATED APPROPRIATIONS ACT OF NOVEMBER 29, 1999 (*113 Statutes-at-Large 1501A-233*)

Provisions:

a. Funded the Health and Human Services, Office of Refugee Resettlement for fiscal year 2000. The program provides temporarily dependent refugees and Cuban/Haitian entrants initial transitional assistance.

b. Extended the so-called Lautenberg amendment for an additional year and reenacted a version of the McCain amendment, relating to Vietnamese refugees, for 2 years.

154. ACT OF DECEMBER 7, 1999 (*113 Statutes-at-Large 1696*)

Amended the INA to increase the age limit from 16 to 18 for adopted alien children who are siblings of children who were themselves adopted under age 16.

Appendix C: Estimates of Emigration

and Illegals

Authors' Note: This section presents estimates of the number of persons who leave the United States to take up residence elsewhere, as well as the number and characteristics of persons residing in this country illegally, and describes the INS's [the Immigration and Naturalization Service's] efforts to develop reliable information on the total number of persons who enter the United States each year.

Although a considerable amount of detailed information is available about immigrants, temporary visitors, and other categories of international migrants to the United States, significant gaps remain in our knowledge about immigration to the United States. In some areas these deficiencies persist because of the inherent difficulty in estimating the numbers, as is the case for emigration and illegal immigration. As a result, no detailed tables on these two categories are included in the *Statistical Yearbook [of the Immigration and Naturalization Service]*, 1996.

Emigration

The collection of statistics on emigration from the United States was discontinued in 1957; no direct measure of emigration has been available since then. Estimates compiled in this country and statistics collected in other countries indicate that emigration from the United States has increased steadily since the 1950s, exceeding 100,000 per year from 1970 to 1990, and surpassing 200,000 in the 1990s. These figures are consistent with U.S. historical experience; between 1900 and 1990, approximately 38 million immigrants were admitted, and an estimated 12 million foreign-born persons emigrated.[1] That is, for every 100 immigrants admitted, roughly 30 returned home (see Estimates Tables A.1, below, and A.2, p. 750).

The U.S. Bureau of the Census currently uses an annual emigration figure of 222,000, which includes both citizens and aliens, for computing national population estimates. Statistics (shown below) on U.S. residents migrating to other countries published by the United Nations and the Economic Commission for Europe indicate that emigration from the United States could be substantially above 200,000 annually.

Accurate, detailed, and timely estimates of emigration are needed to develop and evaluate U.S. immigration policy, to derive accurate national and local population estimates (including estimates of illegal immigration), and to measure coverage of the decennial censuses. The sketchy data that are available indicate that emigration is a large and growing component of U.S. population change. However, partly

Table A.1: Emigration from the United States to Top Ten Countries of Destination: Selected Years in 1980s

All countries	241,000
1. Mexico	55,000
2. United Kingdom	31,000
3. Germany	29,000
4. Canada	20,000
5. Japan	19,000
6. Philippines	19,000
7. Guatemala	13,000
8. Indonesia	9,000
9. Australia	8,000
10. Italy	4,000

Source: *1998 U.N. Demographic Yearbook*, Table 28; Economic Commission for Europe, CES/710/Corr.

---

1. Warren, Robert, and Ellen Percy Kraly, 1985, *The Elusive Exodus: Emigration from the United States*, Population Trends and Public Policy Occasional Paper No. 8, March, Population Reference Bureau: Washington, D.C.

Table A.2: United States Immigration and Emigration by Decade, 1901–1990

Period	Immigrants to the United States in Thousands	Emigrants from the United States in Thousands	Net Immigration in Thousands	Ratio: Emigration/ Immigration
Total 1901-90	**37,869**	**11,882**	**25,987**	**0.31**
1981-90	7,338	1,600	5,738	0.22
1971-80	4,493	1,176	3,317	0.26
1961-70	3,322	900	2,422	0.27
1951-60	2,515	425	2,090	0.17
1941-50	1,035	281	754	0.27
1931-40	528	649	-121	1.23
1921-30	4,107	1,685	2,422	0.41
1911-20	5,736	2,157	3,579	0.38
1901-10	8,795	3,008	5,787	0.34

Source: 1992 *Statistical Yearbook*, Table 1; Robert Warren and Ellen Percy Kraly, 1985, *The Elusive Exodus: Emigration from the United States, Population Trends and Public Policy Occasional Paper No.8*, March, Population Reference Bureau: Washington, D.C.

Source: *Statistical Yearbook of the Immigration and Naturalization Service*, 1996, Table 3.

because of inherent methodological difficulties, data on emigration from the United States are not being collected.

Illegal Immigrants[2]

In 1994 the INS [Immigration and Naturalization Service] released detailed estimates of the undocumented immigrant population residing in the United States as of October 1992.[3] Those estimates were useful for a variety of purposes, including planning and policy development at the national and state level, evaluating the effects of proposed legislation, and assessing the fiscal impacts of undocumented immigration.

---

2. The estimated illegal immigrant population from the Dominican Republic shown in [Estimates Table A.3] was revised from 50,000 (shown in the *1995 Yearbook*) to 75,000 following a review of the estimates for Dominica and the Dominican Republic.

3. Warren, Robert, 1994, *Estimates of the Unauthorized Immigrant Population Residing in the United States, by Country of Origin and State of Residence: October 1992.* Unpublished paper, U.S. Immigration and Naturalization Service.

Over the past two years, the INS has revised those estimates and updated them to October 1996. The estimates presented here incorporate new data on the foreign-born population collected by the Census Bureau, improvements in the methodology recommended by the General Accounting Office (GAO), suggestions provided by outside reviewers, and further analyses of INS's data sources and estimation procedures. Revised and updated estimates of the undocumented population have been computed for each state of residence and for nearly 100 countries of origin.

Data Overview

About 5.0 million undocumented immigrants were residing in the United States in October 1996, with a range of about 4.6 to 5.4 million. The population was estimated to be growing by about 275,000 each year, which is about 25,000 lower than the annual level of growth estimated by the INS in 1994.

California is the leading state of residence, with 2 million, or 40 percent of the undocumented population. The seven states with the largest estimated numbers of undocumented immigrants—California (2 million), Texas (700,000), New York

(540,000), Florida (350,000), Illinois (290,000), New Jersey (135,000), and Arizona (115,000)—accounted for 83 percent of the total population in October 1996.

The 5 million undocumented immigrants made up about 1.9 percent of the total U.S. population, with the highest percentages in California, the District of Columbia, and Texas. In the majority of states, undocumented residents comprise less than 1 percent of the population.

Mexico is the leading country of origin, 2.7 million, or 54 percent, of the population. The Mexican undocumented population has grown at an average annual level of just over 150,000 since 1988. The 15 countries with 50,000 or more undocumented immigrants in 1996 accounted for 82 percent of the total population. The large majority, over 80 percent, of all undocumented immigrants are from countries in the Western Hemisphere.

About 2.1 million, or 41 percent, of the total undocumented population in 1996 are nonimmigrant overstays. That is, they entered legally on a temporary basis and failed to depart. The proportion of the undocumented population who are overstays varies considerably by country of origin. About 16 percent of the Mexican undocumented population are nonimmigrant overstays, compared to 26 percent of those from Central America and 91 percent from all other countries.

National Estimates

The total number of undocumented immigrants residing in the United States in October 1996 is estimated to be 5.0 million [see Estimates Table A.3, p. 753], with a range of about 4.6 to 5.4 million. The estimate for October 1996 is about 1.1 million higher than the revised estimate of 3.9 million for October 1992; this implies that the population grew by about 275,000 annually during the 1992–1996 period, about the same as the annual growth of 281,000 estimated for the previous period. The original INS estimates for October 1992 and October 1988, released in 1994, showed average annual growth of 300,000.

The undocumented population grows at varying levels from year to year, but the data available to make these estimates do not permit the derivation of annual figures to measure year-to-year changes. However, the similar levels of growth for the 1988–1992 and 1992–1996 periods, 281,000 and 275,000, respectively, suggest that the overall level of growth has been fairly constant over the past decade. This also indicates that the rate of growth of the undocumented resident population has declined since 1988.

State of Residence

The estimates for states reflect the well-established pattern of geographic concentration of undocumented immigrants in the United States. As expected, California was the leading state of residence, with 2 million, or 40 percent, of the total number of undocumented residents in October 1996. Seven states—California (2 million), Texas (700,000), New York (540,000), Florida (350,000), Illinois (290,000), New Jersey (135,000), and Arizona (115,000)—accounted for 83 percent of the population in October 1996 (see Estimates Table A.3, p. 753).

The estimated undocumented population of California has grown by an average of about 100,000 annually since the end of the IRCA legalization program in 1988. More than 83 percent of total growth of the undocumented population since 1988 has occurred in the top seven states. With the exception of Massachusetts (6,000), none of the remaining 43 states grew by more than 3,000 undocumented residents annually. In 27 states, the undocumented population grew by an average of 1,000 or less each year.

Country of Origin

Mexico is the leading source country of undocumented immigration to the United States. In October 1996 an estimated 2.7 million undocumented immigrants from Mexico had established residence here (see Estimates Table A.3, p. 753). Mexican undocumented immigrants constituted about 54 percent of the total undocumented population. The estimated population from Mexico increased by just over 150,000 annually in both the 1988–1992 and 1992–1996 periods.

The estimated number of Mexican undocumented immigrants who arrived between 1990 and 1996 is based on data on country of birth and year of immigration collected by the Census Bureau in the March 1994, 1995, and 1996 Current Population Surveys (CPS). Demographic analysis of the CPS data indicates that approximately 230,000 undocumented Mexican immigrants established residence annually between 1990 and 1996. This is the net annual addition of undocumented Mexicans who arrived during the period. Note, however, that it does not reflect the average annual growth of the Mexican undocumented population. To compute average annual growth it is necessary to subtract the number of undocumented Mexicans who lived here in January 1990 and who emigrated, died, or adjusted to legal permanent resident status during the 1990–1996 period. This last step produces the estimate cited above, of just over 150,000 annual growth in the Mexican undocumented population since 1988.

In October 1996, 15 countries were each the source of 50,000 or more undocumented immigrants (see Estimates Table A.3, p. 753). The top five countries are geographically close to the United States— Mexico, El Salvador, Guatemala, Canada, and Haiti. Of the top 15 countries, only the Philippines and Poland are outside the Western Hemisphere. The estimated undocumented population from Poland has declined by more than 25 percent, from 95,000 to 70,000, since 1988, possibly reflecting changed conditions in that country over the last several years.

Although undocumented immigrants come to the United States from all countries of the world, relatively few countries add substantially to the population. The annual growth of the undocumented population can be grouped into four disparate categories: 1) Mexico, with more than half of the annual growth, adds just over 150,000 undocumented residents each year; 2) six countries—El Salvador, Guatemala, Canada, Haiti, Honduras, and the Dominican Republic—each add between 6,000 and 12,000 annually; 3) 13 countries each add about 2,000 to 4,000 annually;

and 4) the remaining approximately 200 other countries add a total of about 30,000 undocumented residents each year [see Estimates Table A.3]. A large majority of the additions each year, more than 80 percent, are from countries in the Western Hemisphere.

Estimation Procedure

Methodology

The estimates were constructed by combining detailed statistics, by year of entry, for each component of change that contributes to the undocumented immigrant population residing in the United States. For most countries of the world, the typical way of entering the undocumented population in the United States is to arrive as a nonimmigrant and stay beyond the specified period of admission. This segment of the population, referred to here as "nonimmigrant overstays," constitutes roughly 40 percent of the undocumented immigrant population residing in the United States. The rest of the population, more widely publicized, enter surreptitiously across land borders, usually between official ports of entry. This part of the population, often referred to as EWIs (entry without inspection), includes persons from nearly every country, but a large majority of them are from Mexico; most of the rest are natives of Central American countries.

Primary Sets of Data

The figures presented here were constructed from five primary sets of data. Each set of data was compiled separately for 99 countries and each continent of origin.

1. *Entered before 1982*—estimates (as of October 1988) of the undocumented immigrant population who established residence in the United States before 1982 and did not legalize under the Immigration Reform and Control Act (IRCA) of 1986. The assumption used to estimate this part of the population is based on estimates developed by the Census Bureau using data from the June 1988 Current Population Survey (CPS).

2. *Net overstays*—estimates for 1982 to 1996 of the net number of nonimmigrant overstays, for 99 countries of origin, derived from INS data bases. Estimates were derived by:

   a. matching INS I-94 arrival/departure records;

   b. adjusting for the incomplete collection of departure forms; and

   c. subtracting the number of nonimmigrant overstays who subsequently either departed or adjusted to legal resident status.

3. *Net EWIs*—estimates of the number from each country who entered without inspection (EWI) and established residence here between 1982 and 1996. A very large majority of all EWIs are from Mexico. Average annual estimates of Mexican EWIs were derived by:

   a. adjusting the CPS count of the Mexican-born population for underenumeration;

   b. subtracting the estimated legally resident population counted in the CPS; and

   c. subtracting the estimated number of net overstays.

4. *Mortality*—estimates of the annual number of deaths to the resident undocumented immigrant population. The estimates were derived using an annual crude death rate of 3.9 per 1,000, which was computed using a modified age distribution of IRCA applicants and age-specific death rates of the foreign-born population.

Table A.3: Estimated Illegal Immigrant Population for Top Twenty Countries of Origin and Top Twenty States of Residence: October 1996

Country of Origin	Population	State of Residence	Population
All countries	5,000,000	All states	5,000,000
1. Mexico	2,700,000	1. California	2,000,000
2. El Salvador	335,000	2. Texas	700,000
3. Guatemala	165,000	3. New York	540,000
4. Canada	120,000	4. Florida	350,000
5. Haiti	105,000	5. Illinois	290,000
6. Philippines	95,000	6. New Jersey	135,000
7. Honduras	90,000	7. Arizona	115,000
8. Dominican Rep.*	75,000	8. Massachusetts	85,000
9. Nicaragua	70,000	9. Virginia	55,000
10. Poland	70,000	10. Washington	52,000
11. Bahamas, The	70,000	11. Colorado	45,000
12. Colombia	65,000	12. Maryland	44,000
13. Ecuador	55,000	13. Michigan	37,000
14. Trinidad & Tobago	50,000	14. Pennsylvania	37,000
15. Jamaica	50,000	15. New Mexico	37,000
16. Pakistan	41,000	16. Oregon	33,000
17. India	33,000	17. Georgia	32,000
18. Ireland	30,000	18. District of Columbia	30,000
19. Korea	30,000	19. Connecticut	29,000
20. Peru	30,000	20. Nevada	24,000
Other	721,000	Other	330,000

* The estimated illegal immigrant population from the Dominican Republic was revised from 50,000 (shown in the 1995 Yearbook) to 75,000 following a review of the estimates for Dominica and the Dominican Republic.

Source: *Statistical Yearbook of the Immigration and Naturalization Service,* 1996.

5. *Emigration*—estimates of the number of undocumented immigrants who resided here at the beginning of a period (either October 1988 or October 1992) and who emigrated from the United States in the following four-year period. Estimates of emigration are based on statistics published by the Census Bureau in *Technical Paper No. 9.*

Construction of the Estimates

Estimates of the undocumented immigrant population were derived for October 1988, October 1992, and October 1996 for 99 individual countries and for each continent of origin. The calculations were carried out separately for overstays and EWIs.

Estimates by State of Residence

In the earlier estimates for October 1992, the state distribution of the undocumented population was based on the U.S. residence pattern of each country's applicants for legalization under IRCA; the results were summed to obtain state totals. This assumed that, for each country of origin, undocumented immigrants who resided in the United States in October 1992 had the same U.S. residence pattern as IRCA applicants from that country. The revised and updated estimates presented here incorporate the same assumption for the October 1988 undocumented population. However, it was necessary to develop new methods of deriving state estimates for October 1992 and 1996 that would reflect more recent patterns of geographic settlement.

As noted, the estimates of the undocumented population were constructed separately for overstays and EWIs. This permitted the distribution of the overstay and EWI populations to states using data most appropriate for the type of population. For overstays, the cohorts that arrived in the 1988–1992 and 1992–1996 periods were distributed to state of residence based on annual estimates of overstays by state of destination for 1986 to 1989. For EWIs who entered during these periods, the totals were distributed to state of residence using INS statistics for the early 1990s on the destination of the beneficiaries of aliens who legalized under IRCA.

Limitations of Data

Estimating the size of a hidden population is inherently difficult. Overall, the figures presented here generally reflect the size, origin, and geographic distribution of the undocumented immigrant population residing in the United States during the mid-1990s. The estimates probably reduce the range of error for the total population to a few hundred thousand rather than a few million, which was the error range during the late 1970s and into the 1980s. The estimates for most countries should be fairly precise because they were constructed primarily from data on nonimmigrant arrivals, departures, and adjustments of status that have relatively small margins of error.

Although the estimates are based on the most reliable information available, they clearly have limitations. For example, the estimates make no allowance for students or other long-term nonimmigrants, and the estimates for some countries could be underestimated because of special circumstances (e.g., Dominicans entering illegally via Puerto Rico; ships arriving undetected from China).

The figures for some countries overstate the actual undocumented population. In general, the net nonimmigrant overstay figures are more likely to be overestimates than underestimates because the collection of departure forms for long-term overstays who depart probably is less complete than for those who depart within the first year.

The estimates include a large number of persons who have not been admitted for lawful permanent residence but are permitted to remain in the United States pending the determination of their status or until conditions improve in their country of origin. This category includes many of the undocumented immigrants from El Salvador, aliens from other countries in a status referred to as "deferred enforced departure," and IRCA applicants whose cases have not been finally resolved.

In a few cases, the estimates appear to be too high, but we have no basis for making downward adjustments. For example, the estimates for the Bahamas appear to be much too large because they imply that a relatively large proportion of the population is residing illegally in the United States, whereas large-scale undocumented immigration from the Bahamas has not been observed previously. In addition, the estimates shown in the *1995 Yearbook (Statistical Yearbook of the Immigration and Naturalization Service,* 1995) for Dominica were considerably higher than would be expected based on the number of IRCA applicants from Dominica. This overstatement could have occurred because of processing problems with I-94 arrival/departure documents, with the result that overstays from Dominica are overestimated and those from the Dominican Republic underestimated. The figures shown in this [1996] edition of the *Yearbook* have been adjusted to account for this anomaly in the data used to estimate overstays.

The number of EWIs is the most difficult component to estimate with precision, and errors in this component have the largest effect on the estimated undocumented population from Mexico. In particular, the shortage of information about two components—emigration of legally resident immigrants and undercount in the CPS— makes it difficult to derive acceptable residual estimates of the number of undocumented immigrants counted in the CPS.

The estimates presented here are based on the most extensive array of figures ever compiled for the purpose; nevertheless, they should be used with caution because of the inherent limitations in the data available for estimating the undocumented immigrant population.

Inspections

The text and table on the estimated number of aliens and citizens admitted by state and port of entry are omitted from this [1996] edition of the *Statistical Yearbook.* The largest component of the admissions is the number of persons who enter at land border ports. Information developed from survey data indicates that the estimation procedures used during the past few years at some land ports have resulted in an overstatement of the total number of entries into the United States. The methodology used to derive estimates of the number of passengers per vehicle and the proportion of aliens and U.S. citizens is being evaluated and revised. Publication of this data series is expected to resume in future years.

Source: *Statistical Yearbook of the Immigration and Naturalization Service,* 1996.

Appendix D: Tips on Genealogy

Authors' Note: For many people, an interest in immigration is closely linked to an interest in family history. Throughout this book, we have included genealogical resources—both Internet and print resources—relating to individual countries and regions. Below are some general tips for people getting started in genealogical research. Drawn and adapted from the genealogy section of the National Archives and Records Administration Web site *(http://www.nara.gov/genealogy/genindex.html)*, these materials include some guidelines for getting started in research, an overview of what information is available from the government, and a guide to the Soundex system of handling names for ready access in census records. Following that are some general genealogical resources, again both Internet and print resources.

Beginning Your Genealogical Research

Talk to your relatives. Begin your family history research by finding out as much information as you can from living family members:

- Names of ancestors, their spouses, and their siblings
- Dates of birth, marriage, death, and divorce
- The places (town, county, state or province, and country) where these events occurred.

Borrow books from your public library on genealogical research. These will tell you what records are available and where they can be found and describe the research process. This is an extremely important step in your research. (Note: A few of the many "how to" books which have been published on the subject are listed at the end of this section.)

Join genealogical societies: the National Genealogical Society, the state genealogical society in the state where you live and the state(s) where your ancestors lived, and the county genealogical society in the county where you live and the counties where your ancestors lived. Membership usually costs relatively little ($5–$50) but you get a lot in return. Most societies publish newsletters and other publications that will provide you with information about genealogical research in the area, often including transcripts of actual records. You can find the names and addresses of genealogical societies in Elizabeth Petty Bentley, *The Genealogist's Address Book* (Baltimore: Genealogical Publishing, 1995). This book can be found in many public libraries. [Note: At the end of this section is a list of on-line sites offering information about key genealogical societies and links to many other genealogical sites.]

Solving Difficult Research Problems

Eventually, every genealogical researcher will "hit a brick wall" or have a knotty problem to solve. You can learn much by reading how other people have solved such problems. The articles listed below show you how others solved their research problems.

From the *National Genealogical Society Quarterly,* Vol. 83, No. 1 (March 1995), see:
Thomas W. Jones, "The Children of Calvin Snell: Primary versus Secondary Evidence."
Joy Reisinger, "Is Mother Genevieve a Greslon or a Fontaine?"

From the *New England Historical and Genealogical Register,* Vol. 151, Whole No. 603 (July 1997), see:
Vernon D. Turner, "Lydia Gaymer, the Wife of Humphrey Turner of Scituate."
Steven E. Sullivan, "Joanna (Adams) Lunt Identified."

From the *New York Genealogical and Biographical Record,* Vol. 128, No. 2 (April 1997), see:
Harry Macy Jr., "The Van Wicklen/Van Wickle Family: Including Its Frisian Origin and Connections to Minnerly and Kranckheyt."

Cynthia B. Biasca, "Jacques Hertel and the Indian Princesses."

Frederick C. Hart Jr., "A Proposed Family for Thomas Jones of Fairfield, Connecticut, and Huntington, Long Island."

The *NGS Quarterly, New England Historical and Genealogical Register,* and the *NYG&B Record* can be found in libraries with a large genealogical collection, or you may be able to purchase back issues from the societies that published them.

Records Available from NARA

The National Archives and Records Administration (NARA) has many records that are useful for genealogical research, such as the Federal population censuses, 1790–1920; military service and pension records, ca. 1776–1900; immigration records, 1820–1957; and naturalization records.

Begin with Census Records

You may wish to begin your research in census records, which are available for 1790–1920. Begin with the 1920 census and work your way backward. Census records are basic building blocks for your genealogical research; they will provide names and ages of family members, state or country of birth, occupations, and other useful information.

Due to staffing limitations, we [NARA] cannot do census research. However, you can get access to census records:

- At the National Archives Building in Washington, D.C.
- At 13 NARA Regional Records Services Facilities
- At State Archives and State Libraries
- At many public libraries, historical societies, and other research facilities
- Through the National Archives Microfilm Rental Program, which many public libraries participate in.

Other Useful Federal Records

For information on other microfilmed Federal records in the custody of NARA that are useful for genealogical research, consult:

- *Microfilm Resources for Research: A Comprehensive Catalog of National Archives Microfilm Publications.* Washington, D.C.: National Archives and Records Administration, 1996. Available on-line or for purchase.
- *American Indians: A Select Catalog of National Archives Microfilm Publications.* Washington, D.C.: National Archives and Records Administration, 1995. Available on-line or for purchase.
- *Black Studies: A Select Catalog of National Archives Microfilm Publications.* Washington, D.C.: National Archives and Records Administration, 1996. Available on-line or for purchase.
- *Diplomatic Records: A Select Catalog of National Archives Microfilm Publications.* Washington, D.C.: National Archives and Records Administration, 1986. Available on-line or for purchase.
- *Genealogical & Biographical Research: A Select Catalog of National Archives Microfilm Publications.* Washington, D.C.: National Archives and Records Administration, 1983. Available on-line or for purchase.
- *Federal Court Records: A Select Catalog of National Archives Microfilm Publications.* Washington, D.C.: National Archives and Records Administration, 1987. Available on-line or for purchase.
- *Immigrant & Passenger Arrivals: A Select Catalog of National Archives Microfilm Publications.* Washington, D.C.: National Archives and Records Administration, 1991. Available on-line or for purchase.
- *Military Service Records: A Select Catalog of National Archives Microfilm Publications.* Washington, D.C.: National Archives and Records Administration, 1985. Available on-line or for purchase.

For information on other Federal records, both microfilmed and unfilmed, in the custody of NARA that are useful for genealogical research, consult:

- *Guide to Genealogical Research in the National Archives.* Washington, D.C.:

National Archives and Records Administration, 1985. Available for purchase.

A Final Word

Do not expect "Star Trek" capabilities in the early 21st century. You will not really be able to "do" your genealogical research on the World Wide Web. Remember, old records are handwritten on paper, and now exist either on paper or on microfilm. It is extremely costly to convert old records to an electronic format.

NARA is, however, committed to increasing public access to historically significant and representative (sample) documents through our Electronic Access Project.

Source: Adapted from National Archives and Records Administration Web site (*http://www.nara.gov/genealogy/genindex.html*).

Genealogy Resources

Internet Resources

Genealogy Instructions for Beginners, Kids and Teenagers (*http://home.earthlink.net/~howardorjeff/instruct.htm*) Web site for getting started in genealogy, including tips on what questions to ask and of whom, blank forms to fill out, research projects, bibliographies, and links.

National Genealogical Society (*http://www.ngsgenealogy.org*) Organization of individuals, family associations, societies, and related institutions; offers tips on research and getting started, library with loan service, and on-line bookstore. (Address: 4527 17th Street North, Arlington, VA 22207-2399; Phone: 800-473-0060 or 703-525-0050)

Federation of Genealogical Societies (*http://www.fgs.org/*) Web site provides information about the organization, its publications and projects, and links to other genealogical societies. (Address: P.O. Box 200940, Austin, TX 78720-0940; Phone: 512-336-2731; Fax: 512-336-2732; E-mail: fgs-office@fgs.org)

Genealogy (*http://www.census.gov/ftp/pub/genealogy/www*) U.S. Census Bureau's genealogy Web site, offering information on research and access to records, including the bureau's search services.

Genealogical Research at the National Archives (*http://www.nara.gov/genealogy/genindex.html*) Official genealogy section of the National Archives and Records Administration (NARA) Web site; provides many finding aids, guides, and research tools to prepare amateur genealogists for a visit to a NARA facility or for requesting records from NARA; includes a discussion of policy issues affecting genealogists, a description of NARA's Washington, D.C., and 13 regional facilities; catalogs of data and microfilm publications; lists of publications, some free; information on the Soundex Machine and genealogy workshops and courses; and links to genealogical resources on the Internet.

Vital Records Information—United States (*http://vitalrec.com/index.html*) Web site containing information about how to obtain vital records from around the country, including birth, death, marriage, and divorce records; provides information about a CD-ROM and links to investigative services and foreign vital records Web sites.

WorldGenWeb Project (*http://www.worldgenweb.org/*) Web site that seeks to connect genealogical researchers worldwide, grouping Web links by region.

USGenWeb Project (*http://
www.usgenweb.org*) Web site that seeks
to connect genealogical researchers
worldwide, grouping Web links by
region; offers links and resources by
individual state; offers tips for
researchers and links to databases.

Cyndi's List (*http://www.cyndislist.com*)
Web site providing links to useful
genealogical sites around the world and
to related information, such as
databases on information about ships
and passenger lists.

World-Wide Genealogy Resources (*http://
www.genhomepage.com/world.html*)
Web site offering links to general and
regional genealogical resources around
the world.

North American Genealogy Resources
(*http://www.genhomepage.com/
northamerican.html*) Web site offers
links to genealogical resources by
country and then by state or province,
for the United States, Canada, and
Mexico.

Genealogy Resources on the Internet
(*http://www-personal.umich.edu/
~cgaunt/gen_int1.html*) Web site
indexing the wide range of materials
available on the Internet through Web

sites, mailing lists, usenet newsgroups,
anonymous file transfer protocol (FTP),
gopher, Telnet, and e-mail.

Family Tree Maker's Genealogy Site
(*http://www.familytreemaker.com/*)
Web site offering help to amateur
genealogists, including advice on
searching; genealogy message boards;
on-line genealogical library; lists of
useful books, articles, and CDs; and
links to useful Web sites.

Genealogy Home Page (*http://
www.genhomepage.com*) Web site
offering general resources, tips, and
links for people researching their
ancestry; includes links to a site
offering genealogical computer
programs and information available for
downloading.

Helm's Genealogy Toolbox—Providing the
Tools to Research Your Family History
Online (*http://
www.genealogytoolbox.com*) Web site
offering resources for family historians,
including news and articles on
genealogical research, guides to
genealogical software, query pages,
bookstore, registration of genealogical
home pages, and thousands of Web
links.

Print Resources

General Works

Allen, Desmond Wallace, and Carolyn
Earle Billingsley. *Beginner's Guide to
Family History Research.* Conway, Ak.:
Arkansas Research (P.O. Box 303,
Conway, AR 72033), 1997. (Available
on-line at *http://biz.ipa.net/
arkresearch/guide.html*)

Crandall, Ralph J. *Shaking Your Family
Tree.* Dublin, N.H.: Yankee Publishing,
1986.

Croom, Emily A. *Unpuzzling Your Past: A
Basic Guide to Genealogy.* Cincinnati:
Betterway, 1995.

Hey, David, ed. *The Oxford Companion to
Local and Family History.* New York:
Oxford University Press, 1993.

Horowitz, Lois. *Dozens of Cousins: Blue
Genes, Horse Thieves, and Other
Relative Surprises in Your Family Tree.*
Berkeley, Calif.: Ten Speed Press, 1999.

Jacobus, Donald Lines. *Genealogy as a
Pastime and Profession.* Baltimore:
Genealogical Publishing, 1968.

Lind, Marilyn. *Immigration, Migration,
and Settlement in the United States: A
Genealogical Guidebook.* Cloquet,
Minn.: Linden Tree, 1985.

Mills, Elizabeth Shown. *Evidence! Citation
and Analysis for the Family Historian.*
Baltimore: Genealogical Publishing,
1997.

Oldfield, Jim, Jr. *Your Family Tree.* Grand
Rapids, Mich.: Abacus, 1997.

Sagraves, Barbara. *A Preservation Guide:
Saving the Past and the Present for the
Future.* Salt Lake City: Ancestry, 1995.

Stryker-Rodda, Harriet. *How to Climb Your Family Tree.* Baltimore: Genealogical Publishing, 1977.

Szucs, Loretto D., and Sandra H. Luebking. *The Source: A Guidebook of American Genealogy.* Rev. ed. Salt Lake City: Ancestry, 1997.

Taylor, Maureen. *Through the Eyes of Your Ancestors: A Step-by-Step Guide to Uncovering Your Family's History.* Boston: Houghton Mifflin, 1999.

Vandagriff, G. G. *Voices in Your Blood: Discovering Identity Through Family History.* Kansas City: Andrews and McMeel, 1993.

Willard, Jim, et al. *Ancestors : A Beginner's Guide to Family History and Genealogy.* Boston: Houghton Mifflin, 1997.

Research Guides

Baxter, Angus. *In Search of Your European Roots: A Complete Guide to Tracing Your Ancestors in Every Country in Europe.* 2d ed. Baltimore: Genealogical Publishing, 1994.

Bentley, Elizabeth Petty. *The Genealogist's Address Book.* Baltimore: Genealogical Publishing, 1995.

Colletta, John P. *They Came in Ships: A Guide to Finding Your Immigrant Ancestor's Arrival Record.* 2d ed. Salt Lake City: Ancestry, 1993.

Drake, Paul. *What Did They Mean by That? A Dictionary of Historical Terms for Genealogists.* Bowie, Md.: Heritage Books, 1994.

————. *What Did They Mean by That? Some More Words.* Bowie, MD: Heritage Books, 1998.

Greenwood, Val D. *The Researcher's Guide to American Genealogy.* Baltimore: Genealogical Publishing, 1990.

Heisey, John W. *A Genealogist's Guide to Washington, D.C., Research.* Indianapolis: Heritage House, 1986.

Neagles, James C., and Lila Lee Neagles. *Locating Your Immigrant Ancestor: A Guide to Naturalization Records.* Rev. ed. Logan: Everton Publishers, 1986.

Parker, J. Carlyle. *Going to Salt Lake City to Do Family History Research.* 3d ed. Turlock, Calif.: Marietta Publishing, 1996.

Redmonds, George. *Surnames and Genealogy: A New Approach.* Boston: New England Historic Genealogical Society, 1997.

Rubincam, Milton. *Pitfalls in Genealogical Research.* Salt Lake City: Ancestry, 1987.

Smith, Jessie Carney, ed. *Ethnic Genealogy: A Research Guide.* Westport, Conn.: Greenwood, 1983.

On Using Computers in Genealogy

Arends, Marthe. *Genealogy Software Guide.* Baltimore: Genealogical Publishing, 1998.

Bonner, Laurie, and Steve Bonner. *Searching for Cyber-Roots: A Step-by-Step Guide to Genealogy on the World Wide Web.* Salt Lake City: Ancestry, 1997.

Crowe, Elizabeth Powell. *Genealogy Online: Researching Your Roots.* New York: McGraw Hill, 1998.

Eastman, Richard. *Your Roots: Total Genealogy Planning on Your Computer.* Emeryville, Calif.: Ziff-Davis, 1995.

Howells, Cyndi. *Netting Your Ancestors: Genealogical Research on the Internet.* Baltimore: Genealogical Publishing, 1997.

Kemp, Thomas Jay. *Virtual Roots: A Guide to Genealogy and Local History on the World Wide Web.* Wilmington, Del.: Scholarly Resources, 1997.

Przecha, Donna, and Joan Lowrey. *Guide to Genealogy Software.* Baltimore: Genealogical Publishing, 1993.

Renick, Barbara, and Richard S. Wilson. *The Internet for Genealogists: A Beginner's Guide.* 3d ed. La Habra, Calif.: Compuology, 1997.

Roberts, Ralph. *Genealogy via the Internet: Tracing Your Family Roots Quickly and Easily: Computerized Genealogy in Plain English.* Alexander, N.C.: Alexander Books, 1998.

For Young People

Beller, Susan Provost. *Roots for Kids: A Genealogy Guide for Young People.* White Hall, Va.: Betterway, 1989.

Cooper, Kay. *Where Did You Get Those Eyes?: A Discover It Yourself Book.* New York: Walker, 1988.

Depue, Anne. *Climb Your Family Tree: A Genealogy Detective's Kit.* New York: Hyperion Paperbacks for Children, 1996.

Perl, Lila. *The Great Ancestor Hunt: The Fun of Finding Out Who You Are.* New York: Clarion, 1989.

Wolfman, Ira, and Michael Klein. *Do People Grow on Family Trees? Genealogy for Kids and Other Beginners.* New York: Workman, 1991.

Note: See also genealogical works following articles on specific countries or ethnic groups.

Appendix E: National Archives and

Records Administration

On-line Catalog

The National Archives and Records Administration Web site (see above) contains much more information on-line for amateur and professional genealogists. These include:
- Census Records
- The Soundex Indexing System [see "Appendix F: Guide to the Soundex System"]
- Immigration and Naturalization Records
- Military Records, including Civil War Records, Confederate Pension Records, Spanish-American War Records, World War I Records, and State-level Lists of Casualties from the Korean Conflict (1951–1957) and the Vietnam Conflict (1957–)
- Miscellaneous Records
- Post Office Records
- Social Security Records
- Freedman's Savings and Trust Company Records
- Genealogical Data in National Archives Information Locator (NAIL), a pilot searchable database with limited NARA genealogical data, part of NARA's Electronic Access Project

NARA offers a number of free publications from the Product Development and Distribution Staff (NWCP), National Archives and Records Administration, Room G-7, 700 Pennsylvania Avenue, NW, Washington, D.C. 20408 (Telephone: 202-501-5235 or 1-800-234-8861; Fax 202-501-7170). Among them are:
- GIL 5. "Using Records in the National Archives for Genealogical Research." 27 pp.
- GIL 7. "Military Service Records in the National Archives." 14 pp.
- GIL 30. "Information About the National Archives for Prospective Researchers." 24 pp. Focuses on

research in the Washington, D.C., area facilities
- "Aids for Genealogical Research" describes publications by NARA and various commercial sources that are available for purchase from NARA

NARA's Publication Program offers for sale many publications for genealogists. These include *The Guide to Genealogical Research in the National Archives*, which provides an excellent introduction to the topic.

NARA also publishes a series of microfilm catalogs on topics of great interest to genealogists. These contain both detailed descriptions of the records and roll-by-roll listings for each microfilm publication. Topics include:
- Census Records
- Military Service Records
- Immigrant and Passenger Arrivals
- Genealogical and Biographical Research
- Federal Court Records
- American Indians
- Black Studies
- Microfilm Resources for Research: A Comprehensive Catalog

Each catalog is also available for purchase in print format. Microfilm is available at the National Archives Building in Washington, D.C., and also in the 13 regional records services facilities:
- Anchorage
- Atlanta (East Point)
- Boston (Waltham)
- Chicago
- Denver
- Fort Worth
- Kansas City
- Laguna Niguel, California
- New York City
- Philadelphia
- Pittsfield, Massachusetts
- San Francisco (San Bruno)
- Seattle

Not all microfilm records are available at all regional facilities. Selected titles are also available through NARA's Microfilm Rental Program. In addition, many large libraries and genealogical societies have purchased all or some of the microfilm sets listed above.

National Archives microfilm publications provide basic documentation for research in the fields of American, European, Far Eastern, African, and Latin American history, as well as in local history and genealogy. Materials relating to immigration are described more fully in the *National Archives and Record Administration Microfilm Catalog*, which is drawn from NARA's on-line Web site.

NARA also offers genealogical workshops and courses for the general public, in Washington, D.C., and also in the regional centers. Topics include an introduction to genealogy and research into records such as census schedules, military service and pension records, and passenger lists.

Microfilm Catalog

Introduction

This catalog lists National Archives microfilm publications of records relating to the arrival of passengers, crew members, and vessels in U.S. ports. Most of the records before 1891 are from the Records of the U.S. Customs Service, Record Group 36. Later records are part of the Records of the Immigration and Naturalization Service (INS), Record Group 85. The publications are arranged by record group and thereunder alphabetically by the name of the port.

The second edition features five new ports of entry: Detroit, Michigan; Galveston, Texas; the St. Albans, Vermont, District, encompassing territory along the Canadian border from Maine to Washington; San Francisco, California; and Seattle, Washington. The catalog now includes complete roll listings for every microfilm publication, providing the researcher with a more thorough understanding of the records each publication contains. In addition, there are three new indexes at the back of the catalog: publications are arranged by port, by title, and by their inclusion in microfilm holdings of each regional archives.

Records of the United States Customs Service, Record Group 36

Early records relating to immigration originated in regional customhouses. An act of March 2, 1819 (*3 Stat. 489*), required the captain or master of a vessel arriving at a port in the United States or any of its territories from a foreign country to submit a list of passengers to the collector of customs. The act also required that the collector submit a quarterly report or abstract, consisting of copies of passenger lists, to the Secretary of State, who was required to submit such information at each session of Congress. After 1874, collectors forwarded only statistical reports to the Treasury Department. The lists themselves were retained by the Collector of Customs. Customs records were maintained primarily for statistical purposes.

Records of the Immigration and Naturalization Service, Record Group 85

In 1882, Congress passed the first Federal law regulating immigration; between 1882 and 1891 the Secretary of the Treasury had general supervision over immigration. The Office of Superintendent of Immigration of the Department of the Treasury was established under an act of March 3, 1891, and was designated a bureau in 1895 with responsibility for administering the alien contract-labor laws. In 1900, administration of the Chinese-exclusion laws was added. In 1903, the Bureau became part of the Department of Commerce and Labor. Functions relating to naturalization were assigned to the Bureau in 1906, and its name was changed to the Bureau of Immigration and Naturalization. It was transferred in 1940 to the Department of Justice.

The records of the Immigration and Naturalization Service listed in this catalog were transferred to the National

Archives on microfilm. The original records were destroyed by the INS. In some instances, there are indexes for which the National Archives has no list. Some of the records were microfilmed as they appeared in volumes and the date spans may overlap. Errors in arrangement or omission cannot be corrected. Not all passenger lists are indexed. Many of the indexes are difficult to read. This catalog describes contents of individual rolls of microfilm.

The Records

In this catalog, passenger arrival records are preceded by their indexes. The date spans for the indexes and the records do not always exactly correspond.

Card Indexes

The quantity of information in each of the indexes varies. They may be simple alphabetical listings or arranged in the Soundex coding system (see "Appendix F: Guide to the Soundex System" on p. 766.) The indexes may contain the name, age, occupation, nationality, and last permanent residence of the passenger; the port of entry; the name of the vessel; and the date of arrival. The Soundex index cards may contain only the passenger's name, age, and sex, and the volume number, page, and line where the name may be found.

Book Indexes

These records consist of alphabetical listings of passengers provided to the Immigration and Naturalization Service by the shipping lines. The lists are usually arranged chronologically by date of arrival. The lists include the passenger's name, age, and destination.

Passenger and Crew Lists

Customs Passenger Lists and Abstracts

Customs passenger lists contain each passenger's name, age, sex, occupation, nationality, and the name of the country in which each intended to reside. Entries are arranged by date of arrival and sometimes by the passenger or crew member's occupation and the port from which he or she sailed. Lists may also include notations as to the number and causes of deaths on board. The abstracts, which are consolidated lists of all the passengers who arrived at a port during the quarter, generally contain the same information as customs passenger lists.

Immigration and Naturalization Service Passenger Lists

Immigration and Naturalization Service passenger lists include the names of U.S. citizens returning from abroad, foreign visitors, and immigrants. The lists usually also contain names of vessels and shipmasters, ports of arrival and embarkation, dates of arrival, and the following information about each passenger: full name; age; sex; marital status; occupation; last residence; port of arrival and final destination in the United States; if the passenger had been in the United States before, when and where; and if the passenger were going to join a relative, the relative's name, address, and relationship. Beginning in 1903, race was included; in 1906, personal description and birthplace; in 1907, the name and address of the alien's nearest relative in the country from which he or she came.

Crew Lists

Crew lists may include the names of both American and alien seamen. Information about each crew member may include his length of service at sea, position in the ship's company, when and where the seaman joined the vessel's crew, whether he was to be discharged at the port of arrival, literacy, age, race, nationality, height, and weight.

Obtaining Single Copies of Passenger Lists

For a researcher who doesn't wish to buy an entire roll of film to look for a single name, the National Archives will provide, for a fee, copies of single pages of passenger lists. If the list is indexed, the Reference Services Branch will consult the index to find the correct page of the passenger list to copy. The minimum information required for a search of the index is the full name of the person being researched, the port of arrival, and the approximate date of arrival. Additional information such as age of passenger and names of accompanying passengers can be useful. More specific information, however, is needed to search unindexed lists. In addition to the facts listed above, it is necessary to provide either the exact date of arrival or the name of the ship on which the person arrived.

Requests for these copies must be made on NATF Form 81, "Order for Copies of Passenger Arrival Records." The fee for this service is $10, payable only when the records requested are found. If it is not possible to find records, no payment is required. The order form can be obtained from the Reference Services Branch (NNRS), National Archives, Washington, D.C. 20408.

This catalog was compiled by Constance Potter with assistance from Anne DeLong.

Source: Adapted from National Archives and Records Administration Web site (*http://www.nara.gov/genealogy/genindex.html*).

Appendix F: Guide to the Soundex System

To use the census Soundex system to locate information about a person, you must know his or her full name and the state or territory in which he or she lived at the time of the census. It is also helpful to know the full name of the head of the household in which the person lived because census takers recorded information under that name.

The Soundex is a coded surname (last name) index based on the way a surname sounds, rather than the way it is spelled. Surnames that sound the same but are spelled differently, like SMITH and SMYTH, have the same code and are filed together. The Soundex coding system was developed so that you can find a surname even though it may have been recorded under various spellings.

To search for a particular surname, you must first work out its code. NARA's on-line Soundex Machine can code surnames automatically (see below). If you wish to understand the process, however, the instructions below should prove helpful.

Basic Soundex Coding Rule

Every Soundex code consists of a letter and three numbers, such as W-252. The letter is always the first letter of the surname. The numbers are assigned to the remaining letters of the surname according to the Soundex guide shown below. Zeroes are added at the end if necessary to produce a four-character code. Additional letters are disregarded.

For example, Washington is coded W-252 (W, 2 for the S, 5 for the N, 2 for the G, remaining letters disregarded). Lee is coded L-000 (L, 000 added).

Soundex Coding Guide

Number Represents the Letters

1. B, F, P, V
2. C, G, J, K, Q, S, X, Z
3. D, T
4. L
5. M, N
6. R

Disregard the letters A, E, I, O, U, H, W, and Y.

Additional Soundex Coding Rules

- Names with Double Letters: If the surname has any double letters, they should be treated as one letter. For example, Gutierrez is coded G-362 (G, 3 for the T, 6 for the first R, second R ignored, 2 for the Z).
- Names with Letters Side-by-Side That Have the Same Soundex Code Number: If the surname has different letters side-by-side that have the same number in the Soundex coding guide, they should be treated as one letter. For example, Pfister is coded as P-236 (P, F ignored, 2 for the S, 3 for the T, 6 for the R). For example, Jackson is coded as J-250 (J, 2 for the C, K ignored, S ignored, 5 for the N, 0 added).
- Names with Prefixes: If a surname has a prefix, such as Van, Con, De, Di, La, or Le, code both with and without the prefix because the surname might be listed under either code. Note, however, that Mc and Mac are not considered prefixes. For example, VanDeusen might be coded two ways: V-532 (V, 5 for the N, 3 for the D, 2 for the S) or D-250 (D, 2 for the S, 5 for the N, 0 added).

If several surnames have the same code, the cards for them are arranged alphabetically by given name. There are divider cards showing most code numbers, but not all. For instance, one divider may be numbered 350 and the next one 400. Between the two divider cards there may be names coded 353, 350, 360, 365, and 355, but instead of being in numerical order they are interfiled alphabetically by given name.

The following names are examples of Soundex coding and are given only as illustrations:

Name	Letters	Code No.
Allricht	l,r,c	A-462
Eberhard	b,r,r	E-166
Engebrethson	n,g,b	E-521
Heimbach	m,b,c	H-512
Hanselmann	n,s,l	H-524
Henzelmann	n,z,l	H-524
Hildebrand	l,d,b	H-431
Kavanagh	v,n,g	K-152
Lind, Van	n,d	L-530
Lukaschowsky	k,s,s	L-222
McDonnell	c,d,n	M-235
McGee	c	M-200
O'Brien	b,r,n	O-165
Opnian	p,n,n	O-155
Oppenheimer	p,n,m	O-155
Riedemanas	d,m,n	R-355
Zita	t	Z-300
Zitzmeinn	t,z,m	Z-325

Native Americans, Asians, and Religious Nuns

Researchers using the Soundex system to locate religious nuns or persons with Native American or Asian names should be aware of the way such names were coded. Variations in coding differed from the normal coding system.

Phonetically spelled Asian and Native American names were sometimes coded as if one continuous name, or, if a distinguishable surname was given, the names were coded in the normal manner. For example, the American Indian name Shinka-Wa-Sa may have been coded as "Shinka" (S-520) or "Sa" (S-000). Researchers should investigate the various possibilities of coding such names.

Religious nun names were coded as if "Sister" were the surname, and they appear in the Soundex indexes under the code "S-236." Within the code S-236, the names may not be in alphabetical order.

Getting and Using a Soundex Code

Genealogical researchers can use the above guidelines to get the Soundex code for the name they are seeking or they can get the number automatically on-line at *http://www.nara.gov/genealogy/coding.html*.

With the Soundex code, researchers can then use it to help track down the person they are seeking. For example, they can go to the Federal Population Census page (*http://www.nara.gov/publications/microfilm/census/census.html*) to locate the census records they need (only 1880–1920 are Soundexed). Within each census you must find the state in which the person lived. Soundex codes are arranged alphabetically by the first letter of the surname. Some immigrant and passenger arrival lists are also coded in Soundex.

Note: The above is partly based on "Using the Census Soundex," General Information Leaflet 55 (Washington, D.C.: National Archives and Records Administration, 1995), a free brochure available from inquire@nara.gov (include your name, postal address, and "GIL 55 please").

Source: Adapted from National Archives and Records Administration Web site (*http://www.nara.gov/genealogy/genindex.html*)

Glossary of Immigration Terms

Acquired Citizenship: Citizenship conferred at birth on children born abroad to a U.S. citizen parent(s).

Adjustment to Immigrant Status: Procedure allowing certain aliens already in the United States to apply for immigrant status. Aliens admitted to the United States in a nonimmigrant or other category may have their status changed to that of lawful permanent resident if they are eligible to receive an immigrant visa and one is immediately available. In such cases, the alien is counted as an immigrant as of the date of adjustment, even though the alien may have been in the United States for an extended period of time.

Adversely Affected: See *Nonpreference Category*.

Agricultural Workers: As a nonimmigrant class of admission, an alien coming temporarily to the United States to perform agricultural labor or services, as defined by the Secretary of Labor.

Alien: Any person not a citizen or national of the United States.

Amerasian Act: Public Law 97-359 (Act of 10/22/82) provides for the immigration to the United States of certain Amerasian children. In order to qualify for benefits under this law, an alien must have been born in Cambodia, Korea, Laos, Thailand, or Vietnam after December 31, 1950, and before October 22, 1982, and have been fathered by a U.S. citizen.

Amerasian (Vietnam): Immigrant visas are issued to Amerasians under Public Law 100-202 (Act of 12/22/87), which provides for the admission of aliens born in Vietnam between January 1, 1962, and January 1, 1976, if the alien was fathered by a U.S. citizen. Spouses, children, and parents or guardians may accompany the alien.

Apprehension: The arrest of a deportable alien by the Immigration and Naturalization Service. Each apprehension of the same alien in a fiscal year is counted separately.

Asylee: An alien in the United States or at a port of entry unable or unwilling to return to his or her country of nationality, or to seek the protection of that country because of persecution or a well-founded fear of persecution. Persecution or the fear thereof may be based on the alien's race, religion, nationality, membership in a particular social group, or political opinion. For persons with no nationality, the country of nationality is considered to be the country in which the alien last habitually resided. Asylees are eligible to adjust to lawful permanent resident status after one year of continuous presence in the United States. These immigrants are limited to 10,000 adjustments per fiscal year.

Beneficiaries: Those aliens who receive immigration benefits from petitions filed with the U.S. Immigration and Naturalization Service. Beneficiaries generally derive privilege or status as a result of their relationship (including that of employer-employee) to a U.S. citizen or lawful permanent resident.

Border Crosser: An alien or citizen resident of the United States reentering the country after an absence of less than six months in Canada or Mexico, or a nonresident alien entering the United States across the Canadian border for stays of no more than six months or across the Mexican border for stays of no more than 72 hours, or a U.S. citizen residing in Canada or Mexico who enters the United States frequently for business or pleasure, or an individual entering the U.S. on any flight originating in Canada or Mexico.

Border Patrol Sector: Any one of 21 geographic areas into which the United States is divided for the Immigration and Naturalization Service's Border Patrol activities.

Business Nonimmigrant: An   alien coming temporarily to the United States to engage in commercial transactions which do not involve gainful employment in the United States, i.e., engaged in international commerce on behalf of a foreign firm, not employed in the U.S. labor market, and receives no salary from U.S. sources.

Certificate of Citizenship: Identity document proving U.S. citizenship. Certificates of citizenship are issued to derivative citizens and to persons who acquired U.S. citizenship (see definitions for *Acquired Citizenship* and *Derivative Citizenship*).

Child: An unmarried person under 21 years of age who is: a legitimate child; a stepchild provided that the child was *under 18 years of age* at the time that the marriage creating the stepchild status occurred; a legitimated child provided that the child was legitimate while in the legal custody of the legitimating parent; a child adopted while *under 16 years of age* who has resided since adoption in the legal custody of the adopting parents for at least 2 *years*; or an orphan, *under 16 years of age*, who has been adopted abroad by a U.S. citizen or has an immediate-relative visa petition submitted in his/her behalf and is coming to the United States for adoption by a U.S. citizen.

Conditional Immigrant: See *Immigration Marriage Fraud Amendments of 1986*.

Country:
Birth: The country in which a person is born.
Chargeability: See *Foreign State of Chargeability*.
Citizenship: The country in which a person is born (and has not rescinded citizenship) or naturalized; the country to which that person owes allegiance and is entitled to its protection.
Former Allegiance: The previous country of citizenship of a naturalized U.S. citizen or of a person who derived U.S. citizenship.
(Last) Residence: The country in which an alien habitually resided prior to entering the United States.
Nationality: The country of a person's citizenship. For nonimmigrant data, citizenship refers to an alien's reported country of citizenship.

Crewman: A foreign national serving in any capacity on board a vessel or aircraft. Crewmen are admitted for 29 days, with no extensions. Crewmen required to depart on the same vessel on which they arrived are classified as D-1s. Crewmen who depart on a vessel different than the one on which they arrived are classified as D-2s. Although these aliens are nonimmigrants, crewmen are not included in nonimmigrant admission data.

Crewman Technical (or Nonwillful) Violator: Any crewman who through no fault of his or her own remains in the United States more than 29 days (e.g., a crewman hospitalized beyond the 29-day admission period).

Cuban/Haitian Entrant: Status accorded 1) Cubans who entered the United States illegally between April 15, 1980, and October 10, 1980, and 2) Haitians who entered the country illegally before January 1, 1981. Cubans and Haitians meeting these criteria who have continuously resided in the United States since before January 1, 1982, and who were known to the INS before that date, may adjust to permanent residence under a provision of the Immigration Control and Reform Act of 1986.

Deferred Enforced Departure: See *Extended Voluntary Departure*.

Deferred Inspection: See *Parolee*.

Departure Under Safeguards: The departure of an illegal alien from the United States which is physically observed by an Immigration and Naturalization Service official.

Dependent: Spouse, unmarried dependent child under 21 years of age, unmarried dependent child under 25 years of age who is in full-time attendance at a postsecondary educational institution, or unmarried child who is physically or mentally disabled.

Deportable Alien: An alien in the United States subject to any of the 5 grounds of deportation specified in the Immigration and Nationality Act. This includes any alien illegally in the United States, regardless of whether the alien entered the country illegally or entered legally but subsequently violated the terms of his or her visa.

Deportation: The formal removal of an alien from the United States when the presence of that alien is deemed inconsistent with the public welfare. Deportation is ordered by an immigration judge without any punishment being imposed or contemplated. Data for a fiscal year cover the deportations verified during that fiscal year.

Derivative Citizenship: Citizenship conveyed to children through the naturalization of parents or, under certain circumstances, to spouses of citizens at or during marriage or to foreign-born children adopted by U.S. citizen parents, provided certain conditions are met.

District: Any one of 33 geographic areas into which the United States and its territories are divided for the Immigration and Naturalization Service's field operations or one of three overseas offices located in Rome, Bangkok, or Mexico City. Operations are supervised by a district director located at a district office within the district's geographic boundaries.

Diversity Transition: A   transition toward the permanent diversity program in fiscal year 1995, allocating 40,000 visas annually during the period 1992– to nationals of certain countries identified as having been "adversely affected" by the Immigration and Nationality Act Amendments of 1965 (P.L. 89-236). At least 40 percent of the visas were reserved for natives of Ireland.

Employer Sanctions: The   employer sanctions provision of the Immigration Reform and Control Act of 1986 prohibits employers from hiring, recruiting, or referring for a fee aliens known to be unauthorized to work in the United States. Violators of the law are subject to a series of civil fines or criminal penalties when there is a pattern or practice of violations.

Exchange Visitor: An alien coming temporarily to the United States as a participant in a program approved by the Secretary of State for the purpose of teaching, instructing or lecturing, studying, observing, conducting research, consulting, demonstrating special skills, or receiving training.

Exclusion: The formal denial of an alien's entry into the United States. The exclusion of the alien is made by an immigration judge after an exclusion hearing. Data for a fiscal year cover the exclusions verified during that fiscal year.

Exempt from the Numerical Cap: Those aliens accorded lawful permanent residence who are exempt from the provisions of the flexible numerical cap of 675,000 set by the Immigration Act of 1990. Exempt categories include immediate relatives of U.S. citizens, refugees, asylees, Amerasians, adjustments under the legalization provisions of the Immigration Reform and Control Act of 1986, and certain parolees from the former Soviet Union and Indochina.

Extended Voluntary Departure (EVD): A special temporary provision granted administratively to designated national groups physically present in the United States because the U.S. State Department judged conditions in the countries of origin to be "unstable" or "uncertain" or to have shown a pattern of "denial of rights." Aliens in EVD status are temporarily allowed to remain in the United States until conditions in their home country change. Certain aliens holding EVD status from Afghanistan, Ethiopia, Poland, and Uganda, who have resided in the United States since July 1, 1984, were eligible to adjust to temporary and then to permanent resident status under the legalization program. The Immigration Act of 1990 established Temporary Protective Status as the mechanism for "blanket" suspensions of deportation. In certain instances an administrative decision has been made to place aliens in deferred enforced departure (DED) rather than Temporary Protective Status.

Fiancé(e)s of U.S. Citizen: A nonimmigrant alien coming to the United States to conclude a valid marriage with a U.S. citizen within ninety days after entry.

Files Control Office: An Immigration and Naturalization Service field office; either a district (including INS overseas offices) or a suboffice of that district where alien case files are maintained and controlled.

Fiscal Year: Currently, the 12-month period beginning October 1 and ending September 30. Historically, until 1831 and from 1843 to 1849, the 12-month period ending September 30 of the respective year; from 1832 to 1842 and 1850 to 1867, ending December 31 of the respective year; from 1868 to 1976, ending June 30 of the respective year. The transition quarter (TQ) for 1976 covers the three-month period July to September 1976.

Foreign Government Official: As a nonimmigrant class of admission, an alien coming temporarily to the United States who has been accredited by a foreign VIA government to function as an ambassador, public minister, career diplomatic or consular officer, other accredited official, or an attendant, servant, or personal employee of an accredited official, and all above aliens' spouses and unmarried minor (or dependent) children.

Foreign Information Media Representative: As a nonimmigrant class of admission, an alien coming temporarily to the United States as a bona fide representative of foreign press, radio, film, or other foreign information media and the alien's spouse and unmarried minor (or dependent) children.

Foreign Medical School Graduate: An immigrant who has graduated from a medical school or has qualified to practice medicine in a foreign state, who was licensed and practicing medicine on January 9, 1978, and who entered the United States as a nonimmigrant on a temporary worker or exchange visitor visa before January 10, 1978.

Foreign State of Chargeability: The independent country to which an immigrant entering under the preference system is accredited. No more than 7 percent of the family-sponsored and employment-based visas may be issued to natives of an independent country in a fiscal year. Dependencies of independent countries cannot exceed 2 percent of the family-sponsored and employment-based visas issued. Since these limits are based on visa issuance rather than entries into the United States, and immigrant visas are valid for four months, there is not total correspondence between these two occurrences. Chargeability is usually determined by country of birth. Exceptions are made to prevent the separation of family members when the limitation for the country of birth has been met.

General Naturalization Provisions: The basic requirements for naturalization that every applicant must meet, unless a member of a special class. General provisions require an applicant to be at least 18 years of age, a lawful permanent resident with five years of continuous residence in the United States, and to have been physically present in the country for half that period.

Geographic Area of Chargeability: Any one of five regions—Africa, East Asia, Latin America and the Caribbean, Near East and South Asia, and the former Soviet Union and Eastern Europe—into which the world is divided for the initial admission of refugees to the United States. Annual consultations between the Executive Branch and the Congress determine the ceiling on the number of refugees who can be admitted to the United States from each area. In fiscal year 1987, an unallocated reserve was incorporated into the admission ceilings.

Hemispheric Ceilings: Statutory limits on immigration to the United States in effect from 1968 to October 1978. Mandated by the Immigration and Nationality Act Amendments of 1965, the ceiling on immigration from the Eastern Hemisphere was set at 170,000, with a per-country limit of 20,000. Immigration from the Western Hemisphere was held to 120,000, without a per-country limit until January 1, 1977. The Western Hemisphere was then made subject to a 20,000-per-country limit. Effective October 1978, the separate hemisphere limits were abolished in favor of a worldwide limit of 290,000. This limit was lowered to 280,000 for fiscal year 1980, and to 270,000 for fiscal years 1981–1991.

Immediate Relatives: Certain immigrants who because of their close relationship to U.S. citizens are exempt from the numerical limitations imposed on immigration to the United States. Immediate relatives are: spouses of citizens, children (under 21 years of age) of citizens, parents of citizens 21 years of age or older, and orphans adopted by citizens who are at least 21 years of age.

Immigrant: An alien admitted to the United States as a lawful permanent resident. Immigrants are those persons lawfully accorded the privilege of residing permanently in the United States. They may be issued immigrant visas by the Department of State overseas or adjusted to permanent resident status by the Immigration and Naturalization Service in the United States.

Immigration Act of 1990: Public Law 101-649 (Act of November 29, 1990), which increased total immigration to the United States under an overall flexible cap, revised all grounds for exclusion and deportation, authorized temporary protected status to aliens of designated countries, revised and established new nonimmigrant admission categories; revised and extended the Visa Waiver Pilot Program; and revised naturalization authority and requirements.

Immigration and Nationality Act: The Act, which along with other immigration laws, treaties, and conventions of the United States, relates to the immigration, temporary admission, naturalization, or removal of aliens.

Immigration Marriage Fraud Amendments of 1986: Public Law 99-639 (Act of 11/10/86), which was passed in order to deter immigration-related marriage fraud. Its major provision stipulates that aliens deriving their immigrant status based on a marriage of less than two years are conditional immigrants. To remove their conditional status the immigrants must apply at an Immigration and Naturalization Service office during the 90-day period before their second-year anniversary of receiving conditional status. If the aliens cannot show that the marriage through which the status was obtained was and is a valid one, their conditional immigrant status is terminated and they become deportable.

Immigration Reform and Control Act (IRCA) of 1986: Public Law 99-603 (Act of 11/6/86), which was passed in order to control and deter illegal immigration to the United States. Its major provisions stipulate legalization of undocumented aliens, legalization of certain agricultural

workers, sanctions for employers who knowingly hire undocumented workers, and increased enforcement at U.S. borders.

Industrial Trainee: See *Temporary Worker*.

International Representative: As a nonimmigrant class of admission, an alien coming temporarily to the United States as a principal or other accredited representative of a foreign government (whether officially recognized or not recognized by the United States) to an international organization, an international organization officer or employee, and all above aliens' spouses and unmarried minor (or dependent) children.

Intracompany Transferee: An alien, employed by an international firm or corporation, who seeks to enter the United States temporarily in order to continue to work for the same employer, or a subsidiary or affiliate, in a capacity that is primarily managerial, executive, or involves specialized knowledge.

IRCA: See *Immigration Reform and Control Act of 1986*.

Labor Certification: Requirement falling on certain persons whose immigration to the United States is based on job skills or nonimmigrant temporary workers coming to perform services unavailable in the United States. Labor certification is awarded by the Secretary of Labor when there are insufficient numbers of U.S. workers available to undertake the employment sought by an applicant and when the alien's employment will not have an adverse effect on the wages and working conditions of U.S. workers similarly employed. Determination of labor availability in the United States is made at the time of a visa application and at the location where the applicant wishes to work.

Legalization Dependents: A maximum of 55,000 visas were issued to spouses and children of aliens legalized under the provisions of the Immigration Reform and Control Act of 1986 in each of fiscal years 1992–1994.

Legalized Aliens: Certain illegal aliens who were eligible to apply for temporary resident status under the legalization provision of the Immigration Reform and Control Act of 1986. To be eligible, aliens must have continuously resided in the United States in an unlawful status since January 1, 1982, not be excludable, and have entered the United States either 1) illegally before January 1, 1982, or 2) as temporary visitors before January 1, 1982, with their authorized stay expiring before that date or with the Government's knowledge of their unlawful status before that date. Legalization consists of two stages— temporary and then permanent residency. In order to adjust to permanent status aliens must have had continuous residence in the United States, be admissible as an immigrant, and demonstrate at least a minimal understanding and knowledge of the English language and U.S. history and government.

Median Age: The age which divides the population into two equal-sized groups, one younger and one older than the median.

Medical and Legal Parolee: See *Parolee.*

Metropolitan Statistical Areas (MSAs): The general concept of an MSA is one of a large population nucleus together with adjacent communities which have a high degree of social and economic integration with that nucleus. Tabulations in the *Statistical Yearbook* include Metropolitan Statistical Areas (MSAs), Primary Metropolitan Statistical Areas (PMSAs), and New England County Metropolitan Areas (NECMAs). MSAs and PSAs are defined by the Office of Management and Budget. PMSAs are components of larger metropolitan complexes called Consolidated Metropolitan Statistical Areas (CMSAs), which are not displayed in the *Yearbook.*

National: A person owing permanent allegiance to a state.

Nationality: The country of a person's citizenship. For nonimmigrant data, citizenship refers to the alien's reported country of citizenship.

NATO Official: As a nonimmigrant class of admission, an alien coming temporarily to the United States as a member of the armed forces or as a civilian employed by the armed forces on assignment with a foreign government signatory to NATO (North Atlantic Treaty Organization), and the alien's spouse and unmarried minor (or dependent) children.

Naturalization: The conferring, by any means, of citizenship upon a person after birth.

Naturalization Court: Any court authorized to award U.S. citizenship. Jurisdiction for naturalization has been conferred upon the following courts: U.S. District Courts of all states, the District of Columbia, and Puerto Rico; the District Courts of Guam and the Virgin Islands; and state courts. Generally, naturalization courts are authorized to award citizenship only to those persons who reside within their territorial jurisdiction.

Naturalization Petition: The form used by a lawful permanent resident to apply for U.S. citizenship. The petition is filed with a naturalization court through the Immigration and Naturalization Service.

New Arrival: A lawful permanent resident alien who enters the United States at a port of entry. The alien is generally required to present an immigrant visa issued outside the United States by a consular officer of the Department of State. Three classes of immigrants, however, need not have an immigrant visa to enter the United States—children born abroad to lawful permanent resident aliens, children born subsequent to the issuance of an immigrant visa to accompanying parents, and American Indians born in Canada.

Nonimmigrant: An alien who seeks temporary entry to the United States for a specific purpose. The alien must have a permanent residence abroad (for most classes of admission) and qualify for the nonimmigrant classification sought. The nonimmigrant classifications are: foreign government officials, visitors for business and for pleasure, aliens in transit through the United States, treaty traders and investors, students, international representatives, temporary workers and trainees, representatives of foreign information media, exchange visitors, fiancé(e)s of U.S. citizens, intracompany transferees, and NATO officials. Most nonimmigrants can be accompanied or joined by spouses and unmarried minor (or dependent) children. Although refugees, parolees, withdrawals, and stowaways are processed as nonimmigrants upon arrival to the United States, these classes, as well as crewmen, are not included in nonimmigrant admission data. See other sections of this Glossary for detailed descriptions of classes of nonimmigrant admission.

Nonpreference Category: Nonpreference visas were available to qualified applicants not entitled to one under the other preferences until the category was eliminated by the Immigration Act of 1990. Nonpreference visas for persons not entitled to the other preferences had not been available since September 1978 because of high demand in the preference categories. An additional 5,000 nonpreference visas were available in each of fiscal years 1987 and 1988 under a provision of the Immigration Reform and Control Act of 1986. This program was extended into 1989, 1990, and 1991 with 15,000 visas issued each year. Aliens born in countries from which immigration was adversely affected by the Immigration and Nationality Act Amendments of 1965 (Public Law 89-236) were eligible for the special nonpreference visas.

North American Free-Trade Agreement (NAFTA): Public Law 103-182 (Act of 12/8/93), superseded the United States–Canada Free-Trade Agreement as of 1/1/94. Continues the special, reciprocal trading relationship between the United States and Canada (see *United States–Canada Free-Trade Agreement*) and establishes a similar relationship with Mexico. See Appendix B [of the *Statistical Yearbook of the Immigration and Naturalization Service,* 1996], Act of December 8, 1993, for specific provisions.

Nursing Relief Act of 1989: Public Law 101-238 (Act of 12/18/89), provides for the adjustment to permanent resident status of certain nonimmigrants who as of September 1, 1989, had H-1 nonimmigrant status as registered nurses; who had been employed in that capacity for at least three years; and whose continued nursing employment meets certain labor certification requirements. It also provides for a five-year pilot program for admission of nonimmigrant nurses under the H-1A category.

Occupation: For an alien entering the United States or adjusting without a labor certification, occupation refers to the employment held in the country of last or legal residence or in the United States. For an alien with a labor certification, occupation is the employment for which certification has been issued.

Orphan: For immigration purposes, a child whose parents have died or disappeared, or who has been abandoned or otherwise separated from both parents. An orphan may also be a child whose sole surviving parent is incapable of providing that child with proper care and who has, in writing, irrevocably released the child for emigration and adoption. In order to qualify as an immediate relative, the orphan must be under the age of 16 at the time a petition is filed on his or her behalf. To enter the United States, an orphan must have been adopted abroad by a U.S. citizen or be coming to the United States for adoption by a citizen.

Panama Canal Act Immigrants: Three categories of special immigrants established by Public Law 96-70 (Act of 9/27/79): 1) certain former employees of the Panama Canal Company or Canal Zone Government, their spouses and children; 2) certain former employees of the U.S. government in the Panama Canal Zone, their spouses and children; and 3) certain former employees of the Panama Canal Company or Canal Zone Government on April 1, 1979, their spouses and children. The Act provides for admission of a maximum of 15,000 immigrants, at a rate of no more than 5,000 each year. They are not, however, subject to the worldwide limitation.

Parolee: A parolee is an alien, appearing to be inadmissible to the inspecting officer, allowed to enter the United States under urgent humanitarian reasons or when that alien's entry is determined to be for significant public benefit. Parole does not constitute a formal admission to the United States and confers temporary admission status only, requiring parolees to leave when the conditions supporting their parole cease to exist. Although these aliens are processed as nonimmigrants upon arrival, parolees are not included in nonimmigrant admission data. Types of parolees include:

1. *Deferred inspection*—Parole may be granted to an alien who appears not to be clearly admissible to the inspecting officer. An appointment will be made for the alien's appearance at another Service office where more information is available and the inspection can be completed.

2. *Advance parole*—authorized at an INS District office in advance of alien's arrival.

3. *Port of entry parole*—authorized at the port upon alien's arrival.

4. *Humanitarian parole*—authorized at INS headquarters, e.g., granted to an alien who has a serious medical condition which would make detention or immediate return inappropriate.

5. *Public interest parole*—authorized at INS headquarters, e.g., granted to an alien who is a witness in legal proceedings or is subject to prosecution in the United States.

6. *Overseas parole*—authorized at an INS district or suboffice while the alien is still overseas.

Per-Country Limit: The maximum number of family-sponsored and employment-based preference visas that can be issued to any country in a fiscal year. The limits are calculated each fiscal year depending on the total number of family-sponsored and employment-based visas available. No more than 7 percent of the visas may be issued to natives of an independent country in a fiscal year; dependencies of independent countries cannot exceed 2 percent. The per-country limit does not indicate, however, that a country is entitled to the maximum number of visas each year, just that it cannot receive more than that number. Because of the combined workings of the preference system and per-country limits, most countries do not reach this level of visa issuance.

Permanent Resident Alien: See *Immigrant*.

Port of Entry: Any location in the United States or its territories which is designated as a point of entry for aliens and U.S. citizens. All district and files control offices are also considered ports, since they become locations of entry for aliens adjusting to immigrant status.

Preinspection: Complete immigration inspection of airport passengers before departure from a foreign country. No further immigration inspection is required upon arrival in the United States other than submission of INS Form I-94 for nonimmigrant aliens.

Preference System (prior to fiscal year 1992): The six categories among which 270,000 immigrant visa numbers are distributed each year during the period 1981–1991. This preference system was amended by the Immigration Act of 1990, effective fiscal year 1992. (See *Preference System [Immigration Act of 1990]* below.) The six categories were: unmarried sons and daughters (over 21 years of age) of U.S. citizens (20 percent); spouses and unmarried sons and daughters of aliens lawfully admitted for permanent residence (26 percent); members of the professions or persons of exceptional ability in the sciences and arts (10 percent); married sons and daughters of U.S. citizens (10 percent); brothers and sisters of U.S. citizens over 21 years of age (24 percent); and needed skilled or unskilled workers (10 percent). A nonpreference category, historically open to immigrants not entitled to a visa number under one of the six preferences just listed, had no numbers available beginning in September 1978.

Preference System (Immigration Act of 1990): The nine categories since fiscal year 1992 among which the family-sponsored and employment-based immigrant preference visas are distributed. The family-sponsored preferences are: 1) unmarried sons and daughters of U.S. citizens; 2) spouses, children, and unmarried sons and daughters of permanent resident aliens; 3) married sons and daughters of U.S. citizens; 4) brothers and sisters of U.S. citizens. The employment-based preferences are: 1) priority workers (persons of extraordinary ability, outstanding professors and researchers, and certain multinational executives and managers); 2) professionals with advanced degrees or aliens with exceptional ability; 3) skilled workers, professionals (without advanced degrees), and needed unskilled workers; 4) special immigrants; and 5) employment creation immigrants (investors). The number of visas issued annually may vary; they are described in Appendix 2 [of the *Statistical Yearbook of the Immigration and Naturalization Service, 1996*].

Principal Alien: The alien from whom another alien derives a privilege or status under immigration law or regulations (usually spouses and minor children).

Refugee: Any person who is outside his or her country of nationality and who is unable or unwilling to return to that country because of persecution or a well-founded fear of persecution. Persecution or the fear thereof may be based on the alien's race, religion, nationality, membership in a particular social group, or political opinion. People with no nationality must be outside their country of last habitual residence to qualify as a refugee. Refugees are exempt from numerical limitation (though worldwide ceilings by geographic area are set annually by the President) and are eligible to adjust to lawful permanent residence after one year of continuous presence in the United States. Although these aliens are considered nonimmigrants when initially admitted to the United States, refugees are not included in nonimmigrant admission data.

Refugee Approvals: The number of refugees approved for admission to the United States during a fiscal year. Refugee approvals are made by Immigration and Naturalization Service officers in overseas offices.

Refugee Arrivals: The number of refugees the Immigration and Naturalization Service initially admits to the United States through ports of entry during a fiscal year.

Refugee Authorized Admissions: The maximum number of refugees allowed to enter the United States in a given fiscal year. As set forth in the Refugee Act of

1980 (Public Law 96-212), the annual figure is determined by the President after consultations with Congress.

Refugee-Parolee: A qualified applicant for conditional entry, between February 1970 and April 1980, whose application for admission to the United States could not be approved because of inadequate numbers of seventh-preference visas. As a result, the applicant was paroled into the United States under the parole authority granted the Attorney General.

Region: Any one of three areas of the United States into which the Immigration and Naturalization Service divides jurisdiction for operational purposes—Eastern Region, Central Region, and Western Region.

Registry Date: Aliens who have continuously resided in the United States in an unlawful status since January 1, 1972, are eligible to adjust to legal permanent resident status under the registry provision. Before the date was amended by the Immigration Reform and Control Act of 1986, aliens had to have been in the country continuously since June 30, 1948, to qualify.

Required Departure: The   directed departure of an alien from the United States without an order of deportation. The departure may be voluntary or involuntary on the part of the alien, and may or may not have been preceded by a hearing before an immigration judge. Data for a fiscal year cover the required departures verified in that fiscal year.

Special Agricultural Workers (SAW): Aliens who performed labor in perishable agricultural commodities for a specified period of time and were admitted for temporary and then permanent residence under a provision of the Immigration Reform and Control Act of 1986. Up to 350,000 aliens who worked at least 90 days in each of the 3 years preceding May 1, 1986, were eligible for Group I temporary resident status. Eligible aliens who qualified under this requirement but applied after the 350,000 limit was met and aliens who performed labor in perishable agricultural commodities for at least 90 days during the year ending May 1, 1986, were eligible for Group II temporary resident status. Adjustment to permanent resident status is essentially automatic for both groups; however, aliens in Group I were eligible on December 1, 1989, and those in Group II were eligible one year later on December 1, 1990.

Special Immigrants: Certain categories of immigrants who were exempt from numerical limitation before fiscal year 1992 and subject to limitation under the employment-based fourth preference beginning in 1992: persons who lost citizenship by marriage; persons who lost citizenship by serving in foreign armed forces; ministers of religion, their spouses and children; certain employees and former employees of the U.S. Government abroad, their spouses and children; Panama Canal Act immigrants; certain foreign medical school graduates, their spouses and children; certain retired employees of international organizations, their spouses and children; juvenile court dependents; certain aliens serving in the U.S. Armed Forces, their spouses and children; and religious workers, their spouses and children.

Special Naturalization Provisions: Provisions covering special classes of persons who may be naturalized even though they do not meet all the general requirements for naturalization. Such special provisions allow: 1) wives or husbands of U.S. citizens to be naturalized in three years instead of the prescribed five years; 2) a surviving spouse of a U.S. citizen who served in the armed forces to file in any naturalization court instead of where he/she resides; 3) children of U.S. citizen parents to be naturalized without meeting the literacy or civics requirements or taking the oath, if too young to understand the meaning. Other classes of persons who may qualify for special consideration are former U.S. citizens, servicemen, seamen, and employees of organizations promoting U.S. interests abroad.

Stateless: Having no nationality.

Stowaway: An alien coming to the United States surreptitiously on an airplane or vessel without legal status of admission. Such an alien is subject to denial of formal admission and return to the point of embarkation by the transportation carrier.

Student: As a nonimmigrant class of admission, an alien coming temporarily to the United States to pursue a full course of study in an approved program in either an academic (college, university, seminary, conservatory, academic high school, elementary school, other institution, or language training program) or a vocational or other recognized nonacademic institution.

Subject to the Numerical Cap: Categories of legal immigrants subject to annual limits under the provisions of the flexible numerical cap of 675,000 set by the Immigration Act of 1990. The largest categories are: family-sponsored preferences; employment-based preferences; and diversity immigrants. See Appendix 2 [of the *Statistical Yearbook of the Immigration and Naturalization Service,* 1996] for a discussion of the limits.

Suspension of Deportation: A discretionary benefit adjusting an alien's status from that of deportable alien to one lawfully admitted for permanent residence. Application for suspension of deportation is made during the course of a deportation hearing before an immigration judge.

Temporary Protected Status (TPS): Establishes a legislative base to the administrative practice of allowing a group of persons temporary refuge in the United States. Under a provision of the Immigration Act of 1990, the Attorney General may designate nationals of a foreign state to be eligible for TPS with a finding that conditions in that country pose a danger to personal safety due to ongoing armed conflict or an environmental disaster. Grants of TPS are initially made for periods of 6 to 18 months and may be extended depending on the situation. The legislation designated El Salvador as the first country to qualify for this program. Deportation proceedings are suspended against aliens while they are in Temporary Protected Status.

Temporary Resident: See *Nonimmigrant.*

Temporary Worker: An alien worker coming to the United States to work for a temporary period of time. The Immigration

Reform and Control Act of 1986, the Immigration Nursing Relief Act of 1989, and the Immigration Act of 1990 revised existing classes and created new classes of nonimmigrant admission. Nonimmigrant worker classes of admission are as follows:

1. H-1A—registered nurses;
2. H-1B—workers with "specialty occupations" admitted on the basis of professional education, skills, and/or equivalent experience;
3. H-2A—temporary agricultural workers coming to the United States to perform agricultural services or labor of a temporary or seasonal nature when services are unavailable in the United States;
4. H-2B—temporary nonagricultural workers coming to the United States to perform temporary services or labor if unemployed persons capable of performing the service or labor cannot be found in the United States;
5. H-3—aliens coming temporarily to the United States as trainees, other than to receive graduate medical education or training;
6. O-1, O-2, O-3—temporary workers with extraordinary ability or achievement in the sciences, arts, education, business, or athletics; those entering solely for the purpose of accompanying and assisting such workers; and their spouses and children;
7. P-1, P-2, P-3, P-4—athletes and entertainers at an internationally recognized level of performance; artists and entertainers under a reciprocal exchange program; artists and entertainers under a program that is "culturally unique"; and their spouses and children;
8. Q—participants in international cultural exchange programs;
9. R-1, R-2—temporary workers to perform work in religious occupations and their spouses and children.

Temporary visitors in the Exchange Visitor, Intracompany Transferee, and U.S.-Canada or North American Free-Trade Agreement classes of nonimmigrant admission also are granted authorization to work temporarily in the United States. See other sections of this Glossary for definitions of these classes.

Transit Alien: An alien in immediate and continuous transit through the United States, with or without a visa, including 1) aliens who qualify as persons entitled to pass in transit to and from the United Nations Headquarters District and foreign countries, and 2) foreign government officials and their spouses and unmarried minor (or dependent) children in transit.

Transition Quarter: The three-month period—July 1 through September 30, 1976—between fiscal year 1976 and fiscal year 1977. At that time, the fiscal year definition shifted from July 1–June 30 to October 1–September 30.

Transit Without Visa (TWOV): A transit alien traveling without a nonimmigrant visa under section 238 of the immigration law. An alien admitted under agreements with a transportation line, which guarantees his immediate and continuous passage to a foreign destination. (See *Transit Alien*.)

Treaty Trader or Investor: As a nonimmigrant class of admission, an alien coming temporarily to the United States, under the provisions of a treaty of commerce and navigation between the United States and the foreign state of such alien, to carry on substantial trade or to direct the operations of an enterprise in which he has invested a substantial amount of capital, and the alien's spouse and unmarried minor (or dependent) children.

Underrepresented Countries, Natives of: The Immigration Amendments of 1988, Public Law 101-658 (Act of 11/5/88) allow for 10,000 visas to be issued to natives of underrepresented countries in each of fiscal years 1990 and 1991. Underrepresented countries are defined as countries which received less than 25 percent of the maximum allowed under the country limitations (20,000 for independent countries and 5,000 for dependencies) in fiscal year 1988.

United States–Canada Free-Trade Agreement: Public Law 100-449 (Act of 9/28/88) established a special, reciprocal trading relationship between the United

States and Canada. It provided two new classes of nonimmigrant admission for temporary visitors to the United States—Canadian citizen business persons and their spouses and unmarried minor children. Entry is facilitated for visitors seeking classification as visitors for business, treaty traders or investors, intracompany transferees, or other business people engaging in activities at a professional level. Such visitors are not required to obtain nonimmigrant visas, prior petitions, labor certifications, or prior approval but must satisfy the inspecting officer that they are seeking entry to engage in activities at a professional level and that they are so qualified. The United States–Canada Free-Trade Agreement was superseded by the North American Free-Trade Agreement (NAFTA) as of 1/1/94. (See *North American Free-Trade Agreement*.)

Visa Waiver Pilot Program: Allows citizens of certain selected countries, traveling temporarily to the United States under the nonimmigrant admission classes of visitors for pleasure and visitors for business, to enter the United States without obtaining nonimmigrant visas. Admission is for no more than 90 days. The program was instituted by the Immigration Reform and Control Act of 1986 (entries began 7/1/88) and extended through fiscal year 1997 by subsequent legislation. Currently, there are 25 countries participating in this program.

Under the Visa Waiver Pilot Program, certain visitors from designated countries may visit Guam for up to 15 days without first having to obtain a nonimmigrant visitor visa. Currently, there are 16 countries participating in this program.

Withdrawal: An alien's voluntary removal of an application for admission to the United States in lieu of an exclusion hearing before an immigration judge. Although these aliens are technically considered nonimmigrants when applying for entry, withdrawals are not included in the nonimmigrant admission data.

Worldwide Ceiling: The numerical limit imposed on immigration visa issuance worldwide beginning in fiscal year 1979 and ending in fiscal year 1991. The ceiling in 1991 was 270,000 visa numbers. Prior to enactment of Public Law 96-212 on March 17, 1980, the worldwide ceiling was 290,000.

Source: *Statistical Yearbook of the Immigration and Naturalization Service,* 1996.

Index